Guide to Antiques
& Fine Arts

A Charles II Two-Handled Porringer and Cover

(*London Mark 1669, 19 ozs., 9 dwt.*)

The Wordsworth
Guide to Antiques
& Fine Arts

—

John R. Bernasconi

Wordsworth Reference

First published as *The Collectors' Glossary of Antiques and Fine Arts*
by the Estates Gazette Ltd, London, 1971.

This edition published 1995 by Wordsworth Editions Ltd,
Cumberland House, Crib Street, Ware, Hertfordshire SG12 9ET.

ISBN 1-85326-343-5

Printed and bound in Denmark by Nørhaven.

The paper in this book is produced from pure wood
pulp, without the use of chlorine or any other substance
harmful to the environment. The energy used in its
production consists almost entirely of hydroelectricity
and heat generated from waste materials, thereby
conserving fossil fuels and contributing little to the
greenhouse effect.

FOREWORD TO THE 1st EDITION

BY

F. CLARE HAWKES, C.B.E., M.A.

*(Late Secretary of the Chartered Auctioneers' and Estate Agents' Institute
and late President of the College of Estate Management)*

THERE is a strong temptation to describe this book as an "Open Sesame" to an enchanted world. Antiques, rarities, works of art—this is the realm in which collectors delight; through its highways and byeways they are led by the treasures auctioneers and dealers have to offer. "Dull must he be of soul" who never lingered at an antique dealer's window, never fingered hopefully an auctioneer's catalogue. Professional or amateur, he who would win the rank of connoisseur must study long his subject in books, museums, shops and sales, and in the homes of high and low. To do so he must learn the terms of art used to describe the objects of his study in their many different aspects, and only those who have tried know how wide is the field. Gold and silver, clocks, porcelain, pottery, furniture, pictures, all have their own language and to few it is given to be familiar with them all. Even those few will find something of value in this Glossary; to the rest of us it is indispensable.

Many of those who use this book will remember with affection and respect the late Mordaunt Rogers and his encyclopaedic knowledge of the arts. The series of lantern lectures which he gave year after year to the members of the Chartered Auctioneers' and Estate Agents' Institute revealed to his hearers the fascination of antiques and works of art, and the happiness a devotion to them can bring to life. Fortunately those lectures were collected together and published by The Estates Gazette, Ltd. in his famous book "The Making of a Connoisseur". It is in that tradition that this Glossary of Antiques and Fine Arts has been compiled.

John R. Bernasconi comes well equipped to the task. Trained in the famous firm of Anderson & Garland under his father and the late Colonel Anderson, once President of the Auctioneers' Institute, he has for more than a quarter of a century had a rich and ever-growing experience of the world of art. As valuer, as auctioneer, he has come to understand not only intrinsic merits and market prices, but also the kind of help collectors and dealers, experts and novices, are likely to welcome. He gave generously of his knowledge in his paper on "The Work of a Chattel Auctioneer and Valuer", which he read at the Chartered Auctioneers' and Estate Agents' Institute in 1956. Now, in his Glossary, he has indeed put deeply in his debt all who are interested in this field.

The appearance of the Glossary is timely, for the College of Estate Management is now offering courses of instruction for those who are sitting for the Chattels Examination of the Chartered Auctioneers' and Estate Agents' Institute. The Glossary cannot fail to be of great value to all young students of those chattels which may be classed as works of art, whether they sit for examinations or not, whether they are gaining their experience in London or the Provinces. And later, when they come to prepare inventories and catalogues or to study those prepared by others, they will find the Glossary an ever-ready counsellor and friend.

Anatole France has said: "We ought rather to envy collectors, for they brighten their days with a long and peaceable joy." If this be true—and few will question it—the author of this book may fairly claim to have added to the happiness of his generation.

F. CLARE HAWKES.

1959.

PREFACE TO THIRD EDITION

WHEN THE Collectors' Glossary was first published it was intended primarily as a handbook for the Professional Valuer and Auctioneer.

The warm response of the reviewers and public led to an early revised edition.

The great surge of interest in antiques in recent years continues, which is evidenced by the number of antique shops and markets which have made their appearance. The popularity of television and radio programmes on the subject continues unabated; it is this great interest which has made this third edition necessary.

The third edition has been revised and brought completely up to date. A new section on French Furniture Terms and another on Stevengraphs have been added.

CONTENTS

FURNITURE   *Page*

Chronological Table of English Periods   1

Characteristics of the English Furniture Periods 3

Characteristics of Adam, Chippendale, Hepplewhite and Sheraton 23

List of Cabinet Makers and Furniture Designers 37

Woods used in Cabinet Work 39

Chronological Table of French Periods 53

Characteristics of the French Furniture Periods 55

French Terms 69

Glossary of Terms 83

SILVER

Description and brief History of the Assay Marks ... 127

GOLD

Description of the Hall Marks 131

FOREIGN GOLD AND SILVER 132

The Worshipful Company of Goldsmiths' Memorandum of the Law relating to the Manufacture and Sale of Gold and Silver Wares 134

The Worshipful Company of Goldsmiths' Notice of Procedure for checking with Offences and Suspected Offences against the Hall Marking Laws 138

SILVER, SHEFFIELD PLATE and ELECTRO PLATE

Glossary of Terms 141

TABLE for converting Avoirdupois weight into Troy ... 150

PEWTER 151

PORCELAIN and POTTERY—Descriptions and Marks ... 153

Page

GLASS 207

CLOCKS and WATCHES with list of Makers 213

OIL PAINTINGS, WATER COLOUR DRAWINGS,
ENGRAVINGS, ETCHINGS, with list of Artists and
dates 229

JEWELLERY 295

FABRICS, CARPETS and RUGS 309

COINS 325

MEDALS 357

ARMS and ARMOUR 369

MUSICAL INSTRUMENTS 387

HERALDRY 397

CHINESE EMBLEMS AND SYMBOLS (with illustrations)
CHINESE DYNASTIES AND PERIODS 415

MYTHOLOGICAL DIVINITIES with index of their
attributes 421

SAINTS with index of their symbols 479

MONASTIC ORDERS 479

STEVENGRAPHS 509

ROMAN NUMERALS 510

GLOSSARY of GENERAL and MISCELLANEOUS
TERMS, not included in previous specialised sections ... 511

SILVER
Tables of Date Letters 536

ILLUSTRATIONS

Page

Charles II Silver two-handled Porringer ... ... *Frontispiece*
CHINESE SYMBOLS AND MARKS 416
FURNITURE:
 English 18th century Tea Table 9
 English 18th century Walnut Chair 10
 English 18th century Cabinet on a stand 11
 Louis XVI Commode of Drawers 12
 Louis XV Writing Table 12
 English Oak Draw Table about 1600 13
 Louis XV Wing Easy Chair 14
 Louis XV Fauteuil 14
 Louis XVI Settee 15
 Louis XV Settee 15
 Louis XVI Chair 16
 Louis XVI Fauteuil... 16
 French mid-18th century Chaise-longue 25
 Chippendale's design for a Library Bookcase 26
 Chippendale's design for a China Table 27
 Chippendale's design for a Writing Table 28
 Chippendale's design for a State Bed 29
 Chippendale's designs for Backs of Chairs 30
 Chippendale's design for Chinese Cabinet 31
 English Armchair about 1760–65 32
 Sheraton's design for a Lady's Cabinet and Writing
  Table 41
 Louis XV Cabinet 42
 Adam Half-Circular Commode 42
 French mid-18th century Commode 43
 French mid-18th century Armchair 44
 French Toilet Secretary about 1765 45
 French Cupboard about 1700 46

xi

FURNITURE—*continued* *Page*

Two Hepplewhite Armchairs with shield-shape backs ... 47
Hepplewhite's designs for Bed Posts ... 48
Early 17th century English Armchair ... 57
English Armchair about 1775 ... 58
Lyre Pattern Armchair—Style of Adam ... 59
Sheraton's design for a Lady's Cabinet Dressing Table ... 60
English Commode about 1775 ... 61
Franco-German Commode about 1785 ... 62
Sheraton's designs for Doors for Bookcases ... 63
Sheraton's designs for Chair Backs ... 64
French Commode about 1774 ... 73
French Secretaire about 1780 ... 74
Mahogany Chair inlaid in Box Wood ... 75
Armchair in Mahogany with Gilt-base mounts ... 76
Hepplewhite's Design for Bureau Bookcase ... 77
Sheraton Inlaid Half-Circular Side Table ... 78
Sheraton Inlaid Satinwood Commode ... 78
Grained and Gilded Armchair 1807 ... 79
Sheraton's design for a Harlequin Pembroke Table ... 80
Acanthus Leaf ... 83
Ball-Flower ... 84
Bulbous Leg ... 87
Cabriole Leg ... 87
Carlton House Table ... 88
Carved Beech Armchair for Marie-Antoinette's apartments 89
Carved Mahogany Chair ... 90
Satinwood English Armchair about 1790 ... 91
Carved Mahogany Claw Table ... 92
Carved Mahogany Armchair 1788 ... 93
Hepplewhite's design for a Pembroke Table ... 94
Hepplewhite's design for a Window Seat ... 94
Chippendale's design for a Pier Glass Frame ... 95
Carved Wood and Gilded Firescreen ... 96
Diaper Work ... 100

FURNITURE—*continued* Page

Girandole 104
Chippendale's design for a Shaving Table 105
Hepplewhite's design for a Sideboard 106
French 19th century Gilded Wood Stool 107
Guéridon 109
Linen-fold Panel 112
Paterae 115
Pie Crust Top 115
"S" Scroll—as used in Furniture 118
Splat Back 120
Teapoy 122
Verre Eglomise 124
Yorkshire Chair 125

GENERAL TERMS NOT INCLUDED IN SPECIALISED
SECTIONS:

Andirons or Handirons 511
Capital 515
Crosses—various styles 518
Entablature 520
Fleur-de-Lys... 521
Lectern 524
Quincunx 530
Trivet... 534
Volute 535

HERALDRY:

Affronté 397
Barry-Pily 398
Bicorporate 399
Checky 400
Chevron 400
Combatant 401
Displayed 403
Dormant 403
Ermine 404

HERALDRY—*continued*   *Page*

Fess or Fesse 404
Flanch 404
Gemel 405
Gyron 406
Impalement 407
Jessant 408
Lion Passant Gardant 408
Mascle 409
Naiant 409
Pale 410
Pile 411
Quarterly Quartered 411
Rompu 412
Saltier or Saltire 412
Vair 414
Voided 414

PORCELAIN AND POTTERY MARKS:

Alcora 154
Anspach 154
Arras 155
Baden-Baden 155
Berlin... 156
Bordeaux 157
Bow 157
Bristol 158
Brussels ... ...₹ 159
Buen Retino (Madrid) 159
Burslem 160
Caffaggiolo 160
Capo-di-Monte 161
Castel Durante 161
Castelli 161
Caughley 162
Chantilly 163

PORCELAIN AND POTTERY MARKS—*continued*   *Page*

Chelsea   163
Clignancourt...   164
Coalport   165
Cobridge   165
Copenhagen   166
Delft   167
Derby   169
Derby Chelsea   169
Doccia   170
Dresden   170
Faenza   171
Florence   172
Frankenthal   173
Fulda...   173
Fürstenberg   174
Gotha   174
Gubbio   175
Hague, The   175
Herend   176
Hispano-Moresque   176
Höchst   176
Kloster-Veilsdorf   177
Korzec   177
Lane End   177
Leeds...   178
Lille   178
Limbach   179
Limoges   179
Liverpool   179
Longport   179
Loosdrecht   180
Lowesby   180
Ludwigsburg...   181
Marieberg   181

PORCELAIN AND POTTERY MARKS—*continued* Page

							Page
Marseilles	...	...	...	...	...	...	182
Milan...	...	...	...	...	...	...	183
Minton	...	...	...	...	...	...	183
Moscow	...	...	...	...	...	...	183
Moustiers	...	...	...	...	...	...	184
Naples	...	...	...	...	...	...	184
Nevers	...	...	...	...	...	...	185
Niderviller	...	...	...	...	...	...	185
Nove Bassano	...	...	...	...	...	...	185
Nymphenberg	...	...	...	...	...	...	186
Nyon...	...	...	...	...	...	...	186
Orleans	...	...	...	...	...	...	186
Paris ...	...	...	...	...	...	...	187
Persian	...	...	...	...	...	...	187
Plymouth	...	...	...	...	...	...	189
Prague	...	...	...	...	...	...	190
Premières	...	...	...	...	...	...	190
Rockingham...	...	...	...	...	...	...	191
Rouen	...	...	...	...	...	...	191
St. Amand	...	...	...	...	...	...	192
Saint Cloud ...	...	...	...	...	...	...	192
St. Petersburg	...	...	...	...	...	...	192
Savona	...	...	...	...	...	...	193
Sceanx-Penthievre	...	...	...	...	...	...	193
Sèvres	...	...	...	...	...	...	194
Shelton	...	...	...	...	...	...	196
Sinceny	...	...	...	...	...	...	196
Spode...	...	...	...	...	...	...	196
Strasbourg	...	...	...	...	...	...	197
Sunderland	...	...	...	...	...	...	197
Swansea	...	...	...	...	...	...	198
Tournay	...	...	...	...	...	...	199
Tunstall	...	...	...	...	...	...	199
Turin...	...	...	...	...	...	...	199

PORCELAIN AND POTTERY MARKS—*continued*   *Page*

    Urbino 200

    Valenciennes... 200

    Venice 200

    Vienna 201

    Vincennes 201

    Wedgwood 202

    Weesp 203

    Worcester 204

    Yarmouth 205

    Zürich 205

SILVER—DATE LETTERS:

    Birmingham 536

    Chester 540

    Dublin 546

    Edinburgh 552

    Exeter 558

    Glasgow 564

    London 568

    Newcastle 576

    Sheffield 580

    York 584

SILVER—MARKS ON FOREIGN PLATE 133

ZODIAC SIGNS 454

NOTE

When looking for any particular term, the reader should refer to more than one section of the book. Many terms are used with the same meaning, in different sections, and in order to keep this book to a handy size, each term is only included once and then in the subject in which it is more generally used.

Acknowledgments

The publishers are grateful to the Victoria and Albert Museum, of South Kensington, London, for their kind permission to reproduce the photographs.

FURNITURE

Chronological Table of the English Periods

TUDOR AND RENAISSANCE PERIOD (1485-1558).
Henry VII	1485-1509
Henry VIII	1509-1547
Edward VI	1547-1553
Mary	1553-1558

ELIZABETHAN PERIOD.
Elizabeth	1558-1603

JACOBEAN OR EARLY STUART PERIOD (1603-1649).
James I	1603-1625
Charles I	1625-1649

CROMWELLIAN PERIOD.
Commonwealth	1649-1660

CAROLEAN OR LATE STUART PERIOD (1660-1689).
Charles II	1660-1685
James II	1685-1689

WILLIAM AND MARY PERIOD.
William III and Mary	1689-1702

ANNE PERIOD (1702-1735).
Anne	1702-1714
George I	1714-1727
George II (part)	1727-onward

GEORGIAN PERIOD (1714-1800).
George I	1714-1727
George II	1727-1760
George III	1760-1820

REGENCY PERIOD (1800-1830).
George IV	1820-1830
William IV	1830-1837

VICTORIAN PERIOD.
Victoria	1837-1901

FURNITURE

Characteristics of the English Periods

TUDOR PERIOD

HENRY VII	...	...	...	1485-1509
HENRY VIII	...	...	...	1509-1547
EDWARD VI	...	...	...	1547-1553
MARY	...	...	...	1553-1558

Tables often had only trestle supports.

Construction was often very crude. Really genuine specimens are rare.

The late chests or coffers were often carved with griffins, grotesque heads, etc.

"Linen fold" was a favourite design for carved panels.

Most of the furniture was made of oak, but chestnut, beech and cypress were also used, some of the pieces being painted.

The design of chairs was at first severe; they had high carved backs and the legs were usually square and plain with carved stretcher rails.

Much of the furniture made during the reign of Queen Elizabeth is classified by many as belonging to the Tudor Period.

The requirements of the Period were very modest and the furniture consisted chiefly of bedsteads, tables, dwarf buffets, marriage-chests, livery hutches, box and X-shaped chairs, benches and cupboards.

The first real advance in making furniture was during the reign of Henry VIII, who encouraged foreign craftsmen to work in England.

The Gothic influence passed slowly and it was probably not before about 1550 that the Renaissance style began to make headway. Much of the furniture followed architectural lines, the transformation first being apparent in the churches.

3

Much furniture was imported from the Continent and was far in advance of that made in the British Isles. Many pieces were carved with female terminal figures, shields, coats of arms, etc., and decorated with gilt. Some of the later pieces were crudely inlaid with agate, coloured marble, tortoiseshell and mother-of-pearl, as well as with other woods, the latter often being about 1/16th inch thick.

ELIZABETHAN PERIOD

ELIZABETH **1558-1603**

(Contemporary French Period—Henri IV, 1589-1610)

Drawers were seldom fitted to Elizabethan furniture.

The X-shaped chair with padded seat prevailed throughout the period.

The Gothic influence remained strong and was often manifest in the furniture of the period.

Oak was the wood generally used in the construction of furniture belonging to this period.

Amongst the woods used for inlay work were beech, box, cherry, ebony, holly, oak, sycamore, walnut, as well as ivory.

Large bulbous legs, often enriched with crudely carved acanthus leaves, were an outstanding feature in Elizabethan furniture.

Archwork was a notable feature in the heads of bedsteads, etc., the arches often being divided by caryatids.

Caryatids, grotesque figures and masks were familiar in the carved work, as was strapwork, gadrooning, guilloche bandings, fluting, etc.

Some of the carved work embodied arabesque designs as well as intricate interlacing strapwork copied from the Flemish and ribbon ornamentation imitated from the French. Backgrounds were sometimes punched to produce a roughened surface.

The articles which probably received most attention were court cupboards, dining tables (including draw-tables), four-poster or tester bedsteads and buffets.

The inlay work was generally very coarse, and often 1/16th inch thick; it became thinner, however, as time advanced.

During the latter part of Elizabeth's reign, wooden seats began to be replaced by stuffed seats, then called " cushioned " chairs.

Wood floors replaced the rush-covered floors, so that carpets came into use. Pillows and cushions were also generally used.

Heraldic designs were often embodied in the chair backs.

Baskets and vases of flowers and fruit were often represented in the inlay work, as was the "Tree of the Knowledge of Good and Evil".

Walls were frequently panelled in oak, which was occasionally inlaid. Chimney corners were made in place of open hearths.

Tables often had massive stretchers between each of the legs, so that feet could be kept off the rush-covered floors.

Panelled chairs were heavily built, but, as designs advanced, the credence or tasting buffet developed into a sideboard and the oak chest into a settle.

EARLY STUART or JACOBEAN, CROMWELLIAN and LATE STUART PERIOD

JAMES I	1603-1625
CHARLES I	1625-1649
COMMONWEALTH	1649-1660
CHARLES II	1660-1685
JAMES II	1685-1689

(Contemporary French Periods—Henri IV, Louis XIII and Louis XIV, 1589-1715)

Gate-leg tables are generally associated with Jacobean times.

Drawers were in more general use.

Oak was the wood chiefly used, but chestnut, pine, walnut and sycamore were also employed.

Designs were occasionally incised or carved in the seats of chairs.

Table-tops were often of round or oval shape.

Back legs of the later chairs were nearly always turned.

Handles and large scroll hinges of wrought-iron "cockshead" design were frequently employed, as were brass drop handles.

Mirrors began to take a more prominent place during the latter part of the 17th century.

The Huguenot silk weavers began to settle in Spitalfields, London, in about 1670, and beautiful fabrics were produced. The Mortlake factory was previously established in 1619.

Lacquer work imported from the East became fashionable.

Ball turning was extensively employed during the period 1625-1660, with square intersections to receive stretchers and other members.

The massive bulbous legs gave way to simple turnery, vase-shaped pillars (sometimes fluted) often being seen.

The wood seats of chairs were often sunk so as to hold squab cushions in the proper place. Stools were the usual seats at meals up to about 1680.

Geometrical designs prevailed in the raised appliqué panel work, as also in the incised and inlay work, the designs for the latter often being cut out of the solid wood.

The carvings were more restrained than in the Elizabethan Period, and included cartouche scrolls, vine leaves, laurelling, fruit, chains of flowers, winged cherubim, shells, etc., and it is thought the later designs were influenced by Grinling Gibbons.

Chequer and "herringbone" inlay work was extensively used, bone, ebony, ivory, and mother-of-pearl being employed.

The backs of Jacobean chairs were sometimes carried out in archwork, the centre part often being inlaid with floral designs and arabesques.

Diaper work was favoured in the carvings, as also was ropework, acanthus leaves, pomegranates, guilloche bandings a crown supported by amorini, etc.

Stretcher rails were lighter in construction and more ornamental, being no longer required for use as foot rests.

The later chairs were often upholstered in velvet or pigskin, with large brass nails, to such an extent as to subordinate the work of the cabinet maker to that of the upholsterer. They sometimes had low padded backs, under a foot in height.

The arm supports of Continental chairs were usually ornamented with carved masks or figures, whereas those produced in this country did not possess this feature.

Grandfather clocks were probably first introduced into this country from Holland, during the latter part of this period, and walnut was more generally used at this time.

"Yorkshire" chairs are a well-known feature of the period. These possess open backs, usually with two carved crescent-shaped rails, a sunk wooden seat, turned legs and front stretcher.

Cane panelling was extensively employed in Carolean times for the seats and backs of chairs, day beds (usually with adjustable heads), etc. Sturdy "S" scrolls or "Flemish curves" often formed the arm supports, besides which they were embodied in the chair backs and legs.

Features of the later pieces (after about 1660) were the spiral or "barley sugar" twist, turned legs and rails, and the pierced and carved backwork and leg rails of the chairs, the tendency being to place these nearer to the seat than hitherto. They often embodied a carved shell design in the centre. The "barley sugar" twist should not be confused with the open twist, which is of a later date.

Genuine articles usually show the heads of wooden pegs securing the tenon into the mortice. Original pieces often have turned wooden knobs to doors and drawers.

Marquetry was considerably used in late pieces, but ornamentation was not allowed to interfere with the practical use of articles.

The oak furniture was often treated with a dark varnish mixed with oil so that it sank into the wood and did not form a surface polish.

Foreign influence was apparent during the late period and workmanship continued to improve; amongst other popular pieces can be included oak dressers, court cupboards, oak cradles, coffin stools, day-beds, monks' benches, X-shaped chairs, intricate table cabinets with secret drawers, etc. It is thought that more elbow chairs were made, at least at the beginning of the period, than occasional chairs, also that few coffers and chests were produced.

WILLIAM AND MARY PERIOD
WILLIAM III AND MARY ... 1689-1702
(Contemporary French Period—Louis XIV 1643-1715)

Needlework coverings were extensively used.

Designs assumed more graceful outlines.

"Oyster pieces" were often employed in the veneer work.

Dutch and French influence was strongly evident in the designs.

Pierced and carved splats were fashionable towards the end of this period, and often embodied "C" scrolls. Other chair backs were entirely filled in with pierced and carved work.

Oak, chestnut and walnut were the woods chiefly used. Some of the pieces, particularly settees, were painted black and ornamented with gilt.

Mirrors were in almost general use, the plates often having bevels up to an inch in width, some being blue-coloured. Other mirrors had painted designs of birds, flowers, etc., and still another form of decoration were intaglio designs cut on the backs.

Dutch marquetry was largely employed, the designs being inlaid in a veneer groundwork and not carved out of the solid as before. They included fruit, flowers, vases and scenes, often being gaily coloured.

The alternate square and turned legs and stretchers gave way to those with the "inverted cup" or "acorn"-shaped swell which is a feature of the furniture of this period. Its use was extended well into the Anne period.

The chairs were much improved and lighter in design, some having cane panels and shaped and removable seats and dragon's foot and pearl feet.

The "cabriole" leg, copied from the Dutch, began to make its appearance, particularly in the later pieces.

A notable feature of this period is found in the arms, which in section are raised in the centre and curl over the arm post in a bulge, the lower parts terminating in scrolls.

Turned spiral supports of chairs and tables were still largely employed, often being thicker at the bottom and tapering to the top.

Tied stretcher work somewhat resembling an "X" was another feature, and often had a finial in the centre. It succeeded the carved stretcher between the front legs.

Grandfather, or long-case clocks, grew in popularity, the cases often being made of oak, veneered with walnut, etc. Some were produced in close and finely executed marquetry in the well-known "bird and bouquet", "spider's web" and seaweed designs. Many of the clocks were surmounted by three brass spiked balls.

QUEEN ANNE PERIOD

ANNE	...	...	...	...	1702-1714
GEORGE I		...	...	...	1714-1727
GEORGE II (part)			...	...	1727-onward

(Contemporary French Period—Louis XV, 1715-1774)

The Queen Anne style was popular all through the reign of George I, and extended well into the reign of George II.

The stretcher rails on chairs and settees were now but little employed.

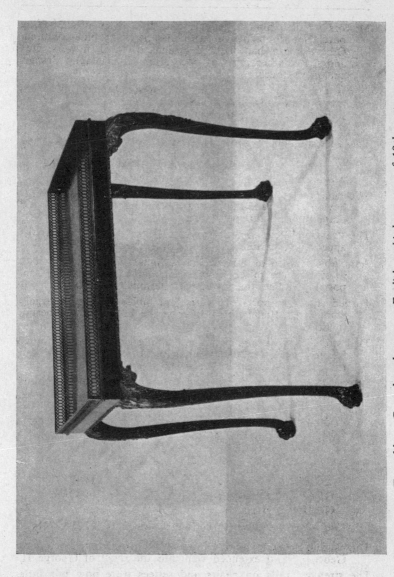

Tea-table. Carved mahogany. English; third quarter of 18th century.
From the Percival Griffiths Collection.

Chair. Walnut with carved lion paw feet. English; early 18th century. One of a pair given by Sir Paul Nakins, Bart.

*Cabinet on stand. Walnut veneer with ash cross banding. English;
early 18th century. Given by Brigadier W. F. Clark, C.M.G.,
D.S.O., D.L., through the National Art-Collections Fund*

A Louis XVI commode inlaid with various woods in geometrical designs. Jones Collection. Victoria and Albert Museum.

A Louis XV writing table

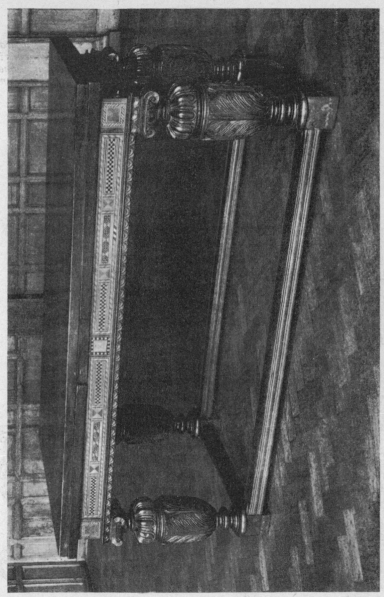

Draw-table. Joined oak, the frieze inlaid with chequer pattern in sycamore, bog oak and other woods. English; about 1600.

A Louis XV
wing easy chair

C.E.B

A Louis XV fauteuil

C.E.B

A Louis XVI carved and gilt settee upholstered in tapestry.
Victoria and Albert Museum

A Louis XV gilt settee with open arms, seat and back in
needlework

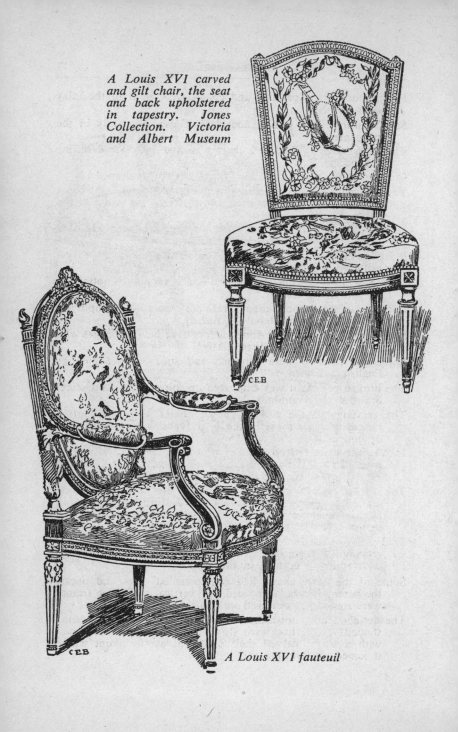

A Louis XVI carved and gilt chair, the seat and back upholstered in tapestry. Jones Collection. Victoria and Albert Museum

C.E.B

C.E.B

A Louis XVI fauteuil

Herringbone, cross-banding and ebony were used in the inlay work.

Spiral turned work was in considerable use, especially in the early pieces.

The well-known "Windsor" chair was first introduced during this period.

Corner cupboards and interior fittings were often domed.

The cabinet work was generally finely executed, great care being taken in matching the grain and figure of the wood at the joints.

Fine needlework and damask materials were produced and used for upholstery and hangings.

Marquetry was still in evidence, but considerably improved, being toned down and quieter in effect.

Carved detail was sometimes gilded and is especially noticeable on late wall mirrors.

Loose seats, sometimes called "Trafalgar" seats, were employed, being either upholstered or rushed.

Many of the early Queen Anne mirrors have bevelled edges with deep borders of coloured glass.

Lacquered cabinets were imported and successfully copied by English craftsmen.

The broken pediment was employed on some pieces, and secret drawers were common.

The crestings of the early types of chairs were more often raised, whereas those of the later types were usually sunk or hooped.

Metal pear-shaped drop handles were in general use; handles with pierced back-plates and plain, engraved and pierced escutcheons were first used on furniture of this period.

The carved work was well executed, escallop shells, lion and satyr heads being favourite forms of ornamentation for the knees of chairs, etc. Eagle heads also appeared in the carvings.

The seats of chairs were narrowed towards the back, the rectangular form disappearing and giving place to a shape with rounded corners in the front.

Some of the early chairs had cane-panelled seats and backs, the latter often being divided by a vertical spar. The frames were sometimes veneered with burr walnut.

The designs tended towards comfort, the backs of chairs being shaped with a backward slope. Many had a plain splat with a single carved shell ornament at the point where it joined the cresting rail.

The "bracket" foot, somewhat similar in shape to the supports used on wall brackets, was extensively used.

On some of the late chairs the splats did not run the full length of the backs, finishing at a secondary rail situated a little below the cresting rail.

"Lovers'" or "drunkards'" chairs were fashionable during this period. In design they were similar to ordinary open elbow chairs, but were of unusually large proportions.

Early 18th-century English marquetry was seldom "sand burnt", whereas that produced in Holland was often embellished in this way. Engraved marquetry is never found in early English work. The early pieces of furniture were in straight forms, but later these gave way to swelled or bombé sides, whilst bouquets, vases of flowers, butterflies, etc., were a feature in the marquetry designs.

Walnut, chestnut, beech and oak were used in the construction of Queen Anne furniture proper, the first mentioned being the most popular. Mahogany was also extensively used in the later stages of this period.

English walnut is usually distinguishable by its rich golden-brown colour and straight grain, foreign varieties being of a darker colour.

Amongst other articles produced were chairs, card and other tables, two-chair-back settees, chests of drawers, marquetry cabinets with numerous drawers, sometimes enclosed by doors and mounted on stands, bureau-bookcases, mirror frames, china cabinets, grandfather clock cases in marquetry and walnut, etc.

Upholstered easy chairs of the "grandfather" type began to be appreciated, their outstanding features being the tall arched backs which stood above the wings or ear guards, and the truncated arms. They were also usually provided with a loose squab cushion.

The backs of the chairs were proportionally tall, with pierced and inlay-work (sometimes heraldic) splats. The designs of some of the former embodied the letter "C" and closely resembled those produced by Chippendale at a later date. The "fiddle back" splat was another favourite form.

A favourite arrangement for drawers in tables, which were usually of small size, was one long drawer occupying the whole width of the front, and two comparatively small drawers below, one on either side of the arched underhanging, making room for the knees of the person using the table.

The "cabriole" leg proper is the outstanding feature of Queen Anne furniture. It was adapted for use on practically all articles, and in the later stages the knee was usually carved, the escallop shell being the most favoured form of decoration. The toes gradually assumed the shape of a claw and were afterwards made to grip a ball (pearl). Sometimes, however, they ended in a scroll or were in the shape of a hoof or "colt's foot".

GEORGIAN PERIOD

| GEORGE II | ... | ... | ... | 1727-1760 |
| GEORGE III | ... | ... | ... | 1760-1820 |

(Contemporary French Periods—Louis XV, Louis XVI and Empire, 1715-1799)

The finer points as to detail, etc., are given under the headings of Chippendale, Adam, Hepplewhite and Sheraton, whose designs were of paramount influence in the period.

Pierced splats came into prominence.

The "cabriole" leg reached its zenith of perfection, gradually giving way to the straight tapering leg.

The elegant style which prevailed during the Queen Anne period gave way to the coarse and over-elaborate baroque style in the late Georgian period.

Oriental lacquer panels of scenes, pagodas, etc., were imported from the East and used in the production of pieces of lacquered furniture which became very fashionable.

The claw-and-ball foot was partly replaced by the lion's paw.

The charm of mahogany began to be appreciated, and this wood was popular during the closing years of George I's reign, although walnut was still extensively used.

It was in the reign of George II that furniture underwent the greatest change, viz., at the time Chippendale first made his influence felt.

The tendency was to build furniture more on architectural lines. The Dutch influence of the Queen Anne period yielded to that of the French.

The coil spring used in upholstery was introduced about the middle of the 18th century.

Gilding was freely used to decorate carved ornamentation.

Veneering was used more and more.

Furniture produced during the reign of George I and the early part of the reign of George II underwent but little alteration, and is regarded as being of the Queen Anne period.

REGENCY PERIOD (1800-1830)

"Regency" is a term applied to English furniture from 1800 to 1830; it is rather loosely applied as it does not coincide with the Regency of George, which was from 1811-1820. This period was partly a reflection of the French Empire designs and many of the designs are Classical.

The Furniture of this period was more useful and smaller than earlier—this is one of the reasons for its recent revival in popularity. Rosewood was the principal wood used. Metal inlay was extensively used, ormolu and brass mounts being popular.

Among the designers of this period were Henry Holland, George Smith, Thomas Hope and Thomas Sheraton, who died 1806.

The sofa and sofa table became fashionable.

VICTORIAN PERIOD

VICTORIA 1837-1901

German influence was discernible in the furniture of this period, the style becoming heavy, massive and ugly, losing the sense of fine proportion which was the outstanding characteristic of the Georgian period.

The fine example set by the master cabinet makers of the middle 18th century was ignored but fortunately pride in craftsmanship was not lost.

Work-tables and teapoys, generally of circular or octagonal form mounted on pillar and tripod supports, were features of the times. Also sarcophagus-shaped wine coolers, loo tables. Pembroke and Sutherland tables, chiffoniers, Davenports, overmantels, etc., mostly in mahogany and rosewood.

FURNITURE

Cabinet Makers and Designers

CHIPPENDALE

Thomas Chippendale was the son of a Worcestershire carver, and established himself in business in Conduit Street, London, in 1749, removing to more prominent premises in St. Martin's Lane in 1752. His book entitled "The Gentleman and Cabinet Maker's Director" was published two years later. After his death in 1779 the business was carried on by his son in partnership with others at several addresses in London.

Chippendale is considered the master of perspective and proportion.

The serpentine front was much employed.

Stretcher rails were used only in chairs, etc., having square legs.

The so-called "Irish Chippendale" presents a heavy appearance by comparison with genuine Chippendale. The carvings are not so sharp or deep, being flat and lifeless.

Chased mounts and bands of brass, etc., were occasionally used as ornamentations.

Many mid-18th century pieces were gilt or japanned.

Cupid as an ornamentation often appeared in the gilt mirrors, console tables, etc.

Wine coolers were produced in varying shapes, a common form being an octagonal brass-bound bucket with lid and zinc liner on a separate stand, usually with square, but sometimes with carved cabriole legs.

Mahogany-framed wall mirrors were sometimes decorated with inlaid shell designs and often had gilt pediments.

"C" scrolls were employed as brackets in the angles between the framing and legs of tables, etc.

The knees of chair and table legs were often decorated with carved scrolls, cabochons, acanthus leaves, crockets, etc.

Wine tables were made with carved edges and centre pieces for holding bottles, and mounted on tripod supports.

21

The anthemion was represented in the cornices of some of the later pieces.

Some of the square legs, particularly those of dining tables, had a sunk beading to their outside edges.

Chippendale furniture was not generally highly polished, being treated with an "oil polish" which left a somewhat dull finish.

The tracery of bookcase doors often had the famous thirteen pane arrangement associated with Chippendale's work.

The lion's-claw-and-ball foot is earlier than the eagle's-claw-and-ball.

Couches were not extensively made by Chippendale, but on those he produced the heads were generally in the form of chair backs and not adjustable. Péché mortels were occasionally made.

The top or cresting rails of dining chairs were seldom, if ever straight, the line usually being broken at the ends, and/or in the centre.

Some of the best chairs had the bottom edges of the front and side members shaped and ornamented.

Chippendale did not produce sideboards, but only side or carving tables, often fitted with marble tops.

The cut through tern or cluster-column legs, chiefly appearing on cabinets and tables, were a feature of some of Chippendale's Chinese designs.

Tables with sunk or dish tops were much favoured. These sometimes had "pie crust" or "raised ribband" tops, the latter so called from the carved edge resembling ribbon.

Mahogany was discovered by Sir Walter Raleigh and was in general use by about 1720. It was the most popular wood in use, but rosewood was sometimes employed, and in some earlier pieces walnut, all on occasion being decorated with carvings.

Many of Chippendale's designs were influenced by the style of the corresponding French period, viz., Louis XV, and were elaborately carved in the rococo style.

Chippendale seldom used inlay in his work but relied on delicate carvings, but such inlay as was used was only in the form of a lining or stringing; its presence usually denotes lateness of production.

"Chinese Chippendale", a style in the Chinese taste, was principally represented in the fret (sometimes appliqué) and carved lattice ornamentations. This style was in vogue from about 1754 to 1770.

A favourite design for chair splats embodied the well-known "ribband" pattern, and others the letter "C" or "C" scroll. The "S" scroll was also employed in the earlier examples. The ladder back is another form. "Cupid's bow" was a favourite form for cresting rails.

Many pieces attributed to Chippendale were made by his contemporaries, such as Edwards and Darley, Ince and Mayhew, and others, especially articles in the Chinese taste. However, they may have been put out by Chippendale to be made, as at the height of his fame it is probable he had more orders to execute than could be carried out in his own workshops.

Chippendale made a great variety of articles, including bureau-bookcases, tripod and dining tables with two fixed and two hinged legs, two- and three-backed settees, card tables, some with five or six legs, commodes, tester or four-poster bedsteads, pole fire-screens, knife boxes, tea caddies, basin or wig stands, etc.

ADAM

Robert and James Adam came of a Scottish family of architects and were born at Kirkcaldy, in Fifeshire. Robert apparently took the leading part in affairs. He was born in 1728 and died in 1792. The brothers' book of designs was published in 1775.

Brass inlay was occasionally used.

The decorations on many tables were on the underframing.

Ormolu escutcheons, knobs, handles and other fittings were largely employed.

The tracery of doors and inlay panels was sometimes of diamond shape.

Circular tapering legs as distinct from the square tapering legs of some of the other masters, were a feature.

The "rainceau" style of decoration was much used by the Adam brothers.

Some of the pieces were painted, others japanned in black and soft shades of slate and green with painted or gilt decorations on the polished surfaces.

The chair backs were often of oval or shield shape, and were usually padded.

Some of the larger side tables have eight or even ten legs.

Brass lattice-pattern grills were sometimes fitted to bookcase doors, in place of glass.

The carvings or garnishments on Adam furniture usually had a centre ornament or patera, the latter being used in a large proportion of their designs.

Papier-maché was employed in some cases in making door panels, candle brackets, etc.

Some of the articles of furniture designed by the Adelphi, as the Adam brothers were sometimes called, were sideboards with taper pedestals, commodes, vase-shaped knife cabinets, bookcases, girandoles, mirror-frames, tables, etc.

The Adam brothers revived the classical style, this class of ornamentation and design being represented in practically all their work.

Celebrated artists such as Angelica Kauffmann, Zucchi, Cipriani and Pergolesi helped them in the decoration of rooms, the panels of furniture, table tops, etc.

The Adam brothers may be said to be among the first to produce sideboards. Tables were first made with separate pedestals en suite, but later these were embodied.

Amongst other forms of ornamentation used by them were painted and Jasper ware (Wedgwood) medallions, Greek and Roman vases, festoons, cord and tassel, anthemion, bows of ribbon, caryatids, rams' heads, cupids, eagle-headed grotesques, winged sphinx lyres, pineapples, etc.

The inverted bell flower or husk was extensively used in the carved and gilt festooned decorations on the mirrors, etc., but apparently not so much on the chair legs, these usually being fluted and sometimes cable fluted.

Mahogany and satinwood were largely used, being decorated with rich inlays, composed of such woods as amboyna, kingwood, tulipwood, etc., or painted by one of the famous artists who assisted in the brothers' work.

HEPPLEWHITE

George Hepplewhite was apparently the founder of the business, which after his death (1786) was carried on by his widow under the style of Hepplewhite & Co. The first book of designs was published in 1788, and at that time they were probably at their best.

Some of the satinwood tables had painted panels.

Chaise-longue. Carved and gilded wood, stamped Tilliard. Traditionally made for the Marquise de Pompadour, whose arms, added at a later date, are carved on the cresting. French: mid-18th century, the upholstery modern. Given by Sir Chester Beatty, F.S.A., LL.D., D.Sc.

Library Bookcase

The Gentleman and Cabinet Maker's Director, 1754—Thomas Chippendale]

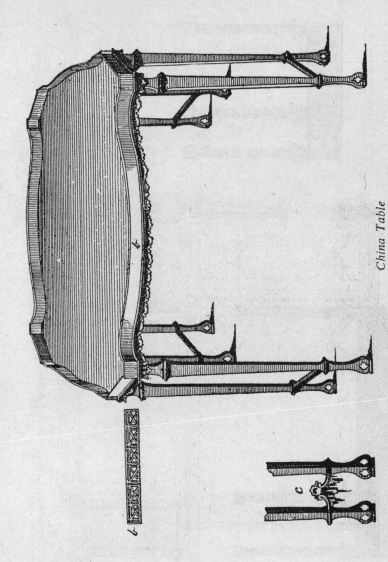

China Table

The Gentleman and Cabinet Maker's Director, 1754—Thomas Chippendale]

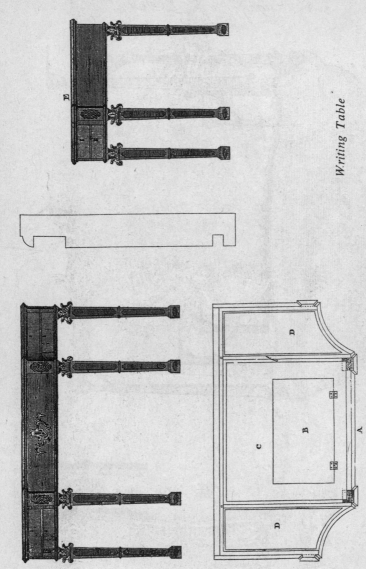

Writing Table

The Gentleman and Cabinet Maker's Director, 1754—Thomas Chippendale]

A Design for a State Bed.

The Gentleman and Cabinet Maker's Director, 1754—Thomas Chippendale]

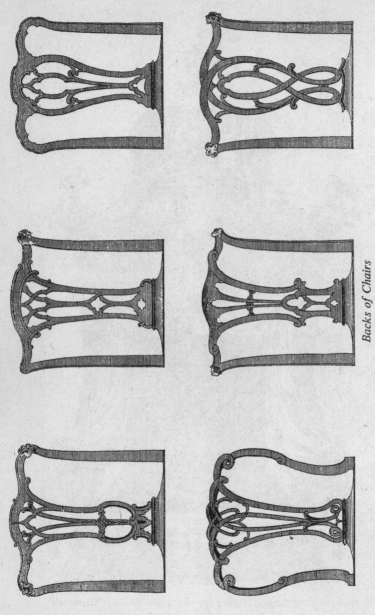

Backs of Chairs

The Gentleman and Cabinet Maker's Director, 1754—Thomas Chippendale]

Chinese Cabinet.

The Gentleman and Cabinet Maker's Director, 1754—Thomas Chippendale

Armchair. Beech with parquetry of walnut and sycamore. English;
about 1760–65.   Given by Mr. Randolph Behrens.

Round-shaped brass handles were largely used.

The arms of the early elbow chairs were often padded.

Mahogany, satinwood, sycamore and chestnut were the principal woods employed.

Straight lines in the chair backs were avoided and decoration on legs kept to a minimum.

The settees were often of the three-chair-back type.

The coverings were sometimes fixed by the aid of close brass nailing.

The square-legged chairs were usually provided with stretcher rails.

Lacquered elbow chairs occasionally had cane-panelled backs with painted centre medallions.

Compared with Chippendale the designs were lighter in style, rather resembling French work.

The anthemion or Greek honeysuckle was a favourite form of ornamentation, both in carvings and inlay work.

Square tapered legs were largely used, often decorated with carved strings of inverted bell flowers (husks).

"Camel back" is the name sometimes given to chair backs, the top rail of which is humped in the middle.

Other chair backs were of oval, ladder and wheel designs; some had carved openwork splats.

A quantity of the furniture, made of beech, had a painted or japanned background decorated with painted medallions. etc.; some was partly inlaid. That coloured black often had gold or copper-coloured shadings or decorations.

Hepplewhite is best known for his chairs and sideboards. A large number of the backs of the chairs were of shield shape.

The chair backs are usually lower than those of Chippendale, and the seat fronts are often of slight serpentine shape. Other seats are "dipped", the lowest part running from front to back.

The backs of Hepplewhite chairs were very seldom upholstered and on the few occasions when this was done the entire backs were filled in. Horsehair and morocco leather were favourite materials.

The strings of tapered bell flowers or husks, the Prince of Wales' feathers, drapery, vases and wheat-ears were features in the carvings, which were, however, never so pronounced as those in Chippendale's work.

The fronts of sideboards often have serpentine centre parts with concave corners. This is important to note, as many sideboards closely resemble those designed by Sheraton except that the corners are usually convex.

Another important point is that the curved top rail of Hepplewhite chairs is practically always unbroken. In Sheraton chairs with shield-shaped backs the curve in this rail is invariably broken by a straight line or panel in the centre.

Among other things designed by 'Hepplewhite were winged easy chairs, the wings of which were usually of scroll shape and extended from the back to nearly the full length of the arms; finely inlaid tea caddies and trays; swing toilet glasses, the mirrors of which were similar in shape to the chair backs; writing tables; night commodes, etc., fitted with tambour fronts; large cabinets, knife urns, tables, grandfather clock cases, fire-screens, etc.

SHERATON

Thomas Sheraton was born at Stockton-on-Tees in 1751 and published a book of designs in London in 1791. He is reputed to have died in poverty in 1806.

Inlay work was extensively employed.

Brass inlay was considerably used in the late English Empire pieces.

Underframing or stretcher rails were seldom used in the chairs.

The French style was lavishly imitated and brass finials were often used.

The curved legs and tripod supports often had a small foot set vertically.

Silver and Sheffield plate handles were occasionally employed, a common form for all handles being the oval.

The oval was largely represented in the inlay work, and the serpentine front was successfully embodied in many pieces.

Deep cresting rails denote lateness of period, as does reeding in the legwork.

The Prince of Wales' feathers, vases and urns, shell designs and drapery were features of the carving, inlay and painted work.

In chairs of the early period the splats did not reach the seats but were supported by a cross rail. The backs were usually composed of four, five or sometimes seven uprights.

A large quantity of the work produced was of the painted or japanned variety, decorated with painted designs. The underframings were often festooned and the leg fronts embellished with strings of flowers. Some pieces with a white ground had gold ornamentation.

In some articles woven materials were used, e.g., in ladies' work tables. These were described by him as "pouch" tables.

Table supports and chair backs in the Empire style were often in the shape of a lyre, fitted with stout brass wire as strings.

Marquetry took the place of much of the carved work seen in previous markers' pieces.

Acanthus leaves often appeared in the carvings, and "acanthus swags" were used to relieve the plainness of some of the members, being chiefly employed on chairs.

The great majority of the legs were square tapered, but a few of the earlier pieces had turned legs. The square legs sometimes had line inlay.

Most of Sheraton's designs mentioned satinwood, this apparently being his favourite wood, decorated with inlay or paintings by Angelica Kauffmann, Cipriani, Pergolesi, etc. Mahogany was also extensively used, and occasionally rosewood and tulipwood.

The inverted bell flower or husk was largely used by Sheraton in carvings, as by his predecessors; strings of them often ornament the fronts of chair legs, etc.

Veneering was resorted to whenever possible, but exposed members such as backs, legs, etc., were usually made of solid satinwood.

Sheraton is reputed to be the inventor of the kidney-shaped table. It is at least evident that a large number in this shape were designed by him to meet various purposes.

His chairs with shield-shaped backs have the line of the top rail broken, either by a straight line or panel in the centre, whereas this line is unbroken in the chairs produced by Hepplewhite. Square backs often have "X" rails in place of splats.

In a large number of cases Sheraton furniture was ingeniously fitted with secret doors and drawers and various semi-mechanical contrivances, such as mirrors fitted to wash-stands and drawers, pivoted pen-troughs, writing slopes, library steps in the form of tables, all of which fold and slide away into concealed places. The " Harlequin " table is a typical example; in this a nest of pigeon holes and drawers can be raised from or lowered into the body of the table.

Sheraton is perhaps most famed for his sideboards. These are chiefly constructed of mahogany inlaid with satinwood, etc., and fitted with sundry conveniences. One style invariably had convex corners, this being the principal feature distinguishing them from those of Hepplewhite, which had concave corners. They were usually mounted on reeded tapered legs, and often had a brass back of "rainceau" design.

LIST OF CABINET MAKERS AND
FURNITURE DESIGNERS

ADAM BROTHERS—John (1721-1792), Robert (1728-1792) James (1730-1794), and William (1739-1822). Robert and James were the most distinguished Architects and Designers of Furniture in the Classic style.

BOROUGHS, JOHN—Cabinet Maker to Charles II. Partner with Wm. Farnborough.

BOULTON, MATTHEW (b. 1728)—Manufacturer of ormolu and metal mounts for furniture.

BRADBURN, JOHN—Cabinet Maker to George III during the period 1765-1775.

BRETTINGHAM, MATTHEW (1688-1768)—Architect and Furniture designer. A pupil of William Kent.

CAMPBELL, ROBERT—Cabinet Maker to George IV when Prince of Wales.

CASBERT, JOHN—Cabinet Maker and Upholsterer to Charles II.

CHAMBERS, SIR WILLIAM (1726-1796)—Architect and Designer of Furniture. Architect of Somerset House.

CHIPPENDALE, THOMAS (1718-1779)—Cabinet Maker: Produced his book of designs "The Gentleman and Cabinet Maker's Director, 1754." From 1771 was senior Partner in Firm of Chippendale, Haig & Co.

CHIPPENDALE, THOMAS, Junior (1749-1822)—Son of Thomas Chippendale; in partnership of Chippendale, Haig & Co.

CIPRIANI, GIOVANNI BATTISTA (1727-1785)—Painter and Decorator. Came to England in 1755. No furniture painted by him but he influenced late 18th-century style of furniture.

COBB, JOHN (d. 1778)—Cabinet Maker to George III in partnership with William Vile. Several examples of his work are in the Royal Collection at Buckingham Palace.

COPELAND, H.—Furniture Designer. Associate with Matthias Lock 1768.

CRUNDEN, JOHN—Architect and Furniture Designer Author of " The Joyner and Cabinet Maker's Darling " 1765.

FARNBOROUGH, WILLIAM—Cabinet Maker to Charles II and William III. Partner of John Boroughs.

FRANCE, WILLIAM—Cabinet Maker and Upholsterer.

GALE, CORNELIUS—Cabinet Maker to William III.

GIBBONS, GRINLING (1684-1720)—Wood Carver and Designer. Engaged at Windsor and Hampton Court Palace.

GILLOW, RICHARD (d. 1811)—Cabinet Maker, son of Robert Gillow (*q.v.*).

GILLOW, ROBERT—Cabinet Maker. Sometimes in the late 18th century and always after 1820, the Firm's productions were stamped with their name.

GOODISON, BENJAMIN (d. 1767)—Cabinet Maker to George II.

GRIFFITHS, EDWARD—Cabinet Maker, at one time assistant to Benjamin Goodison.

GUMLEY, JOHN (d. 1729)—Cabinet Maker and Looking-glass Manufacturer to Queen Anne and George I.

HAIG, THOMAS—Partner of Thomas Chippendale, father and son from 1771 to 1796.

HALLETT, WILLIAM (1707-1781)—Cabinet Maker.

HEPPLEWHITE, GEORGE (d. 1786)—Cabinet Maker. Was an apprentice of R. Gillow. His book "Cabinet Maker and Upholsterer's Guide" was published in 1788, two years after his death.

INCE, WILLIAM—Cabinet Maker and Upholsterer in partner-ship with Thomas Mayhew. Published the "Universal System of Household Furniture."

JOHNSON (or JENSEN) GARRETT—Cabinet Maker to Royalty between 1680 and 1714.

KAUFFMANN, ANGELICA (1741-1807)—Painter. Employed by the brothers Adam.

KENT, WILLIAM (1685-1748)—Furniture Designer, Sculptor, Painter, Architect and Landscape Gardener.

LANGLEY, BATTY and THOMAS—Architects and Designers.

LINNELL, JOHN (d. *c.* 1798)—Cabinet Maker and Designer, specialising in mirrors and wall lights.

LOCK, MATTHIAS—Carver and designer. Between 1752-68 he was probably employed in the preparation of designs for Thomas Chippendale.

MANWARING, ROBERT—Cabinet and Chair Maker. Pub-lished several books including "The Cabinet and Chair Makers' Real Friend and Companion" 1765.

MAYHEW, THOMAS—Cabinet Maker and Partner of William Ince.

MOORE, JAMES (d. 1726)—Cabinet Maker. Partner of John Gumley.

NORMAN, SAMUEL—Cabinet Maker employed by Adam Brothers.

PARRAN, BENJAMIN—Cabinet Maker. Partner of Benjamin Goodison.

PERGOLESI, MICHELE ANGELO—Decorator. Came to England from Italy c. 1758. Employed by the Adam Brothers. His "Original Designs" 1777-1801 inspired much of the painted furniture of this period.

ROBERTS, THOMAS—Joiner and Chair Maker to William III and Queen Anne.

SEDDON, GEORGE (1727-1801)—Cabinet Maker.

SHEARER, THOMAS—Cabinet Maker and Designer.

SHERATON, THOMAS (1751-1806)—Designer. Published "Cabinet Maker's and Upholsterer's Drawing Book" 1791-4, etc.

SMITH, GEORGE—Cabinet Maker and Designer who enjoyed the patronage of George IV. Published a pattern-book entitled "A Collection of Designs for Household Furniture and Interior Decoration " 1808.

VILE, WILLIAM (d. 1767)—Cabinet Maker in Partnership with John Cobb.

WYATT, EDWARD—Carver.

ZUCCHI, ANTONIO PIETRO (1726-1795)—Painter with Robert Adam in Italy, and later worked for him. Married Angelica Kauffmann.

WOODS USED IN CABINET WORK

Acacia—A dull yellow-coloured hardwood with brownish markings, occasionally used for inlay work towards the end of the 18th century. It is strong and durable.

Alder—A wood sometimes used in making chairs of common variety; it grows in England on swampy ground and is of orange yellow colour. The bark is used for dyeing.

Amaranth—*See Purple Heart.*

Amboyna—A West Indian wood of yellowish-brown colour, mottled with "bird's-eye" figurings, used to veneer whole surfaces such as table tops, and also for inlay and marquetry.

Apple—A heavy hardwood, reddish-brown in colour, with straight grain, used as a veneer and inlay.

Ash—A tough white wood largely used for making furniture, particularly chairs; it has light-brown markings and closely resembles oak in appearance and texture.

Beech—A wood much used in making articles of furniture, chairs being the most favoured; also used for other articles that are afterwards painted. It is of brownish white colour, hard and solid, and has a speckled grain.

Birch—A wood once much preferred for the construction of bedroom furniture; when polished it closely resembles satinwood, but is of a somewhat lighter colour with a fine wave-like grain. It is a hardwood and retains its arris.

Black Bean—A richly marked Australian hardwood of rich golden colour, much used for panels and high-class joinery work.

Blackwood—A general title given to numerous hardwoods found in both the East and West Indies. They are all heavy, hard and decorative, and in colour range from dark brown to purplish.

Bog Oak—Oak which has been preserved in peat bogs, black in colour.

Box—A very hard, extremely heavy wood of pale yellow colour, with a fine regular texture, used for making flutes, etc., also for wood-engraving, the lines being as sharp as those produced on a metal plate.

Brazil Wood—A hard, heavy wood resembling mahogany, used as an inlay.

Calamandar—A very hard wood from East India. It is hazel-brown in colour with black streaks, and was much used for making small articles of furniture.

Camphorwood—A wood similar to mahogany both in colour and texture, obtained from Borneo and Kenya. Linen and blanket chests are made, or lined with it because of its moth-resisting properties.

Canary Wood—A species of mahogany of a light yellow colour, much used for veneers and inlay work.

Cedar—A light, soft brown wood with straight grain but little used in cabinet work owing to its poor quality; it is, however, sometimes employed for drawers, linings, etc., owing to its possessing a delicate fragrance which also acts as a deterrent to insects; it is little affected by changes in temperature.

Cherry—A hardwood with a reddish close grain; used for small articles and inlay.

Chestnut—A hard, durable white wood, somewhat resembling oak, but when polished it is not unlike satinwood; it was often used for rails and spars of chairs.

Circassian Walnut—A beautifully figured walnut used for veneers and obtained from Southern Europe.

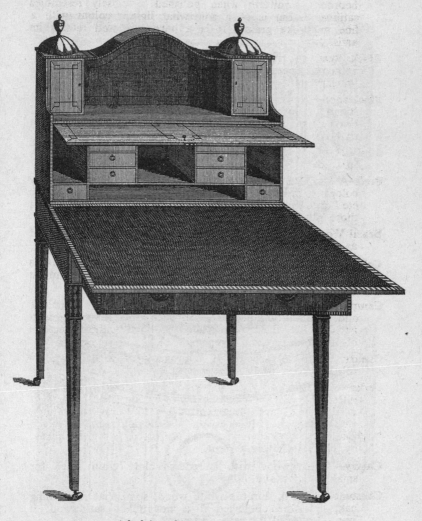

A lady's cabinet and writing table

The Cabinet Maker and Upholsterer's Drawing Book, 1791-94—Thomas
Sheraton]

*A Louis XV Cabinet with Vernis-Martin panels from the
Hamilton Palace Collection. Victoria and Albert Museum*

An Adam half-circular commode

Commode. Marquetry of various woods with gilt-brass mounts and marble top. Style of C. Cressent. French; mid-18th century. Jones Bequest.

Armchair.   Carved and gilded wood.   French; mid-18th century.
(The upholstery of a later date.)

Toilet secretary. Marquetry of various woods with gilt-brass mounts. French; about 1765. Jones Bequest.

Cupboard. Marquetry of ebony and metals, bearing the cipher of Louis XIV. Attributed to A. C. Boulle. French; about 1700. Jones Bequest.

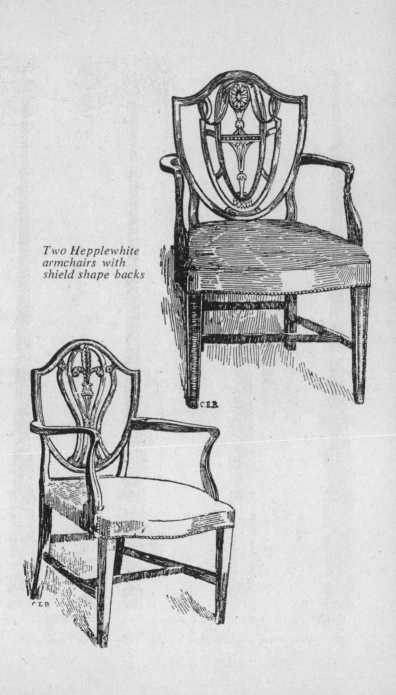

Two Hepplewhite armchairs with shield shape backs

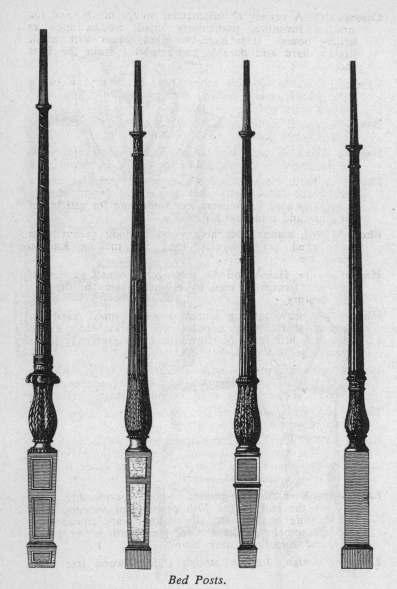

Bed Posts.

The Cabinet-Maker and Upholsterer's Guide, 1788—George Hepplewhite

Coromandel—A variety of calamandar wood; much used for making furniture, particularly small articles such as writing boxes. It is hazel-brown in colour with black streaks, hard and durable and imported from the East Indies.

Cypress—A strong, durable timber used in joinery; it has a fine, durable grain and is of a yellowish colour with reddish markings.

Deal—A general name given to the wood of fir and pine trees, straight grained, easily worked.

Degame Wood—A hardwood found in the West Indies, used for decorative purposes; it is light yellow in colour.

Ebony—A hard, close-grained wood, heavier than water, of deep black colour with dark green and brown stripes; principally used for veneers, but sometimes for articles of furniture and ornamental items.

Elm—A hard, compact, durable wood of light colour with pronounced grain, largely used for making kitchen chairs, etc.

Hare-Wood or Hair-Wood—A green-grey stained veneer of sycamore frequently used by cabinet makers in the late 18th century.

Hickory—A heavy, strong tenacious wood, much used for carriage shafts, whip handles, gun stocks, etc.; it has been very little used for furniture, being peculiarly liable to damage by worms, heat and moisture.

Holly—An ivory white, hard, fine-grained wood, with a small spotted grain, largely used for veneer work, in which it is sometimes dyed various colours.

Kauri—A light yellow straight-grained wood from New Zealand, used for bentwood work.

Kingwood—A Brazilian wood much used for veneer and inlay work; it is similar to rosewood but lighter in colour and more heavily marked in a violet shade; often used as bandings on satinwood veneer.

Laburnum—A hard fine-grained wood considerably used towards the end of the 17th century for veneers, inlay work, knife handles, etc.; the colours vary considerably and are sometimes almost dark green with brown markings, and sometimes dark brown.

Larch—A tough, durable, straight-grained wood free from knots.

Lignum Vitæ—A very hard, tough, close-grained wood of dark greenish-brown colour, imported from Jamaica; used for veneering, particularly in the 17th century, also for making pulleys, balls, pestles, etc.

Lime—A light, soft, but tough and durable white wood, free from knots and cross grain, much used by carvers.

Mahogany—The quality of mahogany varies considerably, some varieties being hard and others soft, but it is probably the most stable of woods when seasoned. The hard variety, known as "Spanish" mahogany, was generally used in England from the early 18th century. It was obtained from Jamaica, Cuba and San Domingo. Honduras mahogany is lighter in colour and softer and was much used from the late 18th century.

Maple—A compact, fine-grained white wood much employed for inlay and marquetry work. The famous "bird's-eye" maple is obtained from the sugar maple tree; its wood is often used for panels, inlay work and picture frames and when polished is of a rich golden-brown colour, with a satiny appearance somewhat resembling sycamore.

Oak—Famous for its strength and durability. In general use for the making of furniture until the late 17th century. Subsequently its use was restricted to the carcase portions of fine veneered furniture, although it continued to be generally employed for simpler, country furniture.

Olive Wood—Of a greenish yellow colour with black cloudy spots and veins; often used for veneering and small ornamental articles, some bearing an inscription in Jewish characters, as travel mementoes.

Padouk—An Australian hardwood, resembles rosewood, greyer in colour.

Palisander—*See Purple Heart.*

Pear—A fine hard-grained wood of reddish colour, without markings, somewhat resembling box in texture; often employed as a body-work for small articles of furniture; it was occasionally used for chair frames and dyed to imitate ebony.

Pine—A white, fairly soft, durable wood; the red pine or deal is the wood most universally used in the construction of houses, cheap furniture, etc.

Pitch Pine—A variety of wood imported from the United States; it is hard and of yellowish colour with brown streaks; it is not very extensively used in making furniture.

Plane—A white close-grained wood often used as a substitute for beech.

Plum—A heavy yellow to reddish brown wood used as inlay.

Pollard Oak and Walnut—The wood of oak and walnut trees that have been polled, cut at the top to give a bushier head. This process alters the grain.

Purple Heart, Amaranth or Palisander—A strong, durable closegrained hardwood obtained from British Guiana. Its colour varies from dark-brown to purplish-violet, with a wavy grain and distinct markings. It is used for veneers and other decorative purposes.

Rosewood—A hard-wood imported from India; it somewhat resembles mahogany in general appearance; the colours vary from a light to almost blackish brown, marked with streaks of dark red and black. It was chiefly used for veneer and inlay work, but during the first half of the 19th century articles were made up entirely from it. When cut it yields an agreeable smell of roses, from which it derives its name.

Sandalwood—A compact, fine-grained wood, remarkable for its fragrance, which is much disliked by insects. The wood is therefore useful in making work-boxes and similar articles. It is imported from the East Indies, and is of a greenish-yellow colour.

Satin Walnut—The English name for American Gum; a light brown sometimes with black stripe markings, used for inexpensive bedroom furniture.

Satinwood—A hard, close-grained, heavy wood of yellow colour varying to a golden hue; some varieties have no markings and are quite plain, others have a distinct rippled figure, and were extensively used by Adam, Hepplewhite and Sheraton. It is imported from Africa and the West Indies.

Snakewood—A rare, very hard heavy wood of warm yellowish brown colour, beautifully mottled with deep brown marks, arranged regularly and bearing a slight resemblance to the markings of a snake; its scarcity makes it valuable and it is used only on very fine inlay work. It is obtained from Guiana.

Sycamore—A species of maple, hard and even-grained; in its natural state is of a light yellowish colour, and often possesses a fine "fiddleback" grain, although it is sometimes found without markings. It is often stained to a greenish grey shade, and in this state is used for veneering whole suites of furniture, when it is sometimes called greywood.

Teak—A heavy, very hard wood of reddish brown colour extensively used for shipbuilding; it is used for making furniture, sinks, etc.

Thuya—A wood occasionally used for inlay work, it is of a golden brown colour, figured with small "birds'-eyes" in a halo or circle.

Tulipwood—A hardwood of yellowish colour with reddish stripes; it is usually cut across the grain and used in veneers for banding. It loses lustre on exposure.

Walnut—A fairly hard fine-grained wood of rich brown colour, veined and shaded with darker brown and black. Considerably used in the making of furniture, particularly of the Queen Anne period. English walnut is usually distinguishable by its rich golden-brown colour and straight grain, foreign varieties being of a darker colour.

Yew—A very hard, tough, pliable wood of orange red or dark brown colour, formerly much used for making bows and the backs of Windsor chairs.

Zebra Wood—Occasionally used for inlay and veneer work; it has pronounced markings of brown stripes on a light brown ground.

FURNITURE

Chronological Table of the French Periods

HENRI QUATRE PERIOD.
   Henri IV 1589-1610

LOUIS TREIZE PERIOD.
   Louis XIII 1610-1643

LOUIS QUATORZE PERIOD.
   Louis XIV 1643-1715

LOUIS QUINZE PERIOD.
   Louis XV 1715-1774

LOUIS SEIZE PERIOD.
   Louis XVI 1774-1792

EMPIRE AND DIRECTOIRE PERIOD.
   Republic 1793-1794
   Directorate 1794-1799

FURNITURE

Characteristics of French Furniture

HENRI QUATRE (IV) 1589-1610
**(Contemporary English Periods—Tudor,
Elizabethan and Early Stuart)**

Oak was the wood chiefly used, but some of the pieces were painted.

French ébénistes of the day imitated furniture produced in Italy, although they imparted into the designs an influence of their own. It was difficult to distinguish whether some of the pieces were of French or Italian origin.

The designs were usually cold and formal, but became more lavish as time advanced.

Tester bedsteads mounted on griffin feet, with carved posts, frames and dossiers (back-boards), were produced.

A type of armoire common to the period had two pairs of doors, placed one above the other, the doors being separated by carved caryatids.

The carvings included war trophies, mythological figures, eagles with spread wings, satyrs, lions' heads, festoons, fruit, flowers and foliage; caryatids and atlantes were the subjects for pilasters and legs.

The ornamentation of some of the panels was in high appliqué relief and consisted of porticos, complete with pillars and pediments.

Ébénistes (cabinet makers) whose names are known in connection with furniture of the period are Bachelier and Sambin, and designers and engravers de L'Auln, du Cerceau and Goujon.

LOUIS TREIZE (XIII) 1610-1643
**(Contemporary English Periods—Early
Stuart and Jacobean)**

Italian, Dutch and German influences were still evident in the furniture produced during the period.

Turned legs and stretchers were in considerable use; many legs were of square section and ornamented with carving.

The upper part of some of the chair backs was completely
covered with upholstery, beneath which was a pierced and
carved rail. Others had cane panels.

Carved "X"-shaped stretchers were employed on chairs, with
pierced and carved front stretcher rails set high up from
the floor.

In some chairs the front legs project above the seat level; others
have upholstered back panels set in a pierced and carved
frame, extending at the top and bottom to join the main
back members.

Arms were carved with masks and figures; tulips were often
represented.

Furniture became more comfortable, some chairs being entirely
covered in material or leather; other pieces were ornamented with bronze mounts.

Carved ornamentation gradually gave way to turnery and inlay
work, the latter being carried out in ivory, stained bone,
tortoiseshell or mother-of-pearl.

Many mirror frames were carved and gilded; others were of
ebony without any decoration.

Ébénistes who produced furniture during the period are Baum-
garter, and Golle. Designers and engravers: Bosse,
Breughels, De Vos and Francks.

LOUIS QUATORZE (XIV)   ...   1643-1715
(Contemporary English Periods—Jacobean,
William and Mary, and Anne)

The greatest advance in the making of furniture, tapestries and
objets d'art generally, followed the establishment in
1663 of the Gobelin Manufacturies, more correctly known
as "Manufacture Royale des Meubles de la Couronne",
under the direction of Le Brun.

The early pieces of this period are mostly of a rectangular
shape, being somewhat massive and severe in design.

Table tops, panels, etc., were sometimes enriched with designs
in pietra-dura, the Italian influence still remaining.

Many pieces were painted, gilded and varnished; others had
gilded claw feet, and some were over-enriched with gilding
and plated and blue metal appliqué mounts.

As the period advanced the demand grew for bigger pieces, with
the result that armoires, cupboards, tables, etc., were
made with much larger proportions.

Masks were often employed in the carvings of legs and under-
hangings. Some legs were carved in the form of figures.

Armchair. Oak, partly covered in knotted woollen pile ('Turkey work').
From Beau Desert, Warwickshire.   English; early 17th century.

Armchair. The frame veneered with rosewood; inlaid decoration and splat of satinwood, the mounts on the legs of gilt bronze. One of a set, probably designed by Robert Adam, from the library at Osterley Park House. English; about 1775.

A lyre pattern armchair, late 18th century.

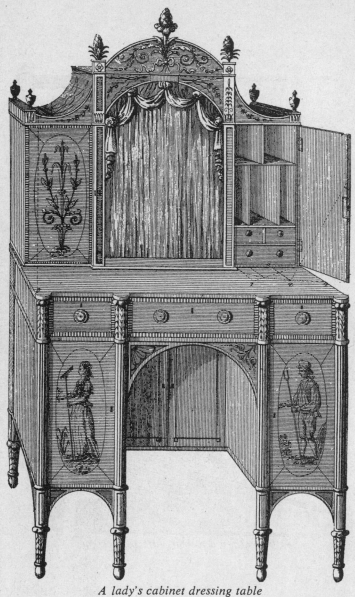

A lady's cabinet dressing table
The Cabinet Maker and Upholsterer's Drawing Book, 1791-94—Thomas Sheraton]

Commode, one of a pair. Hare-wood veneer with marquetry of ebony and other woods. Mounts of pierced and gilt bronze. Probably designed by Robert Adam. From the Drawing Room at Osterley Park House. English; about 1775.

Commode. Marquetry of various woods with gilt-brass mounts and marble top. Attributed to D. Roentgen. the front decorated with a scene from the Commedia dell Arte from a design by J. Zick. Franco-German; about 1785. Bequeathed by Sir Bernard Eckstein, Bart.

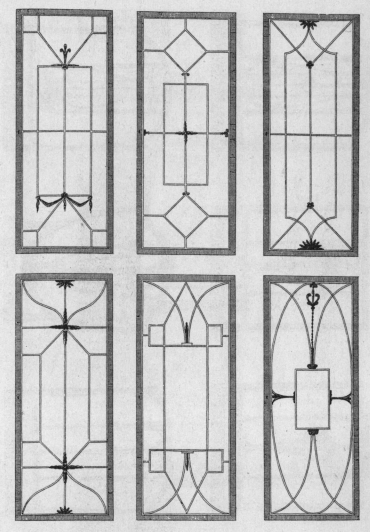

Doors for bookcases

The Cabinet Maker and Upholsterer's Drawing Book, 1791-94—Thomas Sheraton]

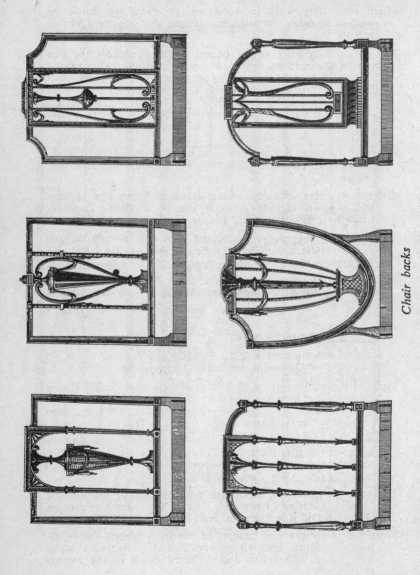

Chair backs

The Cabinet Maker and Upholsterer's Drawing Book, 1791-94—Thomas Sheraton]

Much marquetry work in wood was produced by Boulle as well as by other ébénistes, the designs showing considerable merit.

The outstanding work of the period was undoubtedly the fine marquetry in tortoiseshell and brass perfected and produced by Boulle (*q.v.*); this was often on an ebony base, enriched by chased ormolu masks and reliefs. The marquetry designs were light and tasteful and consisted of foliage, scrolls, arabesques, etc. Boulle was not the inventor of the process, somewhat similar marquetry having been made by Italians in France before his time.

Ébénistes (cabinet makers) who made a name for themselves during the period include Boulle, Cucci, Oppenord and Poitou.

Ciseleurs (carvers or chasers of metal) and sculptors who became well known include Anguier, Fillipo Caffieri, Coustou, Coysevox, Lespagnandel, Taupin, Tuby and Van Cleve.

Designers and engravers associated with the period include Audran, Bérain, Le Clerc, Le Pautre, Marot, Rousselet and Varin.

Artists and painters include Baptiste, Boullognes, Coypel, Jouvenet, Le Brun, Mennoyer, Mignard, Van der Meulen and Yvart.

LOUIS QUINZE (XV)   1715-1774
(Contemporary English Periods—Anne (part) and Georgian, including Chippendale)

Many of the early pieces possessed considerable grace, parquetry work being extensively used. This early work, before the introduction of rococo ornamentation, is sometimes known as the Regency Style.

Lacquer work from the East came into vogue, and French workmen at first imitated it, later designing and producing their own versions, the principal exponents being Huygens and Martin. (*See Vernis-Martin.*)

The reign of Louis XV produced four ébénistes of outstanding merit: Charles Cressent (1685-1768), Jean François Oeben, David Roentgen and Jean François Riesener.

From the fairly graceful designs of the early pieces, the furniture developed into an elaborate and over-ornate style, overloaded with lavish and distorted detail in the rococo style.

The style developed to such an extent that in some pieces no straight lines were employed, the curves and swellings being exaggerated out of all proportion.

Lavish marquetry was extensively used. The designs included musical instruments, bouquets of flowers, trophies of war, etc., some designs competing with painted pictures.

Many different woods were used in the marquetry work, some light varieties being stained or dyed. Tulip, sycamore, laburnum, rosewood and purplewood were all employed.

Tapestries from the looms of Aubusson, Beauvais, Gobelin, etc., assisted in the lavish furnishing of apartments. The bonheur-du-jour was a product of the period.

Carved and chased ormolu mounts in the rocaille style were considerably used.

Parquetry was used extensively, some pieces having no other form of inlay work; the friezes of such articles were often ornamented with key and guilloche patterns.

In the early part of the period Charles Cressent continued the manufacture of tortoiseshell marquetry in the style of Boulle.

Ébénistes (cabinet makers) whose names became famous during the period include Arnoult, Charles Cressent, Gaudereaux, Joubert, Loriot, Migeon, Oeben, Riesener, Roentgen and Sulpice. It became the practice in 1751 for ébénistes to put their names upon their work.

Ciseleurs (carvers or chasers of metal) and sculptors included Jacques Caffieri, Duplesis, Germain, Hervieux and Winant.

Designers and engravers of the period include the Brothers Slodtz and Meissonnier.

Artists and painters, included Bayer, Bernard, Boucher, Boudin, Choquet, Delorme, Denizot, Douvax, Dubois, Filleul, Garnier, Gillot, Gravelot, Guesnon, Hédouin, Hérbert, Hult, Jabodot, Latz, Lazare, Leprince, Levasseur, Petit, Pineau, Pionnier, Pleney and Watteau.

LOUIS SEIZE (XVI) 1774-1792
(Contemporary English Period—Georgian)

The style attributable to Louis Seize actually commenced in the previous reign.

Carved egg-and-tongue mouldings appeared on some of the pieces.

Articles of black and gold lacquer decorated in the Chinese taste were produced during the period.

Pieces made by Riesener were marked with his name either on a panel or on the oak lining.

Furniture of the period is noted for its straight lines, in direct contrast to that produced in the reign of Louis XV.

Though of plainer design, it possessed much ornamentation, but in elegant and refined taste. It is sometimes referred to as the "decorated" style.

The marquetry was finely executed and of great beauty, magnificent panels of vases, flowers, hunting, musical and other trophies being produced; backgrounds were often of diaper or parquetry pattern.

Finely grained, figured and coloured marble tops were fitted to many tables, and festoons of flowers adorned the framings.

Tables, etc., were fitted with ormolu gallery rails; copper was employed in some of the marquetry, and chased ormolu and gilded bronze mounts were in considerable use.

Some legs were of square taper shape, with gilded sunk bead mouldings to their angles; others were fluted and spiral fluted. Festoons of flowers were applied spiral-wise to the legs of some fauteuils.

The inlay work often consisted of geometrical patterns of chess-board marquetry, garlands, ribbons, scrolls and knots. Some pieces embodied Sèvres porcelain plaques.

Many pieces were painted and decorated; Vernis-Martin panels, often executed by Watteau, Pater, etc., were applied to vitrines and commodes. Tambour fronts or panels were occasionally fitted.

Woods used in the marquetry work included holly, kingwood, laburnum, maple, purplewood, rosewood, snakewood, sycamore and tulipwood.

The following ébénistes (cabinet makers) appear to have produced furniture during the period: Benemann, Carlin, Frost, Gouthière, Leleu, Levasseur, Montigny, Pasquier, Richter, Riesener (1735-1806), Roentgen, Saunier, Schmitz, Schwerdfeger, Séverin, Stockel and Weisweiler.

Ciseleurs (carvers and chasers of metal) and sculptors: Bardin, Gouthière, Hauré, Martin, Riesener and Thomire.

Designers and engravers: Boizot, Duplessis and Le Barbier.

Artists and painters: Watteau, Boucher, Fragonard, Lancret, and Pater.

EMPIRE AND DIRECTOIRE   1793-1799
(Contemporary   English   Period—Georgian)

Many pieces were painted white or gilded.

Favourite colours for upholstery were dark blue, crimson, white and gold.

Medallion portraits, classical figures, imperial symbols and figures were employed in the decorations.

Furniture of the period was of a dignified style and carried out mostly in mahogany, rosewood and ebony.

Bronze-gilt mounts were largely employed and brass wires were used in the lyre-shaped table supports.

Furniture was massive in design and construction, with carvings of anthemion, palm, bay, laurel leaves, etc.

Classical figures, caryatids, winged sphinx, animal forms and rams' heads were used in the decorations; claw feet were occasionally employed.

Ébénistes, designers and painters famous during the period included David, Desmalter, Fontaine, Percier, Prud'hon and Thomire.

FRENCH TERMS

accoudoir	Arm of a chair.
ambulante	Portable stand or table.
armoire	Cupboard or press.
armoire à bijoux	Jewel cabinet.
armoire à glace	Cabinet with glazed doors.
armoire basse	Low cabinet.
armoire d'encoignure	Corner cupboard.
atelier	Workshop or factory.
bahut	Chest or trunk.
baldaquin	Canopy over a bed or chair.
banquette	Long stool or bench
banquette de croisée	Window seat.
barbière	Shaving stand.
berceau	Cradle.
bergère	Easy chair with upholstered or canework sides.
bergère à joues	Wing easy chair.
bibliothèque	Bookcase, bookshelves or library.
boîte	Box or case.
boîte à chandelles	Candlebox.
boîte à musique	Music box.
boîte à ouvrage	Work box.
bonheur du jour	A lady's writing table with cupboard over.
bonnetière	Narrow cupboard with single door.
bureau	Writing table or desk.
bureau à cylindre	Cylinder front writing desk.
bureau à pente	Writing desk enclosed by a sloping front.
bureau à pupitre	Table with central writing easel.
bureau-bibliothèque	Writing desk surmounted by bookcase.
bureau de dame	A lady's writing table.
bureau plat	Flat topped writing table.
cabaret	Liquor cabinet.
cadre	Frame for a mirror or picture.
canapé	Settee with upholstered back and ends.

69

canapé à console	Settee with projecting seat front supported by a central leg.
canapé à joues	Wing settee.
cartel	Wall clock.
cartonnier	Filing cabinet, a nest of boxes.
casier	Cupboard, pigeon holes.
casier à musique	Open shelves to hold music.
cassette	Casket.
causeuse	Wide upholstered chair, a love seat.
chaffeuse	Chair with low seat, fireside chair.
chaise à jeu	Chair for use at a gaming table.
chaise à la reine	Chair with flat oval back.
chaise à porteur	Porter's hall chair.
chaise à porteurs	Sedan chair.
chaise en cabriolet	Chair with concave back shaped to the human body, usually with curved top rail.
chaise longue	Day bed.
chauffe-assiette	Plate warmer.
chauffe-lit	Bed warmer.
chauffe-pieds	Foot warmer.
cheminée	Mantelpiece.
chenet	Firedog, andiron.
coffre	Chest or coffer.
coffret	Small chest.
coiffeuse	Dressing table.
commode	Chest of drawers.
commode à encoignure	Chest with cupboard at each end.
commode à l'anglais	Chest with open shelves at each end.
commode à la Régence	Chest of serpentine form.
commode à pieds	Chest of usually two drawers on long legs.
commode à vantaux	Chest of drawers in which doors conceal the drawers.
commode en console	Chest containing a single drawer on long legs, intended to stand beneath a mirror.
commode en tombeau	Chest with protuberant shaped sides and front.
confessionnal	Wing chair.
confident	Small settee for two persons.
console	Pier table, a side table of bracket form.

coquillage	Shell ornamentation.
couche	Couch, or bed.
desserte	Serving table.
dossier	Chair back; headboard of a bed.
duchesse	Day-bed, or *chaise longue*.
duchesse à bateau	Boat-shaped *chaise longue*.
duchesse brisée	*Chaise longue* in two or three parts.
ébéniste	Cabinet maker.
écran	Screen, fire screen.
écran-secretaire	Cheval screen supporting a desk.
écrin	Jewel case or casket.
écritoire	Inkstand, or compartment fitted for pen and ink.
égouttoir	Plate rack with spindle or fret gallery.
encoignure	Corner cabinet.
étagère	Open shelves.
fauteuil	Armchair.
fauteuil en bergere	Armchair with upholstered sides.
fauteuil en cabriolet	Armchair with concave back to fit the body.
fauteuil en confessionale	Armchair with wings.
flambeau	Candlestick.
garde-manger	Livery cupboard, larder.
garde-robe	Wardrobe.
girandole	Wall bracket having a shaped mirror and candle branches.
guéridon	Circular or oval table of small size often fitted a shelf.
jardinière	Flower-stand or table.
liseuse	Reading table.
lit	Bed.
lit à parade	Bed for receiving callers, state bed.
lit à la duchesse	Bed with draperies, the canopy supported independently from the wall or ceiling.
maître ébéniste	Master cabinet maker.
maître menuisier	Master joiner.
marquise	Small seat for two.
médaillier	Cabinet for medals.
meuble	Piece of furniture.
paravent	Screen.
porte-assiette	Plate stand.

porte-montre	Watch stand.
porte-musique	Music stand.
poudreuse	Dressing table.
prie-Dieu	Chair with high back for kneeling at prayer.
pupitre	Desk, table desk.
quenouille	Bedpost.
rafraîchissoir	Wine cooler.
régulateur	Long case clock.
rideau	Curtain, screen.
rouet	Spinning wheel.
sablier	Hourglass.
sabot	Shoe, the applied mounts at the base of a leg.
secrétaire	Writing desk, or bureau.
secrétaire à abattant	Writing desk with fall front enclosing pigeon holes, the lower portion usually fitted cupboard.
secrétaire à panse	Cylinder front desk, *bureau à cylindre*.
secrétaire-bibliothèque	Desk with cabinet over.
secrétaire-chiffonnier	Chest of drawers with writing section.
secrétaire-commode	Chest of drawers with writing section.
secrétaire en tombeau	Desk with slanting writing section.
semainier	Tall chest of seven drawers.
serre-bijoux	Jewel cabinet.
servante	Dumb-waiter.
siège	Seat, bench, chair.
siège de paille	Chair with straw seat.
singerie	A composition incorporating monkeys.
sofa	Couch.
table à coiffeuse	Dressing table. See *poudreuse*.
table à écran	Table fitted with a screen panel.
table à écrire	Writing table.
table à feu	Fireside table.
table à jeu	Gaming table.
table à jeu pliant	Gaming table with folding top.
table à ouvrage	Work table.
table à rafraîchissoir	Dumb waiter with metal lined recess for cooling bottles.
table à rallonge	Telescopic table.

Commode. Marquetry of various woods with gilt-brass mounts and marble top. Made for the apartments of Madame Adelaide, aunt of Louis XVI, at the chateau of Marly. French; about 1774. Bequeathed by Mrs. L. Stephens.

*Secretaire.   Mahogany with gilt-bronze mounts.   Attributed to
Bernard Molitor. French; about 1780. Given by Sir Chester Beatty,
F.S.A., U.D., D.Sc.*

Chair. Mahogany, inlaid with boxwood paterae. The splat is very similar to a design in Hepplewhite's Guide. (1788). Given by Mrs. A. R. Hatley.

Armchair. Mahogany with gilt-brace mounts. French; early 19th century. Bequeathed by the Condesa de Valencia de Don Juan.

Bureau Bookcase

The Cabinet-Maker and Upholsterer's Guide, 1788—George Hepplewhite]

A Sheraton inlaid half-circular side table

A Sheraton inlaid satinwood commode

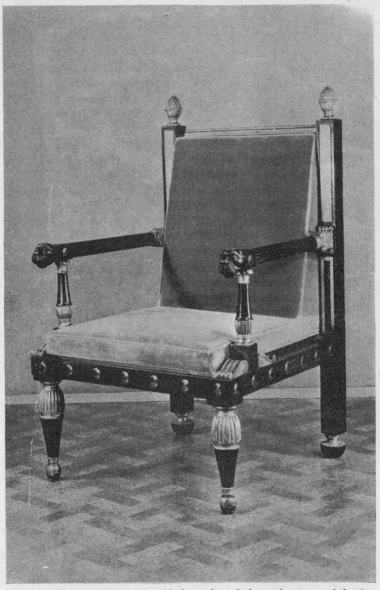

Armchair. Grained and gilded, with upholstered seat and back. One of a pair. Based on a design by Thomas Hope in Household Furniture, 1807.

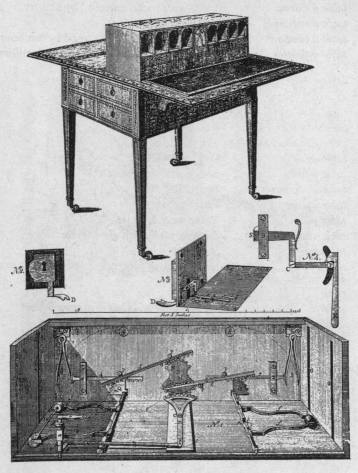

A Harlequin Pembroke table

table à rideau	Table with recess enclosed by shutter.
table à rognon	Kidney-shaped table.
table à tambour	Table with cupboard enclosed by tambour.
table à tirettes	Table with recesses enclosed by sliding panels.
table à trictrac	Backgammon table
table à tronchin	Drawing table with raised top.
table à volets	Table with drop leaves.
table ambulante	Easily portable table.
table de cabaret	Tea or coffee table.
table de lit	Bedside table.
table de nuit	Bedside table or stand.
table de trumeau	Pier table.
table liseuse	Reading table.
table pliant	Table with drop leaves.
table-vitrine	Display table with glass frieze.
tabouret	Stool.
tête-à-tête	Small settee for two persons facing inwards.
tiroir	Drawer.
toilette	Dressing table. *Coiffeuse, poudreuse*
torchere	Candleabrum. Tall Candlestands.
travailleuse	Workstand.
tricoteuse	Knitting table.
trictrac	Backgammon.
trumeau	Pier, pier mirror.
turquoise	Sofa with back and sides designed to fit in an alcove.
veilleuse	Night light.
Vernis Martin	A varnish invented by the Martin brothers who in 1730 were granted a monopoly for all kinds of lacquer work. Vernis Martin was used for furniture panels on which were painted pictures by Lancret, Boucher, etc.
vide-poche	Table which as its name implies was used to take the contents of men's pockets when emptied at night.
vitrine	Display cabinet, usually a china cabinet richly adorned with ormolu mounts.

voyeuse   Conversation chair, with shaped seat
                            narrowing towards the back and padded
                            top rail to back of chair, the user sat
                            astride and rested his arms on the padded
                            top rail.

FURNITURE

A Glossary of Terms

Aaron's Rod—A straight moulding of rounded section from which leafage or scrollwork appears to emerge; in art, a straight rod with serpent entwined around it.

Acanthus—The name given by the Greeks and Romans to certain plants, the beautiful leaves of which led to their artistic application; they are often seen in the capitals of columns of the Corinthian and Composite Orders of Architecture and in the carvings of period furniture, etc. (*See illustration.*)

Acanthus Swags—Small carved rosettes or paterae usually oval or round, embodying the famous acanthus leaves; often used in the decoration of Adam and Sheraton furniture. (*See Patera.*)

A la Grecque—*See Greek Fret.*

Ambry—A small enclosed cupboard used in churches for holding alms before distribution, or ecclesiastical utensils such as chalices, etc. A niche in a church wall enclosed by a door. (*See Armoire.*)

Amorini—Infant Cupid figures—a motif used in 17th and late 18th century—often seen in Italian art of the 16th century. (*See Putti.*)

Anthemion—The Grecian honeysuckle, a favourite form of decoration for carved and inlay work; it was sometimes employed in late Chippendale, Adam and Sheraton furniture.

Applied Mouldings—A 17th-century decoration, called also Jacobean ornament; mouldings fixed to furniture to give the appearance of panelling.

Appliqué—A design put on, or applied, such as fret designs glued to a flat surface on furniture, or patterns of a second material sewn on textiles.

Apron Piece—The valence extension piece between the legs of the seat-framing of a chair; the base between the feet of a cabinet. Also styled **Skirting Piece.**

Aquila—A reading desk or lectern (*q.v.*) used in churches, usually in the form of an eagle.

Arabesque—A style of ornamentation favoured among the Arabians, which excludes animal forms and consists of intertwined foliage and plants and geometrical figures.

Ark—The name sometimes given to a large coffer or dower chest.

Armillary Sphere—A revolving globe fixed in a framing, ringed to represent the starry heavens; sometimes composed of a series of hoops or rings only. (*See Celestial Sphere.*)

Armoire—The name usually given to a large cupboard or wardrobe of French design, often with carved panels representing flowers and trophies. (*See Ambry.*)

Astragal—A beading fixed to the extreme edge of one of a pair of doors. The glazing bars in the door of a bookcase or cabinet made after about 1750.

Backgammon—A game of considerable antiquity in which circular discs or men and dice are used; it was played on tables and folding boards with twelve points specially made for the purpose.

Back-stool—Originally in the early 17th century, a chair with back but without arms, developing from the stool, and allowing for greater comfort. Also used in the 18th century to describe an upholstered single chair.

Bacon Cupboard—Cupboard for holding bacon, sometimes forming the back of a settle. Found in farmhouses at the end of the 17th century.

Bagatelle—A game somewhat resembling billiards, played on a table about 7 ft. in length with a semi-circular end in which are nine numbered depressions to take the balls.

Bail Handles—Drop handles depending from knobs fixed to back plates, used on drawers, cupboards and the like. Iron handles of this sort are very old.

Ball-Flower—A globular flower-shaped ornament, consisting of a ball held in position by three petals. Often employed as an enrichment in mouldings. (*See illustration.*)

Ball Foot—A turned foot round in form. Also **Claw and Ball Foot,** the latter intended to represent a dragon's foot, with jewel in setting; introduced from Holland at the end of the 17th century.

Ball-Frame—A term used to describe the turned framing of chairs, tables, etc., when in the shape of a succession of balls.

Baluster—A turned pillar, may be vase-shaped, twisted or tapered, etc.

Banding—A broad band of coloured inlay contrasting with the surrounding surface.

Banner screen—Very fashionable in the 19th century, having tapestry or needlework forming a banner which was on a pole on tripod legs.

Bar Back—Hepplewhite's term for an open shield-back sofa.

Barber's Chair—A corner armchair having a head rest from the centre portion of the back.

Baroque—A word deriving from the Spanish " barucca ", a deformed pearl. A style which originated in Italy and dominated European taste in the 17th century.

Basset Table—A table made for the game of basset, seating five players; dating from the period of Queen Anne.

Beaconsfield Wardrobe—A style of wardrobe, half of which is fitted with a hat cupboard, a recess and drawers, and the other half as a hanging compartment.

Beehive Chair—A variety of chair, usually made of wicker, with tall enclosed back and sides, resembling half a bee-skip.

Bell Flower—Carved ornamentation on furniture in the form of a bell-shaped flower and/or catkin, used as a chain or pendant.

Bellows—An apparatus for producing currents of air.

Bench—Usually a church seat or pew; any similar seat.

Bergère Chair—A French upholstered easy chair with covered-in arms, often seen with cane panels.

Bevel—A slant or inclination of a surface, as on the edge of mirrors. The date of a mirror may be roughly deduced from the depth of the bevel.

Bible Box—An antique box with a lid, usually made of oak, with incised designs, and sometimes mounted on a stand.

Bidet—A small shaped bath of ware or metal.

Block Foot—A foot to chair or table legs shaped as a cube. When the foot tapers, it is called **Taper Foot, Therm Foot** or **Spade Foot.**

Boasting or Bosting—A rough form of carving.

Boll—A bubble; the name given to any knob-like protuberance fitted to furniture, etc.

Bombé—A term applied to articles of French furniture, particularly commodes, which swell or bulge out at the front and sides.

Bonheur-du-Jour—The French name for a particular style of writing table, popular about 1760; it usually consisted of a small, elegantly shaped table having a drawer with an adjustable writing slope; the upper and back section was made up separately and attached, and comprised an open centre part with shelf, on either side of which was a vertical division for books and a cupboard with shelf and door; three drawers, covering the whole width, were fitted under.

Boss—A raised ornament or stud covering intersections of mouldings, etc., succeeded by the patera.

Bottle-End Glazing—Glazing of doors, etc., with a "blob" in or near the centre of each pane.

Boulle—A process of marquetry (*q.v.*) perfected by André Charles Boulle during the reign of Louis XIV of France. The articles of furniture were usually made of oak or ebony and their surfaces covered with tortoiseshell in which were inlaid the designs in brass and sometimes silver, often chased as a further embellishment. The wood beneath the tortoiseshell was sometimes coloured red, green, etc., to give a heightened effect. To avoid waste in materials the same design was cut out of an equal number of sheets of tortoisehell and vice versa, the former being called boulle or première-partie, and the design having a predominance of brass being called counter-boulle or contre-partie.

Bow-Fronted—A term applied to an article of furniture having a curved front.

Bow-Top—The top rail of a chair having an unbroken curve between the uprights.

Box Bed—A bed which folds against the wall when not in use. Formerly common in Scotland.

Box Settle—A box or chest with a hinged (generally padded) lid forming the seat.

Bracket—A right-angled support for a shelf or similar object fastened to a wall; a fitting fastened to and projecting from a wall. The double-pointed head-dress worn by women in the 17th century.

Bracket Foot—A foot extending each way from the corner of the base of a piece of furniture, sometimes richly ornamented. If the foot is longer than its height. it is usually English; if shorter, with a concave curve, French.

Breakfront—A name often given to bookcases, sideboards, etc., having a vertical part or parts projecting from the main structure.

Breakfast Table—A table made by Chippendale of an elegant type on four legs, often with pierced gallery.

Broken Pediment—A pediment with the mouldings broken at the apex for ornamental purposes.

Buffet—An antique sideboard or dinner-wagon, used for serving or storing food; made in various shapes often somewhat resembling a court cupboard.

Buffet or Boffet Chair—A three-legged triangular chair of Scandinavian origin, with much turned work; mainly 16th century.

Bulbous—Bulblike in shape. The term is often used to describe the large bulb-shaped legs much employed in Elizabethan furniture. (*See illustration.*)

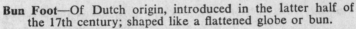

Bun Foot—Of Dutch origin, introduced in the latter half of the 17th century; shaped like a flattened globe or bun.

Bureau—An enclosed writing cabinet fitted with fall front, which, when let down, forms a writing table; it is usually provided with drawers under.

Burnishing—The process which gives carved woodwork the look of modelling, introduced about 1720; it consists of rounding and smoothing the carvings.

Burrs—Rounded knots or irregular growths in trees, giving a beautiful figure in cut timbers, as in burr-walnut, etc.

Butter Cupboard—An oak Jacobean cupboard, perforated for ventilation at both sides and in front.

Button—A fastening for a cupboard door, etc., consisting of a small piece of wood or metal secured by a screw in its centre which allows it to revolve. (*See Turnbuckle.*)

Cabochon—A polished, uncut stone of rounded form. The term is also applied to an ornamental motif of oval, rounded shape, usually surrounded by scrolled leaves, sometimes seen ornamenting the knees of cabriole legs.

Cabriole leg—A chair or table leg curving outward at the knee and inwards towards the foot in an elongated "S" shape. A form frequently used in the first half of the 18th century. (*See illustration.*)

Cage Work—A term sometimes used to describe any kind of work that resembles a cage, as certain pierced brass work.

Camel-back Chair—The original name of the type of chair now known as shield-back.

Canapé—A seat or sofa having a back, large enough to accommodate several people.

Canapé à confidents—A French term for a small settee in which the ends curve inwards in an embracing manner.

Canopy—An overhanging covering, as fixed over a bed.

Canopy Chair—A chair of State (15th and 16th centuries) with canopy over and carved in Gothic fashion. Also called **Dossier.**

Canted—Parts of furniture, etc., described as canted have an inclination from the level; a sloping or tilted position; where the corners of a square are cut off.

Canteen—A cabinet or chest in which wine, spirits and drinking vessels are kept; also for containing complete sets of cutlery and table utensils.

Canterbury—A dwarf stand with divisions, to hold music, or a kind of two-tier table with rails and divisions, called a "supper Canterbury".

Caqueteuse—A 16th-century type of chair, with narrow back and spreading arms.

Carlton House Table—A "D"-shaped writing table containing drawers in the straight front, the top surrounded by a tier of small drawers and crowned with a brass rail. A type popular between 1790 and 1820 and said to have been provided for the Prince Regent at Carlton House.

Cartonnier or Cartonnière—A cabinet for use in keeping or filing papers, often fitted with numerous small drawers; a bureau.

Carton-Pierre—A kind of papier mâché or paste-board and stucco composition, made to represent stone, etc.; it was much used for festoon work on furniture. It consists of paper pulp mixed with glue and whitening with a little plaster-of-Paris added.

Cartouche—A scroll and carvings somewhat resembling the end of a ribbon or strap terminating in a graceful curve, the name is also given to a tablet made for an inscription, the edges or corners of which are folded round.

Caryatid or Caryatide—Carved female figures, often in long robes, used in furniture-making and architecture in the place of columns and pilasters; were much employed in Elizabethan furniture. Male figures are called Atlantes.

One of a pair of armchairs of carved beech, painted white and partly gilded, bearing the monogram of Marie-Antoinette. Made in the Séné workshop for Marie-Antoinette's apartments in the Palace of St. Cloud and delivered in 1788. Given by Sir Chester Beatty, F.S.A., LL.D., D.Sc.

Chair. Carved mahogany. The back based on a plate in Sheraton's Drawing Book (1791–94). Given by Mr. Eric Browett in memory of his wife.

Armchair. Satinwood, painted in colours. Probably made by Seddon, Sons and Shackleton. English; about 1790. Given by Mrs. Simon Green.

Claw-table. Carved mahogany. English; third quarter of 18th century. Given by Brigadier W. E. Clark, C.M.G., D.S.O., D.L., through the National Art-Collections Fund.

*Armchair.   Carved mahogany with the Prince of Wales' feathers:
a motif found in Hepplewhite's Guide (1788).*

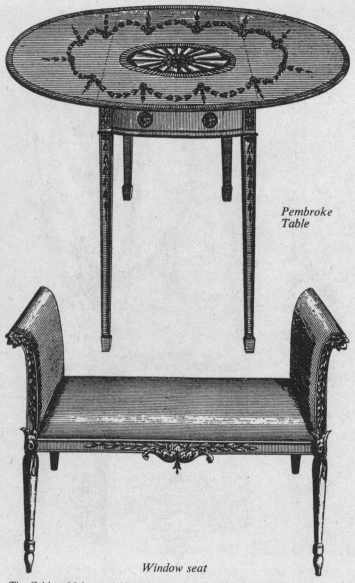

*Pembroke
Table*

Window seat

The Cabinet-Maker and Upholsterer's Guide, 1788—George Hepplewhite]

Pier glass frame

The Gentleman and Cabinet Maker's Director, 1754—Thomas Chippendale]

Firescreen. Carved wood and gilt gesso with panel of tent stitch embroidery. From Bretby Hall, Derbyshire; said to have been made for Philip, 2nd Earl of Chesterfield. English; first quarter of 18th Century. Given by Brigadier W. E. Clark, C.M.G., D.S.O., D.L., through the National Art-Collections Fund.

Casket—A small box or chest often made of precious metals, and chiefly used for jewellery and trinkets.

Cassone—An Italian name for a bridal chest or coffer; the designs are usually very ornate, being richly carved in alta-relievo, and the chests are usually of sarcophagus shape. **Caisson**—The French name for a similar article. **Cassette**—A strong box or coffer usually bound with bands of metal.

Castor—A small wheel on a swivel attached to the legs of furniture.

Causeuse—French term for a small settee.

Celestial Sphere—A revolving globe on which is represented the constellations and other heavenly bodies. (*See Terrestrial Globe.*)

Cellaret or Wine Cooler—An article of furniture in use before sideboards were introduced, for holding wine, etc., usually seen with bottle divisions lined with zinc.

Chair Bed—A kind of lightly constructed iron bedstead which folds into a chair.

Chaise Longue—A kind of elongated seat or couch, usually with only one end and no back. A long chair. It was sometimes made in three parts, a stool forming the centre section between two chairs. (*See Péché Mortel.*)

Chamfer—A bevelled edge; a groove or a channel.

Chasing—A technique used by the metal worker in which the rough surface of a cast bronze or of wrought silver is worked over to sharpen the detail of the ornament. Metal is not removed from the object by the process.

Chenet—An andiron (*q.v.*) or fire-dog of French origin.

Chequer Work or Checker—A pattern of alternating squares of different colours; common in inlay work.

Cherub—A celestial spirit represented as a winged human head (usually a child's).

Chesterfield—A large upholstered settee.

Cheval Glass—A large swing robing mirror mounted on a frame for standing on the floor. **Cheval**—A horse, hence a support or frame. Sometimes called a Psyche mirror.

Chiffonier—A small sideboard usually but not necessarily of simple design, with drawers and cupboards under; a high chest of drawers, often with a mirror.

Chip Carving—Frequently met with in early 17th-century furniture; the term is generic to rough types of carving, as amongst primitive peoples.

Clap Table—The 18th-century term for what is now styled a pier or console table.

Claw-and-Ball Foot—(*See Ball Foot.*) Representing a bird or animal's claw clutching a ball. *c.* 1720.

Claw Table—A small table with circular shaped top and a tripod or claw stand.

Close Caned—A term used to describe cane seats and panels in furniture, when no openings are left in the pattern.

Club Foot—A plain gradually tapering leg with hoof-shaped foot; the foot is sometimes called "Colt's Foot".

Cluster Column—A column formed of several smaller columns, either built up separately or carved to give that effect.

Cock Beading—A bead made to project beyond a surface.

Coffer—A strong chest or trunk for storing valuables.

Coffin Stools—Usually made of oak or elm with rectangular tops about 18 in. long, mounted on sturdy legs with stretcher rails.

Coffre-Fort—An old strong-box, often richly carved and decorated, in which valuables are kept.

Commode—An ornamental chest of drawers often of the bombé shape, and usually enriched with marquetry panels and ormolu mounts. From the 19th century also used to describe a close-stool.

Composition—Whitening, resin and size mixed and cast in moulds for redecoration of ceilings, etc., or for giving the effect of carving on wooden panels; introduced in the second half of the 18th century.

Concave—The term applied to a surface which is inclined to internal roundness, as that of a basin. **Convex**—The corresponding term applied to a surface inclined to external roundness, as opposed to concave.

Concertina Frame—A term sometimes used to describe card tables when the two rear legs pull out concertina-wise as a support for the folding flap.

Confidente—An upholstered settee having seats at each end outside the arms.

Confiture or Comfiture—Any kind of receptacle for holding sweetmeats or confections.

Console Table—Made in the form of a bracket, the back of which is fastened to a wall, the front being supported by one or two scroll-shaped or figure legs (consoles); are usually seen with marble tops and carved gilt frames.

Coquillage (French)—Literally " shell-fish "; used to describe a shell pattern in the ornamentation of frames and mirrors, with additions of birds, flowers, masks, etc., common in French furniture.

Corbeil—An ornamentation consisting of a basket of flowers.

Cordoned—A term used to describe an article having projecting bands to represent a cordon.

Corner Chair—A square-seated chair with a seat fixed diagonally so that one of the corners is at the front.

Corner Cupboards—Corner cupboards became fashionable in the 18th century. They were enclosed by either panelled or astragal glazed panel doors, often made as hanging cupboards.

Cornice—A projecting moulding at the top of a piece of furniture or of a wall or column.

Cornucopia—The Horn of Plenty, usually placed in the hands of emblematical figures, who are represented as pouring from it an abundance of fruit and corn. Sofas with backs and scroll work resembling a cornucopia were made in England early in the 19th century.

Couch—A long settee with supports at the back and at one or both ends.

Counter Boulle—*See Boulle.*

Counter Pool—A small dished cavity sunk in the tops of card tables, to hold counters and money.

Court Cupboard—A stand with three open tiers, supported at the back by plain posts and at the front by bulbous columns. The upper part sometimes contained a recessed cupboard with canted sides. Common from the early 16th to the late 17th centuries.

Credence Table—A small table on which bread and wine are laid before being consecrated; a buffet of early Tudor days on which the meats and drinks were placed and tasted before being served; a cabinet for the display of silver and plate.

Crenate—An edge having rounded projections.

Cresting—An ornamental carving on the top rail of a chair, etc., common in the Restoration period, when it frequently represented a crown and cherubs.

Crib—A child's sleeping cot.

Cricket—A Scottish term for a low stool.

Cricket Table—A Jacobean table on a triangular frame, with three straight legs; the top may be triangular, round, or polygonal.

Crinoline Stretcher—A semi-circular stretcher found on Windsor chairs, attached to the front legs and supported by a short arm from each hind leg.

Cromwellian Chair—A chair popular at the time of the Commonwealth, with seat and low back in leather.

Cross Rail—A horizontal bar connecting uprights of a chair back.

C-Scroll—A characteristic rococo (*q.v.*) motif, often used asymmetrically, in conjunction with flowers, etc., on carved girandoles (*q.v.*), mirror frames, etc. or embossed on silver.

Cup-Turned—A turned tapering leg with a cup-like prominence; 17th- and 18th-century furniture often has this form of leg.

Curio Table—A small table with box top having glazed sides and lid, for displaying bric-à-brac, etc.

Curtain Screen—A skeleton-framed screen, the panels of which are formed by detachable curtains.

Curule—A stool used by high Roman dignitaries, in appearance like a camp stool with curved legs which are often richly ornamented; copied in Empire period furniture.

Cylinder-Fall—The curved solid wood sliding top fitted to writing tables.

Cypress Chests—Chests for clothing or tapestry (early Renaissance), made of cypress wood to resist moth and worm.

Davenport—A small ornamental writing desk with sloping box top and drawers under, which usually pull out from one or both sides.

Day-Bed—A forerunner of the sofa; it had an adjustable head and was frequently richly carved; Eastern in origin; it was common in the Restoration period; a Chaise longue.

Deck Chair—A chair in common use; originally intended for use on the decks of ships. It consists of a canvas hammock on a wooden frame, which can be folded flat when not in use.

Dentil or Dentel—An ornamentation in the shape of a tooth, usually represented by small oblong blocks alternating with an equal space. **Denticulated** (Moulding) with dentils.

Derbyshire Chair—A 17th-century chair, Jacobean in style with straight uprights topped with inward scrolls, the back in open-arcade form, supported by cross rails.

Diaper Work or Diapering—A term used to describe a style of decoration or carving representing small flowers, leaves, arabesques, or geometrical patterns, as upon cloth or linen, in a small closely repeated design. (*See illustration.*)

Dinner Wagon—A table of several tiers, moving on wheels, for use in serving meals.

Dished—The cavities sunk in the tops of card tables to hold counters and money. Sometimes called "counter pools".

Dish Top Table—A table with circular top, having its edge or rim turned up, popular in the 18th century.

Divan—An Eastern type of sofa, upholstered, but without back, for standing against a wall. A bed without head- and foot-boards.

Dole or Bread Cupboard—The name given to old cupboards with carved or fretted panels, or made up with turned spindles, used in monasteries for containing the dole bread.

Double Chair or Two-Back Chair—An open-back settee for two persons; French in origin, it became very popular in the early Queen Anne period.

Dovetail—A mode of fastening wood together by fitting pieces shaped like a wedge, or dove's tail spread out, into corresponding cavities.

Dowel—A pin of wood or iron used for joining two pieces of wood together in place of screws or nails; the method is extensively employed in making furniture.

Dower Chest—A large chest, usually made of oak, having plain, incised or inlaid panels and lid, and sometimes fitted with one or two drawers; supposed to hold the portion of a wife or widow.

Draught Chair—A winged chair to keep off draughts. In Tudor times it was made of wood only, but later was upholstered.

Draw or Withdrawing Table—An Elizabethan or Jacobean table having two leaves which together form the size of the top. When these are pulled out, one from either end, the top sinks to the level of the leaves, thus making a table twice the size of the original.

Dresser—A kitchen fitment, or a sideboard having a tall back and shelves.

Dressing Table—A piece of furniture usually forming part of a bedroom suite and comprising a table with drawers and swing mirror. **Dressing Chest**—A chest of drawers with swing mirror similarly used.

Drop-Front or Fall Front—The lid of a desk which, when open and resting on slides, forms a surface for writing. (*See also Cylinder and Tambour Fronts.*)

Drop-Ornament—An ornament depending from the under-frame of a piece of furniture.

Drunkard's Chair—An elbow chair of ordinary design, except that the proportions are unusually large. Chippendale produced specimens of this chair, which were, however, called "lover's chairs".

Duchesse—A term now applied to a dressing table with a swing glass. Sheraton and Hepplewhite used it to describe two bergère chairs fastened to a stool in the middle. (*See Péché Mortel.*)

Duet Stool—A piano stool capable of accommodating two persons.

Dumb Waiter—A circular revolving two- or three-tier dining room table on pillar and tripod support; a circular revolving stand to support dishes on a dining table. Sheraton designed some of the former with drawers.

Easel—A wooden frame, adjustable to different heights and angles; used for supporting an artist's canvas or a black-board.

Ébéniste—A French cabinet maker.

Ebonised Wood—Wood stained black to resemble ebony.

Egg and Tongue—An architectural ornament or moulding in the form of an egg alternating with a tongue, dart or anchor.

Elbow Chair—A chair of ordinary type but having elbow rests, as a carving chair in a dining-room set.

Empire Style—A rather severe and dignified style of furniture which originated in France during the first Empire. It followed classical lines and much of it was painted white or gilded, and decorated with symbols, pateræ, etc.

Encoignure—A triangular corner cupboard or cabinet; a "corner piece" of furniture.

Endive Marquetry—A fine type of "seaweed" marquetry (*q.v.*), popular in the William and Mary and Queen Anne periods.

Escallop Shell or Scallop—A flat spoon-shaped shell with regular curved indentures, often represented in the carvings of Queen Anne furniture.

Escritoire—A French cabinet or table of elegant design, with conveniences for writing and usually fitted with drawers and pigeon holes.

Escutcheon—The small shield-shaped piece of ware or metal which covers the key-hole in a door; a shield with armorial device.

Etagère—A French word used to describe open or fancy wall shelves or brackets with more than one shelf; they exist in many forms and sometimes have mirror backs; the term is also applied to small, elegant tables of two or more tiers.

Faldstool—A folding stool, the seat of which is covered in a rich material, used by a church dignitary for resting during a service; a small desk in churches in England at which the litany is sung or said.

Farthingale Chairs—Chairs of the Elizabethan and James I periods, having broad seats but no arms, to accommodate hooped dresses or farthingales; it was probably the forerunner of the lady's armless easy chair, common in suites.

Fauteuil—An armchair originally of French design, usually with open arms and upholstered seat and back and of comfortable dimensions.

Festoon—A wreath or garland of flowers or fruit, suspended so as to hang in an elliptical curve.

Fiddleback—The grain in maple and sycamore, so called because of its use in the making of violins. Having a back shaped like a fiddle.

Fiddle-String Back or Stick Back—A back of straight sticks or "fiddle strings" common on Windsor chairs.

Figure—In furniture, used to indicate the natural markings on wood.

Fillet—A flat narrow band or moulding.

Finial—A decorative top for a vertical piece of furniture such as the acorn tops on the supports of 18th-century toilet mirrors.

Flambeau—A flaming torch light or taper; the term is often used in describing articles in this form; sometimes used as a finial.

Flemish Curve—The name sometimes given to the sturdy "S" scroll much employed in furniture of the William and Mary and preceding periods, usually seen in leg and arm supports.

Floreated or Floriated—Decorated with floral ornamentations.

Flutings—The vertical grooves in a column.

Foliaged—When articles are decorated or carved with a design containing an abundance of leaves, they are said to have foliaged decorations.

Foot Stool—In Elizabethan and Jacobean times, foot stools were the usual accompaniment to a chair, later the foot stool became a luxury rather than a necessity.

Form—A long narrow seat or bench.

Four-Poster Bedstead—In Elizabethan times these were very heavy and they had much ornamental carving. By the beginning of the 18th century they became lighter and more graceful.

French Foot—A bracket foot which is concave. It is usually higher than the width of its face.

French Polish—Consists mainly of shellac dissolved in methylated spirit, with various colouring matter. It succeeded oil polish in the second part of the 19th century.

Fretwork—Perforated woodwork much used in the ornamentation of furniture, the designs being cut out with a fine, thread-like saw. **Fret Ornament**—Small fillets intersecting each other at right angles; an interlaced network.

Fuming—A method of darkening the surface of wood, especially oak, by exposing it to the fumes of ammonia in an air-tight container.

Gadroon Edges—A style of decoration often applied to the edges of silver and plated articles, furniture, etc., somewhat resembling an almond-shaped reeding or fluting.

Gallery—A miniature balustrade or railing of metal or wood around the edge of cabinets and small tables.

Games Table—A small table fashionable in the 18th century, often the top was reversible with an inlaid chess board on one side. This top slid out to reveal a Backgammon board below.

Garde du Vin—A brass-hooped tub, cellaret, or wine cooler for standing under a sideboard.

Garde-Robe—The French word for a wardrobe.

Gate-Leg Table—A table with fall leaves supported by folding legs, somewhat resembling a gate.

Gesso—A composition of parchment size and whiting applied to furniture, and, when hardened, used as a ground for carving in low relief and gilding.

Gilding—The art of ornamenting articles with gold leaf; the woodwork was primed with a chalk composition and the gold leaf was applied over a coating of size or varnish.

Gilt Furniture—Furniture overlaid with a composition of size or whiting and gilt. Fashionable in England from the last quarter of the 17th century.
(*See also Gesso.*)

Girandole—A shaped wall mirror in showy carved gilt frame fitted with candle branches; a jewelled pendant having smaller pendants. (*See illustration.*)

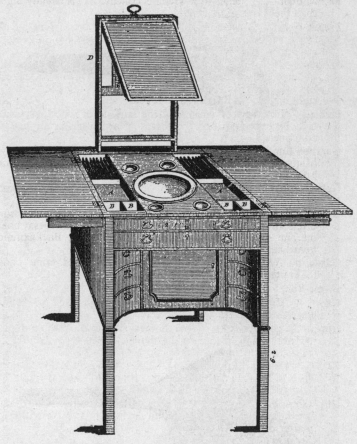

A shaving table
The Gentleman and Cabinet Maker's Director, 1754—Thomas Chippendale]

Sideboard

The Cabinet-Maker and Upholsterer's Guide, 1788—George Hepplewhile]

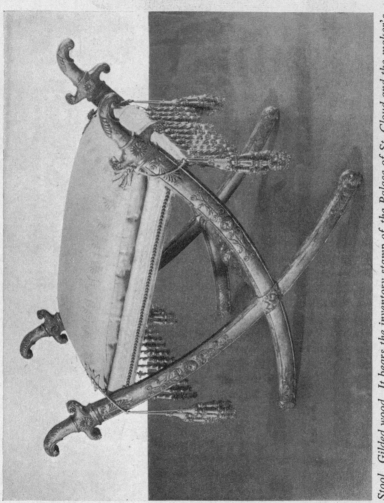

Stool. Gilded wood. It bears the inventory stamp of the Palace of St. Cloud and the maker's stamp of Jacob Desmalter et Cie. Made after 1803, presumably for the redecorations at St. Cloud under Napoleon. Original upholstery French; early 19th century. Given by Messrs. H. Blairman & Sons.

Glastonbury Chairs—A popular term for a chair with X-shaped supports and elbow arms reaching from the top of the back to the seat. Derives from an example at Wells said to have been used by the last Abbot of Glastonbury.

Gorgoneion—A mask or other representation of Medusa's head.

Gossip Chairs—Small circular or tub-shaped easy chairs. Occasionally they are joined together, facing in opposite directions. (*See Causeuse.*)

Gouty Stool—A stool of the Hepplewhite period, with an adjustable top, presumably used by gouty persons for resting their feet at a comfortable angle.

Graduating Screen—A screen in which the folds or panels successively decrease in height.

Grandfather Chair—A winged upholstered chair, developed in the Queen Anne period from the oak winged chairs of earlier date.

Greek Fret—A variety of ornamentation after the Greek fashion, similar to the well-known "key border", resembling a twisted ribbon.

Griffin—A fabled monster with the head and wings of an eagle and the body of a lion. Was much used by Adam Brothers.

Grisaille—Decorative painting in greyish tints.

Grotesque—Decoration composed of fantastic animals, caryatids (*q.v.*) and vase-like motifs, interwoven with foliage and leaf scrolls, derived from Roman mural decoration. Adopted by Renaissance artists and craftsmen and subsequently popular. Inspired some of Adam's designs for wall panels.

Guéridon—A carved gilt torchère (*q.v.*) or pedestal of French design, usually very ornate, sometimes with a figure support. (Literally, round table.) (*See illustration.*)

Handles—Furniture handles were usually of the knob, bail or drop variety. In Jacobean furniture wooden handles and rings of wrought iron were used. Brass was first used for handles during the William and Mary period. In the Queen Anne period a handle had a backplate of metal which was shaped and ornamented, later round and oval handles were made, designed to match the backplate. Sheraton often used a ring handle hanging from a lion's mouth.

Harlequin Table—A combined writing and dressing table designed by Sheraton. The top part folds over in halves and encloses a writing slope. A nest of pigeon holes is made to raise or lower itself into the table, which has a dummy drawer front, also a drawer with division and a cupboard under fitted with two tambour fronts. (*See illustration, page 86.*)

Hassock—A small hard-stuffed cushion for kneeling on in church, or for use as a foot-stool.

Herring-Bone—An inlaid banding or lining, imitating the backbone of a herring. In furniture it was peculiar to the latter part of the 17th and early 18th centuries.

High-Boy—A chest of drawers mounted on a low-boy or dressing table, fitted with a long drawer or two small drawers. Of Dutch origin—William and Mary period. When the chest of drawers is mounted on another chest of drawers of similar design, it is described as a tall-boy or double chest.

Hock-Leg—A cabriole-type leg with a broken curve on the inner side of the "knee".

Hogarth Chairs—The name sometimes given to chairs of the late Queen Anne period, the principal feature being the plain splats (contemporary with Hogarth).

Hoof-Foot—Also styled **Pied de Biche**. Seen on very ancient furniture, as that found in Egyptian tombs; introduced from France into England in the time of Louis XIV.

Horseshoe Table—A dining table shaped like a horseshoe, so as to bring guests closer together, in common use at the end of the 18th century.

Husk—The outer coat or envelope of various seeds and fruits; often represented in string carvings on furniture and in architectural decorations. A favourite design of Adam.

Hutch—Originally a chest, but in the Gothic period developed into a cupboard with doors, a forerunner of the court cupboard; if in two tiers it was called a double hutch.

Incise—To cut into; to engrave. As applied to furniture, is the art of cutting out designs with a sharp-edged knife or tool, the designs as a rule being somewhat crude and irregular.

Inlay—The art of decorating surfaces by the insertion of similar or different materials. It is one of the principal forms of enriching furniture, designs being of coloured woods, ivory or metals. The French produced a very elaborate inlay work called marquetry. Metals are often inlaid with other metals and when steel is inlaid with gold, the technique is known as damascening.

Ivory—Obtained from the tusks of elephant, walrus, etc. Extensively used as an inlay in marquetry work.

Jardinière—An ornamental pot or jar, or piece of furniture made for holding plants.

Joint, Joined, or Joyned—In Tudor and Jacobean tables, stools, etc., indicates that the parts are held together by mortise and tenon joints fixed with wooden pegs, neither metal nor glue being used.

Key Cornered—A description of rectangular panels with the corners broken into squares; when curves replace the squares they are called **Segmental-Cornered.** Popular from Adam days.

Kidney Table—A table shaped like a kidney, designed by Sheraton; frequently with tiers of drawers and knee-hole between.

Knee-holes—Introduced at the beginning of the 18th century in bureaux and writing tables.

Knurr or Knur—A knot in wood; a wooden ball.

Lace Boxes—In the 17th century boxes adorned with marquetry were popular for the keeping of lace; there are still many in existence.

Lacertine Work—A term applied to any kind of decorative work, the design of which is composed of inter-twined lizards or snakes.

Lacquer—An Oriental preparation composed of sand, fine clay, fibre grasses and gums, applied to carcase furniture, screens, etc., then allowed to harden before being blackened or coloured and polished. "Coromandel" lacquer was decorated with incised designs. Many Oriental lacquer cabinets were imported into England in the late 17th century.

Ladder Back—The name given to the backs of chairs with cross-rails arranged above each other like the rungs of a ladder.

Lamp Stand—An easily portable small table upon which to place a lamp.

Lancashire Spindle Back Chair—A chair made in Lancashire in the middle of the 18th century, with turned uprights, the back consisting of two rows of four or five vertical spindles supported by two horizontal rails and a top rail.

Landscape Mirror—The name sometimes given to old wall mirrors; they usually consist of several plates, and have a width much greater in proportion to their height. They were often fitted with candle sconces.

Laurel—The common decoration used in friezes, bands, garlands, etc., for decorative work in architecture and on furniture. Actually it is taken from the leaves of the bay tree.

Legs—In Tudor times the heavy elaborately carved bulbous legs and square legs were prevalent. In the Jacobean period, legs became lighter and baluster legs became usual. From the reign of Queen Anne until Chippendale the cabriole leg was the fashion. During the Queen Anne period the cabriole legs were carved on the knee. Chippendale adopted the cabriole leg until it went out of fashion, when he made the legs straight. Chippendale in his Chinese pieces introduced fretted legs. Adam designed legs of many shapes often decorated with chased brass work or with rams' heads and animal feet, or fluted with husk ornament. Hepplewhite legs were round or square and often fluted and generally tapered. Sheraton preferred round legs generally fitted with a castor. Empire-style legs followed classical lines, the front legs curving forwards.

Linen Fold—A late Gothic style of carving in panels, which represents a folded or pleated napkin, the folds of which run vertically. *c.* 1500. (*See illustration.*)

Linen Press—A cupboard, usually of oak and fitted with shelves, for storing bed- and table-linen. A large chest similarly used.

Lion Mask—Lions' masks and carved furred paws are commonly found on furniture dating between 1720 and 1740. Revived during Regency period.

Livery Cupboard—A Tudor cupboard enclosed by rail doors to allow ventilation; used for the storage of food.

Locker—From the 15th century the term was applied to all cupboards and chests. A cupboard, particularly for personal use.

Log Box—A box with lid for standing beside a fireplace, usually ornamental and often covered with embossed brass panels.

Loo Table—A circular table with tip-up top mounted on centre pillar and tripod support, originally designed for playing the game of loo.

Lounge—The name formerly given to a couch on which a person could recline.

Low-Boy—In America a small table with drawers made to support a chest of drawers (then becoming a **High-Boy**) or used as a dressing table. 18th century.

Love Seat—An upholstered settee made for two persons.

Malachite—A green variety of copper ore used for ornamental purposes, such as table tops. In its fine examples it can be worked up as gems.

Marbled—With a grain resembling that of marble.

Marquetry or Marqueterie—The art of inlaying or veneering elaborate designs in wood, with wood of other colours, or materials such as ivory, shell and metals. (*See Inlay.*)

Marquise Chair—The French original of the English **Love-Seat**; may be regarded as a very wide chair or a small settee.

Mask—A carved design representing a human or animal face usually grotesque; the satyr mask period was about 1740.

Misericord—The name given to an ornamental carved boss or bracket on the under side of a hinged church seat, intended to give support to a worshipper when standing.

Mitre Joint—A joint in which each of the two edges are cut at an angle of 45 degrees (as in a picture frame).

Monk's Bench—A settle in which the back is made to fold over and rest on the arms to form a table; usually seen in carved oak.

Mauresque—An ornament of Moorish derivation, composed only of abstract motifs.

Mortise—A term used in carpentry to denote a hole or slot cut in a piece of wood to receive the end of another piece, called a tenon.

Mother-of-Pearl—The nacreous internal layer of the shells of certain molluscs; largely used as inlay on furniture in the 17th century. There are known to be several suites in oriental palaces entirely overlaid with it.

Moulding—Formed by or in a mould. An ornamental edging on a picture frame or piece of furniture. In architecture, raised above or sunk below the surface of a wall; cornices, jambs, lintels, etc.

Mule Chest—A chest standing on a plinth in which there are sometimes three or four drawers.

Nicking or Notching—Frequently used as an ornament on 17th-century oak furniture.

Nonsuch Chests—Chests dating from the second half of the 16th century, decorated with an inlaid design representing an imaginary building resembling Henry VIII's Palace of Nonsuch. Many of such chests were of German origin.

Nulling—A small projection or recession from the surface in wood carving, usually successions of bosses or beads; when worked along the edge of a flat surface is called also **Gadroon** (*q.v.*).

Nursing Chair—A rather broad low-seated chair, usually made of birch or similar wood with cane-panelled seat and back.

Occasional Table—A light and easily portable table, originating in the 18th century and used for many purposes.

Oil Polish—An old process applied to furniture. The surface was first rubbed down with a brick, linseed oil was then applied and a final polish was given with beeswax and turpentine. The fine surfaces that resulted were mainly due to the exertions of the polisher. Later a mixture of oil and varnish was used.

Onion Foot—A foot turned to resemble that vegetable, once common on furniture; it was but little used after the William and Mary period.

Ormolu—A variety of brass usually made up of 75 parts of copper and 25 parts of zinc. The colour resembles gold more than ordinary brass. Ormolu was largely used for making ornamental decorations for furniture, and was often lacquered to prevent tarnishing. (Literally, ground gold.)

Ottoman—An upholstered box or seat.

Overlay—A method of ornamenting by laying some decorative material over a plain object.

Overmantel—An ornamental structure or mirror placed over a mantelpiece.

Oviform—Having the shape of an egg; a term often applied to vases, etc., which are of egg shape. **Ovate and Ovoid**—Egg-shaped.

Oxford Frame or Corner—A picture or other frame in which the members extend outwards at the corners as in a cross and are not mitred.

Oystershell—A term used to describe veneer work which is made up of a series of pieces cut traversely from saplings, the ring-like grain somewhat resembling an oyster shell.

Panel—A flat surface with raised or sunk margins, or with a surrounding frame; used in furniture as applied mouldings in the latter part of the Jacobean period; panels are formed of wood, cane, marquetry, needlework, upholstery, etc., or are painted; celebrated panel ornamentors were Angelica Kaufmann, Cipriani, Pergolesi, etc., all of the 18th century.

Paper Scroll—The name given to the scroll on the top rails of chairs; also styled spiral whorl, S-scroll, S-volute, conical or helicoidal volute; most favoured in the 18th century.

Papier-Mâché—A material produced by moulding pulped paper into shape, used for making small articles, such as boxes and trays; it is usually varnished and sometimes inlaid with mother-of-pearl. Used extensively in England in the middle of the 18th century.

Parquetry—Inlaid woodwork for floors, composed of blocks of wood laid in geometrical regularity; in finer kinds of work veneer is used and in this form is applied to furniture.

Patera—A round dish with foliaged design copies of which were carved by the Romans in their ceilings. **Paterae.** The name given to small carved rosettes usually of round or oval shape, which cover small holes or joints in furniture. (*See illustration.*)

Patina—The colour and bloom on the surface of furniture, being the result of age, wear and polishing; also the green film on old bronze.

Péché Mortel—The name given by the French to an upholstered couch, the end or ends of which resemble a fauteuil; when taken apart it forms separately a chair, or chairs, and the centre part a stool. (*See Chaise Longue.*)

Pedestal Sideboard—The name given to a sideboard, the top part of which is supported at the ends by fitted pedestals or cupboards.

Pediment—A decorative feature above the cornice of a cabinet or bookcase. There are many variations such as scroll, swan-neck or broken pediment.

Pembroke Table—A table fitted with two hinged flaps, each of about the same width as the top, and a drawer. (*See illustration, page* 100.)

Penthouse—The name sometimes given to the lids of antique boxes when they have a slope on one side only, such as the lid of a desk.

Picture-Board Dummy—Representation generally of wood, sometimes canvas, of a human figure. The dummies are painted in oils and cut out and made to stand up giving the impression of a living person.

Picture Mirror—18th-century mirrors with a painted picture in the upper half of the frame.

Pie Crust Top—The tops of certain mid 18th-century tables were sunk and the edge carved in such a way as to resemble the edge of a pie crust. (*See Dish Top.*) (*See illustration.*)

Pied de Biche—(*See Hoof-foot.*)

Pier-Glass—A large mural mirror, which should, strictly speaking, be fixed between two windows or openings. (*See illustration, page* 101.) **Pier-Table.** A table similarly fixed; a console table (*q.v.*).

Pietra-Dura—Florentine mosaic work, often seen decorating the tops of Italian and French tables; also applied to panels in the form of raised fruit and flowers, made up of coloured marbles.

Pigeon-Hole—One of the small recesses forming the interior fitments of a desk, used for storing papers.

Plateau—A flat surface; as applied to furniture represents the broad undershelf of tables, bases of toilet mirrors, etc., the French also apply the word to a large ornamental table dish.

Pole Screen—A small shaped screen, often with needlework or picture panels, mounted on a tall pole stand. (*See illustration, page* 102.)

Poppyhead—A plain or carved ornamentation, often in the shape of the fleur-de-lys, seen as a finial on the ends of pews and benches.

Pot Board—The shelf just above the floor underneath a dresser.

Pouch Table—Commonly known as a lady's work table, and described by Sheraton in his book of designs as a " pouch table". It usually consists of a small table fitted with a drawer and a well or pouch of fabric suspended from it.

Pouffe Ottoman—A large floor cushion covered in tapestry or other material.

Première Partie—Boulle marquetry of tortoiseshell and metal in which the former predominates, forming the groundwork.

Press—A cupboard or armoire in which clothes and linen were stored; dates from Norman times or earlier.

Prie-Dieu Chair—A low-seated chair with a tall back, used for praying; the back slightly projects on either side at the top to form a rest for the elbows. The term is also applied to desks used in a similar way.

Prince of Wales' Feathers—The badge of the Prince of Wales which comprises three ostrich feathers rising from a crown.

Quartette Tables—Nests of small tables, designed and named by Sheraton. The tables are of light make and fit one under the other.

Rake—An inclination, slope or slant (as in a chair back) from the perpendicular.

Rance—A cross rail between the legs of a chair.

Reading Stand or Reading Desk—Hepplewhite made these for private libraries, somewhat on the lines of those used in churches, but lighter; they were developed by 18th-century craftsmen.

Reeded—A form of decoration much used on furniture, where the surface is raised in thin narrow ridges arranged side by side.

Refectory Table—A table used in a refectory or dining hall of a monastery or college; the term is often applied to any long table.

Reflex Mirrors—Hinged side mirrors fitted to dressing-tables or dressing-chests.

Regency Style—The furniture style in vogue at the time of the regency of George, Prince of Wales, 1810-20.

Restoration Chair—A high-backed cane panelled chair on spiral turned legs and uprights, with carving crown supported by cherub and acanthus leaves.

Riband Back, Ribbon, or Ribband—Chair backs with splats made to represent interlaced ribbon, a form much used by Chippendale.

Riesener Work—An elaborate marquetry introduced by Riesener and much employed in Louis XV and Louis XVI furniture, in which the designs of musical instruments and other objects are represented in bold outline.

Robing Mirror—A full-length mirror as may be seen fixed to walls, or to the doors of wardrobes, etc.

Rococo—From the French "rocaille". A style of decorative art which first developed in France at the beginning of the 18th century, and was ultimately adopted in England by the middle of the century. Lively and often witty, the style exploited an imaginative and ever-varying combination of shell- and rock-forms with foliage, flowers, "C" scrolls and flame-like motifs, linked in asymmetrical harmony.

Rouge Marble—Marble chiefly of a red colour or tint.

Roundabout Chair—A term sometimes applied to a low-backed elbow chair in which the back and arms form a semi-circle.

Roundel—Plain round or oval-shaped centres inlaid in the panels of furniture, etc., anything of a round form.

Rout Stool—A long, somewhat narrow stool, the top of which is usually upholstered but sometimes has cane panels; almost any light-framed and inexpensive seat. **Rout:** A fashionable gathering attended by a large number of people.

Rudd's Table—A table produced by Hepplewhite and others, having three drawers on one side with numerous divisions and fittings, including mirrors and a slide top.

"S" Scroll—A favourite form of arm support and decoration in the carvings of Carolean and William and Mary furniture. (*See illustration.*)

Salt Box—A wooden box usually with a sloping lid which hung in the kitchen to hold salt, sometimes with a fitted drawer to hold spice.

Saltire or Saltier—A St. Andrew's Cross; in furniture, cross-stretchers between the legs of chairs and tables; also called X-shape stretchers. Italian in origin, they were developed and made very elaborate in the time of William and Mary.

Sarcophagus—A stone coffin (originally limestone); a receptacle, usually of oblong shape tapering to a smaller size at the bottom.

Scagliola—A composition made to resemble marble, chiefly composed of powdered gypsum, alum and earthy colouring substances into which are pressed pieces of marble, the composition being rubbed down and polished with pumice stone. Much used in 18th century.

Screen—A piece of furniture intended to secure privacy, protect from draughts, hide fireplaces or shield from heat; of numerous forms and materials, sometimes very elaborate.

Scroll—A term usually applied to a form of ornamentation or article like a loosely rolled or partly rolled piece of paper when viewed from its edge or in section.

Scutcheon—(See Escutcheon.)

Seaweed Marquetry—A style of marquetry popular in the reigns of William and Mary and Anne. The designs consisted of intertwining stalks in light, close, graceful patterns, usually in panels with a centre motif. Sometimes called endive marquetry.

Secretaire—(See Escritoire.)

Sedan Chair—A covered chair for accommodating one person, carried by two men by means of poles. It was invented at Sedan and was in general use by the middle of the 17th century.

Seignurial Chair—A chair of state, used by a great noble or ecclesiastic; Gothic and Renaissance forms exist, both being very high backed, very solid, and sometimes having a canopy.

Serpentine—Resembling the windings of a snake. The term is much used in describing the fronts of furniture having a large bulge or outward curve in the centre and a smaller one at either side

Servante—A French serving-table or dinner-wagon of the Empire or Directoire Period; it usually has a marble top, supported in front by two carved wood or ormolu legs mounted on a plateau, and at the back by the framing of the mirror panel.

Settee—A long seat with arms and back, usually upholstered, capable of seating two or more persons. (*See illustration, page* 15.)

Settle—An antique bench or form with tall back and arms, capable of seating three or more persons; usually seen in carved oak and often with a box seat.

Shaving Table—A small table, the top being hinged and opening to form two small tables, also fitted with a small basin and a looking glass, and was provided with drawers. (*See illustration, page* 111.)

Shoe or Shoe-Piece—The projection on the back seat rail of a chair to receive the bottom of the splat; the disc under the foot of a chair.

Sideboard—Originally a side-table to which pedestals with cupboards were added by the Adam Brothers. The present form of sideboard with drawers, cupboards and cellaret was a development of the late 18th century.
(*See illustration, page* 112.)

Side Chairs—Sometimes called "single" chairs. Before Cromwellian times the principal members of a houschold had armchairs, the rest sitting on stools or benches without a back; thus single chairs were very uncommon before 1650.

Side Table—William Kent designed magnificent specimens which were richly carved and gilt, having marble tops. Later, the side table became an elegant piece of furniture for the Drawing Room.

Skirting Piece—(*See Apron Piece.*)

Slides—Slides for various purposes were made in the 18th century, such as brushing slides in chests of drawers, slides in bureaux for candlesticks and many other purposes.

Sofa—An upholstered day bed or couch with two ends and a back, sometimes with only one end and a partial back. First made in England in the 17th century.

Spindle—A word from the Latin spina, a thorn, indicating anything slender; common in very old furniture as a slender-turned baluster or rod, and now used largely in modern pieces.

Spinning Chair—A simple stool-shaped chair with tall narrow back, which is usually let into the seat and fastened underneath by means of a peg.

Spinning Wheel—A wheel for spinning flax, wool or cotton into threads. It dates from 1530, when it was first made at Brunswick. In the 18th century spinning was a fashionable occupation and spinning wheels became very ornamental.

Splat—The plain, pierced or carved vertical centre panel in the backs of chairs connecting the cresting rail with the seat. (*See illustration.*)

Spoon-Back—The high back of a chair, shaped to fit the back of the occupant; introduced from the Dutch in the William and Mary period, "spooning" became more pronounced in the Queen Anne period and remained in fashion until Chippendale's time.

Springs—Metal springs for seats of chairs and settees were introduced in the middle of the 18th century.

Squab Seats—Loose flat cushions covering the seats of a particular kind of chair. (*See Trafalgar Seat.*)

Standards—As applied to furniture, are the end supports of tables taking the place of legs; may often be seen in an ornamented form and are sometimes connected to each other by means of a stretcher rail or plateau.

Strapwork—An ornament largely used by Elizabethan and Jacobean carvers for panels; bands formed into designs repeated and interlaced; largely used on splats of chairs of about the Chippendale period.

Straw Marquetry—Small articles of furniture, such as boxes and looking-glass frames, were decorated with bleached and coloured straws in formal patterns and representing landscapes and figure subjects in the late 17th century.

Stretchers—The under-rails which support and connect the legs of chairs and tables; originally used as foot rests, to protect the feet from draughts and the dirty rush-strewn floors.

Stringing—The thin fine inlaid lines often employed in cabinet work.

Studs—Copper, brass, gilt-headed and other nails used for decoration of furniture; in general use throughout the 18th century.

Stuff-Over—A method of upholstering chairs by pulling the covering material over the edges and fronts of the seat rails and securing it along the bottom edges.

Stump Bedstead—A bedstead without posts to support a cornice or tester.

Sutherland Table—A small table with a narrow top (useless when shut) and two large folding leaves; when these are let down it occupies but little space.

Swag—A festoon, a chain of flowers, etc., much used by Adam.

Swell Front—A term used to describe a piece of furniture having a bulging or bombé front.

Table Chair—A form of monk's seat (*q.v.*) which forms a table when the back is lowered over the arms.

Table-du-Nuit—A bedside table.

Tabouret or Taboret—A stool of ornamental design supposed to represent a drum (Tabor). The name is often (though not very correctly) applied to Eastern coffee stools, which are usually inlaid with mother-o'-pearl and have pierced and carved panels enclosing the sides. Sometimes called Kursi.

Tall-Boy—A tall chest of drawers made in two parts, one above the other; were often fitted with a slide on which clothes could be brushed and folded. This slide is often erroneously described as being for writing purposes.

Tambour Front—A sliding front fitted to cabinets, etc., as the familiar roll-top to desks. It consists of a number of small strips of wood attached to a canvas backing.

Taper—To become gradually smaller in diameter towards one end.

Teapoy—A kind of table, the hinged top of which encloses tea caddies, etc. It is usually circular and mounted on a centre pillar and triple support. (*See illustration.*)

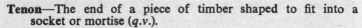

Telamones—(*See Atlantes.*)   Male figures used as caryatides (*q.v.*).

Tenon—The end of a piece of timber shaped to fit into a socket or mortise (*q.v.*).

Terminals—The extreme ends or points, as knobs, applied in much the same way as finials.

Terrestrial Globe—A revolving globe on which is represented a map of the earth. (*See Armillary Sphere.*)

Tester—The flat canopy over a four-poster bedstead. When the canopy extends over only half the bed, it is described as a "half tester".

Tier—One of a number of shelves arranged one above another. The under-shelf of a table or other piece of furniture.

Toilet Mirror—Made its appearance at the end of the 17th century. Consisted of a small mirror supported by two uprights which were generally fixed to a base, having small drawers for toilet requisites.

Torchère—The French name for tall candle stands; they are often distinguishable from tall vase stands by having a gallery rail round the top, or by the fitment of candle holders. (*See Guéridon.*)

Tortoiseshell—The back plates of a sea turtle, flattened, and, where needed, joined together by heat and pressure; a very old veneer for furniture, brought into extensive use by Boulle (Louis XIV era).

Trafalgar Seat—The name given to loose squab seats fitted to chairs.

Tray-Top Table—An 18th-century small table with a skirting round three or all four sides.

Treillage—A term sometimes used to describe articles consisting mainly of light rails and posts; a trellis work, such as might be used to support vines.

Trellis—A wire lattice-work, backed by a fabric, replaces glass in the doors of some of the smaller pieces of Regency (*q.v.*) cabinet furniture.

Trestle—A movable support for tables. Pre-Tudor tables were commonly loose boards on folding trestles; but, between Tudor and Elizabethan times, tables were made chiefly of two fixed trestles united by a strong brace; the trestle disappeared after the introduction of the heavy bulbous-legged tables of Elizabeth's time.

Tri-Darn—A Welsh variety of the court cupboard, comprising an open dresser over two-tier cupboards; when without the dresser it is styled a **Deu-Darn.**

Tripod Table—A small table fashioned in the 18th century, was made with both fixed and hinged tops. This table was popular in the time of Chippendale and afterwards. Generally it had a carved border such as pie-crust. It was supported on a centre pillar with three spreading legs, usually cabriole, with claw and ball feet.

Truckle-Bed—A low bed which can be pushed under another when not in use; in the 18th century castors were added; it was then called a **Trundle Bed.**

Tunbridge Ware—A veneer cut from the ends of small rods of wood, differing in colour, and arranged to form a pattern; made at Tunbridge Wells.

Turnbuckle—A catch for a cupboard door, turning on a central screw. A similar catch on the inside of a door turned by a knob on the outside. (*See Button.*)

Twist—A spiral turning; seen on furniture of the 17th and early 18th centuries.

Upholstery—A branch of the furniture trade which deals with the stuffing or padding and covering of furniture.

Urn (furniture)—A large wooden vessel of vase shape which stood on each pedestal of a side table; several characteristic Adam urns are well known. The name given to any large vase or vessel of rounded or uniform shape.

Urn Stands—Small tables introduced in the mid-18th century upon which stood silver or Sheffield Plate urns. They generally had a pull-out slide to hold the teapot.

Valance—The drapery which hangs down over the top of window curtains or round a bedstead, either from the tester or the mattress.

Veneering—An economical process employed in making furniture, in which a very thin layer of choice wood is glued to the surface of a cheaper kind, giving the article the appearance of being made entirely of the more expensive variety.

Vernis Martin (literally "Martin varnish"). In the early 18th century four brothers Martin were well-known Paris coach- and sedan-chair painters; the third brother (Simon Etienne)

invented a remarkably lustrous varnish, and the brothers
were granted in 1730 a monopoly for all kinds of lacquer
work; three factories were established and, in 1748, these
were by royal decree established as a "Manufacture
Nationale"; Vernis Martin was used for furniture panels,
on which pictures were often painted by Lancret, Boucher,
etc.

Verre Eglomise—A glass border decorated in
the arabesque style, found on some wall
mirrors, particularly of the Anne and
William and Mary periods. It is placed
between the mirror plate and the frame,
following its shape. (*See illustration.*)

Vitrine—An elaborate variety of French china
cabinet usually richly adorned with metal
(ormolu) mounts, the upper parts of the
sides and door being glazed and the lower
parts often decorated with Vernis Martin
panels.

Wardrobe—18th-century wardrobes were usually constructed
with a base of two long and two short drawers, the upper
part being fitted with shelves, enclosed by two solid doors.
Sometimes wardrobes were built in the wall-panelling,
while Sheraton's "Cabinet-Maker's and Upholsterer's Drawing Book" included a design for a break-front wardrobe,
which allowed for hanging space in the wings.

Warming Pan—A shallow brass or copper pan with lid, attached
to a long handle. It was filled with live coals and used
for bed-warming.

Washstand—The first stands for bedroom use date from the
mid-18th century. Hepplewhite and Sheraton included
designs for washstands in their publications.

Wax Polishing—A method of polishing furniture and floors
with beeswax thinned with turpentine.

Wellington Chest—A tall narrow chest of drawers for specimens, often 10 or 12 in number, all of which can be
secured by a hinged flap at the side.

Welsh Dresser—A side table with pot-board and cupboard or
drawers below, and a range of shelves above.

Whatnot—An article of furniture composed of a number of
tiers or shelves, used for displaying ornaments and bric-à-
brac.

Wheat-Ear—Hepplewhite used ears of wheat as a design for
carving on his furniture.

Wheel Back—The name given to the backs of chairs, the design
or tracery of which represents a wheel.

Wig Stand—A short turned wooden standard with mushroom-shaped top, or bulbous knob. A name often given erroneously to a circular washstand.

Window Seats or Window Stools.—Pieces of furniture fitting into the deep window recesses of 18th-century houses. (*See illustration, page* 100.)

Windsor Chair—A popular variety of chair with upright lath backs and wooden seats, for kitchen use; first introduced during the reign of Queen Anne.

Wing Bookcase—A bookcase with the central part projecting beyond the side sections, to accommodate books of greater size.

Wing Chair—An upholstered high-back easy chair with side wings to support the head.

Withdrawing Table—(*See Draw Table*).

Work Box—A small oblong wooden box with or without tray, fitted small compartments for holding cottons, silks, needles, etc.

Work Table—Similar to a work box but generally on a tripod support. Some work tables had tops made for writing or playing games, and a silk pouch underneath to hold the needlework.

Worm Holes—These are made, mostly in the softer woods, by the burrowing activities of the beetle *Anobium domesticum* and its grubs; they were made artificially by the unscrupulous to represent the article in which they appear as being older than it really is. The genuineness of worm holes can be checked by inserting a fine pointed instrument or wire that has been moistened; this will bring away a fine powder; also the natural holes are always crooked, whereas the artificial ones are straight.

X-Shape Chairs—Egyptian, Greek, Roman and most ancient furniture craftsmen made chairs on the principle of the modern folding stool; a 7th-century example is the bronze-gilt chair of Dagobert in the Louvre; in Winchester Cathedral and York Minster may be seen Italian 14th-century chairs of this type, which were largely adopted from the 16th century onward for ecclesiastical furniture.

X-Shape Stretchers—(*See Saltire.*)

Yoke—A shaped piece of wood hollowed out to fit the shoulders, used for carrying two pails, one being suspended from either end.

Yorkshire Chair—A style of chair with rather tall back and two carved semi-circular cross rails, it dates from the early Commonwealth period. (*See illustration.*)

SILVER

A standard for gold and silver was fixed by statute in the year 1300 when silver was first stamped with the Leopard's Head by the Goldsmiths' Company which was established at the Goldsmiths' Hall in London; thus the Leopard's Head was called the "Hall Mark" or "Town Mark".

The Goldsmiths' Company received it's first Charter in 1327 empowering it to assay and stamp articles of gold and silver.

In the early days of marking the punches were made by hand, and in consequence of their small size and the intricacy of some of the designs they were far from uniform; this sometimes resulted in a variation of shapes in letters and shields of the same year, so some latitude must be shown in judging the correct shapes. The punches used by the Assay Offices of to-day are accurately made from master patterns and are thus prefectly produced.

There are usually four, but sometimes five or more marks to be found on silver, the usual four being as follows:—

> The Date Letter. The Hall or Town Mark.
> The Standard Mark. The Maker's Mark or Initials.

THE DATE OR ANNUAL LETTER is applied by the Assay Office. It was introduced in the year 1478 and has continued in use to the present day. Both the letter and the shield which encloses it are distinctive in character and so denote the year of application. The date letters are changed annually by the five Assay Offices still functioning, on the following days:—

> Birmingham, July 1st. Edinburgh, Mid-October.
> Dublin, January 1st. London, May 29th.
> Sheffield, July 1st.

The Date Letters of the Assay Offices are printed at the end of this book.

THE STANDARD MARK. The Lion Passant was first used in 1544 as a mark to show the silver was of sterling standard (that is, 11 ozs. 2 dwts. of silver to 18 dwts. of alloy per pound Troy, or 925 parts silver in every thousand). The Lion appeared passant guardant (head facing the spectator) and was at first crowned until 1550. The Lion Passant was not adopted by the Provincial Assay Offices of England until 1719.

Since 1821 the Lion appears passant only and not guardant on London assayed silver, the same year as the Leopard's head lost its crown on London Silver.

The standard mark for Scotland (Edinburgh) is the flower of a thistle with two leaves; it was used in 1759 and continues to the present time. The Lion Rampant was adopted by the Glasgow Assay Office in 1811, and was obligatory after 1819, but since 1914 it has been accompanied by the thistle.

THE BRITANNIA STANDARD.

The standard of silver was raised in 1697 in order to prevent the practice of melting down silver coins for the purpose of manufacturing utensils for domestic use, and at the same time the Lion Passant and the Leopard's head were replaced by the Lion's head erased (head in profile with neck brisé—torn asunder) and the figure of Britannia. These marks, together with the higher standard, were in use until the year 1719, when the lower standard was revived, but the use of the former marks was permitted on silver reaching the 1697-1719 standard and can still be so used if desired. The Britannia standard of silver being 11 ozs. 10 dwts. silver and only 10 dwts. of alloy.

THE HALL OR TOWN MARK.

Birmingham. The Hall Mark has always been an anchor since the Assay Office was first opened in 1773. The Sovereign's head appeared as a fifth mark from 1784 to 1890.

Chester (discontinued). The City Arms, consisting of three wheatsheaves and a dagger, were adopted in early times as the Hall Mark and are still used at the present time. At one time between the years 1668 and 1700 the Prince of Wales' plume was used, and at others the word "sterling"; also between the years 1701 and 1779 the City Arms and three lions dimidiated (halved) formed a complicated design. In addition, the crowned Leopard's head was used between the years 1719 and 1823, and from this latter year to 1839 it was uncrowned. The Sovereign's head also appeared from 1784 to 1890. Assay Office closed 24th August, 1962.

Dublin. The Hall Mark is a crowned harp, which appeared in 1637 upon the grant of a Charter. The figure of Hibernia has also appeared on Irish silver from the year 1730 to the present time, although it was originally used as a special duty mark. The Sovereign's head appears from 1807 to 1890.

Edinburgh. The Hall Mark is a castle with three towers on a rock and has been used since 1485. From 1457 all plate was stamped with the deacon's mark as well as the maker's mark until 1681, when the date letter was instituted and at the same time the deacon's mark was abolished and the Assay Master's mark substituted. In 1759 the Assay Master's initials were discontinued and replaced by the mark of the thistle. The Sovereign's head was stamped on Edinburgh silver from 1784 to 1890.

Exeter (discontinued). The Assay Office was opened in 1701 and closed in 1883. The Hall Mark was a castle with three towers, but an earlier mark from 1570 to 1701 consisted of a crowned letter X. The Leopard's head was used as an additional mark until the year 1776. The Sovereign's head was in use from 1784 to 1883.

Glasgow (discontinued). The Hall Mark consists of an oak tree with a bird, a salmon and a hand bell, this being the City's arms. The date letter was adopted in 1681 but was discontinued between 1710 to 1819. An Act of 1819 established an Assay Office in Glasgow and prescribed the following marks:—

1. The Lion Rampant (the Standard Mark).
2. The City Arms.
3. The Maker's mark.
4. Date letter.
5. The Sovereign's head (the latter being repealed in 1890).

In 1914 the Thistle mark was added.

The Assay Office closed 31st March, 1964.

London. A Leopard's head. This Hall Mark was first used in 1300 and was then uncrowned, the crown being introduced in 1478. The mark disappeared during the Britannia period (1697 to 1719), to reappear afterwards until 1823, when the crown was finally discarded. At various times the Leopard's head was also used as an additional mark by other Assay Offices, excepting Birmingham and Sheffield.

Newcastle (discontinued). The Assay Office was opened in 1423 and closed in 1884. The Hall Mark was three castles. With a few exceptions prior to 1701 date letters were used from 1658 until the office closed. The Sovereign's head was added between the years 1784 and 1884. The Leopard's head was uncrowned after 1846.

Sheffield. The Hall Mark is a crown, and has been in use ever since the Assay Office was first established in 1773. Gold was not assayed at Sheffield until the year 1904. The date letter and crown sometimes appeared on one punch between the years 1824 and 1844. The Sovereign's head was used between the years 1784 and 1890.

York (discontinued). The Assay Office was opened in 1423 and closed in 1857. Until 1700 the Hall Mark was a fleur-de-lys and a crowned Leopard's Head dimidiated in a circular frame; from 1700 the mark consisted of a cross with five lions, also contained in a plain circle. Date letters were used from 1562 until the close of the Office. No silver assayed here between 1717 and 1778.

There were many other towns in which silver was assayed, Norwich being the most important of these, the Assay Office closing by virtue of the Act of 1697; among others were Barnstaple, Bristol, Hull, King's Lynn, Leeds, Lincoln, Plymouth, Taunton.

In Scotland there were Assay Offices at Aberdeen, Arbroath, Banff, Canongate, Dundee, Elgin, Greenock, Inverness, Montrose, Perth and Wick.

In Ireland there were Assay Offices at Cork, Galway, Kilkenny, Limerick and Youghal.

THE MAKER'S MARK OR INITIALS.

Formerly this was some emblem as a star, a crown or a rose. In 1697, by an Act of Parliament, the maker's mark had to be the first two letters of his name. In 1739 an Act ordered the makers to destroy their existing marks and substitute a new mark with the initials of their Christian and surnames in a different style to those previously used.

OTHER MARKS, ETC.

Sovereign's Head. Between the years 1784 and 1890 a duty was levied on articles of gold and silver, and a special punch depicting the Sovereign's head in profile was impressed on all articles to indicate that duty had been paid.

Jubilee Mark. This was introduced in 1935 to commemorate the Silver Jubilee of Their Majesties King George V. and Queen Mary, and was in official use from February 6th to December 31st of that year. It is a special mark used in addition to the usual ones and consists of the heads of both Their Majesties jugata (overlapping). Its use was sanctioned to appear on articles bearing only the date letters for the years 1933-34, 1934-35 and 1935-36.

Coronation Mark, 1953. The head of Queen Elizabeth II looking to her left, in an oval punch.

GOLD

The Hall Marks for gold until 1798 were identical to those of silver.

In 1798 a new standard of 18 carat for gold was introduced, the marks for this were a Crown and the figure 18, in addition to the town mark, date letter and maker's mark.

The mark for 22-carat gold being the Lion Passant.

In 1844 the Lion Passant disappeared from gold and was replaced by the Crown and the figure 22.

In 1854 three lower standards of 15 carat, 12 carat and 9 carat were introduced and were marked with the figures 15.625, 12.5 and 9.375 respectively (the figures before the decimal point being at right angles to the others).

In 1932, the standards of 15 and 12 carat were abolished and a new standard of 14 carat (58.5 per cent gold) was introduced.

The word carat, when dealing with gold, means a proportion. 24 carats is 100 per cent fine gold, thus 22 carats mean 22 parts fine gold out of 24 parts.

The Standard Marks on Gold are:—

For 22-carat gold:—

London.	22 and a crown.
Birmingham.	22 and a crown.
Chester.	22 and a crown.
Sheffield.	22 and a crown.
Edinburgh.	22 and a thistle.
Glasgow.	22, a thistle and a lion rampant.

For 18-carat gold:—
As for 22 carat except that a stamp marked 18 is used instead.

The less fine standards are marked with the figures:—
14.585 for 14 carat.
 9.375 for 9 carat.

In addition, of course, the Assay Office mark, the date letter and maker's mark are used.

War-time Wedding Rings

In 1942, by order of the Board of Trade, wedding rings were allowed to be made of 9-carat gold and had to be plain and not weigh more than 2 dwts. These rings had an additional mark of two intersected circles in a rectangle. The making of these rings was discontinued in 1952.

The Assay Offices' Marks for Gold

London. The Leopard's head, uncrowned after 1820, as on silver.

Birmingham. The Anchor, as on silver; gold has only been assayed here since 1824.

Chester. The Three Sheaves and a Sword, as on silver.

Sheffield. The York Rose; gold has only been assayed here since 1904.

Edinburgh. The Castle, as on silver.

Glasgow. The City Arms, of a tree with a bird, bell and a fish, with a ring in its mouth as on silver.

The Date Letter Stamp on gold is the same as that found on silver for the respective Assay Office.

Foreign Gold and Silver

Gold and Silver ware manufactured abroad must, when imported into this Country, be sent to an Assay Office for testing and if up to standard, to be marked. This control was first applied in 1842.

Between 1876 and 1904 foreign-made plate, on being assayed in this Country, received the usual mark of the respective Assay Office with the addition of an F in an oval stamp.

From 1904-1906, under the Foreign Plate Act, 1904, the following towns were given these marks for foreign plate:—

London. Phœbus, the sun with rays.

Sheffield. Two arrows crossing another two arrows.

Glasgow. A Bishop's mitre.

Dublin. A shamrock leaf.

For gold these marks appear in a square shield with canted corners.

For silver these marks appear in an oval.

From 1906 onwards the marks of the town assaying foreign plate in this Country are:—

London. The sign of the constellation Leo.

Birmingham. An equilateral triangle.

Chester. An acorn with two leaves. (Closed 1962.)

Dublin. A boujet (a peculiar M-shaped symbol).

Edinburgh. St. Andrew's cross.

Glasgow. The letter F doubled. (Closed 1964.)

Sheffield. The sign of the constellation Libra.

For gold these marks appear in a square shield with canted corners.

For silver these marks appear in an oval.

In addition to the Assay Office mark there is the Standard or Quality Mark and the date letter of the particular office.

If gold the Standard Mark of the article:—

22 .916
18 .750
15 .625 (discontinued since 1932)
14 .585
12 .5 (discontinued since 1932)
9 .375

Antique Foreign Plate

Gold and Silver ware over one hundred years old are exempt from the above hall marking laws (Hall-marking of Foreign Plate Act, 1939).

MARKS ON FOREIGN PLATE

Between 1876 and 1904 foreign plate on being assayed in this Country was marked:—

From 1904–1906 the marks were:

London   Sheffield   Glasgow   Dublin

From 1906 onwards the marks are:

London   Birmingham   Chester   Dublin
                                    (Closed 1962)

Edinburgh   Glasgow   Sheffield
                   (Closed 1964)

For gold the marks appear in a square shield with canted corners as shown.

For silver the same marks appear but in an oval.

MEMORANDUM ON THE LAW
RELATING TO MANUFACTURE AND SALE OF
GOLD AND SILVER WARES

Reproduced by Permission of the
Worshipful Company of Goldsmiths

1. LEGAL STANDARDS. The authorised standards of fineness are:—

for Gold: 22, 18, 14 and 9 carats of fine gold in every pound weight troy of which the decimal equivalents are .9166, .750, .585, .375 respectively.

for Silver: 11 oz. 10 dwts. and 11 oz. 2 dwts. of fine silver in every pound weight troy, of which the decimal equivalents are .9584 and .925 respectively.

In general the law requires that any gold or silver ware made in the United Kingdom or imported and sold shall be of one of the authorised standards and shall be hall-marked before sale. Some permitted exceptions are mentioned in paragraph 12.

Plate Duty Act, 1719; *Plate (Offences) Act*, 1738; *Gold Plate (Standard) Act*, 1798; *Gold and Silver Wares Act*, 1854.

2. Hall-marking is required whatever description or name is given to the wares and whether any other substance than gold or silver is attached thereto or not.

3. Foreign gold and silver wares if imported by a dealer must be hall-marked on arrival by arrangement with the Customs authorities; otherwise such wares may not be removed from bond. But the law permits a private person to import gold and silver wares without having them hall-marked on making a statutory declaration that he does not intend to sell them. If he subsequently wishes to sell them he must have them hall-marked.

Customs Act, 1842, *Section* 59; *Revenue Act*, 1883, *Section* 10; *Hall-marking of Foreign Plate Act*, 1904, *Section* 1.

4. Gold and silver wares sent for hall-marking which are not up to an authorised standard are to be broken by the assayers, but in the case of a foreign ware sent for hall-marking on import (or on proposed sale if imported by a private individual) the option is given to the owner to export it within a month.

Plate (Offences) Act, 1738, *Section* 20; *Revenue Act*, 1883, *Section* 10.

5. (*a*) Where an addition or alteration is intended to any gold or silver ware which has been hall-marked, the law requires that it shall first be brought again to an authorised Assay Office.

(*b*) Additions weighing less than 4 oz. in every pound weight troy of the original ware may be marked with a special additions mark if:—

(i) the original ware is brought to the Assay Office and the assent of the authorities is obtained before the additions are made, and

(ii) the character of the ware is not changed by the additions. The authorities never assent to additions of a standard lower than that of the original ware.

(*c*) Any hall-marked ware which is so altered that its character is changed or which has additions made thereto exceeding the last-mentioned proportion, must be brought again to the Assay Office and shall (if of proper fineness) be marked as a new ware.

Gold and Silver Wares Act, 1844, Section 5.

6. To forge a hall-mark or to transpose a hall-mark from one ware to another is a grave crime punishable with imprisonment for a period not exceeding fourteen years.

Gold and Silver Wares Act, 1844, Section 2; Forgery Act, 1913, Section 5; Criminal Justice Act, 1948, Section 1.

7. Gold and silver wares not properly hall-marked come at times into circulation through some person's illegal act or the previous importation of foreign wares without intent to sell by a person who is not a dealer. The following summary shows what may lawfully be done with such wares and applies generally except where it refers only to dealers:—

(*a*) When a ware bears forged or transposed hall-marks mere possession of it without lawful excuse and with knowledge of the forgery or transposition is a felony. Sale of such a ware with that knowledge generally constitutes the felony of "uttering" a forged or transposed hall-mark. Both such felonies are punishable with imprisonment for a period not exceeding fourteen years.

Gold and Silver Wares Act, 1844, Section 2; Forgery Act, 1913, Sections 6 and 8; Criminal Justice Act, 1948, Section 1.

(*b*) A dealer who without lawful excuse (which he must himself establish) possesses or offers for sale a ware bearing a forged or transposed hall-mark is liable to a penalty of £10 even though it is not proved that he knew of the forgery or transposition. He will be exempted from this penalty if he discloses the name of the person from whom he received the ware.

Gold and Silver Wares Act, 1844, Sections 3 and 4.

(*c*) A dealer is liable to a penalty of £10 if he possesses or sells a hall-marked gold or silver ware which has suffered alteration or addition without being brought again to an Assay Office. He is relieved of liability for the penalty by disclosing the name of the person from whom he received the ware.

Gold and Silver Wares Act, 1844, Sections 5 and 6.

(*d*) A person who sells a foreign gold or silver ware or a British gold ware which has not been hall-marked is liable on summary conviction to a fine not exceeding £100 whether the ware is up to standard or not. He is relieved of the liability in the case of silver which is not up to standard by disclosing the name of the person from whom he received the ware and assisting in his prosecution. A dealer is similarly liable if he sells a British silver ware bearing no hall-marks whether it is up to standard or not. Mere possession of a British or foreign gold or silver ware not up to authorised standard is not an offence.

Plate (Offences) Act, 1738, Sections 1, 3 and 5; Gold Plate (Standard) Act, 1798, Sections 2 and 6; Customs Act, 1842, Section 59; Common Informers Act, 1951.

(*e*) Exposing a ware for sale, exchanging it, or (in the case of a British ware) exporting it, is generally as much an offence as selling it.

8. AUCTIONEERS. The Assay Office authorities consider that the law relating to gold and silver wares applies to an auctioneer whose business includes their sale by auction in the same way as it applies to a dealer in them.

9. PAWNBROKERS. It is considered that a pawnbroker who finds himself in possession of an unredeemed pledge which is not properly hall-marked has no right to break the hall-marking laws by selling it without submitting it to be hall-marked.

10. ERASING OR DEFACING MARKS. Fraudulently to erase or deface an official hall-mark or registered maker's mark (private mark) is an offence.

Gold and Silver Wares Act, 1844, Section 9.

11. WATCHCASES. When a watchcase is brought to an Assay Office, a declaration must show where the case was made. Marks for foreign watch cases are prescribed by Order in Council.

The Merchandise Marks Act, 1887, Section 8.

12. EXEMPTIONS FROM COMPULSORY HALL-MARKING.

(1) The list of exempted gold wares is contained in the Plate (Offences) Act, 1738, Section 6.

(2) The list of exempted silver wares is contained in the Silver Plate Act, 1790, Sections 3, 4 and 5.

(3) Jewellery is affected by both these provisions, and all jeweller's works, viz. the actual settings of jewels or stones, are exempt.

Plate (Offences) Act, 1738, Section 2.

(4) Gold or silver plate manufactured abroad more than one hundred years before being imported or being sold in the United Kingdom is exempt from assay and marking.

Hall-marking of Foreign Plate Act, 1939.

(5) Articles of foreign plate which may be properly described as hand-chased, inlaid, bronzed or filigree work of Oriental pattern are exempt from assay and marking in the United Kingdom.

Revenue Act, 1884, Section 4.

13.   VOLUNTARY MARKING. Many manufacturers and dealers find it expedient to submit for assay and marking articles which are exempt from compulsory marking because members of the public value the standards guaranteed by hall-marking. The Assay Office authorities are glad to assay and mark articles submitted voluntarily, provided that the usual charges are paid.

14.   The following are the Statutes and Orders mainly concerned:—

(a) Statutes.

6 Geo. 1, c. 11.	The Plate Duty Act, 1719.
12 Geo. 2, c. 26.	The Plate (Offences) Act, 1738.
30 Geo. 3, c. 31.	The Silver Plate Act, 1790.
38 Geo. 3, c. 69.	The Gold Plate (Standard) Act, 1798.
5 and 6 Vict., c. 47.	The Customs Act, 1842.
7 and 8 Vict, c. 22.	The Gold and Silver Wares Act, 1844.
17 and 18 Vict., c. 96.	The Gold and Silver Wares Act, 1854.
18 and 19 Vict., c. 60.	The Wedding Rings Act, 1855.
46 and 47 Vict, c. 55.	The Revenue Act, 1883.
47 and 48 Vict., c. 62.	The Revenue Act, 1884.
50 and 51 Vict. c. 28.	The Merchandise Marks Act, 1887
4 Edw. 7, c. 6.	The Hall-marking of Foreign Plate Act, 1904.
3 and 4 Geo. 5, c. 27.	The Forgery Act, 1913.
2 Geo. 6, c. 36.	The Hall-marking of Foreign Plate Act, 1939.
11 and 12 Geo. 6, c. 58.	The Criminal Justice Act, 1948.
14 and 15 Geo. 6, c. 39.	The Common Informers Act, 1951

(*b*)   Orders in Council.

S.R. and O. 1932, No. 653.   The Merchandise Marks (Watch Case Marking) Order, 1932.

S.R. and O. 1932, No. 654.   The Gold Wares (Standard of Fineness) Order, 1932.

S.R. and O. 1932, No. 655.   The Hall-marking of Imported Plate Order, 1932.

NOTICE OF PROCEDURE
FOR DEALING WITH OFFENCES AND
SUSPECTED OFFENCES AGAINST
THE HALL-MARKING LAWS

Reproduced by permission of the
Worshipful Company of Goldsmiths

1.   The following notes are issued for the guidance and assistance of all who co-operate with the Wardens of the Goldsmiths' Company in carrying out their duties relative to the hall-marking of gold and silver wares. If the Wardens suspect deliberate evasion of the law they reserve the right to use their full legal powers.

2.   When a ware is sent to the Assay Office *to be assayed* and is found to be below standard it is broken and either returned to the person submitting it or forwarded to a refiner for melting. In the latter case the value of the metal is recoverable by the person who sends the ware to the Assay Office. In the case of a ware manufactured abroad an opportunity to export it within one month is given before it is broken.

3.   When a ware is submitted to the Wardens *for examination* their Antique Plate Committee first decides whether the ware complies with the hall-marking laws. If it complies, it is returned to the person submitting it as soon as possible after it has been examined. If it does not comply with the law the Wardens decide how it offends and deal with it as follows:—

(1)   If it bears forged or transposed marks, the marks are defaced and the ware is treated as an unmarked ware.

(2)   The owner of an unmarked ware is asked to choose whether he wishes the ware (i) to be assayed and, if up to standard, marked as a modern ware, or (ii) to be returned to him with a caution that it must remain in private ownership. If the owner chooses the first alternative the ware is treated as having been sent to the Assay Office to be assayed and paragraph 2 above applies.

(3)   A ware which has suffered unauthorised alterations or additions is assayed and the Wardens recommend how to bring it within the law (if that is possible) by:—

(i)   Applying the additions' mark if the additions weigh less than one-third of the weight of the original ware and are of proper fineness, or

(ii)   Restoring the ware to its original condition by removing unauthorised additions, or

(iii)   Replacing additions which are below standard with new additions of the appropriate standard and marking the latter with the additions' mark, or

(iv)   Defacing existing marks and marking as a modern ware.

An owner who is *not* a dealer is asked to choose whether he wishes (*a*) to adopt the Wardens' recommendation (if any) for bringing the ware within the law in order that it may be freely sold, or (*b*) to have the ware returned to him with a caution that it must remain in private ownership.

An owner who is a dealer must adopt the Wardens' recommendation. If the ware cannot be brought within the law it is broken and either returned to the owner or forwarded to a refiner for melting. In the latter case the value of the metal is recoverable by the owner.

SHEFFIELD PLATE

The process of making Sheffield Plate was discovered in 1742 by a Cutler named Thomas Boulsover who, when repairing a silver knife, accidentally allowed his work to get overheated, and found that the silver and a piece of copper had fused in one solid piece. Realising the possibilities of this discovery, he succeeded by beating out a thin sheet of silver and placing it on copper, then fusing the two together by the application of heat.

Boulsover set up a factory making small items such as patch and snuff boxes, knife handles, etc. Very soon, his rivals set up factories making teapots, trays, candlesticks, etc.

Sheffield Plate is a method of plating copper with silver by the fusion of the two metals, so that in fact they become one; this was a new method in 1742, but silver plating had existed in one form or another for centuries.

The designs in Sheffield Plate mostly copied those of Silver.

Sheffield Plate had a short life as it began in 1742 and ended about 1840, when Elkington of Birmingham took out a patent for electro-plating.

Electro-plate—A process used to cover objects made of cheap metal with an adherent coating of a more costly metal such as gold, silver or nickel, by placing the articles in a solution of the more costly metal and applying an electric current.

GLOSSARY OF TERMS

used in connection with Silver, Sheffield Plate and Electro-plate

Anointing Spoon—Used for precious ointments and oils; often of quaint shape.

Argyle—A gravy tureen with a spout and has an outer container into which hot water is poured to keep the gravy hot. Late 18th century.

Asparagus Dish—A rectangular shape dish with loose drainer for serving asparagus at table.

Barber's Bowl—A bowl with a piece cut off the rim to fit the neck.

Basins—(*See Ewers and Basins.*)

Beaker—An upright drinking cup without spout or handle, like the present tumbler. Introduced beginning of the 17th century.

Bohemian Glass—An ornamental glass ware from Bohemia noted for its rich colours, often of deep ruby tint, and for its incised and engraved designs.

Bleeding Bowl or Cupping Bowl—A popular but incorrect term for a small circular cup with one or two pierced handles. These cups were really a form of individual porringer.

Brandy Sauce Pan—A small silver sauce pan for warming brandy, fitted with a turned wood handle, about 1750.

Bread Basket—(*See Cake Basket.*)

Breakfast Dish—A tureen-shaped dish on feet, with revolving cover and a chamber for hot water, in which food was kept warm at table.

Cake Basket—Introduced between 1730-1750, and were of very fine work. Paul Lamerie made many: later the work was often cruder.

Candlestick—The early silver candlesticks of the reign of Charles II have fluted columns on square bases. In the reign of Queen Anne the candlesticks had a baluster stem on square base with the corners either recessed or cut off. About 1765 the Corinthian column candlestick appeared which was the first with removable socket pans. Later, candlesticks became ornamented with festoons of flowers, mask heads, etc.

Caster—The straight-sided cylindrical caster was the first type made and dates from about 1680. They were made in sets of three, the two smaller ones for pepper and the larger for sugar. The vase-shaped caster followed about 1700 and was generally part of a cruet stand. The octagonal-shaped caster was popular in reign of George I.

Caudle—A warm beverage of curdled milk flavoured with wine and hot spices.

Caudle Cup—Introduced in the early 17th century for drinking caudle. They are narrower at the top, widening towards the bottom, as the curd floated up into the narrow part and could be removed.

Centre Pieces—Ornamental pieces for decorating the dinner table, often very elaborate.

Chamber Candlestick—Silver chamber candlesticks with and without extinguishers were introduced in the late 17th century.

Chocolate Pot—In Queen Anne's reign these were plain and of tapered cylindrical shape, in George II's reign floral wreaths and gadroons were added.

Coaster—A circular decanter stand with silver sides on wood base, the bottom covered baize to slide decanters and bottles along the table, introduced about 1760.

Coconut Cup—A cup made from a coconut shell mounted on a silver foot with silver rim, and lid. Those of the 15th and 16th centuries are naturally rare but a number were made in Germany in the 18th century.

Coffee Pot—Coffee was introduced into England in the mid-17th century. Silver coffee pots were introduced about 1685. Those of George I's reign were plain and tall, often octagonal.

Cream Jug—Introduced about 1700, when they were generally low.

Cruet—Introduced in Queen Anne's reign and usually contained two-silver mounted glass bottles for oil and vinegar and three silver casters (*q.v.* Warwick Cruet).

Decanter Wagon—Decanter stand on wheels.

Dish Cross—Used to keep dishes warm and were made with four arms moving around a spirit lamp in the centre, with feet which slide along the bars, to fit the size of dish. Were in use from reign of George II until superseded in 1800 by the hot-water dish.

Egg Frame—A frame to hold usually six egg cups and spoons.

Embossing—A method of forming raised ornamental designs which are usually pressed or beaten out from the back.

Engraving—The art of decorating by incising designs.

Entrée Dish—Introduced in reign of George II, usually having detachable handles so that both cover and dish could be used as two dishes. Some earlier ones had an outer container to hold water to keep the contents of the dish warm. Those with stands and spirit lamps were introduced early in reign of George III.

Épergne—A centre piece for decorating the dining table, the centre forming a fruit or flower bowl and had either flower vases or dishes and baskets for sweets which could be detached and handed around.

Ewers—Ewers and basins were used at table. As forks were not used before the later 17th century, the hands were washed before, during and after meals, servants bringing around ewers filled with scented water which they poured over the diners' hands.

Feather Edge—A pattern of table plate being Old English pattern with an engraved feather edge all along the handle.

Fiddle Pattern—A pattern for table plate where the handles have the appearance of fiddles—19th century.

Fish Slice—First made in early 18th century, often with very ornate pierced blades and having silver or ivory handles; later were made to match the other knives and forks.

Forks—Were introduced in the third quarter of the 17th century, the older forks being three-pronged, the four-pronged fork came into fashion about the middle of the 18th century.

Gadroon—A style of decoration often applied, somewhat resembling an almond-shaped reeding or fluting.

Goblet—A drinking vessel without a handle, on a foot.

Gravy Boat—(*See Sauce Boat.*)

Gravy Tureen—(*See Sauce Tureen.*)

Hanap—A name given to large standing cups with cover.

Hanoverian Pattern—A pattern for table plate where the handle has a rounded end turned up, about 1700 until succeeded by the Old English pattern about 1760.

Ice Pail—A pail with a loose lining for cooling a bottle of wine came into vogue in reign of George II, the linings were sometimes of base metal.

Infuser—A small instrument for making a single cup of tea, shaped like a double-perforated spoon, and used in place of a teapot.

Ink Stand—Silver inkstands were introduced about 1700 and were often fitted with taper sticks and pounce boxes. Later, when snuffers trays became obsolete these were frequently made into inkstands.

Jug—Silver jugs were made in reign of George I, coming into general use in George II's reign. Some of the hot water jugs have handles covered with canework and ivory knobs, others have ebony handles and knobs. Jugs were made for claret, beer and hot water, with lids, those for milk without lids.

Kings Pattern—A very ornate form of fiddle pattern table plate, 19th century.

Kettles—(*See Tea Kettles.*)

Lamerie, Paul de—One of the most famous silversmiths whose earliest recorded work dates from 1711-12 and who died in 1751.

Loving Cup—Two-handled cup on a round base with or without cover, introduced in Charles II's reign.

Marrow Scoop—Introduced in reign of Queen Anne with scoop at both ends.

Mazer—A shallow wooden bowl, generally made of maple wood, with a high silver rim. Mazers usually have a silver boss in the bottom, 15th century, later ones were mounted on a silver foot. There are none later than 1540.

Monteith—A circular punch bowl with an escalloped detachable rim designed to hold glasses. These bowls were large and imposing pieces, so called after a Scot named Monteith who always wore his coats with escalloped edges. The Monteith with lion's mask and ring handles came into fashion about 1695.

Muffineer—(*See Casters.*)

Mustard Pot—Mustard has been used at table from reign of George I and mustard pots date from shortly after this period.

Nef—A table ornament in the shape of a ship and generally fitted as a cruet or with a clock.

Nutmeg Grater—18th and 19th century—in many shapes, with steel graters.

Old English—A plain type of table plate, with flat stems, slightly spreading to the rounded ends which are turned down, 18th century.

Pap Boat—A feeding bowl with a lip to drink from; George II.

Parcel Gilt—Partly gilt.

Peg Tankard—A tankard with pegs inside, about eight, so that each person should drink no more than his share, introduced in late 17th century.

Pepperette—(*See Casters.*)

Plates—Silver dinner plates have been in use from earliest times, but large numbers were made in reign of George II and III.

Porringer—A two-handled bowl made for drinking hot spiced beverage; they had wide mouths. Introduced about 1650. Porringers were made with covers.

Posset—A hot drink made from curdled milk with wine or ale flavoured with spices.

Posset Cup—(*See Caudle Cup.*)

Potato Ring—A pierced and usually richly embossed ring of nine to twelve inches in diameter and three to five inches deep. Made only in Ireland between 1740 and 1800; almost always hall-marked in the outside lower rim. The actual method of using the ring is a much-debated point. Some say the ring was a mere stand for a wooden bowl, others say the ring was placed on a wooden platter and the potatoes placed inside it.

Pounce Pot—A container found in old inkstands. Pounce was a fine powder used to sprinkle on writing to dry the ink before the invention of blotting paper.

Punch Bowl—A large imposing bowl introduced during reign of Charles II. (*See Monteith Bowl.*)

Punch Ladle—As the name implies, a ladle for punch usually with whalebone handle and silver bowl.

Quaich—A shallow Scottish drinking bowl with two flat handles which were usually pierced. Found from the early 17th century onwards.

Queen's Pattern—A less elaborate form of table plate than King's Pattern (*q.v.*) which it resembles.

Rat-Tail—A pattern of table plate which at the junction of the stem to the bowl there is a rat-tail. The principal form of late 17th- to early 18th-century spoon.

Repoussé—A French term applied to an elaborate style of embossed ornamentation, the designs being hammered out from the back.

Ring Dish—A circular container or stand for holding a glass or other dish at table.

Rose Water Ewer—A tall, graceful pitcher-shaped ewer, with long slender spout, handle and a terminal lid.

Salts—The salt cellar was first a massive piece and served mainly to differentiate between the nobles and their inferiors, who sat "below the salt". Pedestal salts were first made and hall-marked in middle of the 14th century. Bell-shaped salts followed about 1580. Steeple salts were first made about 1600.

Trencher salts were either circular or hexagonal with a depression to hold the salt; date from James I. The octagonal trencher was introduced in the reign of Queen Anne. Hall marked on side or bottom. Circular salt cellars on feet date from about 1720, later giving way to oval- and boat-shaped ones towards the end of the 18th century.

Salver—Introduced in the time of William and Mary, and at first were quite plain, with a moulded border. Later, in the Georgian period, "Chippendale borders" were used, this gave way to gadroon borders with shell and foliage decoration.

Sauce Boat—The earliest sauce boats dated about 1720 and were oval with handles on both sides and spouts at each end and an oval foot. Early in the reign of George II sauce boats were made with three feet.

Sauce Pan—Plain silver sauce pans with wood handles were made in the mid-17th century and were without stands. Later sauce pans with spout and lid as well as a wood handle were made with a stand which had a spirit lamp.

Sauce Tureen—Sauce tureens with covers were introduced about 1750 and shaped like soup tureens but smaller.

Snuffers—For extinguishing candles, they resemble a pair of scissors with a box on the longer blade. Date from about end of 17th century, generally with a stand or tray; also a cone-shaped candle extinguisher.

Soup Tureen—Generally oval- or boat-shaped with two handles and cover, became very large in 18th century, weighing up to over 600 ozs. Paul Storr made many.

Spoons—Date from the earliest of times. The oldest English spoon known to be in existence is the Coronation spoon, among the Regalia in Tower of London, about 12th century. Spoons were made for many various uses, such as: table spoons, dessert spoons, tea spoons, mustard, etc. which do not require description; but the so-called "olive spoon" with its slender barbed or pointed end and pierced bowl, thought by many for olives, was, in fact, designed for tea making, the pierced bowl for use as a strainer, and the pointed end to clear the teapot spout.

Acorn Knops are spoons, the handles terminating in an acorn, 15th century.

Apostle Spoons are those with handles terminating in figures of the Apostles. 15th century. A complete set numbers thirteen—Christ and twelve Apostles.

Diamond-Points or Spearheads are spoons made in 14th, 15th and early 16th centuries, the shaft terminates in a hexagonal spearhead.

Lion Sejants are spoons topped with a gilt image of a sitting lion, often holding a shield in front. Medieval and later.

Lobed-end. (*See Trefid.*)

Maidenhead is a spoon with the handle terminating in a head and bust, supposed to be the Virgin Mary, 15th century onwards.

Pied-de-Biche are trefid spoons, so called as the end of the handle was supposed to resemble a hind's foot.

Puritan or Stump Tops were spoons with a spade-shaped bowl and long flat stem with a flat end, 1640-1690.

Seal Tops are spoons terminating in a flat top, 15th century.

Strawberry Knops are spoons, the shafts terminating in the form of a strawberry, 15th century.

Trefid or Trefoil topped spoons, the ends terminate in a flat rounded end in which there are two notches.

Wrythen Knops are spoons, the handles ending in a fluted or spiral twisted cone. A rare Medieval type.

Spoon Warmer—A utensil used at table containing hot water to warm gravy spoons before use, often of shell shape—Nautilus pattern.

Standing Cup—A large ornate drinking cup with cover on high stem and foot. Found until the late 17th century.

Standish—A forerunner of the inkstand, was a stand containing an ink well, a holder for pounce, also a holder for shot.

Steeple Cup—A tall cup with conical-shape bowl on baluster stem and tall trumpet-shape foot, the cover having a steeple-shape finial. Early 17th century.

Stoneware Jug—Popular in the 15th and 16th centuries and were of mottled salt-glazed ware with silver or silver gilt cover, neck band, handle and circular base. (*q.v. Tiger Jugs.*)

Storr, Paul—A craftsman of the highest merit of his period. He worked from 1797 until 1821.

Sucrier—A sugar bowl.

Sugar Basket and Basin—Came into use about 1760.

Tankard—A large silver drinking vessel with cover and handle The late 17th-century tankards were plain and had flat lids About 1720 the tankard had a bulbous pot and a dome-shaped lid, with or without a knob.

Taper Holder—Silver taper holders date from about 1660.

Taper Stick—Silver taper sticks with snuffers tray from about 1690. The winding wire taper holders often called Wax Jacks date from about 1770.

Taster—A small shallow circular bowl with a flat handle.

Tazza—An elegant drinking cup on baluster stem and circular foot, not unlike the low open champagne glass. Introduced about 1570. Plural Tazze.

Tea Caddy—The earliest examples date from the late 17th century. Those of Queen Anne's reign were usually plain octagonal in shape. Later they assumed many shapes with loose or hinged covers.

Tea Kettle—Tea kettles on stands with spirit lamp were introduced in the first quarter of the 18th century. At first these were plain, later they were richly decorated with flowers, vine leaves, etc.

Tea Pot—The earliest known silver teapot dates from 1670. Early 18th-century examples were small and plain; in George I's reign they frequently had circular bases, later ones had four feet.

Tea Urn—Began replacing the tea kettle at the end of the 18th century, at first having a spirit lamp, later became vase-shaped with handles and a receptacle to hold an iron heater.

Teapot Stand—Became fashionable in early part of George III's reign.

Tiger Jug—A stoneware jug (q.v.) of German origin from the German word Tigel, meaning a kiln.

Tumbler—A drinking vessel so called as it will not lie on its side but rolls from side to side until it rests upright; introduced about 1670.

Vinaigrette—A small box with a pierced inner lid for holding a sponge steeped in aromatic vinegar, used as a smelling bottle.

Wager Cup—A cup in the form of a woman holding a small cup above her head in upstretched arms, 17th century.

Waiter—A small salver (q.v.).

Warwick Cruet—A well-known design of cruet dating from about 1750 to 1770, and usually containing two silver-mounted glass bottles for oil and vinegar, and three silver casters.

Wassail Horn—A large ornamental drinking horn with silver mounts and lid, used for drinking wassail, a beverage of sweetened and spiced ale or wine.

Wax Jack—A reel on a framework for holding a length of taper, which was fed up through a nozzle in the centre. (*See Taper Holder.*)

Wine Cistern—These range from about 1660 to 1740, some were immense, the largest being one made by Charles Kandler of London, 1734, which weighs 8,000 ozs. and holds 60 gallons.

Wine Cooler—Generally urn shape with two handles on circular foot, often with loose lining of a base metal; the earlier ones were large and oval and were introduced into England in the the reign of Charles I from Italy.

Wine Label—Commonly rectangular, crescent shape or oval, but can be any shape with the name of the wine engraved or pierced, to hang on the bottle by the chain attached to them.

A TABLE FOR CONVERTING
AVOIRDUPOIS WEIGHT INTO TROY

7,000 grains ... 1 lb. avoirdupois
5,760   „   ... 1 lb. troy

AVOIRDUPOIS		TROY			AVOIRDUPOIS		TROY		
lbs.	*oz.*	*oz.*	*dwts.*		*lbs.*	*oz.*	*oz.*	*dwts.*	
—	¼ ...	—	5	approx.	—	15 ...	13	13	approx.
—	½ ...	—	9	„	1	0 ...	14	12	„
—	1 ...	—	18	„	2	0 ...	29	4	„
—	2 ...	1	16	„	3	0 ...	43	16	„
—	3 ...	2	14	„	4	0 ...	58	8	„
—	4 ...	3	12	„	5	0 ...	73	0	„
—	5 ...	4	10	„	6	0 ...	87	10	„
—	6 ...	5	9	„	7	0 ...	102	4	„
—	7 ...	6	7	„	8	0 ...	116	16	„
—	8 ...	7	5	„	9	0 ...	131	8	„
—	9 ...	8	4	„	10	0 ...	146	0	„
—	10 ...	9	2	„	15	0 ...	219	0	„
—	11 ...	10	0	„	20	0 ...	292	0	„
—	12 ...	10	18	„	25	0 ...	365	0	„
—	13 ...	11	16	„	30	0 ...	438	0	„
—	14 ...	12	15	„					

PEWTER

Pewter is an alloy, the best quality being about 112 parts tin to 26 of copper; the ordinary quality 100 parts tin to 17 of antimony and the public house quality, 60 parts tin to 40 of lead.

In 1348 the Worshipful Company of Pewterers was established in London to maintain the standard of the quality of the metal, design, workmanship, etc.

In 1503 it became compulsory in London for the marking of all articles with the maker's mark or touch. Many makers marked their goods before this Act.

There were many guilds in the Provinces.

The most common objects made of Pewter no doubt are the plates and dishes, but practically every article was made, such as soup tureens, vegetable dishes, salt cellars, mustard and pepper pots, tea pots, milk jugs, tea caddies, tobacco jars, snuff boxes, inkstands, porringers, etc.

As the description of these articles are dealt with under Silver, given below is a glossary of terms dealing with those articles which are primarily found made of Pewter.

Chopin—A Scottish wine measure containing 1½ Imperial pints.

Charger—A large flat dish, generally 18 in. in diameter or more.

Double-ended Measure—Looks like an egg cup, the larger end holds half a gill, the small end a quarter gill.

Haystack Measure or Harvester Measure—Spirit measures made in Ireland are baluster shape and without handles. Early 19th century.

Measures—In 1673 a new table of weights was produced and wine measures were mentioned. These range from a half quarter pint (a half gill) to a gallon. Their capacity is the Old English Wine Standard which is five-sixths of the Imperial Measure.

Mutchkin—A Scottish wine measure containing three-quarters of an Imperial pint.

Normandy Flagon—A tall lidded measure not unlike the tappit hen but has a bulbous body, more pronounced curves, a heart-shaped lid; of French origin. 15th century.

Pot Bellied Measures—Scottish measures date from *c.* 1680 to *c.* 1740; are found both with and without lids.

Tappit Hen—A Scottish measure used from 16th to 19th century; a tall jug with graceful lines, is of three types, with a lid, without a lid, and crested, that is, with a knob on the lid, the latter are the later ones. A tappit hen holds a Scots pint which equalled three English Imperial pints. However, tappit hens of other sizes are to be seen.

Thistle Measure—A Scottish spirit measure shaped like a thistle, first made in the first quarter of the 19th century. An Act of Parliament of 1907 made it necessary for all measures to empty, when tilted, to an angle of 120 degrees. Thistle measures could not do this and were destroyed.

PORCELAIN AND POTTERY

CERAMICS is derived from the Greek word "Keramos" meaning clay and is thus used in the description of all articles made of clay. These can be divided into two distinct classes. Porcelain and Pottery.

PORCELAIN commonly called "china" is translucent and breaks with a smooth fracture. Porcelain varies in composition from factory to factory, but is roughly divided into two classes— Hard paste (Pâte Durer) and Soft paste (Pâte Tendre).

Hard paste is made from mixing Kaolin (china clay) with felspar, whilst soft paste is made with Kaolin and silica. Each factory has its own formula. English porcelain, on the whole, is soft paste but three factories made hard paste—Bristol, Plymouth and New Hall.

Porcelain was not made in England until shortly before the middle of the 18th century, but the Chinese have been making it for about 1,000 years.

A test to distinguish between hard and soft paste is to use a fine file on the base of a piece of china; soft paste powders easily under the file, whilst hard paste resists it.

POTTERY is opaque and breaks with a rough fracture. Pottery is divided into two classes: Earthenware and Stoneware.

In the case of Earthenware, the heat of the kiln in firing is sufficient to harden the ware yet leaves it porous. This is overcome by glazing, whilst stoneware is submitted to such intense heat as to vitrify the clay.

PORCELAIN AND POTTERY

Acetabulum—A small Roman cup made to hold vinegar.

Aftaba—A ceremonial water ewer of Persia and India, usually made with a long spout.

Aiguière—A pitcher-shaped ewer, usually very ornate, with long slender handle and spout surmounted with a finial lid. (*See Rose Water Ewer and Buire.*)

Albarello—A 15th century earthenware vessel for holding drugs; the modern counterpart may be seen in chemists' shops.

153

Albert—A terra-cotta ware sold in its natural state for decorating.

Albion Ware—A ware decorated with coloured slip, so named because it was a revival of the old English method of slip decoration.

Alcora—Majolica (*q.v.*) was made at this Spanish factory founded by the Count of Aranda in 1727, the early wares being closely modelled on those produced at Monstiers (*q.v.*). Hard-paste porcelain was also made here from *c.* 1774. The mark is A in brownish red, black or gold, some of the porcelain is un-marked.

$$A \quad AZ$$

Ama—A large vessel used in early Christian churches, in which the wine for the Eucharist was consecrated.

Amphora—An ancient Greek vessel for holding liquids, with a capacity of about 5 to 8 gallons. Usually made of earthenware, with two handles, a narrow neck and a pointed base for insertion in a stand. Sometimes used as a cinerary urn and often richly decorated. **Amphorous**—Of irregular shape.

Amstel—The making of porcelain in Holland started at Weesp near Amsterdam (*q.v.*) in 1764. The works were transferred to Oude Loosdrecht in 1771 and in 1784 to Oude Amstel. Production ceased in 1820. Marks—the word "Amstel".

Anatolian Pottery—A coarse soft glazed pottery ware with brightly coloured decorations, made in Anatolia.

Ansbach—Faience was made here from 1710 and later also cream-coloured earthenware. Hard-paste porcelain was made from 1757, under the patronage of the Margrave of Brandenburg.

Apothecaries' Jar or Drug Pot—A name often given to antique ware jars, usually with an abbreviated Latin inscription, the modern edition of which may be seen in most chemists' shops. (*See Albarello.*)

Aretine Ware—A kind of pottery ware made at Arezzo in Italy.

Arras—From about 1780 to 1786—made excellent soft-paste porcelain.

Askos—A small Greek vase or jug shaped like a leather bottle; probably used by the ancients for oil and, when decorated, as a vase or perfume holder.

Astbury Ware—A general term used to describe a type of pottery made in the manner traditionally initiated by John Astbury of Staffordshire. Little is known of Astbury himself but he is thought to have made red earthenware with white relief decoration and figures. So-called "Astbury ware" includes Staffordshire pottery produced in the second quarter of the 18th century, of both red and white clay, covered in a transparent lead glaze.

Aubergine—The name sometimes given to the creamy-eggshell colour on Chinese porcelain. The name is that of the egg-plant, the colour ranges from orange to purple.

Awaji—A variety of Japanese porcelain.

Baden-Baden—A factory for hard-paste porcelain established in 1753, closed about 1880. Pottery was also made.

Banko Ware—A very light Japanese pottery ware made in moulds.

Basalt Ware—A black stoneware with a dull gloss, made by Wedgwood.

Bekko Ware—An Oriental pottery ware resembling tortoise-shell.

Bellarmine—A stoneware drinking jug which originated in Germany in the 16th century. It has a bearded mask of Cardinal Bellarmine (1542-1621).

Belleek Porcelain—A hard porcelain made at Belleek in Northern Ireland from about 1857. Its feature is a peculiar glaze possessing a nacreous lustre.

Berlin Porcelain—A porcelain factory was started in 1752 by Wegely producing pure white hard porcelain. Ornamental and utility articles were made, including groups and figures, table services, etc. It ceased to exist in 1757. A second factory was started by Gotzkowski in 1761. The works were taken over by Frederick the Great in 1763, when they were called "The Royal Porcelain Manufactory". The marks were a W (Wegely) while Gotzkowski's factory used at first a G, but from 1763 the sceptre mark. In the 1830's, the K.P.M. (Königliche Porzellanmanufaktur), with sceptre and orb, was introduced.

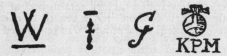

"Bianco Sopra Bianco"—A favourite method of decoration adopted by Bristol and other potteries, whereby the designs were painted in white enamel on a groundwork of a slightly different tone. (*See "En Grisaille".*)

Biberon—An ornate vessel with a spout through which sick persons could drink.

Biscuit Ware—China left in an undecorated state after the first firing, viz., unglazed and of biscuit colour.

Bizen Ware—A hard, whitish-grey unglazed pottery made in Japan. Famed for the excellence of its grotesque figures.

Black Pot—A coarse crockery ware exposed to smoke during the burning process to take the place of glazing; a mug for ale; a toper.

Blanc De Chine—Porcelain of very high quality made at Te-hua in the Fukien Province during the latter part of the Ming dynasty.

Boccaro—A Portuguese name for Chinese brown stoneware, more particularly applied to that produced in the Yi-Hsing potteries during the reign of Wan-Li, 1573-1620. (*See Böttger Ware.*)

Bologna—A factory for Majolica was established here in 1849.

Bombylius—A small Greek narrow-necked vase for holding perfume.

Bordeaux—Porcelain factory commenced about 1785. Mark was A.V. in monogram. Faience also made here. Latens & Rateau established 1829.

Böttger Ware—A reddish-brown stoneware resembling Chinese boccaro ware, made by Böttger at Meissen in 1708.

Bow Porcelain—A patent for the manufacture of porcelain was taken out in 1744 and a second patent in 1749. The porcelain was produced at a factory established at Bromley-by-Bow called "New Canton" but it ceased to operate in 1776 when, it is reputed, the business was purchased by William

Duesbury and transferred to Derby. The porcelain is of the soft-paste variety made from a glassy composition including bone ash. Its quality is far from consistent, although some of the early undercoated work is hardly distinguishable from that made at Chelsea, but generally it is of a coarser texture, the colouring inferior and the modelling

Bow Porcelain—*continued.*

somewhat clumsy by comparison. The glaze is soft, and having a large lead content is prone to discoloration. The earliest pieces were undecorated, but this plain style was soon replaced by painted decorations, both under and over the glaze, in the Oriental style, mostly of Old Japan. These included bamboo, plum branches, partridge designs, etc., executed mainly in red, blue and green with a little gold. Some of the work was made with slightly raised ornaments, brown line edgings and small floral borders. Most of the articles produced were for utility purposes, although many figures and other ornamental items were made. Transfer-printing was not extensively employed, but some pieces have transfer outlines filled in by hand work. Many workmen's marks have been recorded. After 1760, an anchor and dagger in red were sometimes used.

Boyne—The Scottish name for a wide-bottomed bowl or dish.

Breccia—A kind of rock composed of angular fragments, which when cemented together present a variety of colours; used for ornamental items such as bowls and vases.

Bristol Porcelain—The hard-paste porcelain factory transferred from Plymouth was under the control of Richard Champion, and in full production in the years 1773/75, but in 1782 the patent rights for the production of true porcelain were sold to a Staffordshire concern and the works closed

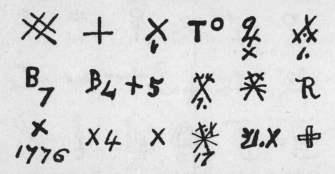

down. Ordinary blue and white ware, without marks, was early produced, as were many articles in the Oriental taste. Ornamental items as well as table services were made and decorated with wreaths and festoons of flowers and laurel with bouquets interspersed; the groundwork

Bristol Porcelain—*continued.*

is milky-white coated with a brilliant glaze. Biscuit portrait medallions were produced, enclosed in porcelain frames enriched in alto-relievo with wreaths of flowers. The marks comprise a plain cross sometimes accompanied with cross swords; the Plymouth mark with a cross; the letter B with a numeral; a cross and a number; the letter B with cross swords and the word "Bristoll". **Bristol Ware**—It is doubtful whether delft was made at Bristol in the 17th century, but there is no doubt it was produced during the first half of the 18th century, as were many other articles of ware, mostly for domestic use. Records show that at least two potteries were in existence, owned by Joseph Ring and Joseph Flower respectively.

Broderie—Design on pottery representing the fine patterns of embroidery.

Bruche—A kind of mug with lid.

Brussels—Hard-paste porcelain was made at a factory established in 1786 near Schaerbeck, Brussels, while a second factory existed at Etterbeck. Faience was made at various workshops from 1650.

Bucchero—An old polished black Etruscan pottery ware with engraved designs.

Buen Retino (Madrid)—A factory originally founded at Capodimonte, Naples, was transferred here by Charles III in 1759. The porcelain is soft paste and a delicate white.

Buire—A pitcher with handle and spout, somewhat resembling the aiguière (*q.v.*). The design is usually less slender.

Burette—An ornamental flask for holding liquids.

Burslem—

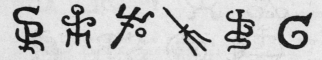

Cadus—An ancient vessel or jar similar to an amphora (*q.v.*).

Caffaggiolo Ware—A variety of Majolica pottery made after 1500, at Caffaggiolo, near Florence.

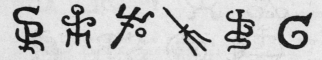

Calphis or **Kalpis**—A hydria. A Grecian water jar with three handles.

Cambrian Pottery—The name given to pottery ware at one time made at Swansea (*q.v.*).

Cameo Ware—Pottery ornamented with figures in relief to represent a cameo, an example of which is Jasper Ware (*See Wedgwood*).

Canette—A German stoneware pitcher with raised ornamental subjects, usually having a handle and metal cover.

Canopic Jars—Etruscan cinerary urns made of terra cotta or bronze, with covers in the form of a human head, and sometimes with handles in the form of human arms. In Egypt they represent the four jars which contained the intestines of a deceased person, buried with the mummy.

Cantharus—A deep cup mounted on a stem, with loop-shaped handles extending above the brim.

Capis—A large earthenware ewer or jack used by the ancient Romans for wine.

Capo-di-Monte—Soft-paste porcelain made at Naples in a factory established in 1743.

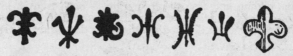

Carpet Balls—Balls made of earthenware of coloured patterns. A set comprises six coloured and one white ball, used for Carpet Bowls, a Victorian game.

Casserole—A French fireproof-ware covered dish.

Castel Durante—A kind of Majolica ware made at Castel Durante in Italy.

Castelli—Majolica was first produced here in the 16th century.

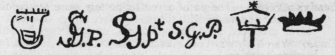

Castleford Ware—Ware of fine quality made in a pottery near Leeds established by David Dunderdale, noted for its Queen's ware and black Egyptian ware.

Caudle Pot—A pot used for preparing a caudle, a warm sweet drink of wine or ale, eggs, spices, etc.; a cup similarly used.

Caughley Porcelain—The original small pottery at Caughley in Shropshire was established about 1754, but was extended when Thomas Turner took it over in 1772 and commenced the making of porcelain. The factory was sold to John Rose, of Coalport, in 1799, who carried on the work until 1814, when the pottery was closed and the plant transferred to Coalport. During its existence porcelain of good quality was produced, mostly decorated in blue floral designs on a white ground. The willow-pattern plate and the blue Broseley dragon were favourite designs, introduced about 1780. Some of the ware

Caughley Porcelain—*continued.*

 resembled that produced at Worcester, with dark blue bands, line gilding and festoon decorations. Both transfer-printing and enamel painting were employed, and a large proportion of the output was devoted to articles for domestic use. Some of

 the pieces were unmarked, but others bore a crescent, which, as time advanced, evolved itself into the letter C, other marks being the letter S, with a cross, also the word "Salopian".

Cauliflower Ware—A glazed earthenware made in the form of cauliflowers and other vegetables by Wedgwood and Whieldon.

Celadon—Chinese porcelain of a particular pale sea-green colour; the colour was mixed with the paste before firing. The earliest colour produced by Chinese Potters, dating from the Sung Dynasty, A.D. 960-1276. Later imitated by the French and English factories.

Cercle Vase—An Egyptian amphora-shaped jar for holding wine; its decoration consists of practically the whole of its outer surface being encircled with horizontal rings.

Chamberlain's Worcester—Robert Chamberlain, a former apprentice at the main Worcester factory, left about 1786 to start on his own. At first he decorated wares purchased from the Caughley works. From 1791 Chamberlain made his own porcelain, mostly tea services and other useful wares. In 1840 combined with Flight, Barr & Barr and in 1852 this company was wound up and Worcester porcelain re-established.

Chantilly Porcelain—A soft porcelain made at a factory established in 1725 by Ciquaire Cirou. Many of the early pieces were produced with designs in the Japanese taste, while others were ornamented with the "Chantilly sprig", consisting of a peculiar

Chantilly Porcelain—*continued.*

shaped leaf placed at the point where the twigs branch. Blue was the predominant colour in later designs. The early pieces were coated with a tin enamel, but this was later displaced by a vitreous glaze. The mark is a hunting horn, in red on the earlier pieces and in blue on the later pieces.

Chelsea Porcelain—There is no clear evidence as to when the pottery was first established, but a few of its products are known to exist bearing the date 1745, although it is believed the factory existed rather before this. All porcelain made at Chelsea comes under the classification of "artificial porcelain", or soft paste, and possesses a glassy appearance which is less apparent in the later pieces. Chelsea is most famous for its figures, although tea-ware, candlesticks, vases, dishes, scent bottles, and many other articles were made. A good deal of the early work was without decoration except for slightly raised sprays, etc., and closely resembled porcelain made at Bow. The general style and workmanship is thought to resemble that produced by contemporary

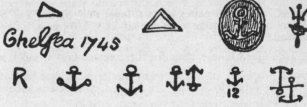

potteries in France, and this is perhaps not surprising when it is remembered that the Chelsea works was under the management of two successive Frenchmen, the second being Nicholas Sprimont, who did much to make its products famous, but owing to his ill-health the plant was sold in 1764, and in 1770 the factory was taken over by William Duesbury, who recommenced making porcelain and continued to do so until 1784, when the workers and plant were removed to Derby. The body of earlier pieces was usually thinner than that which followed, and is consequently liable to distort when fired. About 1755/6 the designs changed materially, and pieces were made in the over-elaborate rococo style with brightly coloured

Chelsea Porcelain—*continued.*

grounds of blue, green and claret and panels of exotic birds, bouquets and scenes, while the handles were very ornate and much gold work was employed. This style did not persist, and by the time the factory was moved to Derby work of a quieter nature was again being produced. The glaze on some of the later work had a tendency to "craze" and in consequence of this and the soft paste it became discoloured. The earliest-known mark is a triangle, but some of the pieces were not marked at all. The triangle was followed by the anchor in an embossed oval, sometimes outlined in colour, usually red. From about 1753 the anchor was painted in red, while a gold anchor was in use between about 1758-70. On the later pieces (1770-1784) the anchor was embodied with the letter "D", and occasionally the letter "D" appeared without the anchor but surmounted by a crown. (*See Derby-Chelsea.*)

Church Gresley Pottery—A small Derbyshire pottery established by Sir Nigel Gresley in 1795 for the manufacture of cream-coloured earthenware and possibly porcelain. It closed in 1808.

Ch'ien Lung (1736-1795)—The potters of this period mastered the control of flambé glaze, which resulted in its extensive use. The porcelain was famed for its chalky-whiteness without any tendency towards yellow or blue tints. It was also noted for its fine smooth glaze, which showed no trace of the potter's wheel. Egg-shell plates were a favourite subject, and many pieces and ornaments were copied from bronzes of an earlier period.

Ching-Tsu—The Chinese name for the greenish-grey **Celadon** ware.

Cistercian Ware—A variety of ware, made in the first half of the 16th century, found in the ruined Cistercian abbeys of Yorkshire.

Cistern—The name given to any large bowl or vessel, especially one used for washing.

Charger—A large flat dish for serving meat. John the Baptist's head was borne on a charger.

Clignancourt—A hard-paste porcelain factory was established in 1771.

Clobbered China—The name given to old china ware that has been touched up or freshened.

Coalport Porcelain (Coalbrookdale)—The Coalport factory was started *c.* 1796 by John Rose, who had previously been at Caughley (*q.v.*), and who, in 1799, also bought up the Caughley works, using it to produce biscuit porcelain which was glazed and decorated at Coalport. The latter factory was moved to Coalport in 1814. Egg-shell tea services (with suké cups), decorated in the Chinese taste were a feature production; in addition a large assortment of both ornamental and useful articles of high quality were made, and are still being made, as the factory continues in production. Sprigs named "Worm", "Chantilly", and

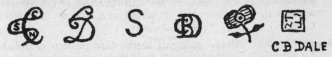

"Tourney" were frequently employed in the decorations, as were fruit and flowers, and panels with floral surrounds. Besides the marks bearing the name of Coalport in one form or another, the following marks were used: a monogram using the letters C.B.D.; the same monogram enclosed in a circular frame containing the words "Daniell and Co., London"; the letters C.S.N. contained in the loops of a peculiarly shaped scroll. Some of the early pieces were unmarked, while others bore imitation marks of Chelsea, Dresden and Sèvres.

Cobridge—

Cockpit Hill Ware—Produced by one of the best-known potteries in Derbyshire, in operation from about the middle of the 18th century until it was closed in 1780. It produced cream-ware, slip and blue-and-white wares. Some of the patterns were in raised outline and the slips coloured orange, white and brown-black. Rims were sometimes notched. Only a few pieces bore the pottery mark.

Combed Ware—The name given to a ware having the surface combed or scratched over to represent catspaw (*q.v.*) or paper mottling.

Compotier—A shallow dish supported on a stem, usually part of a dessert service.

Copeland & Garrett—Copeland and Garrett took over the Spode works in 1833, and produced high grade porcelain, Parian ware and ware. The partnership ended in 1847 and the business was carried on by Taylor Copeland. (*See Spode.*)

Copenhagen—Present factory (hard paste) was established in 1775. In 1779 it became the Royal Copenhagen Porcelain Manufactory, the mark of three wavy lines being adopted in 1775.

Costrel or **Pilgrim's Bottle**—An antique flask made of ware or hide, provided with loops by means of which it could be slung.

Cothon—A Grecian drinking vessel.

Cow Milk Jug—A milk jug made in the form of a cow, the tail being the handle and the mouth the spout. Made in England from 1760.

Crackle Ware—China ware having a fine network of cracks.

Craters—Large earthenware vessels or vases with wide openings and small handles.

Crazing—The accidental fracturing of the glaze in firing.

Crazy China—Earthenware coated with putty or cement into which are pressed fragments of coloured china.

Crock—The name given to almost any large earthenware pot.

Crouch Ware—A term applied to the ware made early in the 18th century from a whiteish Derbyshire clay which had been used by glass makers, the greenish tint being caused by chemical impurities left in the clay.

Crown Derby—(*See Derby Porcelain.*)

Cruse—Any kind of vessel for holding water, honey or the like; a jar or pot.

Cyathus—A long-handled cup or ladle used for filling drinking cups with wine from a crater.

Cylix—A shallow bowl-like drinking cup with two handles, mounted on a stem with base. (*See Kylix*.)

Damassé—The name sometimes given to a type of pottery with a white ground, decorated with flowers in white enamel.

Davenport—An existing pottery at Longport was taken over by John Davenport in 1793. At first only earthenware was made, but porcelain also was produced from the early 19th century.

Delft Ware—Delft became the centre of the Dutch pottery industry in the mid-17th century. It is supposed that Dutch potters introduced the manufacture of tin-glazed earthenware into England at the earlier date (*c.* 1567), where it was long popular and made at many potteries, including Lambeth. It was made of biscuit-coloured clay coated with an opaque white tin enamel on which designs were painted in a variety of colours including blue, purple, yellow and occasionally black, green and red. Before final firing the articles were coated with a transparent glaze. The Dutch ware is softer and thinner than that made in England and generally of greater merit.

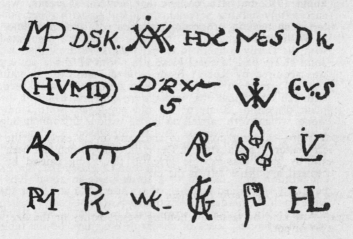

Delft Ware—*continued*.

Demi-tasse—A small coffee cup.

Dentelle Ware—Pottery and porcelain perforated to present a lace-like appearance.

Derby Porcelain—The original pottery was probably established about 1750, but it is certain that William Duesbury was successfully making porcelain in 1756. As with other potteries, changes in proprietorship occurred, and in addition to William Duesbury the following names are associated with the Derby concern in its early days: Andrew Planché, John Heath and Michael Kean. In about 1815 the pottery was acquired by Robert Bloor, who did little to maintain the high tradition which had been previously established, with the result that the works were sold in 1848 and the plant dispersed. Some of the old employees started new works which were carried on under various titles including Locker & Co., Stevenson & Co., Stevenson & Hancock, Sharp & Co., and Courtney. The present Royal Crown Derby Porcelain Works was established in 1876. The early porcelain was largely composed of glassy frit, but its composition was changed to a softer paste in about 1764; bone ash was added some six years after, and still later the paste was made harder and less transparent. The best porcelain was probably produced between the years 1786 and 1796, when fine figures, vases of classic design, jugs, bowls, table

Derby Porcelain—*continued.*

services and many other ornamental and utility articles were made. The decorations and reliefs were well painted and included landscape scenes, roses, sprigs, lace trimmings, borders of blue and gold, festoons in pink, etc., and the patterns of Imari (Japan) ware were successfully imitated. A soft translucent biscuit ware, which included figures, was also produced from about 1770 to 1815; the secret of this is now lost. The first mark is reputed to be the letter "D", in gold and this was followed by the combined "D" and anchor, usually

in gold, at the t me common to both Derby and Chelsea. About 1773 a jewelled crown was placed above the letter "D", and provided another mark, but later the crown was drawn without the representation of jewels, the colours being blue, red or green. To this mark was added in about 1782 two cross staves or daggers with six dots, the colours remaining as before with the addition of black and gold. The D & K mark was first employed in about 1795 and the Bloor mark first used about 1830. There are a number of other marks.

Derby Chelsea Porcelain—*(See Chelsea Porcelain.)*

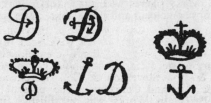

Derby Ware—*(See Cockpit Hill.)*

Deruta Ware—A Majolica made in Deruta, Perugia.

Diaphanie—The art of affixing coloured transparencies to glass to give the effect of staining.

Dinos—A large cistern-like Grecian bowl with a cover.

Diota—A Greek or Roman vessel with two handles or ears, resembling an amphora.

Doccia—This factory was established in 1735 by Carlo Ginori making excellent copies of Capo-di-Monte whose moulds were acquired in 1821. Also made excellent copies of Majolica.

Dollin—The name given in the West of England and Wales to a small earthenware jug.

Doulton—Doulton of Lambeth made a distinctive stone ware. All pieces were marked with the decorator's mark as well as the factory mark. The making of stoneware ceased in 1956. In 1882 Doultons commenced making porcelain of the highest quality at Burslem and still continues.

Dresden (or Meissen)—The factory was founded in 1710 as a result of the researches of J. F. Böttger, in whose laboratory the momentous discovery of the composition and firing of true hard-paste porcelain was first made. The Meissen factory, which still exists today, is just outside the town of Dresden.

Dresden is most famous for its ornamental pieces, which include figures and groups, candelabra, centre pieces and vases, some reaching quite large proportions. Johann Joachim Kandler, one of the finest modellers ever, joined the factory in 1731. Many figures were made for mounting in ormolu, such as those on clocks and candelabra. The famous crinoline

groups belong to this period. Kandler's early work has been termed baroque. Some of the early pieces executed for the king (Augustus the Strong, King of Poland and Elector of Saxony) were marked with a monogram composed of the letters A.R. (Augustus Rex) in blue, and the caduceus (staff of Mercury), and from about 1726 the well-known crossed swords.

Earthenware—The simplest type of baked clay ware, lacking the finish and translucency of china.

Ecuelle—Literally (French) "porringer", applied to a fairly large vessel, generally of ornamental character, in the form of a cup with cover or a casserole, usually on a stand.

Egg-Shell China—A thin, fragile, semi-transparent china ware made in China in the 15th century, since copied elsewhere.

Egyptian Black Ware—(*See Wedgwood.*)

Elers Ware—A red pottery ware made in Staffordshire in the late 17th century by the brothers Elers.

Enamel—A vitrifiable composition used for coating pottery and applied to the glaze after firing. The term is also used to describe that Oriental porcelain in which the colour stands out in slight relief from the surface.

"En Camaieu"—In a single colour, with its varied shades introduced to heighten the effect.

Encaustic Tiles—Decorated paving tiles, the designs of which were formed by coloured clay, largely used in churches during the 15th and 16th centuries.

Encaustic Painting—A style of decoration used in early times, the colours being fixed by heated wax. **Encaustic**—The burning in of colours.

"En Grisaille"—In grey, with its different shades employed to give the effect of relief.

Ewer—A large pitcher or jug.

Faenza (Majolica)—The majolica ware made at the end of the 15th century at Faenza is possibly the most beautiful of all. Generally the pigments are blue and yellow.

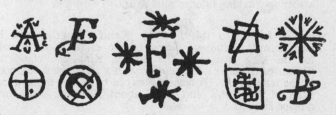

Faenza (Majolica)—*continued*.

Faience or **Fayence**—The name given to coloured earthenware and porcelain believed to have originated at Faenza, in Italy. Properly applied to tin-enamelled wares.

Fairings—Small china groups or figures made during the second half of the 19th century, mostly in Germany, for British fairgrounds. Many are titled.

Famille Rose—A beautiful rose colour used in the decoration of porcelain, particularly oriental. Famille verte, green; famille jaune, yellow; and famille noire, black.

Figuline—A piece of pottery, especially when it bears representations of natural objects. **Figurine**—A pottery figure.

Findjan—A small round coffee cup used in a cone-shaped holder in Turkey and Egypt.

Flagon—A flat-sided, bottle-shaped vessel for holding liquor, usually with a handle and spout.

Flambé—In ceramic art is a term to describe the colouring or glaze when it has been irregularly applied or appears to have run down the sides from the top in flame fashion.

Florence—The first place in Europe to successfully imitate porcelain art. Was a soft paste and translucent, very rare. A modern factory for making faience now exists.

Flux—A glass-like substance containing felspar and bismuth, mixed with the colours used to decorate porcelain, etc., so that it can be fired at a lower temperature.

Fountain—A 17th-century name for a large jar or pitcher to hold water.

Frankenthal Porcelain—A German porcelain made from about the middle to the close of the 18th century.

Frit—The composition from which white soft paste is made; a half-used composition for making glazes; a partly fused material of which glass is made.

Frog Mug—Is a drinking mug with a model of a frog which becomes visible as the contents of the mug are drunk, made at Sunderland, Leeds, Nottingham, etc.

Fuddling Cup—Consists of three, five or six smallware cups shaped like violet bowls and attached to each other in the form of a triangle. It is doubtful if such cups were ever actually used for drinking purposes.

Fulda—A porcelain factory in Germany, 1764 to 1790.

Fulham Pottery—Fine stoneware made of clay and pounded flint with a hard salt glaze (*q.v.*) which was unaffected by fluids and acids. It was first produced at Fulham by John Dwight (d. 1703) in the second half of the 17th century, the patent being granted in 1671. Articles were partly vitrified by firing, and when they reached a white heat salt was applied, the resulting chemical action producing the glaze. Statuettes as well as ordinary domestic and other articles were produced in colours which included marbled-blue, brown, bronze, mouse and white. Some pieces were decorated with hunting scenes, etc., in stamped relief work.

Fürstenberg Porcelain—Made at a German pottery established about the middle of the 18th century for the manufacture of porcelain. Designs follow those of contemporary potteries.

Gallipot—A small earthenware pot used by druggists for ointment, etc., similar to a jam pot but smaller.

Gargoulette—An ornamental earthenware jar with handle and bottle-shaped spout used for cooling water in the East.

Ginger Jar—A globular-shaped jar to contain preserved ginger; often very ornately decorated.

Glare—The name sometimes given to the glaze on earthenware.

Glaze—Silicates used for decoration of pottery and protection against moisture.

Goglet—A long-necked bottle for cooling water, usually made of porous earthenware.

Goss China—A white porcelain ware invented by W. H. Goss (1833-1906) and made at Stoke-on-Trent. It nearly always bore the crest or armorial bearings of a town and was at one time in great demand by collectors.

Gotha—(Thuringia) 1757 onwards. A hard paste.

Graffito or **Graffiato**—Pottery covered with a slip through which the design is scratched.

Grainger-Worcester—Thomas Grainger opened a factory at Worcester in 1801, trading as Grainger & Wood. In 1839 Grainger's son George succeeded and the title was changed to G. Grainger & Co. Produced much fine Parian china. Taken over by the Royal Worcester Co. in 1889 but Grainger shield mark was used until 1902.

Grès de Flandres or Grès Flamand Ware—A blue-coloured stoneware of Flemish origin.

Greybeard—A stoneware drinking jug ornamented with a bearded face in relief on the upper part of the spout.

Gubbio Ware—A variety of Majolica ware made at Gubbio in Italy.

Guldan—A vase of Persian origin, having its perforated top closed in, presumably to hold flowers for better display.

Gutturnium—An old water jug or ewer for pouring water over the hands before and after meals.

Half Moon China—The name sometimes given to porcelain made at Caughley, so named because of the pottery mark.

Hague, The—1775-1785. Hard-paste porcelain only.

Hawthorn China—The name given to certain Oriental china ware of blue ground, decorated with plum-tree (prunus) blossoms in white which resemble the flowers of the hawthorn. The latter was also a favourite subject for the decoration of Bow porcelain.

Hemphill Porcelain—A porcelain made in North America, popular in the 19th century.

Herend—(Hungary). A china factory was commenced here in 1839, specialised in imitations of old Sèvres.

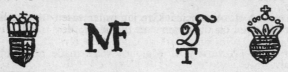

Hispano-Moresque Majolica—

Höchst Pottery—A small German pottery, in operation from early in the 18th century until 1794. Fayence was produced at first and it was not until about the middle of the century that satisfactory porcelain was made. The products best known are probably small figures modelled by Melchior. The mark is a wheel with six spokes which is sometimes crowned.

Hydria—An ancient Grecian water ewer distinguished by having a back and two side handles and a sharp rise in the shape at the neck.

Imari Ware—A glazed porcelain made at Nagasaki in Japan from about the beginning of the 17th century.

Ironstone China—A hard dense pottery ware first produced in 1831, made of ironside (flint), clay and powdered slag.

Isleworth Pottery—Established by Joseph Shore in 1760; existed to 1825.

Ivory Porcelain—A beautiful ivory-white glazed porcelain produced by the Worcester potteries.

Jasper Ware—(*See Wedgwood.*)

Jouy—The name given to Chinese vases with handles or decorations representing emblems of longevity. (*See Ju-i sceptre.*)

Kakiyemon—A 17th-century Japanese potter who invented a process of enamelling porcelain.

Kalpis or **Calpis**—An ancient Grecian water vase with two handles at the shoulder and one at the neck, decorated with red classical figures on a dark ground. (*See Hydria.*)

Kaolin—A fine non-fusible white clay used with petuntse (*q.v.*) to make the hard paste of which true porcelain is composed. It is formed by the decomposition of a granite rock containing quartz, mica and felspar.

Kloster-Veilsdorf—(Thuringia). 1760 onwards.

Korzec—(Poland.) A hard paste of good quality.

Kylix—An ancient Grecian drinking cup with two handles, somewhat similar in shape to a squat-shaped wine glass. (*See Cylix.*)

Lachrymatory—A small vessel for containing the tears of the relatives of a deceased person.

Lagena—Earthenware vessels for holding wine and fruit.

Lambeth Delft—(*See Delft.*)

Lane End—

Lazuli Ware—A Wedgwood pebbleware of blue streaked with gold.

Lecythus—A Grecian ewer-shaped vase, often richly decorated in polychrome.

Lead Glaze—A glaze formed on cheap pottery by the use of lead.

Leeds Ware—Fine cream-coloured ware produced during a period of about one hundred years from 1760; it is thin, uniform in colour and possesses a rich creamy glaze. Many of the pieces have elegantly pierced patterns, as the rims of plates; the borders are often decorated with delicate feather mouldings. Both painted and transfer-printed designs were employed, some of the latter being under-glaze blue. A cheaper white ware, following the general lines of the cream-ware, was also produced, in addition to Egyptian black, surface-marbled lustre ware and some figures.

HARTLEY GREEN & C°   G   LP HAWLEY

Leek Ware—A name sometimes given to Mason's ironstone china owing to its being made at Leek in Staffordshire.

Levigate—To free from grit and make smooth; to smooth as if polished.

Libation—The act of pouring a liquid; consequently, the name sometimes given to Chinese vessels once used to pour wine on a victim in sacrifice or in honour of a deity.

Lille—The pottery was founded in about 1711 for the production of soft porcelain, and later hard porcelain was also made. The early mark is the letter L. The later pieces bear a crowned dolphin. Faience also made.

Limbach—(Thuringia). Commenced 1772.

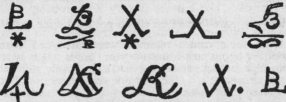

Limoges Porcelain—A famous hard-paste porcelain with a high glaze made at Limoges from about 1773.

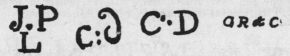

Lithophane—A design or figures impressed on porcelain, made clear by transmitted light.

Liverpool Ware—The 18th century saw a large number of potteries in operation in and around Liverpool, particularly in the district called Herculaneum, resulting in the production of an equally large number and variety of styles of ware, such as Delft, terra-cotta, cream-ware, slipware, stoneware, etc. Transfer-printing was a favourite method for decoration, and was probably at its height in 1760, a popular design being a bird (liver) with a sprig in its beak. A small quantity of porcelain was produced from about 1820 to 1845.

Longport—A porcelain produced by Davenport in 1793.

Longton Hall—William Littler was known to be producing porcelain in the year 1752, but the factory was probably established before then. Its life was short and it is thought it was taken over by William Duesbury and transferred to Derby. In general, the porcelain resembles that made at Chelsea, but flaws are by no means uncommon. Some pieces were made with blue ground panels of a particular shade with reliefs of flowers, insects, etc. Open-work dessert services were also produced. The mark consists of two L's, crossed, with a line of dots from the point of intersection.

Loosdrecht—The porcelain factory originally founded at Weesp, in Holland, was moved here in 1771, where it remained until its removal to Amstel in 1784. A hard paste.

$$M.oL \quad MoL \quad M{:}oL$$

Loutrophorus—A tall black ware vase used in old Grecian marriage ceremonies.

Loving Cup—Wine cups having two or more handles to facilitate passing from person to person.

Lowesby—A pottery established here in 1835.

Lowestoft Porcelain—The pottery is reputed to have been established between the years 1756 and 1760, and although the name of its founder is unknown, Robert Browne is supposed to have had some connection with it. Records show that in 1770 the factory was being operated by Robert Browne & Co., and that manufacture did not cease until 1802. The porcelain was of the soft paste variety, and many pieces closely resemble those produced at Worcester; embossed patterns, inscriptions with dates, designs in the Chinese taste, scenes and floral tributes were all used in the decorations, and a spiral or fluted ware and blue-and-white ware were also produced. There were no regular pottery marks, but it is thought the open crescent moon of Worcester was sometimes employed, as were numerals and workmen's signs.

Ludwigsburg Porcelain—sometimes known as **Kronenburg Ware**—Porcelain was made for about three-quarters of a century before the close of the pottery in 1825. Figures were the most important production. The marks include a shield containing three antlers; also cypher of the reigning duke or king, the latter after 1806; both were sometimes surmounted by a crown.

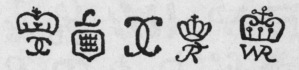

Lustre Ware—A ware having its surface coated with a thin layer of metallic iridescent lustre, made by dissolving metals in chemicals. Copper lustre is more general, but many silver and gold or purple articles exist. The earliest copper lustre ware was probably produced by R. Frank at Brislington in about 1770; others concerned in its manufacture include Wedgwood, Moore & Co., of Sunderland, and Dillwyn of Swansea. Some pieces were decorated with blue bands, and others with floral and foliated designs.

Majolica—Pottery ware produced in Spain and Italy, from the 14th to 16th centuries. It is impossible to give a general description of the ware as it was made all over Italy, most, if not all, of the principal towns having a pottery, each with its own peculiarities in design and workmanship; but it is fairly safe to say that a characteristic of the ware is that it was coated with brilliant warm enamels of tin or lead. The name of Luca della Robbia (about 1400-1481) is associated with some of the earliest pieces.

Marieberg (Sweden)—Both porcelain and pottery made here 1758-1789.

Marseilles—A hard-paste porcelain factory established about 1770 by Joseph Robert. The works closed 1793, Marseilles noted for its potteries.

Marseilles—*continued.*

Martinware—A salt-glaze stoneware produced by the four Martin Brothers between 1873 and 1914. All pieces are incised before firing with their name and place of production (first Fulham and later Southall).

Mason's Ironstone China—This is an earthenware despite its name. Charles Mason, the son of Miles Mason maker of good porcelain at Lane Delph, took out a patent in 1813 for his famous Ironstone. Eventually the firm came to G. L. Ashworth & Bros. of Hanley who today produce this type of ware.

Mazerin—An old name for a porringer.

Medina Jug—Associated with the Armada. It is of ordinary bulbous shape with the top half inclined forward, so that if the serpent handle, with which it is adorned, is suitably held, part of the contents can be poured without lifting the jug.

Meissen—*see Dresden.*

Mennecy-Villeroy Porcelain—The pottery was established by Barbin in 1735 and soft porcelain produced. It was moved to Bourg-la-Reine in 1773. It is most famed for its small statuettes, which were sometimes brightly coloured, though often only coated with a white glaze or left in their biscuit state. The porcelain possessed a fine translucent body with an even and brilliant glaze, and was generally but sparingly decorated with flowers, etc. The mark is the letters D.V.

Mezzina—A 16th century Italian ewer.

Milan—Faience made here from 18th century.

Minton—Thomas Minton was concerned in making only earthenware up to about 1798, when he extended his scope by the manufacture of porcelain and majolica. For about twelve years from this date a semi-transparent china was made, then abandoned until 1821, when its manufacture was resumed. In 1817 he was joined in the business by his two sons, and by John Boyle from 1836 to 1841. The early white earthenware was usually decorated in blue in the Chinese style. Other ware included hard and soft porcelain, parian, majolica, etc. Classical pâte-sur-pâte (*q.v.*) figures and subjects were included in the decorations, as were painted and printed garden and figure scenes, flowers, etc. Sèvres designs were also imitated. The early marks in blue consist of two curved staves crossed with the letter "M", under the intersection; the letters "M & C" (Minton & Co.), sometimes accompanied by the letters "BB"; in 1868 a globe with the word Minton.

Mirror-black glaze—A lustrous and brilliant glaze, used as a monochrome or Chinese porcelain.

Mortlake Pottery—In production from the late 18th to the early 19th century.

Moscow—An Englishman named Gardner started a porcelain factory at Verbilki in 1758, another was founded in 1806 by A. Popoff.

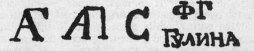

Moustiers Ware—A ware made at Moustiers in the South of France commenced in the 17th century.

Moustiers Ware—*continued.*

$$\mathcal{V}f \quad °OY. \quad \mathcal{BPLL}°° \mathcal{B}$$
$$\mathcal{F.P} \quad B\mathcal{P} \quad \mathcal{B} \quad \mathcal{PA} \quad \mathcal{Sl} \quad \mathcal{Ef}$$

Mug—A large cylindrical drinking vessel with a handle.

Nankin Ware—A general term used to describe Chinese porcelain painted in blue on a white ground, not necessarily made at Nankin.

Nantgarw Porcelain—Ware made at a small pottery near Cardiff founded in 1813 by William Billingsley of Pinxton, with William Young and Samuel Walker. In 1814 William Billingsley and William Young joined the Swansea Pottery and worked there until 1817, after which William Billingsley returned to Nantgarw until 1819, in which year he left for Coalport, where he eventually died. The factory was carried on by William Young until its close in 1820-22. The porcelain produced at Nantgarw is noted for its extreme whiteness and transparency, and was often elaborately and realistically decorated with fruit and flowers by William Billingsley, who was an artist of high repute. The mark was usually the word "Nantgarw" impressed, sometimes followed by the letters C.W., supposed to stand for China Works.

Naples—The Royal Porcelain factory was founded by King Ferdinand IV of Naples in 1771 and remained in existence until 1834. Soft-paste was made. Majolica was also made at Naples from the late 17th century.

Nevers—Faience produced since 17th century.

New Hall—Commenced making hard paste porcelain in 1782. Typical patterns comprise floral sprays and Chinese figures.

Niderviller—A hard paste porcelain factory established here in 1760. Faience was also made.

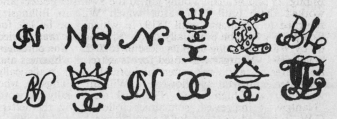

Nivernais Faience—A ware made at Nevers in France in 1608 by the brothers Conrade.

Noggin—A small mug or cup of Scottish origin holding a quarter of a pint (a gill).

Nottingham Ware—A brown stoneware made at Nottingham in the 18th century.

Nove Bassano—In 1728 a factory of earthenware was started. Soft-paste porcelain was made here from 1752 until 1835.

Nuremberg Ware—Brightly coloured ware somewhat resembling majolica, made in the 16th and 17th centuries.

Nymphenberg Porcelain—A German porcelain made at a pottery established about the middle of the 18th century.

Nyon, Lake Geneva—A small factory commenced at end of the 18th century by Jacques Dostu and Charles-Ferdinand Müller.

Oenochoe—A Greek wine pitcher with trefoil top, used to take wine from the crater to fill the cups of guests.

Oiron—It was at one time thought that the so-called Henri Deux ware was made here. Modern research has established that this ware was in fact made at St. Porchaire (*q.v.*)

Olpe—An ancient Greek jug without a lip.

Orleans—Soft-paste porcelain at first and from 1770, hard-paste. (*c.* 1753-*c.* 1810.)

Palissy Ware—A coloured enamelware made by Bernard Palissy at Saintes in France from about the middle of the 16th century to early in the 17th century. He produced several kinds of ware but is probably most noted for that in the "Rustic" style; this had a rough ground decorated in relief with designs of reptiles, fishes, etc. as in water.

Parian—A matt white porcelain, originally called Statuary Porcelain introduced in the early 1840's. Mainly used to make figures, groups and busts by nearly all factories.

Paris—There were a large number of hard-paste factories situated here.

Paris—*continued.*

Pâte-sur-Pâte—In ceramics, a white enamel design or figure in bas-relief, through which its darker groundwork shows, varying in accordance with the thickness of design.

Pebble Ware—A kind of pottery ware made by Wedgwood. The method employed was to mix different coloured clays in the paste, with the result that the finished article resembled serpentine, porphyry, etc.

Pelike—A Grecian amphora with wide mouth and practically no neck.

Persian—

Pesaro Ware—A variety of majolica with iridescent glaze, made at Pesaro in the late 15th century.

Petuntse—A fusible white china stone containing potash and soda, which, when mixed with kaolin (*q.v.*), forms the necessary ingredients for the making of true or hard porcelain. The English word is "Felspar".

Phaleron Pottery—Ancient Greek ware having decorations in the Oriental style.

Piggin—A small wooden or earthenware bowl or pail with an upright handle.

Pilgrim's Bottle—A flat flask-shaped bottle. (*See Costrel.*)

Pinxton Porcelain—A porcelain ware made by William Billingsley in a small factory established at Pinxton in Derbyshire in 1795. The ware closely resembled that made at Derby, being decorated with sprigs of flowers, landscape scenes, etc. William Billingsley left Pinxton in 1801 for Nantgarw, where he established a small pottery, and after his departure the porcelain declined in quality. The pottery was purchased by J. Cutts in 1804, and he continued to manufacture until 1818. The marks are the letter P, or sometimes the word "Pinxton".

Pipkin—A small earthenware pot, usually with a horizontal handle and sometimes having a lid.

Pitcher—An earthenware vessel of simple design with a lip or spout, used for carrying water. Often represented in classical subjects.

Pithos—A large Grecian earthenware vessel in the shape of a cask; a spheroid vessel.

Plymouth Porcelain—The first hard or true porcelain to be made in England was produced by William Cookworthy in his pottery at Coxside, Plymouth, which he opened in 1768, having previously discovered the existence of kaolin and petuntse in Cornwall, both necessary ingredients for the manufacture of porcelain. He obtained a patent for his process in 1768, and although the work produced was satisfactory, the pottery was not a financial success and was transferred to Bristol in 1770, where the concern was carried on under the title of Cookworthy & Co. In 1773 the pottery was taken over and run by Richard Champion, who called the works "The Bristol China Manufactory". The early white pieces were unmarked and had slightly raised decorations, shells, seaweed, etc., being used as ornamentation for bases. Many of the later pieces had raised decorations and were enriched with Oriental patterns, birds and flowers, and were in the style of Sèvres. The principal mark consists of the figure four with the start of the downward stroke curved backwards in a loop, thus representing the sign for tin. The colours used were blue, red and sometimes gold.

Plymouth Porcelain—*continued.*

$$2_4 \quad \leftrightarrow \quad 2_4 \quad 2_1 \quad x \quad {}^{XII}_{2\ell}$$

Pokal—A tall German drinking cup with lid, popular in the 16th and 17th centuries; usually ornamented with a coat-of-arms.

Porcelain—A kind of translucent pottery, believed to have derived its name from a shell (cowrie) noted for its smoothness and whiteness. Although porcelain was made in China many centuries ago, it does not appear to have been produced in any quantity in England until about the middle of the 18th century, although it was made at Meissen in 1709. Opinions seem to differ as to what really constitutes porcelain, but it is now generally divided into two classes called True Porcelain (hard paste) and Artificial Porcelain (soft paste). **True Porcelain** was made from a paste consisting of china stone (petuntse, *q.v.*) and china clay (kaolin, *q.v.*), with sometimes a little siliceous sand added. Its glaze was made from china stone softened by the addition of lime, the whole being fired at one operation at a temperature of about 1400 deg. Centigrade. The enamel designs are bold and clear in appearance, and little impression can be made on the hard paste with a rasp. Porcelain made at Bristol, Plymouth, Dresden and in China, etc., is of the hard-paste variety. **Artificial Porcelain** was made largely from glass with a small proportion of white clay; its glaze was composed of fusible glass made principally from red lead, sand and nitre. The body was fired first at a temperature of about 1100 deg. Centigrade; the design and glaze were then added and the article again fired at a somewhat lower temperature. The designs of enamel appear to sink into and merge with the soft paste, which is easily scratched. **English Bone Porcelain** is made from bone ash, china stone and china clay, and the glaze from china stone and china clay with boracic acid, lead oxide and alkalis added. Two firings take place, as before mentioned.

Posset Cup—A cup of globular shape with deep rim and two or more handles and spouts. Posset is composed of milk curdled by adding wine or some other acidulous liquor.

Potiche—The French name given to a vase decorated in panels, having a cover, rounded shoulders and nearly straight sides with a short neck of smaller diameter.

Pot-Lids—Originally the lids of bear grease and fish pastes which were decorated with multi-coloured prints under glaze. Jesse Austin (1806-1879) perfected this printing.

Pot-pourri Vase or Jar—Made in many shapes and forms, with perforated lids, to contain a mixture of dried sweet-smelling leaves and spices, such as rose petals, violets, lavender, cedar shavings, etc.

Pottery—A ware made of clay shaped when soft and wet and afterwards hardened by heat. In a general sense it is inferior to porcelain, and is distinguished by being opaque.

Powder Blue—A term used to describe the colouring of vases, etc., the main blue colour of which has the appearance of having been sprinkled on the white groundwork in the form of powder, giving a somewhat mottled effect.

Prague—Earthenware.

Pratt Ware—A name given to two different types of ware.

1. A range of relief moulded Toby and other jugs, teapots, etc., decorated in under glaze colours. Originally made by William Pratt and continued by his son Felix, as F. & R. Pratt of Fenton.

2. Multi-coloured print decoration such as Pot-lids and similarly decorated table ware, Jesse Austin, who perfected this printing, was a friend of Felix Pratt.

Premières, near Dijon—A faience factory was established here in 1783.

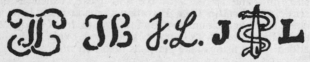

Quaich—A favourite drinking vessel in Scotland during the 16th and 17th centuries; it is a circular bowl with two pronounced ear handles. Reproductions are often used as sugar basins, etc.

Queen's Ware—(*See Wedgwood.*)

Reflet—A term used to describe the peculiar metallic brilliancy seen in lustred pottery.

"Resist" Designs—A method adopted to produce base-coloured patterns on lustre ware. The designs were coated with an easily soluble medium before the whole was lustred; a subsequent washing removed the medium and left the patterns or designs exposed and free.

Rhyton—A Greek earthenware drinking vessel with one handle, the base of which is usually in the form of an animal's head.

Rockingham Porcelain—An almost perfect porcelain ware produced at Swinton in Yorkshire from 1820 to 1842. It was usually heavily decorated with designs of fruit and flowers, with a fairly large amount of gilt in the border patterns. The marks consist of the name of the firm "Brameld" and after 1826 the winged griffin was added.

Rockingham Ware—A factory for the making of pottery was established in 1745 at Swinton, Yorkshire, on the Marquis of Rockingham's estate. After passing through several hands the factory was taken over in 1807 by Messrs. Brameld.

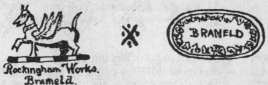

Rörstrandj Ware—Pottery produced at the Rörstrand Pottery at Stockholm, founded in 1726.

Rouen Ware—An enamelled faience ware produced at Rouen in the 17th century. The bodies were made of fairly thick paste and coated with an opaque white enamel which had a tendency to bluishness. Oriental designs in blue and white were early produced, followed by landscape panels with encrusted wreaths of flowers, bouquets, lace patterns, baskets, mythological subjects, etc. A soft porcelain was also made at Rouen by Louis Poterat from about 1673.

St. Amand—A factory of faience was founded here in 1718. A soft-paste porcelain was also made here from 1771, that made since 1800 is similar to that of Tournay.

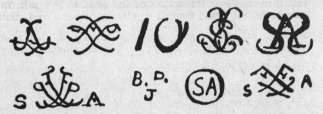

Saint Cloud Porcelain—Soft porcelain was produced at the Saint-Cloud factory by the widow of Pierre Chicanneau from about 1695. Early in the 18th century she married Henri Trou. The ware possessed a milky-white ground and was sparingly decorated with flowers, scrolls, etc., some designs showing an Oriental tendency. Some of the ornaments were raised in low relief and included imbricated patterns. Amongst the marks are a sun in blue and later the letter T (Trou). Closed 1766.

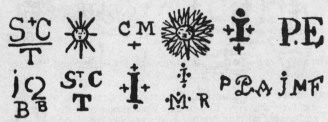

St. Petersburg—Porcelain has been made here since 1744.

Salopian Ware—Porcelain produced at Caughley (*q.v.*) in Shropshire in the late 18th century.

Salt Glaze—A method of coating stoneware (clay and sand or pounded flint) with a fine hard glaze impervious to fluids and acids. The articles were usually kilned to a white heat and salt then applied; the action of the soda in the salt on the silicate in the ware formed a silicate of soda and alumina which coated the surface with glaze. The process was first employed in England in the late 17th century, being used by John Dwight at Fulham and by Astbury and Elers in Staffordshire, as well as by others.

Sang-de-boeuf (Ox blood)—A term used to describe Chinese porcelain, etc., when it is of a blood-red colour.

Sarai—An Eastern vase-shaped vessel for containing liquids; it consists of a flat bulbous-shaped body with tall tapering neck and a lid.

Satsuma Ware—A famous Japanese faience ware made from the late 16th century. A buff-coloured pottery decorated in gold and colours.

Savona—Majolica.

Sceanx-Penthievre—A soft-paste porcelain made between 1748 and 1794.

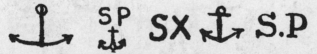

Scinde—An Indian pottery-ware made in the area of the river Scinde in the State of Gwalior.

Scodella—A flat stemmed ware dish used in Italy; a tazza.

Sèvres Porcelain—The pottery was first established at Vincennes in 1740 by two brothers named Dubois, who failed in 1743, when it was taken over by Gravant. The factory was moved to Sèvres in 1753, at which time a Royal decree was granted by Louis XV. Only soft porcelain was made at the factory until 1769, when the manufacture of hard porcelain was introduced, the two kinds being produced side by side until 1804, when the making of the soft variety ceased. Early pieces, up to about 1748, largely followed Oriental designs, but in 1750-52 a white biscuit ware, which included statuettes, was made and its production extended over a period of about a quarter of a century. Other white ware was produced, sometimes with fluted bodies, and decorated with detached blossoms, scattered groups or bouquets of flowers, etc., some of the designs being in high relief. As the reign of Louis XV advanced the designs in pottery, as in furniture, became more decorative in the over-ornate rocaille style, and in some pieces the grounds were entirely covered with bright colours, relieved with pastoral and figure panels in gilded frames, wreaths of flowers, etc., while handles and feet were either gilded or made of ormolu. The best known ground colour is probably the Royal blue (bleu-du-Roi). The turquoise (bleu celeste) is blue by daylight and sea-green by artificial light. A rarer colour is the Rose Pompadour. Jewelled Sèvres is a ware possessing glassy or opaque enamel beads of bright colours, dotted about and forming part of the designs, which include festoons, scrolls and foliaged patterns. This was in vogue for only a short period from about 1780. Several glazes were used on the hard porcelain, but the hard, cold felspathic glaze was the one principally employed from about 1780. This glaze sacrificed art for utility, as the enamel of the designs did not admix with the hard glaze and remained on the surface, presenting a flat appearance. Designs were in step with historical events, and following the Revolution they included military trophies,

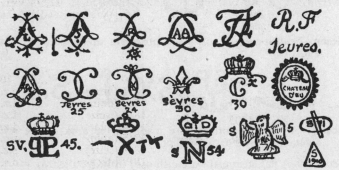

Sèvres Porcelain—*continued.*

battle scenes, thunderbolts, eagles, etc. The marks ordered under the decree of 1753 were the double "L" (King's initial) and a date letter. A single date letter was used to 1777, followed by a double date letter to 1793, and afterwards the word "Sèvres" and the letters R.F. Artists' signs nearly always accompanied the above. The "crowned double L" appears only on pieces of the hard variety. The painted designs on the soft porcelain penetrate the glaze with a tendency to spread, whereas they remain on the surface in the hard variety.

CHRONOLOGICAL TABLE OF SIGNS EMPLOYED IN THE ROYAL
MANUFACTORY OF SÈVRES

by which the exact date of any piece may be ascertained, the date letter being placed within the cipher (interlaced L's), sometimes the double letters were placed one on each side.

A (Vincennes)	1753	O	...	1767	DD	...	1781
B "	1754	P	...	1768	EE	...	1782
C "	1755	Q	...	1769	FF	...	1783
D	1756	R	...	1770	GG	...	1784
E	1757	S	...	1771	HH	...	1785
F	1758	T	...	1772	II	...	1786
G	1759	U	...	1773	JJ	...	1787
H	1760	V	...	1774	KK	...	1788
I	1761	X	...	1775	LL	...	1789
J	1762	Y	...	1776	MM	...	1790
K	1763	Z	...	1777	NN	...	1791
L	1764	AA	...	1778	OO	...	1792
M	1765	BB	...	1779	PP	...	1793
N	1766	CC	...	1780			

During the Revolutionary changes the double letters were rarely used from 1795 to 1800. They were replaced by the following signs:—

Year	IX	1801	...	T9	1807	...	...	7
"	X	1802	...	X	1808	...	...	8
					1809	...	...	9
"	XI	1803	...	11	1810	...	...	10
					1811 (onze)	...		o.z.
"	XII	1804		-//-	1812 (douze)	...		d.z.
					1813 (treize)	...		t.z.
"	XIII	1805		⬆	1814 (quatorze)	...		q.z.
"	XIV	1806		≡	1815 (quinze)	...		q.n.
					1816 (seize)	...		s.z.
					1817 (dix sept)	...		d.s.

Shelton—

Siena Ware—A flesh-coloured majolica ware made at Siena (Italy) from about the middle of the 15th century.

Sigillate—A term applied to pottery when decorated with an impressed pattern as made by stamps or seals.

Sinceny—Faience factory established in 1733.

Slip Ware—Old pottery ware decorated with slightly raised stripes or simple designs with a creamy fluid of clay.

Soma Ware—Soma was a principality of feudal Japan and the crest of its princes was a horse. Soma ware includes porcelain and pottery, netsukes (*q.v.*) and iron tsubas (*q.v.*), all with horses included in their decorations, the carving on the two latter being, as a rule, below the surface.

Spode—Earthenware was first produced at the pottery established at Stoke-on-Trent by Josiah Spode in 1770, but the manufacture of porcelain was commenced in about 1798. Several members of the Spode family were in turn interested in the factory, but upon their decease the concern was taken over by Copelands in about 1833. Willow-pattern plates and dishes were produced in 1784. Ornamental and utility ware was made and decorated with landscape panels, floral tributes, birds and Japanese designs, and dolphin supports are on some pieces. The plates in many of the table services are of octagonal shape, and decorated mesh backgrounds are a feature on others. The marks nearly all contain the word "Spode", so they can easily be recognised; these were impressed or printed, usually in red but sometimes in gold. Similar remarks can, in general, be made in regard to Copeland.

Spurs—The peculiar marks, generally three, frequently found on Chelsea china. These were made by the little pieces of clay used as supports to the article during the firing of the glaze, the marks being left where the spurs are broken away.

Staffordshire Pottery—Different kinds of pottery were produced at the numerous factories here, the better known being Ralph Wood (father and son), Enoch Wood, Aaron Wood, Wedgwood, Turner & Co., Wood & Caldwell, Whieldon, Neale & Co. and others. The group and figures were generally excellent in colour and are quaint—The Parson and Clerk, by Aaron Wood, the bust of Wesley by Enoch Wood, as examples. Toby jugs were also made.

Stamnos—A Grecian urn-shaped vessel for water or wine.

Stoneware—A ware for which German potteries of the 15th century were particularly noted. They produced hunting bottles, canettes and many other articles in blue, brown, etc., usually decorated in relief with masks or shields of arms. (*See Fulham Pottery and Salt Glaze.*)

Strasbourg—A pottery owned by the Hannong family commenced here in 1709, later made hard porcelain.

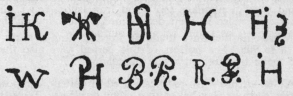

Sunderland—There were several potteries near Sunderland from 1775 onwards, generally mugs and jugs with verses and ships on them.

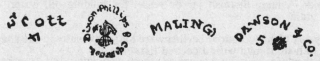

Surahe—A Persian wine bottle with a long neck.

Swansea Porcelain—The date when the factory was established is unknown, but it appears to have been in the hands of L. W. Dillwyn in 1814, when for a while he was joined by William Billingsley and William Young. It was then known as the Cambrian Works. The porcelain first produced was similar

Swansea Porcelain—*continued.*

to that made at Nantgarw and was so marked; this was followed by a porcelain having a stronger and more compact body, marked "Swansea", to which mark was added one or two tridents after about 1817, these marks usually being painted in red or impressed. Another variation occurred in 1818, when the glaze presented a dead-white appearance.

About 1820-24 the moulds, etc., were sold to John Rose of Coalport. The decorations are similar to those of Nantgarw and include insects, butterflies, fruit and flowers, and scenic panels. A little lustre and biscuit ware were also produced. L. W. Dillwyn appears to have carried on with the manufacture of earthenware after 1820-24, as pieces exist marked "Dillwyn's Etruscan Ware", which was introduced in 1848 and usually portrays classical figures in the body terra-cotta, while the rest of the body is filled with colour.

Syntax China—Chinaware made in the early 19th century, so called owing to its decorations consisting of scenes of the adventures of Dr. Syntax in his search of the Picturesque.

Tàng Ware—Earthenware made during the Tàng dynasty from 618 to 906. The potters of this period were also the first to make transluscent white porcelain.

Terra-Cotta—A brownish-red paste used in pottery, composed of brick earth or clay baked to a stony hardness. **Terra-Blue**—A kind of blue earth. **Terra-Verte**—A species of olive green earth used by painters.

Tinaja—A large Spanish jar or vessel for holding oil, water, or grain.

Toby—A highly-coloured earthenware ale jug, usually in the shape of a stout man with a cocked hat.

Toft Ware—A slipware made in the second half of the 17th century by the brothers T. & R. Toft, after whom it is sometimes called. The colour of the grounds varies from buff to red, the designs being worked in brown or black outline filled in with orange-coloured slip; a light ground was obtained by washing with white slip. The process was sometimes reversed, so that articles had a dark ground with decorations in light slip.

Toft Ware—*continued.*

Pieces were coated with a lead glaze which had a yellowish tint. The decorations often consisted of tulips, cockerels, trellis borders and inscriptions.

Tortoiseshell Ware—A ware made to resemble tortoiseshell by colouring the glaze with oxide of copper and manganese.

Tournay—A soft-paste porcelain factory was established here in 1750. Compared with Sèvres it is very coarse.

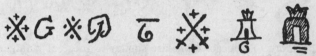

Transfer Printing—John Sadler took out a patent for this in 1756, but the process was first used on enamels at the Battersea enamel factory between 1753-56. Transfer papers engraved from copper plates were applied to the ware, linseed oil being mixed with the ink, the oil evaporated in the kiln, leaving the colour on the article.

Transmutation—A term sometimes used in describing porcelain, etc., in which the colours appear to change.

Truité—A term sometimes used to describe the crackle glaze on Chinese and other vases, as resembling the scale of a trout.

Tumbler—A beaker-shaped drinking glass without stem.

Tureen—A large bowl-shaped vessel to hold soup at table.

Tunstall—There were several potters working here, probably best known was the Adams family. The foundation of the present firm dates from 1757. Wm. Adams made jasper similar to Wedgwood's.

Turin—Faience has been made here since the 16th century.

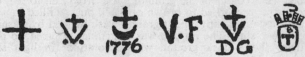

Tyg or **Tig**—An old Staffordshire drinking cup (or loving cup) with numerous handles, often decorated with initials or name and date, or a motto inscription.

Urbino Ware—Probably the most famous of all the Italian majolica wares. It was first made at this factory in 1475 and continued during the 16th and 17th centuries.

Valenciennes—A factory was started here by Fauquez in 1785, the plant was sold in 1809. Faience was made in 18th century by the Dorez family.

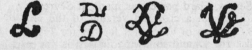

Venice—Majolica was made here from the late 16th century. In 1720 a hard-paste porcelain factory was established by Francesco Vezzi with the help of an arcenist previously employed at Vienna. A second factory, producing soft-paste porcelain, was started in 1765 by Geminiano Cozzi. The factory existed until 1812, the mark being an anchor in red.

Vienna Porcelain—The pottery was started by a Dutchman named du Paquier in 1717 and carried on by several owners until 1864. Hard porcelain was manufactured, following the lines of that produced at Dresden (*q.v.*), probably due to the migration of workmen. Some of the gilded pieces had their patterns worked out in burnished gold from a matt ground of the same material. From 1744 the mark was a shield, usually in blue, applied under the glaze, and from about 1784 this was accompanied by a year mark.

Vincennes Porcelain (*See Sèvres Porcelain.*)—The making of soft-paste porcelain commenced in 1738 by Dubois and the factory was moved to Sèvres in 1756. The double L mark enclosing a date letter was introduced in 1753, the first three letters of the alphabet appearing in pieces made at Vincennes, all subsequent letters being on porcelain made at Sèvres. Hard paste was made at Sèvres from 1769, being marked with a crowned version of the crossed L's.

A,B,C, is that of Vincennes factory for 1753, 1754 and 1755, whilst the D and following letters is the mark of Sèvres. The making of hard-paste porcelain is distinct, P. Hannong commenced making this here in 1767.

Wedgwood Pottery—Josiah Wedgwood was born at Burslem in 1730, and was associated with Whieldon from 1754 to 1759, when he returned to Burslem and opened his own pottery. He was destined to become one of the greatest potters the world has known, and created many kinds of ware, the most famous of which are probably the creamware, called Queen's ware upon his receiving Royal Patronage in 1765; Egyptian black ware, terra-cotta or red ware, white semi-porcelain or stoneware, variegated ware and the most noted of all, Jasper

Wedgwood Pottery—*continued.*

ware. He took into partnership his cousin, Thomas Wedgwood, in 1766, Thomas Bentley in 1768 and five years before his death in 1795, his three sons John, Josiah and Thomas, and his nephew, Thomas Byerley. In 1769 he took over a second and larger factory which he called Etruria. **Cream-ware** or **Queen's ware** varies in colour but is usually of a pale-straw tint with decorations painted in enamel or transfer-printed. A pink lustre was introduced at a later date, as also was a similar white ware called "pearl ware". Figures, vases, busts, etc., as well as articles of utility, were produced; the white ware mainly comprised table sets. **Egyptian black ware** consists of an unglazed stoneware with a smooth surface, fine grain and a rich tone and this ware is supreme and has never been equalled. It was made into medallions, busts, plaques and vases, as well as tea services. It also formed the base for the Etruscan ware, which, decorated with classical figures, was an imitation of the ancient Etruscan ware. **Terra-cotta or red ware** was in vogue for about ten years in the latter half of the 18th century. Its ground varied in colour and included cane, bamboo and chocolate, the reliefs usually

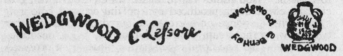

being in black. **White semi-porcelain or stoneware** is slightly transparent with a soft smoothness, and was originally used for the plinths of vases but later for cameos, medallions, etc. **Variegated ware** has a cream-ware base with surface variegations to represent marble, granite and agate which are successfully imitated. **Jasper Ware** is a hard dense stoneware, coloured throughout with metallic oxides in seven tints as follows:—blue, pink, lilac, sage and olive green, black and yellow. The decorations consist of relief ornaments usually in white; vases, plaques, bas-reliefs, intaglios, cameos and portrait medallions were produced, some of the designs being by the renowned Flaxman. It probably reached perfection in about the year 1775, although the body varied in quality, some pieces being opaque and others having a tendency to translucency. The bodies of the later pieces, after about 1780, were surface coloured by staining, the process being referred to as "jasper dip". Besides ornamental items, utility services for tea and coffee, were produced. Jasper ware was successfully imitated by William Adams of Tunstall and by John Turner and was also copied by many others, both at home and abroad, with varying degrees of success. **Porcelain was**

Wedgwood Pottery—*continued.*

made at Etruria between the years 1805 and 1815, and again from 1872. Practically all articles bore a pottery mark, usually the word "Wedgwood" or "Wedgwood & Bentley", impressed on pieces other than porcelain. On porcelain the marks were stencilled in red or blue over the glaze. Sometimes the word "Etruria" was added, and on the small cameos the letters W. and B. were used.

Weesp—The making of porcelain in Holland commenced at Weesp in 1764. The factory was moved to Oude Noosdrecht in 1771.

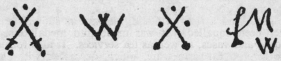

Whieldon Ware—Earthenware made by Thomas Whieldon at Little Fenton, in Staffordshire, where his pottery was established about 1741 to 1780. Whieldon ware was probably best known by the articles produced and coloured to represent tortoiseshell (sometimes called agate ware), the mottling or clouded effect being produced by applying various colouring agents with a sponge on a cream-coloured base. In another type of ware the cream base predominates, being decorated mainly with fruit and floral reliefs; other pieces were profusely decorated, the cream ground being almost obscured. The ware was coated with a fine brilliant lead glaze. Josiah Wedgwood, as a young man, was associated with Whieldon until 1759.

Willow Pattern—A pseudo-Chinese design familiar in blue-and-white china first used about 1780 by the Caughley Pottery.

Wine Pot—A flat openwork teapot-shaped vessel of Chinese porcelain.

Worcester Porcelain—Made at a pottery worked by a Company formed under the direction of Dr. Wall in 1751. The pottery continued to operate until 1783 (seven years after his death) when it was sold. Numerous changes in ownership followed, and in 1783 Thomas Flight, assisted by his sons, Joseph and John, upheld the earlier traditions, and in 1788 received Royal Patronage; in 1791-2 Martin Barr was taken into partnership and the firm became known as Flight & Barr until 1807. In that year it was reconstructed, and for six years carried on as Barr, Flight & Barr. In 1813 a further alteration took place and until 1829 the title was Flight, Barr & Barr;

Worcester Porcelain—*continued.*

following this to 1840 it was Barr & Barr. At about the time the Flights joined the firm, one of the existing partners, Robert Chamberlain, left it, and in 1789 started a new factory and worked in opposition, until the two concerns were amalgamated in 1840 under the title of Chamberlain & Co.

Further changes took place and from 1847-48 the firm became Chamberlain & Lilley, and in 1850, Chamberlain, Lilley & Kerr until 1852, and from 1852 to 1862, Kerr & Binns. A third factory owned by Thomas Grainger (Grainger, Lee & Co.,) was in operation from 1801 to 1889 when it was absorbed by the present Company. The early products were almost entirely based on Chinese designs and consisted mainly of useful articles. Decorations were in quiet taste and often in blue under-glaze, though slightly embossed designs were sometimes employed. More elaborately coloured designs in the Japanese style followed, probably about 1756-57. The early ware was of a creamy tint, the paste containing steatite; the glaze had a large proportion of lead and in some lights possessed a slight greenish tint. A method of printing line-designs from copper plates was evolved in 1756-57 and carried out in black, blue, red and purple, but it was little used after the departure of Robert Hancock in 1774. The process was renewed at a later date in stipple form. The porcelain is thin and ivory-white, and the decorations are all neatly finished whether transfer-printed or carried out by hand. Many of the more decorative designs are thought to be the work of Chelsea artists and include exotic birds with rich plumage, landscapes scenes, bouquets, etc., and grounds of royal blue are not uncommon. Blue-and-white plates and dishes with pierced borders are one of the very large variety of items produced. The first mark to about 1783 is the letter "W". Another early mark is the crescent in outline, later shaded in with blue, probably discontinued about 1793, also square

Worcester Porcelain—*continued.*

maze-like Chinese characters in blue. After about 1783 a considerable number of firm's titles are used in various frames, mostly bearing a crown after 1788. These are but a few of the many marks to be found on Worcester Porcelain.

Wrotham Ware—A slipware made at Wrotham in Kent. It usually has a red body decorated in white slip with fleur-de-lis, rosettes, etc., often with the name of the pottery and year figures between 1627 and 1717. The designs were sometimes incised and the whole coated with a yellowish lead glaze.

Yarmouth—So called "Yarmouth Ware" was made elsewhere such as Staffordshire and decorated by Absolon at Yarmouth.

Zürich—The porcelain factory here commenced in 1763. At first soft paste was produced, but hard paste followed after two years. Pottery was also made here.

GLASS

The history of glass is lost in obscurity but it is known that glass has been made for more than three thousand years.

Glass was made in England in the time of the Roman occupation.

The Venetian glass of the 15th and 16th centuries was envied by noblemen all over but was a close secret.

Jacopo Verzelini (1522-1606), a Venetian glass maker, came to England about 1570, and in 1575 he received a patent for twenty-one years to make glass in England. Frenchmen also came to England and were encouraged to make glass.

Owing to the forests being so devastated, the Government prohibited in 1615 the use of wood as a fuel for glass making. The glass makers had to use coal, which gave a much greater heat. In 1615 Sir Robert Mansell obtained the coal patent and became connected with several glass works including Stourbridge.

The Duke of Buckingham established glass works at Vauxhall and Greenwich and in 1663 obtained a monopoly for making mirrors.

George Ravenscroft (1618–1681) set up glass works in 1673 and produced an improved glass, "the flint glass", the secret of which was oxide of lead; his glasses were distinguished by a seal, a raven's head.

Air Twist—A hollow spiral in the stems of 18th-century wine glasses. An air bubble was admitted so that when the stem was twisted a spiral was formed. (*See Wine Glasses.*)

Ale Glass—A long narrow glass on a foot, often engraved hops.

Amen Glasses—Jacobite glasses generally engraved with a verse ending with "Amen".

Ampulla—A bottle almost globular in shape but becoming smaller towards the neck, used by the Romans for the preservation of anointing liquids.

Aryballos—A globular-shaped bottle having a short neck with small orifice and one handle, often richly decorated, used for containing oils, etc.

Aventurine or **Avanturine**—A variety of glass containing specks of gold colour; the process was discovered accidentally through brass filings being dropped into molten glass; felspar, lacquer. etc., resembling same.

Avoli—The small moulding where the bowl and stem of a wine glass meet.

Baccarat Glass—Glass works in France renowned for its paper weights.

Baluster Stems—The early glasses on baluster stems were generally very thick and heavy. They often contained air bubbles or "tears", which later became the air twist stems. 1680 to 1730. (*See Wine Glasses.*)

Beilby Glass—Glass painted by Wm. Beilby (1740-1819) of Newcastle-upon-Tyne. These glasses usually had heraldic designs.

Bell Bowl—Glasses with bell-shaped bowls, about 1710-1750.

Bohemian Glass—An ornamental glass ware from Bohemia noted for its rich colours, often of deep ruby tint, and for its incised and engraved designs.

Bristol Glass—A factory for the making of coloured glass commenced about 1760 in Bristol; the dark blue glass is well known: decanters, scent bottles, patch boxes, etc., were made. **Bristol Opaque Glass** was painted in enamel colours to represent porcelain; rolling pins, walking sticks were made here.

Cameo Glass—A glass ware consisting of layers of different coloured glass, with the upper layers cut away to form the design, after the manner of a cameo.

Canes—Thin glass rods.

Carafe—A glass water bottle.

Coin Glasses—Glasses with a coin enclosed in the stem; these date from the reign of Charles II.

Constable—A large stemmed glass used in Scotland.

Cordial Glasses—17th-century cordial glasses had very small bowls, smaller than a wine glass, the glasses were five to six inches high.

Cotton Twist Stem—(*See Opaque Stem.*)

Crackle Glass—Glass ware having a fine network of cracks.

Craze—(*See Crackle.*)

Crimping—A fluting giving a wavy effect.

Crisselled—A term sometimes used to describe glass ware having a "crackled" or "crazed" appearance, as in the glaze of porcelain.

Cruse—Any kind of vessel for holding water, honey or the like; a jar or pot.

Crystallo-Engraving—A term sometimes used to describe glass ware engraved to give the clear transparent effect of crystal.

Cut Glass—Glass ornamented by cutting or grinding and polishing with wheels; English glass was first cut about 1720.

Decanter—A glass bottle with stopper for holding decanted wine. Square decanters appeared about 1760. **Decant**—to pour off gently from the edge of a vessel so as not to disturb the sediment.

Drawn Stem—A stem of glass made by pulling out the metal whilst it is molten.

Enamelled Glass—Glass ware ornamented with designs in vitrifiable colours.

Enamel Twist—Enamel twist stems to glasses; date from about 1750.

Engraving—Engraving of glass began about 1720.

Finger Bowl—A small bowl or basin for water, used at table for cleansing the fingers, from about 1760.

Flagon—A flat-sided, bottle-shaped vessel for holding liquor, usually with a handle and spout.

Flint Glass—Glass fused with an oxide of lead.

Folded Foot—The rim of the foot in which the glass is folded double; a general feature with glasses of the late 17th and early 18th century.

Grass or Lily Vases—Tall flower vases, often trumpet shape, about 3 ft. in height.

Ice Plates—Usually of frosted glass with star cut base, or with fluted borders.

Irish Glass—The most famous is Waterford, which was founded about 1783 and closed 1851. The notion that Waterford glass is distinguished by its blue tinge is a fallacy. Glass was also made at Dublin from about 1765, Belfast, 1780, and Cork from 1783.

Keltie—The name given in Scotland to a large glass for holding whisky, etc.

Knop—A bead or bulge on the stem of a glass.

Lachrymatory—A small glass vessel for containing the tears of the relatives of a deceased person.

Latticinio—A lace effect of threads of coloured glass, often used in millefiori paper weights.

Linen Smoothers—Made of solid glass with a handle attached, in appearance not unlike an inverted mushroom.

Lustres—The pendant glass prisms on candelabrum.

Moulded Glass—A glass blown with a mould, giving impressed designs; a poor imitation of cutting.

Mule—The base or foot on which a wine glass stands.

Nailsea—Works were established at Nailsea in the late 18th century and articles of utility were first produced in bottle-glass of a greenish-brown colour, decorated mainly with white threads round the neck with irregular spotting. During the first part of the 19th century the style was changed, when articles were made decorated with loops or wavy patterns of pink, white and other colours.

Newcastle Glass—Glass made at Newcastle-upon-Tyne in the 18th century which was exceptional for its brilliance and whiteness.

Opaque Stems—This group of wine glass stems followed the air twist stem (*q.v.*) and was in vogue from about 1765-1780. This stem was made by using white and clear canes of glass which were heated and molten glass poured on; this mass was then drawn and twisted, forming the patterns. Later in this period, coloured glass was used instead of opaque white glass; often called twisted stem.

Paper Weights—Circular bun-shaped type of clear glass with millefiori flowers, which were made of coloured glass rods. The chief Continental factories were at Baccarat, St. Louis and Clichy. These paper weights date from the mid-19th century. Cone-shape paper weights of bottle green glass in which appears a vase of flowers often made up of innumerable tears, were made at Stourbridge, and practically all other English glass factories. The larger ones are referred to as door stops.

Phial—A small glass bottle or vessel.

Pontil—A metal rod to which the glass was attached for working.

Pontil-Mark—The mark left on the foot of the glass when detached from the Pontil—this is not found on modern glasses.

Pressed Glass—Glass made in a mould under pressure, as opposed to moulded (*q.v.*), which is blown.

Prunts—The small applied buttons of glass on the stems of early glasses.

Rib Twist—A method of decoration employed on stemmed wine glasses by first cutting into the stem and then twisting it.

Römer—A German drinking glass with rounded bowl and thick hollow stem.

Rummer—A tall goblet-shaped glass or drinking cup. About 1770.

Schaper Glass—A cylindrical cup with painted view panels, so-called after Johann Schaper, a German artist of the 17th century, who nearly always used the same type of vessel.

Ship Decanter—A decanter with a very wide bottom.

Sillabub Glass—A shaped and often coloured tumbler, usually in a metal frame with a handle, used for serving sillabub, a confection made of milk, curd or cream flavoured with wine, etc.

Stiegel Glass—An engraved and enamelled glass made in the U.S.A. in the 18th century by Wilhelm Stiegel.

Tear—A bubble in the top of the stem of a glass, from this the air twist stem originated 1715 to 1760.

Toastmaster's Glass—A small glass which held less than it appeared to do so, and had a heavy foot.

Toddy-Lifter—Held a glassful of liquor, it had a hole in the bottom and the top and was used as a pipette to lift the drink from the punch bowl to the glass.

Tot—A small tumbler.

Tumbler—A beaker-shaped drinking glass without stem.

Vauxhall Mirror Glass—Made in a factory at Vauxhall established by the Duke of Buckingham during the reign of Charles II. The plates were made by the process of "blowing" and were consequently not very large. The silvering was effected by depositing a thin layer of quick-silver or mercury on the plate, and the bevelling, which is usually uneven, was "pressed" whilst hot.

Venetian Glass—A variety of ornamental glass made decorative by the fusing of patterns or spiral threads of coloured glass within its mass of clear glass. Slaviati is a well-known variety.

Verre Eglomisé—Glass decorated by having a design at the back in gold and colours.

Vetro-di-Trina—A beautiful Venetian glass made in the 16th century, decorated by a series of opaque wave-like forms embodied in the clear groundwork, giving a lace-like effect.

Waldglas—Glass fused with potash—German.

Wine Glasses—**Baluster** stems were in vogue for some fifty years from about 1680. **Plain** stems with and without tears were in use for about ten years from about 1730. **Air Twist** stems were favoured for about thirty years from 1740. **Opaque Twist** stems were made from about 1755 for about twenty-five years, and **Cut** or **Faceted** stems were fashionable during the last half of the 18th century. The bowls were usually in one of the following shapes:—**Funnel**: with straight slanting sides from about 1670 to 1710; **Waisted**: from about 1710 to 1750,

Wine Glasses—*continued*.

these included, in their variations, the thistle and bell bowls; **Ovoid**: shaped like the lower two-thirds of an egg; **Ogee**: the bowl has sloping shoulders to the stem.

Witch Ball—A blown ball generally silvered or other lustrous colour.

Yard of Ale—Ale glasses about 36 inches long with a bulb at one end with a capacity of about a pint.

CLOCKS AND WATCHES

Methods of recording time have been in use from very early days, one of the earliest forms and the most simple was the sundial.

The Greeks and Egyptians used water clocks (*Clypsedrae*). These worked on the principle of the time taken to empty or fill a vessel with water; there were many various forms of water clocks.

Another method of measuring time was the burning of candles which were graduated, or of oil which was in a marked container.

Later came the sand glass which was a more accurate means of measuring time.

There is no accurate record as to the date of the invention of clocks actuated by weights, but these were in all probability first used in monasteries.

The first clocks in houses were the lantern or birdcage clock, these stood on a bracket and were weight driven.

English watches first appeared about 1580.

CLOCKS AND WATCHES

GLOSSARY OF TERMS

Act of Parliament Clock—A hanging clock which usually had a large wooden circular dial, painted black with gilt numerals and a trunk to allow for a pendulum, so called as an Act of Parliament of 1797 which put a tax of 5s. 0d. per year on watches. Inn-keepers adopted these clocks for the benefit of customers without watches. This Act so nearly crippled the watchmaking industry that it had to be repealed in 1798. Also called Inn Clocks.

Anchor Escapement—This was invented about 1670 by William Clement and is now still the most common type of escapement.

Astronomical Clock—One showing the motions of certain of the planets and stars.

Balloon Clocks—Popular at end of 18th century—so called as they were of that shape, the case was round as was the face, concaving in below and shaping out to a flat base.

Bedpost Clocks—(*See Lantern Clocks.*)

Birdcage Clocks—(*See Lantern Clocks.*)

Bracket Clock—The earliest clocks were true bracket clocks as it was necessary for them to stand on a bracket to allow the weights to fall. During the 17th century the bracket clock was made of wood, with basket-work top which was of chased brass open work, glass front to protect the face, and carrying handles. Later came the "bell top" case, so called from the hollow-curved shape of the top; often the handle was placed on the top instead of the sides. At the end of the 18th century, the bell top case was supplanted by the "balloon", "broken arch" and "lancet" or "gothic" shape. The "broken arch" is an arched top which does not extend the full width of the clock. The "balloon" clock has a circular dial, the case being circular around the dial, concaving in below it and shaping out to a flat base.

Carriage Clock—It has a small rectangular case of brass and glass with handle at top, usually fitted in additional leather outer case.

Cartel Clock—A wall clock of star or scroll design, often in carved gilt wood or ormolu, introduced in the reign of Louis XIV (1643-1715).

Chronograph—This term is generally applied to those watches having a centre seconds hand which may be started, stopped and reset to zero by pressing a knob on the case. A stop watch.

Chronometer—Any exact time keeper, but generally used to mean those used by astronomers, jewellers, and on ships.

Chronometer Escapement—Invented about 1765 by Pierre Le Roy (1717-1785).

Clock—A timekeeper that strikes the hours.

Clock Watch—A watch that strikes the hours.

Cromwellian Clocks—(*See Lantern Clocks.*)

Crown Wheel—The escape wheel of the verge escapement.

Cuckoo Clock—First made by A. Keterer in 1730.

Demi Hunter—A watch case with a glass front of about half the diameter of the case.

French Clocks—In French clocks of the late 17th and 18th century the cases were often of Boulle work with ormolu mounts; the French grandfather clocks differ from the British by a bulge in the centre of the case, and are ornamented with ormolu.

Grandfather Clocks (or Long-Case Clocks)—Introduced after the Restoration (1660) the early clocks had only one pointer and were only thirty-hour clocks. Towards the end of the 17th century these clocks were between six to seven feet high, some of the cases were of seaweed marquetry; about 1710 lacquer work cases were made, after 1750 mahogany was used.

Grandmother Clock—A small edition of the grandfather clock, late 17th century.

Hour Glass—An instrument for measuring periods of time, it consists of two globular-shaped glass containers joined together by a narrow neck and filled with such a quantity of sand as would take an hour to gravitate through the neck.

Hunter—A watch case having a metal cover over the dial.

Inn Clock—(*See Act of Parliament Clock.*)

Keyless—A watch which is wound without a key—there is generally a winding crown in the ring over the watch.

Lantern Clock—This was the earliest type of domestic clock. It was made of brass or wrought iron, was dome shape and had no glass covering the dial. It was mounted on a bracket and driven by weights, and had only one hand. Dated about 1600. One of the characteristics of the lantern clock are the brass frets around the top. Also called Birdcage, Bedpost and Cromwellian clocks.

Long Case Clock—(*See Grandfather Clock.*)

Mantel Clocks—Made their appearance in France about 1700, developed greatly during the latter quarter of 18th century.

Marine Chronometer—A chronometer for use at sea and is suspended in a wooden box on gymbals.

Musical Clocks—Fashionable in early 18th century. They played tunes at the hours.

Night Clocks—Timepieces with a dial lighted from the rear by a candle or night-light.

Pair Case—An old style of casing watches, an inner case contained the movement and a protective outer case which was quite separate.

Pedestal Clock—One which stands on a pedestal, the pendulum of the clock being so long that it extends into the pedestal. These were popular in France.

Pendulum—The pendulum was introduced about 1670, which gave much greater accuracy, and in consequence the minute hand was added to clocks.

Phases of the Moon—Through an opening in the face on some grandfather clocks, the four phases (new, first quarter, full and last quarter) of the moon appear.

Quartz Clock—A clock controlled by a quartz crystal which vibrates at a regular frequency under the effect of an electric field. The action is very accurate.

Repeater—A clock or watch which can be made to strike the past hour, a quarter repeater, strikes the last hour followed by the number of quarters. Repeaters were first made about 1685 being invented by Edward Barlow.

Shelf Clock—American, early 19th century, are in wood, often rosewood, oblong case, with a door, the upper part fitted plain glass to cover the dial, the lower part a painted glass panel.

Spandrils—The corners outside the circle of the dial, the early grandfather clocks had these corners filled with raised gilt ornamentation, cherubs, etc.

Stop Watch—(*See Chronograph.*)

Table Clock—Came into use in the 16th century and were in the shape of a flat drum about 6 inches in diameter and 4 inches or 5 inches high. The face was on the flat top of the clock.

Timepiece—Any timekeeper other than a watch, which does not strike. A clock is one that strikes.

Travelling Watches—Watches of large size, they vary up to about 7 inches in diameter.

Turret Clock—The name given to large public clocks used in bell towers or turrets. The earliest known turret clock is that of Salisbury Cathedral and dates from 1386.

Verge—The Verge escapement was the first escapement to have been used, being first used in the 14th century.

Verge Watch—17th century.

Wag-of-the-Wall Clocks—These usually have a painted dial with no glass, and the works and pendulum are unprotected.

Watch—A timepiece made for wearing either on the person or clothes. The earliest watches only had one hand, the minute hand being added after 1700.

Watch Glasses—Introduced about 1600.

CLOCK-MAKERS

A List of some English Clock-Makers with dates.

fl.—flourished.

ACOTT, William; London, fl. 1810.

ACTON, Thomas; Clerkenwell, fl. 1675.

ADAMS, Francis Bryant; London, fl. 1845.

ADDIS, George; London, fl. 1785-1795.

ADDIS, William; London, fl. 1745-1765.

AGAR, John; York, fl. 1740.

ALCOCK, Thomas; London, fl. 1635-1655.

ALEXANDER, Robert; London, fl. 1707.

ALEXANDER, William; London, fl. 1830.

ALLAWAY, John; London, fl. 1695.

ALLETT, George; London, fl. 1700.

ANDREWS, Thomas; London, fl. 1750.

ANSELL, George; London, fl. 1800-1820.

ARNOLD, John; London, fl. 1760-1795.

ARNOLD, John Roger; London, fl. 1800-1830.

ASHBROOK, John; London, fl. 1700.

ASKE, Henry, London, fl. 1680.

ATKINS, George; London, fl. 1785-1845.

AVENELL, Thomas; London, fl. 1700-1745.

BACON, John; London, fl. 1635.

BADGER, John; London, fl. 1715.

BAGSHAW, William; London, fl. 1720.

BAIRD, John; London, fl. 1780.

BALLANTYNE, William; London, fl. 1830.

BANGER, Edward; London, fl. 1690.

BARBER, Jonas; London, fl. 1680.

BARCLAY, Samuel; London, fl. 1720.

BARLOW, Benjamin; Oldham, fl. 1785. (Invented Repeating Watches.)

BARLOW, Edward; London, fl. 1660-1700.

217

BARNARD, Thomas; London, fl. 1800.

BARR, G.; Bolton, fl. 1790.

BARRAUD, Paul; London, fl. 1790-1810.

BARROW, Samuel; London, fl. 1690-1710.

BARTRAM, Simon; London, fl. 1640-1650.

BARTHROP, G.; Ixworth, fl. 1770.

BATEMAN, Andrew; London, fl. 1800-1820.

BATES, Thomas; London, fl. 1680.

BATTERSON, Robert; London, fl. 1690.

BAULER, James; Leeds, fl. 1800.

BAXTER, Charles; London, fl. 1675.

BAYES, John; London, fl. 1640.

BEAUVAIS, Simon; London, fl. 1680.

BELL, Benjamin; London, fl. 1665.

BENN, Anthony; London, fl. 1760.

BENNETT, Mansell; Charing Cross, fl. 1695.

BENNETT, Thomas; London, fl. 1730.

BERRIDGE, Robert; London, fl. 1790.

BERRY, John; London, fl. 1720-1725.

BEVERLEY, James; London, fl. 1695.

BIRCHELL, William; London, fl. 1830.

BISHOP, Thomas; London, fl. 1815.

BLISS, Ambrose; London, fl. 1650.

BLUNDELL, William; London, fl. 1715.

BOOSEY, Thomas; London, fl. 1810.

BOOTH, Richard; London, fl. 1825.

BOWEN, Thomas; London, fl. 1800.

BOWYER, William; London, fl. 1640.

BRADLEY, Langley; London, fl. 1700-1725.

BRAYFIELD, William; London, fl. 1710-1715.

BROCKBANK, Myles; London, fl. 1775-1800

BROOKS, John; London, fl. 1780.

BROUGH, Samuel; London, fl. 1810.

BROWN, Nathaniel; Manchester, fl. 1780.

BROWN, Thomas; Birmingham, fl. 1765.

BROWNE, John; London, fl. 1675.

BRYANT, John; Exning, fl. 1790

BUCKNELL, James; Crediton, fl. 1785.

BULL, John; London, fl. 1630.
BULL, William; Stratford, fl. 1760.
BUTCHER, Benjamin; London, fl. 1810-1820.

CABRIER, Charles; London, fl. 1724-1750.
CARPENTER, Thomas; London, fl. 1800.
CARRINGTON, Thomas; London, fl. 1770.
CARRUTHERS, George; London, fl. 1790.
CARTER, John; London, fl. 1850-1860.
CARTER, William; Ampthill, fl. 1700.
CHAMBERLAINE, Nathaniel; London, fl. 1685-1715.
CHARLTON, John; London, fl. 1630-1640.
CHATER, E.; London, fl. 1770-1780.
CHILD, Henry; London, fl. 1640-1660.
CHRISTIAN, John; Aylsham, fl. 1750.
CLARKE, Henry; London, fl. 1820-1830.
CLAY, William; London, fl. 1700.
CLEMENT, William; London, fl. 1685-1700.
CLEMENTS, Thomas; Liverpool, fl. 1790.
CLERKE, John; Brentwood, fl. 1780.
CLEWES, James; London, fl. 1680.
COATS, Archibald; Wigan, fl. 1780.
COLLIER, Benjamin; London, fl. 1700-1720.
COLLYER, Benjamin; London, fl. 1710.
COLLINGWOOD, Samuel John; London, fl. 1795.
COMFORT, William; London, fl. 1660.
COOKE, William; London, fl. 1695.
COX, James; London, fl. 1775.
COXETER, Nicholas; London, fl. 1660-1675.
CREAK, William; London, fl. 1750.
CREEKE, Henry; London, fl. 1655.
CROOKE, Benjamin; Hackney, fl. 1805.
CROUCHER, Joseph; London, fl. 1830.
CUMMING, Alexander; London, fl. 1780.
CURTIS, John; London, fl. 1750.
CUTBUSH, Edward; Maidstone, fl. 1705.

DARLING, Robert; London, fl. 1765.
DAWSON, Thomas; London, fl. 1640.

DEBAUFRE, Peter; London, fl. 1690-1700.
DELANDER, Nathaniel; London, fl. 1670.
DENT, Edward John; London, fl. 1740.
DICKER, Thomas; Reading, fl. 1760.
DOOREY, Thomas; London, fl. 1780.
DRURY, James; London, fl. 1725.
DUHAMEL, Isaac; London, fl. 1780.
DUNCOMBE, Richard; London, fl. 1795.
DUNLOP, Conyers; London, fl. 1760.
DUTTON, William; London, fl. 1770.

EARNSHAW, Thomas; London, fl. 1780-1800.
EAST, Edward; London, fl. 1660.
EBSWORTH, John; London, fl. 1680.
EDWARDS, Thomas; Salisbury fl. 1780.
ELEY, James; London, fl. 1785.
ELLICOTT, John; London, fl. 1735.
EMERY, Josiah; London, fl. 1780-1790.
ETHERINGTON, George; London, fl. 1700-1710.
EVANS, James; London, fl. 1780.

FAIRMAN, Thomas Henry; London, fl. 1790.
FAULKNER, Edward; London, fl. 1710.
FENN, Daniel; London, fl. 1765.
FENN, Joseph; London, fl. 1840.
FENN, Samuel; London, fl. 1790.
FINCH, John; London, fl. 1700.
FLETCHER, Robert; Chester, fl. 1795.
FOREMAN, Francis; London, fl. 1640.
FOWLE, Thomas; East Grinstead, fl. 1670.
FRENCH, John; London, fl. 1785.
FRESHFIELD, James William; London, fl. 1810.
FRODSHAM, Charles; London, fl. 1850.
FRODSHAM, William James; London, fl. 1835.
FROMANTEEL, Abraham; London, 1680.
FROMANTEEL, Ahasuerus; London, 1665.
FROMANTEEL, John; London, 1670.

GANTHONY, Richard Pinfold; London, fl. 1840.
GARON, Peter; London, fl. 1700.
GARRET, Ferdinando; London, fl. 1600.
GAUNT, John; London, fl. 1830.
GIBBS, Thomas; London, fl. 1710.
GIBSON, Edward; London, fl. 1800.
GIBSON, James; London, fl. 1680.
GIBSON, John; London, fl. 1800.
GLOVER, Boyer; London, fl. 1765.
GODDARD, Nicholas; Newark, fl. 1715.
GOOD, John; London, fl. 1710.
GOULD, Christopher; London, fl. 1700.
GRAHAM, George; London, fl. 1720.
GRANT, John; London, fl. 1800.
GRANT, Richard; London, fl. 1775.
GRAVELL, William; London, fl. 1840.
GREEN, James; London, fl. 1780.
GREGORY, Jeremy; London, fl. 1660-1670.
GRETTON, Charles; London, fl. 1700.
GRINKIN, Robert; London, fl. 1645.

HACKETT, Simon; London, fl. 1650.
HALEY, Charles; London, fl. 1785.
HALL, Thomas; London, fl. 1695.
HARDING, John; London, fl. 1700.
HARE, Alexander; London, fl. 1800.
HARKER, George; London, fl. 1845.
HARRIS, John; London, fl. 1685.
HARRIS, Thomas; London, fl. 1690.
HARRIS, William; London, fl. 1830.
HARRISON, George; London, fl. 1710.
HARRISON, John; London, fl. 1750.
HEDGE, Nathaniel; Colchester, fl. 1745.
HELDON, Onesiphorous; London, fl. 1645.
HENDERSON, Robert; London, fl. 1785.
HERBERT, Cornelius; London, fl. 1725.
HILL, Abraham; London, fl. 1670.
HILL, Benjamin; London, fl. 1655.
HILTON, Emanuel; Portsmouth, fl. 1775.

HIORNE, John; London, fl. 1740.

HOCKER, John; Reading, fl. 1735.

HODGES, Nathaniel; London, fl. 1695.

HOLLAND, Thomas; London, fl. 1650-1660.

HOLMES, John; London, fl. 1775.

HOLMES, Matthew; London, fl. 1840.

HOOKE, Robert; London, fl. 1670. Invented the Anchor Escapement.

HORNBLOWER, William; London, fl. 1790.

HORNE, Henry; London, fl. 1750.

HOWSE, Charles; London, fl. 1785.

HUGHES, Thomas; London, fl. 1730.

HUYGENS, Christian; Holland, b. 1629, d. 1695. Made the first pendulum.

INGRAM, William; London, fl. 1740.

IRELAND, Francis; London, fl. 1675.

IRVING, Alexander; Westminster, fl. 1700.

JACKSON, John; London, fl. 1790.

JACKSON, Martin; London, fl. 1720.

JAQUES, William; London, fl. 1715.

JARRETT, Richard; London, fl. 1685.

JONES, Henry; London, fl. 1685.

JONES, John; London, fl. 1760.

JOYCE, George; London, fl. 1690.

JOOYCE, Samuel; London, fl. 1820.

KEMP, William; London, fl. 1835.

KENNING, William; London, fl. 1695.

KERSHAW, George; London, fl. 1795.

KIRK, Joseph; Nottingham, fl. 1740.

KNIBB, Joseph; London and Oxford, fl. 1670-1700.

KNOTTESFORDE, William; London, fl. 1680.

LAIDLAU, Thomas; London, fl. 1780.

LAMPE, John; London, fl. 1750.

LAYTON, Thomas; London, fl. 1800.

LEEMING, Edward; London, fl. 1795.

LEES, Thomas; Bury, fl. 1790.

LEFROY, George; Wisbech, fl. 1785.
LEROUX, John; London, fl. 1780.
LEVY, Jonas; London, fl. 1825.
LITHERLAND, Peter; London, fl. 1795.
LOCKYER, John; London, fl. 1750.
LONGFORD, Thomas; London, fl. 1770.
LOOMES, Thomas; London, fl. 1660.
LOUNDES, Jonathan; London, fl. 1690.
LOWNDES, Isaac; London, fl. 1690.
LYONS, Richard; London, fl. 1680.

MABERLY, John; London, fl. 1735.
MACHAM, Samuel; London, fl. 1710-1715.
MACLENNAN, Kenneth; London, fl. 1790.
MAGGS, William; London, fl. 1730.
MAGNIAC, Francis; London, fl. 1780.
MARCHANT, Samuel; London, fl. 1700.
MARGETTS, George; London, fl. 1800.
MARKHAM, Markwick; London, fl. 1750.
MARKWICK, James; London, fl. 1720.
MARRIOTT, John; London, fl. 1795.
MARSDEN, John; London, fl. 1730.
MARSHALL, John; Newark, fl. 1735.
MARTIN, Edmund; London, fl. 1790-1795.
MASTERSON, Richard; London, fl. 1640.
MATHEWS, William; London, fl. 1765.
MATTCHETT, John; London, fl. 1675.
MERRY, Charles; London, fl. 1765.
MERTTINS, George; London, fl. 1715.
MILLION, William; London, fl. 1670.
MOORE, Thomas; Ipswich, fl. 1740.
MOSS, Thomas; London, fl. 1800.
MUDGE, Thomas; London, fl. 1750.
MURRAY, James; London, fl. 1830.

NATHAN, Henry; London, fl. 1685.
NEVE, Henry; London, fl. 1700-1705.
NEWSAM, Bartholomew; London, fl. 1575.
NICASIUS, John; London, fl. 1650.

NORRIS, Edward; London, fl. 1680-1685.
NORTH, William; London, fl. 1650.
NORTON, Eardley; London, fl. 1780.
NORTON, Samuel; London, fl. 1775.

OAKLEY, William; London, fl. 1810.
OLIVER, Thomas; London, fl. 1785.
OVERZEE, Gerard; London, fl. 1685.

PACE, Thomas; London, fl. 1650.
PAINE, William; Trowbridge, fl. 1785.
PARKINSON, William; London, fl. 1820.
PAULL, Philip; London, fl. 1815.
PAYNE, Southern; London, fl. 1775.
PENNOCK, John; London, fl. 1660.
PERIGAL, Francis; London, fl. 1755.
PERRY, J. A.; London, fl. 1850.
PILLING, John; Boothfold, fl. 1800.
PITT, Thyar; London, fl. 1790.
PLAYER, Robert; London, fl. 1725.
PLUMLEY, William; London, fl. 1775.
POISSON, Henry; London, fl. 1710.
POOLE, Robert; London, fl. 1775-1780.
POTTER, Henry; London, fl. 1795.
PRIDEAUX, Edmund; London, fl. 1785.

QUARE, Daniel; London, fl. 1675-1700. Made Repeater Watches.
QUARMAN, Joseph; Temple Cloud, fl. 1770.

RAIRRIER, John; London, fl. 1800.
RAMSEY, David; London, fl. 1610-1650. The First Master of the
    Clock Makers' Co.
REID, Thomas; London and Edinburgh, fl. 1770-1820.
RICHARDSON, James; London, fl. 1785.
RIVERS, David; London, fl. 1770.
ROBINS, William; London, fl. 1800.
ROBINSON, Daniel; London, fl. 1710.
ROBINSON, Francis; London, fl. 1720.
ROBSON, William; London, fl. 1810.

ROGERSON, William; London, fl. 1770.
ROOKER, Richard; London, fl. 1730.
ROSKELL, Robert; London, fl. 1815.
ROWLANDS, William; London, fl. 1855.
RUSSELL, Nicholas; London, fl. 1690.

SANDERSON, John; Wigton, fl. 1725.
SANGSTER, John T.; London, fl. 1825.
SARGEANT, Nathaniel; London, fl. 1780.
SAVAGE, Thomas; London, fl. 1825.
SCAFE, William; London, fl. 1740.
SCHOLEFIELD, James; London, fl. 1760.
SCRIVINER, Richard; London, fl. 1710.
SEIGNOR, Robert; London, fl. 1680.
SEWELL, William; London, fl. 1830.
SHARP, John; London, fl. 1830.
SHAW, John; London, fl. 1710.
SKELTON, Samson; London, fl. 1640.
SHERWOOD, William; London. fl. 1740.
SIDEY, Benjamin; London, fl. 1760.
SINDERBY, Francis; London, fl. 1820.
SKINNER, Matthew; London, fl. 1735.
SMITH, James; London, fl. 1775-1785.
SMITH, John; Houndsditch, fl. 1730.
SNELLING, James; London, fl. 1735.
SPEAKMAN, William; London, fl. 1700.
SPITTLE, Richard; London, fl. 1710.
STAFFORD, John; London, fl. 1735.
STANTON, Edward; London, fl. 1670.
STEINER, Louis; London, fl. 1720.
STEPHENS, Joseph; London, fl. 1760-1770.
STOGDON, Matthew; London, fl. 1720-1770.
STONES, Thomas; London, fl. 1730.
STOPPES, Alymer; London, fl. 1735.
STORER, Robert; London, fl. 1825.
STREET, Richard; London, fl. 1680-1700.
STRIPLING, Thomas; Barwell, fl. 1695.
STYLE, Nathaniel; London, fl. 1750-1770.

TAYLOR, Jasper; London, fl. 1750.

TAYLOR, Thomas; London, fl. 1650-1680.

THACKE, Philip; London, fl. 1690.

THWAITES, Aynesworth; London, fl. 1760.

THWAITES, John; London, fl. 1800.

TOMLIN, Edward; London, fl. 1795.

TOMLINSON, William; London, fl. 1700-1730.

TOMPION, Thomas; The Father of English Clock Making,
   b. 1639, d. 1713; London.

TREGENT, James; London, fl. 1790.

TROUGHTON, Edward; London, fl. 1780-1830.

TUNNELL, John; London, fl. 1825.

TUPMAN, George; London, fl. 1820.

TUTET, Edward; London, fl. 1775.

UNDERWOOD, Robert; London, fl. 1780.

UPJOHN, William; Exeter, fl. 1745.

URSEAU, Nicholas; London, fl. 1555-1590.

VALENTINE, C. F. D.; London, fl. 1810-1825.

VANTROLLIER, James; London, fl. 1640.

VERNON, Samuel; London, fl. 1660.

VICK, Richard; London, fl. 1725.

VIET, Claude; London, fl. 1710.

VINER, Charles E.; London, fl. 1780-1820.

VULLIAMY, Benjamin; London, fl. 1815-1850.

WALDRON, John; London, fl. 1760.

WALLIS, Jacob; London, fl. 1775.

WARD, John; London, fl. 1795.

WARNER, John; London, fl. 1700.

WATKINS, John; London, fl. 1830.

WATSON, Edward; London, fl. 1825.

WEBB, Benjamin; London, fl. 1800.

WEBSTER, Robert; London, fl. 1680-1700.

WEBSTER, William; London, fl. 1730-1750.

WENHAM, John; Dereham, fl. 1750.

WEST, Thomas; London, fl. 1710.

WESTBROOK, William; London, fl. 1700.

WESTCOTT, John; London, fl. 1720.
WHEELER, Thomas; London, fl. 1665-1700.
WHICHCOTE, Samuel; London, fl. 1750.
WHITCHURCH, Samuel; King's Wood, fl. 1770.
WHITEHURST, John; Derby, fl. 1750.
WICKES, John; London, fl. 1790.
WIGSON, William; London, fl. 1800-1825.
WILLIAMSON, Joseph; London, fl. 1720.
WILLIAMSON, Robert; London, fl. 1695.
WILLOWE, John; London, fl. 1635.
WILSON, Joshua; London, fl. 1705-1710.
WILTER, John; London, fl. 1770.
WINDMILLS, Joseph; London, fl. 1690-1700.
WINDMILLS, Thomas; London, fl. 1700.
WISE, John; London, fl. 1670-1700.
WISE, Peter; London, fl. 1720.
WONTNER, John; London, fl. 1790.
WRAGG, Houblon; London, fl. 1730.
WRAY, Hilton; London, fl. 1780.
WRIGHT, Thomas; London, fl. 1780.
WYCKE, John P.; London, fl. 1805.
WYNN, Henry; London, fl. 1685.

YARDLEY, James; Stratford, fl. 1765.
YEATMAN, Andrew; London, fl. 1725.
YOUNG, Charles; London, fl. 1820.
YOUNG, James; London, fl. 1800.
YOUNG, John; London, fl. 1790.

OIL PAINTINGS, WATER COLOUR DRAWINGS, ENGRAVINGS, ETCHINGS, etc.

GLOSSARY OF TERMS USED

Aquatint—A method of etching or engraving on copper by acid.

Artist Proof—A proof of an engraving bearing the signature of the artist, generally in pencil.

Baxter Prints—George Baxter (1804-1867) invented a method of printing in oil colours in about 1835. Baxter's method was to first make an engraving of the picture which was printed, afterwards adding the colours. A separate wood block had to be made for each colour, sometimes more than twenty blocks would be required for each picture, and each block had to be made to fit exactly.

Caricature—A portrait sketch in which characteristic points are exaggerated without destroying the resemblance to the original.

Cartoon—A full size preparatory drawing for a painting or tapestry. A term used later for drawings of a humourous nature.

Chalcography—The art of engraving on copper plates.

Chiaroscuro or **Clare Obscure**—The representation of light and shadow in paintings; employing light and shadow as in monochrome.

Conversation Piece—A variety of genre painting or works of art in which figures are represented in discussion.

Crayon Drawing—(*See Pastel.*)

Counter Proof—An impression taken from a proof just made, and not from the plate. The picture is thus in reverse.

Daguerreotype—A method of taking pictures on metal plates by the light of the sun; a photograph fixed on a plate of copper by a certain process. Invented in 1839.

Drypoint—A method of engraving in which the design is cut direct on to the plate by a graver; the burr which results from the cutting is not removed as in ordinary line engraving; this gives a velvet-like finish, only a limited number of prints can be made by this method.

Diptych—Consisting of two leaves or folds, a folding two-leaved tablet of wood, ivory or metal, the outside of which is usually carved or embossed, enclosing pictures, two pictures hinged together form a diptych. (*See Triptych*).

Engraving—The art of incising designs on wood, metal, etc., for taking off impressions on paper; engraving on wood differs from that on metal, the design projects on the former and is sunk in the latter. (*See Aquatint, Etching, Mezzotint and Stipple.*)

En Grisaille—Grey in flat tints. A term used in painting to describe objects decorated in different tints of grey to give the effect of solid bodies in relief.

Etching—A method of engraving in which the design is composed of a combination of lines drawn by a sharp point on the prepared surface of a metal plate; the acid is then applied which eats into the lines, thus forming the design from which impressions are taken.

Foxed—An engraving spotted with marks due to dampness.

French Prints—The proofs of old French prints are as follows:—
(1) Without letters.
(2) With Coat of Arms of Patron.
(3) With Artist's and Engraver's name.
(4) With full dedication and "Avec Privilege du Roi" or "A.P.D.R."

Fresco—Paintings executed on wet or fresh plaster with earthy colours. (*See Secco.*)

Genre—A term in art applied to compositions possessing an assemblage of species with certain characters in common. Species in distinctive groups with respect to style and purpose In paintings, scenes of everyday life, as opposed to historical, landscape or classical subjects.

Gouache—An opaque water-based paint; a picture painted with this technique.

Graffito—Ancient Roman figure drawings and inscriptions, scratched with a stylus on the plaster of walls.

Grisaille—Decorative painting in greyish tints used largely on satinwood furniture of the late 18th century.

Icon—A sacred representation or image, painted on a panel. Particularly applied to those of the Greek Orthodox Church.

Japanese Prints—A form of Japanese art, coloured prints being produced from wood blocks, each colour requires a separate wood block.

Kakemono—A Japanese wall picture fastened to a roller top and bottom.

Le Blond—A pupil and licensee of George Baxter. Although his prints are similar, they are not as good as those of Baxter.

Line Engraving—A method of engraving in which a combination of lines forms the design, being incised direct on the plate, usually copper.

Lithograph—Produced by drawing with a greasy crayon or ink, on a stone. The stone is saturated with water and printing ink applied. This adheres only to those portions covered with the greasy crayon.

Medium—The base in which the pigment is suspended in a paint, e.g., oil, gum arabic.

Mezzotint—A process of engraving; the plate is prepared by being indented all over with a sharp instrument, a "rocker". The rough surfaces left after the engraver has scraped away the design retain the ink for printing; the parts most scraped or smoothed giving the highest lights.

Miniature—A painting of small size, usually a portrait, enabling it to be carried on the person. Ivory is the commonly used ground for miniatures.

Monochrome—A picture in only one colour, or tints of one colour.

Oil Painting—A method of painting in which the pigments are ground in oil.

Oleograph—A lithograph resembling a painting in oils.

Panorama—A view of the whole surrounding scenery as seen from one point.

Pastel—A chalk mixed with various colouring materials made into crayons, used chiefly for portrait sketches; a sketch so made.

Pentimento, plural **Pentimenti**—Literally repentance, a correction mark in a painting or drawing in the course of work and later visible.

Photogravure—A modern process whereby photographic prints are produced.

Pigment—Powdered colour mixed with a medium to make paint.

Polychrome—Many coloured.

Proof—A trial impression from an engraved plate. "Artist's Proof" is the first impression, "Proof before letters" is the next impression; in this, the artist's name is printed on the left below the engraving and that of the engraver on the right, but there is no title. "Open letter proof" is the next impression, the title being in faint letters.

Proof Before Letters—A proof from an engraved plate which does not bear any inscription or title except the artist's name which is printed on the left below the engraving and that of the engraver on the right.

Remarque—A small design etched on the margin of a plate. An etching or proof so distinguished.

Secco—The name given to a variety of mural painting in which the colours are applied to dry plaster, presenting a dullish appearance, as opposed to Fresco.

Silhouette—A profile portrait or other drawing, the outline of which is filled in with black or other dark colour. Being inexpensive to produce it is supposed that it was named after a French Cabinet Minister in 1759, who attained the reputation of being an "apostle of cheapness".

Silver Point—The name given to a sketch executed with a silver pointed pencil.

Singerie—(literally "monkey-trick")—Mural decorations in which monkeys, squirrels, etc., are depicted; common in the Louis XV period.

Sketch—A quickly made drawing, usually intended as a draft or basis for a painting or other work executed in more detail.

Stencilling—A method of painting or printing by rubbing ink or paint through the designs cut in plate or metal or other suitable material.

Stipple Engraving—A method of engraving in which dots form the design in place of lines, as in line engraving; Bartolozzi excelled in this style.

Triptych—A set of three tablets, leaves, volets (*q.v.*) or pictures hinged together: the outer ones fold over the centre, usually painted with sacred subjects.

Varnish—A resinous solution applied to painted and other surfaces to give a gloss.

Volet—The name given to either of the folding wings of a triptych.

Water Colour—In this method of painting, the pigment is bound with gum and diluted by water.

Woodcut—An early form of engraving, the design being taken out on a wood panel from which impressions were taken.

Alphabetically arranged List of
ARTISTS, ENGRAVERS, SCULPTORS, ETC.
with Dates

This section does not comprise a complete list. Such a list would entail the production of a volume to itself; but it is hoped for general purposes the information given will prove of use.

A.R.A.—*Associate of the Royal Academy.*
R.A.—*Royal Academy or Academician.*
R.H.A.—*Royal Hibernian Academy.*
R.I.—*Royal Institute of Painters of Water Colours.*
R.S.A.—*Royal Scottish Academy.*
R.W.S.—*Royal Society of Water Colours.*
fl.—*Flourished.*

AACHEN, Johann von; German portrait painter, 1552-1615.

AARTSEN, Pieter; Dutch historical painter, 1519-1573.

AARTSZ, Rijkaert; Dutch painter, 1482-1577.

ABANI, Francesco; painter, 1578-1660.

ABBATE, Niccolo dell; Italian painter, 1512-1571.

ABBEY, Edwin Austin; American painter and book illustrator, settled in England, 1852-1911.

ABBOTT, Francis Lemuel; English portrait painter, 1760-1803.

ABEL DE PUJOL, Alexandre Denis; French painter, 1787-1861.

ABEL, Joseph; German painter of portraits, historical and classical subjects, 1768-1818.

ABERCROMBY, Julia Janet Georgiana, Lady; portrait painter, 1840-1915.

ABILDGAARD, Nikolaj Abraham; Danish historical painter, 1744-1809.

ABSOLON, John R.; landscape painter, 1815-1895.

ACHTSCHELLINCK, Lucas; Flemish landscape painter, 1626-1699.

ACKERMANN, Johann Adam; German landscape painter, 1780-1843.

ACTON, John Adams; portrait painter, 1833-1910.

ADAM, Albrecht; German military painter, 1786-1862.

ADAM, Jean Victor; French military painter, 1801-1867.

ADAMS, George Gammon; portrait painter, 1821-1898.

ADAMS, J. C.; landscape painter, 1840-1906.

ADOLPH, Joseph Anthony; painter, 1729-1762.

ADRIAENSSEN, Alexander; Dutch still life painter, 1587-1661.

AEKEN, Hieronymus van; known as Jerom Bosch. Dutch religious painter, 1462-1518.

AERTSEN, Peter; Dutch painter, 1519-1573.

AGASSE, J. L.; animal painter, 1767-1846.

AGLIO, Augustine; Italian painter, 1777-1857. Settled in England.

AGRESTI, Livio; Italian religious painter, fl. 1550-1580.

AIDÉ, Hamilton; painter, etc., 1829-1906.

AIKMAN, William; Scottish portrait painter, 1682-1731.

ALBANI, Francesco; Italian religious painter, 1578-1660.

ALBERELLI, Giacomo; Venetian historical painter, 1600-1650.

ALBERTINELLI, Mariotto; Florentine religious painter, 1474-1515.

ALDEGREVER (or Aldegraff), Heinrich; German portrait painter and engraver, 1502-1558.

ALESIO, Matteo Perez de; Italian painter, 1547-circa 1600, pupil of Michelangelo.

ALEXANDER, William; painter, 1767-1816.

ALFANI, Domenico; Italian religious painter, 1483-1553.

ALFAROY GOMEZ, Juan de; Spanish religious painter, 1640-1680. Pupil of Velazquez.

ALIBRANDO, Girolamo; Sicilian painter, 1470-1524. Pupil of Leonardo da Vinci.

ALKEN, Henry Thomas; Sporting Engraver, 1785-1851.

ALKEN, Samuel Henry; Sporting Engraver, 1810-1894.

ALLAN, David; Scottish landscape and portrait painter, 1744-1796. Settled in Italy.

ALLAN, Sir William; Scottish historical painter, 1782-1850 Settled in Russia.

ALLEGRI, Antonio (Correggio); Italian religious painter, 1494-1534.

ALLEN, Joseph William; English landscape painter, 1803-1852.

ALLORI, Alessendro; Florentine portrait and religious painter, 1535-1607.

ALLORI, Angiolo; Florentine portrait and religious painter, 1502-1572.

ALLORI, Christofano; Florentine portrait and religious painter, 1577-1621.

ALMA-TADEMA, Sir Lawrence, O.M., R.A.; Dutch painter, 1836-1912. Settled in England.

ALOISI, Baldassare; Italian religious painter and engraver, 1578-1638.

ALTDORFER, Albrecht; German landscape and religious painter and engraver, 1480-1538.

AMBERGER, Christoph; German portrait and religious painter, 1490-1563. Pupil of Holbein.

AMIGONI, Jacopo; Venetian historical and portrait painter and engraver, 1675-1752. Settled in England, Germany and Spain.

ANDERSON, Wm.; painter, 1757-1837.

ANDREA D'AGNOLO; known as Andrea del Sarto, Florentine religious painter, 1487-1531. Settled in France.

ANDREA DAL CASTAGNO; Florentine religious painter, 1390-1457.

ANDREWS, G. H.; marine painter, 1816-1898.

ANGELICO, Fra (Fra Giovanni da Fiesole); Florentine religious painter, 1387-1455.

ANGELO DI TADDEO GADDI; Italian painter, 1333-1396.

ANGILLIS, Pierre; Flemish landscape painter, 1685-1734. Settled in England, Germany and Italy.

ANGUISCIOLA, Sofonisba; Italian portrait and historical painter, 1535-1625.

ANNIGONI, Pietro; Contemporary portrait painter, 1910-

ANQUETIN, Louis; water-colour painter, 1861-1931.

ANSDELL, Richard; English animal painter, 1815-1885.

ANSIAUX, Jean Joseph Eléonore Antoine; Flemish historical and portrait painter, 1764-1840.

ANTONIO, Antonello d'; Italian religious painter, circa 1420-1493. Settled in Flanders.

APPIANI, Andrea; Italian painter, circa 1754-1817.

APPIANI, Andrea; (The Younger) 1817-1865.

ARETUSI, Pellegrino de; Italian painter, -1523. Pupil of Raphael.

ARMITAGE, Edward, R.A.; Historical painter, 1817-1896.

ARMFIELD, George; Animal Painter fl. 1836-1867.

ARMSTEAD, Henry Hugh, R.A.; Sculptor, 1828-1905.

AUDINET, Philippe; engraver, 1766-1837.

AUDUBON, John James; painter of birds, 1780-1851.

AUMONIER, James; painter, 1832-1911.

AUSTIN, Samuel; landscape and coastal painter, 1796-1834.

AVERCAMP, Hendrik van; Dutch landscape painter, 1585-1634.

BACHELIER, Jean Jacques; French flower and historical painter, 1724-1805.

BACKER, Jacob; Dutch painter, 1608-1651. Pupil of Rembrandt.

BACON, John, R.A.; sculptor, 1740-1799.

BADALOCCHIO, Sisto; Italian painter and engraver, 1581-1647.

BAGLIONI, Cavaliere Giovanni; Italian religious painter, 1571-1644.

BAILY, Edward Hodges, R.A.; portrait painter 1788-1867.

BAINES, Thomas; English painter, 1822-1875.

BAKER, Thomas, English painter, 1809-1869.

BAKHUYSEN, Ludolf; Dutch marine painter, 1631-1708.

BALDOVINETTI, Alesso; Florentine religious painter, 1427-1499.

BALDUNG, Hans; German religious painter and engraver, circa 1480-1545.

BALLANTINE, James; Scottish painter, 1808-1866.

BALLANTYNE, John, R.S.A.; Scottish portrait painter, 1815-1897.

BALMER, George; Water colours, 1806-1846.

BANDINELLI, Baccio; Florentine sculptor, 1493-1560.

BANKS, Thomas, R.A.; English sculptor, 1735-1805. Settled in Italy and Russia.

BAPTISE, Jean; painter, 1636-1699.

BARBER, Charles Burton; English animal painter, 1845-1894.

BARBER, Charles Vincent; landscape painter, 1784-1854.

BARBER, Joseph; English painter, 1757-1811.

BARBIERI, Giovanni Francesco; Italian religious and mythological painter, 1591-1666.

BARKER, Robert; Irish painter, 1739-1806.

BARKER, Thomas; English landscape painter, 1769-1847.

BARKER, Thomas Jones; English painter, 1815-1882.

BARLOW, Francis; English portrait and animal painter, 1626-1702.

BARLOW, Thomas Oldham; mezzotint engraver, 1824-1889.

BAROCCIO, Federigo; Italian religious painter, 1528-1612.

BARRAUD, Henry; Sporting artist, 1811-1874.

BARRAUD, William; Sporting artist, 1810-1850.

BARRET, George; Irish landscape painter, circa 1728-1784.

BARRY, James, R.A.; Irish historical painter, 1741-1806.

BARTHOLOMEW, Valentine; flower painter, 1799-1879.

BARTLETT, William Henry; English landscape painter, 1809-1854.

BARTOLI, Pietro Santi; Italian painter and engraver, 1635-1700.

BARTOLOMMEO di PAGHOLO del FATTORINO; Florentine religious painter, 1475-1517.

BARTOLOZZI, Francesco, R.A.; Florentine engraver, 1725-1815. Settled in England.

BASIRE, I.; engraver, 1704-1768.

BASIRE, James; engraver, 1769-1822.

BASSANO, Giacomo da Ponte; Italian painter, 1510-1592.

BATES, Harry, A.R.A.; sculptor, 1850-1899.

BATONI, Pompeo Girolamo; Italian religious and portrait painter, 1708-1787.

BAUCHANT, Andre; painter, 1873-1958.

BAUDRY, Paul Jacques Aimé; French painter, 1828-1886.

BAUSE, Johann Friedrich; German engraver, 1738-1886.

BAWDEN, Edward; water-colour painter, 1903-

BAXTER, George; English engraver, 1805-1867.

BAYNES, F. T., R.A.; English still-life painter, 1833-1864.

BAYNES, James; English landscape painter, 1766-1837.

BAZZI, Giovanni Antonio; Italian religious and portrait painter, 1477-1549. Pupil of Leonardo da Vinci.

BEALE, Mary; English portrait painter, 1632-1697.

BEARDSLEY, Aubrey; English black and white artist, 1873-1898.

BEAUMONT, Sir George Howland; English painter, 1753-1827.

BEAUMONT, Sir Albanis; painter and engraver, -circa 1810.

BEAUMONT, John Thomas Barber; miniature painter, 1774-1841.

BEAVIS, Richard; painter, 1824-1896.

BECK, David; Dutch painter, 1621-1656. Pupil of Van Dyck. Settled in England.

BECKET, Isaac; engraver, 1653-1719.

BEECHEY, Sir William, R.A.; English portrait painter, 1753-1839.

BEEK, David; painter, 1621-1656.

BELCHER, George, R.A.; painter, 1875-1947.

BELL, Andrew; English engraver, 1726-1809.

BELL, John Zephaniah; painter, 1794-1883.

BELL, Robert Charles; English engraver, 1808-1872.

BELLANGE, Joseph Louis Hippolyte; French painter, 1800-1866.

BELLERS, William; painter, circa 1730-1780.

BELLINI, Filippo; Italian painter, circa 1550-circa 1604.

BELLINI, Gentile; Venetian portrait and religious painter, 1429-1507.

BELLINI, Giovanni; Venetian religious painter, circa 1430-1516.

BELLINI, Jacopo; Venetian portrait painter, circa 1400-circa 1470.

BENDEMANN, Eduard; German religious and portrait painter, 1811-1889.

BENNETT, William; water-colour painter, 1811-1871.

BENVENUTO, Giovanni Battista; Italian painter, circa 1467-1525.

BERCHEM, Claes Pietersz; Dutch landscape painter, 1620-1683.

BERNINI, Giovanni Lorenzo; Italian sculptor and painter of religious subjects, 1598-1680. Settled in France.

BERRETTINI, Pietro; Italian religious painter, 1596-1669.

BEWICK, John, English engraver, 1760-1795.

BEWICK, Thomas; English engraver, 1753-1828.

BEWICK, William; English painter, 1795-1866.

BIAGGIO, Bernardino di (Pintoricchio); Italian religious painter, 1454-1513.

BIGG, W. R., R.A.; English portrait and landscape painter, 1755-1828.

BIGI, Francesco; Florentine portrait and religious painter, 1482-1525.

BIGORDI, Domenico; Florentine religious painter, 1449-1494.

BIGORDI, Ridolfo; Florentine religious painter, 1483-1561. Assistant to Raphael.

BIRCH, Charles Bell, A.R.A.; portrait painter, 1832-1893.

BIRCH, S. J. Lamorna, R.A.; painter, 1869-1955.

BIRD, Edward, R.A.; English painter, 1772-1819.

BISCAINO, Bartolommeo; Genoese religious painter, 1632-1657.

BLAKE, B.; English landscape and still life painter, 1788-1832.

BLAKE, William; English painter and engraver, 1757-1827.

BLANCHARD, Jacques; French religious painter, 1600-1638. Settled in Italy

BLOEMEN, Peter van; Dutch historical painter, 1657-1719. circa 1740. Settled in Italy.

BLOEMEN, Pieter van; Dutch historical painter, 1657-1719.

BOCCACCINO, Boccaccio; Italian religious painter, 1460-1525.

BODDINGTON, Henry John; English painter, 1811-1865.

BODMER, Karl; painter and etcher, 1805-1893.

BOECKLIN, Arnold; Swiss painter. 1827-1901. Settled in Italy, France and Germany.

BOEHM, Sir Joseph Edgar, R.A.; Austrian sculptor, 1834-1890. Settled in England.

BOEL, Pieter; Flemish still life and animal painter, 1622-1674. Settled in Italy.

BOGLE, John; miniature painter, circa 1746-1803.

BOISSIEU, Jean J. de; French painter and engraver, 1736-1810.

BOND, R. S.; English landscape painter, 1808-1886.

BONDONE, Giotto di; Florentine architect and religious painter, 1276-1337.

BONE, Henry, R.A.; English painter, 1755-1834.

BONE, Henry Pierce; English painter, 1779-1855.

BONE, Sir Muirhead; painter and engraver, 1876-1953.

BONFIGLI, Benedetto; Italian religious painter, circa 1420-1496.

BONHEUR, Maria Rosa; French animal painter, 1822-1899.

BONIFAZIO, Veronese; Italian religious painter, 1487-1533.

BONINGTON, Richard Parkes; English painter, 1801-1828.

BONNARD, Pierre; French painter, 1867-1947.

BONOMI, Joseph, A.R.A.; portrait painter, 1796-1878.

BONVICINO, Alessandro (Moretto); Italian religious and portrait painter, 1498-1555. Pupil of Titian.

BONVIN, F. S.; landscape painter, 1817-1888.

BORDONE, Paris; Venetian painter, 1500-1571.

BORGOGNONE, Ambrogio; Italian architect and painter, circa 1455-1523.

BOTTICELLI, Sandro; Florentine painter, circa 1445-1510.

BOUCHER, François; French painter, 1703-1770.

BOUDIN, Eugene; French painter, 1824-1898.

BOUGH, Samuel; Scottish landscape painter, 1822-1878.

BOUGHTON, George Henry, R.A.; English painter, 1833-1905. Settled in America.

BOUGUEREAU, William; French painter, 1825-1915. Settled in Italy.

BOULANGER, Gustave Rodolphe Clarence; French painter, 1824-1888.

BOURDON, Sebastien; French painter and engraver, 1616-1671. Settled in Sweden.

BOURGEOIS, Sir Peter Francis; English landscape, military and marine painter, 1756-1811. Settled in Poland.

BOUVIER, Augustus Jules; water-colour painter, 1827-1881.

BOWLER, H. A.; painter, 1824-1903.

BOXALL, Sir William, R.A.; English allegorical and portrait painter, 1800-1879.

BOYCE, George P.; English landscape painter, 1826-1897.

BOYDELL, John; English engraver, 1719-1804.

BOYDELL, Josiah; English engraver, 1752-1804.

BOYS, Thomas Shotter; English painter, 1803-1874.

BRABAZON, Hercules B.; English water-colour painter, 1821-1906.

BRADFORD, William; English painter, 1827-1892.

BRADLEY, B.; English water-colour painter, 1842-1904.

BRAMLEY, Frank, R.A.; English painter, 1857-1914.

BRANDARD, R.; engraver, 1805-1862.

BRANGWYN, F., R.A.; English etcher and painter, 1867-1958.

BRANWHITE, C.; landscape painter, 1817-1880.

BRANWHITE, Nathan; portrait and miniature painter, 1813-1894.

BRAQUE, Georges; French painter, 1882-1963.

BRETT, John, A.R.A.; English landscape painter, 1830-1902.

BRIDELL, Frederick Lee; English painter, 1831-1863.

BRIDGMAN, F. A.; American figure painter, 1847-1928.

BRIERLY, Sir Oswald Walters; English painter, 1817-1894.

BRIGGS, Henry Perronet, R.A.; portrait painter, 1793-1844.

BRIGHT, Henry; English painter, 1814-1873.

BROCK, Sir Thomas, R.A.; portrait painter, 1847-1922.

BROCKEDON, William; English painter, 1783-1854.

BROCKHURST, Gerald Leslie, R.A.; engraver, 1890-

BROCKY, Charles; portrait painter, 1807-1855.

BROMLEY, William; English engraver, 1769-1842.

BROOKING, Charles; English painter, 1723-1759.

BROUGH, Robert; English painter, 1872-1905.

BROUWER, Adrian; Dutch painter, 1605-1638.

BROWN, Sir John Arnesby, A.R.A.; English pastoral painter, 1866-1955.

BROWN, Charles Armitage; portrait painter, 1786-1842.

BROWN, Ford Madox; English painter, 1821-1893. Settled in France, Belgium and Italy.

BROWN, Professor Fred; painter, 1851-1941.

BROWNE, Hablot Knight; English water-colour and black-and-white artist, 1815-1882. ("Phiz"; illustrator of Dickens' works.)

BRUNDRIT, Reginald G., R.A., painter, 1883-1960.

BRUEGHAL, Abraham; painted flowers and fruit, 1672-1720.

BRUEGHEL, Jan (The Elder); landscapes, 1568-1625.

BRUEGHEL, Jan (The Younger); 1601- circa 1667.

BRUEGHEL, Peeter (The Elder); painted village scenes, 1530-1569.

BRUEGHEL, Peeter (The Younger); inferior to his father. Painted ecclesiastical subjects, 1564-1638.

BRY, Theodor de; Flemish painter and engraver, 1528-1598. Settled in Germany.

BUCK, Adam; English portrait painter, 1759-1833.

BUCK, Samuel; English engraver, 1696-1779.

BUITENWEG, W.; etcher, 1590-1630.

BUNDY, Edgar; painter, 1862-1922.

BUONACCORSI, Pietro; Florentine religious and mythological painter, 1500-1547. Assistant to Raphael.

BURGESS, John Bagnold; English painter, 1829-1897.

BURNE-JONES, Sir Edward Coley; English painter, 1833-1898.

BURNET, James M.; English painter, 1788-1816.

BURNET, John; English painter and engraver, 1784-1868.

BURNEY, E. F.; English portrait painter, 1760-1848.

BURTON, Sir Frederick William, R.H.A., F.S.A.; English painter, 1816-1900.

BUTLER, Lady Elizabeth (Elizabeth Southerden Thompson); English battle painter, 1850-1933.

BUTLER, Samuel; English painter, 1835-1902.

BYRNE, J.; landscape painter, 1786-1847.

CABANAL, Alexandre; French portrait painter, 1823-1889.

CAGNACCI, Guido; Italian portrait painter, 1601-1681.

CAIRO, Francesco; Italian portrait painter, 1598-1674.

CALAME, Alexandre; Swiss portrait painter, 1810-1864.

CALDARA, Polidoro; Italian portrait painter, 1492-1543. Pupil of Raphael.

CALDECOTT, Randolph; English portrait painter and black-and-white artist, 1846-1886.

CALDERON, Philip Hermogenes, R.A.; English portrait painter, 1833-1898.

CALIARI, Paolo; Italian portrait and religious painter, 1528-1588. (Known as Veronese.)

CALLCOTT, Sir Augustus Wall; English landscape and marine painter, 1779-1844. Settled in Italy.

CALLOT, Jacques; French engraver, 1592-1635.

CALLOW, William; English portrait painter, 1812-1908.

CALTHROP, Claud; English painter, 1845-1893.

CALVERT, Charles; English landscape painter, 1785-1852.

CALVERT, Charles; English landscape painter, 1785-1852.

CALVI, Lazzaro; Italian portrait painter, 1502-1607.

CAMBIASO, Luca, known as Luchetto Da Geneva; Italian painter, 1527-1585.

CAMERON, Sir David Young; Scottish painter and etcher, 1865-1945.

CAMPANA, Pedro; Belgian religious painter, 1503-circa 1570. Settled in Italy and Spain.

CAMPBELL, Thomas; portrait painter, 1790-1858.

CAMPIN, Robert; religious painter, 1375-1444.

CAMPION, George B.; English painter, 1796-1870.

CANALE, Giovanni Antonio da (Canaletto); Italian painter. 1697-1768. Settled in England.

CANALETTO, see CANALE.

CANON, Hans; Dutch artist, 1829-1885.

CANTARINI, Simone; Italian religious painter and engraver. 1612-1648.

CANUTI, Domenico Maria; Italian painter, 1620-1684.

CAPPELLE, Jan van de; Dutch marine and landscape painter, fl. 1650-1680.

CAPPONI, Raffaellino; Florentine religious painter, circa 1476-1524.

CARAVAGGIO, Michelangelo Merisi da; Italian painter, 1569-1609.

CARAVAGGIO, Polidoro Caldara da; Italian painter, 1495-1543.

CARBAJAL, Luis de; painter, 1534-1613.

CARDUCCI, Bartolommeo; Italian painter, sculptor and architect, 1560-1610.

CARDUCCI, Vincenzo; Italian painter, 1568-1638.

CARMICHAEL, James Wilson; marine painter, 1800-1868.

CARMONTELLE, L. C.; portrait painter, 1717-1806.

CARPACCIO, Vittore; Venetian religious painter, fl. 1479-1522.

CARPENTER, Margaret Sarah; English portrait painter, 1793-1872.

CARPENTER, William; English painter and etcher, circa 1820-1899.

CARPIONI, Guilio; Venetian painter, 1611-1674.

CARRACCI, Agostino; Italian engraver and painter, 1557-1602.

CARRACCI, Annibale; Italian mythological and religious. painter, 1560-1609.

CARRACCI, Antonio; Italian painter, 1583-1618.

CARRACCI, Francesco; Italian painter, 1595-1622.

CARRACCI, Lodovico; Italian painter, 1550-1619.

CARRICK, Thomas; miniature painter, 1802-1874.

CARRIERA, Rosalba; Venetian minature painter, 1675-1757.

CARRIERE, E.; French painter, 1849-1906.

CARTER, George; English painter, 1737-1794.

CARTER, Hugh; English painter, 1867-1903.

CARTER, H. B.; English painter, fl. 1821-1830.

CARTER, Samuel John, English animal painter, 1835-1892.

CARTWRIGHT, Joseph; English marine painter, circa 1789-1829.

CARVER, Robert; English painter, circa 1730-1791.

CASANOVA, Francis; painter, 1727-1802.

CASSIE, James; painter, 1819-1879.

CASTAGNO, Andrea del Florentine; Religious painter, 1390-1475.

CASTIGLIONE, Giovanni Benedetto; Italian engraver and religious painter, 1616-1670. Pupil of Van Dyck.

CATLIN, George; American painter, 1796-1872.

CATTERMOLE, Charles; figure painter, 1832-1900.

CATTERMOLE, George; water colour painter, 1800-1868.

CAVALLINI, Pietro; Italian painter, 1279-1364.

CAVALLINO, Bernardo; Italian painter, 1622-1654.

CAVEDONE, Jacopo; Italian religious painter, 1577-1660.

CELLINI, Benvenuto; Italian sculpton and engraver, 1500-1571.

CESAIRI, Giuseppe; Italian religious and historical painter, circa 1568-1640.

CESARE DA SESTO; painter, 1477-1523.

CESI, Bartolommeo; Italian painter, 1550-1629.

CESIO, Carlo; Italian painter and engraver, 1626-1686.

CEZANNE, Paul; French painter, 1839-1906.

CHAGALL, Marc; painter, 1887-

CHALON, Alfred Edward, R.A.; English painter, 1780-1860

CHALON, Henry B.; animal painter, 1770-1849.

CHALON, John James, R.A.; English painter, 1778-1854.

CHAMBERS, George; English marine painter, 1803-1840.

CHAMPAIGNE, Philippe de; Flemish religious, historical and portrait painter, 1602-1674.

CHANTREY, Sir Francis Legatt, R.A.; English sculptor and portrait painter, 1781-1842.

CHAPLIN, Charles; English painter and engraver, 1825-1891.

CHARDIN, Jean Baptiste Siméon; French genre and still-life painter, 1699-1779.

CHARLES, James; English painter, 1851-1906.

CHASSERIAU, Theodore; French painter, 1819-1856.

CHAVANNES, Puvis de; painter, 1824-1898.

CHECA, Ulpiano; Spanish painter, 1860-1916.

CHENAVARD, P.; French historical painter, 1808-1895.

CHERON, Elisabeth Sophie; French portrait painter, 1648-1711.

CHINNERY, George, R.A.; English painter, 1774-1857.

CHISHOLM, A., R.A.; English painter, 1792-1847.

CIGNANI, Conte Carlo; Italian religious painter, 1628-1719.

CIGNAROLI, Giovanni Bettino; Italian portrait painter, 1706-1770.

CIMA, Giovanni Battista; Venetian religious painter, 1487-1517.

CIMABUE, Giovanni; Italian religious painter, circa 1240-1302.

CIPRIANI, Giovanni Battista; Florentine painter and engraver, 1727-1785. Settled in England.

CLARK, Cosmo; contemporary artist, 1897-

CLAUDE OF LORRAIN (Clause Gelée); French landscape painter, 1600-1682.

CLAUSEN, Sir George, R.A.; English painter, 1852-1944.

CLAXTON, Marshall; English historical painter, 1811-1881.

CLEEF, Jan van; Dutch religious painter, 1646-1716.

CLEEF, Joost van, Flemish portrait painter, circa 1520-1556.

CLENNEL, Luke; English painter and engraver, 1781-1840.

CLERISSEAU, Charles L., R.A.; architect and draughtsman, 1722-1820.

CLEVELEY, John; English seascape painter, 1747-1786.

CLEVELEY, Robert, R.A.; English marine painter, 1747-1809.

CLOSTERMAN, John; painter, 1656-1713.

CLOUET, François; French portrait painter, 1510-1572.

CLOUET, Jean; French portrait painter, circa 1485-1541.

CLOVIO, Giorgio Giulo; Croatian miniature painter, 1498-1578.

COATES, Samuel; miniature painter, 1734-1818.

COLE, George Vicat, R.A.; English painter, 1833-1893.

COLE, Thomas; American landscape painter, 1801-1848.

COLLE, Raffaello dal; Italian religious painter, circa 1490-1566, pupil of Raphael.

COLLIER, Hon. John; English portrait painter, 1850-1934.

COLLIER, John; English painter, 1708-1786.

COLLIER, Thomas, R.A.; English painter, 1840-1891.

COLLIER, F. F., R.A.; English painter, exhibited 1856 and 1857.

COLLINS, Charles Allston; English painter, 1828-1873.

COLLINS, William, R.A.; English painter, 1788-1847.

COLLINSON, James; English painter, circa 1825-1881.

CONEGLIANO, Biovanni Battista de, commonly called Cima da Conegliano; Venetian religious painter, 1487-1517.

CONNARD, Philip, R.A.; painter and illustrator, 1875-1958.

CONSTABLE, John, R.A.; English landscape painter, 1776-1837.

CONSTANT, Jean Joseph Benjamin; painter, 1845-1902.

COOK, Henry; English painter, 1642-1700.

COOK, Richard; English painter, 1784-1857.

COOKE, Edward William, R.A.; English marine painter, 1811-1880.

COOKE, George; English engraver, 1781-1834.

COOKE, William Bernard; English engraver, 1778-1855.

COOKE, William John; English engraver, 1797-1865.

COOPER, Abraham; English painter, 1787-1868.

COOPER, Alexander; English miniature painter, 1605-1660.

COOPER, Samuel, English miniature painter, 1609-1672.

COOPER, Thomas Sidney, R.A.; English animal painter, 1803-1902.

COPE, Sir Arthur Stockdale, R.A.; English portrait painter, 1857-1940.

COPE, Charles West, R.A.; English portrait painter, 1811-1890.

COPLEY, John Singleton, R.A.; American portrait and historical painter, 1737-1815.

COQUES, Gonzales; Flemish portrait painter, 1618-1684. Settled in England and Germany.

CORBET, Matthew Ridley, A.R.A.; English painter, 1850-1903.

CORBOULD, Edward H.; English historical painter, 1815-1905.

CORBOULD, Henry; English painter, 1787-1844.

CORBOULD, Richard; English painter, 1757-1831.

CORNELIUS, Peter von; German portrait painter, 1783-1867.

COROT, Jean Baptiste Camille; French landscape painter, 1796-1875.

CORRADI, Domenico; Italian painter, 1449-1498.

CORREGGIO, Antonio Allegri da; Italian painter, 1494-1534.

CORT, Cornelis; engraver, 1536-1578.

COSIMO, Engelo di; Florentine portrait painter, 1502-1572.

COSTA, Giovanni; Italian portrait painter, 1827-1903.

COSTA, Lorenzo; Italian religious painter, circa 1460-1535.

COSWAY, Maria Cecila Louisa; Florentine portrait painter, 1759-1838.

COSWAY, Richard; English miniature painter, 1742-1821

COTES, Francis, R.A.; English portrait painter, 1725-1770.

COTMAN, John Sell; English engraver, 1782-1843.

COURBET, Gustave; painter, 1819-1877.

COURTOIS, Guillaume; French portrait painter, 1626-1679.

COURTOIS, Gustave, C. E.; French painter, 1852-1924.

COURTOIS, Jacques; French military and religious painter, 1621-1676.

COUSIN, Jean; French sculptor, miniature and religious painter, etc., circa 1500-1589.

COUSINS, Samuel, R.A.; English painter and engraver, 1801-1887.

COUTURE, Thomas; French historical painter, 1815-1879.

COWPER, Frank Cadogan, A.R.A.; English painter, 1877-1958.

COX, David, English landscape painter, 1783-1859.

COX, David; English water-colour painter, 1809-1885.

COYPEL, Antoine; French religious painter, 1661-1722.

COYPEL, Charles Antoine; French painter, 1694-1752.

COYPEL, Noel; French religious painter, 1628-1707.

COYPEL, Noel Nicholas; French painter, 1692-1734.

COZENS, Alexander; English painter, circa 1710-1786.

COZENS, John Robert; English painter, 1752-1799.

CRAIG, William Marshall, R.A.; portrait and miniature painter, exhibited 1788-1827.

CRADOCK, Marmaduke; bird painter, circa 1660-1717.

CRANACH, Lucas; German portrait painter, 1472-1553.

CRANACH, Lucas; German religious painter, 1515-1586.

CRANCH, Christopher Pearse; painter, 1813-1892.

CRANE, Thomas; English painter, 1808-1859.

CRANE, Walter; English painter, 1845-1915.

CRAWFORD, Edmund Thornton; English painter, 1806-1885.

CRAWFORD, Thomas; American sculptor, 1814-1857.

CRAWFORD, William; English painter, 1825-1869.

CRAWHALL, Joseph; painter, 1816-1913.

CROSSE, Richard; miniature painter, 1742-1810.

CRESTI, Domenico; Florentine religious painter, 1558-1638.

CRESWICK, Thomas, R.A.; English landscape painter, 1811-1869.

CRISTALL, Joshua; English painter, 1767-1847.

CRIVELLI, Carlo; Venetian painter, circa 1430-1493.

CROFTS, Ernest, R.A.; English historical painter, 1847-1911.

CROKER, John; English engraver, 1670-1741.

CROME, John; English landscape painter, 1769-1821.

CROME, John Bernay; English landscape painter, 1794-1842.

CROMEK, Robert Hartley; engraver, 1770-1812.

CRUIKSHANK, George; English engraver, black-and-white artist and caricaturist, 1792-1878.

CRUIKSHANK, Isaac; English caricaturist and water-colour painter, circa 1756-1811.

CRUIKSHANK, Isaac Robert; English caricaturist and miniature painter, 1789-1856.

CUYP, Aelbert; Dutch landscape, animal and portrait painter, 1620-1691.

CUYP, Jacob, Gerritse; Dutch painter, 1575-1649.

DADD, Richard; English genre painter, 1817-1887.

DADE, Ernest, R.A.; seascape painter, exhibited 1886-1901.

DAEL, Jan Frans van; Dutch flower painter, 1764-1840.

DAHL, Johann Christian; German landscape painter, 1778-1857.

DAHL, Michael; Swedish portrait painter, 1656-1743.

DAL SOLE, G. G.; Italian painter, 1654-1719.

DALI, Salvador; Spanish painter, 1904-

DANBY, Francis; Irish painter, 1793-1861.

DANBY, Thomas; landscape and marine painter, fl. 1841-1886.

DANCE, George, R.A.; portrait painter, 1741-1825.

DANCE, Nathaniel, R.A.; painter, 1734-1811.

DANDINI, Cesare; Florentine painter, 1595-1658.

DANDINI, Pietro; painter, 1646-1712.

DAUBIGNY, Charles François; French landscape painter, 1817-1878.

DAUMIER, Honoré; French painter and caricaturist, 1808-1879.

DAVENPORT, Samuel; English engraver, 1783-1867.

DAVID, Gheeraert; Dutch painter, 1450-1523.

DAVID, Jacques Louis; French portrait painter, 1748-1825.

DAVIDSON, Charles; R.W.S., landscape painter, 1820-1902.

DA VINCI, Leonardo; Florentine painter, architect, sculptor and musician, 1452-1519.

DAVIS, Henry William Banks, R.A.; animal painter, 1833-1914.

DAVIS, John S., R.A.; English painter, 1804-1844.

DAVIS, R. B.; animal painter, 1782-1854.

DAWE, George, R.A.; English painter, 1781-1829.

DAWE, Henry Edward; English painter and engraver, 1790-1848.

DAWSON, Henry; English landscape painter, 1811-1878.

DAYES, Edward, R.A.; landscape and miniature painter and engraver, 1763-1804.

DECAMPS, Alexandre Gabriel; French painter, 1803-1860.

DEGAS, Edgar Hilaire; French impressionist, 1834-1917.

DE HEERE, Lucas; painter, 1543-1584.

DE LA BORDE, Henry, Viscount; French painter, 1811-1899.

DELACROIX, Ferdinand Victor Eugène; French painter, 1798-1863.

DELAMOTTE, William; painter, 1775-1863.

DELAROCHE, Paul Hippolyte; French painter, 1797-1856.

DE LOUTHERBOURGH, P. J., R.A.; painter, 1740-1812.

DEL SARTO, Andrea; Florentine painter, 1486-1531.

DERBY, William; English portrait and water-colour painter, 1786-1847.

DETAILLE, Edouard; French battle painter, 1848-1912.

DEVERELL, Walter Howell; painter, 1827-1854.

DEVIS, Arthur; painter, 1711-1787.

DEVIS, Anthony, R.A.; landscape painter, 1729-1817.

DEVIS, Arthur William; painter, 1763-1822.

DE WILDE, Samuel; portrait painter, 1748-1832.

DE WINT, Peter; landscape painter, 1784-1849.

DIAZ DE LA PENA, Narcisse Virgile; French landscape painter, 1808-1876.

DIBDIN, Thomas C., R.A.; landscape painter, 1810-1893.

DICK, Sir W. Reid, R.A.; contemporary sculptor, 1878-

DICKINSON, William; engraver, 1746-1823.

DICKSEE, Sir Frank, R.A.; classical painter, 1853-1928.

DIEPENBEECK, Abraham van; Flemish historical and mythological painter, 1599-1675. Pupil of Rubens. Settled in England.

DIETRICH, Christian Wilhelm Ernst; German painter, 1712-1774.

DIGHTON, Denis; military painter, 1792-1827.

DIGHTON, William Edward; water-colour painter, 1822-1853.

DOBSON, William; English portrait painter, 1610-1646.

DOBSON, William Charles Thomas, R.A.; English painter, 1817-1898.

DODD, Francis, R.A.; English painter, 1874-1949.

DODD, Robert; English marine painter, 1748-1816.

DODGSON, George Haydock; water-colour painter, 1811-1880.

DOES, Jacobus van der; Dutch painter, 1623-1673.

DOLCI, Carlo; Florentine painter, 1616-1686.

DOMENICHINO; Italian painter, 1581-1641.

DONATELLO; Florentine sculptor, circa 1386-1466.

DORÉ, Louis Christophe Gustave Paul; French historical painter, 1833-1883.

DOSSO DOSSI, Giovanni; Italian religious painter, 1479-1542.

DOU, Gerard; Dutch genre painter, 1613-1675.

DOUGHTY, William, R.A.; portrait painter and etcher, exhibited 1776-1779.

DOUGLAS, Sir William Fettes, P.R.S.A.; Scottish painter, 1822-1891.

DOWNMAN, John, A.R.A.; painter, 1750-1824.

DOYLE, John; English painter and caricaturist, 1797-1868.

DOYLE, Richard; English painter and caricaturist, 1824-1883.

DREVET, Pierre; French engraver, 1663-1738.

DROUAIS, François Hubert; French portrait painter, 1727-1775.

DROUAIS, Jean Germaine; French painter, 1763-1788.

DRUMMOND, James; Scottish historical painter, 1816-1877.

DRUMMOND, Samuel, A.R.A.; painter, 1765-1844.

DUCCIO di BOUNINSEGNA; religious painter and architect, circa 1260-1339.

DUGDALE, Thomas, R.A.; portrait painter, 1880-1952.

DUGHET, Gaspard; see POUSSIN.

DU MAURIER, George Louis Palmella Busson; artist and caricaturist, 1831-1896.

DUNBAR, Evelyn Mary; painter, 1906-1960.

DUNCAN, Edward, R.W.S.; marine painter, 1803-1882.

DUNCAN, Thomas; Scottish painter, 1807-1845.

DUNLOP, Ronald O., R.A.; painter, 1894-

DUPONT, Gainsborough; Nephew of Thomas Gainsborough, 1767-1797.

DUPPA, Richard; English copyist painter, 1770-1831.

DUPRÉ, Jules; French landscape painter, 1812-1889.

DÜRER, Albrecht; German painter and engraver, 1471-1528.

DUVAL, Charles Allen; painter, 1808-1872.

DYCE, William, R.A.; Scottish historical and religious painter. 1806-1864.

DYCK, Sir Anthony van; Flemish religious and portrait painter, 1599-1641. Settled in England.

EAST, Sir Alfred, A.R.A.; English landscape painter, 1849-1913.

EASTLAKE, Sir Charles Locke, P.R.A.; English Scriptural painter, 1793-1865.

EDELINCK, Gérard; engraver, 1640-1707.

EDOUART, Augustin; miniature painter, 1789-1861.

EDRIDGE, Henry, A.R.A.; painter, 1769-1821.

EDWARDS, Edward; English painter, 1738-1806.

EDWARDS, Edwin; painter, 1823-1879.

EDWARDS, Lionel; English sporting artist, 1878-1966.

EGG, Augustus Leopold, R.A.; English historical and genre painter, 1816-1863.

EGINTON, F.; painter on glass, 1737-1805.

ELLIS, Edwin, R.S.A.; land and seascape painter, 1841-1895.

ELLYS, John; painter, 1701-1757.

ELMER, Stephen, A.R.A.; still-life painter, -1796.

ELMORE, Alfred; Irish historical and genre painter, 1815-1881.

ELSHEIMER, Adam; German painter on copper, 1578-1621.

EMES, John, R.A.; English painter, exhibited 1790-1791.

EMPOLI, Jacopo da; (J. Chimenti); Florentine religious painter, circa 1554-1640.

ENGLEHEART, George; English miniature painter, 1750-1829.

ENGLEHEART, Thomas; portrait painter, 1745-1786.

EPSTEIN, Jacob; sculptor and painter, 1880-1959.

ERNST, Max; painter, 1891-

ESSEX, William; English enamel painter, 1784-1869.

ETTY, William, R.A.; English painter, 1787-1849.

EVANS, Richard; portrait painter, 1785-1871.

EVERDINGEN, Allart van; Dutch landscape and marine painter, 1621-1675.

EVES, Reginald G., R.A.; English portrait painter, 1876-1941.

EYCK, Hubert van; Dutch religious painter, 1366-1426.

EYCK, Jan van; Dutch painter, circa 1390-1440.

FABRIANO, Gentile di Niccolò da; see MASSI.

FABRITIUS, Bernhard; Dutch painter, fl. 1650-1672.

FAED, John; Scottish painter, 1819-1902.

FAED, Thomas, R.A.; Scottish painter, 1826-1900.

FAIRLAND, Thomas; English painter, 1804-1852.

FALCONET, Etienne Maurice; French sculptor, 1716-1791.

FANTIN-LATOUR, I.; French painter, 1836-1904.

FARINGDON, Joseph., R.A.; painter, 1747-1821.

FARMER, A., R.A.; painter, exhibited 1855-1867.

FARMER, Emily, R.A.; painter, 1826-1905.

FARQUHARSON, David, A.R.A.; Scottish landscape painter, 1839-1907.

FARQUHARSON, Joseph, R.A.; Scottish landscape and portrait painter, 1846-1935.

FARRIER, Robert, R.A.; English miniaturist, 1796-1879.

FEARNSIDE, W.; landscape painter, exhibited 1791-1801.

FERG, Paul Franz; German painter, 1689-1740.

FERGUSON, James, R.A.; Scottish portrait painter and miniaturist, 1710-1776.

FERNANDEZ, Francisco; painter, 1605-1646.

FERNANDEZ, Louis; painter, 1594-1654.

FERNANDEZ, Navarrete; Spanish painter, circa 1526-1579.

FERNELEY, John; animal painter, 1782-1860.

FERRARI, Gaudenzio; Italian religious painter and sculptor, circa 1481-1547.

FERRARI, Giovanni Andrea; Italian painter, 1599-1669.

FERRI, Circo; Italian engraver and historical painter, 1634-1689.

FETI, Domenico; Italian painter, 1589-1624.

FEUERBACH, Anselm; German historical painter, 1829-1880.

FIELD, John; Miniature painter, 1771-1841.

FIELDING, Anthony Vandyke Copley; English landscape painter, 1788-1855.

FIELDING, Newton Smith; English painter and engraver, 1799-1856.

FIELDING, Theodore Henry Adolphus; English painter, 1781-1851.

FIESOLI; see ANGELICO.

FILDES, Sir Luke, R.A.; English painter, 1844-1927.

FILIPEPI, Sandro (Botticelli); Florentine religious and mythological painter, 1447-1510.

FINCH, Francis Oliver; water-colour painter, 1802-1862.

FINDEN, Edward Francis; engraver, 1791-1857.

FINDEN, William; engraver, 1787-1852.

FINNEY, Samuel; miniature painter, 1721-1807.

FINNIE, John, R.A.; English landscape painter, 1829-1907.

FIORENZO DI LORENZO; Perugian religious painter, circa 1430-circa 1525.

FIORILLO, Johann Dominik; German painter, 1748-1821.

FISCHBACH, Johann; German painter, 1797-1871.

FISCHER, Joseph Anton; German painter, 1814-1859.

FISHER, John, R.A.; painter, 1841-1923.

FISK, William Henry; painter, 1797-1872.

FITTLER, James; English engraver, 1758-1835.

FLANDRIN, Jean Hippolyte; French historical and portrait painter, 1809-1864.

FLAXMAN, John, R.A.; English sculptor, 1755-1826. Settled in Italy.

FLINK, Govert; German painter, 1615-1660.

FLINT, Sir William Russell, R.A.; English painter, 1880-1969.

FOGGO, George; English painter, 1793-1869.

FOGGO, James, English painter, 1789-1860.

FOLEY, John Henry, R.A.; Irish sculptor, 1818-1874.

FONTANA, Lavinia; Italian historical painter, 1552-1602.

FONTANA, Prospero; Italian painter, 1512-1597.

FOPPA, Vincenzo; Italian religious painter, 1427-1492.

FORAIN, Jean Louis; French painter, 1852-1931.

FORBES, Edwin; American painter, 1839-1895.

FORBES, Stanhope Alexander, R.A.; painter, 1857-1947.

FORBIN, Comte de Louis, N.P.A.; painter, 1777-1841.

FORD, Edward Onslow, R.A.; sculptor and portrait painter, 1852-1901.

FOREST, Jean; French landscape painter, 1636-1712,

FORREST, Thomas; English line engraver, 1805-1889.

FORSTER, François; engraver, 1790-1872.

FORTUNY y CARBÓ, Mariano; Spanish painter, 1841-1874. Settled in France and Italy.

FOSTER, Edward Ward; English miniature painter, 1762-1865.

FOSTER, Myles Birket; painter, 1825-1899.

FOUCHIER, Bartram de; Dutch painter, 1609-1674.

FOUQUET, Jean (Foucquet); French painter, 1415-1483.

FRAGONARD, Jean Honoré; French genre painter, 1732-1806.

FRAMPTON, Sir George J.; architect and sculptor, 1860-1928.

FRANCAIS, François Louis; French painter, 1814-1897.

FRANCESCA, Piero della; Italian painter, 1420-1492.

FRANCIA, François L. T., R.A.; Italian painter, 1772-1839.

FRANCKEN, Ambrosius; Flemish religious painter, 1544-1618.

FRANCKEN, Hieronymus; painter, 1540-1610.

FRANCO, Giovanni Battista; Venetian historical painter and engraver, 1510-1580.

FRASER, Alexander, R.S.A.; Scottish painter, 1786-1865.

FRASER, Alexander; Scottish painter, 1827-1899.

FRASER, Charles; painter, 1782-1860.

FREMINET, Martin; French historical painter, 1567-1619. Settled in Italy.

FRÈRE, Charles Édouard; painter, 1837-1894.

FRÈRE, Charles Theodore; painter, 1815-1888.

FRÈRE, Pierre Édouard; painter, 1819-1886.

FRIES, Bernhard; painter, 1820-1879.

FRIESZ, Othon; French artist, 1879-1949.

FRIPP, Alfred Downing, R.W.S.; English painter, 1822-1895.

FRIPP, George Arthur; English water-colour painter, 1813-1896.

FRITH, William Powell, R.A.; English painter, 1819-1910.

FROMENTIN, Eugène; painter, 1820-1876.

FROMMEL, Karl Ludwig; painter, 1789-1863.

FROST, William Edward, R.A.; English painter, 1810-1877.

FRYE, Thomas; painter and engraver, 1710-1762.

FULLER, Isaac; painter, 1606-1672.

FURINI, Francesco; painter, 1604-1649.

FURSE, Charles Wellington, A.R.A.; English painter, 1868-1904.

FUSELI, Johann Heinrich, R.A. (Henry Fuseli); Swiss portrait painter, 1741-1825. Settled in Germany and England.

FYT, Jan; Flemish painter, 1611-1661.

GADDI, Taddeo; Florentine religious painter and architect, 1300-1366.

GAINSBOROUGH, Thomas, R.A.; English portrait and landscape painter, 1727-1788.

GALIMARD, Nicolas Auguste; painter, 1813-1880.

GALLE, Phillipe; Flemish engraver, 1537-1612.

GARDNER, Daniel; English painter, 1750-1805.

GARDNOR, John; painter, 1729-1808.

GARNIER, Etienne Barthélemy; French historical painter, 1759-1849.

GARVEY, Edmund; painter, fl. 1767-1813.

GARZI, Luigi; Italian painter, 1638-1721.

GASTINEAU, Henry, R.A.; English landscape painter, 1797-1876.

GAUGUIN, Eugene Henri-Paul; painter, 1848-1903.

GAULLI, Giovanni Battista; Italian painter, 1639-1709.

GEDDES, Andrew, A.R.A.; Scottish portrait painter, 1783-1844.

GEERAERTS, M.; Flemish portrait painter, 1561-1635.

GEERTGEN, Tot Sint Jans; painter, 1465-1495.

GEGENBAUR, Josef Anton von; painter, 1800-1876.

GEIKIE, Walter; painter, 1793-1837.

GELDER, Arent van; Dutch painter, 1645-1727.

GENNARI, Benedetto; Italian painter, 1570-1610.

GENNARI, Benedetto; Italian painter, 1633-1715.

GENNARI, Cesare; Italian painter, 1637-1688.

GENNARI, Ercolo; Italian painter, 1597-1658.

GENTILE, da Fabriano; Italian religious painter, circa 1360-1450.

GENTZ, Wilhelm; painter, 1822-1890.

GEOFFROY, J.; French portrait painter, 1853-1924.

GERARD, François Pascal Simon; Italian historical and portrait painter, 1770-1837. Settled in France.

GERBIER, Sir Balthasar; Dutch miniature painter and architect, 1592-1667 Settled in England.

GERICAULT, Jean Louis André Théodore; French painter. 1791-1824.

GÉRÔME, Jean Léon; French painter and sculptor, 1824-1904.

GERTLER, Mark; painter, 1892-1939.

GERVEX, Henri; painter, 1852-1929.

GESSNER, J. C.; painter, 1764-1826.

GHIRLANDAIO, Domenico; see BIGORDI.

GIBBON, Benjamin Phelps; English engraver, 1802-1851.

GIBBONS, Grinling; Dutch wood carver and sculptor, 1648-1721. Settled in England.

GIBSON, John, R.A.; sculptor, 1790-1866.

GIBSON, Patrick; painter, circa 1782-1829.

GILBERT, Sir Alfred, R.A.; English sculptor, 1854-1934.

GILBERT, Sir John, R.A.; English water-colour painter and black and white artist, 1817-1897.

GILDER, H., R.A.; water-colour painter, exhibited 1773-1778.

GILES, James William; painter, 1801-1870.

GILL, Eric; English sculptor, 1882-1940.

GILLRAY, James; English caricaturist and engraver, 1757-1815.

GILMAN, Harold; painter, 1878-1919.

GILPIN, Sawrey, R.A.; English painter, 1733-1807.

GINNER, Charles, A.R.A.; painter, 1878-1952.

GIORDANO, Luca (Fa Presto); Italian painter, 1632-1705. Settled in Spain.

GIRTIN, Thomas; English water-colour painter, 1775-1802.

GIULIO-ROMANO (G. Pippi); Italian painter and architect, 1492-1546.

GLOVER, John, R.A.; painter, 1767-1849.

GODDARD, George Bouverie; painter, 1834-1886.

GOES, Hugo van der; Flemish painter, 1419-1482.

GOLDSCHMIDT, Hermann; German painter, 1802-1866.

GOOD, Thomas Sword; painter, 1789-1872.

GOODALL, Edward; English engraver, 1795-1870.

GOODALL, Frederick, R.A.; English painter, 1822-1904.

GOODALL, Walter; English painter, 1830-1889.

GOODWIN, Edward, R.A.; water-colour painter, exhibited 1801-1808.

GOODYEAR, Joseph; engraver, 1799-1839.

GORE, Sir John Watson; painter, 1788-1864.

GORE, Spencer Frederick; painter, 1878-1914.

GOTCH, Thomas Cooper; English painter, 1854-

GOW, Andrew Carrick, R.A.; painter, 1848-1920.

GOYA y LUCIENTES, Francisco José de; Spanish painter and engraver, 1746-1828.

GOYEN, Jan Josefsz van; Dutch landscape painter, 1596-1656.

GOZZOLI, Benozzo; Florentine painter, 1420-1498.

GRAFF, A.; German portrait painter, 1736-1813.

GRAHAM, John; painter, 1754-1817.

GRAHAM-GILBERT, John; Scottish portrait painter. 1794-1866.

GRAHAM, T. A. F.; painter, 1840-1906.

GRANT, Duncan; painter, 1885-

GRANT, Sir Francis, P.R.A.; Scottish portrait painter, 1810-1878.

GRAVELOT, Hubert François Bourguignon; French painter and engraver, 1699-1773.

GRAVES, Robert; English engraver, 1798-1873.

GRAY, Henry Peters; American painter, 1819-1877.

GRECO EL (Domenikos Theotocopoulos); painter, 1541-1614.

GREEN, Amos; painter, 1735-1807.

GREEN, Benjamin, engraver, 1736-1800.

GREEN, Benjamin Richard; painter, 1808-1876.

GREEN, Charles; English black-and-white artist and water-colour painter, 1840-1898.

GREEN, James; English portrait painter, 1771-1834.

GREEN, Valentine; English mezzotint engraver, 1739-1813.

GREENAWAY, Kate; English artist and illustrator, 1846-1901.

GREENHILL, John; portrait painter, circa 1644-1676.

GREENWOOD, John; portrait painter, 1727-1792.

GREGORY, Edward John, R.A.; English painter, 1850-1909.

GREUZE, Jean Baptiste; French portrait and genre painter, 1725-1805.

GRIBBLE, Bernard F.; English marine painter, 1873-1962.

GRIBELIN, Simon; engraver, 1661-1733.

GRIFFIER, Jan; Dutch landscape painter, 1645-1718. Settled in England.

GRIMALDI, Giovanni Francesco; Italian landscape painter and engraver, 1606-1680. Pupil of Carracci. Settled in France.

GRIMALDI, William; miniature painter, 1751-1830.

GRIMM, Samuel Hieronymus; water-colour painter, 1734-1794.

GRISONI, Giuseppe; Italian painter, 1692-1769.

GROS, Antoine Jean, Baron; French military painter, 1771-1835. Pupil of David.

GUARDI, Francesco; Venetian painter, 1712-1793.

GUÉRIN, Pierre Narcisse, Baron; French historical painter, 1774-1833. Settled in Italy.

GUIDO, R.; Italian painter, 1575-1642.

GUILLAUMIN, Jean Baptiste; French painter, 1841-1927.

GULICH, John Percival; water-colour painter and etcher, 1864-1898.

GUTHRIE, Sir James, P.R.S.A.; Scottish painter, 1859-1930.

GWYNNE-JONES, Allan; contemporary painter, 1894-

HAAS, Johannes H. L. de; animal painter, 1832-1880.

HACKER, Arthur, A.R.A.; English figure painter, 1858-1919.

HADEN, Sir Francis Seymour; English etcher, 1818-1910.

HAGHE, Louis, R. I.; Belgian painter, 1806-1885.

HAINES, William, miniature painter and etcher, 1778-1848.

HALL, Charles; English engraver, circa 1720-1783.

HALL, John; English engraver, 1739-1797.

HALS, Frans; Dutch portrait painter, circa 1580-1666.

HALSWELLE, Keeley; painter, 1832-1891.

HAMERTON, George Philip; English painter, 1834-1894.

HAMILTON, Gavin; Scottish painter, 1730-1797.

HAMILTON, Hugh Douglas; Irish painter, 1734-1806.

HAMILTON, William; Scottish historical painter, 1751-1801

HAMON, Jean Louis; French painter, 1821-1874.

HANOTEAU, H.; French painter, 1823-1900.

HARDING, James Duffield; English painter, circa 1797-1863.

HARDY, David, R.A.; English painter, exhibited 1855-1870

HARDY, Heywood; painter, fl. 1861-1903.

HARDY, Thomas Bush; English water-colour painter, 1842-1897.

HARLOW, George Henry; portrait painter, 1787-1819.

HARPIGNIES, H. J.; French landscape painter, 1819-1916.

HARRISON, G. H., R.A.; English painter, 1816-1846.

HARRISON, Mary; flower painter, 1788-1875.

HART, Solomon Alexander, R.A.; English historical painter, 1806-1881.

HARTLAND, Henry Albert; Irish landscape painter, 1840-1893.

HARVEY, Sir George; Scottish historical and landscape painter, 1806-1876.

HARVEY, William; engraver, 1796-1866.

HASENCLEVER, J. P.; painter, 1810-1853.

HASSAN, Childe; American Impressionist, 1859-1935.

HAUGHTON, Moses; painter, 1734-1804.

HAVELL, W., R.A.; water-colour painter, 1782-1857.

HAWARD, Francis; engraver, 1759-1797.

HAYDON, Benjamin Robert; English Scriptural and historical painter, 1786-1846.

HAYES, Edwin, R.A.; English marine painter, 1825-1904.

HAYMAN, Francis, R.A.; portrait painter, 1708-1776.

HAYNES, John; painter and engraver, 1760-1829.

HAYNES-WILLIAMS, John; painter, 1836-1908.

HAYTER, Charles; miniature painter, 1761-1835.

HAYTER, Sir George; historical painter, 1792-1871.

HEAPHY, Thomas; water-colour painter and engraver, 1775-1835.

HEAPHY, Thomas Frank; painter, 1813-1873.

HEARNE, Thomas; water-colour painter, 1744-1817.

HEATH, Charles; English engraver, 1784-1848.

HEATH, James; English engraver, 1756-1834.

HEERE, Lucas de; Flemish historical and portrait painter, 1534-1584. Settled in France and England.

HEIM, François Joseph; French historical painter, 1787-1865.

HELLEU, P.; French painter, 1859-1927.

HELMONT, Segres Jacob van; Dutch painter, 1683-1726.

HELST, Bartholomeus van der; Dutch portrait painter, circa 1611-1670.

HEMY, Charles Napier, R.A.; marine painter, 1841-1917.

HENNEQUIN, Phillipe Auguste; French painter, 1763-1833.

HENNER, Jean Jacques; French (Alsace) historical, landscape and portrait painter, 1829-1905.

HENNESSY, William J.; painter, 1839-1917.

HENSEL, Wilhelm; German historical and portrait painter, 1794-1861.

HERBERT, A., R.A.; English painter, fl. 1844-1861.

HERBERT, Cyril Wiseman; English painter, 1847-1882.

HERBERT, John Rogers, R.A.; English religious and portrait painter, 1810-1890.

HERDMAN, Robert; Scottish painter, 1829-1888.

HERING, George Edwards, R.A.; English painter, 1805-1879.

HERKOMER, Sir Hubert von, C.V.O., R.A.; German painter, 1849-1914. Settled in England.

HERRERA, Francisco de; Spanish painter, 1576-1656.

HERRING, John Frederick; English animal painter, 1795-1865.

HERRING, John Fred. jun.; English animal painter, 1815-1907.

HERSENT, Louis; French painter, 1777-1860.

HESS, Heinrich Maria von; German historical painter, 1798-1863.

HESS, Peter von; German military painter, 1792-1871.

HEYDEN, Jan van der; Dutch painter, 1637-1712.

HICKS, Thomas; American painter, 1823-1890.

HIGHMORE, Joseph; English historical and portrait painter, 1692-1780.

HILDEBRANDT, Eduard; genre painter, 1818-1868.

HILL, David Octavius; Scottish landscape painter, 1802-1870.

HILLEGAERT, P. van; portrait painter, 1595-1640.

HILLIARD, Nicholas; English miniature painter, 1537-1619.

HILLS, Robert; water-colour painter, 1769-1844.

HILTON, William, R.A.; English historical painter, 1786-1839.

HINE, Henry George; English landscape painter and engraver 1811-1895.

HITCHENS, Sydney Ivon; contemporary painter, 1893-

HOARE, Prince; portrait and historical painter, 1755-1834.

HOARE, William, R.A.; English historical and portrait painter 1706-1792.

HOBBEMA, Meindert; Dutch landscape painter, 1638-1709.

HODGES, Charles Howard; English portrait painter, 1764-1837.

HODGES, William, R.A.; English painter, 1744-1797.

HODGSON, John Evan; English painter, 1831-1895.

HODLER, Ferdinand; Swiss painter, 1853-1918.

HOFLAND, Thomas Christopher; English landscape painter, 1777-1843.

HOGARTH, William; English painter and engraver, 1697-1764.

HOLBEIN, Hans; German painter, circa 1460-1524.

HOLBEIN, Hans (the younger); German painter and engraver, 1497-1543.

HOLL, Francis; engraver, 1815-1884.

HOLL, Frank, R.A.; portrait painter, 1845-1888.

HOLLAND, James; landscape painter, 1800-1870.

HOLLAR, Wenceslas; Austrian engraver, 1607-1677.

HOLLINS, John, A.R.A.; English painter, 1798-1855.

HOLLOWAY, Charles Edward, R.I.; English landscape painter, 1838-1897.

HOLLOWAY, Thomas; English engraver, 1748-1827.

HOLMAN-HUNT, William, O.M.; English painter, 1827-1910.

HOLROYD, Sir Charles; English painter and etcher, 1861-1917.

HOMER, Winslow; American painter, 1836-1910.

HONDECOETER, Melchior de; painter, 1637-1695.

HONDT, Josse; Flemish engraver, 1563-1611.

HONDT, Willem; Flemish engraver, 1600-1652.

HONE, Horace; miniature painter, 1755-1825.

HONE, Nathaniel; Irish portrait and miniature painter, 1717-1784.

HONTHORST, Gerard van; Dutch religious painter, 1590-1656. Settled in Italy and England.

HOOCH, Pieter de; painter 1632-circa 1681.

HOOK, James Clark, R.A.; painter, 1819-1907.

HOPPNER, John, R.A.; English portrait painter, 1759-1810.

HORNEL, Edward Adamson; painter, 1864-1933.

HORSLEY, John Callcott, R.A.; English painter, 1817-1903.

HOUBRAKEN, Jacob; Dutch engraver, 1698-1780.

HOUGHTON, Arthur Boyd; English painter, 1836-1875.

HOUSTON, John Adam; English historical and genre painter, 1813-1884.

HOWARD, Henry, R.A.; English historical painter, 1769-1847.

HOWISON, William; engraver, 1798-1850.

HUBER, Jean; Swiss painter, 1722-1790.

HUBER, Johann Rudolf; Swiss painter, 1668-1748.

HUCHTENBURGH, Jan van; Dutch battle painter and engraver, circa 1648-1733.

HUDSON, Thomas; portrait painter, 1701-1779.

HUGGINS, William; animal painter, 1820-1884.

HUGHES, Arthur; painter, 1832-1915.

HUGHES-STANTON, Sir H., R.A.; landscape painter, 1870-1937.

HULL, William; painter, 1820-1880.

HUMPHREYS, Henry Noel; painter, 1810-1879.

HUMPHREYS, Ozias, R.A.; English miniature painter, 1742-1810.

HUMPHRYS, William; engraver, 1794-1865.

HUNT, Alfred William; English landscape painter, 1830-1896.

HUNT, Edgar; English farmyard painter, 1876-1953

HUNT, William Henry; English water-colour painter, 1790-1864.

HUNT, William Morris; American painter, 1824-1879.

HUNTER, Colin, A.R.A.; painter, 1841-1904.

HURLSTONE, Frederick Yeates; English portrait and historical painter, 1800-1869.

HUSSEY, Giles; English painter, 1710-1788.

HUYSUM, Jakob van; Dutch painter, 1686-1740.

HUYSUM, Jan van; Dutch flower painter, 1682-1749.

IBBETSON, Julius Cæsar; English marine and figure painter, 1759-1817.

ILLIDGE, Thomas Henry; portrait painter, 1799-1851.

INCE, J. M.; water-colour painter, 1806-1859.

INCHBOLD, John William; English painter and engraver, 1830-1888.

INGHAM, Charles Cromwell; portrait painter, 1796-1863.

INGRES, Jean Auguste Dominique; French historical painter, 1780-1867. Pupil of David.

INNENBRACH, Franz; German religious and historical painter, 1813-1879.

INNES, James Dickson; water-colour painter, 1887-1914.

INNESS, George; American landscape painter, 1825-1894.

ISABEY, Eugène L. G.; miniature painter, 1804-1886.

ISABEY, Jean Baptiste; miniature painter, 1767-1855.

ISRAELS, Josef; Dutch genre painter, 1824-1911.

JACK, Richard, R.A.; English painter, 1866-1952.

JACKSON, John; English portrait painter, 1778-1831.

JACKSON, John Richardson; English engraver, 1819-1877.

JACKSON, Samuel; landscape painter, 1794-1869.

JACQUEMART, Jules; French painter, 1837-1880.

JAGGER, Charles; miniature painter, 1770-1827.

JAGGER, Charles Sargent; English sculptor, 1885-1934.

JAMES, Edith A.; painter, 1857-1898.

JAMESONE, George; Scottish portrait painter, 1586-1644.

JAMIESON, Alexander; British impressionist, 1873-

JANSSENS, Cornelius; Dutch portrait painter, 1590-1665. Settled in England.

JEENS, Charles Henry; engraver, 1827-1879.

JEFFERYS, James; painter, 1757-1784.

JENKINS, Joseph John; English water-colour painter, 1811-1885.

JENNER, Isaac; engraver, 1750-1806.

JOHN, Augustus, R.A.; English portrait painter, 1878-1961.

JOHN, Gwen; painter, 1876-1939.

JOHN, Sir W. Goscombe, R.A.; 1860-1952.

JOHNS, Ambrose Bowden; landscape painter, 1776-1858.

JOHNSON, Charles Edward; painter, 1832-1913.

JOHNSON, Harry John; water-colour painter, 1826-1884.

JOHNSTON, Alexander; Scottish painter, 1815-1891.

JOHNSTONE, William Borthwick; Scottish painter, 1804-1868.

JOLLIVET, Pierre Jules; French painter, 1794-1871.

JONES, David; contemporary water-colour painter, 1895-

JONES, George; English historical, landscape and military painter, 1786-1869.

JONES, Thomas; landscape painter, 1730-1803.

JOPLING, Joseph Middleton; genre painter, 1831-1884.

JORDAENS, Jacob; Flemish painter, 1593-1678.

JORDAENS, Jans; Flemish painter, 1616-1669.

JOSEPH, George Francis, A.R.A.; painter, 1764-1846.

JOSEPH, Samuel; sculptor,   -1850.

JOUVENET, Jean; French historical and portrait painter, 1644-1717.

JOY, G. W.; English painter, 1844-1925.

JOY, John C.; marine painter, 1806-1857.

JOY, Thomas Musgrave; painter, 1812-1866.

JOY, William; marine painter, 1803-1857.

JUTSUM, Henry; painter, 1816-1869.

KANDINSKY, WARSILY; abstract painter, 1866-1944.

KAUFMANN, Maria Anna Angelica Catherina, R.A.; Swiss painter and engraver, 1741-1807.   Settled in Italy and England.

KAULBACH, Wilhelm von; German historical painter, 1805-1874.

KEARNEY, William Henry; water-colour painter, 1800-1858.

KEELING, William Knight; painter, 1807-1886.

KEENE, Charles Samuel; English caricaturist and black-and-white artist, 1823-1891.

KELLY, Sir Gerald Festus, P.R.A., painter, 1879-

KEMP-WELCH, Lucy Elizabeth; Animal painter, 1869-1958.

KENNEDY, William Denholm; painter, 1813-1865.

KENT, William; English painter, sculptor and architect, 1684-1748.

KERR, Charles; painter, 1858-1907.

KERSEBOOM, Frederick; painter, 1632-1690.

KETEL, Cornelis; Dutch painter and sculptor, 1548-1616. Settled in France and England.

KETTLE, Tilly; portrait painter, 1740-1786.

KEYSE, Thomas; painter, 1722-1800.

KILBOURNE, George Goodwin, R.I.; water-colour painter, 1839-1924.

KILIAN, Philip Andreas; engraver, 1714-1759.

KING, Haynes, R.A.; painter, 1831-1904.

KING, John; painter, 1788-1847.

KIRKUP, Seymour Stocker; painter, 1788-1880.

KLEE, Paul; painter, 1879-1940.

KLINGER, M.; German painter, 1857-1920.

KNELLER, Sir Godfrey; German portrait painter, 1646-1723.

KNIGHT, Charles Parsons; marine painter, 1829-1897.

KNIGHT, John Baverstock; water-colour painter, 1785-1859.

KNIGHT, John Prescott, R.A.; portrait painter, 1803-1881.

KNIGHT, J. W., Buxton; painter, 1842-1908.

KNIGHT, Dame Laura, R.A.; Contemporary painter, 1887-

KNIGHT, Mary Ann; English painter, 1776-1861.

KNIGHT, William Henry; painter, 1823-1863.

KNYFF, Leonard; painter, 1650-1721.

KOCH, Joseph Anton; Austrian historical and landscape painter, 1768-1839.

KOEKKOEK, Barend Cornelius; landscape painter, 1803-1862.

KONINCK, Jacob; painter, 1616-1708.

KONINCK, Philipo de; Dutch landscape painter, 1619-1688.

KOROVIN, K. A.; Russian painter, 1861-1939.

KOTZEBUE, Alexander von; painter, 1815-1889.

KRAFFT, Johann August; German genre painter and engraver, 1798-1829.

KRAFFT, Johann Peter; German genre, portrait and historical painter, 1780-1856.

KRÜGER, Franz; portrait painter, 1797-1857.

KUYCK, Jan Lodewyck van; Belgian animal painter, 1821-1874.

LAAR, Pieter van; Dutch painter, 1582-1642.

LADBROOKE, Robert; landscape painter, 1770-1842.

LADELL, Edward; painter, 1840-1866.

LA FARGE, John; American painter, 1835-1910.

LA FARGUE, P. C.; painter, 1733-1782.

LA FOSSE, Charles de; painter, 1640-1716.

LAGUERRE, Louis; French painter, 1663-1721.

LAMBERT, George; painter, 1710-1765.

LAMBERT, James; landscape painter, 1725-1779.

LAMBORNE, Peter Spendelowe; engraver and miniature painter, 1722-1774.

LANCE, George, R.A.; English still-life painter, 1802-1864. Pupil of Landseer.

LANCRET, Nicolas; French painter, 1690-1743.

LANDI, Gasparo; painter, 1756-1830.

LANDSEER, Charles, A.R.A.; English painter, 1799-1879.

LANDSEER, Sir Edwin Henry, R.A.; English animal and genre painter, 1802-1873.

LANDSEER, George; painter, 1829-1878.

LANDSEER, John; engraver, 1769-1852.

LANDSEER, Thomas; English engraver, 1795-1880.

LANE, John Bryant; painter, 1788-1868.

LANE, Richard James, A.R.A.; engraver, 1800-1872.

LANE, Samuel; portrait painter, 1780-1859.

LANE, Theodore; painter, 1800-1828.

LANFRANCO, Giovanni; Italian religious painter, 1581-1647.

LANGLOIS, Jean Charles; painter, 1789-1870.

LANINI, Bernardino; Italian religious painter, circa 1520-circa 1578.

LAPITO, Louis August; painter, 1805-1874.

LARGILLIÈRE, Nicolas de; French portrait painter, 1656-1746. Pupil of Sir Peter Lely.

LAROON, Mercellus; painter and engraver, 1653-1702.

LASTMAN, Pieter; Dutch religious painter, 1562-1649.

LASZLO, Philip; Hungarian portrait painter, 1869-

LAUDER, James Eckford; Scottish painter, 1812-1869.

LAUDER, Robert Scott; Scottish painter, 1802-1869.

LAURENCE, Samuel; English portrait painter, 1811-1884.

LAURENS, J. P.; French historical painter, 1838-1921.

LAURIE, Robert; mezzotint engraver, 1755-1836.

LAVERY, Sir John, R.A.; English portrait painter, 1856-1941.

LAWES-WITTEWRONGE, Sir Charles; sculptor, 1843-1911.

LAWLESS, Matthew James; painter, 1837-1864.

LAWRENCE, Andrew; engraver, 1708-1747.

LAWRENCE, Sir Thomas, P.R.A.; English portrait painter, 1769-1830.

LAWSON, Cecil Gordon; English painter, 1851-1882.

LEADER, Benjamin William, R.A.; landscape painter, 1831-1923.

LEAHY, Edward Daniel; painter, 1797-1875.

LEAKEY, James; painter and miniaturist, 1775-1865.

LEAR, Edward; English landscape painter, 1812-1888.

LE BLOND, Jean; French historical painter, 1635-1709.

LE BRUN, Charles; French historical painter, 1619-1690.

LE BRUN, Marie Louise Elisabeth Vigée; French portrait painter, 1755-1842.

LEE, Frederick Richard, R.A.; English landscape painter, 1798-1879.

LEE, William; water-colour painter, 1809-1865.

LEECH, John; English black-and-white artist, 1817-1864.

LEES, Charles; Scottish historical painter, 1800-1880.

LEGER, Fernand; painter and sculptor, 1881-1955.

LE GROS, Alphonse; French sculptor and engraver, 1837-1911.

LE GROS, Pierre; French sculptor, 1660-1719.

LEIBL, Wilhelm; painter, 1844-1900.

LEIGHTON, Charles Blair; English painter, 1823-1855.

LEIGHTON, E. B.; English painter, 1853-1922.

LEIGHTON, Lord Frederic, P.R.A.; English painter and sculptor, 1830-1896.

LEITCH, William Leighton; painter, 1804-1883.

LE KEUX, Henry; engraver, 1787-1868.

LE KEUX, John; engraver, 1783-1846.

LE KEUX, John Henry; engraver, 1812-1896.

LELY, Sir Peter; German portrait painter, 1618-1680. Settled in Holland and England.

LENBACH, Franz von; German painter, 1836-1904.

LENS, Andries; Flemish painter, 1739-1822.

LESLIE, Charles Robert, R.A.; English painter, 1794-1859

LESLIE, George Dunlop, R.A.; English painter, 1835-1921.

LESSING, Charles Frederic; painter, 1808-1880.

LE STRANGE, Henry L'Estrange Styleman; painter, 1815-1862.

LE SUEUR, Eustache; French mythological and religious painter, 1616-1655.

LEUTZE, Emanuel; German historical painter, 1816-1868.

LÉVY, Alphonse; French painter, 1843-1918.

LÉVY, Emile; French historical painter, 1826-1890.

LÉVY, Henri Leopold; French historical painter, 1840-1905.

LEWIS, Charles; painter, 1753-1795.

LEWIS, Charles George; engraver, 1808-1880.

LEWIS, Charles James; painter, 1830-1892.

LEWIS, Frederick Christian; engraver and painter, 1779-1856.

LEWIS, Frederick C.; painter, 1813-1875.

LEWIS, George Robert; painter, 1782-1871.

LEWIS, John Frederick, R.A.; English painter, 1805-1876.

LEWIS, Wyndham; English painter, 1884-1957.

LEYDEN, Lucas van Jacobsz; Dutch genre painter and engraver, 1494-1533.

LEYS, Jean Auguste Henri, Baron; Belgian painter, 1814-1869.

L'HERMITTE, L.; French painter, 1844-1925.

LIBRI, Girolamo dai; Veronese religious painter, 1474-1556.

LICINIO, Bernardino; Italian religious and portrait painter, fl. 1524-1541.

LICINIO, Giovanni Antonio (Pordenone); Italian religious painter, 1483-1539.

LIEVENS, Jan; Dutch engraver, portrait and religious painter, 1607-1674.

LIMOSIN, Leonard; Limoges enamel painter, c. 1505-c. 1576.

LINES, Samuel; landscape painter, 1778-1863.

LINNELL, John; portrait and landscape painter, 1792-1882.

LINT, Pieter van; Flemish religious painter, 1609-1690.

LINTON, Sir James Drumgole; water-colour painter, 1840-1916.

LINTON, William; English painter, 1791-1876.

LINTON, William James; English engraver, 1812-1898.

LIOTARD, Jean Michel; Swiss engraver, 1702-1789.

LIPPI, Filippino; Italian religious painter, c. 1457-1504.

LIPPI, Fra Filippo; Italian religious painter, 1412-1469.

LIVERSEEGE, Henry; English genre painter, 1803-1832.

LIZARS, William Home; engraver and etcher, 1788-1859.

LLEWELLYN, Sir W., P.R.A.; British painter, 1863-1941.

LOCKEY, Rowland; painter, fl. 1590-1610.

LOCKHART, William Ewart; Scottish painter, 1846-1900.

LODGE, William; artist and engraver, 1649-1689.

LOGGAN, David; portrait painter and engraver, 1630-1693.

LOMBARD, Lambert; Flemish painter and architect, 1505-1566.

LONG, Amelia, R.A.; water-colour painter, 1762-1837.

LONG, Edwin Longsden, R.A.; English painter, 1829-1891.

LONSDALE, William James; portrait painter, 1777-1839.

LORRAIN, Claude; see CLAUDE OF LORRAIN.

LOTTO, Lorenzo; Venetian portrait painter, 1480-circa 1555.

LOUND, Thomas; landscape painter, 1802-1861.

LOUTHERBOURG, Phillipe Jacques; French painter, 1740-1812, Settled in England.

LOWE, Mauritius; historical painter, 1746-1793.

LOWE, Moses Samuel; German painter and engraver, 1756-1831.

LOWINSKY, Thomas; contemporary painter, 1892-

LOWRY, Lawrence Stephen; contemporary artist, 1887-

LUCAS, Horatio Joseph; painter and etcher, 1839-1873.

LUCAS, John; portrait painter, 1807-1874.

LUCAS, van Leyden; painter and engraver, 1494-1533.

LUCAS, John Seymour, R.A.; historical and portrait painter, 1849-1923.

LUCIANI, Sebastiano; Venetian religious painter, 1485-1547.

LUCY, Charles; English historical painter, 1814-1873.

LUINI, Bernardino; Italian religious painter, 1475-1533.

LUKS, George; American painter, 1867-1933.

LUNY, Thomas; marine painter, 1759-1837.

LUPTON, Thomas Goff; English engraver, 1791-1873.

LUTTI (or LUTI), Benedetto; Florentine religious painter, 1666-1710.

LUTTERELL, Edward; painter and engraver, 1650-1710.

LYNE, Richard; painter and engraver, fl. 1570-1600.

MABUSE, Jan van (Jan Gossaert); Flemish painter, 1470-1532.

MACALLUM, Hamilton; painter, 1841-1896.

MacARDELL, James; mezzotint engraver, c. 1710-1765.

MACBETH, Norman; portrait painter, 1821-1888.

MACBETH, Robert Walker; Scottish painter, 1848-1910.

MacCALLUM, Andrew; Scottish painter, 1821-1902.

MacGREGOR, William Yorke; Scottish painter, 1855-1923.

MACKENZIE, Samuel; portrait painter, 1785-1847.

MACLISE, Daniel, R.A.; Irish portrait, historical and allegorical painter, 1806-1870.

MACNEE, Sir Daniel; painter, 1806-1882.

MACWHIRTER, John, R.A.; Scottish painter, 1839-1911.

MADDOX, Willis; painter, 1813-1853.

MAES, Nicholas; Dutch genre and portrait painter, 1632-1693.

MAHONEY, Charles; contemporary painter, 1903-

MAINARDI, Bastiano; painter, 1450-1513.

MAJOR, Thomas; engraver, 1720-1799.

MAKART, Hans; Austrian painter, 1840-1884.

MANET, Edouard; French painter, 1832-1883.

MANTEGNA, Andrea; engraver and painter, 1431-1506.

MARATTI, Carlo; engraver and painter, 1625-1713.

MARCHAND, Jean; painter, 1883-1941.

MARCHANT, Nathaniel; sculptor, 1739-1816.

MARCUARD, Robert Samuel; engraver, 1751-1792.

MARIS, Jacob; Dutch painter, 1837-1899.

MARIS, MATTHYS; Dutch painter, 1839-1917.

MARIS, WILLEM; landscape painter, 1843-1910.

MARKS, Henry Stacey, English genre and bird painter, 1829-1898.

MARLOW, William, R.A.; water-colour painter, 1740-1813.

MARQUET, Pierre; French painter, 1875-1947.

MARSHALL, Ben; animal painter, 1767-1835.

MARSHALL, Charles; painter, 1806-1890.

MARSHALL, Peter Paul; Scottish painter, 1830-1900.

MARSHALL, Thomas Falcon; painter, 1818-1878.

MARSHALL, William; engraver, fl. 1630-1650.

MARSHALL, William Calder, R.A.; Scottish sculptor, 1813-1894.

MARSTRAND, Wilhelm; Danish painter, 1810-1873.

MARTIN, David; painter and engraver, 1737-1798.

MARTIN, Elias, A.R.A.; painter and engraver, circa 1740-1811.

MARTIN, Homer, D.; American painter, 1836-1897.

MARTIN, John; English landscape and historical painter, 1789-1854.

MARTIN, William; painter, fl. 1765-1821.

MARTINEAU, Robert Braithwaite; painter, 1826-1869.

MARTINI, Simone; Italian religious painter, 1283-1344.

MASON, George Hemming, A.R.A.; English painter, 1818-1872.

MASSI, Gentile (di Niccolò da Fabriano); Italian religious painter, 1360-circa 1450.

MASSUN, Antoine; French engraver, 1636-1700.

MATISSE, Henri; French painter, 1869-1955.

MATSYS, Quentin; Flemish painter, 1466-circa 1531.

MATTEIS, Paolo de; Italian painter and engraver, 1662-1728.

MAUVE, Anton; Dutch landscape painter, 1838-1888.

MAY, Philip William; English painter and black-and-white artist, 1865-1903.

McEVOY, Ambrose, R.A.; English portrait painter, 1878-1927.

McLACHLAN, Thomas Hope; English landscape painter, 1845-1897.

MEADOWS, Joseph Kenny; painter, 1790-1874.

MEDAND, Thomas; engraver, fl. 1777-1822.

MEDINA, John; portrait painter, 1721-1796.

MEDINA, Sir John Baptist; Flemish historical landscape and portrait painter, 1659-1710. Settled in England.

MEDLEY, Samuel; painter, 1769-1857.

MEEN, Margaret, R.A.; painter, exhibited 1775-1810.

MEISSONIER, Jean Louis Ernest; French genre and military painter, 1815-1891.

MELVILLE, A., R.W.S.; painter, 1858-1904.

MEMLINC, Hans; German painter, 1430-1494.

MENGS, Anton Raphael; Bohemian religious, mythological and portrait painter, 1728-1779.

MENGS, Ismael Israel; Danish portrait painter, 1690-1765.

MENZEL; Adolf von; German painter, 1815-1905.

MERCER, A.; miniature painter, 1775-1842.

MERCIER, Phillipe; German portrait painter, 1689-1760. Settled in England.

MERIAN, Matthäus; engraver, 1593-1650.

MERIAN, Matthäus; Swiss portrait painter, 1621-1687.

MERYON, Charles; French engraver, 1821-1868.

MESDAG, Hendrik W.; Dutch painter, 1831-1915.

MESSINA, Antonello Da; Venetian painter, 1430-1479.

METSU, Gabriel; Dutch painter, circa 1630-1667.

MEULEN, Adam Frans van der; Flemish landscape and military painter, 1632-1690.

MEUNIER, Constantin; Belgian sculptor and painter, 1831-1905.

MEYER, Ernst; Danish genre painter, 1795-1861.

MEYER, Henry; painter and engraver, 1782-1847.

MEYER, Jeremiah; miniature painter, 1735-1789.

MICHAEL, Max; German painter, 1823-1891.

MICHAELANGELO, Buonarrotti; Italian sculptor, architect and painter, 1475-1564.

MIDDIMAN, Samuel; engraver, 1750-1831.

MIDDLETON, John; painter, 1827-1856.

MIEREVELT, Michael; Dutch portrait painter, 1567-1641.

MIERIS, Frans van; Flemish painter, 1635-1681.

MIERIS, Frans van (the younger); Flemish painter, 1689-1763.

MIERIS, Willem van; Dutch painter, 1662-1747.

MIGNARD, Pierre; French historical and portrait painter, 1610-1695.

MIGNON, Abraham; painter, 1639-1679.

MILES, George Francis; painter, 1852-1891.

MILLAIS, Sir John Everett, P.R.A.; English painter, 1829-1896.

MILLARD, C. S.; water-colour painter, exhibited 1866-1889.

MILLER, William; painter, circa 1740-1810.

MILLET, Francis Davis; American painter, 1846-1912.

MILLET, François; Flemish painter, 1644-1680.

MILLET, Jean François; French painter, 1814-1875.

MITAN, James; engraver, 1776-1822.

MITCHELL, John; engraver, 1791-1852.

MODIGILIANI, Amedo; Italian painter, 1884-1920.

MOGFORD, Thomas; painter, 1809-1868.

MOLE, John Henry; water colour painter, 1814-1886.

MOLENAER, Jan Miense; Dutch painter, 1610-1668.

MONAMY, Peter; naval painter, 1670-1749.

MONET, Claude; French painter, 1840-1926.

MONNOYER, Jean-Baptiste; French flower painter, 1636-1699.

MONRO, Henry; painter, 1791-1814.

MONTAGNA, Bartolommeo; Italian religious painter, c. 1455-1523.

MOORE, Albert Joseph; English painter, 1841-1893.

MOORE, Henry, R.A.; English marine painter, 1831-1895.

MOORE, J. C.; painter, 1829-1880.

MOORE, Henry; modern sculptor, 1898-

MOORE, William; portrait painter, 1790-1851.

MOORE, Sir Anthony (Antoni Moro); historical and portrait painter, 1512-1582.

MOREAU, Jean Michel; French painter and engraver, 1741-1815.

MOREELSE, Paulus; Dutch architect and engraver, 1571-1638.

MORETTO DA BRESCIA (Alessandro Bonvicino); painter, 1498-1554.

MORGAN, Matthew Somerville; painter, 1839-1890.

MORGHEN, Rafaello; Italian engraver, 1758-1833.

MORISON, Douglas; painter, 1814-1847.

MORISOT, Berthe; French painter, 1840-1895.

MORLAND, George; English genre and landscape painter, 1763-1804.

MORLAND, Henry Robert; English painter and engraver, 1730-1797.

MORRIS, Thomas; engraver, fl. 1780-1800.

MORRIS, William; artist and designer, 1834-1896.

MORTIMER, John Hamilton, R.A.; English painter, 1741-1779.

MORTON, Andrew; English portrait painter, 1802-1845.

MOSCHELES, Felix; English painter, 1833-1917.

MOSER, Mary, R.A.; flower painter, 1744-1819.

MOSSES, Alexander; English portrait and genre painter, 1793-1836.

MOTTRAM, Charles; engraver, 1807-1876.

MOUCHERON, Frederik; painter, 1633-1686.

MÜLLER, Johann Friedrich Wilhelm; German engraver, 1782-1816.

MÜLLER, William James; English landscape painter, 1812-1845.

MULLINS, E. Roscoe; English sculptor, 1849-1907.

MULREADY, M., R.A.; portrait painter, 1808-1889.

MULREADY, William, R.A.; Irish painter and black-and-white artist, 1786-1863.

MUNCH, Edvard; Norwegian impressionist, 1863-1944.

MUNKACSY, Michel de; Hungarian religious and genre painter, 1845-1900.

MUNNINGS, Sir Alfred J., R.A.; English painter, 1878-1959.

MÜNTZ, John Henry; landscape painter, fl. 1755-1775.

MURILLO, Bartolomé Estéban; Spanish religious painter, 1618-1682.

MURPHY, John; engraver, fl. 1780-1820.

MURRAY, Charles Wadsworth; painter, 1894-1945.

MURRAY, Sir David, R.A.; Scottish landscape painter, 1849-1933.

MURRAY, Thomas; portrait painter, 1666-1724.

MUSS, Charles; painter on glass, 1779-1824.

MUZIANO, II Cavaliere Girolamo; Italian religious painter, 1528-1592.

MYTENS, Daniel; Dutch portrait painter, 1590-circa 1656. Settled in England.

NAFTEL, Paul Jacob; English water-colour painter, 1817-1891.

NASH, Frederick; water-colour painter, 1783-1856.

NASH, Joseph; water-colour painter, 1808-1878.

NASH, Paul; English painter, 1889-1946.

NASMYTH, Alexander; Scottish landscape painter, 1758-1840.

NASMYTH, Patrick; Scottish landscape painter, 1787-1831.

NATTIER, Jean Marc; French portrait painter, 1685-1766.

NAVARRETE, Juan Fernandez; painter, 1526-1579.

NAVEZ, Francois Joseph; Belgian genre and portrait painter, 1787-1869.

NEALE, John Preston; English engraver, 1771-1847.

NEEFS, Peter; Dutch painter, circa 1577-circa 1660.

NESFIELD, William Andrew; English water-colour painter, circa 1794-1881.

NETSCHER, Caspar; Dutch genre painter, 1639-1684.

NETTLESHIP, John Trivett; English animal painter, 1841-1903.

NEUVILLE, Alphonse Marie de; French painter, 1836-1885.

NEVE, Cornelius; portrait painter, fl. 1637-1664.

NEWCOME, Frederick Clive; English landscape painter, 1847-1894.

NEWENHAM, Frederick; portrait painter, 1807-1859.

NEWTON, Alfred Pizzi; water-colour painter, 1830-1883.

NEWTON, Algernon, R.A.; landscape painter, 1880-

NEWTON, Francis Milner; portrait painter, 1720-1794.

NEWTON, Gilbert Stuart, R.A.; English painter, 1794-1835.

NEWTON, Mary; painter, 1832-1866.

NEWTON, Sir William John; miniature painter, 1785-1869.

NICHOLL, Andrew, R.H.A.; landscape painter, 1804-1886.

NICHOLSON, Ben; contemporary painter, 1894-

NICHOLSON, Francis; water-colour painter, 1753-1844.

NICHOLSON, Sir William; painter, 1872-1949.

NICHOLSON, Francis; water-colour painter, 1753-1844.

NICOL, Erskine, A.R.A.; painter, 1825-1904.

NIEMANN, Edmund John; landscape painter, 1813-1876.

NOBLE, George; line engraver, fl. 1795-1806.

NOBLE, Samuel, engraver, 1779-1853.

NOBLE, Samuel; English sculptor; 1803-1854.

NOBLE, William Bonneau; water-colour painter, 1780-1831.

NOLLEKENS, Joseph, R.A.; English sculptor, 1737-1823.

NOLLEKENS, Joseph Francis; painter, 1702-1748.

NORDEN, Frederick Ludwig; painter, 1708-1742.

NORTH, John William, A.R.A.; painter, 1824-1924.

NORTH, Marianne; English flower painter, 1830-1890.

NORTHCOTE, James, R.A.; English historical and portrait painter, 1746-1831. Pupil of Reynolds.

OAKES, John Wright; English landscape painter, 1820-1887.

OAKLEY, Octavius; water-colour painter, 1800-1867.

O'CONNOR, James Arthur; landscape painter, 1793-1841.

O'CONNOR, John; Irish painter, 1830-1889.

OKEY, Samuel; mezzotint engraver, fl. 1765-1780.

OLDFIELD, J. Edwin; water-colour painter, exhibited 1825, 1826 and 1854.

OLIPHANT, Francis Wilson; painter, 1818-1859.

OLIVER, Isaac; English miniature painter, 1556-1617.

OLIVER, Peter; English miniature painter, 1594-1648.

OLIVER, Mrs. William, R.I.; water-colour painter, 1819-1885.

OLSSON, Julius, R.A.; English marine painter, 1864-1942.

ONWHYN, Thomas; engraver, 1811-1886.

OOST, James van; Flemish historical and portrait painter, 1639-1713.

OPIE, John, R.A.; English portrait and historical painter, 1761-1807.

OPPENHEIMER, Moritz Daniel; German genre and portrait painter, 1801-1882.

ORAM, William; painter and architect,   -1777.

ORCHARDSON, Sir William Quilter, R.A.; Scottish subject and portrait painter, 1835-1910.

ORLEY, Bernaert van; Flemish religious painter, 1491-1543.

ORPEN, Sir William, R.A.; portrait painter, 1878-1931.

OSBORNE, Walter; water-colour painter, 1860-1903.

OSTADE, Adriæn van; Dutch genre painter, 1610-1685.

OSTADE, Isack van; Dutch genre and landscape painter, 1621-1649.

OSTERLEY, Karl W. F.; painter, 1805-1891.

OUDRY, Jean Baptiste; French portrait, animal and still-life painter, 1686-1755.

OVERBECK, Johann Friedrich; German religious painter, 1789-1869.

OWEN, Rev. Edward P.; etcher, 1788-1863.

OWEN, Samuel; water-colour painter, 1769-1857.

OWEN, William, R.A.; English portrait painter, 1769-1825.

PALIZZI, Filippo; Italian painter, 1818-1899.

PALMA, Jacopo (the elder); Italian religious and portrait painter, c. 1480-1528.

PALMA, Jacopo; Italian religious painter, 1544-1628.

PALMER, Samuel; English water-colour painter, 1805-1881.

PARK, Patric, R.S.A.; portrait painter, 1809-1855.

PARKINSON, Thomas; portrait painter, fl. 1769-1789.

PARMENTIER, Jacques; painter, 1658-1730.

PARRIS, Edmund Thomas; English painter, 1793-1873.

PARROTT, William; English painter, 1813-1893.

PARRY, Joseph; painter, 1744-1826.

PARRY, William; portrait painter, 1742-1791.

PARS, William, A.R.A.; English painter, 1742-1782.

PARSONS, Alfred, R.A.; English landscape painter, 1847-1920.

PARTRIDGE, Sir Bernard; black-and-white artist, 1861-1945.

PARTRIDGE, John; portrait painter, 1790-1872.

PASINI, Alberto; Italian painter, 1826-1899.

PASMORE, Victor; contemporary painter, 1908-

PATER, Jean Baptiste Joseph; French painter, 1696-1736. Pupil of Watteau.

PATON, Sir Joseph Noel; Scottish painter, 1821-1902.

PATON, Walter Hugh; Scottish landscape painter, 1828-1895.

PATTEN, George, A.R.A.; painter, 1801-1865.

PAXTON, Sir Joseph; water-colour painter, 1801-1865.

PEALE, Charles Wilson; American painter, 1741-1825.

PEALE, Rembrandt; American painter, 1778-1860.

PEARCE, Stephen; portrait painter, 1819-1904.

PECKITT, William; English painter on glass, 1731-1795.

PEEL, J.; water-colour painter, 1811-1906.

PEEL, Paul; Canadian painter, 1861-1892.

PEETERS, Bonaventura; Flemish military and marine painter, 1614-1652.

PEETERS, John; painter, 1667-1727.

PENLEY, Aaron Edwin; water-colour painter, 1807-1870.

PENNI, Gianfrancesco; Italian religious painter, 1488-1528.

PENNI, Luca, called ROMANO; Italian painter and engraver, 16th century.

PENNY, Edward; English portrait and historical painter, 1714-1791.

PERANDA, Santo; Venetian painter, 1566-1638.

PERIGAL, Arthur; historical and landscape painter, 1784-1847.

PERIGAL, Arthur; English landscape painter, 1816-1884.

PERUGINO, Pietro (Vannucci); painter, 1446-1524.

PERUZZI, Baldassare; Italian painter and architect, 1481-1536.

PETERS, Matthew William; English painter, 1742-1814.

PETHER, Abraham; English landscape painter, 1756-1812.

PETHER, Sebastian; English painter, 1790-1844.

PETITOT, Jean; Swiss enamel painter, 1606-1691.

PETRIE, George, P.R.H.A.; Irish painter, 1790-1866.

PETTIE, John, R.A.; Scottish historical, portrait and genre painter, 1839-1893.

PHILIPPOTEAUX, Henri E. F.; painter, 1815-1884.

PHILIPPOTEAUX, Paul; painter, 1846-

PHILIPS, Charles; portrait painter, 1708-1747.

PHILIPS, Nathaniel George; English landscape painter and engraver, 1795-1831.

PHILLIP, John, R.A.; Scottish painter, 1817-1867.

PHILLIPS, Charles; engraver, 1738-c. 1780.

PHILLIPS, Elizabeth; painter, 1810-1887.

PHILLIPS, Giles F.; landscape painter, 1780-1867.

PHILLIPS, Henry Wyndham; painter, 1820-1868.

PHILLIPS, Thomas, R.A.; English portrait painter, 1770-1845.

PIAZZETTA, G. B.; religious painter, 1682-1754.

PICASSO, Pablo; contemporary painter, 1881-

PICART, Bernard; engraver, 1673-1733.

PICKERSGILL, Frederick Richard, R.A.; English historical painter, 1820-1900.

PICKERSGILL, H. H., R.A.; painter, 1812-1861.

PICKERSGILL, Henry William, R.A.; painter, 1782-1875

PICOT, François Edouard; French historical painter, 1786-1868.

PICOU, Henri Pierre; French painter, 1822-1895.

PIDDING, Henry James; painter, 1797-1864.

PIDGEON, Henry Clark; English water-colour painter, 1807-1880.

PILLEMENT, Jean; painter, 1727-1808.

PINE, John; engraver, 1690-1756.

PINE, Robert Edge; English painter, 1742-1790.

PINTORICCHIO. *see* BIAGGIO.

PINWELL, George John; English water-colour painter and engraver, 1842-1875.

PIOMBO, Fra Sebastiano del; painter, 1485-1547.

PIPER, John; contemporary water-colour painter, 1903-

PIPPI, Giulio (Romano); Italian religious painter and architect, 1492-1546.

PISSARRO, Camille; French painter, 1830-1903.

PITCHFORTH, Roland Vivian, R.A.; painter, 1895-

PLACE, Francis; English painter and engraver, 1647-1728.

PLIMER, Andrew; English miniature painter, 1763-1837.

PLIMER, Nathaniel; English miniature painter, 1757-1822.

POCOCK, Isaac; painter, 1782-1835.

POCOCK, Nicholas; marine painter, 1741-1821.

POLLAIUOLO, Antonio; Florentine sculptor, engraver and painter, 1429-1498.

POLLARD, James; engraver, 1797-1859.

POLLARD, Robert; engraver, 1755-1838.

POMEROY, Frederick W., A.R.A.; English sculptor, 1856-1924.

PONTORMO, Jacobo da (Carucci); Italian religious painter, 1494-1557.

POOLE, Paul Falconer, R.A.; English historical painter, 1810-1879.

PORDENONE, Giovanni Antonio; Italian painter, 1483-1539.

PORTAELS, Jean François; Belgian painter, 1818-1895.

PORTER, Sir Robert Ker; English military and religious painter, 1777-1842.

POSSO, A.; Italian painter, 1642-1709.

POSTANS, Robert Baxter; etcher, 1787-1892.

POT, Hendrick Gerritsz; Dutch painter, 1585-1657.

POTTER, Frank Huddlestone; English painter, 1845-1887.

POTTER, Paul; Dutch animal painter, 1625-1654.

POURBUS, Frans; Flemish portrait and historical painter, 1545-1581.

POURBUS, Pieter; Flemish historical, allegorical and portrait painter, circa 1510-1584.

POUSSIN, Gaspar Doughet (Le Guaspre); French painter, 1615-1675.

POUSSIN, Nicolas; French historical and religious painter. 1594-1665.

POYNTER, Ambrose; water-colour painter, 1796-1886.

POYNTER, Sir Edward John, P.R.A.; French classical painter, 1836-1919. Settled in England.

PRENTIS, Edward; painter, 1797-1854.

PRICKE, Robert; engraver, fl. 1669-1698.

PRINSEP, Valentine Cameron, R.A.; English painter, 1838-1904.

PRIOR, Thomas Abiel; engraver, 1809-1886.

PRITCHETT, R. F.; painter, 1827-1907.

PROCACCINI, Camillo; Italian religious painter, 1546-1625.

PROCACCINI, Giulio Cesare; Italian painter, 1548-1626.

PROCTER, Dod, R.A.; contemporary painter, 1891-

PROCTOR, Thomas; painter and sculptor, 1753-1794.

PROUT, John Skinner; water-colour painter, 1806-1876.

PROUT, Samuel; water-colour painter and etcher, 1783-1852.

PRUD'HON, Pierre Paul; French historical and portrait painter, 1758-1823.

PRYDE, James; painter, 1869-1941.

PUGH, Herbert; landscape painter, fl. 1758-1788.

PURCELL, Richard; engraver, 1736-1766.

PUVIS de CHAVANNES, Pierre Cécile; French painter, 1824-1898.

PYE, Charles; engraver, 1777-1864.

PYE, John; engraver, 1782-1874.

PYNE, James Baker; painter, 1800-1870.

QUAINI, Luigi; Italian painter, 1643-1717.

QUARTLEY, Arthur; American painter, 1839-1886.

QUARTLEY, Frederick William; engraver, 1808-1874.

QUAST, P. J.; Dutch painter, 1606-1647.

QUELLIN, Erasmus; Flemish sculptor and painter, 1607-1678.

QUELLYN, Artus; Flemish sculptor and painter, 1630-1715.

RADCLYFFE, Edward; engraver, 1809-1863.

RADCLYFFE, William; engraver, 1780-1855.

RAE, Henrietta; English painter, 1859-1928.

RAEBURN, Sir Henry, R.A.; Scottish portrait painter, 1756-1823.

RAIBOLINI, Francesco (Francia); Italian portrait and religious painter, 1450-1517.

RAILTON, Herbert; English black-and-white artist, 1857-1910.

RAIMBACH, Abraham; engraver, 1776-1843.

RAIMONDI, Marc Antonio; Italian engraver, 1488-1534.

RAMSAY, Allan; Scottish portrait painter, 1713-1784.

RAMSAY, James; portrait painter, 1786-1854.

RANKLEY, Alfred; painter, 1819-1872.

RAOUX, Jean; French portrait painter, 1677-1734.

RAPHAEL (Raffaello SANZIO, *q.v.*); Italian painter, 1483-1520.

RATHBONE, John; painter, circa 1750-1807.

RAVEN, John Samuel; landscape painter, 1829-1877.

RAVESTEYN, Jan van; Dutch portrait painter, 1580-1665.

READ. David Charles; painter and etcher, 1790-1851.

READING, Burnet; engraver, fl. 1780-1820.

REDFERN, James Frank; sculptor, 1838-1876.

REDGRAVE, Richard, R.A.; English painter, 1804-1888.

REDOUTE, P. J.; flower painter, 1759-1840.

REED, Joseph Charles; landscape painter, 1822-1877.

REGNAULT, Alexandre Georges Henri; French painter, 1843-1871.

REGNAULT, Jean Baptiste; French historical and allegorical painter, 1754-1829.

REID, Sir George, P.R.S.A.; painter, 1841-1913.

REID, J.; Scottish painter, 1851-1926.

REINAGLE, George Philip; marine painter, 1802-1835.

REINAGLE, Philip, R.A.; English landscape and animal painter, 1749-1833.

REINAGLE, Ramsay Richard, R.A.; painter, 1775-1862.

REMBRANDT, Van Ryn, Harmensz; Dutch portrait painter, 1606-1669.

RENI, Guido; Italian painter, 1575-1642.

RENOIR, Pierre-Auguste; French painter, 1841-1919.

RETHEL, Alfred; German painter, 1816-1859.

REYNOLDS, Frances; English painter, 1729-1807.

REYNOLDS, Sir Joshua, P.R.A.; English portrait painter, 1723-1792.

REYNOLDS, Samuel William; English landscape painter and engraver, 1773-1835.

REYNOLDS, Samuel William; English painter and engraver, 1794-1872.

RIBALTA, Francesco de; Spanish historical painter, 1551-1628.

RIBERA, Jose de (Lo Spagnoletto); Spanish religious painter, 1588-1656.

RIBOT, Augustin T.; French painter and engraver, 1823-1891.

RICCI, Sebastiano (Rizzi); Venetian painter, 1659-1734. Settled in England.

RICCIO, David; painter, 1494-1567.

RICHARDS, John Inigo, R.A.; water-colour painter, -1810.

RICHARDSON, Jonathan; English portrait painter, 1665-1745.

RICHARDSON, Thomas Miles; English landscape painter, 1784-1848.

RICHARDSON, Thomas Miles (Junior); English painter and engraver, 1813-1890.

RICHMOND, George, R.A.; English religious and portrait painter, 1809-1896.

RICHMOND, Sir William Blake, R.A.; English painter, 1843-1921.

RICHTER, Adrian Ludwig; German painter and engraver, 1803-1884.

RICHTER, Gustav Karl Ludwig; German painter and engraver, 1823-1884.

RICHTER, Henry James; painter and engraver, 1772-1857.

RIDINGER, Johann Elias; painter, 1695-1767.

RIEDEL, August; painter, 1802-1883.

RIGAUD y ROS, Hyacinthe; French portrait painter, 1659-1743.

RILEY, John; portrait painter, 1646-1691.

RIMMER, Alfred; painter, 1829-1893.

RIMMER, William; painter, 1816-1879.

RIPPINGILLE, E. V.; painter, 1798-1859.

RIVIÈRE, Briton, R.A.; English painter, 1840-1920.

RIVIÈRE, Henry Parsons; water-colour painter, 1811-1888.

RIVIÈRE, William; painter, 1806-1876.

ROBERT-FLEURY, Joseph Nicolas; French historical and genre painter, 1797-1891.

ROBERT, Hubert; painter, 1733-1808.

ROBERT, Louis Leopold; Swiss painter, 1794-1835.

ROBERTS, David, R.A.; Scottish painter, 1796-1864.

ROBERTSON, Alexander; Scottish landscape painter and miniaturist, 1772-1841.

ROBERTSON, Andrew; Scottish portrait and miniature painter, 1777-1845.

ROBERTSON, Archibald; Scottish portrait and miniature painter, 1765-1835.

ROBINSON, John Henry; engraver, 1796-1871.

ROBINSON, William; portrait painter, 1799-1839.

ROBINSON, W. Heath; humorous artist, 1872-1944.

ROBSON, George Fennel; English landscape painter, 1788-1833.

ROBUSTI, Jacopo (Tintoretto); Venetian religious painter, 1518-1594.

ROCHE, Alexander; Scottish painter, 1861-1921.

RODEN, William T.; English portrait painter, 1817-1892.

RODIN, Auguste; French sculptor, 1840-1917.

ROLL, A.; French painter, 1847-1919.

ROMANELLI, Giovanni Francesco; Italian religious and mythological painter, 1610-1662.

ROMILLY, Amélie Munier; portrait painter, 1788-1875.

ROMNEY, George; English portrait painter, 1734-1802.

ROOKER, Michael Angelo; water-colour painter and engraver, 1743-1801.

ROOS, Johann Heinrich; Dutch animal painter and engraver, 1631-1685.

ROOS, Joseph; landscape painter, 1728-1805.

ROOS, Philipp Peter; German animal painter, 1657-1705.

ROQUEPLAN, Camille Joseph Étienne; French genre and landscape painter, 1800-1855.

ROSA, Salvatore; Italian landscape and religious painter, 1615-1673.

ROSELLI, Matteo; Florentine painter, 1578-1651.

ROSENBERG, George Frederick; painter, 1825-1869.

ROSS, Sir William Charles, R.A.; English historical and miniature painter, 1794-1860.

ROSSELLI, Cosimo di Lorenzo di Filippo; Italian religious painter, 1439-1507.

ROSSETTI, Gabriel Charles Dante; English painter, 1828-1882.

ROSSETTI, Lucy Madox; painter, 1843-1894.

ROSSI, Francesco (il Salviati); Italian painter, 1510-1563.

ROSSI, Giovambattista dei; Florentine painter, 1494-1541.

ROSSI, John Charles Felix, R.A.; English sculptor, 1762-1839.

ROTHENSTEIN, Sir William; painter, 1872-1945.

ROTHWELL, Richard, R.H.A.; painter, 1800-1868.

ROUSSEAU, J.; landscape painter, 1630-1693.

ROUSSEAU, Pierre Étienne Theódore; French landscape painter, 1812-1867.

ROWBOTHAM, Thomas Leeson Charles; landscape painter, 1823-1875.

ROWLANDSON, Thomas; English engraver and caricaturist, 1756-1827.

RUBEN, Christian; painter, 1805-1875.

RUBENS, Sir Peter Paul; Flemish religious and portrait painter, 1577-1640.

RUNCIMAN, Alexander; painter, 1736-1785.

RUSKIN, John; artist and critic, 1819-1900.

RUSSEL, Theodore; portrait painter, 1614-1689.

RUSSELL, John; English portrait painter, 1745-1806.

RUSSELL, Sir Walter, R.A.; painter, 1867-1949.

RUTHERSTON, Albert; painter, 1881-1953.

RUYSDAEL, Jakob; painter and etcher, 1628-1682.

RUYSDAEL, Saloman van; Dutch painter, circa 1602-1670.

RYDER, Thomas; engraver, 1746-1810.

RYLAND, William Wynne; English engraver, 1732-1783.

SABBATINI, Andrea (da Salerno); Italian painter, c. 1480-1545.

SABBATINI, Lorenzo (called Lorenzio Da Bologna); Italian painter, c. 1530-1577.

SACCHI, Andrea; painter, 1591-1661.

SADDLER, John; engraver, 1813-1892.

SADELER, Gillis; Flemish engraver, 1575-1629.

SADELER, Jan; Flemish engraver, 1550-1600.

SADELER, Raphael; Flemish engraver, 1555-1616.

SADLER, Walter Dendy; English painter, 1854-1923.

SALISBURY, Frank; English portrait and historical painter, 1874-1962.

SALTER, William; historical and portrait painter, 1804-1875.

SALVATOR, Rosa; painter, 1615-1673.

SALVI, Giovanni Battista; Italian religious painter, 1605-1685.

SANDBY, Paul, R.A.; English painter and engraver, 1725-1809.

SANDBY, Thomas, R.A.; water-colour painter, 1721-1798.

SANDERS, George; portrait painter, 1774-1846.

SANDYS, Antony Frederick; painter, 1832-1896.

SANT, James, R.A.; English portrait painter, 1820-1916.

SANTERRE, Jean Baptiste; painter, 1658-1717.

SANZIO, Raffaello (Raphael, *q.v.*); Italian religious painter and architect, 1483-1520. Pupil of Perugino.

SARGENT, John Singer, R.A.; Florentine portrait painter, 1856-1925. Settled in England.

SARTAIN, John; painter and engraver, 1808-1897.

SARTORIOUS, Francis; sporting and animal painter, 1734-1804.

SARTORIOUS, J. N.; sporting painter, 1755-1828.

SAUNDERS, J.; miniature painter, 1750-1825.

SAVAGE, William; painter and engraver, 1770-1843.

SAY, William; engraver, 1768-1834.

SCHADOW, Wilhelm Friedrich von; German painter, 1789-1862.

SCHALCKEN, Godfried; Dutch genre painter, 1643-1706.

SCHEFFER, Ary; French painter, 1795-1858.

SCHEFFER, Hendrik; 1798-1862.

SCHETKY, John Alexander; water-colour painter, 1785-1824.

SCHETKY, John Christian; marine painter, 1778-1874.

SCHEUREN, Johann Kaspar; painter, 1810-1887.

SCHINKEL, Karl Friedrich; German classical painter and architect, 1781-1841.

SCHMIDT, Georg Friedrich; engraver, 1712-1775.

SCHRADER, Julius; painter, 1815-1900.

SCHWABE, Randolph; water-colour painter, 1885-1948.

SCHWIND, Moritz von; historical painter, 1804-1871.

SCOTT, David; Scottish historical painter, 1806-1849.

SCOTT, John; engraver, 1774-1827.

SCOTT, Peter; contemporary bird painter, 1909-

SCOTT, Robert; engraver, 1771-1841.

SCOTT, Samuel; marine painter, 1710-circa 1772.

SCOTT, William Bell; Scottish painter, 1811-1890

SCRIVEN, Edward; engraver, 1775-1841.

SEAGO, Edward; contemporary artist, 1910-

SEDDON, Thomas; painter and designer, 1821-1856.

SEEMAN, Enoch; portrait painter, 1694-1744.

SEGANTINI, Giovanni; Italian painter, 1858-1899.

SEGHERS, David; painter, 1590-1661.

SELOUS, Henry Courteney; painter, 1811-1890.

SERRES, Dominic; marine painter, 1722-1793.

SERRES, John Thomas; marine painter, 1759-1825.

SETCHEL, Sarah; water-colour painter, 1813-1894.

SEURAT, Georges; French painter, 1859-1890.

SEVERN, Joseph, R.A.; painter, 1793-1879.

SEYMOUR, James; painter of horses, 1702-1752.

SHALDERS, George; water-colour painter, 1826-1873.

SHANNON, Sir James Jebusa, R.A.; American portrait painter, 1862-1923. Settled in England.

SHANNON, Charles; painter, 1863-1937.

SHARP, M. W., R.A.; painter, 1801-1840.

SHARP, William; English engraver, 1749-1824.

SHAW, J. Byam; Indian black-and-white artist, 1872-1919. Settled in England.

SHAYER, William; animal painter, 1788-1879.

SHEE, Sir Martin Archer, P.R.A.; Irish portrait painter, 1769-1850.

SHELLEY, Samuel; miniature painter, 1750-1808.

SHEPHERD, George; water-colour painter, fl. 1800-1830.

SHERRIN, John, R.I.; water-colour painter, 1819-1896.

SHERWIN, William; engraver, fl. 1670-1710.

SHIELDS, F.; English painter, 1833-1911.

SHORT, Sir Frank, R.A.; engraver and painter, 1857-1945.

SICKERT, Bernard; English painter, 1862-1932.

SICKERT, Walter Richard, A.R.A.; English painter, 1860-1942.

SIDLEY, Samuel; portrait painter, 1829-1896.

SIEVIER, Robert William; engraver and sculptor, 1794-1865.

SIGNAC, Paul; 1863-1935.

SILLETT, James; flower painter, 1764-1840.

SIMMONS, William Henry; mezzotint engraver, 1811-1882.

SIMPSON, John; portrait painter, 1782-1847.

SIMPSON, William; Scottish painter and engraver, 1823-1899.

SIMS, Charles, A.R.A.; English painter, 1873-1928.

SIMSON, William; Scottish painter, 1800-1847.

SISLEY, Alfred; painter, 1839-1899.

SKELTON, William; engraver, 1763-1848.

SKIRVING, Archibald; painter, 1749-1819.

SLOCOMBE, C. P.; etcher, 1832-1895.

SMART, John; Scottish landscape painter, 1839-1899.

SMART, John; English miniature painter, 1741-1811.

SMETHAM, James; English painter and engraver, 1821-1889.

SMIBERT, John; portrait painter, 1684-1751.

SMIRKE, Robert, R.A.; English painter, 1752-1845.

SMITH, Anker; engraver, 1759-1819.

SMITH, Charles; painter, 1749-1824.

SMITH, Charles John; engraver, 1803-1838.

SMITH, Colvin; portrait painter, 1795-1875.

SMITH, Frederick William; sculptor, 1797-1835.

SMITH, George; landscape painter, 1713-1776.

SMITH, John; mezzotint engraver, 1652-1742.

SMITH, John; water-colour painter, 1749-1831.

SMITH, John Raphael; English painter and engraver, 1752-1812.

SMITH, Sir Matthew; painter, 1879-1959.

SMITH, Stephen Catterson; portrait painter, 1806-1872.

SNYDERS, Frans; Dutch animal and still-life painter, 1579-1657.

SOLOMON, Abraham; painter, 1823-1862.

SOLOMON, Solomon Joseph; English painter, 1860-1927.

SOMERVILLE, Andrew; painter, 1803-1833.

SOYER, Elizabeth Emma; painter, 1813-1842.

SPANGENBERG, Gustav Adolf; painter, 1828-1891.

SPENCELAYH, Charles; painter, 1865-1958.

SPENCER, Sir Stanley; contemporary painter, 1892-1959.

SPILSBURY, Jonathan; engraver, fl. 1760-1790.

STANFIELD, George Clarkson; marine painter, 1828-1878.

STANFIELD, William Clarkson, R.A.; English marine and landscape painter, 1793-1867.

STANNARD, Joseph; painter, 1797-1830.

STARK, James; English landscape painter, 1794-1859.

STEELL, Gourlay; Scottish animal painter, 1819-1894.

STEELL, Sir John, R.S.A.; Scottish sculptor, 1804-1891.

STEEN, Jan; Dutch painter, 1626-1679.

STEER, Philip Wilson; painter, 1860-1942.

STEINLEN, T.; Swiss painter, 1859-1923.

STEPANOV, A. S.; Russian painter, 1858-1923.

STEPHENSON, James; engraver, 1828-1886.

STEUBEN, Karl; German painter, 1788-1856.

STEVENS, Alfred; English sculptor and painter, 1817-1875.

STEVENS, Francis; landscape painter, 1781-1823.

STEWARDSON, Thomas; portrait painter, 1781-1859.

STEWART, Anthony; miniature painter, 1773-1846.

STEWART, James; engraver, 1791-1863.

STOKES, Adrian, R.A.; English landscape painter, 1854-1935.

STONE, Marcus, R.A.; English genre painter, 1840-1921.

STORER, James Sargent; engraver, 1781-1853.

STOTHARD, Thomas, R.A.; English painter, 1755-1834.

STOTT, Wm., R.A.; English painter, 1858-1900.

STOW, James; engraver, 1770-1825.

STRANG, W., R.A.; Scottish painter, 1859-1921.

STRANGE, Sir Robert; Scottish engraver, 1721-1792.

STREATER, Robert; painter, 1624-1680.

STUART, Gilbert; American portrait painter, 1755-1828.

STUBBS, George; English animal painter and engraver, 1724-1806.

STUCK, F. von; German painter, 1863-1928.

SUSTERMANS (or Suttermans), Justus; Flemish portrait painter, 1597-1681.

SUTHERLAND, Graham; contemporary painter, 1903-

SWAINE, John; engraver, 1775-1860.

SWAN, Henry; engraver, 1821-1889.

SWAN, John MacAllan, R.A.; English painter and sculptor, 1847-1910.

SWINTON, James Rannie; English portrait painter, 1816-1888.

SYME, John; portrait painter, 1795-1861.

TANNOCK, James; portrait painter, 1784-1863.

TAUNAY, Nicolas Antoine; French painter, 1755-1830.

TAYLOR, Charles; engraver, 1756-1823.

TAYLOR, J. Frederick, R.W.S.; English painter and engraver, 1802-1889.

TAYLOR, Sir Robert; English sculptor and architect, 1814-1888.

TEMPESTA, Antonio; Florentine painter and engraver, 1555-1630.

TENIERS, David (the elder); Flemish painter, 1582-1649.

TENIERS, David (the younger); Flemish landscape painter, 1610-1690.

TER BORCH, Gerard; Dutch genre painter, 1617-1681.

THEW, Robert; engraver, 1758-1802.

THOMAS, George Housman; artist, 1824-1868.

THOMAS, Robert Kent; English engraver, 1816-1884.

THOMAS, William Luson; English painter and engraver, 1830-1900.

THOMPSON, Jacob; landscape painter, 1806-1879.

ARTISTS, ENGRAVERS, SCULPTORS, ETC.

THOMPSON, John; engraver, 1785-1866.

THOMSON, Alfred Reginald, R.A.; painter, 1894-

THOMSON, Henry; painter, 1773-1843.

THOMSON, James; engraver, 1788-1850.

THOMSON, John; Scottish landscape painter, 1778-1840.

THORBURN, Archibald; bird painter, 1860-1935.

THORBURN, Robert, A.R.A.; miniature painter, 1818-1885.

THORNHILL, Sir James; English painter, 1676-1734

THORNYCROFT, Sir William Hamo, R.A.; English sculptor, 1850-1925.

THORVALDSEN, Bertel; Danish sculptor, 1770-1844.

TIDEY, Alfred; English miniaturist and water-colour painter, 1808-1892.

TIDEY, Henry; English genre and portrait painter, 1813-1872.

TIEPOLO, Giovanni Battista; Italian religious painter, 1696-1769.

TILSON, Henry; portrait painter, 1659-1695.

TINTORETTO (Jacopo Robusti); Venetian religious painter, 1518-1594.

TISCHBEIN, Johann Heinrich; German historical painter, 1722-1789.

TISCHBEIN, Johann Heinrich Wilhelm; German painter and engraver, 1751-1829.

TISSOT, James Joseph Jacques; French water-colour painter, 1836-1902.

TITIAN (Tiziano Vecelli); Venetian painter, circa 1487-1576.

TOMKINS, Peltro William; engraver, 1759-1840.

TONGE, Robert; English landscape painter, 1823-1856.

TOPHAM, Francis William; English painter and engraver, 1808-1877.

TORRANCE, James; Scottish painter, 1859-1916.

TOULOUSE-LAUTREC, Henri de; painter, 1864-1902.

TOWNE, Francis; landscape painter, 1740-1816.

TREVISO, Girolamo da; painter, 1508-1544.

TROYON, Constant; French landscape and animal painter, 1810-1865.

TUKE, Henry Scott, R.A.; English painter, 1858-1929.

TURMEAU, John; miniature painter, 1777-1846.

TURNER, Charles, A.R.A.; English engraver, 1773-1857.

TURNER, Joseph Mallord William, R.A.; English painter, 1775-1851.

TURNER, William; English painter, 1789-1862.
TWEEDIE, William Menzies; portrait painter, 1826-1878.
TWOPENNY, W.; English painter, 1797-1873.

UBERTINI, Francesco (Il Bachiacca); 1494-1557.
UDEN, Lucas van; Flemish landscape painter, 1595-1673.
UDINE, Giovanni da (Giovanni Nanni); Italian painter, 1487-1564.
ULFT, Jacob van der; landscape painter, 1627-1688.
UTRILLO, Maurice; painter, 1883-1955.
UUTE WAEL, Joachim; Dutch painter, 1566-1638.
UWINS, Thomas, R.A.; English painter, 1782-1857

VACCARO, Andrea; Italian religious painter, 1598-1670.
VACHER, Charles; water-colour painter, 1818-1883.
VALDES-LEAL, Juan de; Spanish religious painter, 1630-1691.
VAN DER GUGHT, Michiel; engraver, 1660-1725.
VAN DER MYN, Herman; portrait painter, 1684-1741.
VAN DER NEER, Aart; marine painter, 1603-1677.
VAN DER NEER, Eglon Hendik; painter, 1643-1703.
VAN DER VAART, Jan; painter and engraver, 1647-1721.
VANDERVELDE, Wilem (" The Old "); marine painter, 1610-1693.
VANDERVELDE, Wilem; marine painter, 1633-1707.
VAN DER WERFF, Adriaen; historical painter, 1659-1722.
VAN DIEST, Adriaen; landscape painter, 1656-1704.
VAN DYKE, Sir Anthony; portrait painter and etcher, 1599-1641.
VAN EYCK, Hubert; painter, 1366-1426.
VAN EYCK, Jan; Flemish painter, circa 1400-1441.
VAN GOGH, Vincent; Dutch painter, 1853-1890.
VAN HELMONT, Segres Jacob; painter, 1683-1726.
VAN LEMENS, Balthasar; painter, 1637-1704.
VAN LOO, Charles Andre; painter, 1705-1765.
VAN LOO, Jean Baptiste; painter, 1684-1745.
VANNUCCI, Andrea; painter, 1486-1531.
VANNUCCI, Pietro (Perugino); Perugian religious painter, 1446-1524.
VAN OS, Pieter Gerard; painter and engraver, 1776-1839
VAN OSTADE, Adriaen; painter, 1620-1685.
VAN OSTADE, Isaak; painter, 1621-1649.

VAN SOMER, Paul; portrait painter, 1576-1621.

VAN VOERST, Robert; engraver, 1596-1636.

VARGAS, Luis de; Spanish religious painter, 1502-1568.

VARLEY, Cornelius; English water-colour painter, 1781-1873

VARLEY, John; English water-colour painter, 1778-1842.

VAROTARI, Alessandro (Padovanino); Italian painter, 1590-1650.

VASARI, Giorgio; Italian architect and painter, 1512-1574.

VASNETSOV, V. M.; Russian painter, 1848-1926.

VECCHIETTA (Lorenzo di Pietro); Italian painter and sculptor, 1412-1480.

VECELLI, Tiziano (Titian); Venetian religious and mythological painter, 1477-1576.

VEEN, Maerten van (Heemskerk); Dutch religious painter, 1498-1574.

VEEN, Otto van (Venius); Dutch painter, 1558-1629.

VEIT, Philipp; German painter, 1793-1877.

VELAZQUEZ de SILVA, Diego; Spanish portrait painter, 1599-1660.

VELDE, Adriaen van; Dutch animal and landscape painter, 1635-1672.

VENDRAMINI, G.; engraver, 1769-1839.

VERBOECKHOVEN, Eugene Joseph; animal painter, 1798-1881.

VERESTCHAGIN, Vassili; Russian military painter, 1843-1904.

VERMEER, Jan (Van de Meer); Dutch painter, 1632-1675.

VERNET, Antoine Charles Horace; French painter, 1758-1836.

VERNET, Claude Joseph; French landscape painter, 1714-1789.

VERNET, Émile Jean Horace; French military painter, 1789-1863.

VERONESE, Paolo; Venetian painter, 1528-1588.

VERROCCHIO, Andrea del; Florentine sculptor, painter, etc., 1435-1488.

VERWILT, Francis; Dutch portrait painter, 1623-1691.

VICKERS, Alfred Gomersal; marine painter, 1786-1868.

VINCENT, George; painter, 1796-1831.

VINCI, Leonardo da; Italian religious and mythological painter, sculptor and architect, 1452-1519.

VIVARES, François; engraver, 1709-1780.

VIZETELLY, Henry Richard; engraver, 1820-1894.

VIZETELLY, James Henry; engraver, 1790-1838.

VOIS, Adriaen de; Dutch painter, 1641-1698.

VOLPATO, Giovanni; engraver, 1733-1802.

VOS, Cornelis de; Flemish historical and portrait painter, 1585-1651.

VOS, Martin de; Flemish painter, 1531-1603.

VOS, Simon de; Flemish painter, 1603-1676.

VOUET, Simon; French historical painter, 1590-1649.

VRIES, Hans Vredeman de; painter, 1527-1604.

VROOM, Hendrik Cornelisz; Dutch painter, 1566-1640.

VUILLARD, Jean Edouard; painter, 1868-1940.

WADE, Thomas; water-colour painter, 1828-1891.

WAIN, Louis; English artist, cat studies, 1860-

WALES, James; portrait painter, 1747-1795.

WALKER, Anthony; engraver, 1726-1765.

WALKER, Ethel, A.R.A.; painter, 1867-1951.

WALKER, Frederick, A.R.A.; English painter and black-and-white artist, 1840-1875.

WALKER, William; engraver, 1793-1867.

WALLER, Samuel Edmund; painter 1851-1903.

WALLIS, George; English genre and portrait painter, 1811-1891.

WALLIS, Robert; engraver, 1794-1878.

WALMSLEY, Thomas; landscape painter, 1763-1805.

WALTON, C. A.; Scottish painter, 1860-1922.

WALTON, Henry; painter, 1746-1813.

WANE, Richard; English marine and landscape painter, 1852-1904.

WAPPERS, Gustave; Belgian historical painter, 1803-1874.

WARD, Edward Matthew, R.A.; English historical painter, 1816-1879.

WARD, James, R.A.; English animal painter and engraver, 1769-1859.

WARD, Sir Leslie ("Spy"); painter and cartoonist, 1851-1922.

WARD, William, A.R.A.; engraver, 1766-1826.

WARREN, Charles; line engraver, 1767-1823.

WARREN, Henry; religious and Oriental painter, 1794-1879.

WATERLOW, Sir Ernest Alfred, R.A.; English landscape painter, 1850-1919.

WATSON, George; portrait painter, 1767-1837.

WATSON, George Spencer, R.A.; portrait painter, 1869-1934.

WATSON, John Dawson; painter, 1832-1892.

WATSON, Thomas; engraver, 1743-1781.

WATSON-GORDON, Sir John, P.R.S.A., R.A.; portrait painter, 1788-1864.

WATT, James Henry; line engraver, 1799-1867.

WATTEAU, Jean Antoine; French landscape, military and genre painter, 1684-1721.

WATTS, George Frederick, O.M., R.A.; English sculptor, portrait and allegorical painter, 1817-1904.

WATTS, William; line engraver, 1752-1851.

WEAVER, Thomas; painter of cattle, 1774-1843.

WEBB, Philip; English artist, 1831-1915.

WEBBER, John, R.A.; portrait painter, 1752-1793.

WEBER, Otto; painter, 1832-1888.

WEBSTER, Thomas, R.A.; English painter, 1800-1886.

WEEKES, Henry, R.A.; English sculptor, 1807-1877.

WEENIX, Jan; Dutch still-life painter, 1640-1719.

WEHNERT, Edward Henry; water-colour painter, 1813-1868.

WEIR, Harrison William; English painter, 1824-1906.

WELLS, Henry Tanworth, R.A.; English painter, 1828-1903.

WELLS, William Frederick; water-colour painter, 1762-1836.

WERNER, A. A.; German historical painter, 1843-1915.

WERNER, Joseph; Swiss historical, portrait and miniature painter, 1637-1710.

WEST, Benjamin, P.R.A.; American painter, 1738-1820. Settled in England.

WESTALL, Richard; English historical, classical and religious painter, 1765-1836.

WESTMACOTT, Sir Richard; English sculptor, 1775-1856.

WESTMACOTT, Richard, R.A.; English sculptor, 1779-1872.

WEYDEN, Rogier van der; French religious painter, 1399-1464.

WHEATLEY, Francis, R.A.; English painter, 1747-1801.

WHISTLER, James Abbott McNeill; American painter and engraver, 1834-1903. Settled in England.

WHOOD, Isaac; portrait painter, 1689-1752.

WHYMPER, Jonah Wood; English engraver, 1813-1903.

WICAR, Jean Baptiste; French painter and engraver, 1762-1834.

WIERTZ, Antoine Joseph; French painter and sculptor, 1806-1865.

WILD, Charles; water-colour painter, 1781-1835.

WILKIE, Sir David, R.A.; Scottish historical, portrait and genre painter, 1785-1841.

WILLCOCK, George Burrell; painter, 1811-1852.

WILLE, Johann Georg; German engraver, 1715-1808.

WILLEMS, Florent J.; Belgian genre painter, 1823-1905.

WILLIAMS, Hugh Williams; landscape painter, 1773-1829.

WILLIAMS, Robert; mezzotint engraver, fl. 1680-1704.

WILLIAMS, Samuel; engraver, 1788-1883.

WILLIAMSON, Francis John; English sculptor, 1833-1920.

WILLIAMSON, Samuel; landscape painter, 1792-1840.

WILLIS, Henry Brittan; painter, 1810-1884.

WILLISON, George; portrait painter, 1741-1797.

WILSON, Andrew; landscape painter, 1780-1848.

WILSON, Benjamin; English portrait painter, 1721-1788.

WILSON, George; Scottish painter, 1848-1890.

WILSON, John; marine painter, 1774-1855.

WILSON, Richard, R.A.; English landscape painter, 1714-1782.

WILTON, Joseph; English sculptor, 1722-1803.

WIMPERIS, Edmund Monson; English engraver and water-colour painter, 1835-1900.

WINCKELMANN, F. X.; German portrait painter, 1806-1873.

WINGFIELD, Lewis G.; English painter, 1842-1891.

WINSTANLEY, Hamlet; painter and engraver, 1700-1761.

WINT, Peter de; English water-colour painter, 1784-1849.

WINTERHALTER, Franz Xaver; painter and engraver, 1806-1873.

WINTOUR, John Crawford; landscape painter, 1825-1882.

WISSING, Willem; Dutch portrait painter, 1656-1687.

WIT, Jacob de; Dutch painter, 1695-1754.

WITHERINGTON, William Frederick; landscape painter, 1785-1865.

WITTE, Emanuel de; Dutch painter, 1617-1692.

WIVELL, Abraham; portrait painter, 1786-1849.

WOLF, Joseph; German animal painter, 1820-1899. Settled in England.

WOLSTENHOLME, Dean; animal painter, 1757-1837.

WOLSTENHOLME, Dean; animal painter, 1798-1883.

WOOD, John; painter, 1801-1870.

WOOD, S. L.; English painter, 1866-1928.

WOODFORDE, Samuel, R.A.; painter, 1763-1817.

WOODMAN, Richard; engraver, 1784-1859.

WOODS, Henry, R.A.; painter, 1847-1921.

WOODWARD, Thomas; animal painter, 1801-1852.

WOOLLETT, William; English engraver, 1735-1785.

WOOLNER, Thomas, R.A.; portrait painter, 1825-1892.

WOOTON, John; landscape and animal painter, c. 1678-1765.

WORLIDGE, Thomas; painter and etcher, 1700-1766.

WOUVERMAN, Jan; Dutch landscape painter, 1629-1666.

WOUVERMAN, Philip; Dutch painter, 1619-1668.

WRIGHT, John Masey; water-colour painter, 1773-1866.

WRIGHT, John William; water-colour painter, 1802-1848.

WRIGHT, Joseph, R.A.; English painter, 1734-1797.

WRIGHT, Thomas; portrait painter and engraver, 1792-1849.

WYATT, Henry; painter, 1794-1840.

WYATT, Matthew Cotes; English sculptor, 1777-1862.

WYATT, Richard James; English sculptor, 1793-1850.

WYCK, John; painter, 1640-1702.

WYLD, William; English painter, 1806-1889.

WYLLIE, Charles William; painter,

WYLLIE, William Lionel, R.A.; water-colour painter, etcher, etc., 1851-1931.

WYNANTS, Jan; Dutch landscape painter, 1615-circa 1682.

WYNFIELD, D. W.; painter, 1837-1887.

YOUNG, John; mezzotint engraver, 1755-1825.

YVON, Adolphe; historical painter, 1817-1893.

ZAHN, Johann K. W.; painter and architect, 1800-1871.

ZAMACOIS, Eduardo; Spanish painter, 1843-1871.

ZAMPIERI, Domenico (Domenichino); Italian painter, 1581-1641.

ZAUFFELY, Johann, R.A. (Zoffany); German portrait painter, 1733-1810.

ZEEMAN, E.; German portrait painter, 1694-1744.

ZEGHERS, Daniel; Flemish fruit and flower painter, 1590-1661.

ZEGHERS, Gerard; Flemish painter, 1591-1651.

ZEITBLOM, Bartholomaus; German religious painter, 1440-1520.

ZIEGLER, Henry Bryan; English portrait and landscape painter, 1798-1874.

ZINCKE, Christian Friedrich; miniature painter, c. 1648-1767.

ZOFFANY, Johann, R.A.; see ZAUFFELY.

ZOPPO, Marco; Italian religious painter, fl. 1471-1498.

ZOPPO, Paolo; Italian miniature painter, fl. 1492-1530.

ZORN, A. L.; Swedish landscape painter, 1860-1920.

ZUCCARELLI, Francesco, R.A.; Italian historical and landscape painter, 1702-1788.

ZUCCARO (Zuccharo), Federigo; Italian religious and portrait painter, 1542-1609.

ZUCCARO (Zuccharo), Taddeo; Italian painter, 1529-1566.

ZUCCHI, Antonio Pietro; Italian painter, 1726-1795.

ZULOAGA, I. de; Spanish painter, 1870-1945.

ZURBARAN, Francisco de; Spanish painter, 1598-1662.

JEWELLERY

Abraxas—A gem engraved by the ancients with this mystical word.

Acus—A pin; used when referring to the pin or tongue of ancient brooches or buckles.

Agate—A mineral composed of layers of different colours. The agate-forming minerals are chiefly chalcedony, cornelian, quartz, amethyst and jasper. When in stripes or bands it is called "ribband" agate, when the stripes converge towards the centre, "circular agate". "Eye Agate", "Moss Agate", "cloud agate", "rainbow agate" and "fortification agate" are other representative names given to different varieties. The name is probably derived from the river once known as Achates in Sicily.

Aigrette—A diamond head ornament.

Albert—A short watch chain with buttonhole bar (named after the late Prince Consort).

Alexandrite—A variety of chrysoberyl chiefly found in India, remarkable for its prominent hues of green and red. Green usually predominates in the day time, and when the stone is exposed to artificial light a soft columbine red colour prevails. The crystal form is usually six-sided twins and is composed of alumina, glucina, iron oxide, etc.

Almandine—A precious stone named after the town of Alabanda in Caria, where it was first found. It is transparent and of a deep red colour.

Amazonite or Amazon Stone—A variety of microcline possessing a beautiful verdigris-green colour, used as an ornamental stone, chiefly found in Colorado. It is composed of silica, alumina, potash, soda, etc.

Amber—A yellowish translucent and somewhat brittle fossil resin from an extinct tree (conifer) found in alluvial soils on the coasts of the Baltic. Amber becomes slightly magnetic on being warmed by friction. It is chiefly composed of carbon, hydrogen and oxygen. All amber is said to be at least 600,000 years old.

Amethyst—A hard transparent stone much used by jewellers. It is dichoric and under certain conditions displays two distinct tints, one being reddish and the other bluish violet. It is chiefly

Amethyst—*continued.*
composed of silica and is probably tinted by oxide of manganese. Found in company with agates in Brazil, South America, etc.

Amulet—Any object worn as a charm.

Andalusite—A mineral first discovered in Andalusia, Spain, from which province it derives its name. It exists in a variety of colours, green, brown, etc. and is used as an ornamental stone; composed chiefly of silica, alumina, etc.

Anklet—A ring or band of gold, silver or other metal worn on the ankle, often richly engraved or decorated.

Annular or Ring Brooch—A brooch in the shape of a ring.

Aquamarine—A transparent variety of beryl having a bluish-green colour, suggestive of sea-water. It retains its lustre in artificial light, but is not particularly hard, and is, therefore, likely to lose its polish. It is found in Brazil, Europe, America, Australia, etc., and is composed of silica, alumina and glucina. The crystal form is six-sided prisms.

Armil or Armilla—A Roman armlet or bracelet usually consisting of a series of coils of gold or bronze.

Aventurine—A rare quartz somewhat resembling gold-specked glass-ware. It is usually of brownish red or green colour with a vast number of minute points of mica.

Baguette—Term applied when the central stone is in a square setting with supporting stones which are smaller but still rectangular.

Bangle—An ornament worn on the arm or ankle.

Baton Cut—Elongated rectangular-cut diamond.

Beryl—A bluish, green or yellow gem. (*See Aquamarine.*)

Bevelment—A term used when the edges of a crystal or gem are cut as with a bevel, viz., with a slant or inclination of the surface.

Bezel—The part of a precious stone that projects beyond the setting; the expanded top part of a ring that receives the stone; the oblique side of a cut gem.

Bijouterie—Jewellery and relatively small objects, valuable on account of their workmanship or costly materials, or both.

Bloodstone or Heliotrope—A stone consisting of deep green chalcedony interspersed with red spots of jasper resembling drops of blood, hence the name. It is used for signet rings, etc., on which an intaglio monogram or crest is often engraved.

Bob—A loosely hanging pendant, e.g., an ear-ring.

Bolt Ring—A ring with spring-loaded bolt.

Bort or Boart—Diamonds of inferior quality, useless as ornamental stones. They are usually crushed to make diamond dust with which the facets are ground or cut on "first water" stones. They are of greyish colour and slightly harder than ordinary diamonds.

Bracelets—Favourite ornaments of Classical times, revived about 18th century.

Breloque—A seal or charm for a watch chain.

Brequet Chain—A watch guard more commonly known as a fob chain (*q.v.*)

Brilliant—A form in which precious stones are cut with facets, to add to their brilliancy. A split brilliant has 72 facets and a half brilliant 28 or 32 facets. New cuttings have been introduced giving 80 and 88 facets.

Briolette—An oval- or pear-shaped stone, having its entire surface cut with facets, often used as a pendant.

Bristol Diamonds—A misnomer for rock crystal.

Buckles—Shoe buckles were very fashionable in the reign of Charles II.

Cabochon—The name given to highly polished but not faceted stones of convex form; the style itself.

Cacholong—An opaque bluish-white variety of opal.

Cadrans—An instrument with graduated scale, used for measuring angles in cutting and polishing precious stones.

Cairngorm—A variety of quartz found in the Cairngorm peak in the Grampians, yellow or brown in colour.

Cameo—A stone sculptured in relief, the most usual stones used being Agate, Onyx, Sardonyx, Amethyst, Lapis Lazuli, Amber, etc. Generally set in gold or pinchbeck.

Carbonado—A Brazilian opaque diamond, black in colour, used for drills, etc.

Carbuncle—(*See Garnet.*)

Casket—A small box or chest, often made of precious metals, and chiefly used for jewellery and trinkets.

Cat's Eye—A hard, brilliant, luminous gem, giving iridescent reflections from within like the eye of a cat. The shades being

Cat's Eye—*continued*.

brown, green, yellow and black. The Quartz Cat's Eye (which is of comparatively little value) is semi-transparent and similar in appearance, but has no black.

Chains—Have been in use since the earliest times. Long gold chains called "guards" became fashionable in the early 19th century; they usually had a swivel to which a watch was attached and were carried in the waist.

Chalcedony—A translucent variety of quartz, usually of pale blue or grey tint, with waxlike lustre.

Chaplet—A bead necklace.

Châtelaine—A clasp or brooch worn by ladies for carrying keys or trinkets.

Chaton—The part of a ring in which the stone is set, more commonly known as a bezel (*q.v.*).

Chromium—A very hard metal, resistant to corrosion, used for cheap jewellery.

Chrysoberyl—A mineral consisting of a compound of alumina and glucina with a small amount of iron. It is usually found in rolled pieces and is of a yellow or pale green colour, or frequently brownish-yellow to a columbine red. When transparent or translucent it is used as a gem. There are two other varieties of the stone, viz., the Oriental Cat's Eye and the Alexandrite. It is found in the Urals, India, Brazil, America, etc.

Chrysolite—(*See Peridot.*)

Chrysoprase—An apple-green variety of chalcedony found in Silesia, etc. It is transparent and capable of being highly polished, but is affected by heat and sunshine, gradually losing its colour. It is used for signet rings and is composed of silica, oxide of nickel, etc.

Cocktail Ring—A name given in the last thirty years to heavy rings of unusual design.

Coffret—A small jewel box or casket.

Coral—A hard substance, treelike in form and usually red in colour, composed of the skeletons of zoophytes, growing from the sea-bottom and sometimes forming reefs above the water. Used for jewellery. **Coral Lacquer**—A thick red lacquer made to resemble coral.

Cornelian or Carnelian—A variety of translucent chalcedony, usually flesh-red in colour but varying to wax-yellow. The various colours bear different names, thus: pale red (feminine), brown (sard); red stripes into white (cornelian onyx), etc. It is used for signet rings and is found in Germany, the East Indies and other places. It is composed of silica with oxide of iron.

Crocidolite—A lavender-blue or leek-green mineral with the cat's eye effect or sometimes a rich brown deepening to almost black. It often has a ray of lighter colour. It is composed of silica, oxide of iron, soda, magnesia, etc., and is principally found in South Africa.

Crown—The top part of a gem; the upper range of facets in a rose diamond or brilliant.

Culet, Culette, Culasse or Collet—In the cutting of precious stones, the culet is the small flat under-facet parallel with the "table" or top facet.

Damascene Work or Damaskeen—A decoration applied to articles of steel or iron with gold, silver, etc., in delicate Eastern designs. The method adopted was to undercut the lines of the design and then hammer in the more precious metals.

Dextrale—A bracelet worn on the right arm.

Diadem—Another word for Tiara (*q.v.*).

Diamond—The hardest substance or stone known. It is composed of pure carbon, and when cut with facets to form a brilliant (*q.v.*) is much prized. In its purest form it is colourless and transparent, but is sometimes found in shades of pale or greenish yellow, red, green, blue and black (carbonado). The colouring is sometimes faked but can be detected by subjecting the stone to an acid test. Diamonds are found in South Africa, Brazil, India, Borneo, Australia, etc. First-quality stones are said to be of "first water". Common forms of crystals are octahedron, rhombic, etc.

Dichroite—A lustrous mineral of various shades of blue and violet which vary on exposure.

Discoidal Brooch—A brooch having an ornamental face or solid plaque.

Doublet—A counterfeit gem; a piece of glass or paste covered by a veneer of real stone.

Dress Fob—A black silk moire band, or broad fancy chain for carrying a gentleman's pocket watch in evening dress, one end holds the watch, the other usually a seal.

Ecrin—A jeweller's plush-lined box; the term was formerly applied to caskets and frequently to those containing saintly relics, the smaller ones are called écrinets.

Enamel—Vitrified substances applied to the surface of metals, etc., by fusion.

Enamel Work—An art of great antiquity, as is proved by remains found in Egypt. The usual ground for enamel work is copper, but gold and silver were also used; the best known varieties are cloisonné, Limoges, translucent and surface-painted enamel; in the last-named method metal plates were covered with a groundwork of dark enamel on which copies of pictures were painted in lighter colours. This style gave way in the 16th century to miniature painting on a ground of opaque enamel, which was used in decorating small objects such as snuff boxes.

Enamels as used for Jewellery:—

Champlevé: In which the ground is removed leaving a design standing up in the middle between which the enamel is placed.

Cloisonné: In which thin strips of metal are added to contain enamel.

Basse Taille: In which the design is carved at the bottom and shows through the transparent coat of enamel.

Filigree Enamel: In this the containing wires are either twisted or fancy patterns.

Emerald—A transparent mineral composed of silica, alumina, glucina, etc., which probably derives its varying green colour from a small amount of oxide of chromium. Its composition is entirely different from that of the ruby and sapphire, but closely resembles that of the beryl and aquamarine. The stone was well known to the ancients, and is found in South America, Australia, on the Ural Mountains, in Egypt, etc. The crystal form is hexagonal.

Enseigne—A jewel worn in the hat. Very popular during the Renaissance period.

Eslavage—A large ornamental necklace of lace design, popular in 18th century.

Essonite or Hessonite—The cinnamon stone (*See Garnet.*)

Étui—A small box or case in which articles of personal use or toilet are carried.

Euclase—A rare and brittle mineral of pale yellow, straw, green or blue prismatic crystals, possessing considerable lustre. It is found in Brazil and in the Urals, and is composed of silica, alumina, glucina, etc.

Fabergé—Peter Carl (1846-1920). A Russian renowned for his work in precious metals and stones.

Facets—The small plane surfaces of crystals, as cut upon precious stones.

Fermail—A clasp or buckle in the Middle Ages.

Ferronière—A small jewel hanging by ribbon so that the ornament comes in the middle of the forehead.

Fillet—An ornamental band worn on the head.

Filigree—Delicate ornaments made of gold or silver wire twisted into a lace pattern; it is sometimes called Maltese work, being chiefly made in Malta. Beads were originally used.

Fob Chain—(*See Dress Fob.*)

Garnet or Carbuncle—The garnet, of which there are several varieties, was much esteemed by the ancients, and was often engraved, many fine examples being in existence. It is transparent or semi-transparent, brittle, of different colours; chiefly composed of silica, alumina, lime, various oxides, etc. The **Precious Garnet**, sometimes called **Almandine**, is of a rich claret colour. **Pyrope**, or "Bohemian Garnet", a blood-red colour. **Uvarovite or Uwarowite**—an emerald green colour. **Spessartite**—a hyacinth-red to brownish-red colour, or sometimes yellow. **Essonite** varies in colour from yellow to brown. The **Precious Garnet**, when cut *en cabochon*, is called a **Carbuncle**. **Demantoid Garnet**—green in colour.

Guards—Long gold chains popular in the 19th century.

Gem—Any precious stone cut and polished for use as an ornament.

George—The name given to the jewel in The Order of The Garter.

Giardinetto—A jewel with flower-like ornamentation.

Gold—Pure gold is rarely used as it is too soft. It is reckoned at 24 carats, thus, if two parts of alloy are added, the standard is reduced to 22 carats and so on. The rule as to hall mark of gold is not in force with regard to very small items.

Hair Jewellery—Made from the hair of a "dear departed" or lover; chains, rings and bracelets were made of it.

Heliotrope—(*See Bloodstone.*)

Hematite—When polished is of a grey colour with red or reddish-brown streaks, much used for intaglios. It is chiefly composed of iron and oxygen.

Hiddenite—Found in North Carolina and named after its discoverer, W. E. Hidden. It resembles the emerald, being brilliant but inclining in colour towards yellowness; sometimes called "lithia emerald".

Imitation Jewellery—In this, paste stones are used instead of diamonds, and chromium plate instead of platinum.

Imitation Stones—Called "Paste" or "Strass"—used a lot in "costume jewellery".

Intaglio—A subject or design hollowed out of a gem or other substances as a seal. The opposite of cameo (*q.v.*).

Iolite—(*See Dichroite.*)

Jade—A general name given to three hard, tough, compact minerals called nephrite, jadeite and chloromelanite, composed of silica, magnesia, lime, oxide of iron, etc., chiefly found in China, New Zealand and India. Jadeite and nephrite in their rarest and purest form are pure white without a tinge of colour. Such colours as generally exist are due to the admixture of other elements, e.g., green jadeite contains chromium and green nephrite iron. Chloromelanite is naturally a very dark green mineral. Jade was largely used in China for carving into ornaments and was reverenced by Emperors and artists alike, some pieces taking several years to complete. Contrary to popular belief, green is not the only colour in which jade is found, although it is probably the most common; shades of rose, blue, brown and red-brown are by no means rare, and there is a variety known as "mutton fat". The generic name of jade is given to white jade (from China and Turkestan), green jade (New Zealand and Swiss lake dwellings), oceanic jade and jadeite (China), chloromelanite (stone celt), saussurite (Lake of Geneva), and filerolite (Morbihan).

Jaseron Chain—A fine gold neck-chain.

Jasper—The name given to inferior varieties of opaque quartz. The colours are dull and include red, green, yellow, brown, black, etc. Some specimens contain streaks of other colours and are called "ribband" or striped jasper and are used for cameos, etc. It is chiefly composed of silica with a small quantity of oxide of iron.

Jet—A black marble, bituminous coal, capable of being highly polished; became fashionable as mourning jewellery after the death of the Prince Consort.

Keeper Ring—A heavy gold ring to protect the other rings worn.

Labradorite— A felspathic mineral, some specimens of which possess a brilliant iridescent quality resembling that of a peacock's feather. Chiefly found in Labrador and Norway.

Lapidary—Relating to the art of cutting or engraving stones, not necessarily precious stones; as a lapidary ornamentation.

Lapis-Lazuli—The sapphire of the ancients. A stone varying in colour from pale azure to deep blue, often mottled with white or yellow spots; it is brittle, has little lustre and loses its polish by constant use. It is, however, employed for signet rings as well as for larger objects such as caskets, crosses, handles, etc. Found in Siberia, Turkey, China and other places. Mainly composed of silica and alumina.

Locket—A small ornamental case for holding a miniature or lock of hair, usually worn suspended by a chain from the neck.

Malachite—A green variety of copper ore which usually occurs in masses. It is, however, occasionally found in crystal form and is then worked up as gems, although specimens are rare. It is capable of being highly polished and exhibits a variegated pattern of different shades of green.

Marcasite—A mineral which is used as a substitute for diamonds and came into fashion under Louis XIV. The stones are still generally mounted in silver.

Monogram—Two or more initials interwoven, as on a seal.

Moonstone or Adularia—A translucent stone with a pleasing lustre somewhat resembling that of mother-of-pearl. It is of a grey colour and when tinted with green or red is sometimes called **Sunstone**. It is chiefly composed of silica, alumina, potash, etc.

Moroxite—A greenish-blue or bluish variety of apatite.

Morse—A clasp or brooch used to fasten a cape.

Mosaic Gold—An alloy similar to brass and pinchbeck.

Nacre—Mother-of-pearl—the beautiful iridescent substance lining certain shells.

Necklace—A string of precious stones or beads worn around the neck as an ornament.

Necklet—A short necklace.

Nef Jewel—An ornament in the form of a ship.

Negligee—A long necklace of beads, as of coral which apart from being pierced for stringing, are not otherwise prepared.

Niello—Silver inlaid with a black alloy containing lead. Tula, in Russia, was the 19th century centre for such work.

Nephrite—(*See Jade.*)

Obsidian—A black, or dark-coloured volcanic glass or fused lava; in thin pieces it is translucent. There is also a bottle-green variety.

Olivet—An imitation pearl.

Onyx—A variety of agate having its colours arranged in parallel layers; much used for making cameos.

Opal—The opal is a non-crystalline mineral, highly valued as a gem and chiefly composed of silica. It is of amorphous shape, and noted for the remarkable play of its colours. The Common Opal has a milky appearance and is of little value to the jeweller. The Semi-Opal is devoid of colour but has translucency. The Fire-Opal found in Mexico has colours resembling the red and yellow of a flame. The Precious or Noble Opal, usually called Oriental Opal, is the one so much esteemed on account of its unique colours, due to diffraction of light by the layers of the stone. The opal is found in Hungary, Central America, Mexico, Australia, etc.

Opaque—Not transparent, not reflecting light, applied to some precious stones such as turquoise.

Ouch—A brooch, clasp or other setting for precious stones; a personal ornament.

Palladium—Isolated from platinum in 1805 by Wollaston and used for jewellery mounts or rings in the same manner as platinum.

Parure—A set of jewellery or ornaments for personal adornment intended to be worn all at the same time.

Paste—A hard bright glass cut in the same way as diamonds and mounted so as to resemble them.

Pearl—A highly prized gem found in certain molluscs such as the oyster and mussel. It is a dense and shelly abnormal growth composed of nacre in thin concentric layers formed round some foreign particle. The finest pearls have a satiny-silver lustre, but some are tinted black, grey, blue, yellow or pink. They are found chiefly in the Persian Gulf, the Red Sea, the East Indies, Ceylon and Australia. **Cultured Pearls** are produced by artificially inserting a foreign particle into the shell of a living oyster. **Imitation Pearls** are made from glass beads, either solid or hollow, coated with a preparation made from fish scales.

Pectoral—An ornament worn on the breast by bishops, etc., a cross so worn.

Penannular Pin—A pin with a long head on which a shaft moves round. The pin is pushed through material and secured by a half turn.

Peridot, Peridotite or Chrysolite—The peridot was prized by the Ancients. It has a very pleasing yellowish-green colour—the darker the green the more valuable the stone. There are several varieties, including **Olivine, Dunite, Cortlandtite,** etc.

Pinchbeck—An alloy of copper and zinc invented by Christopher Pinchbeck 1670-1732. The early Pinchbeck is very beautifully worked and finished. Brooches, ear-rings, buckles, watches and fob seals were made of this material.

Piqué Work—A minute kind of inlay work, executed with gold, silver and other expensive materials; a variety now much in evidence has a groundwork of tortoiseshell in which designs are inlaid with silver and made into small articles such as trinket boxes.

Platinum—A precious metal which by itself is too soft for jewellery and is generally alloyed with 3% copper.

Pleochroism—The property possessed by some precious stones and crystals of showing different colours when viewed from different angles.

Pomander—A small decorated perforated box containing perfumes hung from the girdle.

Pyrope—(*See Garnet.*)

Quartz—A semi-precious stone of which there are many varieties e.g., Agate, Amethyst, Aventurine, Bloodstone, Carnelian Cat's Eye, Chalcedony, Chrysophase, Heliotrope, Jasper, Onyx, Sard and Sardonyx.

Repoussé Work—A French term applied to an elaborate style of embossed ornament in metals; the design has been hammered out from the back.

Rhinestone—A lead glass employed to imitate diamonds.

Rhodium—A metal discovered by Wollaston, used by jewellers to give untarnishable plating to silver jewellery.

RINGS:—

Banquet—A large and very ornate ring, too ornamental for general use, worn on ceremonial occasions.

Dearest—A ring, the initial letters of the stones used spelling the word "dearest".

Decade—An old-fashioned ring usually having ten projections in addition to the Pater Noster head, used as a rosary.

Episcopal—A ring worn by a Bishop, generally of gold set with a jewel. As they are worn over a glove they are larger than an ordinary ring.

Rings—*continued.*

Eternity—A ring where the jewels encircle the whole ring.

Fede—A ring showing two clasped hands, signifying a betrothal.

Giardinetti—A ring in which the bezel has a group of flowers worked in gold and coloured stones.

Gemmel—These were two rings so made that they formed a perfect ring when placed together.

Half Hoop—A ring with five stones which span the finger.

Jewish Betrothal or Marriage—These were large rings which were not meant to be worn but were simply used at a certain part of the Ceremonial. The little house which forms the bezel representing the Ark of The Covenant.

Keeper—A heavy gold ring with an all-over chased pattern. Was worn with wedding ring. Rarely worn nowadays.

La Semaine—A French ring having seven different stones each having the initial as that of the day of the week.

Lovers'—A ring in the form of two clasped hands.

Marquise—A ring often very large, shape being oval and curved to fit the finger. Came into fashion during the last half of the 18th century.

Memorial—A mourning ring generally of black enamel and gold.

Poison—These were of two kinds, in one the bezel contained a tiny box in which poison could be carried by those who feared torture, the other type had a small projecting pin impregnated with poison.

Puzzle—These rings are in several parts which have to be interlaced before they can be worn. They are favourites in oriental countries.

Signet—The bezel has a flat surface in which the design is worked in intaglio and used for making one's mark.

Solitaire—A ring with a single stone.

Talisman—These have figures of Saints or other Characters engraved upon them. Said to prevent the wearers from peril.

Toplady—One having six diamonds arranged in three pairs one below the other.

Wedding—Nowadays generally a plain circlet of gold or platinum, used to be engraved.

Rock Crystal—A transparent quartz, almost colourless but sometimes having tints of yellow, brown and black. It is used for seals, caskets, intaglios, etc.

Rose Diamond—A diamond cut with twenty-four triangular facets.

Ruby—The ruby was known and much valued by the ancients. It is a transparent stone of the red crystallised variety of corundum found in Burma (clear red); Ceylon (light red); Siam (dark red). It is slightly less hard than the diamond and is composed of alumina. The crystal form is six-sided prisms and pyramids.

Sapphire—A transparent stone similar in composition and hardness to the ruby, but of bright blue colour. Found in Siam, Burma, Ceylon, India and Australia. White, green, yellow and purple varieties are also known. The crystal form is double six-sided prisms and pyramids.

Sard—A brownish-red variety of cornelian, used for cameos.

Sardonyx—Layers of Sard and Onyx.

Sautoir—A very long, narrow necklace often having tassel.

Scarab—A species of beetle held in venerable regard by ancient Egyptians.

Sevigné—A breast ornament of the 17th century consisting of an openwork bow generally set with small diamonds and often enamelled.

Shell Cameos—The modern shell cameo dates from the late 16th and early 17th century and shells from the Indian Ocean, West Indies and Carribean Sea were used. Examples earlier than 1830 are rare but those between that date and 1860 are the best.

Signet—A private seal used either with or instead of a signature.

Signet Ring—A ring containing a signet.

Sphene—A transparent mineral varying in colour from pale yellow to green. Some opaque varieties exist.

Spinel—A hard transparent mineral chiefly composed of alumina and magnesia, and occurring in red, carmine, green, brown, blue and black, some of the darker colours being opaque. Spinels are found in India, Siam and Australia. The crystal form is octahedron.

Spodumene—A silicate of aluminium varying in colour from a greyish to a greenish yellow. Some varieties are transparent (found in Brazil) and others opaque.

Star Stones—Varieties of corundum which when cut in a particular way reflect a star of light from the convex surface. Sometimes called **Asterias**.

Steel Jewellery—Had a great vogue in 18th century. Often the designs were very fine and delicate, used for buttons, buckles, also necklaces and bracelets. An inferior kind of steel jewellery was introduced in 1820 by a Frenchman named Triclot.

Strass—A form of Paste invented by a man called Strass, 1758, to resemble diamonds.

Sunstone—(*See Moonstone.*)

Tang—The tongue of a buckle.

Tassie—A Scotsman in mid-18th century made excellent imitations of antique cameos and intaglios in glass, which became the fashion.

Tiara—A frontal head ornament usually made of costly metals and studded with precious stones.

Topaz—A semi-precious transparent stone varying in colour from canary yellow to a deep orange; white examples are also known. The "true topaz" possesses shades of light blue, light green, pink and straw yellow. The "false" topaz is a variety of quartz. It is found in Brazil, Egypt, Australia and America, and is chiefly composed of alumina, silicon, oxygen, fluorine, etc.

Torque—A twisted ornament worn around the neck or arms.

Tourmaline or Turmaline—The transparent varieties are used as gems and have a large range of soft colours including black (schorl); blue (indicolite); red (rubellite); pink, brown and green. There is also a rare variety which is colourless.

Turquoise—An opaque bright blue gem reputed to have been first discovered in Turkey. The Oriental turquoise of the "Old Rock" does not lose its colour and is scarce. Other varieties known as of the "New Rock" are apt to become green by exposure. The turquoise is chiefly found in Persia and New Mexico, and is composed of phosphate of aluminium with a little copper, iron and manganese oxides. Its form is amorphous.

Uvarovite or Uwarowite—(*See Garnet.*)

Vinaigrette—A small box usually made of gold or silver with a pierced interior lid, containing a sponge steeped in aromatic vinegar.

Wedgwood—Made pottery medallions of all sizes; some were made for setting in rings or clasps.

Zircon—A transparent mineral used as a gem, the colours possessing more lustre than those of the tourmaline; they vary and are red or brown (hyacinth); pale yellow, colourless and smoky varieties (jargoon); Zircon is composed of silica and zinconia, and is found in India and Australia.

FABRICS, CARPETS, etc.

Accordion Pleated—Material pressed into pleats in such a way as to resemble the folds in the bellows of an accordion.

Afghanistan Carpet—One of the most popular today, because of its relative cheapness. Its red colour blends with practically everything. Design is large and small octagons.

Alençon Lace—A French point lace made in the 17th century, with a ground of small mesh of hexagonal brides or network. It was made in small pieces invisibly stitched together and strengthened on the edges with horsehair.

Alpaca—A thin cloth made from the woolly hair of the alpaca (a kind of llama), often mixed with silk or cotton.

Argentan Point—A fine lace made at Argentan in Normandy.

Arras—The name given to a tapestry of loose texture with interwoven figures, made in the town of Arras. A curtain made of such tapestry.

Aubusson—Tapestry and carpets made by hand of fine materials and in elegant designs at Aubusson in France.

Axminster Carpet—Thomas Whitty commenced making carpets at Axminster in 1755; the factory closed in 1835 and moved to Wilton. Axminster is the name given to machine tufted carpets. The process was patented and consisted of inter-weaving coloured pile wools with triple chenille weft threads, or by interweaving with the strong weft threads on a strong jute backing, short pieces of coloured wool to form the pattern.

Baize—(*See Felt.*)

Baluchistan Rug—Made by nomads on Persian borders, colours red, blue, beige or brown. Design varied octagon, diamond and spider.

Batiste—A fine cotton muslin, or material of a similar texture; the name was originally given to linen cambric or lawn.

Beauvais Carpet—A knotted pile carpet made at the end of the 18th century.

Beauvais Tapestry—An old French tapestry (from about 1664) in the manufacture of which the warp threads were placed horizontally, the design being worked in from the top; during the early 18th century the weaving was of a very fine texture.

Beaver Cloth—A heavy woollen cloth used for making overcoats, etc., one side being shorn smooth.

Blond or **Blonde Lace**—A variety of silk lace.

Bobbinet—A fine machine-made lace or netting, having a nearly hexagonal mesh.

Bobbin Lace or **Bone Lace**—Lace made on a pillow with bobbins instead of needles. The bobbins were often made of bone, hence the name "bone lace".

Bokhara Rug—Made by nomads in Southern Turkestan. Colours reddish-brown ground with dark patterns in blue or yellow. Design oblong octagons.

Bombast—A kind of fustian (*q.v.*); a wadding or padding of soft material.

Bough Pot—The bouquet or vase of flowers which often forms the central design in tapestry and other materials used for upholstery; it also appears in marquetry work, wallpapers, curtains, etc.

Bride—A loop, bar or tie in lace or needlework; also a bonnet string.

Brocade—A silken fabric on which the design is formed by projecting gold and silver threads; the word has much the same application to silk textures that damask has to linen textures. A material with a raised design. Now often of man-made fibre.

Broidery—(*See Embroidery.*)

Brussels Carpet—A carpet made of coloured worsted yarns, which form the design and are woven in loops on a foundation; the pattern is traceable from the back. It is usually three-quarters of a yard (27 inches) wide with from 220 to 260 loops in a pick or line. (*See Imperial Brussels.*)

Brussels Lace—Consists of both needle-point and pillow lace, made in several varieties; is of fine quality and costly. **Brussels Tapestry** was made in mural panels during the 15th and 16th centuries; it was the leading centre of tapestry making.

Buckingham Lace—Old pillow lace made at Buckingham.

Buckram—A coarse kind of canvas stiffened with gum; used amongst other things for backing curtain pelmets.

Buckskin—A soft yellowish leather made from deer and sheepskins.

Bullion Fringe—A fringe made up of gold or silver threads, often in Cannetille (*q.v.*) form, sometimes used to decorate furniture coverings, cushions, etc. **Bullion**—Unrefined precious metal.

Caffoy—An 18th-century fabric used for state-room hangings.

Calico—A plain white cotton cloth which originated at Calicut in India, made by interweaving warp and weft threads of equal thickness and weight.

Cambric—A fine, almost sheer, cloth of linen or cotton. Black Cambric is used for tacking under upholstered furniture.

Camlet—Originally an oriental material made of camel's hair, now chiefly of wool and goat's hair. In use since the 14th century. It was styled camelot by the French.

Campaine—A narrow pillow lace made in France and used for edging.

Cannetille—A spirally twisted thread of gold or silver used in embroidery, etc.

Carnival Lace—A variety of 16th-century lace made in France Italy and Spain; the designs represent coats of arms, initials of persons, etc.

Carpets—It is reputed that carpets were first introduced into England during the reign of Edward I by his wife, Eleanor of Castille.

Carrickmacross Lace—The name given to two varieties of lace made at Carrickmacross in Co. Monaghan, one a kind of cambric appliqué and the other a guipure (*q.v.*).

Casement Cloth—A lightweight plain woven fabric, usually cotton.

Cashmere—A soft, silky cloth with a diagonal weave made in India from the wool (not hair) of the Cashmere goat, used for making shawls, scarves, etc., some of which are richly embroidered. There is also a variety of dress fabric known as cashmere, made of wool or wool and cotton, to imitate the original cashmere.

Caterpillar-Point Lace—A needle-made lace popular in Italy during the 17th century, so called because the curls in its design resembled caterpillars in motion.

Chain Stitch—An embroidery stitch resembling a chain.

Chantilly Lace—A delicate French blond-lace, often with a floral pattern in black.

Chenille—A soft tufted material of silk or worsted, much used for table covers, curtains, carpets, etc.; so called from its resemblance to a caterpillar. **Chenille-Embroidery**, popular in France in the 18th century; it was worked either on the surface or by drawing the threads through rough canvas.

Chintz—A fine calico or cambric material with a pattern printed on one side, highly glazed or calendered; used for loose covers on furniture, curtains, etc. Very fine closely woven plain fabrics similarly glazed or semi-glazed are called percales.

Cinq-Trou—A mesh employed in lace-making, where large alternate openings are set in quincunx (*q.v.*).

Cloth of Gold—A costly 14th-century fabric woven of threads of gold with linen, silk or cotton, or wholly of thin wire or strips of gold. Used for vestments, etc.

Cluny Lace—A net lace on which the designs were darned on to a square net background.

Coach Lace—A hand-woven trimming for finishing off the upholstery of carriages.

Coconut Matting—A matting for use as a floor covering, made from the prepared fibre of coconuts. (*See Coir.*)

Coir—The prepared fibre from the husk of coconuts, used for making matting, cordage, etc.; these articles so made.

Cordonnet—A small cord or thread used in making tassels, fringes. etc., and in the edging of point lace.

Cordovan Embroidery—An appliqué in which American cloth is cut in patterns and applied to coarse canvas by means of crewel-work stitches.

Corduroy—A velvet or velveteen with a ribbed surface, made of silk or cotton.

Couching—A method of embroidery in which the thread is laid on the surface of the material and secured by fine stitches.

Counterlined or **Interlined**—A term used in describing heavy curtains, etc., with an inner lining or padding.

Counterpane—A coverlet for a bed.

Couronne—A small ornamental loop added to the cordonnet (*q.v.*) in lace making.

Coutil or **Coutille**—A close-woven fabric used for mattress covers, etc.

Crash—A coarse heavy linen cloth, used for towels and loose covers.

Crêpe—A crinkled material made from raw silk; black crêpe is used for mourning.

Crêpe-de-Chine—A variety of fine silk crêpe.

Cretonne—A strong cotton cloth usually printed on one side with coloured patterns, largely used for furniture coverings, curtains, etc.

Crewel Work—A species of fancy work much in vogue during Stuart and Jacobean days, when it was used for the draperies of tester bedsteads and curtains. It consists of embroidering with coloured wools and silks on a background of coarse canvas, linen or diagonal sheeting. **Crewel**—A twisted yarn.

Crochet—A fancy work which may be described as an extensive system of looping by means of cotton and hooks made for the purpose.

Cross Stitch Embroidery—The stitch is a double one, made by crossing two stitches at right angles. Materials with designs so worked in silk, wool, cotton and gold or silver threads are used to cover chair seats, stool tops, kneelers, hassocks, etc., some rugs are made in cross-stitch by hand.

Cushion-stitch—A short straight stitch used to fill in backgrounds, and on coarse canvas to represent weaving.

Dagastan Rug—Dagastan or Derbend rugs are from North East Caucasus. The ground is usually red or blue with geometrical design ; resemble the Shirvan carpet but are coarser.

Dalecarlian Lace—A lace made by the Swedish peasantry.

Damask—A linen, cotton, wool or silk fabric in which designs of flowers, fruit or figures (excluding small designs of geometrical regularity, which are called diaper, q.v.) are produced by differences of weaving. The material is not necessarily self-coloured, the design sometimes being given a contrasting ground. It was originally made at Damascus from which town it derives its name, and was known in the early 14th century.

Damassin—A damask cloth interwoven with flowers of gold or silver threads.

Danish Embroidery—Consists of part lace and part embroidery worked in white on thin material.

Dhurrie or **Dhurry**—An Indian coarse rug or carpet used as a sofa cover or hanging.

Diaper—In textile manufactures the term is applied to white linen fabrics with simple patterns of geometrical regularity; in appearance it somewhat resembles damask.

Dimity—A stout white cotton fabric, the figures or stripes of which are raised on one side and depressed on the other, chiefly used for bed drapery.

Donegal Carpet—A heavy knotted carpet made by hand in Ireland. The industry was organised by Alexander Morton at the request of the Congested Districts Board in 1898.

Dossal—A rich ornamental hanging placed at the back of a throne, altar, etc., or on walls.

Drawn-thread Work—Needlework in which some of the threads of the materials to be ornamented are drawn out to form an openwork pattern.

Drugget—Originally a coarse linen fabric with woven designs somewhat resembling damask (*q.v.*), later made of cotton and jute; chiefly used as a floor covering and for the protection of fine carpets. It was at one time also in demand for some articles of clothing.

Embroidery—The art of embellishing fabrics with needlework designs; some patterns are formed by cutting holes of different shapes and binding them, as in a button hole. Many different stitches are used, such as cross stitch, solid stitch, basket stitch, stalk stitch, etc.

Escalier Lace—With patterns formed by the filling in of the squares of the net groundwork.

Fagoting—Embroidery work in which horizontal threads are drawn out and the remaining vertical threads tied together in bunches. **Fagot Stitch**—A fancy stitch resembling fagot work.

Feather-stitch—A filling-in stitch much used in embroidery. Also a zig-zag border stitch.

Felt—A material made by pressing hair and wool together, their natural tendency being to cling to each other. Baize is sometimes mistaken for felt; it is, however, woven, whereas felt is not.

Ferret-ribbon—A strong tape used for lacing.

Fimbria—A fringe for a piece of cloth. **Fimbriatus**—fringed clothing.

Flemish Lace—Made on a pillow and known for its large variety of groundwork. **Flemish Point Lace**—A guipure (*q.v.*) lace with no work in relief.

Folk Weave—A fabric loosely woven, having a coarse rough surface, used for loose covers and curtains.

Frieze—A coarse woollen cloth with a nap on one side.

Fringe—An ornamental border to material consisting of loose threads, sometimes of the material itself.

Fustian—A coarse fabric having a linen warp and a thick twilled cotton weft which forms a low pile on one side. It has been known since the 13th century and was first produced at Fustat (Cairo) and used by the Cistercian Abbots, and also by peasantry on account of its hard wearing qualities. It is now chiefly used for pillow and mattress covers.

Galloon—An ornamental edging to curtains and upholstery, being a thick ribbon or braid of gold, silver, etc.; frequently found on 18th-century furniture.

Gauze Point Lace—A Brussels lace of modern manufacture in which braid is applied in patterns to a machine-made net background.

Genoa Point Lace—A fine lace made during the 17th century; some examples are of gold and silver threads.

Georgette—A lightweight, semi-transparent silk crêpe.

Ghiordes Carpets—One of the most valuable of Turkish carpets, generally fine, tightly knotted and close clipped. Prayer rugs are the most common, the prayer niche is generally of one colour.

Gimp—A braid usually formed of a series of flat hairpin-like loops, used for finishing off the upholstery of furniture, etc.

Gingham—A cotton material usually in stripes or checks of two colours, the yarn of which is dyed before being woven. Sometimes used for covering umbrellas, hence the slang name of "gingham" for an umbrella.

Gobelin Tapestry—An old French tapestry in which the warp threads were arranged vertically and the designs worked in from the back, making it unnecessary to cut off the ends of the wool and silk threads on the upper surface as in Beauvais tapestry. Established in 1662.

Grenadine—A light dress material made of silk or of a mixture of silk and wool.

Grogram—A coarse material made of silk and mohair, often stiffened with gum.

Gros-Point—A diagonal stitch used in needlecraft, popular from the days of Elizabeth to those of Anne; largely used on the coverings of chair seats, handbags, samplers, etc., and also as a background work where petit-point (*q.v.*) was employed.

Guipure—A heavy lace both in design and material, the pattern being held together by bars.

Hair Carpet—A carpet composed of hair and yarn, woven in loops and similar in appearance to Brussels, but usually finished in self colours.

Hemp—A fibre obtained from Asiatic plants, used to make cordage, cloth, matting, etc.

Hemstitch—A kind of stitch used in fancywork, particularly for forming a fancy hem or border in which some of the threads have been drawn.

Hessian—A coarse sacking cloth, used for upholstery and for lining the bottoms of chairs, etc.

High-warp (Haute-lisse)—Tapestry looms in which the cylinders are placed vertically.

Hide—A leather made from the dressed skin of the larger animals.

Holland—An unbleached linen cloth; when glazed it is used for window blinds.

Horsehair—A furniture-covering woven from the hair of horses, introduced by Hepplewhite and almost universally used in the Victorian era; loose horsehair is used as a stuffing for mattresses and upholstery.

Huckaback—A strong material of linen or cotton with an uneven surface, sometimes with damask-like figurings, much used for towels. Its rough surface is produced by alternately crossing the weft threads.

Imperial Axminster—A name given to a superior Axminster carpet having about 48 tufts to the square inch as opposed to the usual 30 tufts.

Imperial Brussels—A carpet resembling ordinary Brussels (*q.v.*) except that the looped thread forming the design are cut off so as to form a pile.

India Matting—A woven grass matting made in India.

Insertion—A narrow strip of lace or other material with straight edges "inserted" or let into some other plain material to ornament it.

Jaspé Velours—A term used to describe velvet coverings, etc., of marbled design.

Jean—A twilled cotton cloth.

Kashan Carpet—One of the finest of Persian carpets. Designs are finely wrought medallion, tree, niche and figure subjects and all over floral designs. Colours red, blue or beige.

Kerman Carpet—The most refined carpets produced in Persia. Designs are tree, animal, and figures, medallion and rose patterns. Colours red, blue, pink or beige.

Kidderminster Carpet—A cheap ingrained, two- or three-ply carpet made at Kidderminster; its pattern is formed by the interchange of the plys with the consequent intermingling of their colours.

Kincob—An Indian brocade made of silk and cotton interwoven with gold or silver threads or both.

Kouba Rug—A Caucasian rug, ground is usually ivory, dark blue or dark red.

Kulah Rug—A Turkish rug closely resembling the Ghiordes (*q.v.*) but is coarser and of thicker yarn.

Lacet—An openwork fabric made up with braid and worked into designs with the aid of crochet or lace stitches.

Laid Embroidery—A gimped embroidery in which gold, silver or silken threads are used over a design cut out in parchment.

Lawn—A fine linen material with a rather open texture, used for episcopal robes, etc.

Leatherette—Imitation leather used in upholstery.

Leviathan Canvas—A coarse open canvas used for fancy-work with wool, etc., as for samplers. **Leviathan Stitch**—An elaboration of the cross stitch used on leviathan canvas. **Leviathan Wool**— A soft multi-stranded wool used as above.

Limerick Lace—A variety of appliqué lace made at Limerick.

Linen—A plain woven fabric made of flax and rarely of hemp, formed by interweaving warp and weft threads of equal weight and thickness in regular sequence. It is sometimes woven as twill (*q.v.*) also as cambric and calico. Used largely for household purposes. Fine or sheer linen as used for handkerchiefs, church vestments, etc., is known as lawn (*q.v.*).

Low-warp (Basse-lisse)—Tapestry looms in which the cylinders are placed horizontally, and are parallel to the ground, as in Aubusson tapestry.

Macramé Work—A species of fancy work made of string or cord, usually in the form of fringes, sometimes decorated with glass beads or small pieces of cane.

Matelassé—Material which has its surface marked by depressed lines forming squares or other geometric designs; a kind of quilting effect.

Mechlin Lace, sometimes called **Malines**—A costly pillow lace made near Brussels. It is delicate and transparent and is distinguished by the flat threads forming the designs.

Mihrab—A prayer niche in the design of a rug with a pointed arch. The Mohammedan, when praying, places some dried earth from Mecca in the corner of the mihrab and kneels so that his head touches the earth.

Mirzapore Carpet—A cheap quality of Indian carpet made for selling in England; is coarse and often of poor material.

Mohair—A fine, soft silky wool obtained from the Angora goat, used for making rugs, table covers, curtains, etc.

Moiré—A French word applied to silk material figured with waved lines, and made by the process known as "watering"; of watered or clouded appearance. **Moiré Antique**—Silk watered to resemble the stuffs worn in ancient times.

Moorfield Carpets—Thomas Moore of Moorfields made hand-woven carpets for Adam, the designer.

Moquette—A fine pile material largely used for furniture coverings and the like. Made of wool or cotton.

Moreen or **Morine**—A woollen material (later mixed with cotton) used by 17th- and 18th-century upholsterers.

Morocco Leather—A leather made from goat skins; an imitation is made from sheepskin.

Mortlake Tapestry—The Mortlake factory, said to be the first in England, for making silk tapestry was established about 1619 by James I, Sir Francis Crane directing.

Mull—A soft muslin.

Muslin—A thin, fine, soft cotton cloth originally made at Mosul.

Nankeen—A brownish yellow cloth originally made in China.

Nap—The fine surface or pile running in one direction, as of cloth, carpets, etc.

Napery—Household linen, especially table linen.

Napkin—A hand-cloth used at table.

Needlepoint Lace—Made entirely with the needle, as distinct from pillow lace in which bobbins were employed.

Numdah—The name given to Indian rugs and mats with needlework designs worked on white blanket-like material.

Nylon and **Terylene** are man-made fibres. Nylon was announced in 1938, followed later by Terylene, Orlon and Acrilan; produced under many differing trade names.

    Acrilan: An Acrylic plastic used for blankets, it is mothproof warm and porous and can be washed. It does not shrink or mat.

    Melamine Formaldehyde: Can be used as a surface treatment for fabrics.

    Nylon: As a material of elastic fibres it can be used for reinforcing other materials such as carpets; also used for curtains, laces, velvet, etc.

    Polyvinyl Chloride [P.V.C.]: Is used by itself for floor tiles and linoleum but is also used as a coating to make materials waterproof, e.g., kitchen and bathroom curtains—tablecloths.

Terylene [Polyethyleneterephthallate]: Terylene used as a curtain material, does not rot in sunlight.

Oriental Carpets and Rugs: The following very brief notes on oriental carpets may be helpful:—

Persian designs are generally of a floral pattern with flowing lines and curves, and have a very short pile.

Chinese designs are generally the same symbols as found in Chinese porcelain, often the pile is clipped round the design.

Turkish designs are a combination of floral and geometrical.

Caucasian designs are geometrical and angular, the scorpion and crab are popular designs; as a rule, has a long pile.

Ghileem Rugs are fadeless and are the same on both sides.

Sumakh Rug is not knotted and is also pileless, the loose threads are left hanging at the back.

Turkoman designs are geometrical; the ground is generally of a deep red colour, with black or dark blue and ivory patterns.

Orphery—An elaborate embroidery of gold and silver.

Orris—The name given to practically any kind of gold or silver lace or braid.

Percale—A kind of chintz (*q.v.*).

Petit-Point—An embroidery dating from Tudor times, fashionable in the days of William and Mary and Queen Anne; used for the coverings of chairs, etc.; consists of a slanting stitch across a single thread of canvas; sometimes called **Tent Stitch.**

Picot—One of the small edging loops on lace or in needlework.

Pile—The thick nap (*q.v.*) as of carpets, velvet, etc.

Pile-upon-Pile Velvet—A variety of velvet in which the design is composed of longer pile, this being relieved on the shorter pile groundwork.

Pinking—A method of decorating the edges of fabrics, etc., with serrations. **Pink**—To stab or pierce.

Piqué—A form of quilting; a ribbed material in which the pattern consists of raised rows and depressions.

Plush—A textile fabric made of silk or cotton, or a mixture of them with a nap that is longer and softer than velvet, which it somewhat resembles.

Point Lace—A lace wrought entirely with the needle. **Point Appliqué**—A "point lace" design attached to a net groundwork which is often machine made.

Poplin—A corded fabric, chiefly made in Ireland, of silk and worsted, in which the weft threads are thicker than the warp, thus giving a ribbed appearance across the fabric; largely used for dresses, casement curtains, etc.

Prayer Rugs—These are small, easily portable rugs; distinguished by its Mihrab (*q.v.*) the prayer niche.

Quilting—The name given to a method of stitching layers of material together, usually with some soft thick material between, as down in making quilts.

Reefing—A term applied to materials when festooned, as in reefing a sail.

Regency Point—A pillow lace made in Bedfordshire during the Regency Period.

Rep or **Repp**—A fabric with alternating thick and thin warp and weft threads, giving a close corded finish; much used for curtains and upholstery.

Réseau—A term used in lacemaking for the ground or foundation when formed of a regular net-like mesh.

Reticella—A kind of lace made on a frame, the threads being interlaced with a needle to form the patterns. **Reticle**—A system of wires or threads; a small net.

Rouleau—A small roll; or as applied to fabrics, a piping.

Ruche—A frill or short frieze of silk or cotton used as an edging in upholstery.

Saddle Bag—A pile furniture covering in the form of squares, supposed to represent the bags carried by Persian horsemen.

Samite—A heavy silk fabric interwoven with gold, etc., used for upholstery, particularly in the Middle Ages; a cushion of this material.

Sampler—Ornamental embroidery, worsted work, etc., containing names, figures, texts and the like; worked generally by young girls, from the 17th to the 19th centuries.

Sateen—A cotton material having a glossy surface resembling that of satin.

Satin—A silk material with a smooth, glossy finish.

Savonnerie—Knotted pile carpets made from 1627 in the old soap works on the Quai de Chaillot, Paris, called The Savonnerie. The workshop was amalgamated with the Gobelins in 1825.

Scallop—One of a series of small curves imitating the edge of a scallop shell, used as an ornamental edging for materials.

Scrim or **Scrimp**—A light coarse canvas made of linen or cotton, used for embroidery work.

Selvage or **Selvedge**—The woven edge of a fabric, made to prevent fraying; it sometimes bears the weaver's mark.

Shetland Lace—A knitted woollen lace made in the Shetland Isles.

Shirvan Rug—A Caucasian rug, tightly knotted with practically no pile. The pattern is of triangles, hooks and stars in many colours.

Silk—A strong, fine lustrous fibre produced by silkworms. The Chinese were the first to use silk for textiles; it was introduced into Europe in the 6th century, and into England in the 15th century.

Silk [Artificial], Rayon—Is made from threads of cellulose, obtained by pressing a solution of cellulose acetate in acetone through fine holes. Cellulose is the structural tissue forming the cell-walls of plants and is pulped before use.

Silk Damask—(*See Damask.*)

Sisal—A particular kind of hemp grown at Sisal, in tropical climates; it is strong and durable.

Skein—A quantity of yarn, wool, thread or the like when twisted into a hank.

Smyrna Carpets—Smyrna carpets are Turkey carpets with a deep pile, made for export to Europe.

Soho Tapestry—A tapestry made at Soho in London in the 17th century.

Sparta Carpet—A Turkish carpet with a deep pile, generally imitating the Persian design.

Tabaret or **Taberray**—A heavy silk fabric with satin stripes, used for upholstery.

Tabinet—A material resembling fine damask or poplin, made of a mixture of silk and wool, at one time largely used for curtains and upholstery.

Taffeta or **Taffety**—The name given to materials of silk or wool having a lustre, and in which raised spots often appear in regular formation, much used for upholstery, curtains, dresses, etc. Now of man-made materials.

Tambour Stitch—A stitch used in crochet work.

Tapestry—Tapestry has been defined as painting by weaving. The art of making tapestry is an ancient one and was originally carried out by hand, the weaving being based on warp threads

Tapestry—*continued.*

strung vertically as in a loom, the tapisier interpreting the designs or cartoons by interweaving the coloured weft threads, thus building up and producing the picture as in painting. It is probable that the best and most famous tapestry was produced during the second half of the fifteenth, and the first half of the sixteenth centuries in the form of mural panels and coverings for furniture. The designs were at first comparatively simple but later the mural panels developed into elaborate pictures of historical and other scenes. The making of tapestry flourished in France until it was disturbed by the Hundred Years War (1337-1453) and afterwards in Flanders. The names of some of the better known tapestries are Flemish, Gobelins, Beauvais, Aubusson and Mortlake. Tapestry was first made in England at Mortlake early in the 17th century and individual artists also made their tapestries at Windsor, Merton, Hatton Garden and other places. Modern tapestry is a worsted material made by machinery.

Tapestry Carpet—A cheap Brussels carpet, woven in loops, usually of one colour, the design being afterwards printed on and consequently not visible from the back.

Tapis—A heavy woollen tapestry-like material used for curtains, etc.

Tarpaulin—A large sheet or cloth coated with tar to render it waterproof, used as a temporary covering for ricks, wagons, etc.

Tartan—A checkered wool material worn by Scottish clans, each clan having its own distinctive design.

Tatting—Fancy work popular in Victorian times, consisting of a knotted lace made from cotton or linen threads with hand spindles.

Tent Stitch—A stitch used in embroidery and woolwork, the stitches being placed diagonally and parallel. (*See Petit Point.*)

Ticking—A strong closely woven fabric, usually striped, from which ticks or cases are made to contain the wool, etc., of mattresses. **Tick**—The cover or case of a mattress.

Ticking Work—Embroidery work on ticking.

Tow—The coarse residue of flax after passing through the carding machine.

Turkey Work—Is an English imitation of the carpets woven with a knotted pile in the Middle East, either woven or knotted on canvas.

Twill—A linen or cotton fabric with a diagonal ribbed finish, produced by passing the weft threads over one and under more than one of the warp threads, instead of over and under alternating single threads.

Valenciennes Lace—A fine bobbin lace made in France and Belgium, the pattern being worked into a net foundation.

Velvet—A woven silk fabric with a cut pile on one side; when cotton is mixed it is called "velveteen".

Venetian Embroidery—A variety of work in which the designs are cut out of linen, net, etc., and finished with buttonhole and other lace stitches.

Venetian Flat Point Lace—A needle-point lace which presents a generally flat appearance, having no prominent raised work. Delicate designs are usually employed.

Verdure—A term sometimes applied to tapestry when the design is chiefly composed of green foliage.

Warp—A term used in weaving to denote the length-wise threads first laid down.

Weft or Woof—In weaving is the name given to the threads carried by the shuttle, which are passed backwards and forwards through the warp, or from selvage to selvage.

Wilton Carpet—A carpet with a velvet pile, so called because it was first made at Wilton. Like the Brussels it is woven in loops, which, however, are afterwards cut, thus forming a pile. Wilton carpet has between 50 to 150 tufts per square inch according to the quality.

COINS

[NUMISMATICS—The science of coins and medals]

NOTE:—Where values are given below, these, of course, are not the present values, but at the time of issue.

Abbey Counter—A medal or disc stamped with sacred emblems, given to pilgrims in olden times.

Accolated Coin—A word sometimes used to describe coins on which there are two heads overlapping. (*See Jugata.*)

Agnel—A French gold coin of Louis IX reign, bearing the figure of a lamb.

Alliance Coin—A coin struck by a number of independent states but bearing a common symbol or device to show an alliance. Fairly common in Ancient Greece.

Angel—A gold coin introduced by Edward IV in 1465 and issued during successive reigns up to and including that of James I (1603-1625). It bore no date, but on the obverse depicted the Archangel Michael with wings and a nimbus, spearing a dragon and the inscription HENRICVS. DI. GRA. REX. ANGL. Z. FRANCIE, and on the reverse a ship, the arms of England and France surmounted by a cross and the inscription PER. CRVSE. TVA. SALVA. NOS. XPE. REDET. The quarter-angel was introduced during the reign of Henry VIII (1509-1547).

Angelet—A half-angel. (*See Angel.*)

Angel Gold—Gold pieces presented by English monarchs to persons whom they touched to cure the "king's evil". (*See Touch Piece.*)

Angelot—A French gold coin of the reign of Louis XI; also a gold piece struck in Paris by Henry VI.

Anna—An Indian coin, the sixteenth part of a rupee; equal to one penny.

Argento—An early 14th-century silver coin struck by Clement V.

As—A Roman bronze coin.

Assarion—A Roman copper coin, so called by the Greeks.

Augustal—An Italian gold coin struck in the 13th century and during the reign of Emperor Frederick II.

Aureus—A Roman gold coin which was decreased in weight under successive rulers.

Bagattino—An old Venetian bronze coin worth less than a farthing.

Bahadry—An old Italian coin sometimes called a "pagoda" from the design it bore.

Baiocco—A Papal coin worth something less than a half-penny.

Baiochetto—A small Italian coin of the 16th century.

Balboa—A silver coin issued in Panama, about equal in value to an American dollar.

Barbaric Coin—A crude copy of established coinages struck by primitive tribes.

Bath Metal—A mixture of silver, brass, copper and spelter invented by William Wood and used for certain coinage. (*See Rosa Americana.*)

Batz—A small coin composed of copper and silver, having the image of a bear, once current in Germany and Switzerland; also a Swiss nickel coin value about one penny.

Bawbee—A billon coin first issued in Scotland by James V (1514-1542) worth three halfpence. On the obverse is the crowned head of a thistle and the inscription ICOBVS. D. G. REX. SCOTORVM, and on the reverse a St. Andrew's cross with a crown and fleur-de-lys and the inscription OPPIDVM. EDINBVRGI. A half-bawbee was also issued.

Bell Dollar—A silver coin struck in Germany in 1643, with a bell represented on both sides.

Bezant—A gold coin issued in Constantinople, circulated in Europe from the 6th to the 15th centuries; also a silver coin (the "white" bezant).

Billon—An alloy of silver and copper; silver with more than its weight of copper; used extensively by the Roman mint at Alexandria and has been used for making Scottish coins.

Billon-Lion—(*See Lion.*)

Blanc—A French silver coin used in the time of Henry VI.

Bodle—A copper coin worth twopence, issued in Scotland by Charles I (1625-1649).

Bolivar—A silver coin in circulation in Venezuela.

Boliviano—A silver coin issued in Bolivia.

Bonnet Penny—A silver penny of William II's reign (1087-1100) depicting on the obverse a head with full face wearing a "bonnet" crown together with the inscription PILLEMVS REX, and on the reverse a cross within a circle formed by the inscription of a particular moneyer.

Bonnet Piece— or **Ducat** (*q.v.*)—A gold coin issued during the reign of James V of Scotland (1514-1542), value about fourteen shillings, so named because the king is featured wearing a bonnet.

Breeches Money—The name given to certain coins issued during the Commonwealth (1649-1660) owing to the arrangement of two shields appearing on the reverse. The gold and larger silver pieces have on the obverse a shield with the cross of St. George and branches of laurel and palm, and the inscription THE COMMONWEALTH OF ENGLAND; on the reverse, two shields placed side by side, with the cross of St. George and the Irish Harp, and the inscription GOD WITH US.

Britannia—First appeared on the copper coins of Great Britain during the reign of Charles II (1660-1685).

British Dollar—A silver coin struck in 1895 at Bombay for use in certain British colonies, having on the obverse a figure of Britannia and on the reverse the value in Chinese and Malay characters.

Broad—An English gold coin of the Stuart and Commonwealth periods, value almost twenty shillings. (*See Unite.*)

Brockage—A coin imperfectly struck.

Bronze—The British standard for coinage is 95½ parts of copper, 3 parts of tin and 1½ parts of zinc.

Cardecue—An old French silver coin; a quarter of a crown.

Carlino—Italian gold or silver coins first introduced in 1287.

Carolin—A gold coin issued in Germany in 1732, worth a little over one pound; also a Swedish gold coin.

Carolus—An English gold coin of the reign of Charles I, worth twenty shillings.

Cash—A coin of small value used in India and China; the Chinese cash has a hole in the centre.

Castillon—A Spanish gold coin bearing the arms of Castile.

Cavallo—An old French copper coin.

Cavallotto—A 15th-century silver coin used in Italy and Switzerland, bearing the figure of a horse on the reverse.

Cent—A coin representing a one-hundredth part of an American dollar or a Dutch guilder.

Centesimo—The hundredth part of an Italian lira or a Spanish peseta.

Centime—The hundredth part of a French, Swiss or Belgian franc.

Chaise d'or—A large gold coin issued in France in the 14th century.

Christiana—A 17th-century silver coin issued in Sweden, worth about 7d.

Cinquina—An Italian coin of the 16th century.

Clementino—An old Italian silver coin.

Contorniate—Having a furrow round its edge like a coin or medal; a Roman bronze piece issued in the 4th century, not as a coin but a token in connection with the public games.

Copeck or **Kopeck**—A Russian copper coin worth about one-third of a penny.

Counter Mark—An additional mark or surcharge stamped on a coin to increase or alter its value or for greater security.

Crown—A gold crown and half-crown were first issued during the reign of Henry VIII (1509-1547). The silver crown and half-crown were first issued by Edward VI (1547-1553) and have continued in use ever since.

Crusade or **Crusado**—A Portuguese gold coin of various values; it bears the figure of a cross.

Couronne—A French gold coin used in the first half of the 14th century.

Daric—An ancient gold coin of Persia, having an archer depicted on one of its sides; also a silver coin named after Darius I.

Decadrachm—An ancient Greek silver coin.

Décime—A French coin value one-tenth of a franc.

Denarius—A Roman silver coin, first issued under the Republic and continuing in use in the Empire until the third century A.D. The Denarius is a 25th part of the gold Aureus (*q.v.*).

Demy—(*See Lion.*)

Denier—A silver coin struck in French towns and provinces when under the control of English sovereigns. (*See Mouton.*)

Device—An emblematic design, usually with a motto or legend.

Didrachma—A Greek silver coin; a double drachma, issued in two standards.

Dime—A silver coin in use in the U.S.A., value ten cents.

Dinar or **Dinara**—The name given to several old Oriental coins in use by the Arabs and Persians.

Dobra—A gold coin issued in Portugal in the 18th century.

Doit—A small copper coin once used in Holland and its Dependencies.

Dollar—More commonly in use in North America, Canada, and the U.S.A., but a unit used in other parts of the world. American dollars have been struck in silver and gold; the present dollar is a silver piece.

Dolphins—Bronze coins struck in the shape of dolphins at Olbia on the Black Sea in Classical times.

Doppia—An old Italian gold coin.

Double—A copper coin issued in the Channel Islands by William IV (1830-1837). Eight-, Four- and Two-double pieces were later issued.

Double Cent—A coin once issued in the United States.

Double-Crown—An English gold piece issued during the reigns of James I and Charles I, value about ten shillings.

Double Ducat—A gold coin formerly used in several European countries.

Double Ducatoon—A silver coin issued in Italy.

Double-Eagle—A gold coin of the U.S.A. worth 20 dollars.

Doubloon—A Spanish gold coin.

Drachm—An ancient Greek silver coin, weighing one drachm and being worth six obols.

Drake—An Elizabethan shilling bearing as a mint mark a martlet, which was mistaken for a drake.

Ducat—The ducat was current in several European countries at various times and was first coined in Venice in 1284. A gold ducat, worth forty-shillings, was issued in Scotland by James V (1514-1542). It was made from native gold and was the first Scottish coin to bear a date. On the obverse, a bearded bust of the king in profile wearing a broad bonnet, with the inscription ICOBVS. 5. DEI. G. R. SCOTRV and the date figures. On the reverse, a crowned shield containing the lion rampant, with the inscription HONOR. REGIS. IVDICIVM. DILIGIT. Two-thirds and one-third ducats were also issued. The ducat was issued by other Scottish sovereigns, when the value was increased.

Ducatoon—A silver coin at one time in circulation in Italy and Holland, worth between four and five shillings.

Dupondius—An old Roman copper coin, value two asses.

Ecclesiastical Mints—Until the reign of Henry VIII (1509-1547) certain high dignitaries of the church had the right to coin money and to retain the profits so derived. The coins were similar to those issued by the realm but were distinguished by mint and other marks.

Ecu—The name given to various gold and silver coins having different values, issued in France during the 17th and 18th centuries.

Edward Shovelboard—A shilling current in the reign of Edward VI, so named from its use in playing shovelboard.

Eight, Piece of—The name given to an old Spanish dollar owing to its being equal in value to eight reals (about four shillings).

Eight-Shilling Piece—(*See Merk.*)

Electrum—An amber-coloured alloy of gold and silver formerly used for making coins.

Exergue—The small space beneath the base line or design of a coin in which the date figures, etc., are usually placed.

Fanam—Small Indian gold and silver coins, worth between two and three pence.

Farthing—The smallest British bronze coin, worth one-fourth of a penny. Production ceased 1956.

Field—The area or surface of a coin.

Fippenny Bit—A Spanish silver coin equal to a half-real.

Florin—A coin issued in several countries. A Florentine gold coin first struck in 1252. An English gold coin of Edward III's reign (1327-1377) value six-shillings. On the obverse of this coin the crowned king, holding the sceptre and orb, is seated on a throne with a canopy; two leopards are also shown, and a number of lys, the inscription being EDWR. D. GRA. ANGL. Z. FRANC. DNS. HIB. On the reverse, a cross with crowned ends enclosed in a frame with four lions gardant and the inscription IHC TRANSIENS PER MEDIVM ILLORVM IBAT. A half-florin was also issued. The modern two-shilling piece (florin) was first coined in 1849. An Austrian silver florin was last minted in 1892.

Forty-Shilling Piece—A Scottish silver coin issued during the reign of James VI (1567-1625). On the obverse, a half-length crowned figure of the king with sword and the inscription IACOBUS. 6. DEI. GRATIA. REX. SCOTORVM. On the reverse, a crowned shield with the lion rampant, the letters I and R and the value XL & $, also the inscription HONOR. REGIS. IVDICIVM. DILIGIT and the date figures. Thirty-shilling, twenty-shilling and ten-shilling pieces were also issued with similar designs.

Four-Pound Piece—(*See Hat-Piece.*)

Four-Shilling Piece—A British silver coin minted in the reign of Queen Victoria; sometimes called a double-florin.

Four-Shilling Piece [Scottish]—(*See Merk.*)

Franc—A silver coin in use in several countries of Europe. Normally worth a little less than a shilling.

Gazette or **Gazetta**—A Venetian coin worth something less than one penny.

George Noble—A gold coin issued by Henry VIII (1509-1547), worth one-third of a pound. On the obverse, a ship with the Tudor rose surmounted by a cross and the initials H and K and the inscription HENRIC. DI. G. R. ANGL. Z. FRANC. DNS. HIBERNI. On the reverse, the armoured and mounted figure of St. George spearing a dragon, and the inscription TALI. DICA. SIGNO. MES. FLVCTVARI. NEQVIT. The Half-George-Noble is somewhat similar in appearance.

Godless Florin—Issued in England in the years 1848-9; so called because the words Dei Gratia (by the grace of God) were omitted.

Gold Penny—Only during the reign of Henry III (1216-1272) have gold pennies ever appeared in English currency. On the obverse the king appears seated on a throne holding the sceptre and orb, with the following inscription: HENRIC REX III. On the reverse, a cross with a rose and three dots in each angle and the inscription WILLEM ON LVNDE.

Groat—An English silver coin worth fourpence, in circulation from the time of Edward III (1327-1377) to the reign of Charles II (1660-1685). It was also issued during the reigns of William IV (1830-1837) and Victoria (1837-1901). The groat issued by Richard III (1483-1485) shows on the obverse the bust and full face of the sovereign with crown, enclosed in a tressure with nine arches, around which is the inscription RICARD. DI. GRA. REX. ANGL'Z FRANC. On the reverse, a long cross with splayed ends and three pellets in each of the angles. The inscriptions are in two circles as follows: POSVI DEVM ADIVTORE. MEVM and CIVITAS LONDON. Half-groats were also issued. The groat was current in several European countries, where it had different values.

Gros—A silver coin at one time current throughout W. Europe.

Groschen—A German silver coin.

Grosso—A silver coin formerly current in Switzerland.

Guilder—A silver coin used in Holland; at one time a gold coin current in Germany.

Guinea Pieces—Gold guinea pieces were first issued in 1670, during the reign of Charles II (1660-1685), and remained in circulation until 1813. They consisted of five-, two- and one-guinea pieces, as well as a half-guinea piece. All the

Guinea Pieces—*continued.*

coins followed the same design, which showed on the obverse a laurelled bust of the king and the inscription CAROLVS II DEI GRATIA, and on the reverse four shields with the arms of England, Scotland, Ireland and France, interspersed with the double letter C and a sceptre in each angle, and the inscription MAG. BR. FRA. ET. HIB. REX. The five-guinea piece had an additional inscription on the edge, the edges of the other pieces being milled. The name "guinea" was given to these coins owing to the gold from which they were made being obtained from Guinea. The guinea was intended to be worth twenty-shillings, but due to the inferiority of the silver coins of the time its value was increased to twenty-one shillings.

Gulden—An Austrian florin; a Dutch silver coin equal to 100 cents.

Gun Money—Money partly made of metal from old cannons issued in Ireland in the time of James I (1689).

Half-Crown—An English silver coin woith two shillings and six-pence, first issued in the reign of Edward VI, and was withdrawn from circulation 1st January, 1970. A golden half-crown was issued by Henry VIII.

Half-Dime—An American silver coin worth 5 cents, in use until 1866, when it was replaced by one made of copper and nickel.

Half-Dollar—An American silver coin, worth 50 cents.

Half-Eagle—An American gold coin, worth 5 dollars.

Half-Farthing—Issued during the reign of Victoria, from 1843 to 1856, for use in Great Britain and the Colonies.

Halfling—The name given in Scotland to a silver coin issued in the Middle Ages.

Half-Penny—A British bronze coin of which there were four hundred and eighty to the pound. The half-penny was withdrawn on 1st August, 1969.

Hardhead—(*See Lion.*)

Hardie—The name given to varieties of gold and silver coins in use at the time of the Black Prince.

Harper—An Irish coin in use during the 16th and 17th centuries, showing a harp on one side.

Harrington Farthing—A copper coin in use during the reign of James I, the patent for which was granted to Lord Harrington in 1613.

Harry Groat—A coin worth fourpence, in use during the reign of Henry VIII.

Hat Piece—A gold coin worth four pounds issued by James VI of Scotland (1567-1625). On the obverse, a profile bust of the king wearing a tall round-topped hat, a thistle appearing behind his head, and the inscription IACOBVS. 6. D. G. R. SCOTORVM. On the reverse, a crowned lion rampant holding a sceptre with the word IEHOVAH in Hebrew characters and the inscription TE. SOLVM. VEROR and the date figures.

Heller—A small copper coin, worth about one farthing, from the 17th to the 19th centuries in use in many German states.

Hemidrachm—An old Grecian coin; a half-drachma.

Hog-Money—The name given to a series of coins issued in Bermuda in the 17th century, bearing the figure of a hog.

Hook Money—Hook-shaped pieces of silver used as currency in Ceylon in the 17th century.

Horseman—A famous series of coins of Tarentum, showing a young horseman and Cupid riding on a Dolphin; issued in Classical times.

Incuse—To impress by sinking; the earliest method used in the making of coins.

Imperial—A Russian gold coin worth about 10 roubles, in use during the 18th century.

Irish Penny—A silver coin in use during the late 10th century.

Joachimsthaler—A Bohemian coin issued in the early part of the 16th century by the Count of Schlick.

Jacobus—An English gold coin issued during the reign of James I in 1603. It was originally worth twenty shillings but its value was afterwards raised to twenty-two shillings.

James Royal—A Scottish silver coin in use during the reign of James VI; sometimes called a sword dollar.

Johannes—A gold coin current in Portugal from 1722 to 1835.

Judas Penny—A coin of ancient Rhodes which has often been preserved in European churches as symbolising the crucifixion. It bears a radiate facing head of Helios which is taken to represent Christ wearing the crown of thorns.

Jugata or **Jugate**—A term used when two or more heads are shown on a coin, side by side or overlapping. (*See Accolated Coin.*)

Julio—An Italian silver coin current in the 16th century.

Knife Money—Ancient Chinese bronze money in the form of knives.

Kobang—An oblong gold coin once current in Japan.

Kran—A Persian silver coin, worth a little over fourpence.

Kreuzer—A small copper coin worth about a farthing, once used in Austria and Germany.

Krone—A silver coin used in Denmark and Sweden; also a gold coin once current in Germany and Austria.

Latten—A yellow alloy of copper and zinc used for making tokens, church utensils, etc.

Laurel—A gold coin issued during the reign of James I, on which he was represented as wearing a laurel wreath. Half and quarter laurels were also issued.

Legend—The inscription on a coin.

Leopard—A gold coin bearing a crowned lion, issued for use in France by Edward III.

Leopoldino—A Tuscan gold coin, value five paoli.

Lepton—An ancient coin of Greece, worth about one farthing; a modern coin equal to the French centime—plural **Lepta.**

Leu—A Roumanian silver coin equal to 100 bani, also to the French franc.

Lev—A Bulgarian silver coin equal in value to one hundred statinki.

Liard—A small silver coin first issued in France in the 15th century afterwards made of copper and worth three deniers.

Lion Noble—A Scottish gold coin worth seventy-five shillings, issued by James VI (1567-1625). On the obverse, a cross composed of four pairs of the letters I and R, each pair being crowned, and the inscription DEVS. IVDICIVM. TVVM. REGIS. DA. and the date figures. On the reverse, a crowned lion sejant with sword and sceptre, and the inscription POST. 5. & 100. PROAINVICTA. MANENT. HEC. Two-thirds and one-third-lion nobles were also issued with similar designs.

Lion, St. Andrew or **Demy**—A gold coin first issued in Scotland by Robert III (1390-1406), worth five shillings; sometimes called the "gold mail" and the "copper hardhead". On the obverse, a shield with crowned lion rampant and the inscription ROBERTVS: DEI : GRACIA: REX: SCOT: On the reverse, the figure of St. Andrew with fleur-de-lys, and the inscription DNS. P. TECTO. MS & LIB. Demi-lions or Half-St. Andrews or Half-demies were also issued. Billon-lions or Hardheads worth three-halfpence were current during the reign of Mary (1542-1567).

Lira—A silver coin of Italy.

Lis—A French gold coin in use during the reign of Raymond IV in the late 14th century.

Litra—An ancient silver coin once current in Sicily.

Livre—An old French silver coin having different values at different times. It was superseded in 1795 by the franc.

Lorraine—The name sometimes given to the Scottish testoon (*q.v.*) issued during the reign of Mary and Francis.

Louis—A gold coin worth about sixteen shillings, used in France during the reign of Louis XIII.

Manx Coins—Copper coins were minted in the Isle of Man first of all by the Earl of Derby in 1709, Duke of Atholl in 1758, and George III in 1786. These consisted of pennies, half-pennies and farthings. The reverse has the well-known figure of the "three legs" indicating the three capes of the island. The symbol is, however, of classical derivation and not particular to the Isle of Man.

Maria Theresia Thalers—Coins bearing the portrait of Queen Maria Theresia of Austria, and dated 1780, struck for circulation in Arabia, Abyssinia and East Africa; they are still regularly minted with this portrait and date.

Mark—A German silver coin introduced in 1873 in place of the **Thaler** (*q.v.*); it was worth a little under one shilling. There was also a gold mark.

Massachusetts Pieces—Silver coins struck in 1652 in America by the Pilgrim Fathers or their descendants. They consist of shillings, sixpences and threepences and depict a tree on the obverse, with the inscription MASATHVSETS. IN. On the reverse is shown the date in figures and the value in Roman numerals, and the inscription NEW ENGLAND. AN. DO.

Maundy Money—A series of specially minted silver coins presented by English sovereigns on Maundy Thursday to certain of their aged and needy subjects, who in number equal the years of the sovereign's age. Maundy money was first distributed by Charles II (1660-1685) and the practice has continued to the present time. The nominal value of the coins is fourpence or groat, threepence, twopence or half-groat, and one penny. The designs, in general, follow those of the ordinary coins of the time.

Medino—An Egyptian bronze coin worth about one-fortieth of a piastre.

Medio—A Mexican coin worth half-a-real.

Medjidie—A silver coin issued in Turkey, worth twenty piastres.

Merk—A Scottish silver coin worth thirteen shillings and fourpence, issued by James VI (1567-1625). On the obverse, a crowned shield of arms and the inscription IACOBVS. 6. DEI. G. REX. SCOTORVM. On the reverse, a two-leaved thistle with the letters I and R, and the inscription NEMO. ME. IMPVNE. LACESSET and the date figures. A two-merk piece and half- and quarter-merk pieces were issued. The two-merk piece was sometimes known as the Thistle dollar. Four- and two-merk pieces were also issued in Scotland by Charles II (1649-1685). Designs employed on the one-merk piece were also used on sixteen-, eight-, four- and two-shilling pieces.

Milled—A term used to describe the grooved edge, as on English gold and silver coins. Milling was first introduced during the reign of Elizabeth I, but was not regularly employed until and after the reign of Charles II (1660-1685), to prevent debasement of the coinage by shaving off the edges.

Milreis—A Portuguese gold coin of 1,000 reis, worth about one dollar (4s. 2d.); a Brazilian coin worth about two shillings and threepence.

Mint Marks—This method of indicating the place of mintage of a coin was regularly employed by the Romans during the latter half of the Empire, by giving an abbreviated form of the mint name. Other symbols or devices, such as the sun, rose, boar's head, etc., were used for the early English coinage.

Mocenigo—An old Venetian coin.

Mohur—An Indian gold coin worth about fifteen rupees or twenty shillings.

Moidore—A Portuguese gold coin, formerly worth about one guinea.

Mouton—A gold coin struck in French towns and provinces when in the possession of English Sovereigns. A mouton of Edward III (1327-1377) had on the obverse a lamb with nimbus, bearing a staff and banner, surrounded by the inscription ANG: DEI: QVI: TOLL: PECA MVDEI: MSERE: NOB. On the reverse, a cross, a cinquefoil with a lys in each angle enclosed in a tressure with four rounded and four pointed arches, and the inscription XPE VINCIT. XPE REGNET. XPE MPERAT. (*See Denier.*)

Mule—A coin having two obverse or two reverse sides either intentionally or by mistake.

Napoleon—A French gold coin worth twenty francs, first used by Napoleon I.

Newark Pieces—Obsidional silver coins of lozenge shape in values of half-crown, shilling, ninepence and sixpence, issued at Newark in Nottinghamshire during the Civil War. On the obverse, a crown with the letters C. and R., and beneath, a Roman numeral indicating the value of the piece. On the reverse, the inscription OBS: NEWARK: 1646. (*See Obsidional Coin.*)

Nibu—A small rectangular-shaped silver coin current in Japan in the 19th century. **Nishu**—A similar coin.

Nickel—The popular name for the American 5-cent piece.

Nishu—A Japanese oblong silver coin minted in the 19th century.

Noble—A gold coin worth six shillings and eightpence issued in the reign of Edward III (1327-1377). The design on the obverse is very similar to that of the Rose Noble (*q.v.*), but that on the reverse consists of a cross with fleur-de-lys ends and a crown and lion in each angle, the whole enclosed in a tressure with eight arches surrounded by the inscription IHC. TRANSIENS. PER. MEDIVM. ILLORVM. IBAT. Half- and quarter-nobles were also issued, the half-noble similar to the noble, with varying inscription, but the quarter-noble having a shield on the obverse with the arms of England and France.

Nonsunt—A Scottish billon coin first issued during the reign of Francis and Mary, equal in value to twelve penny placks. On the obverse, the crowned monogram F. & M. with a crowned dolphin and thistle, and the inscription FRAN. ET. D. G. R. R. SCOTOR. D. D. VEN. On the reverse, the inscription IAM. NON. SUNT: DVO. SED. VNA. CARO and two small crosses.

Obsidional Coin—Coins struck during sieges and other emergencies from plate, gold or silver; this particularly applies to issues during the reign of Charles I.

Obol—Small silver coin of ancient Greece. The basic denomination of the early coinages. They were also issued in the Ionian Islands in recent times when under the protection of Great Britain.

Obverse—That side of a coin bearing the principal inscription.

Octadrachm—An old gold coin used in Egypt, equal in value to eight drachmae.

Octagon—An eight-sided coin issued at San Francisco in 1851, worth fifty dollars.

Onza—A South American gold coin issued during the 19th century; also a coin issued in Spain.

Ore—A Swedish coin worth a one-hundredth part of a krone, cast in bronze or silver according to the face value.

Ormonde—The name given to certain silver coins issued in Ireland during the reign of Charles I. A money of necessity issued during the Civil War.

Pagoda—An Indian gold coin worth about seven shillings; half- and quarter-pagodas were issued in silver.

Paolo—A 16th-century Italian silver coin.

Para—A Turkish coin equal to one-fortieth of a piastre, used also in Egypt, Cyprus, etc.

Parado—An old coin worth about two shillings and sixpence, formerly used in Portuguese-India.

Pataca—A Portuguese silver coin worth about four shillings.

Pavillon—A gold coin issued by Philip VI of France (1328-50); imitated and circulated in France by the Black Prince.

Penny—Previous to 1797 (George III, 1760-1820) pennies were made of silver. After this date until 1860 they were made of copper; afterwards bronze was employed. A penny made of billon was first issued in Scotland by James I (1406-1437). The penny was in circulation until 31st August, 1971. (*See Silver Penny and Gold Penny.*)

Penny-yard Penny—A silver penny first produced in Penny-yard Castle, Ross.

Peseta—A Spanish silver coin equal to one hundred centimos.

Peso—The Spanish or Mexican dollar; a silver coin of several Central and South American countries.

Pfennig—A small bronze German coin worth one-hundredth part of a mark.

Pice—An Indian copper coin worth about one penny.

Pie—An Indian copper coin worth about one-twelfth of a penny.

Pineapple Penny—A coin struck in Barbados in 1788 bearing a design showing a pineapple.

Pine-Tree Money—American silver coins issued during the 17th century, bearing a design of a pine-tree.

Pistole—A gold coin worth twelve pounds issued in Scotland by William III (1694-1702). On the obverse, a profile bust of the king below which the sun is rising from the sea, and the inscription GVLIELMVS. DEI. GRATIA. On the reverse, a crowned and quartered shield of arms with the crowned letters W. and R., the inscription MAG. BRIT. FRA. ET.

Pistole—*continued.*

HIB. REX., and the date figures. Half-pistoles were also issued. Pistoles were also current in Spain and France, the Spanish being a gold coin equal in value to a quarter-doubloon.

Plack—A Scottish billon coin worth threepence and later twopence, first issued by James III (1460-1488). On the obverse, a shield with the lion rampant enclosed by a four-arched frame, with the inscription ICOBVS: D: GRA: REX: SCOTTORVM: On the reverse, a lozenge containing the cross of St. Andrew over an ornate cross with a crown in each division, and the inscription VILLA: EDIN: BVRGH. Half-placks were also issued.

Planchet—A disc of metal; a coin before the design is stamped upon it.

Pontefract Shilling—A coin struck by the Royalists at Pontefract in 1648.

Portcullis—The name given to a series of silver coins struck during the reign of Queen Elizabeth for use by the East India Company, so named from the portcullis appearing on the reverse. On the obverse was a crowned shield and the letters E. and R.

Postboy's Groat—A coin issued during the reign of Charles I, worth about fourpence.

Pound—The pound-sovereign is a gold coin issued in several reigns, commencing with that of Henry VIII (1509-1547) and worth about twenty shillings. During the reign of Charles I (1625-1649) twenty-shilling pieces or pounds and half-pound pieces were made of silver. These coins with various obverse designs were minted at Oxford, etc. One such design showed the king seated on horseback with sword and armour strewn on the ground, with the inscription CAROLVS D. G. MAG. BRIT. FRAN. ET HIBER REX. On the reverse, the inscription RELIG. PROT. LEG. ANG. LIBER. PAR. in two lines across the field, with plumes and the date figures, surrounded with the inscription EXVRGAT DEVS DISSI-PENTVR INIMICI. The pound or sovereign is now the monetary gold unit of Great Britain, and contains .916 grain of fine gold; this standard was fixed as long ago as 1575.

Profile—The head on coins had always appeared full face until towards the end of the reign of Henry VII (1485-1509), when it was represented in profile.

Quadrans—Copper and bronze coins used by the ancient Romans, worth a quarter of an as.

Quart or **Quarto**—A copper coin worth 1/192nd of a Spanish dollar, issued in Gibraltar by Victoria (1837-1901). Two-quart and half-quart pieces were also struck.

Quinarius—An ancient Roman silver coin worth about five asses; an early British coin.

Quarter—A silver coin issued in the U.S.A., worth twenty-five cents.

Rap—An Irish coin worth about one-eighth of a penny; it passed for one half-penny.

Rappen—A Swiss coin worth one centime.

Real—A former Spanish silver coin worth twopence half-penny.

Reverse—The side of a coin on which the subordinate inscription or type appears. Commonly known as the "Tail" side.

Rial—A Spanish coin used in England in the 16th century.

Rider—A gold coin worth twenty-three shillings, first issued by James III of Scotland (1460-1488). On the obverse, the king on horseback with sword and the inscription IACOBVS: DEI: GRA: REX SCOTRO. On the reverse, a shield with the lion rampant over a cross, and the inscription SALVVM FAC POPVLVM TVVM DNE. Half- and quarter-riders were also issued in the same reign and a two-thirds and a one-third rider were struck in the reign of James IV (1488-1513). The Dutch also issued a gold rider in the 16th century.

Rix-Dollar—A Dutch silver coin current in the 18th century. An English minted rix-dollar was used in Ceylon.

Rosa Americana—Before the Declaration of Independence in 1776 a number of coins were struck for use in North America. The best known are probably the Rosa Americana series made of Bath metal (*q.v.*), consisting of twopence, penny and half-penny (sometimes spoken of as penny, half-penny and farthing), issued during the reign of George I (1714-1727). On the obverse, the laurelled head of the king and the inscription GEORGIVS. D: G: MAG: BRI: FRA: ET: HIB: REX., or a variation. On the reverse, a rose or a crowned rose with the inscription ROSA AMERICANA and UTILE DULC., and the date figures.

Rose Noble—A gold coin worth ten shillings, introduced by Edward IV in 1465. On the obverse, a three-quarter-length crowned figure of the king standing in a ship holding a sword and shield of arms; a rose appears on the side of the ship and a flag bearing the letter E. The following is the inscription: EDWARD DEI GRA REX ANGL Z FRANC DNS HYB. On the reverse is the sun with sixteen rays, four

Rose Noble—*continued.*

of which are decorated with a lys; a crown and a lion also appear, together with the inscription IHS AVT''TRANSIENS PER MEDIVM ILLORVM IBAT. A Rose Noble or Ryal was also issued by Henry VII (1485-1509). The obverse of this is similar to that described above, with some variations, but the reverse consists of a double rose with shield bearing a triple fleur-de-lys, and the inscription IHC. AVTEM. TRANSIENS. PER. MEDIV. ILLORV. IBAT.

Rose Ryal—A gold coin issued by James I (1603-1625), worth about thirty-shillings. It shows on the obverse the king robed and enthroned with sceptre and orb, and a portcullis and a double-rose with shield of arms on the reverse.

Rouble—A Russian silver coin worth about two shillings, in use prior to the Revolution.

Royal—(*See Ryal.*)

Rupee—An Indian silver coin worth one shilling and fourpence, first introduced in the 16th century.

Ryal or Royal—A gold coin worth ten shillings issued by Edward IV (1461-1483). Gold and silver ryals were also issued in Scotland during the 16th century, as were two-third and one-third ryals.

St. Andrew—(*See Lion.*)

Saltire Plack—A Scottish billon coin worth fourpence, issued by James VI (1567-1625). On the obverse are two crossed (saltire) sceptres with a thistle, etc., and on the reverse a lozenge with a thistle at each angle.

Salute—A gold coin used in France, issued by Charles VI of France and by Henry V and Henry VI of England.

Sceatta—An Anglo-Saxon silver coin in use from about the 7th century, thick and crude in design. It is known to have been made of gold as well as of silver.

Scudo—An Italian silver coin worth about four shillings, in use from the 16th to the 18th centuries. A gold coin of about the same value.

Sceptre—(*See Unite.*)

Semibracteate—A German silver penny of the 12th century.

Semis—An ancient Roman gold or copper coin, the latter being of large size and depicting the head of Jupiter, etc., on one side, and the prow of a boat on the other.

Sen—A Japanese copper or bronze coin, equal to a one-hundredth part of a yen.

Sequin—A Turkish coin; popular name, derived from the Venetian *zecchino*.

Sestertius—An ancient Roman coin of silver or brass, worth a quarter denarius.

Seven-Shilling Piece—(*See Third-of-guinea*.)

Sextans—An ancient Roman copper coin worth one-sixth of an as.

Shekel—An old Hebrew coin of gold or silver; half- and quarter-shekels were made of copper.

Shereefee—A Turkish gold coin.

Shilling—An English silver coin worth twelve pennies, first issued during the reign of Edward VI (1547-1553). It was the first English coin to bear a date. On the obverse, a crowned bust of the king with the inscription EDWARD VI D. G. ANGL. FRA. Z. HIB. REX. On the reverse, an oval shield with the arms of France and England and the letters E. and R. and the inscription TIMOR DOMINI FONS VITE and the Roman date letters. The shilling first appeared in its present form during the reign of Henry VIII (1485-1509); the edge was first milled during the reign of Charles II (1660-1685). Shilling is an old English word meaning "thin slice". (*See Testoon*.)

Sicca—A seal or coining die. An Indian silver rupee.

Siglos—An ancient Persian silver coin.

Silver Penny—Silver pennies were the only coins issued in England from the time of the early Saxon kingdoms, commencing during the first half of the 8th century A.D. until 1279, when under Edward I the coinage was reorganised. Silver pennies are still struck, but only for issue as "Maundy Money".

Six-Angel Piece—A rare gold coin issued during the reign of Edward VI (1547-1553), worth something over two pounds. Upon it was represented an angel spearing a devil, and a three-masted ship.

Sixpence—A silver coin first issued during the reign of Edward VI (1547-1553). The designs are similar to those on the shilling (*q.v.*) of the same period.

Sixteen-Shilling Piece—(*See Merk*.)

Sixty-Shilling Piece—A silver coin issued in Scotland during the reign of William and Mary (1689-1694).

Skilling—A Scandinavian coin, worth less than one penny. It is no longer in use.

Soho Penny—A copper penny struck at Soho, Birmingham, by Matthew Boulton. The word "Soho" in minute characters appears on the reverse, hence its name. The design is similar to the twopence (*q.v.*)

Solidus—An ancient Roman gold coin, first issued in the reign of Constantine the Great. The earlier gold denomination was the Aureus (*q.v.*).

Sou—A French coin, worth 5 centimes, which is equivalent to a half-penny.

Sovereign—An English gold coin first issued during the reign of Henry VII (1485-1509), worth twenty shillings. There were several types. On the obverse appears a full-length figure of the king, robed and crowned, seated on a throne, holding a sceptre and orb, surrounded by the inscription HENRICVS DEI·GRACIA REX ANGLIE ET FRANCIE DNS IBAR. On the reverse, a shield with the arms of England and France placed in the centre of a double rose with five points between its petals; this is surrounded by a ten-arched tressure with a lion and a lys in alternating arches, and the inscription IHESVS. AVTEM. TRANSIENS: PER MEDIVM: ILLORVM: IBAT. A half-sovereign was first issued during the reign of Henry VIII (1509-1547).

Spade Guinea—An English gold coin worth twenty-one shillings, issued during the reign of George III (1760-1820), so called from the spade-shaped shield on the reverse. On the obverse, a draped and laurelled bust of the king with the inscription GEORGIVS III DEI GRATIA. On the reverse, a crowned and pointed spade-shaped shield with the arms of England, France, Ireland and Scotland, with the inscription M.B.F. ET H. REX F.D. B. ET L.D.S.R.I.A.T.ET. E.

Spur Royal—An English gold coin in use during the reign of James I (1603-1625). Its value was 15s. 0d. On the obverse the king is crowned standing in a ship. Reverse has a rose on spur rowel in centre of royal cross, hence the name.

Star Pagoda—An Indian gold coin issued at Madras, with a device of a star on one side.

Stater—A gold or silver coin issued by the ancient Greeks and Persians.

Sterling—The lawful money of England. A Scottish silver penny first issued during the reign of David I (1124-1153). On the obverse, a crowned bust in profile and the inscription ER : TIVAD. On the reverse, a cross fleury and the inscription HVGO : ON : ROCH.

Stiver—An obsolete Dutch silver coin worth one-twentieth of a guilder.

Styca—A small copper coin issued in Northumberland and current from the 7th to 9th centuries.

Sword & Sceptre Piece—A gold coin worth six pounds, issued in Scotland by James VI (1567-1625). On the obverse, a crowned shield of arms with the inscription IACOBVS. 6. D.G.R. SCOTORVM. On the reverse, a sword and sceptre crossed and in the angles a crown; also the date figures and two thistles, with the inscription SALVS. POPVLI. SUPREMA. LEX. Half-sword-and-sceptre pieces were also issued.

Sword Dollar—The name sometimes given to the Scottish silver ryal, worth thirty-shillings, issued during the reign of James VI (1567-1625), so named from the down-pointed sword depicted on the reverse.

Ten-Shilling Piece—(See *Forty-shilling piece*.)

Testoon—A silver shilling worth twelve pence, issued during the reign of Henry VII (1485-1509). It was the first English silver coin to bear a portrait of the sovereign. On the obverse, a head of the king in profile with arched crown, and the inscription HENRIC' SEPTIM' DI'. GRA'. REX. ANGL' Z. FR' On the reverse, a shield with the arms of France and England, quartered by the arms of a long cross fleury, and the inscription POSVI DEVM. ADIVTORE' MEVM. A silver testoon worth five-shillings and a half-testoon were first issued in Scotland in 1553 by Mary (1542-1567).

Teston—A silver coin used in France during the reign of Louis XII.

Tetradrachm—An old Greek silver coin.

Thaler—A German coin worth three marks or three shillings; it superseded the mark which was introduced in 1873.

Third-of-Guinea—A gold coin worth seven-shillings, issued during the reign of George III (1760-1820); its design was similar to the guinea of the period, often called the spade-guinea (*q.v.*).

Thirty-Penny Piece—A silver coin issued by James VI (1567-1625) in Scotland. On the obverse, a bareheaded bust of the king, with the inscription IACOBVS. 6. D. G. R. SCOTORVM. On the reverse, a three-flowered thistle with two leaves and a small crown, and the inscription NEMO. ME. IMPVNE. LACESSIT and the date figures. A twelve-penny piece was also issued with similar designs.

Thirty-Shilling Piece—Was the first English coin to bear its currency value. It was made of gold and issued in the reign of James I (1603-1625). (*See Forty-shilling piece*.)

Thistle Crown—A gold coin issued by James I (1603-1625) for use in Scotland as well as in England; worth about four shillings. On the obverse, a crowned rose with leaves and the letters I and R and the inscription IA : D : G : MAG : BR : F : ET : H : REX. On the reverse, a crowned thistle with the letters I and R and the inscription TVEATVR. VNITA. DEVS.

Thistle Dollar—(*See Merk*.)

Thistle Merk—A silver coin worth thirteen-shillings and four-pence issued in Scotland by James VI (1567-1625). On the obverse, a crowned shield of arms and the inscription IACOBVS. 6. D. G. R. SCOTORVM. On the reverse, a crowned two-leaved thistle, and the inscription REGEM. IOVA. PROTEGIT. and the date figures. Half-, quarter- and one-eighth thistle-merks were also issued with similar designs.

Thistle Noble—A Scottish gold coin issued by James VI (1567-1625), worth seven pounds, six shillings and eightpence. On the obverse, a ship with two flags, a shield of arms and a thistle, with the inscription IACOBVS. 6. DEI. GRATIA. REX. SCOTORVM. On the reverse, two crossed sceptres with crown terminals and a thistle with a crowned lion in each angle, and the inscription FLORENT. SCEPT. PIIS. REGNA. HIS. IOVA. DAT. NUMERATO.

Three-Farthing Piece—A thin silver coin issued during the reign of Elizabeth (1558-1602). On the obverse, a head of the Queen with a rose and the inscription E. D. G. ROSA SINE SPINA. On the reverse, a shield of arms and the inscription CIVITAS LONDON.

Threehalfpence—A silver coin first issued by Elizabeth I. Commonly known from the coins of William IV and Victoria, when issued for the Colonies.

Threepence—A silver coin first issued during the reign of Edward VI (1547-1553). The designs are similar to those on the shilling (*q.v.*) of the same period. In 1937 a twelve-sided nickel-brass coin was issued and was currency until 31st August, 1971.

Three-Pound Piece—An English gold coin produced during the Civil War.

Tin Money—Coins of small value, usually farthings and tokens, were made of tin or pewter during the reigns of several English sovereigns. Such coins issued in the time of Charles II (1660-1685) followed the designs of the copper coins (then first issued) and had a small inset of copper as a protection against counterfeiting.

Tokens—During the reign of Henry VIII (1509-1547) and afterwards, the need for small change among the poorer classes was great, so that tradesmen and others issued coin-like tokens of tin, lead and other base metals for spending at the place of issue. The practice extended so that the tokens could be exchanged for coins of the realm. The use of tokens was forbidden in 1672. Tokens were re-issued by tradesmen in 1786 and continued to 1797; they were again issued in 1811-1812.

Touch Piece or **Touch Money**—In former times persons suffering from a scrofulous disease called "king's evil" were touched by the sovereign to effect a cure. A gold piece was always presented to the sufferer as a charm against a recurrence, the angel (*q.v.*) usually being the coin chosen for this purpose.

Treble-Sovereign—A rare gold coin issued by Edward VI (1547-1553), worth sixty shillings. On the obverse, the king seated on a throne, crowned and holding a sceptre and orb, and on the reverse, a shield with the arms of France and England, supported by a dragon and a lion with crown.

Tressure—An ornamental border or frame enclosing the principal device of a coin.

Twelve-Penny Piece—(*See Thirty-penny piece.*)

Twenty-Pound Piece—A gold coin issued by James VI of Scotland (1567-1625). On the obverse, a half-length crowned figure of the king holding a sword and an olive branch, with the words IN. VTRVNQVE. PARATVS, the date figures and the inscription IACOBVS. 6. DEI. GRA. REX. SCOTOR. On the reverse, a crowned shield of arms and the inscription PARCERE. SVBIECTIS & DEBELLARE. SUPERBOS.

Twenty-Shilling Piece—(*See Forty-shilling piece.*)

Twopence—A pure copper coin issued only during the reign of George III (1760-1820). On the obverse, a draped and laurelled bust of the king, with incuse inscription GEORGIUS III. D. G. REX., and on the reverse the figure of Britannia, the date letters and the inscription BRITANNIA.

Two-Shilling Piece (Scottish)—(*See Merk.*)

Turner—A copper coin worth twopence, issued in Scotland by Charles I (1625-1649).

Unicorn—A gold coin worth between ten and thirteen shillings, issued in Scotland by James III (1460-1488). On the obverse, a unicorn with a crown about its neck, supporting a shield with a lion rampant, and the inscription ICOBVS: DEI : GRACIA : REX : SCOTO : On the reverse, a wavy star over a cross fleury, and the inscription EXVRGAT : DE : ET : DISIPENT : NIMICI : E : Half-unicorns were also issued.

Unite or Unity—A gold sovereign sometimes known as a "sceptre", issued by James I (1603-1625), worth about twenty shillings, used in Scotland and England alike. On the obverse, a half-length figure of the king with beard, wearing a crown and holding the sceptre and orb, with the inscription IACOBVS D. G. ANG. SCO. FRAN. ET. HIB REX. On the reverse, a crowned shield bearing the arms of England, France, Scotland and Ireland, and the inscription EXVRGAT DEVS DISSI-PENTVR INIMICI. A later issue, sometimes known as the laurel, showed on the obverse a bust of the king with beard and wearing a laurel wreath, and on the reverse a cross fleury with a crowned shield of arms. Also issued for Charles I.

Yen—Gold coins of five, ten and twenty yen current in Japan; formerly made of silver.

York Half-Crown—A silver coin minted at York during the reign of Charles I.

Zecchino—A Venetian gold coin.

ENGLISH COINS

List of Denominations and Reigns of Issue

NOTE—The figures given in brackets are the approximate values at the times of issue.

WILLIAM I (1066-1087).
Silver—Penny.

WILLIAM II (1087-1100).
Silver—Penny.

HENRY I (1100-1135).
Silver—Penny.

STEPHEN (1135-1154).
Silver—Penny.

HENRY II (1154-1189).
Silver—Penny.

RICHARD I (1189-1199).
Silver—Penny.

JOHN (1199-1216).
Silver—Penny.

} Struck in the name of Henry II.

HENRY III (1216-72).
Silver—Penny.

EDWARD I (1272-1307).
Silver—Groat (4d.); Penny; Half-penny and Farthing.

EDWARD II (1307-1327).
Silver—Penny; Half-penny and Farthing.

EDWARD III (1327-77).
Gold—Noble (6s. 8d.); Half and Quarter Nobles; Florin (6s. 0d.); Half and Quarter Florins.
Silver—Groat; Half Groat; Penny; Half-penny and Farthing.

RICHARD II (1377-99).
Gold—Noble; half and quarter.
Silver—Groat (4d.); Penny; Half-penny and Farthing.

349

HENRY IV (1399-1413).

 Gold—Noble (6s. 8d.); Half- and Quarter-nobles.

 Silver—Groat (4d.); Half-groat; Penny; Half-penny and Farthing.

HENRY V (1413-1422).

 Gold—Noble (6s. 8d.); Half- and Quarter-nobles.

 Silver—Groat (4d.); Half-groat; Penny; Half-penny and Farthing.

HENRY VI (1422-1461).

 Gold—Noble (6s. 8d.); Half- and Quarter-nobles; Angel (6s. 8d.); Angelet or Half-Angel.

 Silver—Groat (4d.); Half-groat; Penny; Half-penny and Farthing.

EDWARD IV (1461-1483).

 Gold—Rose Noble; Royal or Ryal (10s. 0d.); Noble (6s. 8d.); Half- and Quarter-ryals; Angel (6s. 8d.); and Angelet or Half-angel.

 Silver—Groat (4d.); Half-groat; Penny; Half-penny and Farthing.

EDWARD V (1483-1483).

 Gold—Angel (6s. 8d.); Angelet or Half-angel.

 Silver—Groat (4d.).

RICHARD III (1483-1485).

 Gold—Angel (6s. 8d.); Angelet or Half-angel.

 Silver—Groat (4d.); Half-groat; Penny; Half-penny and Farthing.

HENRY VII (1485-1509).

 Gold—Sovereign or Double-ryal (20s. 0d.); Rose Noble or Ryal (10s. 0d.); Angel (6s. 8d.); Angelet or Half-angel.

 Silver—Testoon (1s. 0d.); Groat (4d.); Half-groat; Penny; Half-penny and Farthing.

HENRY VIII (1509-1547).

 Gold—Double Sovereign (44s. 0d.); Sovereign (20s. 0d.); Pound Sovereign (20s. 0d.); Half-sovereign or Ryal; Angel (6s. 8d.); Angelet or Half-angel; Quarter-angel; George Noble (6s. 8d.); Half-george-noble; Crown and Half-crown.

 Silver—Testoon (1s. 0d.); Groat (4d.); Half-groat; Penny; Half-penny and Farthing.

EDWARD VI (1547-1553).

Gold—Treble Sovereign (60s. 0d.); Six-angel piece (48s. 0d.); Double Sovereign (48s. 0d.); Sovereign (24s. 0d.); Pound Sovereign (20s. 0d.); Half-sovereign (10s. 0d.); Quarter-sovereign or Crown (5s. 0d.); and Half-crown.

Silver—Crown (5s. 0d.); Half-crown; Shilling; Sixpence; Groat (4d.); Half-groat; Threepence; Penny; Half-penny and Farthing.

MARY (1553-1558).

Gold—Sovereign (30s. 0d.); Ryal (15s. 0d.); Angel (10s. 0d.).

Silver—Groat (4d.); Half-groat and Penny.

ELIZABETH I. (1558-1603).

Gold—Sovereign (20s. 0d. to 30s. 0d.); Half-sovereign; Ryal (10s. 0d. to 15s. 0d.); Angel (6s. 8d. to 10s. 0d.); Angelet or Half-angel; Quarter-angel; Crown and Half-crown.

Silver—Crown (5s. 0d.); Half-crown; Shilling; Sixpence; Groat (4d.); Threepence; Three-half-pence; Penny; Three-farthings and Half-penny.

JAMES I (1603-1625).

Gold—Rose Ryal (30s. 0d. to 35s. 0d.); Pound Sovereign (30s. 0d.); Unite or Laurel (about 20s. 0d.); Spur Royal (15s. 0d. to 16s. 6d.); Half-sovereign (15s. 0d.); Angel (11s. 0d.); Double Crown or Half-laurel (about 10s. 0d.); Crown (7s. 6d.); Angelet or Half-angel; British Crown (5s. 0d.); Thistle Crown (about 4s. 0d.); Half-crown and Half-British Crown.

Silver—Crown; Half-crown; Shilling; Sixpence; Groat (4d.); Half-groat; Penny; Half-penny.

Copper—Farthing.

CHARLES I (1625-1649).

Gold—Treble Unite or Three-pound piece (60s. 0d.); Twenty-shilling piece, Broad or Unite (about 20s. 0d.); Double-Crown or Half-broad or Ten-shilling piece (10s. 0d.); Crown or Britain Crown and Angel (10s. 0d.); Unite and Half-Unite.

Silver—Pound or Twenty-shilling piece (20s. 0d.); Half-Pound; Crown; Half-crown; Shilling; Sixpence; Groat (4d.); Threepence; Half-groat; Penny and Half-penny.

Copper—Farthing.

COMMONWEALTH (1649-1660).

Gold—Fifty-shilling piece (50s. 0d.); Broad (20s. 0d.); Ten-shilling piece or Half-broad and Five-shilling piece.

Silver—Crown: Half-crown; Shilling; Sixpence; Half-groat (2d.); Penny and Half-penny.

CHARLES II (1660-1685).

Gold—Five-guinea piece (£5); Two-guinea piece (£2); Guinea (20s. 0d.); Half-guinea (10s. 0d.); Twenty-shilling piece or Broad; Half- and Quarter-broads.

Silver—Crown; Half-crown; Shilling; Sixpence; Groat (4d.); Threepence; Half-groat and Penny.

Copper—Half-penny and Farthing.

JAMES II (1685-1689).

Gold—Five-guinea piece (£5); Two-guinea piece (£2); Guinea (20s. 0d.); and Half-guinea (10s. 0d.).

Silver—Crown; Half-crown; Shilling; Sixpence.

Tin—Half-penny and Farthing.

WILLIAM & MARY (1689-1695).

Gold—Five-guinea piece (£5 7s. 6d.); Two-guinea piece (£2 3s. 0d.); Guinea (£1 1s. 6d.); and Half-guinea (10s. 9d.).

Silver—Crown; Half-crown; Shilling and Sixpence.

Copper—Half-penny and Farthing.

Tin—Half-penny and Farthing.

WILLIAM III (1695-1702).

Gold—Five-guinea piece; Two-guinea piece; Guinea and Half-guinea.

Silver—Crown; Half-crown; Shilling and Sixpence.

Copper—Half-penny and Farthing.

ANNE (1702-1714).

Gold—Five-guinea piece (£5 7s. 6d.); Two-guinea piece (£2 3s. 0d.); Guinea (£1 1s. 6d.); and Half-guinea (10s. 9d.).

Silver—Crown; Half-crown; Shilling and Sixpence.

Copper—Farthing.

GEORGE I (1714-1727) and GEORGE II (1727-1760).

Gold—Five-guinea piece (£5 5s. 0d.); Two-guinea piece (£2 2s. 0d.); Guinea (£1 1s. 0d.); Half- and Quarter-guinea.

Silver—Crown; Half-crown; Shilling and Sixpence.

Copper—Half-penny and Farthing.

GEORGE III (1760-1820).

> **Gold**—Guinea; Half-guinea; Third-of-guinea or Seven-shilling piece; Quarter-guinea; Sovereign (20s. 0d.) and Half-sovereign.
>
> **Silver**—Crown; Half-crown; Shilling and Sixpence.
>
> **Copper**—Twopence; Penny; Half-penny and Farthing.

GEORGE IV (1820-1830).

> **Gold**—Double Sovereign; Sovereign and Half-Sovereign.
>
> **Silver**—Crown; Half-crown; Shilling and Sixpence.
>
> **Copper**—Penny; Half-penny and Farthing.

WILLIAM IV (1830-1837).

> **Gold**—Sovereign and Half-sovereign.
>
> **Silver**—Half-crown; Shilling; Sixpence and Groat.
>
> **Copper**—Penny; Half-penny and Farthing.

VICTORIA (1837-1901).

> **Gold**—Five-pound piece; Double Sovereign; Sovereign and Half-sovereign.
>
> **Silver**—Crown; Half-crown; Double Florin; Florin; Shilling; Sixpence; Groat and Threepence.
>
> **Copper**—Penny; Half-penny; Farthing and Half-farthing.

EDWARD VII (1901-1910).

> **Gold**—Five pounds; Two pounds; Sovereign and Half-sovereign.
>
> **Silver**—Crown; Half-crown; Florin; Shilling; Sixpence and Threepence.
>
> **Copper**—Penny; Half-penny; Farthing and Third-farthing.

GEORGE V (1910-1936).

> **Gold**—Five pounds; Two pounds; Sovereign and Half-sovereign.
>
> **Silver**—Crown; Half-crown; Florin; Shilling; sixpence and Threepence.
>
> **Copper**—Penny; Half-penny and Farthing.

EDWARD VIII (1936, abdicated).

> No coins issued for currency in England bearing the name or portrait of Edward VIII. Coins were issued for the Colonies.

GEORGE VI (1936-1952).

Gold—Five-pounds; Two-pounds; Sovereign and Half: sovereign.

Silver—Crown; Half-crown; Florin; Shilling; Sixpence and Threepence.

Cupro-Nickel—Half-crown; Florin; Shilling and Sixpence.

Nickel-Brass—Threepence.

Copper—Penny; Half-penny and Farthing.

ELIZABETH II (1952-   ).

Gold—Sovereign.

Cupro-Nickel—Crown; Half-crown; Florin; Shilling and Sixpence.

Nickel-Brass—Threepence.

Copper—Penny; Half-penny and Farthing.

Britain changed over to Decimal currency on the 15th February 1971, which meant the issue of the following new coins:

Cupro-Nickel—50 new pence, a seven-sided coin first issued October 1969.

Ten new pence and five new pence, both issued 1968.

Bronze—Two new pence, one new pence and a half new pence.

The half-penny was withdrawn on 1st August, 1969, and the half-crown was withdrawn on 1st January, 1970.

The penny and the threepenny piece were both withdrawn on 31st August, 1971.

Chronological Order of
ENGLISH SOVEREIGNS

William I - - -	1066 to 1087
William II - - -	1087 to 1100
Henry I - - -	1100 to 1135
Stephen - - -	1135 to 1154
Henry II - - -	1154 to 1189
Richard I - - -	1189 to 1199
John - - - -	1199 to 1216
Henry III - - -	1216 to 1272
Edward I - - -	1272 to 1307
Edward II - - -	1307 to 1327
Edward III - - -	1327 to 1377
Richard II - - -	1377 to 1399
Henry IV - - -	1399 to 1413
Henry V - - -	1413 to 1422
Henry VI - - -	1422 to 1461
Edward IV - - -	1461 to 1483
Edward V - - -	1483 to 1483
Richard III - - -	1483 to 1485
Henry VII - - -	1485 to 1509
Henry VIII - - -	1509 to 1547
Edward VI - - -	1547 to 1553
Mary - - - -	1553 to 1558
Elizabeth I - - -	1558 to 1603
James I - - -	1603 to 1625
Charles I - - -	1625 to 1649
Commonwealth - -	1649 to 1660
Charles II - - -	1660 to 1685
James II - - -	1685 to 1689
William and Mary -	1689 to 1695
William III - - -	1695 to 1702
Anne - - - -	1702 to 1714
George I - - -	1714 to 1727
George II - - -	1727 to 1760
George III - - -	1760 to 1820
George IV - - -	1820 to 1830
William IV - - -	1830 to 1837
Victoria - - -	1837 to 1901
Edward VII - - -	1901 to 1910
George V - - -	1910 to 1936
Edward VIII - - -	1936 to 1936
George VI - - -	1936 to 1952
Elizabeth II - - -	1952 to

MEDALS

Medals are divided into four classes:—

1. Medals for gallantry in action, or for saving life in peace.

2. Medals for War Service.

3. Commemoration Medals.

4. Medals for long service and good conduct.

Of these, those under Class 1 are the type most in demand by collectors, and consequently are of higher value. Collectors generally demand medals awarded to Army, Navy or Air Force personnel. They also generally collect those of a specific regiment, and consequently those medals awarded to a more famous regiment in a glorious action can realise high prices, i.e., a medal awarded to a man known to have been in the Charge of the Light Brigade during the Crimean War.

It is impossible in this work to describe every type of medal and it must be stressed that medals are a specialised subject.

Most medals bear an inscription round the edge giving the Rank, Name and Regiment of the recipient.

A short description of the campaign medals mostly in demand is given hereunder.

In addition to the types to be described, collectors are also interested in Decorations, such as the following:—

The Most Noble Order of the Garter.

The George Cross.

The Most Honourable Order of the Bath.

Order of Merit.

Order of the British Empire, etc., etc.

Medals for Gallantry and for War Service

Victoria Cross—The most highly coveted decoration instituted in 1856. Issued to all ranks and all three services. Consists of a Bronze Cross, 1½ inches across, with Lion standing upon a Crown, beneath which the words "FOR VALOUR".

Distinguished Service Order—For rewarding individual instances of service in war. Recipient must be holding a commission in one of the services. Consists of a gold cross, enamelled white, edged gold, with laurel wreath in centre, within which Royal Cypher.

Distinguished Service Cross—Awarded to all Naval and Marine Officers below the rank of Lieutenant-Commander, with proviso that recipient must have been mentioned in despatches. Consists of a plain silver cross, in centre Royal Cypher surmounted by Crown.

Military Cross—Entirely an army decoration, recipient must be a Captain, a commissioned officer of a lower grade or a Warrant Officer. Can be awarded to officers and warrant officers of R.A.F. for services on the ground only. Consists of an ornamental silver cross, on each side of which an Imperial Crown, with Imperial Cypher in centre.

Distinguished Conduct Medal—Exclusively for non-commissioned officers and men of the Army. Bears on one side an effigy of the Sovereign, and on the other the words "FOR DIS-TINGUISHED CONDUCT IN THE FIELD".

Conspicuous Gallantry Medal—For Petty officers and men of the Royal Navy and non-commissioned officers and men of the Royal Marines. On one side the effigy of the Sovereign, on the other the words "FOR CONSPICUOUS GALLANTRY".

Distinguished Service Medal—Awarded to petty officers and men of the Royal Navy, non-commissioned officers and men of the Royal Marines, and all other persons holding corresponding positions in the naval services. It bears on one side an effigy of the Sovereign, and on the other the words "FOR DIS-TINGUISHED SERVICE".

The Military Medal—Awarded to non-commissioned officers and men of the Army. On one side is an effigy of the Sovereign, on the reverse the words "FOR BRAVERY IN THE FIELD".

Naval General Service Medal (1793-1840)—The obverse shows the diademed head of Queen Victoria, the usual legend and the date 1848. The reverse shows figure of Britannia seated on a sea-horse.

Engagement bars for no fewer than 230 different engagements were authorised. These bear the name of the action, or the name of a vessel capturing or defeating an enemy's ship, or the words "BOAT SERVICE" with the date.

Naval General Service Medal—*continued.*

Among some of the bars are the following:—
"1st JUNE 1794": "CAMPERDOWN"; "NILE": "COPEN-HAGEN": "TRAFALGAR".

The last bar to be issued, and the most common, is that described "SYRIA", for the operations of November, 1840.

Military General Service Medal (1793-1814)—The obverse shows the diademed head of Queen Victoria. Reverse an upright figure of Queen Victoria standing on a dais, crowning the kneeling figure of Wellington with a wreath of laurel.

Round the top circumference are the words "TO THE BRITISH ARMY"; "1793-1814" at the bottom. 29 different bars were issued.

The following is a list of those bars issued:—
"EGYPT": "MAIDA": "ROLEIA": "VIMIERA": "SAHA-GUN": "BENEVENTE": "CORUNNA": "MARTIN-IQUE": "TALAVERA": "GUADELOUPE": "BUSACO": "BARROSA": "FUENTES D'ONOR": "ALBUERA": "JAVA": "CIUDAD RODRIGO": "BADAJOZ": "SALAMANCA": "FORT DETROIT": "CHATEAU-GUAY": "CHRYSTLER'S FARM": "VITTORIA": "PYRENEES": "ST. SEBASTIAN": "NIVELLE": "NIVE": "ORTHES": "TOULOUSE".

Waterloo Medal—Obverse bears effigy of H.R.H. the Prince Regent, with the words "George P. Regent", and on the reverse a winged figure of Victory seated on a plinth, the base of which bears the word "WATERLOO". Round the top is the word "WELLINGTON", and at the bottom the date "June 18th, 1815".

No engagement bars were issued as the medal bears the name of the battle. Bestowed on officers and men who fought at Waterloo, and also those who fought at the Battle of Ligny on 16 June, and at Quatre Bras on 16 June.

First Burma Medal—One side shows the white elephant of Ava kneeling before a victorious lion, with the Union Jack and palm trees in background. Below, a Persian inscription. On the obverse is shown an attacking party advancing toward a pagoda.

Given in gold to officers, and in silver to others, and no engagement bars were issued.

First India Medal (1799-1826)—Obverse head of Queen Victoria. Reverse seated winged figure of Victory in the foreground. Above appears the inscription "To the Army of India" and

First India Medal—*continued.*

below the dates 1799-1826. Issued in 1851 at request and expense of East India Co.

Bars for the following battles were issued:—

"ALLIGHUR": "BATTLE OF DELHI": "ASSYE": "ASSEEGHUR": "LASWAREE": "ARGAUM": "GAWIL-GHUR": "DEFENCE OF DELHI": "BATTLE OF DEIG": "CAPTURE OF DEIG": "NEPAUL": "KIRKEE": "POONA": "KIRKEE AND POONA": "SEETABUL-DEE": "NAGPORE": "SEETABULDEE AND NAG-PORE": "MAHEIDPOOR": "CORYGAUM": "AVA": "BHURTPOOR".

Several other medals for special battles were issued, including: "GHUZNEE": "JELLALABAD": "CANDAHAR, GHUZNEE AND CABUL": "DEFENCE OF KELAT-I-GHILZIE": "SINDE": and Stars issued for the Gwalior Campaign, with round the centre of the star "MAHARAJ-POOR 1843" or "PUNNIAR 1843".

China Medal (1842)—Obverse head of Queen Victoria, reverse a palm tree, oval shield with the Royal Arms and a trophy of weapons.

Given to men of the Navy and Army who had taken part in the following operations in China:—

Chusan 1841. Canton River 1841. Amoy, Nigpo, Chinpae, Tsekee Chapoo: in the Yang-tse-Kian; Woosung River; assault upon Ching-Kiang-Foo. No engagement bars were issued.

Medal for Sutlej Campaign (Sikh War) 1845-6—Obverse head of Queen Victoria, reverse a figure of Victory holding a laurel wreath and a palm branch.

The words "ARMY OF THE SUTLEJ" round top, and at bottom the name and date of the battle for which the medal was struck.

The following battles were inscribed on medals:—

"MOODKEE 1845": "FEROZESHUHUR 1845": "ALIWAL 1846": "SOBRAON 1846".

For a first medal a soldier received one with the corresponding battle inscribed, and if he took part in another engagement later he was given an engagement bar bearing the name of the second battle.

New Zealand Medal—Obverse diademed head of Queen Victoria, reverse a wreath of laurel, inside which appears the dates of service of the recipient. The words "NEW ZEALAND" above, and "VIRTUTIS HONOR" below.

New Zealand Medal—*continued.*

Issued to officers and men of Navy and Army for services against the Maoris between 1845 and 1847, and again for operations carried out from 1860 to 1866. No bars were issued. Some medals have only a single date inscribed, and some have no date.

Punjab Medal (1848-9)—Obverse head of Queen Victoria, reverse a party of Sikhs laying down their arms to General Sir Walter Raleigh Gilbert who appears on horseback. Words "To the Army of the Punjab" at the top, and round the bottom MDCCCXLIX. Given to officers and men of the Navy and Army.

Three engagements bars were issued: "MOOLTAN": "CHILIANWALA" and "GOOJERAT".

India General Service Medal (1854)—Obverse head of Queen Victoria, reverse shows winged figure of Victory crowning a seated warrior with a wreath of laurel.

Medal was issued for a number of small wars and expeditions, with the following bars:—

"PEGU": "PERSIA": "NORTHWEST FRONTIER": "UMBEYLA": "BHOOTAN": "LOOSHAI": "PERAK": "JOWAKI 1877-8": "NAGA 1879-80": "BURMA 1885-7": "SIKKIM 1888": "HAZARA 1891": "BURMA 1887-89": "CHIN-LUSHAI 1889-90": "SAMANA 1891": "HAZARA 1891": "N. E. FRONTIER 1891": "HUNZA 1891": "BURMA 1889-92": "LUSHAI 1889-92": "CHIN HILLS 1892-93": "KACHIN HILLS 1892-93": "WAZIRISTAN 1894-5".

Medals for South Africa (1834-5, 1846-7, 1850-3, 1877-9)—Obverse diademed head of Queen Victoria, reverse crouching British lion behind a bush with the words "SOUTH AFRICA" above. No engagement bars were issued.

Crimea Medal (1854-6)—Obverse head of Queen Victoria, reverse flying figure of Victory crowning with a laurel wreath a Roman warrior armed with a shield and sword. The word "CRIMEA" is inscribed vertically to the left of the warrior.

The following engagement bars were issued:—

"INKERMAN": "ALMA": "BALAKLAVA": "SEBAS-TOPOL": with a bar for "AZOFF" awarded to the Navy.

Medals issued to the 17th Lancers, 13th Light Dragoons, 11th Hussars, 4th Light Dragoons and 8th Hussars are most highly prized by collectors owing to the historic charge of the Light Brigade.

Baltic Medal (1854-5)—Obverse head of Queen Victoria, reverse seated figure of Britannia holding a trident, with the word "BALTIC" above and the dates "1854-1855" below. No engagement bars were issued. Issued to officers and men on board H.M. Ships which were in the Baltic in those years, and also to two officers and ninety men of the Sappers and Miners who served on board the flagship.

Indian Mutiny Medal (1857-8)—Obverse head of Queen Victoria, reverse a standing figure of Britannia with a shield. The British lion appears in the background. The word "INDIA" at the top, and below the dates "1857-1858". Awarded to British troops employed in the mutiny and also to officers and men of H.M.S. "Pearl" and "Shannon", and to the crews of the Hon. East India Co. vessels "Calcutta" and "Sans Peril".

The following engagement bars were issued:—

"DELHI": "DEFENCE OF LUCKNOW": "RELIEF OF LUCKNOW": "LUCKNOW": "CENTRAL INDIA".

China Medal (1857-60)—Obverse head of Queen Victoria, reverse a palm tree, oval shield with Royal Arms and a trophy of weapons.

Given to officers and men of the Navy and Army, and the following engagements bars were issued:—

"CHINA, 1842" to those entitled to the new medal who were already in possession of the one for 1842.

"CANTON 1857": "TAKU FORTS 1858": "TAKU FORTS 1860": "PEKIN 1860": "FATSHAN 1857".

Canada General Service Medal (1866-70)—Obverse head of Queen Victoria, reverse Canadian flag surrounded by a wreath of maple. Presented to soldiers of British Army and to those of the Canadian Militia by the Canadian Government. The following three bars were issued:—

"FENIAN RAID 1866": "FENIAN RAID 1870": "RED RIVER 1870".

Abyssinian Medal (1867-8)—Obverse small bust of Queen Victoria within a beaded circle, forming the centre of a nine-pointed star. Word "ABYSSINIA" spaced out in the triangular spaces between each point of star. Reverse a laurel wreath inside of which are the name, rank and ship or regiment of the recipient.

Ashantee Medal (1873-4)—Obverse head of Queen Victoria, reverse a scene in high relief, representing a fight in the bush between British soldiers and natives. An engagement bar inscribed "COOMASSIE" was awarded.

East and West Africa Medal (1887-1900)—The Ashantee medal was again made use of for the many expeditions in East and West Africa, and it is impossible to mention all the campaigns. Issued to officers and men of the Navy and Army, and the following are some of the bars issued:—

"WITU 1890": "JUBA RIVER 1893"; "LIWONDI 1893": "LAKE NYASSA 1893": "GAMBIA 1894": "BENIN RIVER 1894": "BRASS RIVER 1895": "NIGER 1897": "BENIN 1897": "DAWKITA 1897": "SIERRA LEONE 1898-99".

Medal for Afghanistan (1878-80)—Obverse head of Queen Victoria, reverse a column of British troops shown on the march, accompanied by native cavalry, and an elephant. The word "AFGHANISTAN" appears on the reverse.

The following engagement bars were issued:—

"ALI MUSJID": "PEIWAR KOTAL": "CHARASIA": "AHMED KHEL": "KABUL": "KANDAHAR".

Kabul to Kandahar Star (1880)—Consists of a five-pointed star, in bronze. In centre the imperial cypher "V.R.I." encircled by, words "KABUL TO KANDAHAR". Back of star generally inscribed with name, rank and regiment of the recipient.

Cape of Good Hope General Service Medal—Obverse head of Queen Victoria, reverse arms of Cape Colony, with the words "Cape of Good Hope" around.

Three bars were awarded:—

"BASUTOLAND": "TRANSKEI" and "BECHUANA-LAND".

Egyptian Medal (1882-9)—Obverse head of Queen Victoria, reverse shows a representation of the Sphinx, with word "EGYPT" above. Medal issued in 1882 bears date below, but later medals omit date.

The following engagement bars were issued:—

"ALEXANDRIA 11th JULY": "TEL-EL-KEBIR": "SUAKIN 1884": "EL TEB": "TAMAAI": "EL TEB. TAMAAI": "THE NILE 1884-85": "ABU KLEA": "KIRBEKAN": "SUAKIN 1885": "TOFREK": "GEMAI-ZAH 1888": "TOSKI 1889".

North West Canada (1885)—Obverse head of Queen Victoria, reverse words "NORTH WEST CANADA" surrounded by a wreath of maple. The medal was given to Canadian troops engaged in Riel's rebellion, and no British troops were present. One bar "SASKATCHEWAN" was awarded.

India Medal (1895)—Obverse head of Queen Victoria, reverse shows a British and an Indian soldier each supporting a British standard. At the sides the word "INDIA" and the date 1895.

The following engagement bars were issued:—

"DEFENCE OF CHITRAL 1895": "RELIEF OF CHITRAL 1895": "PUNJAB FRONTIER 1897-98": "MALAKAND 1897": "SAMANA 1897": "TIRAH 1897-8".

In 1903 it was issued with effigy of King Edward VII and the bar "WAZIRISTAN 1901-2".

Central Africa Medal (1891-8)—Obverse and reverse same as Ashantee Medal, 1874, but as ribbon is different it is held to be a separate decoration. No bars were given, but in 1899 the same medal was again issued for operations in Central Africa and a bar inscribed "CENTRAL AFRICA 1894-1898" was given.

Sudan Medal (1896-7)—Obverse half-length figure of Queen Victoria, on reverse a seated figure of Victory and draped flags. Below the word "SUDAN". No engagement bars were awarded.

East and Central Africa Medal (1897-9)—Obverse as for Sudan Medal, reverse a standing figure of Britannia with trident and with British lion standing at side. The words "EAST & CENTRAL AFRICA" appear below.

The following bars were issued:—

"LUBWA'S": "UGANDA 1897-98": "UGANDA 1899".

South African Medal (1899-1902)—Obverse head of Queen Victoria, reverse standing figure of Britannia, extending right hand with laurel wreath towards a party of soldiers.

The following bars were issued:—

"CAPE COLONY": "NATAL": "RHODESIA": "RELIEF OF MAFEKING": "DEFENCE OF KIMBERLEY": "TALANA": "ELANDSLAAGTE": "DEFENCE OF LADYSMITH": "BELMONT": "MODDER RIVER": "TUGELA HEIGHTS": "RELIEF OF KIMBERLEY": "PAARDEBERG": "ORANGE FREE STATE": "RELIEF OF LADYSMITH": "DRIEFONTEIN": "WEPENER": "DEFENCE OF MAFEKING": "TRANSVAAL": "JOHANNESBURG": "LAINGS NEK": "DIAMOND HILL": "WITTEBERGEN": "BELFAST": "SOUTH AFRICA 1901": "SOUTH AFRICA 1902".

The last two bars were awarded to those officers and men who had served in South Africa during those years, but who were not eligible for the medal subsequently given by King Edward.

King Edward's South African Medal—Obverse head of King Edward VII with reverse same as South African Medal. Given to all officers and men actually serving in South Africa on or after January 1st, 1902, with bars inscribed "SOUTH AFRICA 1901" and "SOUTH AFRICA 1902". Those who did not qualify for the King's medal were eligible to receive the bars with their Queen's medals.

China Medal (1900)—Obverse head of Queen Victoria, reverse as for China medal of 1842. The following bars were issued:—
"TAKU FORTS": "DEFENCE OF LEGATIONS": "RELIEF OF PEKIN".

Ashanti Medal (1901)—Obverse bust of King Edward, reverse British lion looking towards rising sun with native spear and shields at feet. A bar inscribed "KUMASSI" was awarded to those who took part in its defence and relief.

Africa General Service Medal (1902)—Obverse as Ashanti Medal, reverse as for East and Central Africa medal, with word "AFRICA" below. The following engagement bars were awarded:—

"N. NIGERIA": "N. NIGERIA 1902": "N. NIGERIA 1903": "N. NIGERIA 1903-4": "N. NIGERIA 1904": "N. NIGERIA 1906": "S. NIGERIA": "S. NIGERIA 1902": "S. NIGERIA 1902-3": "S. NIGERIA 1903": "S. NIGERIA 1903-4": "S. NIGERIA 1904": "S. NIGERIA 1904-5": "S. NIGERIA 1905": "S. NIGERIA 1905-6": "EAST AFRICA 1902": "EAST AFRICA 1904": "EAST AFRICA 1905": "EAST AFRICA 1906": "WEST AFRICA 1906": "WEST AFRICA 1908": "WEST AFRICA 1909-10": "SOMALILAND 1902-04": "SOMALILAND 1908-10": "JUBALAND": "UGANDA 1900": "B.C.A. 1899-1900": "GAMBIA": "ARO 1901-1902": "LANGO 1901": "JIDBALLI": "KISSI 1905": "NANDI 1905-6".

Another medal for Africa with effigy of George V was issued in 1916. This medal was not issued without bars, and the following bars were awarded:—

"SHIMBER BERRIS 1914-15": "NYASALAND 1915": Recipients already in possession of King Edward's medal only received the new bars.

Further new bars were sanctioned:—"EAST AFRICA 1913-14": "EAST AFRICA 1913": "EAST AFRICA 1914": Again only officers and men already in possession of King Edward's medal received the new bars.

Africa General Service Medal—*continued.*

Bars subsequently issued were:—"EAST AFRICA 1915": "JUBALAND 1917-18"; "NIGERIA 1918": "EAST AFRICA 1918": "SOMALILAND 1920".

The African General Service Medal is never seen without a bar.

India General Service Medal (1908)—Obverse bust of King Edward VII, reverse a hilltop fort with mountains in background, and word "INDIA" below. One bar was granted:—"NORTH WEST FRONTIER 1908", but the medal was re-issued with the bust of George V, and the following bars were awarded:— "ABOR 1911-12", issued only to those in possession of the King Edward medal. Bars issued later were: "AFGHANI-STAN N.W.F. 1919": "WAZIRISTAN 1919-20": "MAHSUD 1919-20": "MALABAR 1921-22": "WAZIRISTAN 1921-24": "WAZIRISTAN 1925"—R.A.F. only: "NORTH-WEST FRONTIER 1930-31": "BURMA 1930-32": "MOH-MAND 1933": "NORTH-WEST FRONTIER 1935".

Naval General Service Medal (1915)—Obverse head of King George in naval uniform, reverse a representation of Britannia and two sea-horses travelling through the sea.

Bars issued were:—

"PERSIAN GULF": "IRAQ 1919-20": "NORTH-WEST PERSIAN 1920".

In 1940 it was announced that the bar "PALESTINE" would be issued, with medal bearing effigy of King George VI.

General Service Medal (Army and R.A.F.)—Instituted in 1918. Obverse head of King George V or King George VI, reverse winged figure of Victory.

The following bars have been issued:—

"IRAQ": "KURDISTAN": "N.W. PERSIA": "S. PERSIA": "SOUTHERN DESERT IRAQ": "NORTHERN KURDIS-TAN": "PALESTINE".

India General Service (1936)—Obverse crowned head of King, reverse a tiger to the left, with the word "INDIA" above, and a view of the N. W. Frontier.

The following bar has been issued:—

"NORTH-WEST FRONTIER 1936-37".

It is not necessary to describe here the issue of the usual Stars and Medals during the wars of 1914-18, and 1939-45. All serving members of the Forces received issues depending on what zone of operations they were in, and the medals themselves are not of any high value.

In addition to the above-described medals, others are also issued which are in demand by collectors, such as:—

Long Service and Good Conduct Medals, all services.

Meritorious Service Medals.

Volunteer Long Service Medals.

Efficiency Medals, Territorial, etc.

Royal Naval Reserve Decorations and **Long Service Medals.**

Police Medals.

Lloyd's Medals,

and many other similar medals, including foreign issues to British personnel, such as the **Turkish Crimea Medal** and the **Khedives Bronze Star.**

ARMS and ARMOUR

Acketon—A quilted jacket worn beneath armour in the 13th and 14th centuries.

Acinaces—A short straight dagger used by the Medes and Persians.

Acontium—An ancient Grecian javelin or dart of light weight, thrown by means of the **Amentum** (a thong), and used by cavalry.

Agraffe—A hook-and-eye clasp fastening used on armour and on costumes.

Ailette or **Aillette**—Leather shoulder appendages to armour worn by knights in the 13th and 14th century; the shapes vary and include circular, lozenge and cruciform; also represented in stained glass windows, etc.

Ala—The feather affixed to an arrow.

Alcato—Collar of mail worn as a protector for the throat by the Crusaders.

Allecret—A half suit of light armour used by the Swiss in the 16th century.

Almayne—The name given to a rivet sliding in slot holes in overlapping plates of armour.

Amgarn—A stone implement or weapon of primitive times.

Andrea Ferrara—A Scottish broadsword of the 16th and 17th centuries.

Anjou—An old spear-like weapon mounted on a long shaft.

Anlace or **Anelace**—A very broad dagger worn at the girdle.

Antyx—The ornamental rim of a shield, etc.

Arbalest—A cross-bow consisting of a steel bow and a wood stock with a trigger for releasing the bow string. (*See Quarrel.*)

Armet—Modern writers intend by this term an early form of the close-helmet (*q.v.*). The cheek-pieces were hinged and fastened at the chin, with a roundel on a short stem at the back.

369

Armour—A protective clothing worn in battle; generally made of metal but also of skins, hardened leather, etc. The type varied from time to time as weapons developed and became more effective. A full suit of armour plate probably consisted of the following parts:—helmet with beaver, gorget, pauldron, breast-plate, rerebrace, coudière, gauntlets, vambrace, skirt of taces, cingulum, tuilles, guisse, genouillère, jambes and sollerets.

Arquebuse or Harquebus—A hand gun; one of the earliest firearms, fired by applying a match at the touch-hole, and afterwards by a trigger.

Arrow—A missile weapon shot from a bow, usually a slender barbed and feathered shaft.

Assagai or Assegai—A South African native spear made from the assagai tree, usually tipped with iron and used as a missile and for stabbing.

Ataghan—(*See Yatagan.*)

Avant-Bras—A piece of armour which protected the forearm.

Bainberg—Plate armour for protecting the shins.

Balarao—A large two-edged dagger used in the Philippines.

Baldric—An ornamental belt worn over one shoulder and across the breast, to support a sword or other weapon.

Ballista, Balista, or Balister—An ancient engine of war in the form of a cross-bow for hurling large missiles.

Ballok—An ornamental dagger worn at the girdle in the 14th century.

Balteus—A Roman girdle or baldric (*q.v.*).

Bancal—A French sabre as used by Napoleon's officers.

Bandoleer or Bandolier—A belt worn either over one shoulder and under the opposite arm, or round the waist, to carry cartridges, gunpowder, etc.

Barb—Armour used for a horse. (*See Bard.*)

Barbet—A 16th-century beaver or the lower part of a visor when made to operate separately.

Barbute—A steel helmet worn by infantrymen during the 15th and 16th centuries.

Bard or Barde—Plate armour worn by horses and men-at-arm, in the 16th century. (*See Barb.*)

Barette—The crossbar on the hilt of an old fencing foil or rapier.

Barong—A leaf-shaped knife with a thin back and cutting edge.

Bar-shot—A dumb-bell-shaped missile, once used to destroy the rigging of ships in naval combat.

Basinet—A light steel head covering worn under a battle helmet in the Middle Ages.

Baston—A Norman cudgel.

Battle Axe or **Ax**—An offensive weapon; a halberd, broadaxe or bill; made in many shapes and sizes.

Bayonet—A dagger-like weapon made to fit on the muzzle of a rifle or musket (named from Bayonne, France).

Beaver—The hinged part of a battle helmet which protects the lower part of the face, as distinct from the visor (*q.v.*).

Bec-de-Corbin—The pointed end of the martel-de-fer (*q.v.*); a crow's beak.

Besague—Usually in the form of a roundel of steel, employed for protecting a joint in plate armour.

Besague—A double-edged axe.

Bident—An ancient two-pronged weapon, similar to a trident.

Bilbo—A Spanish rapier or sword.

Bill—A weapon of medieval times, consisting of a hook-shaped blade with a pike at the top and back, mounted on a pole.

Bipennis—A double-bladed axe.

Bistoury—A dagger or knife.

Blunderbuss—A short musket with a very large bore, used in the 17th century.

Bolas—A missile weapon consisting of two or three thongs, to the ends of which are attached balls of iron, stone or other materials. Used by South American gauchos for entangling cattle. (*See Goupillon.*)

Bolo—A large single-edged knife or dagger.

Bolt—A blunt-pointed arrow used with a crossbow.

Bombard or **Lombard**—An ancient cannon or mortar; a primitive firearm consisting of a tube with a touch-hole.

Boomerang—An Australian native weapon made of hard wood and bent in form, about 22 ins. long; when properly thrown returns behind the thrower if it fails to strike its objective.

Bouche—A small aperture in a shield to accommodate the sword blade or lance shaft.

Bouchette—In medieval armour, a buckle fastening the lower part of the breastplate to the upper part.

Bourrelet—A wreath worn on a helmet by a knight.

Bracelet—A piece of armour for the wrist or arm; the vambrace (*q.v.*).

Bracer—A guard for the arm or wrist, as in archery.

Brachiale—A protective piece of armour for the upper arm. (*See Brassard.*)

Braconnière—In 16th-century armour, a protection for the thighs, consisting of a series of overlapping hoops which were free to move. Also called Brayette. It succeeded the tasset.

Braguette—A piece of 15th-century armour, corresponding to the codpiece of ordinary attire.

Brassard—A piece of armour for the protection of the upper arm from the shoulder to the elbow. (*See Brachiale.*)

Breastplate—A piece of armour worn as a protection to the breast. Some old examples are particularly ornate. A few cavalry regiments still wear breastplates as ornaments.

Brigandine—A medieval coat of body armour consisting of metal plates, scales or rings sewn on leather.

Broigne—A garment on which metal rings or plates were sewn as a protection.

Brown Bess—The popular nickname given to the old smooth bore musket with flint lock, at one time used by the British army.

Brown Bill—The popular name for the bill or halberd.

Buckler—An old shield of varying shape but usually with a boss in the centre, worn on the left arm by spearmen.

Buffe—A vizor.

Burgonet—A light helmet with cheek pieces and sometimes a nose guard.

Burr—The broad ring towards the base of a tilting lance to prevent the hand slipping.

Cabasset—A 16th-century helmet worn by both cavalry and infantry.

Calcotte—A close-fitting helmet without brim or vizor; a skull cap.

Caldric—A leather bandolier with a bullet pouch and a number of tin containers, each to hold a charge of powder.

Caliver—A harquebus or musket used in the 16th century.

Caltrop—A four-pronged instrument of iron, one point of which always stands upright, used to check the advance of cavalry.

Camail—A neck guard of chain mail, especially one hanging from a head piece.

Camisade or **Camisado**—A white shirt once worn by soldiers over their armour as a means of recognition.

Campilan—A straight two-edged sword used in the Philippines.

Canberia—Pieces of armour to protect the legs and feet.

Canjar—A short Indian dagger.

Cap-à-pie—From head to foot; armed cap-à-pie, i.e., wearing a full suit of armour. (*See Panoply*.)

Capeline—A 13th-century helmet with neck and cheek pieces and a nose-guard.

Capellum—A flap at the base of the handle of a sword to act as a rain guard.

Capularis—The ornamental handle of a sword or knife.

Carbine—A short gun for use by mounted troops.

Cargan—A medieval collar of mail.

Carronade—A Scottish light cannon distinguished by having no trunnions, principally used on ships.

Cascabel—A knob or loop projection at the breech of a cannon.

Casque or **Cask**—Any metal helmet worn in battle; the steel hats worn by soldiers in the Great and World Wars may be described as casques.

Casquetel—A casque or helmet having no vizor or beaver.

Catchpole—A medieval weapon comprising a two-pronged fork mounted on a long handle, used for catching an enemy by the neck.

Cavalot—An old rampart gun.

Cerebrerium—An iron skull-cap of medieval times.

Chain-Mail—Suits of armour made up of small interlocking rings or links; worn during the 12th and 13th centuries.

Chanfron, Chamfron, Chamfrain or **Chaffron**—The armour mask at one time worn by horses in battle, from the front of which an iron spike projects.

Chape—The metal mountings to a scabbard, particularly the end cap or crampit (*q.v.*), and the part by which it is attached to the belt.

Chausses or **Chausson**—Long chain-mail stockings to cover the legs and body below the waist; short skirts of armour covering the thighs.

Cheek-Piece—Fixed or hinged pieces of a helmet which protect the cheeks.

Chevaux-de-frise—A series of spikes attached to a beam, used by military to impede cavalry.

Chirotheca—An armour gauntlet.

Cingulum—A belt or girdle; in armour, a belt from which weapons were suspended.

Clavain—An armour covering for the neck and shoulders.

Claymore—A large Scottish two-edged sword; it sometimes had a two-handed haft.

Cleddyo—A bronze leaf-shaped sword of Celtic origin.

Clich—A Turkish broad-bladed sabre.

Clothyard Shaft—An arrow the length of a yard of cloth, used with the English longbow.

Coat of Mail—A close-fitting coat of leather upon which interlaced rings or plates were sewn. (*See Brigandine.*)

Cocker—A quiver for arrows.

Colletin—A piece of plate-armour to protect the neck, sometimes attached to the helmet.

Contus—A long Roman spear used in hunting.

Copis—A Greek curved sword used for cutting rather than for thrusting.

Corazine—A defensive garment worn by Norman soldiers.

Corselet—The name given to a piece of armour, particularly of the 16th century, consisting of the breastplate and the back-piece joined together.

Corytus—A Roman case for arrows; a quiver.

Costile or **Custile**—A short sword or dagger in use during the Middle Ages.

Coudiere or **Coude**—A piece of plate armour to protect the elbow; it could be worn over mail.

Couse—A 14th-century glaive (*q.v.*).

Couteau—The French word for knife, but particularly applied to one that is long and double-edged.

Crampit—The metal protective cap or chape (*q.v.*) at the base of a sword scabbard.

Creese, Crease or **Kris**—A Malay dagger with a blade of serpentine shape.

Crinet—The piece of protective armour covering a horse's neck and mane.

Crista—A crest worn on helmets by the Romans.

Croc—A weapon with hooked points resembling a halberd (*q.v.*).

Cross-bow—An antique weapon formed by placing a bow across a stock. (*See Quarrel and Arbalest.*)

Crouper—Armour covering the croup or rump of a horse.

Crowbill—A battle-axe with a stiletto hidden in its handle.

Cue—A rest or support for the lance when charging. (*See Faucre*).

Cuirass—An old armour breastplate, originally made of leather but later of metal.

Cuisse—A piece of armour for the thighs.

Culet—In medieval armour, the part that hangs from the waist at the back.

Cultel—A long knife carried by the attendant of a knight.

Culverin—Like a serpent; the name given at first to a kind of musket and later to a long cannon having serpent-shaped handles.

Curtana—The pointless sword carried before English kings at their coronation; the sword of mercy.

Cuspis—The sharp point of a spear or lance; a cusp.

Custile—A dagger or large knife.

Cutlass—A broad, curved naval sword.

Dag or **Dagg**—A large pistol used in the 15th and 16th centuries.

Dagger—A short stabbing weapon.

Dague-a-Roelle—A dagger with a disc-shaped guard.

Darloch or **Dorlach**—A Scottish name for a bundle of arrows.

Dart—A small throwing spear or javelin or as used in blow-guns by natives.

Derringer—A short-barrelled pistol firing a large ball.

Dhar—A long-handled Siamese sword.

Dirk—A Scottish dagger-shaped sword or poniard, the sheath for which is often ornamented with silver and amethysts, topazes, etc.

Dolphin—One of the handles by which an old cannon was lifted.

Dossière—A backplate.

Doublet of Defence—A coat of linen or leather covered with scales of metal.

Dragon—A short 17th-century musket carried hooked to the belt by dragoons.

Dudgeon—A dagger having its handle made of dudgeon, a kind of boxwood.

Dusack—A roughly-made sword with the blade and hilt in one piece, used in Germany in the 16th century.

Ear Lap or **Ear Piece**—That part of a helmet which covers and protects the ears.

Ecu—A triangular shield carried by mounted men-at-arms in the 14th and 15th centuries.

Emerasse—An escutcheon or ailette worn on the shoulder by an armed knight.

Enarme—The arrangement of straps by which a shield was held on the arm.

Epaulière—A piece of plate armour worn to protect the shoulder.

Epinglette—A priming wire used for old cannon.

Escopette—A name formerly given to a short musket or carbine.

Espadon—A long two-handed sword used by foot soldiers in the late Middle Ages.

Estoc—A small sword, at one time worn in place of a dagger; it varied in different periods.

Estocade—A heavy thrusting sword used in the 16th and 17th centuries.

Estramacon—A straight heavy sword used principally for cutting.

Falarica—A Roman throwing-spear.

Falchion—A slightly curved broad-bladed sword, used in the Middle Ages.

Falcon—A light cannon used in the 15th century. **Falconet**—A small type of falcon.

Falcon Bill—A weapon of the battle-axe type curved to represent a falcon's beak.

Fauchard—A long-handled weapon with a concave edge.

Faucre—An attachment fixed to a breastplate to steady a lance or spear when charging. (*See Cue.*)

Feltrum—A quilted jacket worn by medieval soldiers.

Feuter—The rest for a lance used by medieval horsemen.

Finger Guard—An extension to the hilt of a sword as a protection for the fingers.

Flamberg—The name once given to a rapier-like sword.

Flanchard or **Flancard**—A piece of armour used for protecting the flanks of a horse.

Flintlock—An old musket fired by means of a flint fixed in the hammer-head striking the steel pan, thus causing a spark to fire the charge.

Foil—A thin bar of pliable steel made up as a rapier and used in fencing, the blunt point being covered by a small ball of leather; a leaf or thin plate of metal.

Fowling Piece—A light gun for shooting birds, etc.

Framea—A spear of Germanic origin having an iron head, used as a pike or a javelin.

Francisc or **Francisca**—A long slender battle-axe used by the Franks.

Frontal—The name given to a piece of armour for covering the face of a knight or a horse's forehead.

Fusil—A small musket with a flintlock.

Gad—A spike attached to a gauntlet.

Gambeson—A garment of cloth or leather worn under armour in the Middle Ages.

Garde-Bras or **Garde-Brace**—An additional piece of armour covering the elbow joint. **Garde-Collet**—A ridge piece worn at the neck as a protection against glancing blows. **Garde-Faude**—A kind of skirt hanging below the tassets. **Garde-Reine**—A protective piece for the lower part of the back.

Gauntlet—A steel glove formerly worn by knights, etc.

Genouillères—The knee pieces in a suit of plate armour; sometimes separate pieces strapped to the jambes. (*q.v.*)

Giberne—A pouch in which soldiers once carried grenades.

Gladius—The Latin name for a sword.

Glaive—Is a broad-bladed pole arm in which the edge curves backwards to the point. 12th and 13th centuries.

Godendag—A poleaxe with a spike at the end, used in the 13th and 14th centuries.

Gorget—A piece of armour, either plate or chain, used to protect the throat.

Goupillon—A weapon consisting of a handle to which several short chains with spiked balls at the ends were attached. (*See Bolas*.)

Grand Guard—A piece of plate armour attached to the breastplate to give additional protection.

Greaves—Pieces of plate armour to protect the legs below the knees.

Guard—A protection on the hilt of a sword for guarding the hand.

Guige—A leather strap used by medieval knights to sling their shields when not in use.

Guisarme or **Gisarme**—A battle-axe mounted on a long pole, carried by medieval soldiers; the heads are of numerous shapes.

Guissette—A piece of plate armour for covering the thigh.

Habergeon or **Haubergeon**—A short sleeveless jacket of mail or armour which reached only half-way down the thighs. 14th century. (*See Hauberk*.)

Habena—A thong used on a spear or lance.

Hache—A soldier's axe; in heraldry, an axe when depicted as a charge.

Hake—A pike or similar weapon.

Halberd—A 16th-century weapon similar to a double-headed axe but with a spike projecting from the centre, mounted on a pole 5ft. or 6ft. long.

Hand Buckler—A 16th-century small shield worn on the left arm to parry sword thrusts.

Handseax—A knife formerly carried by Celtic warriors.

Hanger—A light, slightly curved sword once used by seamen.

Harquebus—Also **Harquebuse** and **Harquebuss**. (*See Arquebuse*.)

Hasta—A Roman spear.

Haubergeon—A short hauberk; a coat of mail extending to the thighs.

Hauberk—In armour, a long coat-of-mail. (*See Haubergeon*.)

Hausse-Col—A piece of armour similar to the plastron, in use during the 14th century; later, a protective piece for the throat or as a badge of rank.

Haute-de-Barde—A piece of plate-armour forming a shield and encircling a horse's body in front of the saddle.

Hautepiece—A piece of armour fixed to the breastplate, designed to protect the face.

Helm—A heavy headpiece or helmet carried at the saddle and worn only when in battle.

Helmet—A headpiece of lighter construction than the helm, made in many forms.

Heumat—An old name for a helmet.

Heilaman—A shield used by Australian aborigines.

Hilt—The handle of a sword, usually protected by a guard.

Hobitz—An old name for a mortar or howitzer.

Holster—A leather case for carrying a pistol, shaped to facilitate quick withdrawal.

Imbricate—To lay pieces in order, one overlapping another, as the scales of fish.

Iztle—A kind of obsidian used by Indians for making arrow heads.

Jack—A defensive coat worn by archers in the Middle Ages, made of leather or stout canvas lined with small metal plates between the stitchings or folds.

Jamb, Jambe or **Jambeau**—A piece or pieces of armour used to protect the leg.

Japanese Armour—Was originally made of a strong lacquered material finished in black.

Javelin—A light spear for throwing or thrusting; the shaft was made of tough wood with a barbed pyramidal head, the weapon being of a total length of about 5ft. to 6ft.

Javelot—A small javelin or throwing spear.

Jazerant or **Jesserant**—Suits of armour made of metal plates mounted on linen or other lining and linked together with steel wire.

Jedburgh Axe or **Jeddart Staff**—A battle-axe with a handle or staff about 9ft. in length.

Jesserant, Jesseraunte or **Jazerant**—A coat of mail in which splints or small metal plates were mounted on material so as to overlap.

Jingal—A large musket for which a rest was required during firing.

Jupon—A long sleeveless surcoat worn over armour in the 15th century.

Kabuto—A large helmet worn by old-time Japanese warriors.

Kargas—A curved Indian dagger.

Katana—A single-edged Japanese sword, usually about 3ft. in length.

Kettle Hat—An iron helmet worn by soldiery in the 14th and 15th centuries.

Knapskull—A name formerly given to a helmet.

Knobkerri—A short club with a knobbed end, used by Kaffirs as a missile weapon.

Kris or **Kriss**—(*See Creese.*)

Kukri—The famous weapon of the Gurkhas, similar in shape to the scimitar, but smaller; used only for striking.

Kuttar or **Katar**—A short Indian dagger with a handle consisting of two parallel bars joined by a crosspiece.

Lambel—A screen-shaped piece of armour used to protect the breast or flanks of a horse, usually made of cuir bouilli (*q.v.*).

Lamboys—A flexible steel shield worn by soldiers in the Tudor period.

Lamina—A thin plate or scale as used in armour; a piece of armour so made.

Lancegay—A name formerly given to a spear or javelin.

Langue de boeuf—A short Italian sword with broad blade somewhat resembling an ox tongue; a French pike of the 15th century similarly shaped.

Languet—The small stiffening tongue which extends down the blade of a sword from its hilt.

Lascaree—An Indian hunting spear.

Linstock—An iron-pointed staff or pike with branches or forks for holding a lighted match with which to fire a cannon.

Lochaber Axe—An old Scottish battle-axe with a narrow blade and a hook.

Locket—The strengthened part of a sword scabbard to which the belt hook is attached.

Longbow—The national weapon of England from the 14th century until replaced by firearms, made of ash or yew, and as high as the bowman using it.

Lumière—The eye-slit in the visor of a helmet.

Mace—A strong short wooden staff with a spiked iron ball-shaped head, at one time a favourite weapon.

Machete or **Machette**—A heavy, broad knife about 2ft. long, used by Spanish Americans in husbandry and as a weapon.

Mail—As applied to armour, represents the flexible fabric made up of a series of small metal rings interlinked so as to form a protective covering.

Manifer—A heavy iron gauntlet used by knights when tilting.

Mall—A medieval hammer-shaped weapon.

Malkin—A mop attached to a hinged rod, used for cleaning the barrels of cannons.

Manubalist—A crossbow or similar weapon.

Martel-de-fer—A hammer-like weapon with one end pointed, used by horsemen in the Middle Ages. (*See Bec-de-Corbin.*)

Mascled—Describing armour made up of small lozenge-shaped pieces.

Matchlock—An old musket with touch-hole, the charge being fired with a lighted match.

Maximilian Armour—A 15th-century armour in which the larger pieces are fluted.

Merai—A club-like weapon once used by the Maoris.

Mere—A short flat Maori club of bone, wood, etc., now represented by charms made of jade and similar materials.

Mesail—The visor of a medieval helmet.

Misericord—A thin dagger of medieval times.

Mitrailleuse Pistol—An old pistol having four or six barrels.

Morion or **Morrion**—An iron or steel helmet worn by men-at-arms, distinguished from the helmets worn by knights by having no visor or beaver.

Morne—The blunted end of a tilting lance.

Morning Star—The name given to a medieval weapon having a ball-shaped head studded with spikes.

Mortar—A kind of cannon for high-angle firing.

Mortier—A kind of mortar-shaped helmet worn by the French.

Musket—A 17th-century firearm which succeeded the arquebuse (*q.v.*); the original musket was a matchlock (*q.v.*).

Nasal—A piece of armour attached to a helmet so as to form a protection to the nose.

Ocrea—An old Greek name for a greave or shin-guard.

Oreillet—A piece of armour to protect the ear.

Overplate—A piece of medieval plate-armour added to protect the shoulder or elbow.

Palette—A small plate to protect a join or gusset in a suit of armour.

Panoply—A full suit of armour as distinct from one of mail. (*See Cap-à-pie.*)

Paunce or **Pansière**—A piece of plate-armour used as an extra protection to the lower part of the body.

Paraling—A sword used by the natives of Borneo; its handle is usually decorated with a tuft of victim's hair.

Parma—An old circular Roman shield

Partisan—A kind of halberd.

Passegarde—A ridge fitted to the shoulder of a suit of armour as a protection against lance thrusts.

Patu—A Maori's club weapon.

Pauldron—A piece of plate-armour covering the shoulder joint, where the body and arm pieces meet, consisting either of splints or of one pivoted plate.

Pavis or **Pavise**—A large body-shield used by cross-bow men in medieval times.

Pectoral—Armour for the breast.

Pelta—A Greek javelin.

Petronel—A 15th- 16th-century firearm resembling a horse-pistol of large bore.

Pike—A thrusting weapon mounted on a long shaft, much used by infantry in the 16th and 17th centuries.

Pile—The point of an arrow or similar weapon.

Pisan or **Pisane**—A piece of armour to protect the neck and chest.

Pistol—A short firearm intended for use with one hand.

Plastron—A detachable breastplate used with medieval suits of armour.

Plombée—A French weapon consisting of a staff with a weight suspended by short chains from its head.

Pogamoggan—A North-American Indian weapon, consisting of a stone or bone fastened to the end of a slender rod.

Poitrel or **Poitrail**—A breastplate for a horse.

Poleaxe—A weapon having an axe head mounted on a long pole, similar to a halberd.

Pommel—The knob- or globular-shaped body on the hilt of a sword to prevent the hand from slipping.

Poniard—A small slender dagger.

Quarrel—An arrow having a square pointed head, used with a crossbow.

Quillon—One of the arms of the cross-guard of a sword.

Quiver—A case or sheath, usually of leather, in which to carry arrows. It is supported by a strap passing over the right shoulder.

Ranseur—A halberd (*q.v.*) or partisan.

Rapier—A light, highly tempered steel blade, used only for thrusting, as in duels.

Rerebrace—In medieval armour, a piece of plate-armour to protect the upper part of the arm.

Revolver—A small firearm with a revolving cartridge cylinder.

Rifle—A firearm having its barrel rifled (spiral grooves cut in its barrel) to increase the straight line travel of the bullet.

Ring Armour—A type of armour consisting of numerous metal rings sewn on a garment made of leather, used in the Middle Ages.

Rondache—A round shield used by foot soldiers in the Middle Ages.

Rondelle—A small shield, usually round, attached to a lance to protect the hand.

Roundel—A round shield used by Norman soldiers in battle.

Sabre or **Saber**—A heavy sword used by cavalry, sometimes curved towards the point.

Sabre-tache—An ornamental pocket accoutrement which hangs from the sword belt, often enriched with the regimental coat-of-arms.

Sagitta—An arrow with a bronze head used by the ancients.

Sallet or **Salade**—A light, simple 15th-century helmet with a protection for the neck.

Scabbard—A sheath for swords, daggers, bayonets, and the like.

Scale Armour—Composed of a large number of small steel plates riveted or fastened together in such a way as to resemble fish scales.

Scimitar—A curved sword of Eastern origin, used only for striking and of no use for thrusting.

Sclopus—A 14th-century hand gun.

Sconce—A name given to helmets generally.

Scutum—A Roman leather shield, often bound with metal.

Seax—A curved one-edged sword used by Germanic and Celtic peoples.

Secret—A steel cap worn under a hat or other head covering as a protection.

Sica—An ancient curved dagger, in shape resembling a wild boar's tusk.

Siege Cap—A large heavy medieval helmet worn by soldiers besieging a fortress.

Skean-dhu—A small dirk or dagger worn by Highlanders in their stockings. **Skean**—An ancient dagger of Irish origin.

Snaphaunce—The name given to an old flintlock pistol.

Solleret—A flexible steel shoe, usually with long pointed toe, worn by medieval warriors.

Splint Armour—Armour composed of narrow strips of metal riveted to one another.

Stiletto—A small dagger with a narrow blade.

Studded Armour—Made of small pieces of leather fastened together with large-headed rivets.

Taaweesh—A war club used by North American Indians.

Taces, Skirt of—The steel splints forming a short skirt or kilt on which the tuilles (*q.v.*) usually hung.

Taiaha—A Maori club or spear-like weapon carried as a sign of authority.

Targe—A small medieval shield, the large centre boss of which is supposed to resemble a target.

Tegulated Armour—Consists of small overlapping plates, as roofing tiles, sewn on a leather foundation.

Tiller—The handle of a crossbow.

Tomahawk—A light war hatchet made of steel, used by the North American Indians; early examples were made of stone.

Tsuba—A Japanese sword-guard of Soma ware bearing a design cut with a knife by native craftsmen into the hard iron; the design often represents a horse, usua lly bucking and with a halter attached.

Tuck—The name given to any long rapier-like sword.

Tuille—A hinged piece of plate armour to protect the thigh.

Tulwar—A curved sword or sabre used in Northern India.

Umbo—The projecting knob or spike at the centre of a shield.

Umbrel—A movable piece attached to a helmet as a protection to the face.

Vambrace—A piece of medieval armour to protect the arm from the wrist to the elbow, either by enclosing the arm as in a sleeve, or like a shield to the front only.

Vamplate—A funnel-shaped piece of iron fitted to a lance above the grip, to protect the hand.

Visor or Vizor—The adjustable perforated part of a battle helmet, used as a protection for the upper part of the face. (*See Beaver.*)

Voider—A contrivance in armour for covering an unprotected part of the body.

Voulage—A medieval weapon consisting of a large pointed blade mounted on a staff.

Yataghan—A sabre with in-curved blade used in Turkey and adjoining countries; often the entire hilt is of silver and the scabbard often covered in silver.

MUSICAL INSTRUMENTS

Accordion—A box-shaped instrument which produces its tones by the vibration of metallic tongues with wind supplied by its bellows.

Accordoir—A tuning key for the piano or harp, with a wooden head and an iron shank.

Acocotl—A musical instrument used by the ancient Mexicans. It consisted of a thin tube made from the stalk of a plant, and was about eight feet in length.

Aeolian Harp—An instrument usually consisting of 10 catgut strings stretched over a wooden sound box, which produces harmonic sounds when placed in a current of wind.

Alpenhorn—A long curved wooden horn with cupped mouthpiece used by Swiss cowherds.

Althorn—Is of the saxhorn family and replaces the French horn in military bands.

Amati—The name of a family of Cremona, famous for making violins in the 16th and 17th centuries.

American Organ—A reed organ in which the air is drawn in through the reeds by a suction bellows, as opposed to another type in which the air is forced out through the reeds, e.g., the harmonium.

Archet—A fiddler's bow.

Aulos—A Greek wood-wind instrument with a vibrating reed in the mouthpiece, as in a clarinet. It was commonly, but incorrectly, called a flute.

Autoharp—A zither on which chords are played by pressing keys that allow the desired strings to sound.

Bagpipe—An instrument consisting of a leather wind-bag with three or four sounding-pipes, one of which is the chanter with eight holes and produces the melody; the others are drones and produce a continuous low tone.

Balafo—Resembles a xylophone and consists of a number of pieces of wood placed over gourds.

Balalaika—A Russian stringed instrument, the sounding board of which is triangular.

Bamboula—A primitive drum or tambourine made of bamboo, used by negroes.

Bandonion—A kind of concertina.

Banjo—An instrument with five strings, a neck like that of a guitar and a body like that of a tambourine.

Banjoline—An instrument similar to a banjo but having a shorter neck and only four strings.

Banjulele—An instrument similar to the banjo, but having four strings only.

Barbitos or **Barbiton**—An ancient Grecian lute.

Barrel Organ—A small portable instrument which produces music by a revolving cylinder studded with pegs acting upon valves which admit air to a set of pipes.

Bass Drum—The largest kind of drum, having two heads.

Basset Horn—A wood-wind instrument similar to a clarinet.

Bassoon—A wood-wind instrument of the double reed type.

Bass Viol—A stringed instrument for playing bass.

Bell—The curved spreading mouth with which brass instruments terminate.

Bell Harp—A box-shaped harp instrument swung like a bell, sometimes called "fairy bells".

Bichordon—Similar in appearance to a mandoline, but having two strings tuned in unison for each note.

Bishero—The tuning pegs of a violin.

Bombard—An old instrument, a predecessor of the bassoon.

Bombardon—A large deep-toned wind instrument of brass with valves.

Bonang—An instrument consisting of a series of gongs, used in Java.

Buccina—A Roman "C"-shaped trumpet; trumpet-like.

Calamus—An old instrument similar in appearance to the more familiar panpipes (*q.v.*).

Calascione—A two-stringed guitar used in Southern Italy.

Capo-Tasto—A screw stop or bar attached to a guitar or similar instrument to raise the pitch of all strings in uniformity.

Castanets—Small spoon-shaped pieces of ivory or wood used by dancers as a time-beating accompaniment; they are of Moorish origin.

Celesta—An instrument invented in Paris by Mustel in 1886. In form it resembles a piano.

Cembalo—A dulcimer or similar instrument the strings of which are struck with hammers.

Cetra—A guitar having two single and four double strings; of the English 18th century.

Chalil—An ancient Hebrew flute of simple design.

Chalumeau—A 17th-century name for an oboe; chantler of a bagpipe.

Che—An old Chinese harp instrument of large size with twenty-five strings.

Chelys—An old Roman or Grecian form of lyre of improved design.

Cheng—A Chinese wind instrument consisting of a number of graduated tubes fitted with reeds and attached to a gourd base.

Cheville—The adjusting peg to which the string of a musical instrument is attached.

Chitarra—An Italian 16th-century guitar with wire strings.

Chitarrone—A 16th-century instrument resembling a lute.

Cithara—An ancient instrument similar to a lyre.

Citole—A kind of dulcimer played in the Middle Ages.

Cittern—An ancient instrument with metal strings, played with a plectrum.

Clarinet—A wood-wind instrument with a single reed.

Clarion—A trumpet having clear and shrill tones.

Clavecin—A harpsichord.

Clavichord—The forerunner of the modern piano, the wires being struck by brass tangents at the ends of the keys.

Clavicitherium—A keyed instrument of the 17th century.

Clavier—The keyboard of a musical instrument; a stringed key-board instrument (as the piano).

Claviharp—A harp struck with keys like a piano.

Concertina—An instrument similar to, but smaller than, the accordion, with buttons at each end for playing.

Cor Anglais—An English tenor horn.

Cor-de-Chasse—A ring-shaped French hunting horn.

Cor-de-Postillion—The long coaching horn blown by postillions.

Cornet—A brass wind instrument much used in bands, with three pistons or valves.

Crowd—An ancient Celtic instrument with six strings played with a bow.

Cymbal—A circular plate of brass with handle at the back. Used in pairs as a band instrument of percussion.

Diaulos—A Grecian double flute.

Dichord—An old lyre-shaped instrument with two strings, or with two strings to a note.

Double Bass—The largest instrument played with a bow; it has three or four strings.

Dulcimer—A musical instrument consisting of taut wires struck by "hammers" held in the hand.

Dulcitone—A small keyboard instrument in which tuning forks are struck by hammers.

Euphonium—A small brass instrument of the saxhorn class with a range of about three octaves.

Fagotto—A small bassoon.

Fescue—A plectrum for the harp.

Fiddle—A stringed instrument; a violin.

Fidicula—A small lute.

Fife—A woodwind instrument of the piccolo and flute class; it has a shrill note and is principally used to accompany drums in military music.

Finger Board—The part of a stringed instrument against which the strings are pressed by the fingers to vary the tone.

Flageolet—A flute-like instrument, usually made of wood and having six or more holes and a detachable mouthpiece.

Flügel Horn—A brass instrument resembling a cornet.

Flute—A woodwind instrument, the tone of which is controlled by finger holes or by keys.

Flutina—A reed musical box invented 1820.

French Horn—A brass wind instrument with a wide flaring bell.

Gekkim—A Japanese instrument of the guitar type.

Gigue—A kind of violin used in the Middle Ages.

Giraffe—An upright spinet.

Gittern—An old instrument, strung with wire, like a guitar.

Glockenspiel—An instrument consisting of a number of metal bars or bells attached to a frame and played by striking with a mallet.

Gotto—A Japanese instrument with thirteen strings, played with an ivory plectrum.

Gudok—A Russian fiddle with three strings.

Guitar—A six-stringed instrument played with the fingers, somewhat resembling the lute.

Harmonica—The musical glasses. Graded glasses played by the moistened finger; metal plates played with a small mallet; the mouth organ.

Harmoniphone—An old wind instrument with keys, notes being produced by the vibration of thin metallic reeds or plates.

Harmonium—An instrument played with keys and worked by wind supplied by its foot bellows; in general outline it somewhat resembles a piano or small organ. (*See American Organ.*)

Harp—A tall, stringed instrument played by "plucking" with both hands; probably the oldest musical instrument and usually highly decorative.

Harp-Lute—A kind of guitar in which the pitch could be raised by pressing a key, in use about the middle of the 19th century.

Harpo Lyre—A three-reeded 21-stringed guitar invented by Salomon 1827.

Harpsichord—A keyed instrument in the form of a small grand piano, extensively used from the 16th to 18th centuries. It was strung like a harp and the wires were plucked with small pieces of leather or quill.

Helicon—An instrument played in a brass band.

Horn—A wind instrument made in many forms; some are simple and used only for producing calls, whilst others are more elaborate and are used in orchestras.

Hunting Horn—A brass wind instrument without valves.

Hurdy-Gurdy—Originally a stringed lute-like instrument played by the friction of a wheel turned by a cranked handle. The name is now more popularly applied to a street piano played by turning a crank.

Jew's Harp or **Guimbard**—A small instrument with a metal tongue, played by placing between the teeth and vibrating the metal tongue with the finger.

Kantelet—A Finnish harp.

Kettledrum—A small drum which can be tuned to a definite pitch by means of thumb-screws.

Kit—A small violin carried by dancing masters.

Krummhorn—An old wind instrument consisting of a curved tube with finger holes and a reed.

Lali—A native drum made by hollowing out a tree trunk.

Lute—A stringed instrument like the guitar, except that the body is inclined to be pear-shaped; it was popular in Europe in the late 16th and early 17th centuries.

Lyre—An ancient Grecian gut-stringed instrument with the framing projecting outwards and resembling the tail feathers of the lyre bird.

Lyrichord—An instrument resembling the harpsichord, in which the strings were played by moving wheels instead of being plucked.

Mandola—An instrument of the mandoline type but larger and tuned to a lower pitch.

Mandoline—An instrument having a deep pear-shaped body, fretted neck and four to eight strings. It is played with a plectrum.

Manjairah—A Syrian flute with six finger holes.

Maraca—A dried gourd with beans inside and a handle with which it is shaken, used for Latin American music.

Marimba—A primitive kind of xylophone, used in South Africa and Central America; some have gourds as resonators.

Metronome—An instrument with a pendulum for indicating the correct time or speed at which a musical composition should be played.

Mouth Organ or **Harmonica** (*q.v.*)—A small wind instrument fitted with reeds and played with the mouth.

Musette—A small bagpipe popular in France in the 18th century.

Mute—A contrivance to deaden the sound of an instrument. A three-pronged grip fixed over the bridge, is used for string instruments and a pear-shaped piece of wood or metal to be placed in the bell of brass instruments.

Nabla or **Nablum**—A medieval harp-like instrument with ten or twelve strings.

Nay—A reed flute with finger holes used by the Egyptians.

Nebel—An old Hebrew triangular-shaped harp or lute.

Nefer—A long-necked lute with three strings, used by the ancient Egyptians.

Noursingh—An Indian trumpet.

Oboe—A woodwind instrument slightly flared at the lower end, with numerous keys and a slender mouthpiece.

Ocarina—A toy wind instrument made of earthenware; it is oblong in shape with finger noles, and gives soft whistling tones.

Octave—In music, an eighth or an interval of twelve semitones.

Octo-Bass—A large instrument similar to the double-bass, having three strings and played with a bow.

Oliphant—A simple ivory horn for calls, used in the Middle Ages.

Ophicleide—A large brass keyed wind instrument invented in the 19th century; supplanted by the tuba.

Organ—The largest and most powerful of wind instruments, usually operated by compressed air from bellows. The notes are obtained from sets of pipes of different sizes controlled by one or more keyboards and foot pedals. Chiefly used in churches and cinemas.

Organistrum—An old lute-like hurdy-gurdy operated by two people, one keeping a wheel in motion whilst the other presses the strings against it by the use of keys.

Orpharion—A lute or cittern having its strings in pairs and played with a plectrum, used during the 16th and 17th centuries.

Panpipes—A musical instrument comprising a series of short graduated pipes or reeds, with the lower ends stopped, tied together and operated by wind. (*See Calamus.*)

Percussion Instrument—An instrument which is struck to produce its sound, as a drum or cymbals.

Pianoforte, popularly shortened to **Piano**—A stringed instrument of percussion, music being obtained by the vibration of wires struck by hammers operated from a keyboard. First introduced by Cristofori, an Italian, in 1709.

Piano Player—A mechanical instrument contained in a cabinet for attaching to a piano; it is operated by bellows, and a perforated roll of music.

Piccolo—A small woodwind instrument of the flute type with sounds an octave higher.

Plectrum—A small contrivance fitted to the finger, used to pluck the strings of musical instruments.

Psaltery—An instrument of the zither type used in the Middle Ages; its strings were plucked either with the fingers or with a plectrum.

Quinterne—An early guitar related to the lute.

Rebab—An ancient Persian stringed instrument, played by plucking and later with a bow; sometimes regarded as the original violin.

Recorder—A flute with whistle mouthpiece, popular in the 16th and 17th centuries, now having a revival.

Reed Organ—A portable instrument in which the notes are obtained by the vibration of reeds by a current of air supplied by bellows.

Regal or Rigole—A small portable organ, at one time used in churches; it was played with one hand, the other supplying wind by means of bellows.

Resonophone—The name often given to cylindrical or flagon-shaped gongs with dulcimer tops. **Resonator**—A hollow resounding body, as of a fiddle.

Rote—A musical instrument similar to the lyre.

Ruana—A viol-like two-stringed instrument used in India.

Sackbut—An old brass wind instrument resembling a trombone.

Sambuke—An ancient stringed instrument resembling the harp.

Samisen—A Japanese three-stringed musical instrument resembling a banjo.

Sancho—A rough guitar-like instrument of hollowed wood with long neck and strings of vegetable fibre, played by American negroes.

Santir—An Oriental dulcimer played with small curved sticks as plectrums.

Sarinda—A Tibetan stringed instrument played with a bow.

Sarrusophone—A brass instrument of the oboe class, named after Sarrus, a Parisian bandmaster.

Saxhorn—A brass wind instrument invented in the middle of the 19th century by Adolphe Sax.

Saxophone—A brass wind instrument largely used in dance and military bands.

Serinette—A small hand organ used for training song birds.

Seringhi—An instrument of the viol class; the native violin of India.

Serpent—A French brass wind instrument of the trumpet class, of serpentine form.

Shawm—An instrument resembling the oboe, with a double-reed.

Spinet—An old musical instrument which preceded the pianoforte. It was wing-shaped, the strings being arranged horizontally and played by plucking by means of pointed quills and a keyboard. It was smaller in size than the harpsichord but similar in appearance to the virginal (*q.v.*).

Sultana—An old-fashioned instrument of the viol type with wire strings.

Swanee-Sax—An instrument of the saxophone class with a slide.

Tabl—A Mohammedan single-handed drum.

Tabour or **Tabor**—A small drum, resembling the tambourine but without jingles, played with a stick.

Tabret—A small barrel-shaped drum.

Tambour—A small shallow drum. **Tambourine**—A similar instrument, except that it has only one skin and is fitted with jingles.

Tamboura—An Asiatic guitar-like instrument.

Tam-Tam or **Tom-Tom**—A native drum.

Theorbo—An obsolete musical instrument of the 17th century, shaped like a lute, but with a double neck and two sets of strings.

Timbal—A Spanish kettledrum. **Timbrel**—A Hebrew tambourine.

Triangle—A percussion instrument consisting of a rod of steel bent into the form of a triangle and struck with a small metal rod.

Trigon—An ancient Eastern lyre of triangular shape.

Trombone—A brass wind instrument without valves or keys; the tone is varied by sliding the centre part.

Trumpet—A brass wind instrument with valves.

Tuba—A brass wind instrument of the saxhorn type having a deep tone and three to five valves.

Tuning Fork—A small steel instrument with two prongs which when sharply struck vibrates with a note of definite frequency.

Ukulele—An Hawaiian instrument similar to the guitar.

Vina—A Hindu seven-stringed instrument similar to a guitar but having two gourds on which rests the bamboo finger board.

Viol—The forerunner of the violin.

Viola—A stringed instrument similar to but larger and lower in tone than the violin. **Viola da Gamba**—A bass viol, sometimes called Knee Lyre.

Violin—A modern treble instrument, evolved from the viol and brought to perfection by Niccolo Amata, Stradivari and Guarneri in the 17th century.

Violoncello—A bass violin.

Virginal—A musical instrument fashionable in the 16th and 17th centuries; it had four octaves and a single string to each note, and was played by means of a keyboard and quills as in a spinet, although of smaller size; one of the three forms of the harpsichord.

Xylophone—A percussion instrument consisting of a series of wooden bars graduated in length to the musical scale and struck by hammers.

Yukin—A Chinese instrument with four strings played by plucking.

Zither—A flat-shaped instrument with 30 to 40 strings played with a plectrum.

Terms used in
HERALDRY

Abased—Said of a charge when placed lower than its customary position.

Abyss—The centre of an escutcheon or shield, also called the fesse-point or coeur.

Accollee—Placed side by side.

Accosted—Supported on both sides by other charges.

Achievement—The coat-of-arms fully emblazoned.

Addorsed—Set or turned back to back. (*See Aversant*.)

Affronté—Facing to the front; front to front. (*Opposite to Addorsed*.) (*See illustration*.)

Aisle—A name sometimes given to winged animals which are usually wingless.

A la Cuisse—The leg of a bird or animal cut off at the thigh.

Alant or Aland—Represents a mastiff with short ears.

Allerion—An eagle with outstretched wings but without beak or feet.

Allusive Arms—A charge which figuratively represents the office of the bearer.

Amethyst—The purple colour in a nobleman's escutcheon.

Anchored—A charge having its extremities turned back like the flukes of an anchor.

Annodated—Twisted into the shape of the letter S.

Annulet—A small circle borne as a charge.

Annulated—Any bearing whose extremities terminate in rings.

Antique Crown—A golden-coloured crown consisting of a circular band with an indefinite number of pointed rays.

Appaumée or Apaumy—A hand opened out to show the palm.

Appointé—Placed point to point or end to end.

Argent—Silver or white.

Armed—Blazoned animals or birds having talons, horns, beaks or teeth.

397

Assis—Said of an animal depicted in a sitting position.

Augmentation—An honourable additional charge to a coat-of-arms.

Avellane—Shaped like a filbert or hazel-nut. The avellane cross comprises four unhusked filberts as arms.

Aversant—A term meaning the back, as the back of a hand. (*See Addorsed.*)

Aylet—A representation of the Cornish chough (*bird*).

Ayrant—A bearing depicting a bird upon its nest.

Azure—The colour blue indicated by horizontal lines.

Badge—A device without motto, worn by servants, retainers.

Banner—A square flag with the bearer's arms used as a charge.

Bar—An ordinary or stripe crossing a shield horizontally.

Barb—A small leaf which projects from the calyx of a rose.

Bar Gemels—Barrulets borne in pairs.

Barnacle—An instrument for pinching the noses of horses, etc. In heraldry, a charge depicting such an instrument.

Barrulée or Barruly—The field when traversed by ten or more barrulets.

Barrulet—A diminutive having one fourth of the width of a bar.

Barry—A field divided into an even number of bars, of two colours.

Barry-Nebuly—Barry with wavy lines.

Barry-Pily—A field traversed by equal piles arranged barry. (*See illustration.*)

Bar Wise—Horizontally.

Basilisk—An imaginary animal represented like the cockatrice, and with a head of a dragon at the end of its tail.

Baston—A bendlet sinister restricted so that it does not reach the edge of the field.

Baton-Cross—A cross on a field having crosslets at the ends of each arm.

Beacon—A cresset or fire basket, usually depicted inflamed and mounted on a pole against which a ladder leans.

Bearer—A supporter, usually an animal, as in the Royal Coat-of-Arms.

Bearing—Armorial Insignia, borne on shields.

Bend—Formed by two diagonal lines drawn from dexter chief to sinister base.

Bendy—A charge divided into an equal number of bends.

Bend Sinister—A charge taking the form of a wide diagonal, from the sinister chief to the dexter base.

Bevel—A term used to describe a line broken at an angle and continued in the same direction.

Bezant—A circle, supposed to be of gold, to represent the coin of the same name.

Bicorporate—Double-bodied. (*See illustration.*)

Billet—Oblong figures set upright.

Billetée—A term used to describe a field decorated with at least ten billets.

Blazon—A shield; a coat-of-arms or armorial bearings.
   Blazoned—Emblazoned; delineating armorial bearings.

Bordure—The border round a shield; when plain it is usually one-fifth of the width of a shield, but wider when charged.

Botteroll—The chape or crampit used as a charge.

Bottony—Extremities of charges having knobs or buds.

Bottony Fitchée—A cross with its lower arm ending in a sharp point.

Bouget—A leather water-carrier. In heraldry, a conventional charge representing a pair of bougets suspended from a pole.

Bourdonné—A charge of bourdon staffs terminating in knobs or balls. **Bourdon**—A prior's staff or a cudgel.

Braced—Said of a charge when it is interlaced.

Bray—A charge depicting barnacles.

Bretessé—A charge in which embrasures oppose each other.

Brisé—A bearing depicted as torn asunder.

Brochant or Bronchant—Overlapping; one charge overlapping another.

Brusk—Orange-coloured.

Caboshed—An animal's head affronté or full face.

Cabré—A charge which represents a rearing horse.

Cadence—Charges used to distinguish different members of the same family.

Cannet—A duck represented without feet or bill.

Cantellus—The fourth part of a shield. **Cantle**—A corner part of a shield.

Canton—A rectangular division of a shield occupying either of the top corners.

Caparisoned—Depicting a warhorse fully clothed in armour.

Carbuncle—A charge with eight rays springing from a centre rose.

Castellated—Having battlements like a castle.

Celestial Crown—A bearing representing a rayed crown with each ray terminating in a star.

Chamber Piece—A charge representing a short cannon.

Chaplet—A garland or wreath of flowers and leaves.

Charge—A figure or bearing borne on a field.

Checky—A shield divided into squares of different colours. (*See illustration.*)

Chevelure—A charge depicting a wig.

Chevron—A chevron-shaped figure represented upon a shield often in such a way as to call for numerous sub-titles, as, Abased, alaisé, broken, counter-pointed, couched, couped, enhanced, enarched, engrailed, interlaced, in chief, ployé, per chevron, rompu, reversed, removed or undy. (*See illustration.*)

Chevronel—A bearing similar to a chevron but of only half its width.

Chevronny—A shield divided into equal chevrons.

Chief—One of the ordinaries which occupy the upper third part of a field.

Cleché—A bearing charged with another of similar shape so that only a narrow border of the first remains visible.

Close—A term used to describe a bird with wings folded to the body; with the vizor of a helmet down.

Closet—A diminutive of the bar, being half the usual width.

Cloué—A charge usually in the form of a trellis studded with nails.

Coat-of-Arms—The escutcheon of a person, family or company, embodying a number of charges, crest, motto, etc.

Cockatrice—A figure with a reptile's body and the head, wings and legs of a cockerel.

Coeur—The heart or centre of an escutcheon, the fesse point, or abyss.

Cognizance—A family crest or badge worn by knights in armour or their servants.

Combatant—Two animals rampant and face to face as a charge upon a shield. (*See illustration.*)

Combel—A diminutive of the chief, being about half its width.

Compartment—A panel or mount below the shield on which the supporters rest.

Componé—The border of a shield divided into squares of two alternate colours.

Confronté—(*See Affronté.*)

Conjoined—Joined together, as two animals with one head; linked as rings or annulets. **Conjoined in Lure,** said of two wings joined together with tips downwards.

Coppé—Depicting an animal or bird with its head raised above a natural position.

Cotise—A diminutive of the bend, being a quarter of its width.

Cottised, Cotised or Coticed—An ordinary set between two cottises, said of a fess, chevron, etc.

Couchant—An animal lying down with the head raised or wakeful.

Couché—A charge inclined and not erect as it is usually.

Counter-Changed—Having a charge or colour reversed; a charge separated by a partition line.

Counter-Compony—An ordinary composed of a double row of small squares of two colours alternating.

Counter-Couchant—Animals depicted on a shield lying down with their heads in opposite directions.

Counter-Courant—Said of animals on a shield when running in opposite directions.

Counter-Embattled—Embattled on opposite sides, the embrasures on one side being opposite to the solids on the other.

Counter-Embowed—A charge when shown in reverse or contrary to its true position.

Counterfessed or Counter-fessy—A shield divided into bars and cut palewise, the half-bars being of alternate colours.

Counter-Flory or Counter-Fleury—A charge having fleur-de-lys set opposite to each other.

Counter-Naiant—Said of a charge bearing fishes swimming in opposite directions.

Counter-Paled or Paly—A shield divided palewise and then fesswise so that each pale is cut into two.

Counter-Point—Meeting at the points, as a charge of two chevrons, one being inverted so that the points of each meet.

Counter-Potent—A charge arranged base to base.

Counter-Quarterly—A shield quartered and having one or more of its quarters again quartered.

Counter-Salient—Animals depicted on a shield as leaping from each other.

Counter-Trippant—Said of animals of the chase when represented on a shield as tripping or trotting past each other in opposite directions.

Counter-Vair—A row of bells or shields of the same colour, arranged in horizontal rows. A fur.

Couped—The head of an animal cut off evenly as opposed to erased.

Couple Close—One of a pair of diminutives of the chevron, each being a fourth of its surface.

Courant—Said of a beast running.

Courlett—A breastplate depicted as a charge.

Coward—A charge depicting an animal with its tail between its legs.

Crenelé—A shield with a device having the upper edge embattled or crenelated.

Crest—A device or bearing usually worn above the shield or separately on liveries, etc. It is also engraved upon silver-plate, etc.

Crined—A charge having hair or with a mane.

Crosslet—A cross whose limbs, of even breadth, end as trefoils.

Dancetté—A bar with large indents or zigzags.

Dancetté Couped—A dancetté with its ends not reaching the sides of a shield.

Debased—A term used to describe a charge when inverted or reversed.

De-Bruised—A charge crossed by an ordinary.

Declinant—An animal or serpent having its tail hanging straight down.

Decrescent—A moon in its wane, the horns of which point to the sinister side.

Defamed—An animal depicted without its tail.

Demembré—A term applied to animals whose heads, tails and feet are severed from their bodies but left in position.

Device—An heraldic composition which is emblematical and usually includes a text or motto.

Dexter—Pertaining to the side of a shield at the right of a person wearing it, as opposed to sinister or left.

Diademed—A charge when ringed with a circle or halo.

Dimidiated—Cut in halves per pale, and one half removed.

Diminutive—A smaller form of any one of eighteen ordinaries.

Disclosed—With expanded wings, in the case of birds which are not birds of prey; the opposite of Close.

Displayed—Said of an eagle or other bird of prey with its wings spread. (*See illustration.*)

Dormant—A charge depicting an animal in a sleeping posture with its head on its fore-paws. (*See illustration.*)

Doubling—The ermine or other lining of a mantle.

Dragonné—An animal represented as having the hinder parts of a dragon.

Duciper—The heraldic name for the Cap of Maintenance.

Elevated—The wings of a bird when they point upwards.

Embattled—A line of battlements across a field.

Embowed—Anything bent or curved, like a bow, an arm embowed has the elbow to the dexter.

Endorse—A subordinary of the pale of which it is one fourth or one eighth its width.

Enfiled or **Enpiled**—An arrow, sword or other weapon when transfixing a coronet, animal's head or other object.

Engouled—Being swallowed, or having partly disappeared.

Engrailed—A term used when the edges of a bend, etc., or a bordure are indented with small concave curves.

Enhanced—When a charge is borne in a higher position than is usual.

En Pied—A bear on its hind legs.

Enpiled—(*See Enfiled.*)

Ensigned—Adorned, having some charge placed above, e.g., a coronet above a shield.

Entoyer or **Entoire**—Said of a field when charged with bearings of an inanimate nature, usually eight in number, as on a bordure.

Entrailed—A cross in outline with looped flourishes at its angles.

Enveloped—Said of a charge when one object has another twined about it, e.g., the caduceus entwined with snakes.

Eradicated—A tree showing its roots; rooted out.

Erased—When the base of an animal's head is left rough-edged as if torn asunder (opposed to couped).

Ermine—A representation of the ermine or stoat, or its white fur studded with black tails. (*See illustration.*)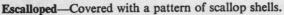

Erminois—A representation of ermine fur on a golden field.

Escalloped—Covered with a pattern of scallop shells.

Escarbuncle—A charge with eight ornamental rays springing from a centre boss, supposed to represent the iron bands on an old shield.

Escroll—The long ribbon-like strips of parchment bearing a motto.

Escutcheon—The shield or diamond-shaped surface upon which arms are emblazoned and displayed.

Estoile—A star with wavy rays.

Fess or Fesse—A bar placed horizontally across a shield, being one third of its width. It is borne in a variety of forms, each having its particular title. (*See illustration.*)

Fesse Point—The central point of a shield.

Fesse-wards—Said of a charge when its head or point is directed to the centre of a shield.

Fetterlock—A handcuff.

Field—The entire surface of a shield upon which charges are placed.

Figured—A term used to describe the sun, moon, etc., when depicted with human faces.

Fimbriate—A charge that is edged on all sides.

Fitchée—A cross pointed at the base.

Flanch—A bearing composed of two circular segments projecting from either side of a shield. (*See illustration.*)

Fleece—The skin of a ram borne as a charge.

Fleury—Decorated with fleur-de-lys.

Fluke, Fleuk or Flook—A flounder when appearing as a bearing.

Fondant—A falcon when depicted as swooping for prey.

Fracted—A charge having a part displaced as though broken; a charge that is fractured or broken.

Frasier—A strawberry leaf or cinquefoil depicted on a shield.

Fusil—A lengthened and sharper lozenge; a distaff. **Fusilly**—Covered with fusils.

Fylfot—A Greek cross with its arms bent at right angles; the swastika.

Gad—A spike or knob projecting from the knuckles of gauntlets.

Gamb or Gambe—The foreleg of an animal when depicted as a charge.

Garb—A charge representing a sheaf of wheat.

Gardant—Said of a beast when its face only is turned towards the spectator.

Garnished—Said of a charge when ornamented.

Gaze—Said of an animal with its face turned to the spectator, or gardant (*q.v.*).

Gemel—Twins or in pairs; any ordinary represented in pairs. (*See illustration.*)

Gemmed—A term depicting a ring when set with a stone or stones and used as a charge.

Genuant—A charge when in a kneeling position.

Gillyflower—A carnation or a clove when used as a charge.

Gobony—(*See Componé.*)

Golpe—A roundel purpure.

Gorged—An animal with its neck encircled by a coronet, collar or ring.

Goutte—A drop-shaped figure to represent water, tears, blood, etc.

Gradient—A charge depicted as walking, usually said of a tortoise represented as moving.

Grady—Cut into steps.

Grafted—A shield divided into three parts, two being in the upper half with vertical division and the other below; inserted into another piece.

Grain Tree—A charge representing a tree or shrub with berries used for dyeing.

Grappe de Raisin—A term used to describe a bunch of grapes when represented in a bearing.

Green—A wild man with a club over his shoulder when used as a charge; the tincture vert; indicated by lines drawn diagonally downwards across the shield from sinister to dexter.

Grelier—A hunting horn when used as a charge.

Griece—One of the steps forming the base to a Calvary cross.

Grilleté—Representing a falcon which has grelots (small bells) on its feet.

Griotte—A cherry tree or a cluster of cherries when used as a charge.

Grove—A number of trees when used as a bearing.

Grue—A crane when used as a charge.

Gules—Denoting the tincture red.

Gumène—A cable rope when attached to an anchor.

Gurges—A spiral representing a whirlpool.

Gusset—An abatement of the shield.

Gyron—A subordinary, triangular in shape and having one of its angles at fess-point and the opposite side at the edge of the escutcheon. (*See illustration.*)

Gyronny—A shield divided into gyrons.

Habeck or **Habick**—A term used for an old instrument for dressing cloth when used as a charge.

Habillé—Clothed, as a man, or a ship with sails.

Hafted—A hammer or other instrument when the handle is of a different colour.

Haie—An enclosure when formed with brambles and used as a bearing.

Hanger—A short curved sword when used as a charge.

Hame—A horse's collar when depicted as a charge.

Hamecon—A cross with its arms terminating in barbs or fish hooks.

Haméide—A charge depicting three bars with pointed ends placed one above the other.

Hanchet—A bugle-horn when represented as a charge.

Haurient—A fish depicted as rising in the air or in an erect position.

Haut—A sword when in a vertical position.

Herse—A portcullis when represented as a charge.

Herissé—Bristling, as of an animal with its fur bristling.

Herisson—A hedgehog when shown as a charge; **Herissoné**—A cat with its back arched.

Hew—A pickaxe when depicted as a charge.

Hilted—Said of a sword when the hilt is of a different colour from the blade.

Hirondelle—A swallow used as a bearing.

Homme d'Armes—A man clothed in armour.

Honoured—Said of an animal when crowned, appearing as a charge.

Houlette—A shepherd's crook used as a bearing.

Humet—A bar couped at the ends; a short bar not touching the edges of the shield.

Humetty—Said of any ordinary that does not touch the edges of a shield.

Huppé—The plover, peewit or lapwing when used as a charge.

Hure—The head of a boar represented as a charge.

Impalement—A term used when two or more escutcheons or coats-of-arms are set side by side and palewise on a shield. (*See illustration.*)

Incensed—When fire is issuing from the mouth or eyes of an enraged animal.

Inclave—The border of an ordinary or any other charge with a dovetail pattern.

Incontrant—A term used of creatures facing each other.

Increscent—A new and increasing moon when the points are towards the dexter.

Indented—A notched or serrated line or border.

Indentilly—A partition line with deep indentures.

Inescutcheon—A small escutcheon, as within a shield.

Ingulphant—Swallowed.

Invexed—Having one side curved or bowed inward; concaved.

Involute—Coiled as in a spiral; rolled inwards.

In Quadrangle—Having a charge in each quarter of the shield.

Irradiated—A charge decorated by rays.

Issuant—Emerging: said of an animal with only the upper part visible.

Issuant and Revertant—Said of a charge when one half of a beast is appearing at the base of a shield and the other half is disappearing at the top.

Jaune—A term indicating gold represented by dots.

Jelloped—The wattles of a cockerel when of a different tincture from its body.

Jessant—Rising from the bottom line of a field or the upper line of an ordinary. Issuing forth as an animal from an ordinary. (*See illustration.*)

Julian's Cross (Saint)—A cross having its extremities crossed.

Label—A carrulet with three or five pendants to distinguish an elder son.

Lambeauxed—Dovetailed.

Langued—A term used to describe a beast when its tongue is of a distinct tincture.

Limaçon—A snail appearing as a charge.

Lioncel—A young lion or one of several when borne on a shield and not separated by an ordinary.

Lion—Represented in heraldry as follows:—**Coward,** with its tail doubled between its legs. **Dormant,** asleep with its head resting on its fore-paws. **Passant,** walking with its dexter paw raised. **Passant gardant,** walking with its head affronté. (*See illustration.*) **Passant regardant,** walking with its head looking behind. **Rampant,** reared on one hind leg with its head in profile. **Rampant gardant,** rampant but with its face affronté. **Rampant regardant,** rampant but with its head looking back over its shoulder. **Salient,** in a leaping position with both its hind legs on the ground. **Sejant,** in a sitting position. **Statant,** with all its legs on the ground. **Statant gardant,** in a standing position with all four feet on the ground.

Lion-Poisson—A creature half-lion and half-fish.

Lion-Tricorporate—Three lions with one head common to them all.

Liston—A ribbon bearing a motto.

Lodged—A term used to describe a beast of the chase when it is couchant.

Lolling—A term used to describe an eagle when actually feeding on its prey.

Loutre—An otter appearing as a charge.

Lozengy—A shield or bearing divided into lozenges (diamonds).

Lucy—A pike (fish) when depicted as a charge.

Lunel—Four crescents when they are united point to point.

Lymphad—A small vessel with a mast used as a charge.

Masoned—A charge which resembles masonry.

Majesty—A charge representing a crowned eagle holding emblems of royalty.

Manche, Maunche or Maunch—Represents a lady's sleeve with long lappet of the 14th century.

Marcassin—A young wild boar when it appears in armorial bearings.

Marshalling—A term used when several coats-of-arms are depicted on one shield to denote the alliance of a family.

Martlet—A bird of the swallow class depicted as having thighs or thickened legs.

Mascle—A lozenge voided, viz., with its centre removed, supposed to represent a link of chain armour. (*See illustration.*)

Masculy or Masculé—A charge made up of a series of lozenges or mascles; covered with mascles.

Miniver—A parti-coloured fur.

Mi-Parti—Having two equal parts of two shields with their charges joined to make one.

Moile—An ox's head without horns.

Morne—Said of a lion without claws, teeth or tongue.

Mouchetté—A charge having tufts of ermine.

Mount—When earth or a hillock is shown at the base of a shield.

Moussu—A cross having rounded ends.

Mullet—A five- or six-pointed star, sometimes pierced in the centre.

Naiant—A fish depicted horizontally in fesse. (*See illustration.*)

Naissant—Issuing from the middle of an ordinary.

Nebulé—An undulating division across a shield intended to represent a cloud.

Nourri—A rootless plant or tree.

Nowed—A charge when knotted, as a serpent or the tail of an animal.

Nowy—Said of a line which rises or has a curvature in or near the middle.

Opincus—A dragon when depicted with a beak and ears.

Or—Gold or yellow.

Orbicular—A charge when represented by a number of stars arranged in a circle.

Ordinary—A term for charges or bearings in most common use, as the bend, chevron, chief, cross, fesse, pale, etc.

Oreiller—A pillow or cushion when depicted as a charge.

Orle—A number of small charges set round a central charge.

Overt—A bird having its wings spread.

Pale—A perpendicular division of the shield, being one-third of its width. **Palet**—Having half the width of a Pale. (*See illustration.*)

Palisade—One of the projections of a crown.

Palisee—A shield divided so as to represent battlements pointing both upwards and downwards.

Pall—Bands arranged in the form of the letter "Y" charged with crosses.

Paly—When a shield is divided into equal parts by perpendicular lines with alternative tinctures.

Paly Bendy—Divided into lozenges by bendwise (diagonal) and palewise (perpendicular) lines.

Pamé—A fish with its mouth agape.

Pampre—A shoot or branch of a vine when represented as a charge.

Panache—A plume when appearing as a charge.

Papilloné—A term used when the field is mascled or covered with an overlapping pattern as fish scales.

Party—Said of an escutcheon divided into parts.

Passant—A term used to denote the attitude of an animal in a walking position with the head in profile; when the head is turned sideways it is described as "passant gardant", and with the head turned backwards as "passant regardant". The "lion passant" is the English Standard Mark for silver. **Passant-Counter-Passant**—Two animals passing in opposite directions.

Patte—The paw of a beast.

Pean—A term which denotes one of the furs, the ground being sable with tufts or.

Pellet—A black roundel.

Perclose—The part of a garter which bears the buckle when borne as a charge.

Pheon—The barbed head of a dart or arrow when represented as a bearing.

Pile—A wedge-shaped ordinary with its point downwards. (*See illustration.*)

Pily—A shield divided into an equal number of piles.

Plentitude—A term applied to the moon when depicted at its full.

Point—One of the nine positions in the shield, i.e., dexter chief, dexter base, fesse, honour, middle chief, middle base, nombrie, sinister chief and sinister base. A bearing which usually occupies the lower part of the shield.

Pommetté—A cross having one or more balls at each extremity.

Port—The porch of a church or the gateway of a castle when represented as a charge.

Posé—An animal statant with its four feet resting on the ground.

Potent—A term for one of the furs when potents, crutches or "T"-like figures cover the field.

Proper—Denotes the charges appear in their natural colour.

Purpure—A tincture of purple.

Quartering—The bearing of two or more coats-of-arms on a shield divided by horizontal and perpendicular lines, denoting the alliances of the family; one of the additions thus formed.

Quarterly Quartered—When the lines which quarter a field are divided. (*See illustration.*)

Queue—The term for an animal's tail, especially that of a lion. **Queued**—A term used when a tail is of a different tincture from the body or when it is not bending over the back.

Radiant—A term used to describe a bearing when rays are issuing from it.

Raguly—An ordinary notched in regular oblique breaks representing a tree trunk lopped of its branches.

Rampant—A term used to denote a lion or other animal when in an upright position on one hind leg, with the head in profile; when the head is turned presenting a full face it is described as "rampant gardant", such as is embodied in the Royal coat-of-arms, and with the head turned backwards as "rampant regardant". The "lion rampant" is the Scottish Standard Mark for silver. (*See Passant.*)

Rangier—The blade of a scythe.

Rapin—An animal or bird when depicted in the act of feeding on another creature.

Rebate—A term when part of a charge is broken off, as for a difference.

Rebus—Represents a pictorial suggestion in a coat-of-arms.

Recursant—An eagle with its back displayed.

Reflected—A term used to describe a charge or part of a charge which is turned back, as an animal's tail.

Regardant—A term applied when a lion or other animal is looking backwards.

Renne—A reindeer when used as a charge.

Reremouse—An heraldic term for a bat (mammal.)

Respectant—Animals or fishes when upright and facing each other.

Roc—A chess rook when represented as a charge.

Rompu—A term used when the point of a chevron is broken. (*See illustration.*)

Roundel—Said of a charge when circular in shape.

Rousant—Said of a bird when depicted as rising on the wing.

Rustre—A lozenge-shaped charge with a circular perforation in the centre.

Sable—Black.

Salient or Saltant—A term for a wild beast when depicted as leaping or springing into the air.

Saltier or Saltire—An ordinary consisting of a cross formed by a bend dexter and a bend sinister (*See illustration.*)

Sang—Blood, usually represented by sanguine tear-shaped drops. **Sanguine**—Red like blood.

Sanglant—Bleeding.

Sanglier—A wild boar when it appears as a charge.

Scarp—A diminutive of the bend sinister.

Seax—A curved sword or sabre with a semi-circular notch in its back.

Segreant—A griffin when depicted in a rampant position.

Sejant or Sejeant—Animals when in a sitting posture.

Sepurture—Wings when displayed as a charge.

Sinister—The left side.

Slipped—A leaf or flower represented as having a stalk torn off from the stem.

Soleil—The sun when depicted as a charge.

Souche—A tree stump showing its roots.

Sparling—A smelt when used as a charge.

Sparver or **Sperver**—A tent when used as a charge.

Statant—A term used to describe an animal when represented as standing still with all its feet on the ground.

Subordinary—A charge which is considered to be of less importance than an ordinary, as bordure, canton, flanch, fret, gyron, inescutcheon, orle, pile, tressure and border.

Sun—When represented as a charge and only part is visible it is described as "rising" or "issuant" and when fully shown as in "splendour".

Surgeant—A bird of prey when represented as rising on the wing.

Talbot—A sporting or hunting dog when it appears as a charge.

Tenné—Having an orange tincture.

Tertre—A hillock when represented as a charge.

Tiercé—A shield divided into three parts of different tinctures.

Tierce-Feuille—A trefoil without a stem.

Timbre—The external ornamentations of a crest.

Tinctures—The colours—seven in number:

GOLD or YELLOW	...	Or
SILVER or WHITE	...	Argent
RED...	...	Gules
BLUE	...	Azure
BLACK	...	Sable
GREEN	...	Vert
PURPLE	...	Purpure

In uncoloured illustration the colours are indicated by the use of lines and dots:

GOLD	...	A powdering of dots.
SILVER	...	Is left plain.
GULES	...	Upright lines.
AZURE	...	Horizontal lines.
SABLE	...	Cross hatching of upright and horizontal lines.
VERT	...	Diagonal lines from dexter to sinister.
PURPURE		Diagonal lines from sinister to dexter.

Torteau—A roundel gules.

Tortilly—A wreathed ordinary.

Traverse—A triangle having one side flush either with the dexter or the sinister edge of a shield. **Traversed**—Lying across; when two charges are so placed.

Tressure—An ornamental border or sub-ordinary enclosing the main device.

Trippant—A term applied to stags when they are as other animals passant (*q.v.*).

Undy—A division line when drawn to represent the waves of the sea.

Urinant—A fish with its head pointing downwards.

Vair—The skin of the squirrel represented in heraldry by a series of small shields of argent and azure tincture placed close together. (*See illustration.*)

Vambraced—A term denoting a bended arm clothed in armour with a gauntlet, clutching a sword a little below the hilt.

Vane—A small pennant or flag.

Verdox—A bordure (border) charged with leaves, fruit or flowers.

Vert—Of green tincture.

Vetu—A diamond or lozenge with its four points touching the edges of the shield: clothed as an arm.

Vires—A term denoting several annulets, one within the other.

Viure—A narrow ribbon usually arranged nebuly.

Voided—A term applied to a simple charge when the inner part is cut away. (*See illustration.*)

Vorant—Said of a dolphin or fish when depicted as swallowing something whole.

Vulned—Said of a charge when it is represented bleeding or wounded.

Wreath—A twist of two silken cords or two cloth rolls of two colours, used to support a crest or charge.

Yale—An antelope when appearing as a charge.

Emblems and Symbols used in
CHINESE ART

Almond—An emblem of good fortune.

Autumn—Represented by chrysanthemums, also by birds, butterflies, rivers in spate, gatherers of fruit, etc.

Bamboo—An emblem of durability.

Bat—An emblem of felicity and happiness.

Butterfly—An emblem of conjugal felicity.

Carp—An emblem of longevity, a dispeller of evil spirits.

Cherry—A double-cherry is the emblem for the month of April.

Chrysanthemum—An emblem of pleasure, enjoyment and of the month of October.

Conch Shell—Indicates a prosperous journey.

Coral—Together with feathers, indicates promotion in the official classes.

Crane—Indicates promotion in the official classes.

Crow—A bird of ill omen.

Deer—An emblem of longevity and prosperity.

Ducks—An emblem of conjugal affection.

Elephant—An emblem of power and energy.

Fan—Used to revive the souls of the dead.

Fishes—An emblem of domestic happiness, they frighten away evil spirits.

Flywhisk—Used to revive the souls of the dead.

Fox—Controls the seals of high office.

Fungus—An emblem of longevity, fertility and immortality.

Gardenia—The emblem for the month of November.

Geese—An emblem of conjugal affection.

Gourd—An emblem of longevity.

Hare—A mythical animal that lives in the moon and prepares the Elixir of Life. An emblem of longevity.

Knot—An emblem of longevity.

Land Citron—A votive offering for an abundance of happiness.

Leopard—An emblem of power and energy.

415

CHINESE SYMBOLS AND MARKS
The Eight Precious Things. (Pa pao)

The Jewel (Chu)

The "cash" symbol of riches. (Ch'ien).

The lozenge, symbol of victory. (Fang-Sheng).

The two books, a dual symbol. (Shu).

The mirror or painting. (Hua).

The musical bell-plate. (Ch'ing).

The pair of Rhinoceros horns. (Chüch).

The arthemisia leaf. (Ai yeh).

SYMBOLICAL MARKS

The hare, symbol of longevity.

A brush-pencil, cake of ink and ju-i septre. Pi ting ju-i = "May it be as you wish."

Lotus Flower—A sacred emblem of purity, creative power and the month of July.

Lute—An emblem of harmony.

Magpie—A bird of good omen.

Mallow—The emblem for the month of September.

Magnolia—The emblem for the month of May.

Narcissus—An emblem of good fortune.

Nelumbium—The lotus (*q.v.*).

Olive—A symbol of study and sweetness.

Parrot—Instructs wives to be true to their husbands.

Peach—The Fruit of Life; an emblem of immortality and longevity; a symbol of marriage and prosperity; a votive offering for an abundance of years. **Peach Blossom**—The emblem for the month of February.

Peacock—The tail feathers portray rank.

Pear—The emblem for the month of August.

Peony—An emblem of good fortune.

Pheasant—An emblem of beauty, symbolises love and the beauty of women.

Pine—An emblem of longevity.

Pomegranate—The emblem for the month of June; a votive offering for an abundance of sons.

Poppy—The emblem for the month of December.

Prunus or Plum—An emblem of longevity and good fortune; the emblem for the month of January.

Quail—Displays fighting ability.

Spring—Represented by peony; also by prunus or peach in flower without leaves; white magnolia; mountains; willow tree, etc.

Stag—An emblem of longevity.

Stork—An emblem of longevity.

Summer—Depicted by lotus; also by poplars, pinks, flags, pines, reeds, etc.

Sword—An emblem of supernatural power.

Tiger—An emblem of power and energy.

Tortoise—An emblem of longevity and strength.

Tree Peony—The emblem for the month of March.

Winter—Represented by prunus; also by early roses and winter scenes.

CHINESE SYMBOLICAL MARKS
(*continued*)

 A palm leaf	 Two fishes, symbol of domestic happiness
  Peaches and bat, symbol of longevity and happiness.	 A conch shell, symbol of a properous journey
  Lotus flower, symbol of purity and creative power.	 Sacred fungus, symbol of longevity and fertility.
 PA KUA. The trigrams on which a Chinese philosophy is founded. YIN-YANG. Dualism of nature.	 Incense burner.

CHINESE DYNASTIES AND PERIODS

HAN DYNASTY	206 B.C.-A.D. 220
THE SIX DYNASTIES	220-589
SUI DYNASTY	589-618
T'ANG DYNASTY	618-906
THE FIVE DYNASTIES	907-960
SUNG DYNASTY	960-1280
YUAN DYNASTY	1280-1368
MING DYNASTY	1368-1644
HUNG WU PERIOD	1368-1398
CHIEN WÊN PERIOD	1399-1402
YUNG LO PERIOD	1403-1424
HUNG HSI PERIOD	1425
HSÜAN TÊ PERIOD	1426-1435
CHÊNG T'UNG	1436-1449
CHING T'AI	1450-1457
T'IEN SHUN PERIOD	1457-1464
CH'ÊNG HUA PERIOD	1465-1487
HUNG CHIH PERIOD	1488-1505
CHENG TÊ PERIOD	1506-1521
CHIA CHING PERIOD	1522-1566
LUNG CH'ING PERIOD	1567-1572
WAN LI PERIOD	1573-1620
T'IEN CH'I PERIOD	1621-1627
CH'UNG CHÊN PERIOD	1628-1644
CH'ING DYNASTY	1644-1912
SHUN CHIH PERIOD	1644-1661
K'ANG HSI PERIOD	1662-1722
YUNG CHÊNG PERIOD	1723-1735
CH'IEN LUNG PERIOD	1736-1795
CHIA CH'ING PERIOD	1796-1821
TAO KUANG PERIOD	1821-1850
HSIEN FÊNG PERIOD	1851-1861
T'UNG CHIH PERIOD	1862-1873
KUANG HSÜ PERIOD	1874-1908
HSÜAN T'UNG PERIOD	1909-1912
CHINESE REPUBLIC	1912 onwards

A CLASSICAL DICTIONARY

of

Greek and Roman, Indian, Egyptian, Chinese and Japanese mythological deities

and of

Symbolic and other Figures

with a

Supplement

indexing their attributes

to facilitate identification in works of art

Aah—The Egyptian moon god, often represented with a moon above his head and sometimes with an animal face and sometimes with a human face.

Aapep or **Apepi**—The great serpent of Egyptian mythology who led attacks against the sun but was daily overcome, thus symbolizing the struggle between darkness and light.

Achilles—Son of Peleus and Thetis; famous Greek warrior who fought against the Trojans; was made invulnerable by being dipped in the river Styx, except for one heel by which his mother held him; was slain by Paris whose arrow pierced the vulnerable heel.

Actæon—A huntsman who, having surprised Diana bathing, was changed by the goddess into a stag and was killed by his own hounds.

Adonis—A young hunter beloved by Aphrodite (Venus); was killed by a wild boar; afterwards changed into an anemone by Aphrodite and later restored to life by Proserpina.

Ægis—The storm cloud enveloping the thunderbolt of Zeus, but later, the shield of Minerva which bore Medusa's head.

Æneas—A prominent defender of Troy; he carried his father on his shoulders from the burning city.

Æolus—The happy ruler of the winds, which he kept confined in caves for release at the bidding of Jove.

Æsculapius—The Greek god of medicine, in the form of an old man with staff encircled by a serpent.

Æthra—The mother of Theseus, carried off by Helen, whose slave she became.

Agamemnon—The leader of the Greeks in the expedition against Troy. He quarrelled with Achilles and was murdered by his own wife, Clytemnestra.

Agni—The Vedic god of the altar fire, usually represented in red with two faces.

Ajax, called **Aias** by the Greeks—Represented in the Iliad as second only in bravery to Achilles, was the son of Telamon. A second Ajax, son of Oileus, called the lesser Ajax, is the more familiar character, and is usually depicted "defying the lightning". After shipwreck, he reached a rock by the assistance of Neptune, but as he boasted that he would escape in defiance of the immortals, Neptune split the rock with his trident and he was thrown back into the sea and drowned.

Alcinous—King of the Phaeacians and father of Nausicaa; celebrated for his beautiful gardens in Scheria.

Alecto—One of the Furies, represented with flaming torches, head covered with serpents.

Amalthea—Daughter of Melisseus, king of Crete. She fed the infant Jupiter with goat's milk and is sometimes represented in art as a goat.

Amazons—A race of female warriors of Asia Minor who frequently fought the Greeks. Penthesilea, their Queen, went with her warriors to the assistance of the besieged Trojans, where she was slain by Achilles.

Ambrosia—The fabled food of the gods, which to its consumers gave immortality.

Amen-Ra (more correctly Ra alone)—The Egyptian sun god, usually represented as a man wearing on his head a disc with two tall ostrich plumes. The chief of Egyptian gods.

Amor—(*See Cupid.*) The God of Love.

Amphion—A son of Jupiter (Zeus), who became a great musician, and playing his lyre charmed into position the stones of the wall surrounding Thebes.

Amphitrite—A Greek goddess of the sea, wife of Neptune

Ancile, Ancilia or Ancilla—The sacred shield of the Romans, said to have fallen from heaven; was guarded by the Salii (priests) in Rome.

Androcles—A slave who was thrown to the lions in the Roman arena, but was saved owing to one of the animals recognising him as having extracted a thorn from its foot when in the African desert.

Andromache—Wife of Hector; after his death she became the prize of Pyrrhus, and later married Helenus.

Andromeda—To appease Neptune's anger, she was chained to a rock to be devoured by a sea monster; was rescued by Perseus and became his wife.

Andro-sphinx—An ancient male deity with a human head on a lion's body, representing the union of intellectual and physical power.

Antæus—A Grecian giant, defender of the Pygmies; was invulnerable while his feet were in contact with the ground. When Hercules encountered him he lifted him in his arms and crushed him to death.

Antiope—The mother of Amphion and Zethus, who were brought up as shepherds; Dirce ordered the young men to tie her to the horns of a bull, but upon discovering Antiope was their mother they so treated Dirce.

Anu—One of the ancient gods of Babylon, who controlled the heavens and the sky.

Anubis—The Egyptian god of graves and burial rites; with head of dog or jackal; was one of the conductors of the dead to the Judgment Chamber where their hearts were weighed against the feather of Truth.

Aphrodite (the Greek name for **Venus**)—The Grecian goddess of love and beauty, sometimes represented as riding on a swan; sparrows and doves were especially sacred to her.

Apis—An Egyptian god in the form of an ox, with a black body with a square white mark on the forehead, a white crescent-shaped spot on its side, a knot under the tongue like a beetle, an eagle figure on its back and double hairs in its tail.

Apollo—Son of Zeus and Latona. God of manly youth and beauty, of poetry, music and healing; later became identified with the sun. Was banished to the world of men for attempting to avenge the death of Aesculapius. Represented in art with a solar disc around his head and often with a lyre or bow. Associated with Helios (*q.v.*).

Aspsara—Nymphs in Hindu mythology depicted in the form of mist, cloud or spray; the last named due to the churning of the ocean by the gods.

Aquarius—The Water Carrier. The eleventh sign of the Zodiac (*q.v.*).

Arachne—In Greek mythology, was turned into a spider by Minerva for competing with her in the art of weaving; another version is that she hanged herself, the rope afterwards turning into a cobweb and Arachne into a spider.

Ares—The Greek god of war, son of Zeus and Hera and lover of Aphrodite. He is represented as a warrior, clad in armour with spear and torch.

Arethusa—The daughter of Oceanus, who was transformed into a fountain in order that she might avoid Alpheus.

Argo—The fifty-oared ship in which the Argonauts sailed to recover the Golden Fleece.

Argus—Was possessed of one hundred eyes, only two of which slept at a time; was slain by Mercury and his eyes were transferred to the tail of Juno's sacred peacock.

Ariadne or **Ariadna**—In love with Theseus; she assisted him to escape from the Minotaur, which he afterwards slew.

Aries—The Ram. The first sign of the Zodiac (*q.v.*).

Arion—A famous poet and musician of Methymna. Being menaced by the murderous crew of a ship, he is fabled to have thrown himself into the sea, but was saved by a dolphin which had been attracted by his sweet music, and was carried on its back to the shore.

Artemis (The Greek name for **Diana**)—An Olympian goddess with various attributes. Usually represented as the virgin huntress. In her earliest phase she was goddess of lakes, rivers and woods and the wild life of these places. Associated with the moon.

Astræa—The goddess of Justice, who lived among men during the Golden Age, but was disgusted with the wickedness of mortals, returned to heaven and became the constellation Virgo. She is usually portrayed as being blindfolded and holding a pair of scales in one hand and a sword in the other.

Astræus—In Greek mythology is the father of the winds and the stars.

Astyanax—The son of Hector and Andromache. He was murdered by the Greeks, who threw him from the walls of Troy, to prevent his restoring the kingdom, as predicted by Calches.

Asuras—Hindu demons or evil spirits, represented in art in varying forms.

Atalanta—A beautiful heroine who was fleet of foot. In Greek legend she required her suitors to outrun her, death being the penalty of defeat and her hand the prize. Hippomenes defeated her by dropping three golden apples in her path, which she stopped to pick up.

Ate—The Greek goddess of evil and mischief.

Athena, Pallas or **Athene** (The Greek name for **Minerva**)—The patron deity of Athens, wise in the industries of peace and the arts of war, represented as holding a lance in her left hand and in her extended right hand a Nike (image of the goddess of victory); also with lance in right hand and shield in left.

Atlas—Changed by Perseus with the aid of the Medusa's head into the Atlas mountain for refusing him assistance; the mountain is so lofty that it gave rise to the notion that Atlas carried the world on his shoulders, as he is often represented in art as doing.

Attis—A god of vegetation and young life. He may have been slain by a boar; another version is that he died from loss of blood due to self-inflicted wounds and that violets grew from the blood so spilt.

Atys—A beautiful, but mad, Greek shepherd.

Aurora (In Greek, **Eos**)—Daughter of Hyperion, usually represented as a veiled figure riding in a rose-coloured chariot drawn by white horses, opening the gates of day, or as rising out of the sea in a chariot with rosy fingers dripping dew.

Ba—In Egyptian art, the soul depicted as a bird.

Bacchanals and **Bacchantes**—(*See Bacchus.*)

Bacchus (In Greek, **Dionysus**)—God of wine and revelry; was crowned with grape-vine and bore the vine-encircled wand (thyrsus); educated by Silenus; his chariot drawn by leopards or panthers; his attendants, (male) called bacchanals, (female) bacchantes, and nymphs, fauns and satyrs; married Ariadne, who wore a crown with seven stars.

Balder—The son of Odin, god of the good, eloquent and wise, as well as of light and peace. Killed by Hoder with a dart of mistletoe.

Basilisk—A fabulous serpent, lizard or other reptile whose hissing would drive other creatures away and whose breath or glance was fatal.

Bast, also styled **Pakht** and **Sekhet**—An Egyptian goddess "the lady of life", usually represented as having the head of a lion and wearing the solar disc. Identified in monuments with both Hathor and Isis.

Bellerophon—A Greek hero who succeeded in bridling the winged horse Pegasus and with its aid slew the fire-breathing monster, the Chimera.

Bellona—The Roman goddess of war, usually depicted preparing the chariot of Mars, and with dishevelled hair driving horses, sometimes armed with a bloody scourge.

Bes—An Egyptian god of pleasure and recreation, sometimes represented as a grotesque bandy-legged dwarf and at other times as wearing the skin of an animal, probably a cat.

Boreas—The north wind; a man with cheeks outblown; carried off Orithyia.

Brahma—An Indian god, the spiritual head of the Brahman (or Brahmin) cult; usually depicted as having four heads, and sometimes five.

Briareus—A Greek giant having fifty heads and one hundred hands; he is supposed to have aided Zeus in his war with the Titans.

Briseis—A captive of Achilles, taken away by Agamemnon, thus causing the feud between them.

Buddha—The term means "the awakened", "the enlightened". The Buddha was the founder of the cult of Buddhism; usually represented as a serene human being in a squatting position.

Cacus—Son of Vulcan represented as a three-headed monster vomiting flames, a giant who stole the divine cattle of Geryon and hid them in a cave. It was the tenth Labour of Hercules to recapture these cattle and in doing so he slew Cacus with his club.

Cadmus—A king of Phoenicia, who killed a dragon that guarded the well of Ares, afterwards sowing its teeth, which produced armed men who fought among themselves until only five were left.

Caduceus—The winged staff of Mercury, comprising a staff with two snakes entwined and surmounted by a pair of wings.

Calliope—The Muse of Heroic (epic) Poetry; wore a laurel crown and held a tablet.

Callisto—A nymph beloved by Zeus, who transformed her into a bear; she was attacked by the huntsman Arcas, but was saved by Zeus and placed as a constellation in the sky.

Calypso—In Greek mythology, a sea-nymph who, by her charms, kept Odysseus (Ulysses) on her island Ogygia.

Cancer—The Crab. The fourth sign of the Zodiac (*q.v.*).

Capaneus—In Greek legend, one of the seven heroes who marched against Thebes. He was killed by lightning whilst scaling the walls.

Capricornus—The Sea Goat. The tenth sign of the Zodiac (*q.v.*).

Cassandra—A daughter of Priam, King of Troy. Was beloved by Apollo who bestowed upon her the gift of prophecy, but afterwards decreed that her predictions should be disbelieved. At the fall of Troy she was taken by Agamemnon, and later slain with him.

Castor—A horse-trainer, twin brother of Pollux. (Together called the Disocuri or Gemini) the deities of boxing, wrestling and equestrian exercises.

Centaur—A monster, half horse, half man.

Cepheus—A king of Ethiopia, father of Andromeda, who was placed amongst the stars after his death.

Cerberus—The three-headed dog which guarded Hades. It was the twelfth Labour of Hercules to capture it.

Ceres (In Greek, Demeter)—The goddess of agriculture; represented with a sheaf of wheat and poppies in one hand and a lighted torch in the other. Symbolises Autumn in representations of the Seasons.

Charybdis—A whirlpool between Italy and Sicily below Scylla (*q.v.*) which three times a day sucks in the sea and discharges it again in a terrible whirlpool.

Charon—Son of Erebos, ferried the souls of the dead over the waters of the Styx to the lower world.

Chepera—An Egyptian solar deity; god of the rising sun; often represented by the scarabæus, the sacred beetle of ancient Egypt.

Chimera—A monster usually represented as breathing fire, having the head of a lion, the body of a goat and the tail of a dragon.

Chinese and Buddhist Divinities.

> **Amitâbha**—The ideal Buddha of Boundless Light, stands on a lotus-decorated pedestal, with a triple nimbus round his head, under a jewel-enriched canopy.

> **Avalokita**—Usually depicted squatting in typical Buddha fashion, with one pair of hands clasped in an attitude of devotion; other hands holding a lotus flower and a rosary. Sometimes represented with a multiplicity of hands, up to forty, each holding a symbol or a weapon, and with eleven heads in cone formation.

Chinese and Buddhist Divinities—*continued.*

Bôdhidharma or **Bodhisat**—One who has attained the highest degree of saintship; usually represented with shoe in hand or ferrying a stream on a reed.

Chêêng Wang—Depicted in a sitting position with an umbrella over his head.

Chieh Kuei—Is usually armed with a ko (halberd).

Chung-Li Ch'üan—Leader of the Taoist genii; carries a fan which he wields to revive the souls of the dead.

Dharmatrata—A member of the laity, usually represented with long hair, a bundle of books on his back, and a fly-whisk and vase in his hands; gazing at a small image of Amitâbha.

Eight Genii, The—The Taoist Immortals. (Pa Hsien.)

> **Chang Kuo**—Carries a bamboo tube and rods in his right hand.
>
> **Chung-Li Ch'üan**—Supposed to have discovered the Elixir of Life; lived to a great age; represented with a fan.
>
> **Han Hsiang Tzū**—Carries a tieh (flute) in his right hand.
>
> **Ho Hsien Ku**—Carries a lotus flower or willow branch.
>
> **Lan Ts'ai-Ho**—Stands on a basket of flowers.
>
> **Li T'ieh-Kuai**—Sits on his pilgrim's gourd.
>
> **Lü Tung-Pin**—Represented with a sword.
>
> **Ts'ao Kuo-Ch'iu**—Depicted riding on a log or with castanets.

Four Maharajas, The (Ssū Ta T'ien Wang)—Four great kings who each guarded a quarter of the temple.

Fu Hsi—In human form but with body terminating like a dragon's; a mason's square held in one hand. (*See Nü Wa.*)

Ho-Shang—The familiar "Bonze (monk) with the Hempen Bag".

Hsi Wang Mu—Usually depicted bestride a lion-like monster, with two females in attendance.

Huang Ch'u-P'ing—A hermit shepherd, who, with his magic wand, changes stones into sheep.

Kuan Ti—The god of war. Represented as a seated warrior figure in mail, with long drooping moustache and narrow beard.

Chinese and Buddhist Divinities—*continued.*

Kuan Yin—The goddess of mercy and maternity, the Queen of Heaven. Depicted as seated or standing, often with two maiden attendants and sometimes with a child in her arms.

Lao-Tzu—The founder of Taoism, usually represented riding on an ox or buffalo with book in hand.

Maitreya—An obese Buddhist figure, with smiling features and bare chest and stomach; usually seated on a throne supported by three demons.

Manjusri—A Buddha, seated on a lotus pedestal.

Mu Wang—Usually depicted with a chariot drawn by eight horses.

Nirvana—The final liberation of the soul from evil; represented by a recumbent figure upon a bench with head on a lotus pillow.

Nü Wa—In human form, but with body terminating in the form of a dragon's or serpent's; usually wears a crown and holds a pair of compasses in one hand. (*See Fu Hsi.*)

Sakyamuni—The Gautama Buddha, usually represented on a lotus throne with incense-burning utensils. Or as a child, standing on a lotus pedestal with his right hand pointing up to heaven and his left downwards to the earth.

Sakya—A benevolent figure having a beard and shaven head, enlarged ear lobes (a sign of wisdom) and the luminous mark (urna) of Buddha. Clad in flowing robes with hands clasped as though in prayer.

Sakya, The All Wise—A Buddha seated on a lotus throne with legs crossed, his left hand resting upon the knee, his right hand raised as though preaching. A jewel or third eye in the centre of his forehead, with which he sees the past, present and future, and with hair in short close curls.

Sakyamuni Trinity—Sakya, either standing or seated between his two sons, Bodhisattvas Manjusri and Samantabhadra, in an attitude of meditation and with alms bowl in his hands.

Shou Lao—Usually represented with a high forehead and long beard, and holding a ju-i-sceptre. Is often accompanied by two attendants, one holding a branch and the other a peach.

Twin Genii—Representing harmony and union. One usually carries a gourd and palm leaf and the other a scroll and broom.

Chinese and Buddhist Divinities—*continued.*

Vajrapani—A Buddha seated on a lotus pedestal.

Wên Kung—The star god. Patron of literature; usually represented wielding a brush.

Yu—Depicted with a pronged spade.

Chione—In Greek mythology, was slain by Artemis for daring to compare her own beauty with that of the goddess.

Chiron—(*See Centaur.*)

Circe—A sorceress who offered a poisoned cup to Ulysses and changed his men into swine.

Cleopatra, Queen of Egypt—Her lover, hearing a false report of her death, fell upon his own sword, thereupon the grief-stricken Cleopatra killed herself by the bite of an asp.

Clio—The Muse of History; represented with laurel wreath, book and stylus.

Clytemnestra—Conspired with Aegisthus to assassinate her husband Agamemnon.

Clytie—A water nymph, whom Helios changed into a plant (heliotropium) so that her face would always be turned towards him in his daily journey across the heavens.

Comus—The god of joy and mirth, usually represented as a winged youth flushed with drinking.

Creon—In Greek mythology, became the king of Thebes and condemned Antigone to be buried alive.

Cressida—The beautiful daughter of Calchas, notorious for her infidelity.

Creusa—A daughter of Priam and Aeneas's wife.

Crio-Sphinx—A sphinx with a ram's head.

Cronus—A god of the forests; he dethroned his father Uranus and was in turn dethroned by his son Zeus.

Cupid or **Amor** (In Greek, **Eros**)—The god of love; a charming winged boy armed with bow and quiver of arrows.

Cybele—(*See Rhea.*)

Cyclopes—A race of giants with only one eye, which was in their foreheads. They were the workmen of Vulcan.

Cryene—A nymph, the daughter of Hypseus, beloved by Apollo.

Dædalus—An architect who was expelled to Crete, where he built a labyrinth in which he was imprisoned by Minos. He escaped with his son Icarus, by means of wings made of feathers and wax; the latter melted in the sun, so that he fell into the sea and was drowned.

Dæmon—A spirit who presided over births and destiny.

Dagon—The national idol of the Phillistines, represented by a figure with the head and body of a woman or man and the tail part of a fish.

Danae—A daughter of Acrisius, King of Argos, and mother of Perseus. Zeus visited her in the form of a golden shower when she was imprisoned in a brazen tower.

Danaides—The fifty daughters of Danaus. With one exception (Hypermnestra) killed their husbands, for which crime they were in Hades compelled to fill with water a vessel full of holes or to draw water with a sieve.

Daphne—A Grecian nymph pursued by Apollo, from whom she escaped by being turned into a laurel tree.

Daphnis—A shepherd of Sicily, son of Mercury. Was educated by the nymphs; Pan taught him to play upon the pipes, and the Muses inspired him with a love of poetry. He, with Chloe, formed a pair of lovers in pastoral romance.

Deianeira—Wife of Hercules, was carried off by the centaur Nessus, who was slain in the act by an arrow from the bow of Hercules.

Delphi—A small town in Phocis but one of the most famous in Greece, on account of its oracle of Apollo.

Demeter—(*See Ceres.*)

Diana (In Greek, **Artemis**)—The goddess of the Moon and the Chase; wore a crescent in her hair and was armed with a bow and arrows. **Actæon,** discovering her bathing, was forthwith transformed into a stag by the goddess. As the Moon, she was captivated by the beauty of the sleeping shepherd Endymion and came down from heaven every night to visit him

Diogenes—A Greek cynic who lived in a tub. He searched in day-time with a lighted lantern for an honest man.

Diomedes—A king of Thrace who fed his horses on human flesh. It was the seventh labour of Hercules to capture these steeds of Diomedes.

Dionysus—(*See Bacchus.*)

Dirce—The second wife of Lycus; was tied to a bull by Amphion and Zethus for ill-treating their mother Antiope.

Discobolus—The athlete throwing the discus.

Dog of Fô or **Corean Lion**—A Buddhist symbol of power and energy. Of dog-like appearance with fearsome expression, bristling mane, sharp teeth and claws and bushy tail. The male plays with a ball between its fore-paws; the female plays with a cub.

Dolphin—A sea-monster represented in art as a fish with large head and mouth, and body tapering towards its tail.

Dona Dea—An ancient Roman goddess whose worship was confined to women; she represented the fertility of fields and the chastity of women.

Doryphorus—A statue of a nude athlete bearing a spear.

Dragon—A fabulous winged monster, powerful and ferocious, having a scaly body, a crested head and large claws.

Dragon Horse—A horse with the head of a dragon, sometimes carrying a scroll on its back.

Dryades—Nymphs who presided over the woods. For other nymphs, see Nymphæ, and Myths, Earth and Sea.

Echo—A nymph who was transformed by Juno into an echo for her deception in shielding Jupiter in his love-making.

Electra—(1) Daughter of Agamemnon and Clytemnestra. Incited her young brother Orestes to avenge the murder of their father by their mother. Also called Laodice. (2) The mother of Iris and the Harpies. (3) Daughter of Atlas, and one of the seven Pleiades.

Elysian Fields or **Elysium**—In classical mythology, the dwelling place of happy and virtuous souls after death.

Endymion—A beautiful shepherd beloved by the moon goddess, Selene (Diana) who caused him to sleep for ever so that he might be unconscious of her caresses.

Eos (The Roman goddess **Aurora**)—The Greek goddess of the dawn.

Ephialtes—In Greek mythology, giants who confined Ares in a jar for over a year; they were killed by Apollo while trying to pile Mount Pelion on to Mount Ossa.

Epimetheus—He accepted Pandora as his wife from Zeus, in spite of a warning from his brother, Prometheus, not to do so, and thus brought misfortune to the mortal world.

Equus Bipes—A fabulous monster with the head of a horse and the tail of a fish; Neptune's seahorse.

Erato—The Muse of Lyric Poetry; crowned with myrtle and roses and holding a lyre.

Erebus—The gloomy space of nether darkness through which souls passed on their way to Hades; its entrance was guarded by Cerberus, the three-headed dog.

Eris—A Greek goddess emblematic of discord.

Eros—The Greek God of Love. (*See Cupid.*)

Eteocles—A king of Thebes. An agreement with his brother, Polnnices, to reign in alternate years led to their killing each other.

Euphrosyne—In Greek mythology, one of the Three Graces.

Europa—Daughter of Agenor; beloved by Jupiter who, assuming the form of a white bull, swam off with her to Crete (The Rape of Europa.)

Eurynome—The mother of the Three Graces.

Euterpe—The Muse of Music; with flute and garlands of flowers.

Fama—The goddess of Fame, attendant of Jupiter; with a long trumpet and a leaf or wreath of laurel.

Fates, The Three—Represented in art as three women; **Clotho** (attribute—a distaff), the spinning fate; **Lachesis**, the one who assigns to man his fate; and **Antropus** (attribute—shears), the fate that cannot be avoided.

Faun—One of a class of Latin rural deities with horns and tail. With nymphs, satyrs, bacchanals and bacchantes, formed the train of Bacchus. Identified with the Greek god, Pan.

Fêng-Hwang—(*See Ho-Ho Bird.*)

Flora—The goddess of flowers and spring, in whose honour feasts were held in the springtime; represented with upheld drapery filled with flowers.

Fortuna—The goddess of Fortune and Plenty. Represented with a horn of plenty, sometimes blindfolded, and holds a wheel in her hands as an emblem of her inconstancy.

Furies, The Three—Alecto, Megaera and Tisiphone, usually represented as winged figures of threatening demeanour, with serpents hanging from their arms and blood dropping from their eyes. Their work was to carry out the vengeance of the gods. Called by the Romans, Furiæ and Diræ; and by the Greeks, Eumenides and Erinyes.

Gaea—The Greek goddess of the Earth.

Galatea—A statue of a maiden made by Pygmalion, with which he fell in love; in response to his prayer Aphrodite gave it life.

Ganesha or **Ganesa**—The Hindoo god of wisdom and prudence and the remover of obstacles; represented with a human body and an elephant's head.

Ganymede—A goddess of eternal youth, better known as Hebe.

Garuda—A Hindoo god represented as half man and half bird, with golden body and red wings.

Gemini—The Twins. The third sign of the Zodiac. (*q.v.*)

Geryon—A monster having three bodies and three heads and powerful wings. He was killed by Hercules.

Glaucus—A sea divinity, originally a fisherman but usually represented in art as a vigorous old man of the sea.

Gnome—A fabled race of diminutive beings, supposed to inhabit the inner parts of the earth and to be the guardians of quarries, mines, etc.

Golden Fleece—In Greek mythology, the fleece of gold taken from the ram that carried Phrixus through the air to Colchis. It was stolen by the Argonaut Jason from the sacred grove in which it was guarded by a sleepless monster.

Gorgoneion—A mask or head of the gorgon Medusa as represented in classical art.

Gorgons or **Gorgones**—In Greek mythology, three sisters whose heads were covered with serpents and whose glance turned mortals to stone. They were named Euryale, Medusa (*q.v.*) and Stheno.

Graces, The Three—Euphrosyne, Aglaia and Thalia, represented the perfect form of grace, beauty of body and mind; usually represented as beautiful girls in light attire, crowned with flowers. Styled by the Romans, Charites, and by the Greeks, Gratiæ.

Graiæ Sisters, The—Three old Greek women, grey-haired from birth and possessing between them only one eye and one tooth, of which they were robbed by Perseus when searching for nymphs whose whereabouts were known to the Graiæ Sisters.

Griffin or **Griffon**—A fabulous animal usually represented with the body and legs of a lion and the wings and beak of an eagle. Also Gryfon, Gryphon.

Hades—The lower world, abode of departed spirits. Its entrance was guarded by Cerberus, the three-headed dog which was captured by Hercules. Pluto, whose attribute was a two-pronged fork, was its king, and he carried off Proserpina to be his queen.

Hamadryad—A tree nymph.

Ham Hit—An Egyptian goddess, the Lady of Heaven and queen of other gods, usually depicted with a fish on her head.

Harpy—A mythical monster usually represented as having a woman's head and body and the wings, tail and legs of a bird.

Hathor, also **Athor** and **Hat-har**—The Egyptian goddess of love, the female principle or counterpart of Osiris, usually represented as having a cow's head or ears, the cow being sacred to her.

Hebe (the Roman goddess, **Juventas**)—The goddess of youth and a cup-bearer of the gods; daughter of Juno; wife (after Deianeira) of Hercules. Attributes, cup and/or pitcher and/or bowl.

Hecate—The goddess who presided over magic, one of the Titans; often represented in art as having three bodies and three heads. Her dominion included heaven, earth, hell and the sea, in which she was known as Selene or Luna, Artemis or Diana, and Proserpina or Persephone respectively. She generally carries a dagger, a whip, a torch and a key.

Hector—A valiant leader of the Trojan forces; slain by Achilles and tied to the wheel of his chariot to be dragged three times round the city of Troy.

Helena, also **Helene** (Helen of Troy)—Famed for her beauty and had many suitors; eventually married Menelaus; was carried off by Paris to Troy (The Rape of Helen), and to avenge this insult the Trojan war was fought.

Heliades—Three sisters, the daughters of Helios, who were turned into poplar trees through mourning the death of their brother Phaeton.

Helios (The Roman god, **Sol**)—The god of the sun; also called Hyperion; represented as a man's head from which spring points representing rays, also in a chariot drawn by four horses coming from the East, or with the horses at rest in the Islands of the Blessed.

Helle—A Greek maiden who was drowned when trying to cross the Hellespont. She is sometimes represented with a golden fleece which was presented to her by Hermes.

Hephæstus (The Roman god **Vulcan**)—The Greek god of fire, the smith of the gods.

Heqet—The Egyptian frog-headed goddess.

Hera —(*See Juno.*)

Hercules (The Roman **Heracles**)—The Samson of mythology and god of all athletic games. Son of Jupiter and Alcmene. Depicted as a big, usually bearded, muscular man, either naked or wearing over his shoulder the skin of the Nemean lion and armed with a huge club. As a baby he strangled two serpents with his hands; as a boy he was trained by the learned centaur Chiron, whom he accidentally killed; as a youth he met two women, Arete, the goddess of virtue, and Kakia, the goddess of vice, and chose to be guided by the former. He married Megara and whilst temporarily insane slew his own children. To expiate his crime he entered the service of Eurystheus and undertook the following twelve labours:— (1) To kill the Nemean lion. (2) To kill the Hydra of Lerna. (3) To capture the Cerynean stag. (4) To capture the Erymanthian boar. (5) To clean the Augean stables. (6) To capture the Cretan bull. (7) To capture the divine horses of Diomedes. (8) To obtain the girdle of Hippolyte. (9) To destroy the Stymphalian birds. (10) To capture the oxen of Geryon. (11) To procure the golden apples of the Hesperides, and (12) To capture Cerberus, the three-headed dog. All of these labours he accomplished. Renouncing his wife Megara, he set off on other adventures, which included the rescue of Hesione from a sea-monster, and the killing of the giant Antæus. He also assisted Lapithæ against the Centaurs. He married Deianeira after slaying her suitor, the river-god Achelous, who had assumed the shape of a bull. His wife was treacherously carried off by the centaur Nessus, but was in the act slain by Hercules with an arrow. In his later years, and as a further penance, he was condemned to serve Omphale, who compelled him to submit to occupations unworthy of a man and made him wear woman's attire, whilst she decked herself in his lion's skin and brandished his club. In the end, he was poisoned through wearing the robe of Nessus, and expired upon a pyre of his own building. After death he was immortalised by Jupiter, who gave him Hebe in marriage.

Hermes identified with the Roman god **Mercurius** or **Mercury**— The messenger and herald of the Greek gods. Also the god of eloquence, prudence and cunning, and even of fraud, perjury and theft. Later became the god of roads and travellers. In art he is depicted as soaring in flight with an arm outstretched above his head. His broad-brimmed hat was adorned with two small wings and was called Petasus; his serpent-circled wand, Caduceus; and his winged sandals, Talaria. Sometimes paired with Mercury in works of art is Iris, the personification of the rainbow, attendant of Juno, and her swift messenger.

Hermione—The daughter of Menelaus and Helen and the wife of Neoptolemus.

Hero—(*See Leander.*)

Hesione—The daughter of Laomedon, rescued by Hercules, who gave her in marriage to Telamon.

Hesperides, also **Atlantides**—The daughters (3, 4 or 7) of Atlas and Hesperis, who with the hundred-headed dragon Ladon were the guardians of the golden apples, which Ge (Earth) gave to Hera at her marriage with Zeus. It was one of the labours of Hercules to obtain these apples.

Hestia (The Roman goddess **Vesta**)—The Greek goddess of the hearth.

Hieracosphinx—A hawk-headed sphinx of the ancient Egyptians.

Hipparchus—The tyrant of Athens.

Hippocampus—A fabulous seahorse having the forepart of a horse and the tail of a fish.

Hippocerous—A fabulous creature, half-horse and half-goat.

Hippodamia—Her father Ænomaus offered her as a prize to the first suitor who could defeat his horses in a race. Pelops succeeded in so doing, as Hippodamia bribed her father's charioteer to remove a spoke from the wheel of his chariot.

Hippolyte—A queen of the Amazons.

Hippolytus—He publicly flouted Phædra, who was in love with him. As a result she hanged herself. His father, Theseus, ordered Poseidon to take his son's life, which he did by sending a sea-monster to frighten the horses of Hippolytus so that they dragged him to death.

Hippomenes—(*See Atalanta.*)

Hob—An old name for a hobgoblin, elf or sprite.

Ho-Ho Bird or **Fêng-Hwang**—An emblem of the Chinese Empress, typifying benevolence. Pheasant-like in appearance, with grotesque head sometimes not unlike a dragon's, it has brilliantly coloured plumage, and its tail resembles long leaves rather than feathers. Being the "bringer of good tidings", it sometimes carries a scroll.

Horæ—Children of Zeus. The seasons; in art represented as maidens (or sometimes as youths) carrying the products of the seasons.

Horus—The most important of the Egyptian gods bearing this name was the hawk-headed sun or day god, the son of Isis and the slayer of Set.

Hyacinthus—A beautiful Greek boy beloved by Apollo; was accidentally killed whilst throwing the discus.

Hydra—A moster which inhabited the lake and marshes of Lerna. It had nine heads, any of which when cut off was at once replaced by two others. It was killed by Hercules, the task being one of his twelve labours.

Hydriad—A water nymph.

Hygiea, Hygea or **Hygia**—The goddess of health, usually represented in classical subjects as feeding a serpent from a cup.

Hylas—A beautiful youth who was drawn into the spring-waters at Mysia by enamoured nymphs.

Hymen or **Hymenæus**—The god of marriage; son of Apollo. His attribute is a flaming torch crossed with a quiver of arrows (Hymen's trophy).

Hyperion—The father of Helios, the sun god; Selene, the moon; and Eos, the goddess of the dawn. Later he was associated with Apollo.

Hypnos—The Greek god of sleep.

Icarus—With his father Dædalus, escaped from Crete by means of imitation wings made of feathers and fastened with wax. (*See Dædalus.*)

Idas—He defeated Apollo and carried off the nymph Marpessa. He took part in the Argonautic expedition and the Calydonian boar hunt, and was eventually killed by the lightning of Zeus.

Iduna—A Norse goddess who kept a box of golden apples by which the gods were rejuvenated.

Indra—The great Vedic national god, often represented as riding on an elephant and holding a thunderbolt.

Ino—A daughter of Cadmus. She threw herself and her son into the sea, but was rescued by the gods and became a sea-goddess.

Io—Daughter of Inachus. Jupiter became enamoured of her and, in order to deceive his wife, changed her into a beautiful heifer.

Iphigeria—A daughter of Agamemnon; disappeared in a cloud when about to be sacrificed by Calchas, a stag taking her place.

Iris—The attendant of Juno, and her swift messenger. Personification of the rainbow. In works of art is depicted holding a festoon of drapery above her head, and is sometimes paired with Mercury.

Isis, also **Hes**—An Egyptian goddess, the consort of Osiris. Second only to Hathor, with whom she is frequently identified; represented as a woman bearing on her head her emblem, the throne, or the solar disc and cow's horns.

Ixion—As a punishment for making love to Juno he was bound to a wheel which never ceased to revolve.

Janus—God of the past, present and future, and of gates and entrances. Patron of all beginnings, as the month of "January". Sometimes depicted with two faces, because every lock has two ways and with four faces, because he presided over the four Seasons. Sometimes represented with a key in his right hand and a rod in his left or with the number 300 in one hand and 65 in the other.

Japanese Divinities—Included among the large number of deities worshipped in Japan are the following Seven Gods of Luck, to whom many temples are dedicated. Special fetes and celebrations are held in their honour, particularly in the New Year:

Benten—The maiden goddess who represents art, literature, music and eloquence; devoutly worshipped by maidens desirous of attaining those accomplishments. She is always represented in company with a sea serpent, and sometimes playing the musical instrument called the biwa.

Bishamon—A god with the dual role of warrior and religious missionary. Usually represented clad in armour, carrying a spear and a toy pagoda. His mission is to conquer the world through the virtues of his attributes.

Daikoku—The god of happiness, humour, and riches; patron saint of farmers. Usually represented as seated or standing on two bales of rice, a large bag of treasure on his shoulder, and the hammer of luck in his hand. His wealth and beneficence are so great that he does not object to a rat feeding from one of his bales.

Fuku-Rokujin—The god of prophecy, who performed miracles for the betterment of mankind. He lived on the mists of heaven and earthly dews. Represented as a grotesque dwarf-like figure with a short body, shorter legs, and an elongated head, even longer than his legs.

Hotei—The god of wisdom, which he acquired from Buddha. Seated and smiling, he is distinguished by his large stomach, usually bare, which is supposed to represent an inner resourcefulness and a greatness of soul.

Jurojin—The god of longevity. Usually represented as an old man with a long white beard, carrying a shaku (holy staff) to which is attached a scroll, setting out the wisdom of the world. He is associated with the crane, stag and tortoise, emblems of longevity.

Japanese Divinities—*continued.*

Yebisu—The god of fishermen and traders; often represented as carrying a rod and line and a large tai (fish).

Jason—A leader of the Argonauts who secured the Golden Fleece from Æetes of Colchis after carrying out the tasks of harnessing two fire-breathing and brazen-hoofed bulls to a plough, sowing the teeth of dragons, and destroying the crop of armed men that grew up.

Jene—A four-headed Japanese god who presides over the souls of married or aged persons.

Joss—A Chinese idol.

"Judgment of Paris, The"—(*See Paris.*)

Jugudhatri—The Hindoo goddess of destruction; she is often represented as a yellow woman with four hands holding a shell, a club, a lotus flower and a discus, seated on a lion.

Juno (the Greek goddess **Hera**)—Queen of Heaven and the jealous wife of Jupiter; she worked vengeance on those and theirs with whom Jupiter became enamoured.

Jupiter or **Jove** (The Greek god **Zeus**)—The King of Heaven and the presumed father of the gods and men; he became master of the world after conquering the Titans; he gave the empire of the sea to Neptune, the infernal regions to Pluto and installed himself King of Heaven. Often represented seated on a throne, wearing a wreath of olive and myrtle, with thunderbolts in one hand, a sceptre in the other, and an eagle in attendance.

Kama—In Hindoo mythology, the Cupid god of love, usually depicted riding on a parrot.

Kartikeya—In Hindoo mythology, the god of war, usually represented as riding on a peacock.

Ketu—In Hindoo mythology, a god usually represented as a frog with a human head issuing from its back.

Kiau—The Chinese dragon of mountains and fens.

Kylin—A Chinese monster of hideous aspect but of a kind and gentle nature, typifying longevity and sound rulership. Like a horse or deer in appearance, with dragon's head and ox's tail. A scroll or other emblem sometimes in its mouth.

Ladon—In Greek mythology, an Arcadian river god; the monster which guarded the golden apples of the Hesperides.

Lakshmi—In Hindoo mythology, the goddess of good fortune.

Lamia—Monsters who appeared as beautiful women to ensnare young men. In true form they were supposed to have the head and breast of a woman and the body of a serpent.

Laocoön—A Trojan priest. Minerva, resenting an insult, caused two monster serpents to issue from the sea and attack his two sons. Laocoön went to their aid but all three were crushed to death.

Laomedon—The king who founded Troy, father of Priam and Hesione.

Lapithæ—The inhabitants of Thessaly. Their king, Peirithous, married Hippodamia. The Centaurs were invited to the wedding feast. One of them, becoming intoxicated, offered violence to the bride, whereupon a fight ensued ("The Battle between the Lapithæ and Centaurs"), the former being assisted by Hercules and Theseus.

Lares and **Penates**—Inferior gods of Rome, mainly connected with household belongings, but also concerned with public and state affairs.

Leander—Loved Hero, a priestess of Venus, to whom he swam across the Hellespont every night; he was eventually drowned on one of these expeditions, whereupon Hero threw herself into the sea. Represented in art as a youth removing his sandals before making the plunge.

Leda—A charming nymph who, when bathing, was surprised by Jupiter. In order not to alarm her he transformed himself into a swan, in which guise he approached, wooed and won her.

Leo—The Lion. The fifth sign of the Zodiac. (*q.v.*)

Li—The Chinese dragon of the sea.

Liber—The Italian god of wine.

Libra—The Balance. The seventh sign of the Zodiac (*q.v.*).

Lips—The south-west wind.

Loadamia—The wife of Protesilaus, who after his death kept his image always before her, and when it was burned she threw herself into the flames.

Lucifer or **Phosphorus**—(1) the bringer of light; the name of the planet Venus when seen before sunrise. (2) The church fathers attached this name to Satan, founding their decision upon Isaiah xiv, 12.

Lucina—The Roman goddess of childbirth and light.

Luna—The goddess of the moon.

Lung—The Chinese dragon of heaven.

Maat—The Egyptian goddess of truth.

Maia—In Greek mythology, the eldest and most beautiful of the Pleiades, after whom the month of May was named.

Manticore—A monster having the head of an old man, the body of a lion and the tail of a dragon.

Mars (The Greek god **Ares**)—The god of war, whose love for Venus led him into many adventures. He was a formidable warrior, and is sometimes represented as riding in a chariot drawn by horses.

Marsyas—A flute player of Phrygia. Matched his skill against Apollo, and losing the contest was tied to a tree and flayed alive by his opponent.

Medea—A Grecian enchantress who assisted Jason to win the Golden Fleece. Being subsequently deserted by him she killed their two children and fled through the air in a chariot drawn by winged dragons.

Medusa—A beautiful maiden whose hair was transformed into snakes and who became the leader of the Gorgones (of whom she was the only mortal). Was beheaded by Perseus when asleep, and he carried her head with him on his adventures. Subsequently, it adorned Minerva's shield—The Ægis.

Megaera—One of the Three Furies (*q.v.*).

Meleager—Leader of the Calydonian Hunt; killed a boar in rescuing Atalanta. Sometimes represented with a hound and the head of a boar.

Melpomene—One of the Nine Muses, daughter of Jupiter and Mnemosyne. She presided over tragedy, and is represented wearing a tragic mask, and sometimes with a dagger and buskins.

Memnon—A king of Ethiopia. Assisted his uncle Priam in the Trojan war and killed Antilochus, Nestor's son. Was afterwards slain by Achilles.

Menelaus—A king of Sparta and husband of Helen.

Mentor—A friend to whom Ulysses entrusted the care of his estates and affairs before setting out for the Trojan war.

Mercurius (Mercury)—(*See Hermes.*)

Mermaid—A fabulous creature of the sea, having the upper part of a woman and the lower part of a fish.

Midas—A king of Phrygia. In return for good service rendered to Silenus, Bacchus granted his wish that everything he touched should turn to gold. The result was disastrous, as even the food he ate became gold in his mouth. Usually represented as having the ears of an ass.

Milo—A celebrated athlete who carried a four-year-old heifer on his shoulders, and afterwards ate the whole of it in a single day.

Minerva (The Greek goddess **Athena**)—The goddess of wisdom, who presided over the liberal arts, peace and defensive war. The victor of dullness. Usually represented wearing a helmet and a coat of mail, and carrying a shield (ægis) which was adorned with Medusa's head.

Minos—A lawgiving king of Crete, who after death was made a judge in Hades.

Minotaur—A monster, half bull and half man, who every year devoured seven youths and seven maidens; ultimately slain by Theseus.

Mithras—A Persian god, defender of the truth, who slew the divine bull from whose body sprang all plants and animals beneficial to man.

Mnemosyne—The Greek goddess of memory; mother of the nine Muses by Jupiter.

Moiræ or **Mœra** (The Roman goddess **Parcæ**)—The Greek goddess of fate.

Morpheus—Son of the god Somnus or Sleep. Often represented as a chubby child with poppies in his hand.

Mors (Death)—The Greek god **Thanatos**, one of the infernal deities born of Night, without a father.

Muses, The Nine—Calliope, Muse of Heroic Poetry, wore a laurel crown; Clio, Muse of History, with laurel wreath, book and stylus; Erato, Muse of Lyric Poetry, with lyre; Euterpe, Muse of Music, with flute and garland of flowers; Melpomene, Muse of Tragedy, with tragic mask and dagger; Polyhymnia, Muse of Rhetoric, with sceptre; Terpsichore, Muse of Dancing, treading an airy measure; Thalia, Muse of Comedy, with comic mask, shepherd's crook and crown of wild flowers; Urania, Muse of Astronomy, with mathematical instruments and/or globe.

Mut—An Egyptian goddess, consort of Amen-Ra, sometimes represented with the head of a lion.

Naga—Among the Hindoos a deified cobra.

Naiades or **Naides**—Nymphs who presided over rivers, springs, wells and fountains.

Narcissus—A beautiful Greek youth, who fell in love with the reflection of his own face, which he saw in the water of a fountain. He could not bear to leave it and so pined away and died, his blood being changed into the flower which bears his name. His infatuation was a punishment for despising the love of Echo.

Narada—In Hindoo mythology, the messenger of the gods.

Nemesis—One of the infernal deities, daughter of Nox. The goddess of retributive justice and moderation, always prepared to punish excess. Represented with a helm and a wheel, and sometimes in a chariot pulled by griffins.

Neoptolemus—A son of Achilles. After his father's death he assisted in the capture of Troy and was one of the heroes of the wooden horse; he slew Priam and afterwards married Hermione.

Neptune (The Greek god **Poseidon**)—God of the seas. Represented sitting in a chariot made of a shell and drawn by sea-horses or dolphins, and holding his trident in his hand.

Nereides—The fifty daughters of Nereus and Doris; nymphs of the sea. They are usually represented in human form but sometimes with the tail of a fish and often riding on a sea-monster. One of the most famous was Thetis.

Nereus—A deity of the sea, son of Oceanus and Terra. He married Doris, by whom he had fifty daughters called the Nereides. Represented as a man having the tail of a fish, with eyebrows and beard of seaweed.

Nessus—A centaur who carried off Deianeira, the wife of Hercules, across the river Evenus. Hercules slew him with an arrow.

Nestor—In his youth a distinguished warrior; as an old man he gave wise counsel to Agamemnon in the Trojan war.

Nike (The Roman goddess **Victoria** or **Victory**)—The goddess of victory; usually represented as winged and carrying a wreath and a palm branch.

Nilus—A personification of the River Nile, represented as an old man in a reclining position, holding a reed in one hand and a cornucopia in the other, indicating the wealth obtained from the river.

Niobe—A daughter of Tantalus. Married Amphion, by whom she had six sons and six daughters. The former were killed by the darts of Apollo and the latter were slain by Diana. Niobe, struck at the suddenness of her misfortunes, was changed into a statue of stone.

Notus—The South wind; represented in art as a deity pouring water from a jar.

Nox—One of the most ancient deities, daughter of Chaos. From her union with her brother Erebus she gave birth to the Day and the Light.

Nut—The Egyptian goddess of heaven; consort of Seb.

Nymphæ (Nymphs)—Female deities. Sea nymphs, Oceanides; fresh-water nymphs, Naiades or Naides; mountain nymphs, Oreades; nymphs of glens, Napæae; nymphs of woods, Dryades and Hamadryades.

Nyroothey—In Hindoo mythology, one of the gods who protect the eight divisions of the world, usually depicted as being carried on the shoulders of a man.

Nyx—The Greek personification of night.

Oceanides—Sea nymphs, daughters of Oceanus and Tethys.

Oceanus—The Greek god of the sea.

Odin—The king of the Norse gods.

Œdipus—Son of Laius, king of Thebes, who exposed him on Mount Cithæron, with his feet pierced, immediately after birth, to nullify a prophecy that Laius should be killed by his son. The child was rescued by a shepherd, and given a name having reference to his swollen feet. He grew up to kill his father and marry his own mother, in both cases unknowingly. On learning that it was his mother Jocasta whom he had married, he put out his own eyes (Jocasta having hanged herself) and wandered from Thebes with his daughter. The tragic fate of Œdipus and his family formed the subject of many Greek tragedies. Œdipus also answered the riddle of the Sphinx.

Oenone—A nymph. Wife of Paris before he carried off Helen.

Ogre—A hideous giant who lived on human beings.

Olympus—A mountain range of Macedonia and Thessaly. The ancients believed that its highest point touched the heavens and so made it the abode of the gods and the court of Jupiter.

Omphale—A queen of Lydia, whom Hercules was condemned to serve in his latter years. She clothed him in female attire and made him submit to occupations unworthy of a man, and decked herself in his lion's skin and brandished his club.

Oreades—Nymphs of the mountains.

Orestes—A son of Agamemnon, who, at the command of Apollo, avenged his father's murder and was pursued by the Furies.

Orion—A giant who sought the hand of Hero, whose father, with the assistance of Bacchus, put out his eyes; later his sight was recovered and he became a great hunter. After his death Orion was placed amongst the stars, where he appeared as a giant with a girdle, a sword, a lion's skin and a club.

Orithyia—A daughter of Erechtheus, king of Athens. She was courted and carried away by Boreas, king of Thrace, and became the mother of Cleopatra, Zetes and Calais.

Orpheus—A son of Oeagrus by the Muse Calliope. He received a lyre from Apollo upon which he played exquisite music. Married Eurydice who, however, died through a misadventure. Resolved to recover her he so charmed Pluto with his music that he secured her return to earth upon the condition that he did not look upon her until clear of the region of Hades. The temptation proved too great and she was lost to him for ever.

Osiris—A deity of the Egyptians, who typified good in perpetual conflict with evil. It was to him that prayers and offerings for the dead were made, and all sepulchral inscriptions, except those of the oldest period, were addressed directly to him. He is depicted as a mummy wearing the royal cap of Upper Egypt.

Pales—The Roman goddess of sheepfolds and of pastures. She was worshipped with festivals, called Parilia.

Palladium—A statue (or shield) of Pallas. It fell from heaven near the tent of Ilus, as that prince was building the citadel of Ilium. On its preservation depended the safety of Troy, and therefore Ulysses and Diomedes were commissioned to steal it away.

Pallas—The Roman goddess Minerva (*q.v.*).

Pan—The goat-footed Arcadian god of nature, shepherds, flocks, woods and pastures. Though of a pleasant disposition his appearance often caused groundless "panic". He loved the nymph Syrinx, but fleeing from him into a stream, she was changed into a clump of reeds. Pan took seven pieces of the reed, of unequal length, and tying them together made a musical instrument (Pan-pipes) which he named after the fair nymph. He is usually represented as a sensual being having horns and a puck nose, with a pine garland round his mis-shaped head, a shepherd's crook in his hand and playing the syrinx.

Panch Mukhti—In Hindoo mythology, a five-headed god.

Pandora—The first woman to tread the earth. She married Epimetheus, to whom she gave a box which Jupiter had given her. When it was opened there issued from it a multitude of evils which dispersed all over the world, Hope alone remaining.

Parche—Goddess who presided over birth and life of mankind.

Paris—The son of Priam, king of Troy. At a marriage feast he was appointed to bestow an apple upon the fairest woman (The Judgment of Paris). He gave it to Venus, who was one of the three chief contestants, the others being Juno and Minerva. Later, he carried off Helen to Troy and thus caused the Trojan war. Usually he is depicted as a beautiful shepherd lad wearing a Phrygian cap.

Parnassus—A mountain of Phocis, sacred to the Muses, and to Apollo and Bacchus.

Pasht—An Egyptian goddess, usually represented with the head of a lioness crowned with the solar disc and an asp.

Pavana—The Hindoo god of the wind, usually represented riding on a deer.

Pax (the Greek goddess **Irene**)—The goddess of peace, represented by the Athenians as holding the infant Plutus (god of wealth) in her lap, sometimes also depicted holding the "horn of plenty".

Pegasus—A winged horse, sprung from the blood of Medusa, when Perseus had cut off her head. Becoming the favourite of the Muses it was given to Bellerophon to conquer the Chimæra. Was placed among the constellations by Jupiter.

Pelops—A son of Tantalus, who served him as food to the gods.

Penelope—The faithful wife of Ulysses. Being pestered by suitors she promised to make a choice when she had finished the weaving of a garment, but each night she unravelled that which she had woven during the day.

Peri—In Persian mythology, an elf or fairy, originally of either sex and regarded as evil, but later as benevolent and beautiful and of female sex.

Persephone (The Roman goddess **Proserpina**)—Was carried off by Pluto to become queen of Hades.

Perseus—Rendered himself invisible with the aid of Pluto's helmet, and with the assistance of other gods flew to the land of the Gorgones, whom he found asleep; he cut off Medusa's head which later he gave to Athena, who placed it in the middle of her shield or breastplate.

Petasus—The winged hat of Mercury.

Phaethon—The son of Helios, the sun god, who was killed by Zeus with a thunderbolt for mishandling the chariot of the sun, depicted as driving a chariot of light.

Philoctetes—A Greek bowman bitten in the heel by a snake when attacking Troy.

Philomela—The daughter of Pandion, king of Athens; her tongue was cut out by Tereus, but with her two sisters she obtained revenge and was afterwards transformed into a swallow.

Phoebe—The Greek moon goddess. She bequeathed the Delphian oracle to her brother Apollo.

Phoenix—A mythological bird which lived for hundreds of years, then after consuming itself on a funeral pyre, sprang from the ashes again into new life; the symbol of immortality.

Pirithous—Married Hippodamia. After her death, with the aid of Theseus he endeavoured to carry off Persephone from Hades, but failed, and was kept in torment by Pluto.

Pisces—The Fishes. The twelfth sign of the Zodiac (*q.v.*).

Pleiades—The name given to seven of the daughters of Atlas. They were placed in the heavens after death, where they formed a constellation called Pleiades.

Pluto—King of Hades. (*See Hades.*)

Pollux—One of the twin sons of the Greek god Zeus; brother to Castor (*q.v.*).

Polyhymnia—The Muse of Rhetoric.

Polyphemus—In Greek mythology, a giant with only one eye who dwelled in Sicily.; he killed and ate some of Ulysses' men, the remainder escaping by first putting out his eye whilst he slept.

Pomona—The Roman goddess of gardens and fruit trees.

Poseidon—Greek god. (*See Neptune.*)

Priapus—The god of fertility, especially in gardens. Represented carrying fruit in his garments and with a sickle or cornucopia in his hand.

Prometheus—Stole fire from the chariot of the sun and brought it to earth for the benefit of mankind. Jupiter caused him to be secured to a rock, where a vulture fed upon his liver, which never diminished. Was eventually delivered by Hercules. Depicted carrying a vase of fire.

Proserpina—(*See Persephone.*)

Proteus—A sea deity who received the gift of prophecy from Neptune. Presided over seals, sea-lions, etc.

Psyche—A beautiful nymph, the personification of the soul, whom Cupid married and carried away to a place of bliss, where he loved her in the darkness of the night. Venus in her jealousy kept them apart but after years of affliction the lovers were again united. Represented in art as a maiden with the wings of a butterfly.

Pygmalion—A sculptor of Cyprus. Became enamoured of the statue of a woman which he had made and prayed that it might be endowed with life. Upon his prayer being granted he married the maiden, whom he called Galatea.

Pyramus—(*See Thisbe.*)

Python—A serpent sprung from the mud which remained on the surface of the earth after the deluge of Deucalion. Apollo attacked the monster with arrows and killed him.

Ra—The Egyptian god of the Sun. (*See Amen-Ra.*)

Remus—(*See Romulus.*)

Rhea or **Cybele** (The Roman goddess Ops)—A Greek goddess of the earth; represented as seated on a throne, adorned with a mural crown, from which a veil falls, and with lions crouching right and left of the throne; sometimes she is seen riding in a chariot drawn by lions.

Romulus—As a child, was thrown into the Tiber to drown with his twin brother Remus, but their lives were preserved and they were reared by a she-wolf. They decided to build a city but quarrelled as to its situation. In the fight Remus lost his life leaving Romulus his choice, whereupon he founded Rome.

Sabini—An ancient people of Italy. They united with Romulus at Rome, under their king Tatius.

Sagittarius—The Archer. The ninth sign of the Zodiac (*q.v.*).

Salamander—A small lizard-like reptile; the name is also applied to a mythical dragon that lived in fire.

Salmoneus—Deemed himself equal to Zeus and imitated thunder by driving his chariot over a brazen bridge and darting lighted torches on every side to imitate lightning. This angered Jupiter, who killed him with a thunderbolt.

Sani—A Hindoo god usually depicted astride a vulture and holding a sword, arrows and daggers.

Saraswati—The Hindoo goddess of the arts, usually represented holding a musical instrument.

Saturnus (Saturn)—The god of agriculture and seed sowing, usually represented as a bent old man holding a child by one hand and a scythe in the other. Father Time.

Satyrs—Sylvan deities, half-man and half-goat, attendants of Bacchus. Represented in art with bristling hair, round nose, ears pointed at the top, two small horns and the tail of a horse or goat.

Sciron—A Greek robber who induced travellers to wash his feet and then kicked them into the sea. Was killed by Theseus.

Scorpio—The Scorpion. The eighth sign of the Zodiac (*q.v.*).

Scylla—A rock between Italy and Sicily, peopled by tradition with Scylla, a monster barking like a dog, with twelve feet and six long necks and heads, each with three rows of sharp teeth. (*See Charybdis.*)

Sea-horse—A horse with body terminating in the tail of a dolphin.

Seb—An Egyptian god usually represented with a goose upon his head.

Sebek—An Egyptian god represented in human form but with the head of a crocodile.

Sekhet—An Egyptian goddess having the head of a cat or a lioness.

Seraph—A celestial being of high order, in human form, having three pairs of wings, two pairs of which are used to cover the face and body and the other to fly.

Sesha—The Hindoo god of snakes.

Set—The Egyptian god of darkness and night, usually represented in human form but with the head of an animal.

Shu—An Egyptian goddess who supported the sun and the horizon.

Silenus—Described as the oldest of the Satyrs, usually represented as a short fat old goat-man with a flat nose and often tipsy.

Sinon—A son of Sisyphus, accompanied the Greeks to the Trojan war. Failing to subdue the city of Troy after prolonged siege, the Greeks ostensibly withdrew their troops, leaving behind a great wooden horse, which the Trojans, persuaded by Sinon, dragged into the city as a gift from the gods. In the night Greek soldiers hidden within the horse crept out and opened the gates of Troy to their returning comrades, who entered and captured the city.

Sirens—Sea nymphs who charmed so well with their voices that all forgot their employments to listen, and at last died for want of food. Ulysses escaped their blandishments by blocking his ears with wax.

Sisyphus—A king of Corinth who in the underworld was condemned to roll a huge stone to the top of a hill. It always rolled back again, thus making his task never-ending.

Siva—One of the three principal Hindoo gods, with power over destruction and regeneration; usually represented with four hands. His symbol is the linga.

Sol—The sun, identified with Apollo and Helios.

Soma—A Hindoo god representing the moon.

Somnus (The Greek god Hypnos)—The Roman god who presided over sleep. He was the son of Night (Nox), and the brother of Death (Mors).

Sphinx—A female monster with a lion's body and the head and bust of a woman; propounded a riddle which was solved by Œdipus. The Egyptian Sphinx is the figure of a lion without wings, the upper part of the body human; the Greek Sphinx is a winged lion with the breast and head of a woman. (*See Andro-Sphinx.*)

Stentor—A Greek who went to the Trojan war. His voice alone was louder than those of fifty men's together.

Stymphalus—An Arcadian lake, the neighbourhood of which was infested with voracious birds which fed upon human flesh and were called Stymphalides. It was the ninth Labour of Hercules to destroy them.

Styx—The principal river of the lower world across which Charon ferried the shades of the dead.

Syrinx—An Arcadian nymph, beloved of Pan. (*See Pan.*)

Sukra—A Hindoo god, usually represented as riding on a camel and holding a hoop.

Talaria—The winged sandals of Mercury.

Tantalus—A king of Lydia and the son of Jupiter. Punished in hell with an unquenchable thirst which he was unable to slake, although standing up to the chin in a pool of water, whilst over his head a huge rock was suspended which threatened to crush him.

Taurt—An Egyptian goddess who usually resembles a hippopotamus.

Taurus—The Bull. The second sign of the Zodiac (*q.v.*).

Telemachus—The son of Ulysses and Penelope; he journeyed without success to find his father and returned home in time to assist in the killing of his mother's suitors.

Terminus—The Roman god of rights and boundaries.

Terpsichore—One of the Muses, daughter of Jupiter and Mnemosyne. She presided over dancing. Sometimes represented with the lyre and plectrum.

Terra—The wife of Uranus and mother of Oceanus.

Teucer— The best archer in the Greek army attacking Troy.

Thalia—The Muse of Comedy. Her attribute is a comic mask, a shepherd's staff or a wreath of ivy.

Theseus—One of the Argonauts. He slew the Minotaur, overcame the Amazons and Centaurs, and carried off Minos's daughter Ariadne.

Thetis—One of the sea deities. Daughter of Nereus and Doris. Married Peleus and became the mother of Achilles.

Thisbe—Arrived late at a tryst with her lover Pyramus, losing her cloak on the way while watching a lion killing an ox. Pyramus, finding the bloodstained cloak, supposed her dead and killed himself; and Thisbe, finding his body, followed his example.

Thor—The Norse god of thunder and strength, conceived as having a red beard and hair (the colour of lightning), riding in a chariot drawn by goats (the rumbling of which represents thunder) and bearing a magic hammer (thunderbolt).

Thoth or **Tauut**—The moon god; the Egyptian god of letters, wisdom and magic; usually represented with the head of an ibis.

Tisiphone—One of the Furies (*q.v.*).

Titans—Giants who were at war with Jupiter for ten years. They were eventually beaten and imprisoned in a cave. The name is also given to their descendants, six brothers and six sisters.

Triptolemus—In Greek mythology, the patron of agriculture, often represented seated in a winged chariot drawn by two dragons, in which he travelled from land to land.

Triton—A son of Neptune by Amphitrite. He was powerful among the sea deities and could calm the ocean and abate storms. His body above the waist is like that of a man, and below, that of a dolphin. His trumpet is the conch shell.

Trojan War, The—Waged for ten years between the Greeks and Trojans. It was caused through the abduction of Helen by Paris and ended in the destruction of Troy.

Ulysses (The Greek hero **Odysseus**)—A hero of the Trojan war, but better known through his later adventures, which form the subject of Homer's "Odyssey". Appears in art in many forms, but principally in a ship beset by sirens.

Unicorn—A fabulous animal in the form of a horse with a straight horn projecting from its forehead. The figure was embodied in the Royal Coat of Arms by King James I.

Uræus—The serpent emblem of ancient Egyptian divinities and kings, placed on the head-dress.

Urania—One of the Muses. She presided over astronomy. Her attributes are a globe and mathematical instruments.

Uranus—Father of the Titans; he confined them in Tartarus until they revolted and overthrew him.

Varuna—In Hindoo mythology, the god of the heavens and bestower of rewards and punishments; sometimes represented as riding on a sea monster.

Venus—The Roman goddess of beauty, called Aphrodite by the Greeks. She married Vulcan and was the mother of Cupid.

Vesper—A name applied to the planet Venus when it is the evening star.

Vesta (the Greek goddess **Hestia**)—Daughter of Rhea and Saturn, sister to Ceres and Juno. She was goddess of the hearth and home. At Rome a fire was continually kept lighted in her temple by a number of virgins who had dedicated themselves to the service of the goddess.

Virgo—The Virgin. The sixth sign of the Zodiac (*q.v.*).

Vulcanus (**Vulcan**) (The Greek god **Hephæstus**)—A god who presided over fire and was the patron of all artists who worked in metal. He was the son of Jupiter and Juno. The Cyclops of Sicily assisted him in making the thunderbolts of Jupiter and arms for the gods. His forges were situated under Mount Etna in the island of Sicily.

Wyvern—A fabulous monster having the head and body of a dragon with extended wings, the tail of a scorpion and the feet of a bird.

Yama—In Hindoo mythology, the god of departed spirits, being a deification of the first mortal to die.

Zephyrus (Roman **Favonius**)—The west wind.

Zeus—(*See Jupiter.*)

Zodiac—An imaginary belt of the heavens, as known to the ancients, in which all apparent positions of the sun and planets as they pass in their annual course are indicated. Divided into twelve equal parts, each having a name and sign. (*See illustration on following page.*)

SIGNS OF THE ZODIAC

1	**ARIES**—The Ram	♈
2	**TAURUS**—The Bull	♉
3	**GEMINI**—The Twins	♊
4	**CANCER**—The Crab	♋
5	**LEO**—The Lion	♌
6	**VIRGO**—The Virgin	♍
7	**LIBRA**—The Balance	♎
8	**SCORPIO**—The Scorpion	♏
9	**SAGITTARIUS**—The Archer	♐
10	**CAPRICORNUS**—The Goat	♑
11	**AQUARIUS**—The Water-Carrier	♒
12	**PISCES**—The Fishes	♓

SUPPLEMENT

to the preceding

CLASSICAL DICTIONARY

Indexing the attributes of the subjects to facilitate identification in works of art.

Attributes, etc.	Subject.
Angel, Dog, Boy ...	The legend of Tobias and the Angel.
Antlers...	Actæon, the hunter, changed into a stag by Diana.
Anvil	Vulcan, god of the forge.
Apple	Bestowed upon Venus by the shepherd, Paris. ("The Judgment of Paris".)
Apples	To search for the Golden Hesperian Apples was the eleventh Labour of Hercules.
Apples, three golden ...	Dropped by Hippomenes in the path of Atalanta during his race with her for the prize of her hand.
Archer	Sagittarius, the ninth sign of the Zodiac.
Armour, man in ...	Mars, god of war.
Armour, woman in ...	Bellona. War personified in the figure of a woman.
Armour, woman in ...	Minerva (Pallas Athene); presided over defensive war, peace and the liberal arts.
Armour, man in. Spear. Toy pagoda in hand.	Bishamon, the Japanese god of militarism.

Arrow	Paris slew Achilles, whose vulnerable heel was pierced by an arrow.
Arrow	Hercules slew the centaur Nessus with an arrow.
Arrows, quiver of. Bow.	Cupid's attributes.
Arrows, quiver of, crossed with flaming torch.	Hymen's trophy.
Asp	The sting of an asp caused the death of Cleopatra.
Ass	Silenus, the tutor of Bacchus, is usually depicted riding an ass.
Ass	Midas. A man with the ears of an ass.
Bamboo tube. Rods ...	The Chinese Chang Kuo.
Barrel	Diogenes once lived in a tub.
Bear	Callisto. The nymph transformed into a bear.
Beetle	Chepera, the Egyptian solar deity, often represented by the scarabæus, the sacred beetle of ancient Egypt.
Besom. Manuscript roll. Palm leaf. Gourd.	The Chinese Twin Genii of Union and Harmony.
Bird (half bird, half man).	Garuda.
Bird (half bird, half woman).	Harpy.
Bird, with pheasant-like plumage.	Ho-Ho bird, a Chinese symbol.
Bird (vulture)	Fed on the liver of Prometheus.
Bird	In Egyptian art—the soul depicted as a bird.
Birds	The ninth Labour of Hercules was to destroy the Stymphalian Birds.
Bison. Red Indian ...	Symbolical of the continent of America.
Biwa (Japanese musical instrument). Sea-serpent.	Benten, the Japanese maiden deity; the only woman among the seven gods.

Blindfolded woman. Sword. Scales.	Astræa, goddess of Justice.
Boar	Meleager killed a boar in rescuing Atalanta.
Boar	Killed Adonis, a young hunter beloved by Venus.
Boar	The fourth Labour of Hercules was to capture the Erymanthian Boar.
Boat	Argo, the fifty-oared ship in which the Argonauts sailed to recover the Golden Fleece.
Boat	Charon ferried the souls of the dead across the waters of the Styx.
Book. Stylus. Laurel wreath.	Clio, the Muse of History.
Book, or roll of paper, or tablet. Stylus.	Calliope, the Muse of Epic Poetry.
Books, bundle of. Vase. Fly-whisk.	The Chinese Dharmatrata.
Bow. Crescent in her hair.	Diana, goddess of the moon and the chase.
Bow	Apollo is sometimes depicted with a bow.
Bow. Quiver of arrows	Cupid, the boy-god of Love.
Bow, in the hands of a centaur.	Sagittarius, the Archer. Ninth sign of the Zodiac.
Box (or casket) ...	From Pandora's box issued evils which spread all over the world.
Boy, extracting thorn from foot.	The Spinario.
Boy, with wings. Bow. Quiver of arrows.	Cupid, the god of Love.
Boy. Angel. Dog ...	The legend of Tobias and the Angel.
Branches	(*See Trees.*)
Brazier, burning. Broken column.	Constancy.
Brush, wielded by a man	Wên Kung, the Chinese star god of Literature.

Buddha. Standing on lotus pedestal under a jewelled canopy. Wearing three-fold nimbus.	The Chinese Amitâbha.
Buddha. Standing. With many hands, or, with eleven heads.	The Chinese Avalokita.
Buddha. Seated on lotus pedestal.	The Chinese Manjusri.
Buddha, of various aspects.	(*See the Chinese Sakyamuni.*)
Buddhist Messiah. Obese, seated figure with smiling features and exposed stomach and chest.	The Chinese Maitreya. The prototype of the Japanese Hotei.
Bull	Symbolical of the continent of Europe.
Bull	Dirce ordered Amphion and Zethus to tie Antiope to a bull. But they, discovering that Antiope was their mother, so treated Dirce.
Bull	Taurus, the second sign of the Zodiac.
Bull	Jupiter assumed the form of a bull to carry off Europa. (The Rape of Europa.)
Bull	It was the sixth Labour of Hercules to capture the Cretan Bull.
Bull	Hercules slew Achelous, who, in a struggle for Deianeira, assumed the form of a bull.
Bull. Half bull, half man.	Minotaur.
Buskins	Melpomene is sometimes depicted wearing buskins.
Camel	Symbolical of the continent of Asia.
Camel. Man with hoop, on back of.	Sukra, the Hindu god.
Casket	(*See Box of Pandora.*)
Castanets, man playing.	The Chinese Ts'ao Kuo-Ch'iu.

Cattle	It was the tenth Labour of Hercules to capture the Divine Cattle of Geryon. (On this expedition he slew the giant Cacus with his club. *See Cacus*.)
Centaur	Nessus, the centaur, was slain by Hercules with an arrow in the act of carrying off Deianeira.
Centaur	Chiron, a learned centaur, tutor and friend of the gods, especially of Hercules. Was accidentally killed by Hercules. Was transferred to the sky where he is known as the constellation Sagittarius, the Archer, the ninth sign of the Zodiac.
Centaurs	Centaurs tried to kidnap Hippodamia but were frustrated by the Lapithæ, assisted by Hercules and Thesus. (The Battle between the Centaurs and Lapithæ.)
Chained to rock ...	Andromeda. Was rescued by Perseus.
Chained to the Caucasian Mountains. Vulture feeding upon his liver.	Prometheus. Was delivered by Hercules.
Chained in the dark abyss called Tartarus (Hades).	Titans and Titanides, the six sons and six daughters of Uranus and Gaea.
Chariot	Hector was slain by Achilles and tied to the wheel of his chariot.
Chariot	Mars' chariot was drawn by horses.
Chariot	Nemesis' chariot was drawn by griffins.
Chariot	Phæton, son of Apollo, drove the sun chariot.
Chariot	The chariot of Triptolemus was drawn by two dragons.
Chariot	Thor's chariot was drawn by goats.
Chariot	Rhea's (Cybele) chariot was drawn by lions.
Chariot	Bacchus's chariot was drawn by leopards.
Chariot	Cybele's chariot was drawn by two lions.

Chariot	Venus's chariot was a pearl shell drawn by snow-white doves.
Chariot	Aurora's chariot was drawn by white horses.
Chariot	Medea's chariot was drawn by winged dragons.
Chariot	Neptune's shell-chariot was drawn by sea-horses, or by dolphins.
Chariot	Galatea's pearl-shell chariot was drawn by dolphins.
Chariot	The chariot of the Chinese Mu Wang was drawn by eight horses.
Child (chubby) ...	Morpheus was sometimes so represented.
Child, or children clinging to her skirts.	Charity.
Club. Lion's skin across his shoulder. Muscular, bearded man.	Hercules, the Samson of mythology; god of all athletic games.
Column, broken. Burning brazier.	Constancy.
Compasses. Mirror ...	Prudence.
Compasses in her hand. Coronet on head. Body terminating in a dragon or serpent.	The Chinese Nü Wa.
Cornucopia	Priapus sometimes carried one.
Cornucopia; stuffed with fruit.	Fortuna, the goddess of Plenty.
Crescent in her hair. Bow.	Diana, goddess of the moon and of the chase.
Crook (Shepherd's) ...	Pan sometimes carried one.
Crown with seven stars	Ariadne, wife of Bacchus.
Crown of laurel. Tablet	Calliope, the Muse of Epic Poetry.
Crown (coronet) on her head. Compasses in her hand. Her body terminating in dragon or serpent.	The Chinese Nü Wa.

Cup	Circe, the sorceress who offered a drugged cup to Ulysses and changed his men into swine.
Cup. Eagle	Ganymede, a beautiful youth, beloved by Jupiter, who assumed the form of an eagle to carry him off to become the cup-bearer of the gods.
Cup	Hebe, goddess of youth; cup-bearer of the gods.
Cup	Hygiea, goddess of health.
Dagger. Tragic Mask	Melpomene, the Muse of Tragedy.
Dagger. Whip. Torch. Key.	Hecate, one of the Titans. She presided over magic.
Dancing. A nymph treading an airy measure.	Terpsichore, the Muse of Dancing.
Deer, with man on its back.	Pavana, the Hindu god of the wind.
Deer	(*See also Stag.*)
Diadem. Sceptre. Peacock.	Hera, the Roman goddess Juno, Queen of Heaven.
Disc with two tall ostrich plumes on his head.	Amen-Ra, the Egyptian sun god.
Disc, solar, around her head.	Bast, the Egyptian goddess, "The Lady of Life".
Disc, solar, around his head. Lyre.	Apollo, god of the sun, of music, and of medicine.
Discus, athlete throwing.	Discobolus.
Discus	Hyacinthus, a beautiful Greek boy, beloved by Apollo. Was accidentally killed while throwing the discus.
Distaff	The attribute of Clotho, one of the Three Fates.
Dog, of fearsome appearance.	Dog of Fo, a Buddist symbol.
Dog. Heart	Fidelity.
Dog. Angel. Boy ...	The legend of Tobias and the Angel.

Dog with three heads ...	Cerberus. Guarded the entrance to Hades. It was the twelfth Labour of Hercules to capture it.
Dog's head on man ...	Anubis, the Egyptian god of graves and burial rites.
Dolphin. Man with body terminating in the tail of a dolphin.	Triton.
Dolphin. Woman with body terminating in the tail of a dolphin.	Nereide. Siren.
Dolphin. Horse with body terminating in the tail of a dolphin.	Sea-horse.
Dolphin	Arion was saved by a dolphin when he threw himself into the sea.
Dolphins	Drew the pearl-shell chariot of Galatea.
Dolphins	Or sea-horses, drew the shell-chariot of Neptune.
Doves, snow white ...	Drew Venus's pearl-shell chariot.
Doves and sparrows ...	Were especially sacred to Aphrodite, the Roman goddess Venus.
Dragon	Cadmus slew a dragon.
Dragon	Was slain by St. George, patron saint of England.
Dragon that lived in fire	Salamander.
Dragon, winged ...	Drew Medea's chariot.
Dragon with extended wings, tail of scorpion, and feet of bird.	Wyvern.
Dragon, five-clawed ...	The Imperial dragon of China. Emblem of the Emperor, and of Princes of high rank.
Dragon, four-clawed ...	Emblem of Princes of lower rank.
Dragon of lesser degree, or snake with four claws.	Emblem of Princes of lowest rank, and of Mandarins.
Dragon, three-clawed...	The Imperial dragon of Japan.
Dragon	Lung, the Chinese dragon of heaven.
Dragon	Li the Chinese dragon of the sea.

Dragon	Kiau, the Chinese dragon of mountains and fens.
Dragons, two	Drew the chariot of Triptolemus.
Dragons	Drew the chariot of Medea.
Eagle	Ganymede was carried off by Jupiter who assumed the form of an eagle. ("The Rape of Ganymede".)
Eagle	Sometimes depicted in attendance upon Jupiter.
Elephant	Symbolical of the continent of Africa.
Elephant	Indra, the great Vedic national god, often portrayed riding an elephant.
Eye, one only, in forehead.	Cyclops.
Fan, in man's hand ...	Chung-Li Ch'üan, leader of the Taoist Genii.
Feathers. Two tall ostrich plumes in the disc he wore on his head.	Amen-Ra, the Egyptian sun god.
Fire	Vesta, the goddess of fire, and of the hearth and home.
Fishes	Pisces, the twelfth sign of the Zodiac.
Fishing rod. Sea bream	The Japanese Yebisu, deity of fishermen and tradesmen.
Flaying alive	Marsyas, a Phrygian flute player: flayed alive by Apollo.
Flowers	Flora, goddess of flowers.
Flowers. Fruit ...	Pomona, the Roman goddess of flowers and fruit trees.
Flowers. Flute ...	Euterpe, the Muse of Music.
Flowers, with basket of	The Chinese Lan Ts'ai-Ho.
Flute. Flowers ...	Euterpe, the Muse of Music.
Flute	Han Hsiang Tzü. One of the Eight Genii of China.
Fly-whisk. Vase. Bundle of books.	The Chinese Dharmatrata.
Forge	Vulcan, god of the forge.
Fork, two-pronged ...	Pluto, king of Hades.

Fork, three-pronged ...	Neptune, god of the seas.
Fountain	Arethusa was turned into a fountain.
Fountain nymphs ...	Naiades.
Frog with human head on back.	Ketu, the Hindu god.
Fruit. Flowers ...	Pomona, the Roman goddess of fruit trees and flowers.
Giant	Ogre who lived on human beings.
Gladiator, lying down and mortally wounded.	The Dying Gaul.
Gladiator, in an aggressive attitude, with one arm stretched upward and forward, and one arm stretched out behind.	The Borghese Gladiator.
Globe (terrestrial) on shoulders.	Atlas.
Globe (terrestrial) ...	Jupiter's footstool.
Globe (celestial). Mathematical instruments.	Urania, the Muse of Astronomy.
Goat	Amalthæ. Sometimes represented in art as a goat, feeding the infant Jupiter.
Goat with head of lion and tail of dragon.	Chimera.
Goats	Drew Thor's chariot.
Goat. Half goat, half man.	Satyr.
Goat. Half goat, half man.	Pan, the Arcadian satyr; god of nature, of shepherds, and of the universe.
Gourd, man with ...	The Chinese Li T'ieh-Kuai.
Gourd. Palm leaf. Besom. Manuscript roll.	The Chinese Twin Genii of Union and Harmony.
Grapes...	Bacchus, god of wine and revelry, crowned with grape vine.
Halberd in man's hand	The Chinese Chieh Kuei.
Hammer. Anvil ...	Vulcan, god of the forge.

Hammer. Rice bales. Sack.	The Japanese Daikoku, the happy god of wealth and patron saint of farmers.
Hammer	A magic hammer was carried by Thor.
Hands, four	Siva, the Hindu god.
Head, woman's, with serpents in hair.	Medusa, the Gorgon slain by Perseus.
Head, decapitated ...	Judith with head of Holofernes.
Head, decapitated ...	Salome with head of St. John the Baptist.
Head surrounded with sunrays.	Helios, god of the sun.
Heads, two or more. Sometimes with key in his right hand and a rod in his left; or with the number 300 in one hand and 65 in the other.	Janus, god of the past, present, and future.
Heads, three	Hecate, one of the Titans; the goddess presiding over magic.
Heads, four or five ...	The Indian god Brahma.
Heads, nine	(See Hydra.)
Heads, fifty, and a hundred hands.	The Greek god Briareus.
Heart. Dog	Fidelity.
Heifer	Io was changed into a heifer by Jupiter.
Heifer	Milo, a celebrated athlete, carried a heifer on his shoulders.
Helm. Wheel ...	Nemesis, goddess of moderation.
Helmet...	Minerva (Pallas Athene) is always depicted wearing a helmet.
Helmet, winged ...	Rendered Perseus invisible.
Hoop in the hand of a man riding a camel.	Sukra, the Hindu god.
Horn (cornucopia) stuffed with fruit.	Fortuna, goddess of plenty.
Horns	(See Pan and Satyrs.)
Horse with dragon's head and ox's tail.	Kylin, a Chinese monster.

Horse (half horse, half man).	Centaur.
Horse with tail of a dolphin.	Sea-horse.
Horse with straight horn projecting from forehead	Unicorn.
Horse with head of a dragon.	The Chinese Dragon Horse.
Horse, winged... ...	Pegasus, given to Bellerophon to conquer the Chimeræ.
Horse, white	Seen with one or other of the twin brothers Castor and Pollux (together called the Dioscuri or Gemini), the deities of boxing, wrestling and equestrian exercises.
Horses, a prancing pair, each with a man holding its bridle.	The Marly Horses.
Horses, white ...	Drew the chariot of Aurora.
Horses, eight	Drew the chariot of the Chinese Mu Wang.
Horses, fed on human flesh.	The Steeds of Diomedes, a king of Thrace.
Jackal. Man with the head of.	Anubis, the Egyptian god of graves and burial rites.
Ju-i sceptre, in the hand of a man with protuberant brow and flowing beard.	The Chinese Shou Lao.
Key in the hand of two-headed man. Sometimes the numerals 300 in one hand and 65 in the other.	Janus.
Key. Dagger. Whip. Torch.	Hecate, the goddess who presided over magic.
Lamb with banner across its shoulder.	Agnus Dei (The Lamb of God), a Christian emblem.
Lance in one hand, and Niké (Winged Victory) in the other.	Athene, the Roman goddess Minerva.

Lantern	Diogenes used a lighted lantern when looking for an honest man.
Lath	The attribute of Harlequin, the buffoon of pantomime.
Leopards	Drew the chariot of Bacchus.
Lion with head and bust of a woman.	Sphinx. (Sphinx with ram's head— Crio-Sphinx.)
Lion with head of an old man and tail of dragon.	Manticore.
Lion with wings and head of eagle.	Griffin.
Lion	Samson slew a lion with his hands.
Lion	It was the first Labour of Hercules to kill the Nemean Lion.
Lion's skin across his shoulder. Club.	Hercules.
Lion	Leo, the fifth sign of the Zodiac.
Lion, killing ox ...	(See Thisbe.)
Lion. Woman with four hands, seated on a lion.	Jugudhatri, the Hindu goddess of destruction.
Lion	Androcles, a slave thrown to the lions in a Roman arena, was saved by one of the animals.
Lion's head on a woman	Bast, the Egyptian goddess.
Lions crouching beside her throne.	Rhea, a Greek goddess of the earth.
Lions	Drew Rhea's chariot.
Lions	Drew Cybele's chariot.
Lion-like monster. Man on its back. Two female attendants.	The Chinese Hsi Wang Mu.
Lotus flower in hand ...	One of the Eight Genii, a Taoist Immortal.
Lyre	Apollo, god of the sun, of music, and of medicine.
Lyre	Orpheus charmed Pluto with the music of his lyre which had been bestowed upon him by Apollo.

Lyre	Terpsichore, one of the Muses, sometimes carried a lyre.
Lyre	Amphion, playing his lyre, charmed into position the stones of the wall surrounding Thebes.
Lyre. Crown of myrtle and roses.	Erato, the Muse of Lyric Poetry.
Man with hawk's head	The Egyptian god Horus.
Man with pointed ears, horns, and short tail.	Faun.
Man with elephant's head.	The Indian god Ganesha.
Man with antlers ...	Actæon.
Man with two or more faces.	Janus.
Man with tail of fish ...	Nereus.
Man, in woman's clothes.	Hercules was made to wear woman's attire by Omphale.
Man with two faces ...	Agni. Janus.
Man with jackal's or dog's head.	The Egyptian god Anubis.
Man with four or five heads.	Brahma.
Man with fifty heads and one hundred hands.	Briareus.
Man with only one eye, in his forehead.	Cyclops.
Man with three bodies and three heads.	Geryon.
Man with five heads ...	Panch Mukhti.
Man with body terminating in dragon or serpent.	The Chinese Fu Hsi.
Man-eating giant ...	Ogre.
Mask, comic	Thalia, the Muse of Comedy.
Mask, tragic. Dagger	Melpomene, the Muse of Tragedy.
Mason's square. Body terminating in a dragon or serpent.	The Chinese Fu Hsi.

Mathematical instruments (compasses). Mirror.	Prudence.
Mathematical instruments. Celestial globe.	Urania, the Muse who presided over astronomy.
Mermaids	Nereides, nymphs of the sea.
Mermaids	Sirens, nymphs of the sea.
Mermen	Tritons.
Mirror. Compasses ...	Prudence.
Moon above his head ...	Aah, the Egyptian moon god.

Musical Instruments:

Lyre	Apollo's attribute.
Mandolin	Attribute of the Chinese Dhritarashtra.
Syrinx	Pan's pipes.

Nimbus, three-fold, round his head.	The Chinese Amitâbha.
Numerals 300 in one hand, 65 in the other.	Janus, god of the past, present, and future.

Nymphs:

Fountain	Naiades.
Mountain	Oreades.
Plant	Dryades.
Sea	Oceanides. Nereides. Sirens.
Tree	Hamadryades.
Valley	Napæae.

Oar	Charon, the boatman who ferried the souls of the dead across the river Styx.
Oars	Argo, the fifty-oared ship in which the Argonauts sailed to recover the Golden Fleece.
Ox	Hercules slew the river god Achelous who had assumed the form of a bull.
Ox	Apis, the Egyptian god.
Ox	The Chinese Lao-Tzü rode a black ox.
Pagoda (toy), in the hand of an armour-clad Japanese.	The Japanese Bishamon, the god of militarism.
Palm Branch. Wreath.	Niké, the winged goddess of Victory,
Parrot	Kama, Hindu the Cupid, god of love. bestrode a parrot.

Peacock. Diadem. Sceptre. Cuckoo.	Juno, queen of heaven, jealous wife of Jupiter.
Peacock	Kartikeya, the Hindu god of war, rode a peacock.
Pick-a-back	Aeneas carried Anchises on his back from the burning ruins of Troy.
Pitcher. Cup or bowl	Hebe, goddess of youth, cup-bearer to the gods.
Pomegranate. Torch ...	Hecate, queen of Hades.
Poppies	Ceres sometimes carried poppies.
Poppies	Morpheus sometimes carried poppies.
Quiver of arrows. Bow	Cupid, god of love.
Quiver of arrows. Bow	Diana, goddess of the moon and of the chase.
Quiver of arrows crossed with a flaming torch.	The trophy of Hymen, god of marriage
Ram	Aries, the first sign of the Zodiac.
Ram	Phrixus rode the golden-fleeced ram to Colchis.
Ram-headed Sphinx ...	Crio-Sphinx.
Rape	The Rape of Europa. Jupiter, in the form of a bull, carried her off.
Rape	The Rape of the Sabines. Women of an Italian race who were raped by Roman soldiery.
Rape	Pluto carried off Proserpina.
Rape	Boreas, the North Wind, carried off Orithyia.
Rape	Nessus, the centaur, carried off Deianeira, wife of Hercules.
Rape	Paris carried off Helen of Troy.
Rape	The Rape of Ganymede. A beautiful youth carried off by Jupiter who assumed the form of an eagle.
Red Indian. Bison ...	Symbolic of the continent of America
Reflection in water ...	Narcissus was attracted by his reflection in the water of a fountain.
Rice bales. Hammer. Sack.	The Japanese Daikoku, the happy god of Wealth.

Rods	Fasces—a bundle of rods bound round the helve of an axe and borne before the Roman magistrates as an emblem of authority.
Rod. Key	Janus, god of the past, the present and the future.
Rod. Bamboo tube ...	The Chinese Chang Kuo.
Sack. Rice bales. Hammer.	The Japanese Daikoku, the god of Wealth.
Sandals	Leander, famous for his love of Hero, divested himself of his sandals before plunging into the Hellespont.
Sandals	Mercury's sandals were winged, and were called Talaria.
Satyrs	Monsters, half man, half goat.
Scales. Sword ...	Astræa, the blindfold figure symbolic of justice.
Scales (balance) ...	Libra, the seventh sign of the Zodiac.
Sceptre. Diadem. Peacock. Cuckoo.	Juno. queen of Heaven, jealous wife of Jupiter.
Sceptre. Thunderbolt ...	Jupiter, or Jove, the Greek Zeus. King of the gods and personification of the sky.
Sceptre	Polyhymnia, the Muse of Rhetoric.
Sceptre. (Ju-i sceptre)	A Chinese symbol of longevity.
Scorpion	Scorpio, the eighth sign of the Zodiac.
Scroll. Laurel crown ...	Calliope, the Muse of Heroic Poetry.
Scroll or book. Stylus. Laurel wreath.	Clio, the Muse of History.
Scythe, in the hand of a bent and bearded old man.	Saturn (Time.)
Sea divinities: ...	Oceanus, a powerful deity of the sea; son of Uranus and Gaea; married Tethys. Oceanides, nymphs of the ocean; daughters of Oceanus. Neptune (Poseidon); god of the sea; married Amphitrite.

Sea divinities—*contd.*	Triton, son of Neptune and Amphitrite, and father of the Tritons. Nereides, nymphs of the sea. One of the most famous was Thetis. Sirens, nymphs of the sea who allured mariners by their wondrous songs. Glaucus, a fisherman changed into a sea-god. Loved Scylla who was changed into a six-headed sea monster. Galatea, a sea nymph in pearl-shell chariot drawn by dolphins. Loved by Polyphemus and Acis.
Sea bream. Fishing rod	The Japanese Yebisu, the deity of fishermen and tradesmen.
Sea horses	Drew Neptune's chariot.
Sea monster with six heads.	Scylla.
Seaweed	Nereus had eyebrows and beard of seaweed.
Serpent	Aapep or Apepi. In Egyptian mythology, a large snake, symbolic of evil.
Serpent	Apollo slew the monster serpent Python.
Serpent	Basilisk, a fabulous serpent whose hissing would drive other creatures away and whose breath or glance was fatal.
Serpent	Cleopatra poisoned herself with the bite of an asp.
Serpent. Heart. Dog	Symbolic of Fidelity.
Serpent with seven heads.	It was the second Labour of Hercules to kill the Hydra of Lerna.
Serpent. Mirror ...	Symbolic of Prudence.
Serpent	Python, destroyed with arrows by Apollo.
Serpent	Salamander, a small lizard-like reptile. Also, a mythical dragon that lived in fire.
Serpent, sea. Musical instrument.	The Japanese Benten, the maiden deity of art, literature, music and eloquence.

Serpents, two	Crushed to death in the hands of the infant Hercules.
Serpents, two	Issued from the sea and crushed to death Laocoön and his two sons.
Serpents, two	Entwined about Mercury's wand—the Caduceus.
Serpents	The three Furies were snake-locked.
Serpents in hair ...	Medusa, the Gorgon slain by Perseus. Her head subsequently adorned Minerva's shield—the ægis.
Shell. Nymph standing on one in the sea.	The Birth of Venus.
Shells, conch ...	The trumpets of the sea tritons and sirens.
Shield. Sword. ...	Achilles, the Greek warrior.
Shield. Armour ...	Mars, the Roman god of war.
Shield. Armour ...	Minerva, presided over peace, defensive war, and the liberal arts. Her shield, called the ægis, bore Medusa's head.
Shield	Ancile, Ancilia, or Ancilla—the sacred shield of the Romans. Was guarded by the Salii (priests) in Rome.
Ship	Argo. (*See Oars.*)
Shoe in hand	The Chinese Bodhidharma.
Sickle	Priapus, the god of fertility, especially in gardens.
Snake	(*See Serpent.*)
Solar disc	Apollo was sometimes represented with a solar disc.
Spade, man with pronged.	The Chinese Yu.
Sparrows and doves ...	Were especially sacred to Aphrodite, the Roman goddess Venus.
Spear, borne by a nude athlete.	Doryphorus.
Spear. Toy pagoda in hand.	The Japanese Bishamon, armour-clad god of militarism.
Spider	Arachne was turned into a spider by Minerva.

Staff, vine-encircled ...	The Thyrsus, the wand borne by the attendants of Bacchus.
Staff, serpent entwined	The Caduceus, Mercury's wand.
Staff borne by bearded man.	The Japanese Jurojin, god of longevity.
Stag	Actæon, the hunter, changed into a stag by Diana.
Stag	Iphigenia's place was taken by a stag when she was about to be sacrificed by Calchas to appease the gods.
Stag	It was the third Labour of Hercules to capture the Ceryneian Stag.
Star, on heads	Dioscuri, or sons of Jupiter, a name given to Castor and Pollux.
Statue of a maiden ...	Sculptured by Pygmalion. In answer to his prayer it became animate.
Stomach, protuberant and exposed.	The Chinese Maitreya, prototype of the Japanese Hotei.
Stylus. Laurel wreath. Scroll or book.	Clio, the Muse of History.
Sunrays around head ...	Apollo, god of the sun.
Swan	Jupiter, in the form of a swan, approached, wooed and won Leda.
Swan	Cycnus intimate friend of Phæton, was turned into a swan.
Swan	Aphrodite, the Roman Venus, rode a swan.
Swine	Circe changed Ulysses' men into swine.
Sword, Scales	The blindfold Astræa, symbol of justice.
Sword. Shield	Achilles, the Greek warrior.
Sword	The Chinese Lü Tung-Pin.
Syrinx	Pan's pipes, fashioned from seven reeds of unequal length.
Tablet or book. Stylus. Laurel wreath.	Clio, the Muse of History.
Tazza or cup	Hebe, goddess of youth, cup-bearer of the gods.
Throne	Rhea (Cybele) sits on a throne with a lion on each side.

Throne borne on a woman's head.	The Egyptian goddess Isis.
Thunderbolt. Sceptre ...	Jupiter, or Jove, the Greek Zeus. King of the gods and personification of the sky.
Torch, flaming, crossed with quiver of arrows.	Hymen's trophy. The god of marriage.
Torch. Dagger. Whip. Key.	Hecate, one of the Titans; presided over magic.
Torch	Ceres sometimes carried a torch.
Tree	Heliades, three sisters, were turned into poplar trees.
Tree	Cyparissus, son of Telephus. Killed a favourite stag, and in his remorse was changed into a cypress tree.
Tree	Daphne, a Grecian nymph who transformed herself into a laurel tree to escape the pursuing Apollo.
Trident...	Neptune's three-pronged fish-spear.
Triton. Half man, half dolphin.	Sea divinities. Their trumpets were conch shells.
Trumpet. Laurel leaf or wreath.	Fama, the goddess of Fame; attendant of Jupiter.
Tub	Diogenes once lived in a tub.
Twins	Gemini, the third sign of the Zodiac.
Umbrella over head of seated man.	The Chinese Ch'êng Wang.
Vase. Fly-whisk. Bundle of books.	The Chinese Dharmatrata.
Venus, half draped; no arms.	Venus de Milo. (The Aphrodite of Melos.)
Venus, standing, nude; with hands screening body.	Venus de Medici.
Venus, in a crouching posture.	The Crouching Venus.
Vine, grape	Attribute of Bacchus, Silenus, and the bacchantes and bacchanals in their train. Depicted in scenes of bacchanalian revels.

Virgin	Virgo, the sixth sign of the Zodiac.
Vulture	Gorged on the liver of Prometheus, who was chained to a rock and was delivered by Hercules.
Vultures	Gorged on the liver of the giant Tityus as he lay stretched over nine acres on the ground.
Wand, vine-encircled ...	The Thyrsus, borne by Bacchus and his crew of bacchanalian revellers.
Wand, serpent-circled...	The Caduceus, given to Mercury by Apollo.
Wand, in the hand of a shepherd hermit.	The Chinese Huang Ch'u-P'ing.
Wand, or staff, in the hand of a bearded man.	Jurojin, the Japanese god of longevity.
Warrior (male) ...	Mars, god of war.
Warrior (male) ...	Achilles. Generally portrayed in the nude, with sword and shield.
Warrior (male). Spear. Toy pagoda in hand.	Bishamon, the Japanese god of militarism.
Warrior (male). Long drooping moustache and long narrow beard.	Kuan Ti, the Chinese god of war.
Warrior (female) ...	Bellona. War personified in the figure of a woman.
Warrior (female) ...	Minerva. Presided over defensive war, peace and the liberal arts.
Warriors (female) ...	Amazons. A race of famous women who employed their lives in wars and manly exercises.
Water carrier... ...	Aquarius, the eleventh sign of the Zodiac.
Wheat, sheaf of, in a woman's hand.	Ceres, the goddess of agriculture. Symbolises autumn in representations of the seasons.
Wheel	Hector, slain by Achilles and tied to the wheel of his chariot.
Wheel	Ixion was bound to a wheel which never ceased to revolve.
Wheel. Helm ...	Nemesis, the goddess of moderation, always prepared to punish excess.

Whip. Dagger. Torch. Key.	Hecate, one of the Titans.
Wind	Boreas, the North Wind. Generally depicted with cheeks outblown. He carried off Orithyia.
Wind	Zephyrus, the West Wind.
Wings (butterfly) ...	Psyche, a fair, winged princess, beloved of Cupid. Emblem of the soul.
Wings on feet	Mercury, the messenger of the gods.
Wings	Iris, the personification of the rainbow. Attendant of Juno, and her swift messenger. Sometimes paired with Mercury in works of art.
Wings on his helmet ...	Perseus.
Wings	Dædalus. Made wings of feathers and wax for himself and his son Icarus.
Wolf	A she-wolf suckled the twin babes Romulus and Remus. ("The Capitoline Wolf.")
Woman with cow's head or ears.	Hathor.
Woman with three heads	Hecate.
Woman with body terminating in a fish tail.	A mermaid or nereide.
Woman with frog's head.	Heqet.
Woman with lion's head.	Bast.
Woman with four hands	Jugudhatri.
Woman with head of lioness crowned with solar disc.	Pasht.
Woman with body terminating in dragon or serpent, coronet on head, compasses in hand.	The Chinese Nü Wa.
Wreath of laurel, Stylus. Book or scroll.	Clio, the Muse of History.
Wreath or leaf of laurel. Trumpet.	Fama, the goddess of fame; attendant of Jupiter.
Wreath. Palm branch...	Niké, the winged goddess of Victory.

SAINTS AND THEIR SYMBOLS

with a preliminary description of

MONASTIC ORDERS

and the Habits by which they are distinguished

(HAGIOLOGY - A History of Saints.)

MONASTIC ORDERS

The oldest and most important Order is that of—

THE BENEDICTINES,

founded by S. Benedict, and distinguished by a habit entirely black. This Order, having been reformed at different times, embraces the following branches:—

The *Camaldolesi*, founded by S. Romualdo.

The *Carthusians*, founded by S. Bruno.

The *Cistercians*, founded by S. Bernard of Clairvaux.

The *Olivetani*, founded by S. Bernard dei Tolomei.

The *Oratorians*, founded by S. Philip Neri.

The *Vallombrosans*, founded by S. John Gualberto.

Of these the Camaldolesi, the Carthusians, the Cistercians, and the Olivetani are habited in white; the Oratorians in black; and the Vallombrosans in light grey.

THE AUGUSTINE ORDER,

claiming S. Augustine as its founder, comprises the minor Orders of—

The *Brigittines*, founded by S. Bridget of Sweden; habit, black.

The *Premonstratesians*, founded by S. Norbert: habit, black or brown, with a white cloak.

The *Servi*, founded by S. Philip Benozzi: habit, black.

The *Trinitarians*, founded by S. John de Matha: habit, white, with a blue and red cross on the breast.

The *Order of Mercy*, founded by S. Peter Nolasco: habit, white, with a badge of the arms of the King of Aragon.

479

THE CARMELITES,

claim as their founder the prophet Elijah, but were first definitely formed into an Order by S. Albert of Vercelli. The habit of the Order is dark brown with a long scapulary, and a white mantle. The reformed branch, known as—

The *Scalzi,* or barefooted Carmelites, was founded by S. Theresa.

THE DOMINICAN ORDER,

founded by S. Dominic, is distinguished by a white habit under a long black cloak with a hood.

THE FRANCISCAN ORDER,

founded by S. Francis of Assisi, and distinguished by a brown or grey habit bound by a knotted cord, embraces the following reformed branches:—

The *Capuchins,* dark brown habit, with a long pointed hood.

The *Cordeliers,* brown habit.

The *Minimes,* founded by S. Francis de Paula: brown habit, short scapulary with rounded ends, and a knotted cord.

The *Observants,* founded by S. Bernardino of Siena: grey habit, and cord.

The *Poor Clares,* Franciscan nuns, founded by S. Clara: grey or brown habit, and cord.

THE JERONYMITES,

claim S. Jerome as their founder.

THE JESUITS,

founded by Ignatius Loyola, are distinguished by a straight black cassock and square cap.

THE ORDER OF THE VISITATION OF S. MARY,

was founded by S. Francis de Sales and S. Jeanne Françoise de Chantal.

SAINTS AND THEIR SYMBOLS

M. = *Martyr*

V.M. = *Virgin Martyr*

Symbols	Saints
Anchor. Sometimes three balls, or three children in a tub. Bishop's robes.	S. Nicholas of Myra, A.D. 342. Patron saint of Russia, and many seaports; also of children, especially schoolboys, of sailors, merchants, and travellers, and against thieves.
Anchor at his side, hung round his neck, or held in his hand. Pope's or Bishop's robes.	S. Clement, M., A.D. 100. Third Bishop of Rome.
Angel or Man.	S. Matthew, Apostle, Evangelist, M.
Angel holding a book. Benedictine habit.	S. Francesca Romana, A.D. 1440.
Angel. Crown of red and white roses. Musical instruments. Palm.	S. Cecilia, V.M., A.D. 280. Patron saint of music and musicians.
Angel holding a flame-tipped arrow. Dove. Carmelite habit.	S. Theresa, A.D. 1582. Patron saint of Spain. Foundress of the Scalzi, reformed Carmelites.
Angel leading captives. White habit. Blue and red cross on his breast.	S. John de Matha, A.D. 1213. Founder of the Order of Trinitarians, for the redemption of captives.
Angel with pyx or chalice. Franciscan habit. Cardinal's hat on a tree or at his feet.	S. Bonaventure, A.D. 1274.
Angel holding fruit or flowers. Crown. Palm.	S. Dorothea of Cappadocia, V.M., A.D. 303.
Angel and Lily. Not represented before 1622.	S. Philip Neri, A.D. 1595. Founder of the Order of the Oratorians.
Angel holding a shield on which are three fleurs-de-lys.	S. Clotilda of Burgundy, A.D. 534.

Angel ploughing, in the background. Spade. In Spanish pictures only.	S. Isidore the Ploughman, A.D. 1170. Patron saint of Madrid and of agriculture.
Angels crowning her with roses.	S. Rosalia of Palermo, A.D. 1160.
Anvil at his feet or in his hand. In armour. Lion.	S. Adrian, M., A.D. 290. Patron saint of Flanders and Germany, of soldiers, and against the plague.
Anvil. Bishop's robes, or as a blacksmith.	S. Eloy, Lo, or Eligius, A.D. 665. Patron saint of Bologna, and of goldsmiths, blacksmiths and horses.
Armour and crown lying at his side. Benedictine habit.	S. William of Aquitaine, A.D. 812.
Armour, girl in. Sword. Banner.	S. Joan of Arc, A.D. 1412-1431.
Arrow. Banner with a red cross. Crown. Sometimes surrounded by many virgins. Palm.	S. Ursula, V.M. Dates vary from 237 to 451. Patron saint of young girls, and women engaged in the education of their own sex.
Arrow transfixing his breast or hand, or a hind near pierced by an arrow. Old and in Benedictine habit.	S. Giles, Hermit, A.D. 725. Patron saint of Edinburgh, and of woods, lepers, cripples, and beggars.
Arrows, pierced by. Bound to a tree or column.	S. Sebastian, M., A.D. 288. Patron saint against the plague and pestilence.
Arrows. Millstone. Crown. Palm.	*S. Christina, V.M., A.D. 295. Patron saint of Bolsena, and one of the patron saints of Venice.
Arrow; sometimes piercing a crown. Wolf near. Royal robes.	S. Edmund, M., A.D. 870. Patron saint of Bury St. Edmunds.
Awl, or shoemaker's knife. Two men together. Palms.	S. Crispin, M., and S. Crispianus, M., A.D. 300. Patron saints of Soissons.

* It is difficult to distinguish this saint from S. Ursula, but when found in early Italian art and without signs of royalty, it is S. Christina.

Axe.

S. Matthias, Apostle, M.

Axe in his hand; or sometimes in his head. In armour.

S. Proculus, M., *circa* 303. Patron saint of Bologna.

Axe, lictor's; also a two-pronged fork.

S. Martina, V.M., A.D. 230.

Bag of money. Book. Pen and inkhorn.

S. Matthew, Apostle and Evangelist, M.

Balls, three. Bishop's robes.

S. Nicholas of Myra, A.D. 342. Patron of Russia, and many seaports; also of children, especially schoolboys, of sailors, merchants, and travellers, and against thieves.

Banner with black Imperial eagle. Royal robes. Palm.

S. Wenceslaus of Bohemia, M., A.D. 938.

Banner, with red cross. Arrow. Crown. Sometimes surrounded by many virgins.

S. Ursula, V.M. Dates vary from 237 to 451. Patron saint of young girls, and women engaged in the education of their own sex.

Banner with red cross on a white ground. Crown. Palm. Sometimes in a red and white mantle.

S. Reparata, V.M., 3rd century. Formerly patron saint of Florence.

Banner, white, with a red cross. Classical armour. Only found near Pisa.

S. Torpé, M., A.D. 70. Patron saint of Pisa.

Banner. Sword. Girl in armour.

S. Joan of Arc, A.D. 1412-1431.

Banner. Sword. Palm. Young and richly dressed.

S. Julian of Cilicia, M. Patron saint of Rimini.

Beasts, surrounded by. Palm. Dark grey or brown mantle.

S. Thecla, V.M., 1st century. Patron saint of Tarragona.

Beds in the background. Dark brown habit and hood.

S. Juan de Dios, A.D. 1550. Founder of the Order of Hospitallers or Brothers of Charity.

Beehive. Inkhorn, pen, and papers. White habit, with a cowl and large sleeves. Sometimes demon bound.

S. Bernard of Clairvaux, A.D. 1153. Founder of the Cistercian Order of reformed Benedictines.

Beehive at his feet. Books. Bishop's robes.

S. Ambrose, A.D. 397. One of the Four Latin Fathers of the Church. Patron saint of Milan.

Beggar, half naked, at his feet, or receiving part of his cloak.	S. Martin of Tours, A.D. 397. Patron saint of Tours, Lucca, and penitent drunkards.
Beggar at his feet. Dark brown habit and hood.	S. Juan de Dios, A.D. 1550. Founder of the Order of Hospitallers or Brothers of Charity.
Beggar with a dish, old and very ragged. Sometimes palm and cross.	S. Alexis, A.D. 400. Patron saint of pilgrims and beggars.
Beggars at her feet. Carrying roses in her mantle. Royal robes or Franciscan habit.	S. Elizabeth of Hungary, A.D. 1231.
Beggars, giving alms to. Widow's veil. Crown. Franciscan habit.	*S. Elizabeth of Portugal, A.D. 1336.
Bell, sometimes suspended from the top of a crutch. Hog.	S. Anthony, Hermit, A.D. 357.
Bell. Sometimes loaf and cruse.	S. Pol de Léon, A.D. 573.
Bishop's robes and crozier. Chalice.	S. John Fisher, A.D. 1459-1535.
Blacksmith with anvil, hammer, and bellows, or Bishop's robes with blacksmith's tools.	S. Eloy, Lo, or Eligius, A.D. 665. Patron saint of Bologna, and of goldsmiths, blacksmiths and horses.
Blood flowing from his head. Generally pierced by a sword or axe. Dominican habit.	S. Peter Martyr, A.D. 1252.
Blood flowing from his head. Bishop's robes, or Benedictine habit.	S. Thomas à Becket, A.D. 1170.
Bones, two human. Scourge. Beehive. Bishop's robes.	S. Ambrose, A.D. 397. One of the Four Latin Fathers of the Church. Patron saint of Milan.
Book. Lord Chancellor's robes with chain of office.	S. Thomas More, A.D. 1478-1535.

* S. Elizabeth of Portugal is distinguished from S. Elizabeth of Hungary by her venerable appearance.

Book transfixed by a sword, or stained with blood. Bishop's robes over the Benedictine habit.

S. Boniface, A.D. 754. Archbishop of Mayence. Apostle and first Primate of Germany.

Books at his feet, or in his hand. Sometimes a heart, flaming or transfixed by an arrow. Bishop's robes.

S. Augustine, A.D. 430. One of the Four Latin Fathers of the Church.

Books, trampling under his feet. Bishop's robes. Palm. Sword.

S. Cyprian of Antioch, M., A.D. 258.

Bottle on the end of a staff. Scallop shell.

S. James the Great, Apostle, M. Patron saint of Spain.

Bottles. Giving alms to the poor. Fur-trimmed tunic and cap.

S. Omobuono. Patron saint of Cremona and of tailors.

Box, or vase, of alabaster. Long, fair hair.

S. Mary Magdalene, A.D. 68. Patron saint of Provence, Marseilles, and of penitent women.

Box of ointment. Surgical instruments. Two men together in red robes.

S. Cosmo, M., and S. Damian, M., A.D. 304. Patron saints of the Medici and of medicine.

Branch of olive. White habit. Only found in late pictures.

S. Bernard of Tolomei, A.D. 1319. Founder of the Order of Olivetani, reformed Benedictines.

Branch of olive. Sword at his feet. Loose physician's robe. Palm.

S. Pantaleon of Nicomedia, M., 4th century. Patron saint of physicians.

Branch of olive. Lamb. Palm.

S. Agnes, V.M., A.D. 304.

Branch twisted round his body. Old and half naked, and with long hair.

S. Onofrio, 4th or 5th century. Hermit of Thebes.

Bread and cruse of water. Bell.

S. Pol de Léon, A.D. 573.

Buildings, in his hand.

S. Petronius, A.D. 430. Patron saint of Bologna.

Candle on his head, or in his hand. Bishop's robes. Wheel.

S. Erasmus or Elmo, M., A.D. 296.

Candle lighted. A demon trying to blow it out with bellows.

S. Genevieve, A.D. 509. Patron saint of Paris.

Captive kneeling at her feet. Broken fetters in her hand.

S. Radegunda, A.D. 587. Protectress of the Order of Trinitarians, for the redemption of captives.

Cardinal, barefooted, with a rope round his neck.

S. Charles Borromeo, A.D. 1584. Archbishop of Milan.

Cardinal. (Only in a group of Vallombrosan saints.)

S. Bernard degli Uberti, Abbot of Vallombrosa.

Cardinal's hat, on a tree or at his feet. Franciscan habit.

S. Bonaventure, A.D. 1274.

Cardinal's hat, at his feet or near him. Emaciated, old, and ragged, or in Cardinal's robes. Lion. Church in his hand.

S. Jerome, A.D. 420. One of the Four Latin Fathers of the Church. Founder of Monachism in the West. Patron saint of scholars.

Carpenter's or builder's square.

S. Thomas, Apostle, M. Patron saint of builders and architects.

Cauldron of oil. A boy with the palm. Generally a cock; sometimes lion or wolf.

S. Vitus, M., A.D. 303. Patron saint of Saxony, Bohemia, Sicily, of dancers and actors, and of those who find a difficulty in early rising.

Censer. Benedictine habit. Generally accompanying S. Benedict.

S. Maurus, A.D. 584.

Chain and fetters in her hand. Peculiar to Rome.

S. Balbina, A.D. 130.

Chain of office and robes (Lord Chancellor's). Book.

S. Thomas More, A.D. 1478-1535.

Chains and fetters. Benedictine habit, or deacon's robes.

S. Leonard, A.D. 559. Patron saint of prisoners and slaves.

Chalice. Bishop's robes and crozier.

S. John Fisher, A.D. 1459-1535.

Chalice or Pyx. Franciscan habit. Cardinal's hat on a tree or at his feet.

S. Bonaventure, A.D. 1274.

Chalice. Dominican habit. Star on his breast.

S. Thomas Aquinas, A.D. 1274.

Chequered Habit. Franciscan cord. Dog at her feet.

S. Margaret of Cortona, A.D. 1297.

Child on his shoulders. Walking through water.	S. Christopher, A.D. 364.
Child-Christ in his arms, or on a book. Franciscan habit.	S. Antony of Padua, A.D. 1231.
Child in his arms, or at his feet.	S. Vincent de Paule, A.D. 1660. Founder of the Sisters of Charity.
Children, three in a tub. Bishop's robes.	S. Nicholas of Myra, A.D. 326. Patron saint of Russia, and many seaports; also of children, especially schoolboys, of sailors, merchants, travellers, and against thieves.
Church with two towers in his hand. Pilgrim with wallet and shell.	S. Sebald, A.D. 770.
Church in her hand. Royal robes. Walking over plough-shares.	S. Cunegunda of Bavaria, A.D. 1040.
Church in his hand. Royal robes. Sometimes in armour.	S. Henry of Bavaria, A.D. 1024.
Church in his hand. Emaciated, old, and ragged, or in Cardinal's robes. Cardinal's hat near. Lion.	S. Jerome, A.D. 420. One of the Four Latin Fathers of the Church. Founder of Monachism in the West. Patron saint of scholars.
Cloak, dividing with beggar.	S. Martin of Tours, A.D. 397. Patron saint of Tours, Lucca, and of penitent drunkards.
Club.	S. James the Less, Apostle, M.
Cock. A boy with the palm. Sometimes lion or wolf.	S. Vitus, M., A.D. 303. Patron saint of Saxony, Bohemia, Sicily, and of dancers and actors, and of those who find a difficulty in early rising.
Comb, of iron. Bishop's robes.	S. Blaise, M., A.D. 289. Patron saint of Ragusa, of wool-combers, of wild animals, and against diseases of the throat.
Comb, of iron. In armour. Keys at his girdle.	S. Hippolytus, M., A.D. 258. The gaoler of S. Laurence.

Cross, transverse, or X-shaped.

S. Andrew, Apostle, M. Patron saint of Scotland and Russia.

Cross at the end of a staff, or sometimes small in his hand, or T-shaped.

S. Philip, Apostle, M.

Cross. Light grey habit. Beardless. Sometimes a crutch.

S. John Gualberto, A.D. 1073. Founder of the Vallombrosan Order of reformed Benedictines.

Cross, blue and red on his breast. White habit. Sometimes angel leading captives.

S. John de Matha, A.D. 1213. Founder of the Order of Trinitarians for the redemption of captives.

Cross. Lily. Pyx. Franciscan habit. Black veil.

S. Clara, A.D. 1253. Founder of the Order of Franciscan Nuns called Poor Clares.

Cross. Dragon. Crown. Palm.

S. Margaret, V.M., A.D. 306.

Cross, T-shaped, Javelins. Lily. Crown. Palm.

S. Miniato, M., A.D. 254.

Cross, black, embroidered on a white robe.

S. Apollinaris of Ravenna, M., A.D. 79.

Cross, red, on his breast. In armour. Sometimes as a Moor, or with eagle on banner and shield.

S. Maurice, M., A.D. 286. Patron saint of Austria, Savoy, and Mantua, and of foot soldiers.

Cross large. Royal robes.

S. Oswald, A.D. 642.

Crown and sceptre at his feet. Franciscan habit, or Bishop's robes embroidered with the fleur-de-lys.

S. Louis of Toulouse, A.D. 1297.

Crown and sceptre at his feet. Hermit's garb. A doe by his side.

S. Procopius, A.D. 1053.

Crown and sceptre at his feet, or by his side. Lily. Young and in royal robes.

S. Casimir of Poland, A.D. 1483.

Crown.   Benedictine habit, Palm.

S. Flavia, M., A.D. 540.

Crown of Thorns in his hand. Franciscan habit, or royal robes embroidered with the fleur-de-lys.

S. Louis IX, King of France, A.D. 1270.

Crown of Thorns. Stigmata. Lily. Dominican habit. — S. Catherine of Siena, A.D. 1380.

Crowns, three, embroidered on his robe. Globe and Cross. In armour. Ermine mantle. — S. Charlemagne, A.D. 814.

Crozier. Bishop's robes. Chalice. — S. John Fisher, A.D. 1459-1535.

Crucifix, sometimes a crutch. Light grey habit. Beardless. — S. John Gualberto, A.D. 1073. Founder of the Vallombrosan Order of reformed Benedictines.

Crucifix, wreathed with the lily. Star on his breast or above his head. Benedictine habit. — S. Nicholas of Tolentino, A.D. 1309.

Crucifix. Dominican habit. Sometimes wings. — S. Vincent Ferraris, A.D. 1419.

Crucifix. Pyx. Dominican habit. — S. Hyacinth, A.D. 1257.

Crucifix. Lily. Surplice over black habit. — S. Francis Xavier, A.D. 1552. Patron saint of India.

Crucifix. Ragged clothes, and long loose hair. — S. Rosalia of Palermo, A.D. 1160.

Crutch, sometimes with a bell hanging from it. Hog. — S. Anthony, Hermit, A.D. 357.

Crutch. Long beard. White habit. — S. Romualdo, A.D. 1027. Founder of the Order of Camaldolesi, reformed Benedictines.

Crutch, Cross, or Crucifix. Light grey habit. Beardless. — S. John Gualberto, A.D. 1073. Founder of the Vallombrosan Order of reformed Benedictines.

Cup, with serpent. Eagle. — S. John, Apostle, Evangelist.

Cup, broken. Benedictine habit. — S. Benedict, A.D. 543. Founder of the Benedictine Order.

Cup, broken. Palm. — S. Donato of Arezzo, M.

Cup and wafer. Tower. Feather. Sword. Crown. Palm. — S. Barbara, V.M., A.D. 303. Patron saint of Mantua and Ferrara; of arms, armourers and fortifications, and against thunder and lightning.

Cup and sponge, with drops of blood.	S. Pudentiana, A.D. 148.
Dates, cluster of, on palm. Cross. Young and richly dressed.	S. Ansano, M. Patron saint of Siena.
Demon, bound. Inkhorn, pen, and papers. White habit. Sometimes bee-hive.	S. Bernard of Clairvaux, A.D. 1153. Founder of the Cistercian Order of reformed Benedictines.
Demon, bound, at his feet. White over black habit. Monstrance or Cup.	S. Norbert, A.D. 1134. Founder of the Order of Premonstratesians.
Demon, holding bellows, and trying to blow out a torch or candle.	S. Genevieve, A.D. 509, Patron saint of Paris.
Demon, trying to blow out a lantern.	S. Gudula, A.D. 712. Patron saint of Brussels.
Dish, breasts on. Shears. Palm.	S. Agatha, V.M., A.D. 251. Patron saint of Malta and Catania.
Dish. Old and dressed as a beggar or pilgrim. Sometimes Cross or Palm.	S. Alexis, A.D. 400. Patron saint of pilgrims and beggars.
Dish, eyes on. Sword or wound in her neck. Lamp. Palm.	S. Lucy, V.M., A.D. 303. Patron saint of Syracuse, and against diseases of the eye.
Distaff. Sheep. Sometimes basket of loaves.	S. Genevieve, A.D. 509. Patron saint of Paris.
Doe by his side. Hermit's garb. Crown and sceptre at his feet.	S. Procopius, A.D. 1053.
Dog, with a torch in its mouth. Star on forehead. Lily. Dominican habit.	S. Dominic, A.D. 1221. Founder of the Dominican Order.
Dog by his side. Pilgrim's shell and staff. Pointing to a wound in his leg.	S. Roch, A.D. 1327. Patron saint of the sick, particularly the plague-stricken.
Dog at her feet. Chequered habit.	S. Margaret of Cortona, A.D. 1297.
Dove on his shoulder, or hovering over his head. Pope's robes.	S. Gregory, A.D. 604. One of the Four Latin Fathers of the Church. Pope.

Dove. Benedictine habit. Lily. Generally accompanying S. Benedict.

S. Scholastica, A.D. 543. Sister of S. Benedict.

Dove. Heart with I.H.S., or Angel holding flame-tipped arrow. Carmelite habit.

S. Theresa, A.D. 1582. Patron saint of Spain. Foundress of the Scalzi, reformed Carmelites.

Dragon at his feet. In armour. Standard. Palm.

S. George, M., A.D. 303. Patron saint of England, Germany, and Venice, and of soldiers and armourers.

Dragon in his hand, its mouth bound with threads. Pope's or Bishop's robes, with an ox at his feet.

S. Sylvester, Pope, A.D. 335.

Dragon at his feet. Bishop's robes.

S. Mercuriale, 2nd century. Bishop of Forli.

Dragon at his feet. In armour.

S. Theodore, M., A.D. 319. Patron saint of Venice.

Dragon under her feet. Cross. Crown. Palm.

S. Margaret, V.M., A.D. 306.

Dragon, bound at her feet. Pot of holy water. Keys at her girdle. Ladle.

S. Martha of Bethany, A.D. 84. Patron saint of cooks and housewives.

Dragon, driving into the sea.

S. Pol de Léon, A.D. 573.

Eagle. Sometimes a cup and serpent.

S. John, Apostle, Evangelist.

Eagle by her side. Lion. Palm.

S. Prisca, V.M., A.D. 275.

Eyes on a book. Benedictine habit.

S. Ottilia, M., A.D. 720.

Eyes on a dish. Sword or wound in her neck. Lamp. Palm.

S. Lucy, V.M., A.D. 303. Patron saint of Syracuse, and against diseases of the eye.

Face of Christ on a cloth.

S. Veronica, M.

Falcon. In armour.

S. Bavon, A.D. 657. Patron saint of Ghent and Haarlem.

Feather. Tower. Chalice and wafer. Sword. Crown. Palm.

S. Barbara, V.M., A.D. 303. Patron saint of Ferrara and Mantua; also of arms, armourers and fortifications, and against thunder and lightning.

Fetters and chains, Benedictine habit, or Deacon's robes.

S. Leonard, A.D. 559. Patron saint of prisoners and slaves.

Fetters in his hand, or at his feet. White habit. Blue and red cross on his breast.

S. John de Matha, A.D. 1213. Founder of the Order of the Trinitarians for the redemption of captives.

Fetters and chains in her hand. Peculiar to Rome.

S. Balbina, A.D. 130.

Fetters, broken, in her hand. A captive kneeling at her feet.

S. Radegunda, A.D. 587. Protectress of the Order of Trinitarians for the redemption of captives.

Finger on his lip. Five stars over his head.

S. John Nepomuc, A.D. 1393. Patron saint of silence, bridges, and running water.

Fire in hand. Bishop's robes.

S. Brice or Britius, A.D. 444. Bishop of Tours.

Fire near him, or under his feet. Crutch with bell. Hog.

S. Anthony, Hermit, A.D. 357.

Fire. Throwing water on a burning house.

S. Florian, M. A patron saint of Austria.

Fish and keys.

S. Peter, Apostle, M. The first Pope.

Fish. Bishop's robes.

S. Ulrich, A.D. 973. Patron saint of Augsburg.

Fish with a key in its mouth. Bishop's robes.

S. Benno, A.D. 1100.

Fish suspended from the crozier. Bishop's robes.

S. Zeno, A.D. 380. Patron saint of Verona.

Fish at his feet. Bishop's robes.

S. Corentin of Brittany, A.D. 495.

Flame of fire in his hand, or on his breast. Lily. Franciscan habit.

S. Antony of Padua, A.D. 1231.

Fleur-de-lys embroidered on royal robes. Crown of thorns.

S. Louis IX, King of France, A.D. 1270.

Fleur-de-lys embroidered on Bishop's robes. Sometimes Franciscan habit. Crown and sceptre at his feet.

S. Louis of Toulouse, A.D. 1297.

Flowers in her hand, or crowned by. Palm.

S. Dorothea of Cappadocia, V.M., A.D. 303.

Flowers, three. Swan. Carthusian habit.

S. Hugh of Lincoln, A.D. 1126.

Fork, two-pronged. Lictor's axe.

S. Martina, V.M., A.D. 230.

Fountain. Sword. Sometimes head in his hand.

S. Alban, A.D. 305. England's protomartyr.

Globe, surmounted by cross, three crowns on robe. In armour. Ermine mantle.

S. Charlemagne, A.D. 814.

Goose by his side. Sometimes Bishop's robes.

S. Martin of Tours, A.D. 397. Patron saint of Tours and Lucca, and of penitent drunkards.

Grate or gridiron. Sometimes only embroidered on his robe.

S. Laurence, M., A.D. 258. Patron saint of Nuremburg and Genoa.

Hair, long, fair. Vase or box of alabaster.

S. Mary Magdalene, A.D. 68. Patron saint of Provence and Marseilles, and of penitent women.

Hair and beard long. Very old and half naked. Sometimes a raven near.

S. Paul the Hermit of Thebes, A.D. 344.

Hair and beard long. Very old and clothed only with branches.

S. Onofrio, 4th or 5th century. Hermit of Thebes.

Halberd (in Germany).

S. Jude Thaddeus, Apostle, M.

Hammer, anvil, tongs, etc. Bishop's robes, or sometimes as a blacksmith.

S. Eloy, Lo, or Eligius, A.D. 665. Patron saint of Bologna, and of goldsmiths, blacksmiths and horses.

Harrow. Bishop's robes.

S. Frediano of Lucca, A.D. 560.

Hat, Cardinal's, near. Old and emaciated. Sometimes Cardinal's robes. Lion.

S. Jerome, A.D. 420. One of the Four Latin Fathers of the Church. Founder of Monachism in the West. Patron saint of scholars.

Hat, cardinal's, at his feet or on a tree. Franciscan habit.

S. Bonaventure, A.D. 1274.

Hawk. Shield with nine balls.

S. Quirinus the Tribune, A.D. 130.

Head, blood flowing from, or pierced by a sword. Bishop's robes, or Benedictine habit.

S. Thomas à Becket, A.D. 1170.

Head, blood flowing from, or pierced by a sword or axe. Dominican habit.

S. Peter Martyr, A.D. 1252.

Head of a man under her feet. Wheel. Crown. Palm.

S. Catherine of Alexandria, V.M., A.D. 307. Patron saint of Venice, and places of education, of science, philosophy, and eloquence, and against diseases of the tongue.

Head, carrying his own. Sometimes sword. Bishop's robes.

S. Denis, M., 1st century Patron saint of France.

Head, carrying his own. Only found in Rouen.

S. Clair, M., 3rd century.

Head, carrying half, with a mitre on it. Bishop's robes.

S. Nicasius, M., A.D. 400. Bishop of Rheims.

Head, carrying her own. Palm.

S. Valerie, M. Patron saint of Aquitaine.

Head, carrying her own, accompanied by a:

S. Grata, A.D. 300.

Roman soldier with Palm.
King.
Queen with a veil.

S. Alexander.
S. Lupo.
S. Adelaide.

Head, carrying his own. In armour. Axe in his hand or head.

S. Proculus, M., *circa* 303. Patron saint of Bologna.

Head in his hand. Fountain in background. Sword.

S. Alban, A.D. 305. England's protomartyr.

Heart, flaming, or transfixed with an arrow. Bishop's robes. Book at his feet or in his hand.

S. Augustine, A.D. 430. One of the Four Latin Fathers of the Church.

Heart, crowned by thorns. I.H.S. in the sky.

S. Ignatius Loyola, A.D. 1556. Founder of the Society of Jesuits.

Heart with I.H.S. Carmelite habit. Sometimes Crucifix and Lily or Dove.

S. Theresa, A.D. 1582. Patron saint of Spain. Foundress of the Scalzi, reformed Carmelites.

Hermit praying in a hollow tree.

S. Bavon, A.D. 657. Patron saint of Ghent and Haarlem.

Hermit. Very old, with long hair, and half naked. Sometimes a raven near.

S. Paul the Hermit of Thebes, A.D. 344.

Hind pierced by an arrow, sometimes through his hand. Benedictine habit.

S. Giles, Hermit, A.D. 725. Patron saint of Edinburgh, and of woods, lepers, cripples and beggars.

Hog. Bell and crutch.

S. Anthony, Hermit, A.D. 357.

Horn, drinking. Bishop's robes.

S. Cornelius, Bishop of Rome.

Horses, tied to wild. In armour. Keys at his girdle.

S. Hippolytus, M., A.D. 258. The gaoler of S. Laurence.

House, throwing water on a burning.

S. Florian, M. A patron saint of Austria.

Huntsman. Stag with a crucifix between its horns. (Hardly ever found in Italy.)

S. Hubert, A.D. 727. Bishop of Liège. Patron saint of dogs and the chase.

I.H.S. on heart. Carmelite habit. Sometimes crucifix and lily or dove.

S. Theresa, A.D. 1582. Patron saint of Spain. Foundress of the Scalzi, reformed Carmelites.

I.H.S. in the sky. Heart crowned by thorns.

S. Ignatius Loyola, A.D. 1556. Founder of the Society of Jesuits.

I.H.S. on a tablet surrounded by rays. Franciscan habit. Sometimes three mitres.

S. Bernardino of Siena, A.D. 1444. Founder of the Order of Observants, reformed Franciscans.

Ink-horn, pen, and papers. White habit. Bee-hive. Bound demon.

S. Bernard of Clairvaux, A.D. 1153. Founder of the Cistercian Order of reformed Benedictines.

Instruments, surgical. Two men in red robes. Palms.

S. Cosmo, M., and S. Damian, M., A.D. 301. Patron saints of the Medici, and of medicine.

Javelin with the point reversed. Lily. Palm.

S. Filomena, M., A.D. 303.

Javelin or lance at his feet. Bishop's robes. Palm.

S. Lambert, M., A.D. 709.

Javelins. T-shaped cross. Lily. Crown. Palm. Red robe.

S. Miniato, M., A.D. 254.

Judge or Doctor of Laws. Sometimes surrounded by widows and orphans.

S. Ives of Bretagne, A.D. 1303. Patron saint of lawyers.

Keys.

S. Peter, Apostle, M.

Keys at his girdle. In armour. Sometimes an iron comb or bound to horses.

S. Hippolytus, M., A.D. 258. The gaoler of S. Laurence.

Keys at her girdle. Pot of holy water. Ladle. Dragon at her feet.

S. Martha of Bethany, A.D. 84. Patron saint of cooks and housewives.

Knife.

S. Bartholomew, Apostle, M.

Knife, shoemaker's, or awl. Two men together. Palm.

S. Crispin, M., and S. Crispianus, M., A.D. 300. Patron saints of Soissons.

Labarum, or Standard of the Cross. Classical costume.

S. Constantine, A.D. 335.

Ladle. Dragon at her feet. Pot of holy water.

S. Martha of Bethany, A.D. 84. Patron saint of cooks and housewives.

Lamb, Crucifix.

S. John the Baptist.

Lamb. Olive-branch. Palm.

S. Agnes, V.M., A.D. 304.

Lamb. Lily. Franciscan habit. Stigmata.

S. Francis of Assisi, A.D. 1226. Founder of the Franciscan Order.

Lamp. Sword or wound in her neck. Eyes on dish. Palm.

S. Lucy, V.M., A.D. 303. Patron saint of Syracuse, and against diseases of the eye.

Lance (in Italian pictures).

S. Matthias, Apostle, M.

Lance, or halberd.

S. Jude Thaddeus, Apostle, M.

Lance at his feet. Bishop's robes. Palm.

S. Lambert, M., A.D. 709.

Lantern. Demon trying to blow it out.

S. Gudula, A.D. 712. Patron saint of Brussels.

Leg, pointing to a wound in. Pilgrim's shell and staff. Sometimes dog.

S. Roch, A.D. 1327. Patron saint of prisoners and the sick, especially the plague-stricken.

Lictor's axe.

S. Martina, V.M., A.D. 230.

Lily.

S. Joseph.

Lily. Dominican habit. Star on his forehead.	S. Dominic, A.D. 1221. Founder of the Dominican Order.
Lily. Franciscan habit. Stigmata.	S. Francis of Assisi, A.D. 1226. Founder of the Franciscan Order.
Lily. T-shaped cross. Javelins. Crown. Palm. Red robe.	S. Miniato, M., A.D. 254.
Lily. Franciscan habit. Flame of fire in his hand or on his breast.	S. Antony of Padua, A.D. 1231·
Lily. Young and in royal robes. Crown and sceptre at his feet or by his side.	S. Casimir of Poland, A.D. 1483.
Lily. Crucifix. Surplice over black habit.	S. Francis Xavier, A.D. 1552. Patron saint of India.
Lily and Angel. (Not represented before 1622.)	S. Philip Neri, A.D. 1595. Founder of the Order of the Oratorians.
Lily. Dove. Benedictine habit.	S. Scholastica, A.D. 543. Sister of S. Benedict.
Lily. Cross. Pyx. Franciscan habit.	S. Clara, A.D. 1253. Founder of the Order of Franciscan nuns called Poor Clares.
Lily. Crown of thorns. Dominican habit. Stigmata.	S. Catherine of Siena, A.D. 1380.
Lily. Sword. Lion. Palm.	S. Euphemia, V.M., 307.
Lily. Javelin with point reversed. Palm.	S. Filomena, V.M., A.D. 303.
Lion, generally winged.	S. Mark, Evangelist, M.
Lion. Emaciated, old, and ragged, or in cardinal's robes. Cardinal's hat near.	S. Jerome, A.D. 420. One of the Four Latin Fathers of the Church. Founder of Monachism in the West. Patron saint of scholars.
Lion. A boy with the palm. Generally a cock. Sometimes a wolf and cauldron of oil.	S. Vitus, M., A.D. 303. Patron saint of Bohemia, Saxony, and Sicily, of dancers and actors, and of those who find a difficulty in early rising.

Lion. Anvil. Sword or axe. in armour.	S. Adrian, M., A.D. 290. Patron saint of Flanders and Germany, of soldiers, and against the plague.
Lion. Eagle. Palm.	S. Prisca, M., A.D. 275.
Lion. Lily. Sword. Palm.	S. Euphemia, V.M., A.D. 307.
Loaves, three small, at her side. Old and worn. Long hair.	S. Mary of Egypt, A.D. 433. Patron saint of penitents and anchorites.
Loaves in a basket. A shepherdess's dress and a distaff.	S. Genevieve, A.D. 509. Patron saint of Paris.
Lord Chancellor's robes with chain of office. Book.	S. Thomas More, A.D. 1478-1535.
Man, or angel.	S. Matthew, Apostle, Evangelist, M.
Man under his feet. In armour. Standard and Palm.	S. Gereon, M. One of the Theban Legion.
Man's head under her feet. Wheel. Crown. Palm.	S. Catherine of Alexandria, V.M., A.D. 307. Patron saint of Venice, and places of education, of science, philosophy, and eloquence, and against diseases of the tongue.
Millstone. In armour.	S. Victor of Marseilles, M., A.D. 304.
Millstone.	S. Florian. A patron saint of Austria.
Millstone. Arrows. Crown. Palm.	S. Christina, M., A.D. 295. Patron saint of Bolsena, and one of the patron saints of Venice.
Mitres, three, on a book, or at his feet. White habit.	S. Bernard of Clairvaux, A.D. 1153. Founder of the Cistercian Order of reformed Benedictines.
Mitres, three. Franciscan habit.	S. Bernardino of Siena, A.D. 1444. Founder of the Order of Observants, reformed Franciscans.
Monstrance of the Blessed Sacrament. White over black habit. Sometimes demon bound.	S. Norbert, A.D. 1134. Founder of the Order of Premonstratesians.

Moor, in armour, red cross on his breast.	S. Maurice, M., A.D. 286. Patron saint of Austria, Savoy, and Mantua, and of foot soldiers.
Moor in armour.	S. Victor of Milan, M., A.D. 303.
Mounds, three, surmounted by a cross or flag. Franciscan habit.	S. Bernardino of Siena, A.D. 1444. Founder of the Order of Observants, reformed Franciscans.
Mountain, burning, in the background. Bishop. Palm.	S. Januarius, A.D. 303. Patron saint of Naples.
Mule, kneeling. Flame in his hand. Franciscan habit.	S. Antony of Padua, A.D. 1231.
Musical instruments. Palm.	S. Cecilia, V.M., A.D. 280. Patron saint of music and musicians.
Neck, sword or wound in, rays issuing from it.	S. Lucy, V.M., A.D. 303. Patron saint of Syracuse, and against diseases of the eye.
Nun kneeling at his feet.	S. Vincent de Paul, A.D. 1660. Founder of the Sisters of Charity.
Nun. Black and white habit, with red band across her forehead. Crosier. Pilgrim's staff.	S. Bridget of Sweden, A.D. 1373. Founder of the Order of Brigittines.
Olive-branch, White habit. Only found in late pictures.	S. Bernard of Tolomei, A.D. 1319. Founder of the Order of Olivetani, reformed Benedictines.
Olive-branch. Lamb. Palm.	S. Agnes, V.M., A.D. 304.
Organ.	S. Cecilia, V.M., A.D. 280. Patron saint of music and musicians.
Otter by his side. Bishop's robes.	S. Cuthbert of Durham, A.D. 687.
Ox.	S. Luke, Evangelist, M.
Ox at his feet. Pope's or Bishop's robes. Dragon in his hand.	S. Sylvester, Pope, A.D. 335.

Padlock on his mouth, or in his hand. Five stars over his head.

S. John Nepomuc, A.D. 1393. Patron saint of silence, bridges, and running water.

Papers and seals. Rich attire.

S. Eleazar of Sabran, A.D. 1300.

Picture of the Blessed Virgin.

S. Luke, Evangelist, M.

Pig. Crutch and bell. Old.

S. Anthony, Hermit, A.D. 357.

Pincers or shears. Palm.

S. Agatha, V.M., A.D. 251. Patron saint of Malta and Catania.

Pincers holding a tooth.

S. Appolonia of Alexandria, V.M., A.D. 250. Patron saint against the toothache.

Pincers, holding tongue in. Bishop's robes.

S. Lieven, M., A.D. 656.

Ploughshares, walking over. Royal robes. Church in her hand.

S. Cunegunda of Bavaria, A.D. 1040.

Pomegranate surmounted by a cross. Dark brown habit.

S. Juan de Dios, A.D. 1550. Founder of the Order of Hospitallers, or Brothers of Charity.

Pot of holy water, and asperges. Dragon at her feet. Ladle.

S. Martha of Bethany, A.D. 84. Patron saint of cooks and housewives.

Pots, earthenware. Two young girls with palms.

S. Justa, M., and S. Rufina, M., A.D. 304.

Priests, two. Palms.

S. Peter Exorcista, M., and S. Marcellinus, M., A.D. 304.

Purse. Pen and inkhorn. Palm.

S. Matthew, Apostle, Evangelist, M.

Purses, three. Bishop's robes.

S. Nicholas of Myra, A.D. 342. Patron saint of Russia and many seaports; also of children, especially schoolboys, of sailors, merchants, and travellers, and against thieves.

Pyx. Franciscan habit, cardinal's hat near.

S. Bonaventure, A.D. 1274.

Pyx. Crucifix. Dominican habit.

S. Hyacinth, A.D. 1257

Pyx. Lily. Cross. Franciscan habit and cord.

S. Clara, A.D. 1253. Founder of the Order of Franciscan nuns called Poor Clares.

Raven with a loaf in its beak. Benedictine habit.

S. Benedict, A.D. 543. Founder of the Benedictine Order.

Raven on a stone. Palm. Deacon's robes.

S. Vincent, M., A.D. 304. Patron saint of Lisbon, Valencia, Saragossa, Milan, and Chalons.

Raven. Very old and half naked. Long hair and beard.

S. Paul the Hermit of Thebes, A.D. 344.

Ring. Sceptre surmounted by a dove. Royal robes.

S. Edward the Confessor, A.D. 1066.

Rod, or Asperges. Benedictine habit.

S. Benedict, A.D. 543, Founder of the Benedictine Order.

Rod. Crutch and bell. Hog near him.

S. Anthony, Hermit, A.D. 357.

Rope round his neck. Cardinal's robes. Barefooted.

S. Charles Borromeo, A.D. 1584. Archbishop of Milan.

Roses, red and white, in her robe. Franciscan habit or royal robes.

S. Elizabeth of Hungary, A.D. 1231.

Roses, crown of, or holding them in her hand. Palm.

S. Dorothea of Cappadocia, V.M., A.D. 303.

Roses, crown of, red and white. Musical instruments. Angel. Palm.

S. Cecilia, V.M., A.D. 280. Patron saint of music and musicians.

Roses, crown of. Franciscan habit.

S. Rosa di Viterbo, A.D. 1261.

Roses falling from his mouth. White over brown habit.

S. Angelus the Carmelite, A.D. 1220.

Rule, builder's.

S. Thomas Apostle, M. Patron saint of builders and architects.

Saw. Sometimes Fishes.

S. Simon Zelotes, Apostle, M.

Scourge, with three knotted thongs. Bishop's robes.

S. Ambrose, A.D. 397. One of the Four Latin Fathers of the Church. Patron saint of Milan.

Scourge, with lead on the thongs. Sword at his feet.

*S. Gervasius, M., A.D. 69.

Sea, walking over, or in the background. Dominican habit.

S. Raymond of Penaforte, A.D. 1275.

Serpents at her side, or feeding from a basket.

S. Verdiana, A.D. 1242.

Seven youths surrounding her. Veil. Palm.

S. Felicitas and her seven sons, M., A.D. 173. Patron saint of male heirs.

Shears. Palm.

S. Agatha, V.M., A.D. 251. Patron saint of Malta and Catania.

Sheep. Distaff. Basket of loaves.

S. Genevieve, A.D. 509. Patron saint of Paris.

Shell. Long staff and wallet. Sometimes bottle on staff.

S. James the Great, Apostle M. Patron saint of Spain

Shield with black eagle. Royal robes. Palm.

S. Wenceslaus of Bohemia, A.D. 938.

Shield with nine balls. Hawk.

S. Quirinus the Tribune, M., A.D. 130.

Ship. Anchor. Three balls. Bishop's robes.

S. Nicholas of Myra, A.D. 342. Patron saint of Russia, and many seaports, also of children, especially school-boys, of sailors, merchants, and travellers, and against thieves.

Shoemakers, two.

S. Crispin, M., and S. Crispianus, M., A.D. 300. Patron saints of Soissons.

Sieve, broken. Benedictine habit.

S. Benedict, A.D. 543. Founder of the Benedictine Order.

Skin, carrying his own. Knife.

S. Bartholomew, Apostle, M.

Skull. Franciscan habit. Stigmata.

S. Francis of Assisi, A.D. 1226. Founder of the Franciscan Order.

Soldier. Red cross on his breast. Sometimes as a Moor. Palm.

S. Maurice, M., A.D. 286. Patron saint of Austria, Savoy, and Mantua, and of foot soldiers.

* The companion with whom he is often represented is S. Protasius.

Spade. Old.	S. Phocas of Sinope, M., A.D. 303. Patron saint of gardens and gardeners.
Spade. Labourer's dress. Sometimes an angel ploughing in the background. (In Spanish pictures only.)	S. Isidore the Ploughman, A.D. 1170. Patron saint of Madrid and agriculture.
Spear. Roman soldier's dress.	S. Longinus, A.D. 45. The centurion at the crucifixion. Patron saint of Mantua.
Spear at his feet. Bishop's robes.	S. Lambert, M., A.D. 709.
Spider over a cup. White over black habit. Sometimes demon bound.	S. Norbert, A.D. 1134. Founder of the Order of Premonstratesians.
Spit. In armour.	S. Quintin, M., A.D. 287.
Sponge, with drops of blood. Cup.	S. Pudentiana, A.D. 148.
Staff, long, with wallet or bottle. Scallop shell.	S. James the Great, Apostle, M. Patron saint of Spain.
Staff. Old. Franciscan habit.	S. Francis de Paule, A.D. 1508. Founder of the Order of Minimes, reformed Franciscans.
Stag. Rich secular attire. Sometimes a boat in the background.	S. Julian Hospitator, A.D. 313. Patron saint of travellers, boatmen, and wandering minstrels.
Stag with crucifix between its horns. In armour.	S. Eustace, M., A.D. 118.
Stag with crucifix between its horns. Huntsman's dress or bishop's robes. (Hardly ever found in Italy.)	S. Hubert, A.D. 727. Bishop of Liège. Patron saint of the chase and dogs.
Star on his forehead. Lily. Dominican habit.	S. Dominic, A.D. 1221. Founder of the Dominican Order.
Star on his breast. Dominican habit.	S. Thomas Aquinas, A.D. 1274.
Star on his breast or above his head. Crucifix wreathed with lily. Benedictine habit.	S. Nicholas of Tolentino, A.D 1309.
Star, holding up, in both hands.	S. Swidbert, A.D. 713.

Stars, five, over his head. Finger on his lip or padlock.

S. John Nepomuc, A.D. 1393. Patron saint of silence, bridges and running water.

Stigmata. Franciscan habit. Sometimes a lamb.

S. Francis of Assisi, A.D. 1226. Founder of the Franciscan Order.

Stigmata. Lily. Crown of thorns. Dominican habit.

S. Catherine of Siena, A.D. 1380.

Stone, beating his breast with.

S. Jerome, A.D. 420. One of the Four Latin Fathers of the Church. Founder of Monachism in the West. Patron saint of scholars.

Stone (millstone). Arrows. Crown. Palm.

S. Christina, V.M., A.D. 295. Patron saint of Bolsena, and one of the patron saints of Venice.

Stone (millstone). In armour.

S. Victor of Marseilles, A.D. 303.

Stone (millstone). Sometimes a burning house in the background.

S. Florian, M., a patron saint of Austria.

Stones. Deacon's robes. Palm.

S. Stephen, Protomartyr.

Stones, carrying, in his chasuble.

S. Alphege, Archbishop of Canterbury.

Swan. Flowers. Carthusian habit.

S. Hugh of Lincoln, A.D. 1126.

Sword.

S. Paul, Apostle, M.

Sword and scales.

S. Michael the Archangel.

Sword at his feet. Olive or palm. Sometimes hands nailed to a tree over his head.

S. Pantaleon of Nicomedia, M., 4th century. Patron saint of physicians.

Sword. Banner. Girl in armour.

S. Joan of Arc, A.D. 1412-1431.

Sword. Books at his feet. Bishop's robes. Palm.

*S. Cyprian of Antioch, A.D. 304.

Sword in his hand, or piercing his head. Bishop's robes.

S. Thomas à Becket, A.D. 1170.

Sword, pierced by, or in his head. Dominican habit.

S. Peter Martyr, A.D. 1252.

* Generally seen in company with S. Justina, *see* Unicorn.

Sword. Tower. Cup and wafer. Feather. Crown. Palm.	S. Barbara, V.M., A.D. 303. Patron saint of Mantua and Ferrara, arms, armourers and fortifications, and against thunder and lightning.
Sword in her neck. Eyes on dish. Lamp. Palm.	S. Lucy, V.M., A.D. 303. Patron saint of Syracuse, and against diseases of the eye.
Sword. Lion. Lily. Palm.	S. Euphemia, V.M., A.D. 307.
Sword. Crown. Palm.	S. Justina of Padua, V.M., A.D. 303. Patron saint of Padua and Venice.
T, blue, on his shoulder. Sometimes crutch with bell, and hog.	S. Anthony, Hermit, A.D. 357.
Tongs, holding tongue in. Bishop's robes.	S. Lieven, M., A.D. 656.
Tongs, or pincers. Palm.	S. Agatha, V.M., A.D. 251. Patron saint of Malta and Catania.
Tooth held in pincers.	S. Apollonia of Alexandria, V.M., A.D. 250. Patron saint against toothache.
Tower. Feather. Chalice and wafer. Sword. Crown. Palm.	S. Barbara, V.M., A.D. 303. Patron saint of Mantua and Ferrara, of arms, armourers, and fortifications, and against thunder and lightning.
Tower, leaning, in a city, held in his hand.	S. Petronius, A.D. 430. Patron saint of Bologna.
Towers in his hand, or in the background. Young and richly dressed. Palm with dates.	S. Ansano, M. Patron saint of Siena.
Tree, foot on prostrate. Bishop's robes over Benedictine habit.	S. Boniface, A.D. 755. Archbishop of Mayence. Apostle and first Primate of Germany.
Tree, hands nailed to, over his head. Sword at his feet.	S. Pantaleon of Nicomedia, M., 4th century. Patron saint of physicians.
Tree, hollow, hermit praying in.	S. Bavon, A.D. 657. Patron saint of Ghent and Haarlem.

Tree coming into leaf, in the background. Bishop's robes.

S. Zenobio of Florence, A.D. 417.

Two men in red robes and caps, with surgical instruments.

S. Cosmo, M., and S. Damian, M., A.D. 301. Patron saints of the Medici and of medicine.

Two men in armour. Palms.

S. John, M., and S. Paul, M., A.D. 362.

Two priests. Palms.

S. Peter Exorcista, M., and S. Marcellinus, M., A.D. 304.

Two men, one old, the other young. Palm and sword.

S. Nazarius, M., and S. Celsus, M., A.D. 69. Patron saints of Milan.

Unicorn at her feet. Palm.

S. Justina of Antioch, V.M., A.D. 304.

Unicorn. Crown. Palm.

*S. Justina of Padua, V.M., A.D. 303. Patron saint of Padua and Venice.

Vase, or box of alabaster. Long fair hair.

S. Mary Magdalene, A.D. 68. Patron saint of Provence, Marseilles, and of penitent women.

Wallet and long staff. Scallop shell.

S. James the Great, Apostle, M. Patron saint of Spain.

Wallet, large, over the shoulder, dark-brown habit, peaked hood.

S. Felix de Cantalice, A.D. 1587.

Wheel. Sometimes head of a man under her feet. Crown. Palm.

S. Catherine of Alexandria, V.M., A.D. 307. Patron saint of Venice, and of places of education, of science, philosophy, eloquence and against diseases of the tongue.

Wheel, small. Bishop's robes. Candle on his head or in his hand.

S. Erasmus or Elmo, M., A.D, 296.

Wings. Dominican habit. Crucifix.

S. Vincent Ferraris, A.D. 1419.

Wolf. Sometimes holding a crowned head. Royal robes.

S. Edmund, M., A.D. 870. Patron saint of Bury St. Edmunds.

* She is easily confused with S. Justina of Antioch, but if the picture is by a Venetian painter, or at Venice, it would be S. Justina of Padua.

Wolf. A boy with palm. Generally a cock. Sometimes a lion or cauldron of oil.

S. Vitus, M., A.D. 303. Patron saint of Sicily, Saxony, and Bohemia, of dancers and actors, and those who find difficulty in early rising.

Wound, pointing to, in his leg. Pilgrim's shell and staff. Sometimes dog near.

S. Roch, A.D. 1327. Patron saint of Sicily, of prisoners and the sick, especially the plague-stricken.

Wound in her neck, rays coming from it. Sometimes eyes on a dish. Lamp. Sword. Palm.

S. Lucy, V.M., A.D. 303. Patron saint of Syracuse, and against diseases of the eye.

Acknowledgment is given to "Saints and their Symbols" by E. A. Greene.

STEVENGRAPHS

STEVENGRAPHS was a trade name used by Thomas Stevens in 1863 to describe his woven silk articles. Today it refers to his mounted silk pictures.

Thomas Stevens was born in Coventry in 1828 and worked in the silk weaving trade. In 1854 he set up in business on his own at first making silk bookmarkers.

These bookmarkers depicted various scenes and greetings. Such as Greetings for Christmas, New Year, Easter and birthday greetings. Portraits of Royalty, politicians and notabilities. Views of Exhibitions, such as Crystal Palace.

Texts from the Bible with suitable illustrations were very popular.

In 1879 Stevens commenced producing his silk pictures in cardboard mounts ready for framing, these were an enormous success and sold by the thousand.

Stevens died in 1888 and the business was carried on by the family until 1908 when it was made into a limited company.

Some of the subjects for Stevengraphs were:

Portraits of both British and Foreign Royalty, Sportsmen, Politicians, Jockeys, Military Heroes, Religious subjects and Classical subjects. Exhibitions, Castles, Bridges, Railway trains and many other subjects.

All types of sport including Horse racing, Fox hunting, Cricket, the Boat Race.

Stevengraphs must be in their original cardboard mounts to be of value and should be protected from damp and sunlight.

ROMAN NUMERALS

These are expressed by letters of the alphabet, i.e.: I, V, L, C, D, X and M. A line over any letter increases it a thousandfold, thus $\overline{V} = 5,000$; $\overline{M} = 1,000,000$, etc.

I	... ...	1
II	... ...	2
III	... ...	3
IV	... ...	4
V	... ...	5
VI	... ...	6
VII	... ...	7
VIII or IIX	...	8
IX or VIIII	...	9
X	... ...	10
XI	... ...	11
XII	... ...	12
XIII or XIIV	...	13
XIV or XIIII	...	14
XV	... ...	15
XVI	... ...	16
XVII	... ...	17
XVIII or XIIX	...	18
XIX or XVIIII	...	19
XX	... ...	20
XXV	... ...	25
XXX	... ...	30
XXXV	... ...	35
XL or XXXX	...	40
XLV	... ...	45
L	... ...	50
LV	... ...	55
LX	... ...	60
LXV	... ...	65
LXX	... ...	70
LXXV	... ...	75
LXXX or XXC	... ...	80
LXXXV	... ...	85
XC or LXXXX	... ...	90
C	... ...	100
CI	... ...	101
CC	... ...	200
CCC	... ...	300
CD	... ...	400
D or IƆ	... ...	500
DC or IƆC	... ...	600
DCC or IƆCC	... ...	700
DCCC or IƆCCC	... ... '	800
CM or DCCCC or IƆCCCC		900
M or CIƆ	... ...	1,000
MI	... ...	1,001
MC	... ...	1,100
MD	... ...	1,500
MCM	... ...	1,900
MM or CIƆCIƆ	... ...	2,000
MMM	... ...	3,000
MMMM	... ...	4,000
$\overline{V}$ or IƆƆ	... ...	5,000
$\overline{X}$	... ...	10,000
$\overline{L}$	... ...	50,000
$\overline{C}$	... ...	100,000
$\overline{D}$	... ...	500,000
$\overline{M}$	... ...	1,000,000

NOTE:—Each repetition of the character Ɔ has the effect of multiplying the preceding characters by ten, e.g., D or IƆ = 500 ∴ IƆƆ = 5,000.

GLOSSARY OF TERMS

(Not included in the Specialised Sections)

Abacus or **County Frame**—A frame with beads on which elementary counting is sometimes taught. **Swanpan**—a similar device used in China.

Alabaster—A white granular semi-transparent variety of Gypsum, much used for small objects of sculpture, vases, mantelpieces, etc.

Allegorical—A term sometimes used for a subject or article in which a higher spiritual order is dealt with in terms of a lower.

Alto-Relievo, Alto-Rilievo or **High Relief**—A term used in sculpture when the figures are made to project bodily from the background; usually part of the figures stand quite free. (*See Bas-Relief and Demi-Relievo.*)

Ammonite—A fossil shell, the spiral form of which resembles a ram's horn.

Amorini—Infant Cupid figures, a motif used in the 17th and late 18th century, often seen in Italian art of the 16th century. (*See Putti.*)

Andirons or **Handirons**—Large iron firedogs used in olden times for burning logs of wood on an open hearth; the fronts are sometimes ornamented with copper, etc., but are more often plain. The iron bars laid across a pair of andirons are called "creepers." (*See illustration.*)

Aneroid Barometer—An instrument for recording the variations of atmospheric pressure, in which an almost airtight metal box is used instead of mercury.

Antimacassar—A protective cover for the backs of chairs and couches.

Antimony—A brittle, crystalline, unoxidizable metal, tin-white in colour, largely used by the Japanese in a covering process for ornamental embossed articles of their manufacture; also used for type metal.

Antlers—Branches of the horns of an animal of the deer family.

Apiary—A place where bees are kept.

Aquarium—A tank, receptacle, or artificial pond for fishes and water plants.

Aquiline—Like an eagle; curved or hooked like the beak of an eagle.

Armorial—Relating to crests, escutcheons or family arms.

Bain Marie—A set of small saucepans contained in a deep metal dish holding boiling water.

Bakelite—A plastic substance which can easily be moulded into complicated shapes by the action of heat and pressure. It is made in a variety of colours and is much used in the production of articles for ornamental and utilitarian purposes.

Baldachin—An umbrella-shaped canopy made of costly materials and richly adorned, usually supported by pillars or fastened to a wall over a throne, altar, pulpit or other special object.

Baldric—A belt or sash, worn over one shoulder and under the opposite arm, usually richly ornamented, used to carry a bugle, sword, etc., a girdle similarly worn.

Baleen or Balene—The substance commonly known as whalebone.

Barograph—An automatic instrument used in meteorology for recording on paper the variations in atmospheric pressure over a period of time.

Barometer—An instrument for measuring the weight or pressure of the atmosphere, so indicating changes in the weather. Also used for determining altitudes. It consists of a long glass tube closed at one end, filled with mercury and inverted in a cup containing mercury. The column of mercury in the tube descends until balanced by the weight of the atmosphere.

Basalt—A tough, heavy basic rock of volcanic origin, black or dark in colour.

Bas-Relief—A term used in scculpture when the figures are only slightly raised from the background. (*See Alto-Relievo and Demi-Relievo.*)

Basse Taille—A French term sometimes used to describe a variety of transparent enamel work with bas-relief background.

Bast or Bass—The inner bark of certain trees from which rope and matting are made. Old vases, etc., having their surfaces decorated with rope or matting patterns are sometimes so described, e.g., an alabaster "bast" vase.

Battersea Enamel—A factory at Battersea was commenced by Stephen Theodore Janssen in 1753, but closed in 1756. Later factories commenced at Wednesbury, in Staffordshire, Bilston and elsewhere. Their products are often erroneously described as Battersea.

Beetle—A heavy wooden mallet.

Bell Metal—An alloy of copper (about 80 per cent) and tin (about 20 per cent).

Benares—An engraved ornamental brass ware which derives its name from the Indian town whose natives excel in its manufacture.

Betel Box—Betel nuts are used as a masticatory by Indians, and are often carried or kept in ornamental metal boxes, some having suspensory chains. Betel nut cutters and mortars are also in use.

Biddery Ware or Bedery—An Indian metal ware from the town of Bidar, in which base metals are damascened or inlaid with silver. (*See Tutenague Work.*)

Bifront—A term describing objects having two fronts or faces as on some vases and statues; it particularly applies when these represent Janus.

Biga—In ancient Roman times, a chariot drawn by two horses abreast.

Bijouterie or Bijoutry—Jewellery and relatively small objects, valuable on account of their workmanship or costly materials, or both.

Bilston Enamel—A name given to decorated enamel ware made in Staffordshire at Bilston, Wednesbury and elsewhere. Often erroneously described as Battersea enamel.

Bombard—A leather bottle for carrying beer, or a large drinking vessel.

Boot Jack—A board with a crotch to hold the heel of a field boot to assist in taking off the boot.

Bouchard—A mallet-shaped tool used by sculptors for roughing the surface of marble.

Bouge—A wallet or leather bag.

Bracteate—A thin piece of metal usually of gold or silver, found in Teutonic graves from the 6th century. **Bracteated** —a term applied to an article that is plated over with a more costly metal.

Brazier—An utensil in which coals and charcoal are burned; some examples are very ornate.

Bronze or **Gun Metal**—An alloy of copper (90 per cent) and tin (10 per cent).

Brougham—A closed horse-drawn carriage.

Brûle Parfum—Incense burner, originally made of marble, bronze or precious metal in the form of a tripod, often with pierced cover.

Buckhorn—Rough horn handles of table cutlery, made from the horns of deer.

Bulla—A round locket-like charm worn by Roman children and dedicated to a deity; a leaden seal attached to documents.

Bullescence—A term to describe articles and materials having the blister-like appearance of some leaves, notably the cabbage.

Burin—An engraver's tool for use on a metal plate.

Buskin or **Greave**—A kind of half boot lacing tight to the leg, representative of tragedy and sometimes seen richly ornamented in statues of Melpomene.

Byzantine Art—The name given to the ornamental style of art which commenced in Byzantium (Constantinople) in the first half of the 6th century, prevailing in the East down to the year 1453, when the Empire of the East was destroyed.

Cache Pot—The name sometimes given to jardinières and similar ornamental pots of ware or metal, when used for holding plants that are already in rough garden pots, thus hiding the latter.

Cadenas—An ornate casket in which noblemen of the Renaissance kept their personal table cutlery.

Calabash—The hard skins of the fruit of the calabash tree, often polished and engraved and converted into ornamental articles, pipes, etc.

Calathus—An ancient vase-shaped basket for holding a lady's fancy work; in art it sometimes represents maidenhood.

Calliper or **Caliper**—A measuring instrument used by engineers and others consisting of two legs pivoted together; employed in determining the diameters or thickness of tubes and other objects.

Calorimeter—An apparatus for measuring heat as distinct from temperature, often seen on the radiator cap of a motor car.

Candelabrum—A frame for branching lights, usually fitted for candles, but sometimes having Roman lamps suspended by chains; a large candlestick. Plural: **Candelabra.**

Canister—A box or case, often of tin, for holding cereals, etc., an ornamental box used in Roman Catholic churches.

Canton Enamel—An enamel ware often of light blue or yellow ground on a copper base, decorated in China at the Canton enamelling workshops.

Capital—The head or uppermost portion of a column or pilaster, crowning the shaft and supporting the weight of the entablature. (*See illustration.*)

Carboy—A very large bottle, usually made of green glass, protected by a wicker or basket covering and generally used for the transport or storage of acids and other chemicals.

Carillon—A set or suite of bells, upon which tunes are played, in France it is the name given to the tunes themselves.

Carrara Marble—A well-known Italian marble, often called Sicilian marble; it is the stone usually employed for statues, being white and free from dark veins, and it also weathers well.

Cartonnage—Pasteboard; the outer covering of a mummy

Carton Pierre—A kind of papier-mâché or pasteboard and stucco composition made to represent stone, etc., it was much used for festoon work on furniture. It consists of paper pulp mixed with glue and whitening with a little plaster of paris added.

Catspaw—The name given to the irregular mottling or marbling on the edges of a book showing as an ornamentation when the volume is closed.

Cauldron, Chalder or **Caldron**—A large kettle of globular shape, usually with swing handle and three feet; now reproduced for use as coal containers.

Cave Relievo—A sunk carving in which the border and highest parts of the design are left as the original plane of the material.

Cavetto—A term used to describe articles that have a design pressed in. (*See Intaglio.*)

Cellophane—A proprietary name for a thin transparent material in which food and many other commodities are wrapped.

Celluloid—A highly-inflammable substance made to imitate ivory, tortoiseshell, etc.

Censer or Thurible—A vase or other vessel for burning incense or perfumes, varied in form and often suspended by chains.

Cerograph—An engraving or writing in or on wax. **Ceroplastic** —modelled in wax.

Chafing Dish—A heated metal or ware dish in which hot food is served at table; live coals were used until superseded by electricity, etc.

Chamois—A species of antelope from whose skin chamois leather was originally made.

Champ—The groundwork or field on which work of the decorative arts is carried out; a flat surface.

Champ Levé—A variety of enamel ware produced by the early Limoges school. In this process the design was cut into the copper base in such a way as to leave a thin partition of metal wherever two colours met, thus preventing the colours running into each other by fusion when fired. As the name implies, the designs usually had plain field groundwork—Champ being the French word for a field. Sometimes also called " pit " and " imbedded " enamel.

Chandelier—A frame suspended from the ceiling with branches for candles; usually very ornamental, some being composed of prismatic glass drops.

Chariot—An ancient two-wheeled vehicle used in war drawn by two or four horses. (*See Biga.*)

Chaufferette—An old-time foot or hand warmer, consisting of a perforated metal container to hold glowing charcoal. **Chauffer**—A small stove or furnace.

Chess—A game of great antiquity played with thirty-two pieces or men; some specimens are very ornate and made of ivory, etc.

Chestnut Roaster—A brass box-shaped container with handle and perforated hinged lid, sometimes in the form of a flat perforated ladle.

Chinoiserie—An imaginative rendering in Western terms, of what was popularly thought to be the Chinese style.

Chronological Table—A register of dates and events in the order of time, such as a "family tree".

Cinerary Urns—Used to contain the ashes of the cremated dead; they vary greatly in shape and are often decorated.

Circa—About. Often used in conjunction with the numerals of a year to denote approximate accuracy.

Ciseleur—A French carver or chaser of metal. **Ciselure**—Carving or chasing. **Ciseler**—To chisel.

Clapdish—A wooden dish with a lid, used by beggars or lepers; sometimes called a **Clackdish.**

Clapper—The hinged piece or tongue of a bell.

Clasp—A bar of metal across the ribbon by which a medal is hung; a hook or catch, usually ornamental, for holding the ends of a belt or the covers of a book.

Clip Candlestick—A metal support on a weighted base with clips to hold a rushlight.

Cloisonné Ware—An enamel ware on copper ground, decorated with elaborate designs, the outlines of which are formed by thin strings of brass. The Chinese and Japanese excel in its manufacture.

Cloisons—Partitions, as, e.g., the fine brass wire used in cloisonné enamel ware to separate the different colours.

Codex—An ancient manuscript or manuscript book.

Comptometer—A calculating machine.

Coracle—A small boat used by the ancient Britons, consisting of a wicker frame covered with skin.

Cordelle—A large cord and tassel, as a cord curtain holder; a tow line.

Cordovan—A soft fine-grained leather, originally made at Cordova in Spain from goatskin, now made in England from various skins, particularly from horsehides.

Cork Carpet—A thick floor cloth or linoleum, made principally of ground cork.

Corona Lucis—A large candle ring or hoop suspended by chains; as used in churches.

Cresset—An iron cage or basket used to contain a flaming light as a torch, either mounted on a pole or suspended as a lantern.

Crimping—To give a regular wavy appearance to material, effected by folding or by heating with tongs called a goffer (*q.v.*).

Crosses—(*See illustrations, page* 518.)

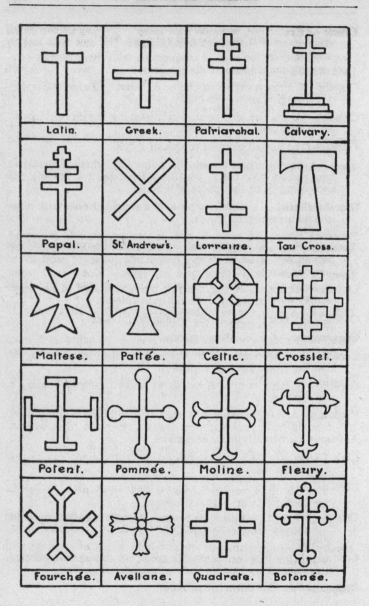

Latin.	Greek.	Patriarchal.	Calvary.
Papal.	St. Andrew's.	Lorraine.	Tau Cross.
Maltese.	Pattée.	Celtic.	Crosslet.
Potent.	Pommée.	Moline.	Fleury.
Fourchée.	Avellane.	Quadrate.	Botonée.

Crusie or Cruisie—A wrought-iron lamp consisting of two small shallow trays suspended from a stand. At one time largely used in Scotland.

Cuir Bouilli—A variety of ornamental leather work, in which the leather is first softened by boiling in oil, and then impressed or moulded into shape; when dry it becomes very hard and retains its form.

Culverhouse—A dove cote. **Culvertail**—A dove's tail.

Curb—A raised moulding or edging round a fireplace, following the line of the hearth.

Daguerrotype—A method of taking pictures on metal plates by the light of the sun; a photograph fixed on a plate of copper by a certain process. Invented in 1839.

Demi-Relievo—A term used in sculpture and modelling when the figures are in the half relief. (*See Alto-Relievo and Bas-Relief.*)

Dendrometer—An instrument for the measurement of the height and girth of trees.

Dieu Et Mon Droit—(God and my right.) The motto which appears on the Royal Coat of Arms. It was adopted by Richard I.

Diffuser—A reflector or other device attached to a lamp to distribute its light more evenly.

Distaff—The staff to which flax or wool is attached and from which threads are drawn when spinning; often represented in art, chiefly as a woman's symbol.

Dog Grate—A movable iron frame used on the open hearth for burning fuel, often highly ornamented. **Dog**—An andiron.

Dorlach—The Scottish name given to a knapsack, a portmanteau and a quiver.

Dosser or Dossal—(From dorsum, "back")—A basket carried on the back; a draping on the back of a throne or altar; the headboard to a bedstead, etc.

Doublet—A close-fitting garment worn by men from the 14th to 17th centuries; it extended from the neck to below the belt, with or without sleeves.

Doublure—The lining to the cover of a book, especially when of unusual pattern or material.

Electrolier—An ornamental electric-light fitting or pendant with provision for more than one lamp, usually suspended from the ceiling.

Elliptical—In the form of an oval.

Enchiridion—A handbook or manual.

Engrailed—Having an edge formed of concave curves.

En Suite or **Ensuit**—Belonging to a series.

Entablature—A term applied to that part of a structure which surmounts a column and rests upon the capital; the term came into use in the 17th century and comprises the cornice, frieze and architrave. (*See illustration.*)

Entablement—A platform above the dado for supporting a statue.

Epaulet or **Epaulette**—A shoulder piece, usually on the tunic of a uniform.

Ephod—The robe of a Jewish high priest, having shoulder pieces mounted with onyx stones engraved with tribal names, the breastplate of judgment being worn above the girdle; a plain linen garment worn by priests.

Equestrian—Pertaining to horses. An equestrian figure is a representation of a man on horseback.

Ermine—A species of weasel; its fur, brown in summer and white with black tipped tail in winter; in the latter phase it is used for the robes of judges and other eminent personages.

Espagnolette—The long bar or tower bolt fitted to french doors. operated by turning a handle in the centre.

Espion—A hinged mirror fixed outside a window so that happenings without can be seen from within.

Ex Libris—Any inscription, label or the like, pasted inside the front cover of a book with the name of the owner. A book plate.

Facsimile—An exact copy or likeness of the original; a duplicate.

Fasces—A roman symbol of authority represented by a bundle of sticks with an axe, bound together. **Fascine**—A number of sticks bound together.

Faucet—A pipe with movable plug or valve (a tap), inserted into a cask or barrel for drawing off liquids.

Fender—A low guard or frame of metal or other material placed in front of a fireplace to prevent burning coal falling into the room.

Ferrule—A ring of metal fastened to articles to strengthen them and prevent splitting, as the bands on the handles of cutlery, or the metal cap on the end of a walking stick.

Figurine—Small carved or sculptured image or statuette with painted or gilded ornamentation.

Fire-Dogs—(*See Andirons.*)

Flabellum—The feather-shaped fan carried before the Pope on state occasions.

Flared—Opening or spread outwards, like the end of a trumpet.

Fleur-de-Lys—A flower-shaped ornamentation made up of three vertical parts held together by a band a little below the centre; it represents a conventionalised lily, and was the national emblem of France up to 1789. (*See illustration.*)

Florentine Frame—Beautifully carved and openwork gilt frames made in Florence, used for pictures and mirrors.

Footman—A pierced brass hearth or kettle stand mounted on feet or on a centre support.

Forceps—A small pair of pincers or tongs for holding tiny objects difficult to hold with the fingers.

Foxed—Said of the edges or pages of books, when discoloured brown by age or decay.

Fusil—The steel of a tinder box.

Fustanelle—A stiffened white linen skirt or kilt worn by Greek soldiers.

Garniture de Cheminée—A set of five porcelain or faience vases. Adopted from Chinese example, sets of vases were made by European factories in the 18th century. In the 19th century the term was used to describe a clock and two bronze figures for the decoration of an overmantel.

Gavel—A small mallet used by the chairman or presiding officer at a meeting; an auctioneer's mallet.

Gimbal—A contrivance which allows such articles as a compass, etc., to remain in their true plane, when their supports are inclined out of that plane. It consists of a ring in which the object is suspended pivoted on two projecting dowels or pegs.

Gladstone Bag—A travelling bag made in two sections hinged together with a centre division; when closed it is secured by straps.

Gnomon—The style or triangular piece which casts the shadow on the face of a sun dial. **Gnomonic Column**—The stone pillar of a sun dial bearing the gnomon.

Goffer or **Gouffer**—To crimp or flute material by means of a heated goffer or pleating iron; the instrument itself.

Gondola—An Italian long narrow boat, propelled by oars and used on the canals of Venice; the prow and stern curve high out of the water.

Gonfalon—An ensign or standard with streamers. A pennon attached to a lance.

Gong—An instrument of percussion used as a call to meals etc. A saucer-like bell.

Gourd—A term used to describe the shape of ornamental articles or drinking vessels which resemble a pumpkin or other similar fruit; the dried fruit of a gourd; hollow dice used by cheating gamblers.

Greave—(*See Buskin.*)

Gridiron—An iron grating used for broiling food over an open fire.

Gun Metal or **Bronze**—An alloy of copper (90 per cent) and tin (10 per cent).

Haft—The handle or helve of a cutting instrument; the handle of a knife or dagger; the long wooden handle of a pick axe.

Hagiology—A history of saints.

Hammered Work—Iron or other metal, hammered or wrought into shape or design.

Handirons—(*See Andirons.*)

Hasp Fastening—A hinged clasp passing over a staple; sometimes the staple is attached to the clasp and fits into the lock.

Hastener—A large semi-circular tin shield in which a joint of meat is placed for roasting in front of an open fire, so that the heat is reflected on to the meat to hasten its cooking.

Hermetical—A term often used to describe a case or other object that is perfectly closed and air-tight, viz., a specimen case containing medals, etc.

Hibernia—The Latin name for Ireland.

Hob—The flat side-part of an open stove on which to stand cooking utensils to keep the contents warm.

Hookah, Hooka or **Haka**—A Turkish apparatus for smoking tobacco, the smoke being drawn through water contained in a glass vessel, by means of a long tube.

Hornbook—A child's primer. A piece of vellum on which the alphabet or other matter was written; it was covered with a piece of transparent horn and mounted on a rectangular-shaped piece of wood with a handle.

Houdah or **Howdah**—A seat fixed on the back of an elephant.

Ibis—A wading bird common in the district of the Nile, much venerated by the Egyptians and often represented in their art. Its plumage is chiefly white and black, but some specimens are scarlet and also white.

Icon, Ikon or **Eikon**—A sacred representation or image; more particularly applied to those of the Greek Church.

Ideogram or **Ideograph**—A picture-writing or heiroglyph.

I.H.S.—Letters meaning Jesus Hominum Salvator (Jesus Saviour for Men), taken from the three initial letters when written in Greek. There are variations of the letters and different interpretations.

Impress—To make a design or pattern by means of pressure. A design made by such means.

Inaurated—Gilded or golden.

Incavo—The part of an intaglio (*q.v.*) which is cut in or hollowed out.

Incinerator—Any kind of receptacle or furnace for burning substances so that they are reduced to ashes.

Incrusted also **Encrusted**—A term used in describing articles with surfaces covered with a crust or coat of another material, often to give a rustic effect.

Indented—Having a dent, depression or furrow struck into a surface.

Ingot—A mass of cast metal. Gold and silver ingots are known as "bars"; copper as "bricks" or "pigs"; tin as "blocks"; zinc as "cakes"; and iron as "pigs".

I.N.R.I.—Letters meaning Jesus Nazarenus Rex Judacorum—Jesus of Nazareth—King of the Jews.

Inro—A small receptacle or set of receptacles used by the Japanese to hold perfumes, etc., carried at the girdle.

Insignia—Distinguishing badges and emblems, as of royalty, regiments, or of an order or office.

Insulators—Non-conducting substances; the circular pieces of glass on which pianofortes stand.

Intaglio—A subject or design hollowed out of a gem or other substance, as a seal.

Intarsia—(*See Tarsia.*)

Inverted—Having a contrary or reversed position to that which is the more usual; upside down.

Iridescent—Having bright colours blended like those of a rainbow.

Jack—A large ewer; a clockwork device used to rotate joints of meat before an open fire for roasting; a figure which strikes the bell of a clock.

Jack Boot—A large riding boot reaching above the knee. A kind of Wellington boot.

Japanning—An imitation of Japanese lacquer work, later a mere coating of colour with figures; introduced to this country by the Dutch in the Restoration period; the commoner japanned goods came chiefly from Birmingham.

Jaspure—Marble mottled to resemble jasper.

Joss Sticks—Small perfumed incense rods which the Chinese burn before images.

Kapok or **Java Cotton**—The silky fibre obtained from the seeds of the Japanese silk cotton tree (*cebia pentandra*) and much used for stuffing cushions, mattresses, etc.

Kicking Plates—Shaped plates of metal screwed to the bases of doors to prevent their being kicked.

Koro—A Japanese globular bowl, usually on three feet with perforated lid often made of bronze and embossed with flowers and mythological beasts.

Kuft-Gori or **Koftgari**—A variety of Indian inlay work, in which the inlaid metal, usually gold, occupies more of the finished surface than the groundwork.

Lambrequin—An ornamental hanging from a shelf or over a window; a pelmet. A term used to describe border decorations on porcelain, etc., representing pelmets.

Lazy Tongs—A series of bars joined together in lattice fashion and capable of great extension and leverage.

Lectern—A reading desk or stand on which the larger books are placed during church services. They are made of wood, brass or stone, sometimes in the form of an eagle with spread wings. (*See illustration.*)

Lepidoptera—Appertaining to an order of insects which includes butterflies, moths, etc.

Limoges Enamel—A Medieval enamel ware, usually on a copper ground, made at Limoges; in this process the whole article was covered with enamel and the design painted on with enamel. The groundwork is usually of dark colour relieved in white with mythological figures, etc. (*See Champ Leve.*)

Lincrusta—A thick paper with embossed designs, used for covering dados, etc.

Long Arm—The name given to a hook on a long pole, used for many purposes, as by a butcher, or for the opening and closing of high windows or fanlights.

Lorgnette—An eyeglass or pair of eyeglasses on a long handle: An opera glass.

Lota—A large ornamental metal pot used in India for holding water.

Lotus—The Egyptian water lily; much used in Eastern art and decoration.

Lozenge—In the shape of a rhombus or in a diamond form.

Lunette—Crescent shaped, as the moon.

Mace—An ornamental staff borne before officers of the state as a symbol of authority.

Madonna—The Virgin Mary, especially as seen in works of art.

Magi—The three Wise Men from the East who were guided by a star to the Infant Jesus.

Magot—A small grotesque figure in Chinese or Japanese taste, often seen as a knob or finial to covers of jars, etc.

Manacles—A pair of joined metal rings with lock for securing the hands of a prisoner. Handcuffs.

Marionette—A puppet or figure made to move by means of a wire.

Marly Horses—The name given to statuary or bronze figures of rearing horses. The originals are at the entrance to the Champs-Elysees in Paris and were sculptured by Coustou.

Maulstick or **Mahlstick**—A small stick with a padded top used by painters to steady the hand.

Medallion—A large medal; a circular or oval panel or tablet usually bearing a figure or figures in bas-relief.

Memento Mori—A reminder of death, e.g., a skull-shaped ornament.

Mesh—The open spaces of a net or network.

Miniver—Fur used in the Middle Ages for lining garments; an old name for ermine.

Missal—A book of devotions. A Mass book.

Mitre—A tall tongue-shaped crown or head-dress worn by Bishops in ceremonial church services.

Monogram—Two or more initial letters interwoven as on a seal.

Monograph—A treatise written on one particular subject, or any branch of it.

Monolith—A stone or pillar of large size, set up as a monument, e.g., those at Stonehenge.

Monstrance—A receptacle in which sacred relics are exposed to view; or in which the consecrated Host is presented for adoration.

Mortar—A utensil of marble or brass, in which substances are pounded with a pestle; a kind of cannon.

Mosaic—The art of producing designs with small pieces of stone, marble or glass of different colours cemented into a ground of stucco, to imitate paintings. The ancient Greeks and Romans excelled in the art, which is still extensively practised for floors, etc.

Mottled—Marked in an irregular way with spots or blotches of colours of a different shade.

Mount—The background to which anything is fastened for more convenient use or exhibition; metal or other materials used to enrich furniture, as ormolu; Tudor mounts were often enriched by piercing and engraving. Originally used to give added strength, mounts later became purely ornamental.

Muff—A soft thick cover, usually cylindrical in shape, formerly worn by women to protect their hands in cold weather. A similar article used in vehicles for the feet.

Mull—A snuff box made of horn.

Mural—Pertaining to a wall. The term is often used in describing tapestry panels, etc., intended to be hung on a wall. A Roman golden crown in the form of battlements.

Muranese—An obscure glass used for windows, of a kind of shell pattern.

Mutoscope—An animated picture machine consisting of a series of pictures printed on pieces of paper attached to a spindle. When this is turned the pictures are brought rapidly into view, giving the effect of subjects in motion.

Nautilus—A shellfish found in Southern seas, once believed to sail by means of an expanded membrane. Frequently represented in art.

Navicula or **Navette**—A boot-shaped vessel for holding incense; a small ship.

Neolithic—Pertaining to the later stone age.

Netsuke—A small Japanese object carved in ivory or wood often pierced with holes for a cord, and used as a button.

Nickel Silver—An alloy of copper (60 per cent), nickel (20 per cent) and zinc (20 per cent).

Niello Work—A method of ornamenting metal cases by engraving designs and rubbing in black and sometimes coloured compositions so as to fill up the incised lines and give effect to the intaglio design. The process is of Italian origin. (*See Biddery Ware.*)

Norfolk Latch—A fastening for a door or gate consisting of a fall iron operated by a sneck or lift.

Obelisk—A word derived from the Greek, applied to monuments which taper as they rise and have four faces and pyramidal tops, e.g., Cleopatra's needle.

Onyx Marble—A beautiful variety of limestone having streaks of dark colours, found in Algeria. Made into ornamental articles, such as cameos.

Opalescent—Reflecting a milky iridescence or light from the interior.

Orb—A symbol of sovereignty, comprising a globe surmounted with a cross.

Oxidised—The term given to metals to which oxygen has been applied with the effect as of tarnishing; fenders and other fittings are often treated in this way.

Paktong—A Chinese alloy of copper, zinc and nickel, used in England from the 18th century for making fire grates, fenders, fire-irons, and candlesticks. It is very hard and has the appearance of German silver.

Palanquin—A covered vehicle used in India and China. It is fastened to a pole and carried on the shoulders of four or six native bearers.

Pailiasse or **Palliasse**—An under-mattress stuffed with straw, usually in two parts.

Palma—In classic art, the palm leaf or branch of victory.

Pampas Grass—A species of ornamental grass introduced from South America, where it grows on the plains and pampas; it bears large silvery white plumes of down-like appearance.

Panache—A plume or bunch of feathers, especially when worn on a helmet.

Panic Bolt—A kind of espagnolette (*q.v.*) bolt fitted to exit doors of theatres and public halls; it is instantly released upon pressure being applied to a bar fitted horizontally

Pannier—A large wicker provision basket carried on the back of a horse or donkey, or· on the back of a person; in architecture, a sculptured basket; a corbel; a frame of whale bone for distending a woman's skirt at the hips.

Pantile—An old-fashioned curved roof tile.

Pantograph—A simple instrument by which drawings and plans can be copied, enlarged or reduced.

Papeterie—A word from the French, denoting a case or box with writing materials.

Papyrus—A reed from which the ancient Egyptians made paper. Chairs and stools have been found covered with this reed similar to the rush-covered wicker chairs of the present day.

Parchment—Used for written documents before printing was invented; made chiefly from the skins of the sheep and goat; later a vegetable parchment was introduced and extensively used.

Parian Marble—The marble for which the Isle of Paros is famous; also the name given to a kind of fine clay ware which closely resembles it, much used for statuettes.

Passe-Partout—A mounting for photographs and pictures, in which the glass front is fixed by means of an adhesive binding.

Pastoral Staff—A long staff of metal or wood, the metal top of which is made in the shape of a shepherd's crook, borne by bishops on special occasions.

Patch Box—Small boxes usually made of papier-mâché and lacquered in which "beauty spots" or "patches" were kept; the lids were often decorated with hand-painted views or pictures. Enamelled patch boxes were made in the late 18th and late 19th centuries.

Paten—A small plate or salver used in Eucharistic services on which the consecrated bread is placed; it is usually made to fit the chalice as a cover.

Patina—The green film on old bronze; or the rich shades or hues seen on the prominent parts of old bronzes, the result of continued handling and dusting. Also applied to the prominent edges of old furniture which possess a hard and brilliant surface occasioned by constant use.

Pectoral—An ornament worn on the breast by bishops, etc.; a cross so worn.

Pelmet—A shaped piece of material covering the cornice board over window curtains, often enriched with applique designs or fringe.

Pelt—The skin of a fur-bearing animal; the name is usually applied to an undressed skin.

Pendant—A hanging appendage; a suspended ornament.

Pennant—A small, long, narrow flag. **Pennon**—a lance flag.

Peruke—An artificial cap of hair; a wig; a periwig.

Pestle—An instrument for pounding substances in a mortar.

Planchette—A small heart-shaped board supported on castors at two points and by a pencil at a third point. It is reputed to move when the fingers of one or more persons are placed lightly upon it, so that the pencil traces words or sentences.

Plaque or **Plaquette**—A flat, shaped piece of metal or earthenware, upon which a design is embossed, painted or enamelled.

Plaster of Paris—Derives its name from the fact that it originated in a suburb of Paris. A white powder formed from calcium sulphate which, when mixed with water, forms a paste which sets and hardens rapidly. Used for casts and mouldings.

Plate and Dish Rack—A wooden framework, usually fixed above a sink, in which plates and dishes are placed to drain after washing.

Plummet—A metal weight attached to the end of a plumb line in order to determine a true vertical direction.

Poker Work—A picture made on wood by a heated metal instrument.

Portfolio—A portable case, sometimes mounted on an easel stand, for holding drawings and papers.

Portière Curtain—A curtain over a door.

Portmanteau—A flat trunk used to contain clothes when travelling.

Pricket—A spike projecting vertically from the top of a candlestick, on which the candle is stuck; it preceded the sconce.

Prismatic—The glass drops with which lustres and chandeliers are formed, so named from the shape in which they are cut. **Prism**—A triangular piece of glass with three planes intersecting in three parallel straight lines.

Psalter—Book of Psalms.

Pumice—A greyish buoyant lava substance erupted from volcanoes, used for rubbing down the surfaces of paintwork. Sometimes called **Rotten-Stone.**

Purdonium—A closed coal scuttle, so named after the inventor, Purdon.

Putti—Nude cupid-like figures of children, often used in sculptures and paintings. (*See Amorini.*)

Queue—A tail-like plait of hair; a pigtail.

Quicksilver—The common name for fluid mercury.

Quilt—A coverlet for a bed; a counterpane; a cover filled with down (from the eider duck) and quilted, hence an eiderdown quilt.

Quilting—Hand or machine stitching in an ornamental design or interlined material.

Quincunx—A pattern or arrangement by which five objects are arranged one in each corner and one in the middle. (*See illustration.*)

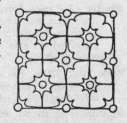

Rabbet—A groove cut longitudinally in a piece of wood to receive the edge of another piece, such as a panel. Also called **Rebate.**

Radiator—An appliance for diffusing heat, which may be supplied by hot water, steam, gas, electricity, etc.

Raffia—The fibre obtained from a palm which grows in Madagascar, used for making baskets and mats.

Refrigerator—A box-shaped apparatus usually lined with metal and fitted with a receptacle for ice or water, and used for keeping eatables, etc., cool. Modern examples are controlled by gas or electricity.

Relief—(See *Alto-Relievo, Bas-Relief and Demi-Relievo.*)

Reliquary—A small box or casket used to contain relics usually of saints. They are made in a large variety of materials and often ornamented with precious stones. **Relic**—an object or part of an object, kept in memory of a deceased person, or of an event.

Renaissance—(New Birth)—The name given to the revival of the classic style of art, which superseded that of the Byzantine and Gothic, and prevailed throughout Europe from the end of the 15th century; or to other similar revivals, in these cases preceded by some descriptive word.

Reredos—An ornamental screen placed against the east wall of a church, behind the altar, usually decorated with statues, paintings or tapestry.

Rocaille—An artificial rockwork made up of rough stones, such as a rockery; rocklike; a rococo system of scroll ornament of the 18th century.

Roulette—A well-known gambling game played with a revolving disc divided into thirty-nine compartments, and a ball. In philately, separating incisions without any of the paper actually being removed as used for some postage stamps in place of the more familiar perforating.

Round—Said of a piece of sculpture when it is carved on all sides, as distinct from reliefs.

Roxburghe—A half leather binding for books in which the back is of leather and the covers of paper or cloth, introduced by the third Duke of Roxburghe.

Rucksack—A waterproof canvas satchel with straps, carried on the back.

Ruff or Ruffle—A crimped or fluted collar as worn in the reign of Queen Elizabeth.

Sabot—The familiar wooden shoe with turned up toe, worn by Dutch, French and Belgian peasantry.

Saké—The chief alcoholic beverage of Japan. The name given to cups used in drinking it.

Salve—An inscription sometimes woven into door mats, meaning "Hail".

Sampler—Small piece of embroidery worked by ladies. Popular in the 17th and 19th centuries.

Satin-Brass—The name given to brass having a dull or antique finish; with the soft tone of satin.

Scaling—Ornamentation resembling tiles or the scales of fish used to fill in the background of small panels.

Sceptre—The gold staff or baton borne by kings as an emblem of their supreme authority.

Scorpion—A large spider-like insect with elongated hind part, often represented in art.

Sculpture—The art of carving or hewing figures or groups out of stone or other solid material.

Scuttle—A container for coals.

Seal—A piece of paper, wax or other material upon which an impression has been made.

Sequins—Small shining metal discs or spangles used to ornament costumes and draperies.

Serrated—Notched or toothed, as a saw.

Shagreen—Leather prepared from the skins of horses, asses, camels and sharks. The surface is dotted with small raised elevations caused by small seeds being pressed into it during preparation. It is dyed in a variety of colours (chiefly green) and used for covering small articles such as boxes and dagger handles.

Shako—A tall military hat with plume and metal plate in front, worn by old-time foot guards.

Sitz Bath—A portable hip bath in which a bath can be taken in a sitting position.

Skittles or **Ninepins**—A game played with nine skittles or pins of hard wood (somewhat resembling bottles) and a ball.

Snuff Bottles and Boxes—Are often very ornate, and are made in many varieties and of many materials. Spoons are sometimes fixed to the stoppers.

Snuff Rasp—A small file, usually in ornamental case, carried by old-time snuff-takers for "rasping" off sufficient snuff as required for use from rappee (tobacco leaves), which they also carried.

Soapstone—A variety of soft stone with a soapy feel, used by the Chinese and Japanese for small carved objects; it is usually streaked with brown or greyish-green.

Spigot—A peg used to stop the vent hole in a cask.

Stalactite—A deposit of calcium carbonate resembling an icicle, depending from the roof or sides of a cavern.

Stalagmite—A deposit similar to an inverted stalactite formed by calcareous water dropping on the floors of caverns.

Stalagmite Marble—A kind of onyx marble resembling a stalagmitic deposit.

Steelyard or Scalebeam—A weighing machine in which the article to be weighed is hung from the shorter part of a suspended lever or bar which moves on a fulcrum; the longer part of the bar is graduated and upon this slides a weight to produce equilibrium or balance. **Stiliarde**—A similar scale but with a platform.

Stiliarde—(*See Steelyard*).

Stirrup—A support for the foot of a rider on horseback.

Strigil or Flesh Brush—Often made of ivory in the shape of a hand with long handle, a back-scratcher; also a slightly curved reeding found on flat surfaces in Roman architecture as an ornamentation.

Sundial—A device for telling the time of day by a gnomon or style which casts a shadow on a plane marked in divisions.

Surcoat—The long cloak worn by knights over their armour, popular during the 13th and 14th centuries; also an outer garment for men and women.

Tabard—A sleeveless or short-sleeved cape, as worn by heralds, emblazoned with the arms of their employers; a military coat of the 15th and 16th centuries.

Tantalus—A stand, usually of oak, with silver or plated mounts, holding one or more (usually three) spirit bottles, the top part being hinged and fitted with a lock.

Tarsia—A mosaic or inlay of vari-coloured woods, ivory, etc., common in the Italian Renaissance and often representing architectural designs in perspective; sometimes styled **Intarsia**.

Tassel—A pendant ornament made of silk or other material attached to curtains, cushions.

Taxidermy—The art of preserving the skins of, and stuffing animals, so as to represent them in the natural form.

Thurible—A vase-shaped censer with perforated lid, often suspended by three chains fixed to its body. Made of metal and usually richly embossed.

Tinder Box—A small metal box made to contain tinder (scorched linen); it was usually provided with a flint and steel for igniting it.

Tondo—A plate or dish having a small centre part as compared with its wide brim.

Tooling—A term usually applied to leather work, such as the covers of books, with a design carried out by the use of small hand tools.

Translucent Enamel—An almost transparent enamel work which originated in Italy; the designs were often slightly raised and carried out in a large variety of colours, usually on a groundwork of silver. **Translucent**—Permitting the passage of light without allowing objects to be clearly seen, e.g., frosted glass.

Tree Calf—A bright brown polished calfskin binding for books ornamented with a tree-like design.

Trencher—A platter, usually made of wood, on which bread is placed at table.

Trivet—A small pierced metal stand for attaching to the bars of a grate as a rest for a kettle; often made with three feet. (*See illustration.*)

Trug Basket—A Sussex name for a boat-shaped basket used for collecting garden produce, made of thin laths of wood bent to shape and mounted on feet.

Tutenague Work—A Chinese and Indian variety of metal inlay work; the groundwork is usually of copper alloy, the designs being cut out and filled in with gold or silver. (*See Biddery Ware and Kuftgari.*)

Unguent—Antique vases used for storing ointment, particularly for embalming purposes, often made of alabaster; an ointment.

Vane—An ornamental plate of metal fixed on the spires of churches, etc., and made to turn by, and to show the direction of the wind; a flag or banner; one of the blades of a windmill.

Vellum—A thin parchment made from calfskin; after treatment it becomes clear and white and is then used for writing upon.

Venetian Blind—A window blind made of a large number of thin laths or slats of wood.

Verdigris—A corrosive green rust or pigment often seen on old copper and brass.

Vignette—A term originally applied to a small engraved embellishment of vine leaves and tendrils with which the capital letters on ancient manuscripts were often surrounded; also a running ornamentation in the hollow mouldings of Gothic architecture; as applied to photographs or engravings, it implies that the edges gradually fade away and are not enclosed in any definite border.

Volute—The spiral or "rolled-up" scroll ornament in the capital of the Ionic, Corinthian and Composite Orders of architecture. (*See illustration.*)

Wafer Box—Occasionally seen fitted to old inkstands, a wafer being a thin disc of dried paste or wax used for sealing envelopes and attaching postage stamps before the use of gum.

Water Mark—A maker's mark impressed on paper during manufacture. The design has greater pressure applied to it than the paper itself, with the result that the paper is thinner where the design exists and this can be seen when it is held to the light.

Weathercock—(*See Vane.*)

Wimple—The white linen head-dress covering the head and neck, as worn by nuns.

Windbell—Composed of a number of shaped pieces of glass suspended by threads from a framing. When placed in a current of wind, these swing and make a musical tinkling.

Zarf—A metallic vase-shaped stand for holding Oriental coffee cups without handles. (*See Saké.*)

BIRMINGHAM DATE LETTERS

Letter	Year
Ⓐ	1849 – 0
Ⓑ	1850 – 1
Ⓒ	1851 – 2
Ⓓ	1852 - 3
Ⓔ	1853 – 4
Ⓕ	1854 – 5
Ⓖ	1855 – 6
Ⓗ	1856 – 7
Ⓘ	1857 - 8
Ⓙ	1858 – 9
Ⓚ	1859 – 0
Ⓛ	1860 – 1

Letter	Year
ⓐ	1824 – 5
ⓑ	1825 – 6
ⓒ	1826 – 7
ⓓ	1827 – 8
ⓔ	1828 – 9
ⓕ	1829 – 0

William IV

Letter	Year
ⓖ	1830 – 1
ⓗ	1831 – 2
ⓘ	1832 – 3
ⓚ	1833 – 4
ⓛ	1834 – 5

Letter	Year
ⓐ	1798 – 9
ⓑ	1799 – 0
ⓒ	1800 – 1
ⓓ	1801 – 2
ⓔ	1802 – 3
ⓕ	1803 – 4
ⓖ	1804 – 5
ⓗ	1805 – 6
ⓘ	1806 – 7
ⓙ	1807 – 8
ⓚ	1808 – 9
ⓛ	1809 –

George III

Letter	Year
Ⓐ	1773 – 4
Ⓑ	1774 – 5
Ⓒ	1775 – 6
Ⓓ	1776 – 7
Ⓔ	1777 – 8
Ⓕ	1778 – 9
Ⓖ	1779 – 0
Ⓗ	1780 – 1
Ⓘ	1781 – 2
Ⓚ	1782 – 3
Ⓛ	1783 – 4

Year	Letter
1862 – 3	N
1863 – 4	O
1864 – 5	P
1865 – 6	Q
1866 – 7	R
1867 – 8	S
1868 – 9	T
1869 – 0	U
1870 – 1	V
1871 – 2	W
1872 – 3	X
1873 – 4	Y
1874 – 5	Z

Victoria

Year	Letter
1836 – 7	A
1837 – 8	C
1838 – 9	D
1839 – 0	E
1840 – 1	F
1841 – 2	G
1842 – 3	H
1843 – 4	I
1844 – 5	K
1845 – 6	L
1846 – 7	M
1847 – 8	N
1848 – 9	Z

George IV

Year	Letter
1811 – 2	n
1812 – 3	o
1813 – 4	p
1814 – 5	q
1815 – 6	r
1816 – 7	s
1817 – 8	t
1818 – 9	u
1819 – 0	v
1820 – 1	W
1821 – 2	X
1822 – 3	y
1823 – 4	Z

Year	Letter
1786 – 7	O
1787 – 8	P
1788 – 9	Q
1789 – 0	R
1790 – 1	S
1791 – 2	T
1792 – 3	U
1793 – 4	V
1794 – 5	W
1795 – 6	X
1796 – 7	Y
1797 – 8	Z

BIRMINGHAM DATE LETTERS

Letter	Year		Letter	Year		Letter	Year		Letter	Year
a	1875 – 6		a	1900 – 1		A	1925 – 6		A	1950 – 1
b	1876 – 7			Edward VII		B	1926 – 7		B	1951 – 2
c	1877 – 8		b	1901 – 2		C	1927 – 8			Elizabeth II
d	1878 – 9		c	1902 – 3		D	1928 – 9		C	1952 – 3
e	1879 – 0		d	1903 – 4		E	1929 – 0		D	1953 – 4
f	1880 – 1		e	1904 – 5		F	1930 – 1		E	1954 – 5
g	1881 – 2		f	1905 – 6		G	1931 – 2		F	1955 – 6
h	1882 – 3		g	1906 – 7		H	1932 – 3		G	1956 – 7
i	1883 – 4		h	1907 – 8		J	1933 – 4		H	1957 – 8
k	1884 – 5		i	1908 – 9		K	1934 – 5		J	1958 – 9
l	1885 – 6		k	1909 – 0		L	1935 – 6			1959 – 0
m	1886 – 7			George V			George VI			

Year	Letter	Year	Letter	Year	Letter	Year	Letter
	L	1937 – 8	N	1911 – 2	m		
1961 – 2	M	1938 – 9	O	1912 – 3	n	1888 – 9	o
1962 – 3	N	1939 – 0	P	1913 – 4	o	1889 – 0	p
1963 – 4	O	1940 – 1	Q	1914 – 5	p	1890 – 1	q
1964 – 5	P	1941 – 2	R	1915 – 6	q	1891 – 2	r
1965 – 6	Q	1942 – 3	S	1916 – 7	r	1892 – 3	s
1966 – 7	R	1943 – 4	T	1917 – 8	s	1893 – 4	t
1967 – 8	S	1944 – 5	U	1918 – 9	t	1894 – 5	u
1968 – 9	T	1945 – 6	V	1919 – 0	u	1895 – 6	v
1969 – 0	U	1946 – 7	W	1920 – 1	v	1896 – 7	w
1970 – 1	V	1947 – 8	X	1921 – 2	w	1897 – 8	x
		1948 – 9	Y	1922 – 3	x	1898 – 9	y
		1949 – 0	Z	1923 – 4	y	1899 – 0	z
				1924 – 5	z		

CHESTER DATE LETTERS

Letter	Years	Letter	Years	Letter	Years	Letter	Years
Anne		A	1726 – 7	a	1751 – 2	a	1776 – 7
B	1702 – 3	**George II**		b	1752 – 3	b	1777 – 8
C	1703 – 4	B	1727 – 8	c	1753 – 4	c	1778 – 9
D	1704 – 5	C	1728 – 9	d	1754 – 5	d	1779 – 0
E	1705 – 6	D	1729 – 0	e	1755 – 6	e	1780 – 1
F	1706 – 7	E	1730 – 1	f	1756 – 7	f	1781 – 2
G	1707 – 8	F	1731 – 2	g	1757 – 8	g	1782 – 3
H	1708 – 9	G	1732 – 3	h	1758 – 9	h	1783 – 4
I	1709 – 0	H	1733 – 4	i	1759 – 0	i	1784 – 5
K	1710 – 1	J	1734 – 5	**George III**		k	1785 – 6
L	1711 – 2	K	1735 – 6	k	1760 – 1	l	1786 – 7
M	1712 – 3	L	1736 – 7	l	1761 – 2	m	1787 – 8
N	1713 – 4						

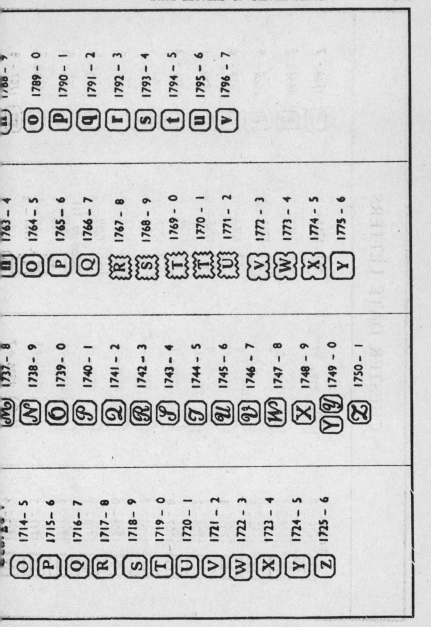

CHESTER DATE LETTERS

Year	Letter	Year	Letter	Year	Letter	Year	Letter
1797 – 8	A	1818 – 9	A	1839 – 0	A	1864 – 5	a
1798 – 9	B	1819 – 0	B	1840 – 1	B	1865 – 6	b
1799 – 0	C	George IV		1841 – 2	C	1866 – 7	c
1800 – 1	D	1820 – 1	C	1842 – 3	D	1867 – 8	d
1801 – 2	E	1621 – 2	D	1843 – 4	E	1868 – 9	e
1802 – 3	F	1822 – 3	D	1844 – 5	F	1869 – 0	f
1603 – 4	G	1823 – 4	E	1845 – 6	G	1870 – 1	g
1604 – 5	H	1824 – 5	F	1846 – 7	H	1871 2	h
1805 – 6	I	1825 – 6	G	1847 – 8	J	1872 – 3	i
1806 – 7	K	1826 – 7	H	1848 – 9	K	1873 – 4	k
1807 – 8	L	1827 – 8	I	1849 – 0	L	1874 – 5	l
1808 – 9	M	1628 – 9	K	1850 – 1	M	1875 – 6	m

Year	Letter
1877 – 8	O
1878 – 9	P
1879 – 0	Q
1880 – 1	R
1881 – 2	S
1882 – 3	T
1883 – 4	U

Year	Letter
1852 – 3	Q
1853 – 4	B
1854 – 5	C
1855 – 6	R
1856 – 7	S
1857 – 8	T
1858 – 9	U
1859 – 0	V
1860 – 1	W
1861 – 2	X
1862 – 3	Y
1863 – 4	Z

William IV

Year	Letter
1830 – 1	M
1831 – 2	N
1832 – 3	O
1833 – 4	P
1834 – 5	Q
1835 – 6	R
1836 – 7	S

Victoria

Year	Letter
1837 – 8	T
1838 – 9	U

Year	Letter
1810 – 1	O
1811 – 2	P
1812 – 3	Q
1813 – 4	R
1814 – 5	S
1815 – 6	T
1816 – 7	U
1817 – 8	V

CHESTER DATE LETTERS

A	1951 – 2 Elizabeth II
B	1952 – 3
C	1953 – 4
D	1954 – 5
E	1955 – 6
F	1956 – 7
G	1957 – 8
H	1958 – 9
J	1959 – 0

🅐	1926 - 7
🅑	1927 - 8
🅒	1928 - 9
🅓	1929 - 0
🅔	1930 – 1
🅕	1931 – 2
🅖	1932 – 3
🅗	1933 – 4
🅙	1934 – 5
🅚	1935 – 6
	George VI 1936 - 7

Ⓐ	Edward VII 1901 – 2
Ⓑ	1902 – 3
Ⓒ	1903 – 4
Ⓓ	1904 – 5
Ⓔ	1905 – 6
Ⓕ	1906 – 7
Ⓖ	1907 – 8
Ⓗ	1908 – 9
Ⓘ	1909 – 0
Ⓚ	George V 1910 – 1

A	1884 – 5
B	1885 – 6
C	1886 – 7
D	1887 – 8
E	1888 – 9
F	1889 – 0
G	1890 – 1
H	1891 – 2
I	1892 – 3
K	1893 – 4
L	1894 – 5

Letter	Year
L	
M	1962
Office Closed 1962	

Letter	Year
A	1938 – 9
O	1939 – 0
P	1940 – 1
Q	1941 – 2
R	1942 – 3
S	1943 – 4
T	1944 – 5
U	1945 – 6
V	1946 – 7
W	1947 – 8
X	1948 – 9
Y	1949 – 0
Z	1950 – 1

Letter	Year
M	1912 – 3
N	1913 – 4
O	1914 – 5
P	1915 – 6
Q	1916 – 7
R	1917 – 8
S	1918 – 9
T	1919 – 0
U	1920 – 1
V	1921 – 2
W	1922 – 3
X	1923 – 4
Y	1924 – 5
Z	1925 – 6

Letter	Year
O	1897 – 8
P	1898 – 9
Q	1899 – 0
R	1900 – 1

DUBLIN DATE LETTERS

William III	1700 – 1	
	1701 – 2	
Anne	1702 – 3	
	1703 – 4	
	1704 – 5	
	1706 – 7	
	1708 – 9	
	1710 – 1	
	1712 – 3	
George I	1714 – 5	

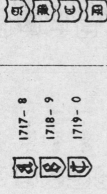

Date	Letter
1717 – 8	
1718 – 9	
1719 – 0	

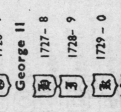

	1720 – 1	
	1721 – 2	
	1722 – 3	
	1723 – 4	
	1724 – 5	
	1725 – 6	
	1726 – 7	
George II	1727 – 8	
	1728 – 9	
	1729 – 0	
	1730 – 1	

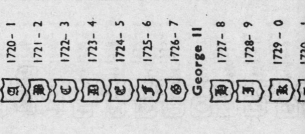

Date	Letter
1747 – 8	A
1748 – 9	B
1749 – 0	C
1750 – 1	D
1751 – 2	E
1752 – 3	F
1753 – 4	G
1754 – 5	H
1757 – 8	I
1758 – 9	K
1759 – 0	L

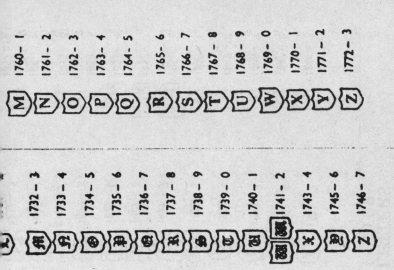

1760 – 1	1761 – 2	1762 – 3	1763 – 4	1764 – 5	1765 – 6	1766 – 7	1767 – 8	1768 – 9	1769 – 0	1770 – 1	1771 – 2	1772 – 3
M	N	O	P	Q	R	S	T	U	W	X	Y	Z

	1732 – 3	1733 – 4	1734 – 5	1735 – 6	1736 – 7	1737 – 8	1738 – 9	1739 – 0	1740 – 1	1741 – 2	1743 – 4	1745 – 6	1746 – 7

1716 – 7

DUBLIN DATE LETTERS

A	1773– 4
B	1774– 5
C	1775– 6
D	1776– 7
E	1777– 8
F	1778– 9
G	1779– 0
H	1780– 1
I	1781– 2
K	1782– 3
L	1783– 4
M	1784– 5

A	1797– 8
B	1798– 9
C	1799– 0
D	1800– 1
E	1801– 2
F	1802– 3
G	1803– 4
H	1804– 5
I	1805– 6
K	1806– 7
L	1807– 8
M	1808– 9

A	1821– 2
B	1822– 3
C	1823– 4
D	1824– 5
E	1825– 6
F	1826– 7
G	1827– 8
H	1828– 9
I	1829– 0
K	William IV 1830– 1
L	1831– 2

a	1846– 7
b	1847– 8
c	1848– 9
d	1849– 0
e	1850– 1
ff	1851– 2
gg	1852– 3
hh	1853– 4
j	1854– 5
k	1855– 6
l	1856– 7
m	1857– 8

1859 - 0	1860 - 1	1861 - 2	1862 - 3	1863 - 4	1864 - 5	1865 - 6	1866 - 7	1867 - 8	1868 - 9	1869 - 0	1870 - 1
O	P	Q	L	S	T	U	V	W	X	Y	Z

1833 - 4	1834 - 5	1835 - 6	1836 - 7	1837 - 8 Victoria	1838 - 9	1839 - 0	1840 - 1	1841 - 2	1842 - 3	1843 - 4	1844 - 5	1845 - 6
N	O	P	Q		R	S	T	U	V	W	X	Y	Z

1810 - 1	1811 - 2	1812 - 3	1813 - 4	1814 - 5	1815 - 6	1816 - 7	1817 - 8	1818 - 9	1819 - 0	George IV 1820 - 1
O	P	Q	R	S	T	U	W	X	Y	Z

1786 - 7	1787 - 8	1788 - 9	1789 - 0	1790 - 1	1791 - 2	1792 3	1793 - 4	1794 - 5	1795 - 6	1796 - 7
O	P	Q	R	S	T	U	W	X	Y	Z

DUBLIN DATE LETTERS

Letter	Date	Letter	Date	Letter	Date	Letter	Date
A	1871 – 2	C	1898 – 9	h	1923 – 4	**Elizabeth II** K	1952
B	1872 – 3	D	1899 – 0	I	1924 – 5	L	1953
C	1873 – 4	E	1900 – 1	K	1925 – 6	M	1954
D	1874 – 5	**Edward VII** F	1901 – 2	L	1926 – 7	N	1955
E	1875 – 6	G	1902 – 3	m	1927 – 8	O	1956
F	1876 – 7	H	1903 – 4	n	1928 – 9	P	1957
G	1877 8	I	1904 – 5	O	1929 – 0	Q	1958
H	1878 – 9	K	1905 – 6	P	1930 – 1	R	1959
I	1879 – 0	L	1906 – 7	Q	1932	S	1960
K	1880 – 1	M	1907 – 8	R	1933	T	1961
L	1881 – 2		1908 9	S	1934	U	1962
M	1882 – 3			T	1935	V	1963
						W	1964

1966	1967	1968	1969	1970	1971	1972
	Z	a	b	c	d	e

1936	1937	1938	1939	1940	1941	1942	1943	1944	1945	1946	1947	1948	1949	1950	1951
U	V	W	X	Y	Z	A	B	C	D	E	F	G	H	I	J

	George V 1910–1	1911–2	1912–3	1913–4	1914–5	1915–6	1916–7	1917–8	1918–9	1919–0	1920–1	1921–2	1922–3
	P	Q	R	S	T	U	A	b	C	D	e	F	S

1884–5	1885–6	1886–7	1887–8	1888–9	1889–0	1890–1	1891–2	1892–3	1893–4	1894–5	1895–6	1896–7	1897–8
O	P	Q	R	S	T	U	V	W	X	Y	Z	&	℞

EDINBURGH DATE LETTERS

William III			George I		Anne
1700 – 1	1705– 6	1730 – 1	1755 – 6		
1701 – 2	1706– 7	1731 – 2	1756 – 7		
	1707– 8	1732 – 3	1757 – 8		
Anne	1708– 9	1733 – 4	1758 – 9		
1702 – 3	1709– 0	1734 – 5	1759 – 0		
1703 – 4	1710– 1	1735 – 6	**George III**		
1704 – 5	1711– 2	1736 – 7	1760 – 1		
	1712– 3	1737 – 8	1761 – 2		
	1713– 4	1738 – 9	1762 – 3		
	George I	1739 – 0	1763 – 4		
	1714– 5	1740 – 1	1764 – 5		
	1715– 6	1741 – 2	1765 – 6		

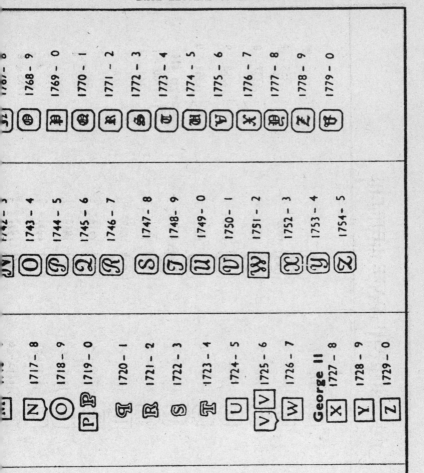

EDINBURGH DATE LETTERS

Letter	Year	Letter	Year	Letter	Year	Letter	Year
A	1780 – 1	a	1806 – 7	a	1832 – 3	A	1857 – 8
B	1781 – 2	b	1807 – 8	b	1833 – 4	B	1858 – 9
C	1782 – 3	c	1808 – 9	c	1834 – 5	C	1859 – 0
D	1783 – 4	d	1809 – 0	d	1835 – 6	D	1860 – 1
E	1784 – 5	e	1810 – 1	e	1836 – 7	E	1861 – 2
F	1785 – 6	f	1811 – 2	f	Victoria 1837 – 8	F	1862 – 3
G	1786 – 7	g	1812 – 3	g	1838 – 9	G	1863 – 4
G	1787 – 8	h	1813 – 4	h	1839 – 0	H	1864 – 5
H	1788 – 9	i	1814 – 5	i	1840 – 1	I	1865 – 6
I/U	1789 – 0	j	1815 – 6	k	1841 – 2	K	1866 – 7
K	1790 – 1	k	1816 – 7	l	1842 – 3	L	1867 – 8
1	1791 – 2	l	1817 – 8			M	1868 – 9

Year	Letter
	N
1870 – 1	O
1871 – 2	P
1872 – 3	Q
1873 – 4	R
1874 – 5	S
1875 – 6	T
1876 – 7	U
1877 – 8	V
1878 – 9	W
1879 – 0	X
1880 – 1	Y
1881 – 2	Z

Year	Letter
1844 – 5	F
1845 – 6	G
1846 – 7	H
1847 – 8	I
1848 – 9	K
1849 – 0	S
1850 – 1	T
1851 – 2	U
1852 – 3	Y
1853 – 4	W
1854 – 5	X
1855 – 6	Y
1856 – 7	Z

Year	Letter
1819 – 0	n
George IV	
1820 – 1	O
1821 – 2	P
1822 – 3	q
1823 – 4	r
1824 – 5	s
1825 – 6	t
1826 – 7	u
1827 – 8	v
1828 – 9	W
1829 – 0	X
William IV	
1830 – 1	y
1831 – 2	Z

Year	Letter
1792 – 3	M
1793 – 4	N
1794 – 5	O
1795 – 6	P
1796 – 7	Q
1797 – 8	R
1798 – 9	S
1799 – 0	T
1800 – 1	U
1801 – 2	V
1802 – 3	W
1803 – 4	X
1804 – 5	Y
1805 – 6	Z

EDINBURGH DATE LETTERS

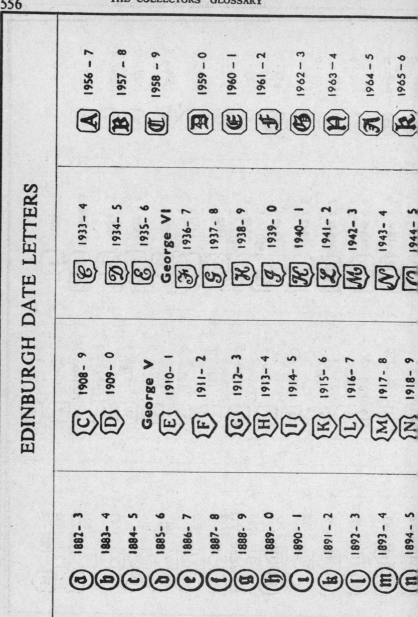

1882 – 3	ⓐ	1908 – 9	Ⓒ	1933 – 4	Ⓔ	1956 – 7	Ⓐ
1883 – 4	ⓑ	1909 – 0	Ⓓ	1934 – 5	Ⓓ	1957 – 8	Ⓑ
1884 – 5	ⓒ	George V		1935 – 6	Ⓔ	1958 – 9	Ⓒ
1885 – 6	ⓓ	1910 – 1	Ⓔ	George VI		1959 – 0	Ⓓ
1886 – 7	ⓔ	1911 – 2	Ⓕ	1936 – 7	Ⓕ	1960 – 1	Ⓔ
1887 – 8	ⓕ	1912 – 3	Ⓖ	1937 – 8	Ⓖ	1961 – 2	Ⓕ
1888 – 9	ⓖ	1913 – 4	Ⓗ	1938 – 9	Ⓗ	1962 – 3	Ⓖ
1889 – 0	ⓗ	1914 – 5	Ⓘ	1939 – 0	Ⓘ	1963 – 4	Ⓗ
1890 – 1	ⓘ	1915 – 6	Ⓚ	1940 – 1	Ⓚ	1964 – 5	Ⓘ
1891 – 2	ⓚ	1916 – 7	Ⓛ	1941 – 2	Ⓛ	1965 – 6	Ⓚ
1892 – 3	ⓛ	1917 – 8	Ⓜ	1942 – 3	Ⓜ		
1893 – 4	ⓜ	1918 – 9	Ⓝ	1943 – 4	Ⓝ		
1894 – 5	ⓝ			1944 – 5	Ⓞ		

1967 – 8   1968 – 9   1969 – 0   1970 – 1

1946 – 7   1947 – 8   1948 – 9   1949 – 0   1950 – 1   1951 – 2   Elizabeth II   1952 – 3   1953 – 4   1954 – 5   1955 – 6

1920 – 1   1921 – 2   1922 – 3   1923 – 4   1924 – 5   1925 – 6   1926 – 7   1927 – 8   1928 – 9   1929 – 0   1930 – 1   1931 – 2   1932 – 3

1895 – 6   1896 – 7   1897 – 8   1898 – 9   1899 – 0   1900 – 1   Edward VII   1901 – 2   1902 – 3   1903 – 4   1904 – 5   1905 – 6   1906 – 7   1907 – 8

EXETER DATE LETTERS

	William III			George II			George III		A	1773 – 4
A	1701 – 2		@	1725 – 6		A	1749 – 0		B	1774 – 5
	Anne			George II		B	1750 – 1		C	1775 – 6
B	1702 – 3		b	1726 – 7		C	1751 – 2		D	1776 – 7
C	1703 – 4		c	1727 – 8		D	1752 – 3		E	1777 – 8
D	1704 – 5		d	1728 – 9		E	1753 – 4		F	1778 – 9
E	1705 – 6		e	1729 – 0		F	1754 – 5		G	1779 – 0
F	1706 – 7		f	1730 – 1		G	1755 – 6		H	1780 – 1
G	1707 – 8		g	1731 – 2		H	1756 – 7		I	1781 – 2
H	1708 – 9		h	1732 – 3		I	1757 – 8		K	1783 – 4
I	1709 – 0		i	1733 – 4		K	1758 – 9		L	1784 – 5
K	1710 – 1		k	1734 – 5		L	1759 – 0		M	1785 – 6
L	1711 – 2		l	1735 – 6			George III		N	1786 – 7
M			M	1736 – 7		M	1760 – 1			

Year	Letter
1787 – 8	O
1788 – 9	P
1789 – 0	Q
1790 – 1	R
1791 – 2	L
1792 – 3	T
1793 – 4	U
1794 – 5	W
1795 – 6	X
1796 – 7	Y

Year	Letter
1761 – 2	N
1762 – 3	O
1763 – 4	P
1764 – 5	Q
1765 – 6	R
1766 – 7	S
1767 – 8	T
1768 – 9	U
1769 – 0	W
1770 – 1	X
1771 – 2	Y
1772 – 3	Z

Year	Letter
1738 – 9	
1739 – 0	O
1740 – 1	P
1741 – 2	Q
1742 – 3	R
1743 – 4	S
1744 – 5	T
1745 – 6	U
1746 – 7	W
1747 – 8	X
1748 – 9	Y
	Z

Year	Letter
1713 – 4 George I	N
1714 – 5	O
1715 – 6	P
1716 – 7	Q
1717 – 8	R
1718 – 9	S
1719 – 0	T
1720 – 1	U
1721 – 2	W
1722 – 3	X
1723 – 4	Y
1724 – 5	Z

EXETER DATE LETTERS

Letter	Date
A	1797 – 8
B	1798 – 9
C	1799 – 0
D	1800 – 1
E	1801 – 2
F	1802 – 3
G	1803 – 4
H	1804 – 5
I	1805 – 6
K	1806 – 7

Letter	Date
a	1817 – 8
b	1818 – 9
c	1819 – 0

George IV

Letter	Date
d	1820 – 1
e	1821 – 2
f	1822 – 3
g	1823 – 4
h	1824 – 5
i	1825 – 6

Victoria

Letter	Date
A	1837 – 8
B	1838 – 9
C	1839 – 0
D	1840 – 1
E	1841 – 2
F	1842 – 3
G	1843 – 4
H	1844 – 5
J	1845 – 6
K	1846 – 7

Letter	Date
A	1857 – 8
B	1858 – 9
C	1859 – 0
D	1860 – 1
E	1861 – 2
F	1862 – 3
G	1863 – 4
H	1864 – 5
I	1865 – 6
K	1866 – 7

Year	Letter
1867 – 8	L
1868 – 9	M
1869 – 0	N
1870 – 1	O
1871 – 2	P
1872 – 3	Q
1873 – 4	R
1874 – 5	S
1875 – 6	T
1876 – 7	U

Year	Letter
1847 – 8	L
1848 – 9	M
1849 – 0	N
1850 – 1	O
1851 – 2	P
1852 – 3	Q
1853 – 4	R
1854 – 5	S
1855 – 6	T
1856 – 7	U

Year	Letter
1826 – 7	k
1827 – 8	l
1828 – 9	m
1829 – 0	n
William IV 1830 – 1	o
1831 – 2	P
1832 – 3	q
1833 – 4	r
1834 – 5	s
1835 – 6	t
1836 – 7	u

Year	Letter
1807 – 8	L
1808 – 9	M
1809 – 0	N
1810 – 1	O
1811 – 2	P
1812 – 3	Q
1813 – 4	R
1814 – 5	S
1815 – 6	T
1816 – 7	U

EXETER DATE LETTERS

OFFICE CLOSED 1883

A	1877 – 8
B	1878 – 9
C	1879 – 0
D	1880 – 1
E	1881 – 2
F	1882 – 3

GLASGOW DATE LETTERS

Letter	Year	Letter	Year	Letter	Year	Letter	Year
George III				A	1871 – 2	A	1897 – 8
A	1819 – 0	a	1845 – 6	B	1872 – 3	B	1898 – 9
George IV		b	1846 – 7	C	1873 – 4	C	1899 – 0
B	1820 – 1	c	1847 – 8	D	1874 – 5	D	1900
C	1821 – 2	d	1848 – 9	E	1875 – 6	**Edward VII**	
D	1822 – 3	e	1849 – 0	F	1876 – 7	E	1901 – 2
E	1823 – 4	f	1850 – 1	G	1877 – 8	F	1902 – 3
F	1824 – 5	g	1851 – 2	H	1878 – 9	G	1903 – 4
G	1825 – 6	h	1852 – 3	I	1879 – 0	H	1904 – 5
H	1826 – 7	i	1853 – 4	J	1880 – 1	J	1905 – 6
I	1827 – 8	j	1854 – 5	K	1881 – 2	I	1906 – 7
J	1828 – 9	k	1855 – 6	L	1882 – 3	K	1907 – 8
K	1829 – 0	l	1856 – 7	M	1883 – 4	L	1908 – 9
William IV		m	1857 – 8				

Column 1	Column 2	Column 3	Column 4
1909 – 0	1884 – 5 N	1858 – 9	1831 – 2 M
George V	1885 – 6 O	1859 – 0	1832 – 3 N
1910 – 1 N	1886 – 7 P	1860 – 1	1833 – 4 O
1911 – 2 O	1887 – 8 Q	1861 – 2	1834 – 5 P
1912 – 3 P	1888 – 9 R	1862 – 3	1835 – 6 Q
1913 – 4 Q	1889 – 0 S	1863 – 4	1836 – 7 R
1914 – 5 R	1890 – 1 T	1864 – 5	Victoria
1915 – 6 S	1891 – 2 U	1865 – 6	1837 – 8 S
1916 – 7 T	1892 – 3 V	1866 – 7	1838 – 9 T
1917 – 8 U	1893 – 4 W	1867 – 8	1839 – 0 U
1918 – 9 V	1894 – 5 X	1868 – 9	1840 – 1 V
1919 – 0 W	1895 – 6 Y	1869 – 0	1841 – 2 W
1920 – 1 X	1896 – 7 Z	1870 – 1 Z	1842 – 3 X
1921 – 2 Y			1843 – 4 Y
1922 – 3 Z			1844 – 5 Z

GLASGOW DATE LETTERS

Letter	Year
a	1923 – 4
b	1924 – 5
c	1925 – 6
d	1926 – 7
e	1927 – 8
f	1928 – 9
g	1929 – 0
h	1930 – 1
i	1931 – 2
j	1932 – 3
k	1933 – 4
l	1934 – 5

Letter	Year
𝔄	1949 – 0
𝔅	1950 – 1
ℭ	1951 – 2
Elizabeth II	
𝔇	1952 – 3
𝔈	1953 – 4
𝔉	1954 – 5
𝔊	1955 – 6
𝔥	1956 – 7
𝔍	1957 – 8
𝔎	1958 – 9

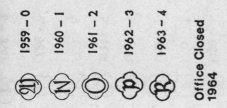

1959 – 0	
1960 – I	
1961 – 2	
1962 – 3	
1963 – 4	
Office Closed 1964	

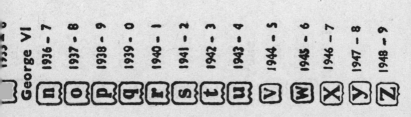

George VI	
1936 – 7	
1937 – 8	
1938 – 9	
1939 – 0	
1940 – I	
1941 – 2	
1942 – 3	
1943 – 4	
1944 – 5	
1945 – 6	
1946 – 7	
1947 – 8	
1948 – 9	

LONDON DATE LETTERS

William III

	1700 - 1
	1701 - 2

Anne

	1702 - 3
	1703 - 4
	1704 - 5
	1705 - 6
	1706 - 7
	1707 - 8
	1708 - 9
	1709 - 0
	1710 - 1

Letter	Year
A	1716 - 7
B	1717 - 8
C	1718 - 9
D	1719 - 0
E	1720 - 1
F	1721 - 2
G	1722 - 3
H	1723 - 4
I	1724 - 5
K	1725 - 6
L	1726 - 7

Letter	Year
a	1736 - 7
b	1737 - 8
c	1738 - 9
d	1739 - 0
p	1739 - 0
e	1740 - 1
f	1741 - 2
g	1742 - 3
h	1743 - 4
i	1744 - 5
k	1745 - 6
l	1746 - 7

Letter	Year
a	1756 - 7
B	1757 - 8
c	1758 - 9
D	1759 - 0

George III

Letter	Year
e	1760 - 1
f	1761 - 2
g	1762 - 3
h	1763 - 4
i	1764 - 5
k	1765 - 6
l	1766 - 7
	1767 - 8

1768 – 9 1769 – 0 1770 – 1 1771 – 2 1772 – 3 1773 – 4 1774 – 5 1775 – 6

1747 – 8 1748 – 9 1749 – 0 1750 – 1 1751 – 2 1752 – 3 1753 – 4 1754 – 5 1755 – 6

1727 – 8 1728 – 9 1729 – 0 1730 – 1 1731 – 2 1732 – 3 1733 – 4 1734 – 5 1735 – 6

M N O P Q R S T V

1712 – 3 1713 – 4 George I 1714 – 5 1715 – 6

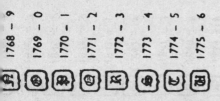

LONDON DATE LETTERS

	1776 – 7	1796 – 7	1816 – 7	1836 – 7
a / A / a / Z	1777 – 8	1797 – 8	1817 – 8	Victoria
b / B	1778 – 9	1798 – 9	1818 – 9	1837 – 8
c / C	1779 – 0	1799 – 0	1819 – 0	1838 – 9
d / D	1780 – 1	1800 – 1	George IV	1839 – 0
e / E	1781 – 2	1801 – 2	1820 – 1	1840 – 1
f / F	1782 – 3	1802 – 3	1821 – 2	1841 – 2
g / G	1783 – 4	1803 – 4	1822 – 3	1842 – 3
h / H	1784 – 5	1804 – 5	1823 – 4	1843 – 4
i / I	1785 – 6	1805 – 6	1824 – 5	1844 – 5
k / K	1786 – 7	1806 – 7	1825 – 6	1845 – 6
l / L	1787 – 8	1807 – 8	1826 – 7	1846 – 7
m / M				

Year	Letter
1848 – 9	𝕬
1849 – 0	𝕭
1850 – 1	𝕮
1851 – 2	𝕯
1852 – 3	𝕰
1853 – 4	𝕱
1854 – 5	𝕲
1855 – 6	𝕳

Year	Letter
1828 – 9	n
1829 – 0	O
William IV 1830 – 1	P
1831 – 2	q
1832 – 3	r
1833 – 4	S
1834 – 5	t
1835 – 6	u

Year	Letter
1808 – 9	N
1809 – 0	O
1810 – 1	P
1811 – 2	Q
1812 – 3	R
1813 – 4	S
1814 – 5	T
1815 – 6	U

Year	Letter
1788 – 9	n
1789 – 0	O
1790 – 1	P
1791 – 2	q
1792 – 3	r
1793 – 4	S
1794 – 5	t
1795 – 6	u

LONDON DATE LETTERS

Letter	Year
George VI	
Ⓐ	1936 – 7
Ⓑ	1937 – 8
Ⓒ	1938 – 9
Ⓓ	1939 – 0
Ⓔ	1940 – 1
Ⓕ	1941 – 2
Ⓖ	1942 – 3
Ⓗ	1943 – 4
Ⓘ	1944 – 5
Ⓚ	1945 – 6
Ⓛ	1946 – 7
Ⓜ	1947 – 8

Letter	Year
ⓐ	1956 – 7
ⓑ	1957 – 8
ⓒ	1958 – 9
ⓓ	1959 – 0
ⓔ	1960 – 1
ⓕ	1961 – 2
ⓖ	1962 – 3
ⓗ	1963 – 4
ⓘ	1964 – 5
ⓚ	1965 – 6

1966–7

1967–8

1968–9

1969–0

1970–1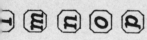

1948 – 9

1949 – 0

1950 – 1

1951 – 2

Elizabeth II

1952 – 3

1953 – 4

1954 – 5

1955 – 6

LONDON DATE LETTERS

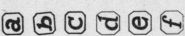

1956 – 7	ⓐ
1957 – 8	ⓑ
1958 – 9	ⓒ
1959 – 0	ⓓ
1960 – 1	ⓔ
1961 – 2	ⓕ

George VI

1936 – 7	Ⓐ
1937 – 8	Ⓑ
1938 – 9	Ⓒ
1939 – 0	Ⓓ
1940 – 1	Ⓔ
1941 – 2	Ⓕ
1942 – 3	Ⓖ
1943 – 4	Ⓗ
1944 – 5	Ⓘ
1945 – 6	Ⓚ
1946 – 7	Ⓛ

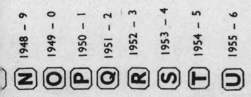

1948 – 9	1949 – 0	1950 – 1	1951 – 2	1952 – 3	1953 – 4	1954 – 5	1955 – 6
Ⓝ	Ⓞ	Ⓟ	Ⓠ	Ⓡ	Ⓢ	Ⓣ	Ⓤ

NEWCASTLE DATE LETTERS

Anne		
1702 – 3	Ⓐ	
1703 – 4	Ⓑ	
1704 – 5	Ⓒ	
1705 – 6	Ⓓ	
1706 – 7	Ⓔ	
1707 – 8	Ⓕ	
1708 – 9		
1709 – 0		
1710 – 1		
1711 – 2		
1712 – 3	Ⓗ	
1713 – 4		
George I		

1730 – 1	Ⓜ
1731 – 2	Ⓑ
1732 – 3	Ⓒ
1733 – 4	Ⓓ
1734 – 5	Ⓔ
1735 – 6	Ⓕ
1736 – 7	Ⓖ
1737 – 8	Ⓗ
1738 – 9	Ⓢ
1739 – 0	Ⓣ
1740 – 1	Ⓐ
1741 – 2	Ⓑ
1742 – 3	Ⓒ

1759 – 0	Ⓐ
George III	
1760 – 8	Ⓑ
1769 – 0	Ⓒ
1770 – 1	Ⓓ
1771 – 2	Ⓔ
1772 – 3	Ⓕ
1773 – 4	Ⓖ
1774 – 5	Ⓗ
1775 – 6	Ⓘ
1776 – 7	Ⓚ
1777 – 8	Ⓛ
1778 – 9	Ⓜ
1779 – 0	

1791 – 2	Ⓐ
1792 – 3	Ⓑ
1793 – 4	Ⓒ
1794 – 5	Ⓓ
1795 – 6	Ⓔ
1796 – 7	Ⓕ
1797 – 8	Ⓖ
1798 – 9	Ⓗ
1799 – 0	Ⓘ
1800 – 1	Ⓚ
1801 – 2	Ⓛ
1802 – 3	Ⓜ
1803 – 4	Ⓝ
1804 – 5	Ⓞ

1806— 7
1807— 8
1808— 9
1809— 0
1810— 1
1811— 2
1812— 3
1813— 4
1814— 5

1781 — 2
1782 — 3
1783 — 4
1784 — 5
1785 — 6
1786 — 7
1787 — 8
1788 — 9
1789 — 0
1790 — 1

1745 — 6
1746 — 7
1747 — 8
1748 — 9
1749— 0
1750— 1
1751 — 2
1752 — 3
1753— 4
1754— 5
1755 — 6
1756— 7
1757 — 8
1758 — 9

1716 — 7
1717 — 8
1718 — 9
1719— 0
1720— 1
1721 — 2
1722— 3
1723— 4
1724— 5
1725— 6
1726— 7
George II
1727— 8
1728— 9
1729 — 0

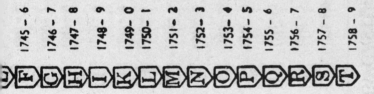

NEWCASTLE DATE LETTERS

Letter	Year	Letter	Year	Letter	Year
A	1815–6	A	1839–0	a	1864–5
B	1816–7	B	1840–1	b	1865–6
C	1817–8	C	1841–2	c	1866–7
D	1818–9	D	1842–3	d	1867–8
E	1819–0	E	1843–4	e	1868–9
George IV		F	1844–5	f	1869–0
F	1820–1	G	1845–6	g	1870–1
G	1821–2	H	1846–7	h	1871–2
H	1822–3	I	1847–8	i	1872–3
I	1823–4	J	1848–9	k	1973–4
K	1824–5	K	1849–0	l	1874–5
L	1825–6	L	1850–1	m	1875–6
M	1826–7	M	1851–2	n	1876–7

1878 – 9	
1879 – 0	
1880 – 1	
1881 – 2	
1882 – 3	
1883 – 4	

OFFICE CLOSED 1884

1854 — 5	
1855 — 6	
1856 – 7	
1857 – 8	
1858 – 9	
1859 – 0	
1860 – 1	
1861 – 2	
1862 – 3	
1863 – 4	

1829 – 0 William IV	
1830 – 1	
1831 – 2	
1832 – 3	
1833 – 4	
1834 – 5	
1835 — 6	
1836 – 7 Victoria	
1837 – 8	
1838 – 9	

SHEFFIELD DATE LETTERS

Year	Letter	Year	Letter	Year	Letter	Year	Letter
George III							
1773 – 4	C	1799 – 0	E	1824 – 5	a	1844 – 5	A
1774 – 5	f	1800 – 1	N	1825 – 6	b	1845 – 6	B
1775 – 6	P	1801 – 2	H	1826 – 7	c	1846 – 7	C
1776 – 7	R	1802 – 3	M	1827 – 8	d	1847 – 8	D
1777 – 8	D	1803 – 4	F	1828 – 9	e	1848 – 9	E
1778 – 9	S	1804 – 5	G	1829 – 0	f	1849 – 0	F
1779 – 0	A	1805 – 6	B	**William IV**		1850 – 1	G
1780 – 1	C	1806 – 7	A	1830 – 1	g	1851 – 2	H
1781 – 2	B	1807 – 8	S	1831 – 2	h	1852 – 3	I
1782 – 3	G	1808 – 9	P	1832 – 3	k	1853 – 4	K
1783 – 4	P	1809 – 0	K	1833 – 4	l	1854 – 5	L
1784 –				1834 – 5	m	1855 – 6	M

Letter	Year
N	1856 – 7
O	1857 – 8
P	1858 – 9
R	1859 – 0
S	1860 – 1
T	1861 – 2
U	1862 – 3
V	1863 – 4
W	1864 – 5
X	1865 – 6
Y	1866 – 7
Z	1867 – 8

Letter	Year
p	1835 – 6
q	1836 – 7
Victoria	
r	1837 – 8
s	1838 – 9
t	1839 – 0
u	1840 – 1
v	1841 – 2
x	1842 – 3
z	1843 – 4

Letter	Year
C	1811 – 2
D	1812 – 3
R	1813 – 4
W	1814 – 5
O	1815 – 6
T	1816 – 7
X	1817 – 8
I	1818 – 9
V	1819 – 0
George IV	
Q	1820 – 1
Y	1821 – 2
Z	1822 – 3
U	1823 – 4

Letter	Year
a	1785 – 6
b	1786 – 7
c	1787 – 8
d	1788 – 9
e	1789 – 0
f	1790 – 1
g	1791 – 2
h	1792 – 3
o	1793 – 4
m	1794 – 5
q	1795 – 6
Z	1796 – 7
X	1797 – 8
V	1798 – 9

SHEFFIELD DATE LETTERS

Letter	Year	Letter	Year	Letter	Year	Letter	Year
A	1868 – 9	c	1895 – 6	d	1921 – 2	E	1947 – 8
B	1869 – 0	d	1896 – 7	e	1922 – 3	F	1948 – 9
C	1870 – 1	e	1897 – 8	f	1923 – 4	G	1949 – 0
D	1871 – 2	f	1898 – 9	g	1924 – 5	H	1950 – 1
E	1872 – 3	g	1899 – 0	h	1925 – 6	I	1951 – 2
F	1873 – 4	h	1900 – 1	i	1926 – 7	Elizabeth II	
G	1874 – 5	Edward VII		k	1927 – 8	K	1952 – 3
H	1875 – 6	j	1901 – 2	l	1928 – 9	L	1953 – 4
J	1876 – 7	k	1902 – 3	m	1929 – 0	M	1954 – 5
K	1877 – 8	l	1903 – 4	n	1930 – 1	N	1955 – 6
L	1878 – 9	m	1904 – 5	o	1931 – 2	O	1956 – 7
M	1879 – 0	n	1905 – 6	p	1932 – 3	P	1957 – 8
		o	1906 – 7	q	1933 – 4	Q	1958 – 9

Year	Letter		Year	Letter		Year	Letter		Year	Letter
1960 – 1	S		1934 – 5	r		1908 – 9	q		1881 – 2	O
1961 – 2	T		1935 – 6	s		1909 – 0	r		1882 – 3	P
1962 – 3	U		George VI			George V			1883 – 4	Q
1963 – 4	V		1936 – 7	t		1910 – 1	s		1884 – 5	R
1964 – 5	W		1937 – 8	u		1911 – 2	t		1885 – 6	S
1965 – 6	X		1938 – 9	v		1912 – 3	u		1886 – 7	T
1966 – 7	Y		1939 – 0	w		1913 – 4	v		1887 – 8	U
1967 – 8	Z		1940 – 1	x		1914 – 5	w		1888 – 9	V
1968 – 9	A		1941 – 2	y		1915 – 6	x		1889 – 0	W
1969 – 0	B		1942 – 3	z		1916 – 7	y		1890 – 1	X
1970 – 1	C		1943 – 4	A		1917 – 8	z		1891 – 2	Y
			1944 – 5	B		1918 – 9	a		1892 – 3	Z
			1945 – 6	C		1919 – 0	b		1893 – 4	a
			1946 – 7	D		1920 – 1	c		1894 – 5	b

YORK DATE LETTERS

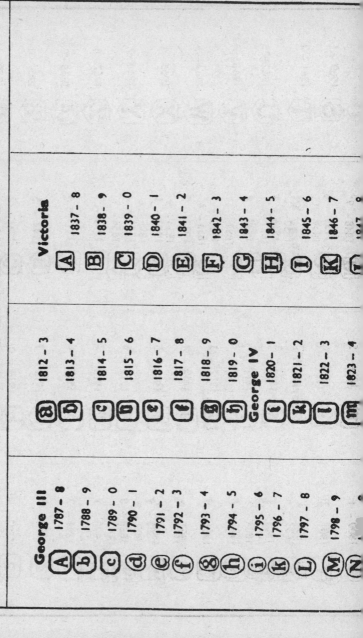

George III
Ⓐ	1787 – 8
ⓑ	1788 – 9
ⓒ	1789 – 0
ⓓ	1790 – 1
ⓔ	1791 – 2
ⓕ	1792 – 3
Ⓖ	1793 – 4
ⓗ	1794 – 5
ⓘ	1795 – 6
Ⓚ	1796 – 7
Ⓛ	1797 – 8
Ⓜ	1798 – 9
Ⓝ	

Ⓐ	1812 – 3
ⓓ	1813 – 4
ⓒ	1814 – 5
ⓓ	1815 – 6
ⓔ	1816 – 7
ⓕ	1817 – 8
ⓖ	1818 – 9
ⓗ	1819 – 0

George IV
ⓘ	1820 – 1
Ⓚ	1821 – 2
ⓛ	1822 – 3
Ⓜ	1823 – 4

Victoria
Ⓐ	1837 – 8
Ⓑ	1838 – 9
Ⓒ	1839 – 0
Ⓓ	1840 – 1
Ⓔ	1841 – 2
Ⓕ	1842 – 3
Ⓖ	1843 – 4
Ⓗ	1844 – 5
Ⓘ	1845 – 6
Ⓚ	1846 – 7
Ⓣ	1847 – 8

Letter	Year
O	1800 – 1
P	1801 – 2
Q	1802 – 3
R	1803 – 4
S	1804 – 5
T	1805 – 6
U	1806 – 7
V	1807 – 8
W	1808 – 9
X	1809 – 0
Y	1810 – 1
Z	1811 – 2

Letter	Year
m	1824 – 5
o	1825 – 6
p	1826 – 7
q	1827 – 8
r	1828 – 9
s	1829 – 0
	William IV
t	1830 – 1
u	1831 – 2
v	1832 – 3
w	1833 – 4
x	1834 – 5
y	1835 – 6
z	1836 – 7

Letter	Year
M	1848 – 9
N	1849 – 0
O	1850 – 1
P	1851 – 2
Q	1852 – 3
R	1853 – 4
S	1854 – 5
T	1855 – 6
V	1856 – 7

OFFICE CLOSED 1857

INDEX

INDEX

	Page
Adam, Characteristics in Furniture of...	23
Anne Period, Characteristics in Furniture of	8
Armour, Names and Descriptions of	369
Arms, Names and Descriptions of	369
Artists, Names and Dates of	233
Assay Marks of Gold and Silver	125
Attributes of Mythological Divinities	421
Attributes of Saints	479
Cabinet Makers	37
Carpets, Description of	309
Ceramics	153
China, Description and Marks of	153
Chinese Divinities	421
Chinese Dynasties and Periods	419
Chinese Symbols and Emblems...	415
Chippendale, Characteristics in Furniture of	21
Classical Dictionary with Index Attributes	455
Clocks	213
Clock-Makers, Names and Dates of	217
Coins, Description and Names of	325
Coins, Schedule of English	349
Cromwellian Period, Characteristics in Furniture of... ...	5
Crosses, Types of...	518
Date Letters of Silver Plate	536
Denominations of English Coins	349
Directoire Period, Characteristics in Furniture of	68
Earthenware, Description and Marks	153
Elizabethan Period, Characteristics in Furniture of	4
Emblems:—	
Chinese	415
Classical	421
Saints	479

	Page
Empire Period. Characteristics in Furniture of	68
English Furniture, Chronological Table of	1
English Sovereigns, Chronological Table of	355
Engravers, Names and Dates of	233
Engravings	229
Etchings	229
Fabrics, Description of	309
Foreign Gold and Silver...	132
French Furniture, Chronological Table of	53
French Terms	69

Furniture:—

Cabinet Makers and Designers, list of	37
Chronological Table of English Periods	1
Characteristics of Adam Style	23
Characteristics of Anne Period	8
Characteristics of Chippendale Style	21
Characteristics of Cromwellian Period	5
Characteristics of Directoire Period...	68
Characteristics of Early Stuart Period	5
Characteristics of Elizabethan Period	4
Characteristics of French Empire Period	68
Characteristics of Georgian Period	19
Characteristics of Henri Quatre Period	55
Characteristics of Hepplewhite Style	24
Characteristics of Jacobean Period	5
Characteristics of Louis Quatorze Period	56
Characteristics of Louis Quinze Period	65
Characteristics of Louis Seize Period	66
Characteristics of Louis Treize Period	55
Characteristics of Regency Period	20
Characteristics of Sheraton Style	34
Characteristics of Tudor Period	3
Characteristics of Victorian Period	20
Characteristics of William and Mary Period	5
Furniture Designers	37

	Page
Gems, Description of	295
General and Miscellaneous Terms	511
Georgian Period, Characteristics in Furniture of	19
Glass, Description of	207
Glossary of Terms:—	
Arms and Armour	369
Clocks	213
Coins	325
Engravings and Etchings	229
Fabrics and Carpets	309
Furniture	75
General and Miscellaneous	511
Glass	207
Heraldry	397
Jewellery	295
Musical Instruments	387
Mythological Divinities with their attributes	421
Oil Paintings and Water Colour Drawings...	229
Pewter	151
Porcelain and Pottery with marks	153
Saints and their attributes	481
Silver and Sheffield Plate	141
Symbolical Figures and their attributes	421
Terms not included in specialised sections	511
Textiles	309
Woods used in Cabinet work	39
Goldsmiths' Company's Memoranda, etc.	134
Hall Marks on Gold	131
Hall Marks on Silver Plate	127
Henri IV Period, Characteristics in Furniture of	55
Hepplewhite, Characteristics in Furniture of	24
Heraldry, Terms used in...	397
Jacobean Period, Characteristics in Furniture of	5
Japanese Divinities	421

	Page
Jewellery	295
Lace, Description of	309
Louis XIII Period, Characteristics in Furniture of	55
Louis XIV Period, Characteristics in Furniture of	56
Louis XV Period, Characteristics in Furniture of	65
Louis XVI Period, Characteristics in Furniture of	66
Medals	357
Miscellaneous and General Terms	511
Monastic Orders	479
Musical Instruments, Description of	387
Mythology, Dictionary of	421
Numismatics	325
Oil Paintings	229
Painters, Names and Dates of	233
Periods of Furniture	1
Pewter	151
Pottery, Description and Marks of	153
Porcelain, Description and Marks of	153
Precious Stones, Description of	295
Prints and Engravings	229
Regency Period	20
Roman Numerals	510
Rugs	309
Saints, Attributes of	479
Semi-Precious Stones, Description of	295
Sheffield Plate	140
Sheraton, Characteristics in Furniture of	34
Silver Marks	127
Sovereigns, Chronological Table of English	355
Stevengraphs	509
Stuart Period, Characteristics in Furniture of	5
Symbols:—	
Chinese	415
Classical	421
Saints	479

Page

Table for Converting Avoirdupois weight into Troy 150

Tapestries, Description of 309

Textiles, Description of 309

Tudor Period, Characteristics in Furniture of 3

Watches 213

Water Colour Drawings 229

Weapons, Description of 369

William and Mary Period, Characteristics in Furniture of ... 7

Woods used in Cabinet work 39

Zodiac, The Signs of 454

DISTRIBUTORS
for the Wordsworth Reference Series

**AUSTRALIA, BRUNEI,
MALAYSIA & SINGAPORE**

Reed Editions
22 Salmon Street
Port Melbourne
Vic 3207
Australia
Tel: (03) 646 6716
Fax: (03) 646 6925

**GERMANY, AUSTRIA
& SWITZERLAND**

Swan Buch-Marketing GmbH
Goldscheuerstraße 16
D-7640 Kehl am Rhein
Germany

GREAT BRITAIN & IRELAND

Wordsworth Editions Ltd
Cumberland House
Crib Street
Ware
Hertfordshire SG12 9ET

INDIA

Om Book Service
1690 First Floor
Nai Sarak, Delhi - 110006
Tel: 3279823/3265303
Fax: 3278091

ITALY

Magis Books
Piazza della Vittoria 1/C
42100 Reggio Emilia
Tel: 0522-452303
Fax: 0522-452845

NEW ZEALAND

Whitcoulls Limited
Private Bag 92098, Auckland

SOUTHERN AFRICA

Struik Book Distributors (Pty) Ltd
Graph Avenue
Montague Gardens
7441
P O Box 193
Maitland
7405
South Africa
Tel: (021) 551-5900
Fax: (021) 551-1124

USA, CANADA & MEXICO

Universal Sales & Marketing
230 Fifth Avenue
Suite 1212
New York, NY 10001 USA
Tel: 212-481-3500
Fax: 212-481-3534